AF207938

The Sultan's Anthologist – Ibn Abī Ḥaǧalah and His Work

Edited by
Nefeli Papoutsakis – Syrinx von Hees

ARABISCHE LITERATUR UND RHETORIK – ELFHUNDERT BIS ACHTZEHNHUNDERT (ALEA)

Herausgegeben von

Thomas Bauer – Syrinx von Hees

Band 3

ERGON VERLAG

The Sultan's Anthologist –
Ibn Abi Ḥaǧalah and His Work

Edited by

Nefeli Papoutsakis – Syrinx von Hees

ERGON VERLAG

Umschlagabbildung:
Dinār des Sultans al-Malik an-Nāṣir Nāṣiraddin Ḥasan,
Kairo 750/1349-1350 (25mm, 6,85g) © Thomas Bauer

Bibliografische Information der Deutschen Nationalbibliothek
Die Deutsche Nationalbibliothek verzeichnet diese Publikation in der Deutschen
Nationalbibliografie; detaillierte bibliografische Daten sind im Internet über
http://dnb.d-nb.de abrufbar.

www.ergon-verlag.de

ISSN 2365-8878
ISBN 978-3-95650-282-8

Inhalt

The Sultan's Anthologist –
Ibn Abī Ḥaǧalah and His Work

Introduction

Nefeli Papoutsakis / Syrinx von Hees

Born in Tlemcen and educated in Damascus, the fourteenth-century Arab litterateur Ibn Abī Ḥaǧalah (725-776/1325-1375) spent most of his adult life in Mamluk Cairo. His best-known works are *Sukkardān as-sulṭān* (The Sultan's Sugar Box) and *Dīwān aṣ-ṣabābah* (The Register of Passionate Love), two anthologies that he dedicated to his patron, the Mamluk Sultan Ḥasan, during the latter's second reign (755-762/1354-1361). A prolific author and master of the *maqāmāt* genre, Ibn Abī Ḥaǧalah also penned numerous other prose works, many of which are lost or still unedited. An acclaimed poet during his own time, he mainly composed panegyric and religious poetry. Even though he is one of the most important litterateurs of the Mamluk era, his work has so far received little scholarly attention.

The present volume, a collection of studies on Ibn Abī Ḥaǧalah and his oeuvre, seeks to remedy this and to stimulate further research on this author and, more generally, Mamluk literature. Most of the works discussed and analysed in the volume are still unpublished or are partly or fully edited here for the very first time. The arrangement of the thirteen contributions roughly follows the chronology of Ibn Abī Ḥaǧalah's writings. These writings characterize Ibn Abī Ḥaǧalah as an anthologist, a writer of *maqāmāt* and a poet.

The first contribution is by Emil Homerin: "Ibn Abī Ḥaǧalah and Sufism" sheds light on Ibn Abī Ḥaǧalah's career as a sheikh of a Sufi chantry as well as on his relationships with patrons and colleagues; in the context of this book, it serves as an introduction to the life and personal network of Ibn Abī Ḥaǧalah. Homerin further focuses on Ibn Abī Ḥaǧalah's views on Sufism, especially his hostile attitude towards monism and speculative theosophy as were associated with the great mystics Ibn ʿArabī (d. 637/1240) and Ibn al-Fāriḍ (d. 632/1235), and discusses Ibn Abī Ḥaǧalah's *Ġayt al-ʿāriḍ fī muʿāraḍat Ibn al-Fāriḍ*. In this late (written probably after 769/1368) and still unpublished work, Ibn Abī Ḥaǧalah included his own *muʿāraḍāt* to famous poems by Ibn al-Fāriḍ. By dedicating his *muʿāraḍāt* to praising the prophet Muḥammad, Ibn Abī Ḥaǧalah aimed at discrediting Ibn al-Fāriḍ's doctrines and at countering the influence of his popular poetry, while portraying himself as a piously inspired poet.

Apart from religious poetry in praise of the prophet, Ibn Abī Ḥaǧalah composed several panegyric poems on persons belonging to his social network in both the military-courtly and the scholarly-urban milieus. In his "The Micro-Qaṣīdah: A Formal Experiment from the 8th/14th Century", Thomas Bauer examines a poetic form that occurs remarkably often in Ibn Abī Ḥaǧalah's *Dīwān*, namely the seven-line long panegyric poem, which he aptly dubs a 'micro-qaṣīdah'. Besides discussing several of Ibn Abī Ḥaǧalah's seven-liners and showing how this form economically accommodates the traditional themes of panegyric in a condensed space, he traces the invention of this form to Ibn Nubātah al-Miṣrī (686-768/1287-1366), the leading poet of that era, whom Ibn Abī Ḥaǧalah deeply admired and who served him as a model.

Sukkardān as-sulṭān, a literary anthology on the number seven, which Ibn Abī Ḥaǧalah dedicated to Sultan Ḥasan in 757/1356, to celebrate his patron's seventh year in office, is one of his most important and intriguing works. Beatrice Gruendler's study "Literary Sweets: Interlacing Motifs in the *Sukkardān as-sulṭān* of Ibn Abī Ḥaǧalah (1325-1375)" explores the way in which the work is structured and especially how recurring themes and motifs serve to bring out the author's deeper concerns and hold together what might at first sight appear as a random gathering of narrative material on the number seven.

A relatively early work (composed prior to 760/1359), is *Sulūk as-sanan fī waṣf as-sakan* (The Right Path in the Description of Dwellings), an anthology on housing and dwellings, which is still unpublished. In her "Urban Architecture and Poetry: Two Medieval Arabic Anthologies as Manuals of Mapping Urban Space", Alev Masarwa presents this work and compares it with *Maṭāliʿ al-budūr*, the better-known anthology on the same subject by al-Ġuzūlī (d. 815/1411-12), showing that the latter work was based on that by Ibn Abī Ḥaǧalah. Masarwa further elaborates on the relation between literature and architecture commenting on the poetic descriptions of wind towers cited in the relevant chapter of Ibn Abī Ḥaǧalah's *Sulūk as-sanan*.

The *Dīwān aṣ-ṣabābah*, Ibn Abī Ḥaǧalah's famous anthology on passionate love, which he completed in 760/1359, attracted early the attention of Western scholars. In her study "Friedrich Rückerts Übersetzungen aus Ibn Abī Ḥaǧalahs *Dīwān aṣ-ṣabābah*", Anke Osigus discusses how the renowned German poet and linguist Friedrich Rückert (1788-1866) became acquainted with this text, extracts of which he then translated. Osigus analyses Rückert's working method as a translator of Arabic literature and shows how he sought to make oriental poetry accessible to German readers. Rückert's translations of love poems from the *Dīwān aṣ-ṣabābah*, which Osigus edits here for the first time, derive from the poet's archive kept at the University Library (ULB) at Münster.

The subject of Remke Kruk's "A Courtier's Chess Book: Ibn Abī Ḥaǧalah's *Unmūḏaǧ al-qitāl fī naql al-ʿawāl*" is a treatise on chess which Ibn Abī Ḥaǧalah probably composed in connection with his other works for the Mamluk court. Kruk compares this work with other classical Arabic treatises on chess and thus throws its belletristic qualities into relief. As Kruk shows, besides defending the legitimacy of the game and spotlighting its benefits both as an intellectual exercise and as a form of recreation, Ibn Abī Ḥaǧalah produced a text that is itself instructing and entertaining in the best tradition of *adab* literature.

Ibn Abī Ḥaǧalah is also known as an author of *maqāmāt*. In his contribution "A *Maqāmah* on the Book Market of Cairo in the 8th/14th Century: The 'Return of the Stranger' of Ibn Abī Ḥaǧalah (d. 776/1375)", Maurice Pomerantz edits and translates into English a *maqāmah* composed around 762/1362-3, in which Ibn Abī Ḥaǧalah describes the book market of Cairo as flourishing after a period of decline. Apart from popular literature and the occult sciences, in his comments on the various kinds of books sold on the market, which he puts into the mouth of his hero Abū r-Riyāš, Ibn Abī Ḥaǧalah singles out for critique the works of the monist Sufis, which he deemed unscholarly and most harmful to the wider public.

In 764/1363 the Black Death broke out once again in Egypt and the death toll in Cairo rose into the thousands per day during its peak. Among the victims of this plague outbreak was a son of Ibn Abī Ḥaǧalah, who in the following years thematized the plague and the death of children in several of his writings.

In "Ibn Abī Ḥaǧalah und sein Traktat „Das Feien gegen jedwede Widerwärtigkeit mittels des Bittgebets für den Propheten der Gnade (*Dafʿ an-niqmah bi-ṣ-ṣalāh ʿalā nabī ar-raḥmah)*", Andreas Herdt presents and analyses the contents of *Dafʿ an-niqmah* (Repelling Affliction by Praying for the Prophet of Mercy), a still unedited work composed in the aftermath of that plague. Because of the rich historical and medical information it contains, *Dafʿ an-niqmah* has previously been discussed in connection with other plague treatises, but, as Herdt points out, Ibn Abī Ḥaǧalah's primary concern here was of a religious and ethical nature. Trying to come to terms with the Black Death tragedy, he pleaded for spiritual purification and therefore viewed the prayer for the prophet Muḥammad as the most efficacious remedy against this and similar tribulations.

At-Ṭibb al-masnūn fī dafʿ aṭ-ṭāʿūn (The Well-Proved Medicine Against the Plague) is an abridgement (*muḫtaṣar*) of *Dafʿ an-niqmah* made by Ibn Abī Ḥaǧalah himself. In this work Ibn Abī Ḥaǧalah focuses on what offers protection against the epidemic, be that prayer and spiritual purification or prophetic and professional medicine, and leaves out the historical information and literary presentations of the plague included in *Dafʿ an-niqmah*. In his "Edition des Traktats *aṭ-Ṭibb al-masnūn fī dafʿ aṭ-ṭāʿūn* des Ibn Abī Ḥaǧalah (Die bewährte Medizin zum Schutz vor der Pest)", Stephan Tölke provides a complete edition of this work.

Having dealt with the plague and the death of children in *Salwat al-ḥazīn fī mawt al-banīn* (Consolation of the Mourning over the Death of Children), Ibn Abī Ḥaǧalah revisited these topics in *Ǧiwār al-aḫyār fī dār al-qarār* (Dwelling near the Best in the Permanent Abode), in which he explicitly mentioned the death of his son as a reason for its composition. In her study "Ein Trauergedicht auf Muḥammad im Kontext des Werkes *Ǧiwār al-aḫyār*", Syrinx von Hees presents the contents of this still unpublished work and shows that here Ibn Abī Ḥaǧalah interrelates three genres: a manual on visiting the graves, a book on death and the dead, and an anthology of his elegies on the prophet, itself a remarkably rare poetic genre. She then edits, translates into German and analyses one of these elegies by reference to three poetic kinds: the elegy, the Kindertotenlied and the praise of the prophet.

After the Franks' devastating attack on Alexandria in 767/1365, Ibn Abī Ḥaǧalah wrote a poem lamenting this event. In "Der Fall Alexandrias in den Städteklagen Ibn Abī Ḥaǧalahs und seiner Zeitgenossen", Alev Masarwa scrutinizes the historical context and studies this ode in connection with other poems composed on that occasion by contemporaries as well as with an earlier poem by Ibn Abī Ḥaǧalah on the recapture of Ṭarābulus al-Ġarb that took place in 755/1354. Contrasting poetic with historical narratives, she illustrates the different literary strategies used in dealing with the distress caused by this and similar military setbacks.

Hakan Özkan's "Die Makame *Dawr az-zamān fī ṭaḥn al-ǧulbān* – Eine sehr persönliche Schmähschrift" is a study, edition and translation into German of a *maqāmah* composed by Ibn Abī Ḥaǧalah on the revolt of the Mamluk soldiers against the emir Yalbuġā al-Ḥāṣṣakī, the de facto ruler of the Mamluk state in 762-768/1361-1366. Ibn Abī Ḥaǧalah describes Yalbuġā's career and morals and the events that led to the revolt of December 768/1366, the emir's assassination and the subsequent period of unrest. The study offers a thorough presentation of the historical background and an analysis of Ibn Abī Ḥaǧalah's portrayal of the events that demonstrates how this text complements the existing historical narratives. In addition, Özkan discusses the peculiarities of the author's prose style.

In his later years Ibn Abī Ḥaǧalah started working on a comprehensive anthology of contemporary prose and poetry, *Muǧtabā al-udabā'* (The Litterateurs' Pick), a work that remained unfinished and does not survive. For that purpose, he composed an open letter asking contemporary litterateurs to send him specimens of their works to include in the *Muǧtabā*. In "The Anthologist's Agenda and Concerns in Ibn Abī Ḥaǧalah's *Maġnāṭīs ad-durr an-nafīs*", Nefeli Papoutsakis evaluates the information that this open letter, the 'Magnet for Precious Pearls', offers on the unfinished and now lost anthology. She also edits three extracts from the 'Magnet', including an autobiographical note that Ibn Abī Ḥaǧalah inserted in this work by way of a calling card.

With one exception, earlier versions of these studies were presented at a conference that bore the same title as the volume and took place in Münster on 1-2 April 2015. The conference was convened by Thomas Bauer, the director of the Münster-based research unit Arabic Literature and Rhetoric, Twelfth to Eighteenth Centuries (German abbreviation: ALEA), with a view to examining in depth the multifaceted oeuvre of this major figure of Mamluk literature. We therefore wish to cordially thank Thomas Bauer for his catching enthusiasm and his generous sharing of knowledge that provoked the research presented in this book, as well as for entrusting us with its editing. Like all other ALEA activities, both the conference and the volume have been funded by means of the DFG Leibniz-Prize that was awarded to Thomas Bauer in 2013. We also thank all ALEA-researchers for the work done collectively on the Arabic texts of Ibn Abī Ḥaǧalah at our weekly meetings; we are especially grateful to Samir Mubayd for his help in elucidating several difficult passages in the Arabic texts. Last but not least, we would like to thank Anna Kortmann, who standardized the footnotes and made a final check of all formalities.

Ibn Abī Ḥaǧalah and Sufism

Th. Emil Homerin

In 725/1325, Aḥmad ibn Yaḥyā ibn Abī Bakr entered the world of Sufism the moment he was born in a Sufi lodge in Tlemcen (Tilimsān). This lodge (*zāwiyah*) belonged to his great grandfather ʿAbd al-Wāḥid, who was known popularly as Abū Ḥaǧalah ("father of the partridge"), because a partridge had once come to him and laid an egg on his sleeve. The account of this strange, if not miraculous, event suggests that ʿAbd al-Wāḥid had a gentle and saintly nature, and several sources refer to him as "one of the virtuous" (*min aṣ-ṣāliḥīn*).[1] In a North African, urban, Sufi context, the term *ṣāliḥ* tended to designate a devout Sunni Muslim who carried out pious acts for the benefit of the larger community in accord with the Qurʾān, the example of the prophet Muḥammad (*sunnah*), and the injunctions of Islamic law (*šarīʿah*).[2] Growing up in such an environment, the young Aḥmad undoubtedly studied the Qurʾān, the traditions of the Prophet (*ḥadīṯ*), and the major rituals of Islam, as well as such Sufi practices as *ḏikr* (recollection). He may also have begun his study of the law of the Ḥanafi school, to which his family belonged.

As a teenager, Aḥmad accompanied members of his family eastward to Cairo and then on to Mecca and Medina as part of the annual Hajj pilgrimage. By 743/1342, Aḥmad had resumed his studies in Damascus where he would live and work for the next eight years. Perhaps, during this period, Aḥmad acquired the title Ibn Abī Ḥaǧalah, in honor of his great grandfather. Among his teachers in Damascus were Yūsuf ibn Yaʿqūb al-Maqdisī (d. 8th/14th c.), the noted hadith scholar ʿAlāʾaddīn Muġulṭāy (d. 762/1361), the hadith scholar, historian, and theologian Šamsaddīn aḏ-Ḏahabī (d. 748/1348), the historian and Qurʾānic commentator ʿImādaddīn Ibn Kaṯīr (d. 774/1373), and the legal scholar and theologian Ibn Qayyim al-Ǧawziyyah (d. 751/1350).[3] Both Ibn Kaṯīr and Ibn Qayyim al-Ǧawziyyah had been students of the controversial Ḥanbalī theologian and le-

---

[1] Ibn Ḥaǧar al-ʿAsqalānī, *Inbāʾ al-ġumr bi-anbāʾ al-ʿumr*, ed. Muḥammad ʿAbd al-Muʿīd Ḫān, 9 vols. in 5, Beirut ²1986, 1:107-10; *idem, ad-Durar al-kāminah fī ʿayān al-miʾah aṯ-ṯāminah*, ed. Muḥammad Sayyid Ǧād al-Ḥaqq, 5 vols., Cairo 1966, 1:350-52 (#826); Ibn Taġrībirdī, *an-Nuǧūm az-zāhirah fī mulūk Miṣr wa-l-Qāhirah*, 16 vols., Cairo 1963, 11:131-32; *idem, al-Manhal aṣ-ṣāfī wa-l-mustawfī baʿd al-Wāfī*, ed. Muḥammad Muḥammad Amīn, 13 vols., Cairo 1986-2005, 2:259-61. For more recent biographies of Ibn Abī Ḥaǧalah, see Muǧāhid Muṣṭafā Bahǧat and Aḥmad Ḥamīd Muḫlif, "Introduction" to *Dīwān Ibn Abī Ḥaǧalah*, ed. Muǧāhid Muṣṭafā Bahǧat and Aḥmad Ḥamīd Muḫlif, Amman 2010, pp. 11-58, and Gruendler, Beatrice, "Ibn Abi Hajalah (1325-75)", in: Lowry, Joseph E. and Devin J. Stewart (eds.,), *Essays in Arabic Literary Biography: 1350-1850*, Wiesbaden 2009, pp. 118-26.

[2] Cornell, Vincent J., *Realm of the Saint: Power and Authority in Moroccan Islam*, Austin 1998, pp. 3-9.

[3] Bahǧat and Muḫlif, "Introduction", *Dīwān*, pp. 12-14, 17-23.

gal scholar Aḥmad Ibn Taymiyyah (d. 728/1328), and their conservative views and opinions on religion greatly impressed Ibn Abī Ḥaǧalah, such that some came to regard him as a Ḥanafī in law, but a Ḥanbalī in doctrine.[4]

This was clearly the case with Islamic mysticism as Ibn Abī Ḥaǧalah took a prudent and cautious approach toward Sufi doctrine and practice. Like Ibn Taymiyyah, Ibn Abī Ḥaǧalah was an outspoken critic of monism and speculative theosophy, often associated with Muḥyiddīn Ibn al-ʿArabī (d. 637/1240), and ʿUmar Ibn al-Fāriḍ (632/1235).[5] Neither Ibn Taymiyyah nor Ibn Abī Ḥaǧalah, however, was anti-Sufi, *per se*, and Ibn Taymiyyah concisely presented his own position on the subject, and one shared by Ibn Abī Ḥaǧalah, in several works, including his epistle *aṣ-Ṣūfiyyah wa-l-fuqarāʾ* (*The Sufis and the Mendicants*). There, Ibn Taymiyyah noted that a moral, ethically based mysticism could restrain pride and hypocrisy, while promoting patience and religious sincerity. Further, a faith informed intuition (*aḏ-ḏawq al-imānī*) and religious ecstasy (*al-waǧd ad-dīnī*) were valuable internal, affective components of a virtuous life based on love and law. Ibn Taymiyyah expressed his admiration for many Sufis of the past, particularly the righteous Sufis who practiced constant vigilance in their personal behavior and relationships, thereby attaining mystical truths and states comparable to those mentioned in the Qurʾān and *sunnah*. Nevertheless, such righteous folk were rare, and many more who wore the garb of the Sufis were charlatans or fools. Between the two ranks were the "funded Sufis" (*ṣufiyyat al-arzāq*) who were supported by religious bequests (*awqāf*), and who were generally attached to mosques, madrasahs, chantries, and other religious institutions. Ibn Taymiyyah accepted this professional class as long as these Sufis carried out their religious obligations, followed proper rules of conduct, and renounced worldliness. Like-wise, whenever possible, they must avoid states of swooning, unconsciousness, and other forms of excess when performing their rituals, lest they commit sin. In sum, this was a kind of juridical Sufism with a guarded acceptance of certain mystical beliefs and practices within a proper legal and doctrinal framework.[6]

Besides Sufism and other religious subjects, Ibn Abī Ḥaǧalah avidly pursued the study of poetry and the literary arts, and among his teachers in Damascus was the chancery official and celebrated poet Ǧamāladdīn Ibn Nubātah (d. 768/1366).[7] Indeed, by all accounts, Ibn Abī Ḥaǧalah excelled in *belles lettres*, and one of his first forays into a professional career as a poet and writer occurred

---

[4] Ibn Ḥaǧar al-ʿAsqalānī, *Inbāʾ*, 1:108.

[5] Ibn Ḥaǧar al-ʿAsqalānī, *Inbāʾ*, 1:108, and below.

[6] Homerin, Th. Emil, "Ibn Taimiya's *Al-Ṣūfiyah wa-al-Fuqarāʾ*", *Arabica* 32 (1985), pp. 219-44. Regarding the use of the term *ṣūfī* as a professional, occupational category during the Mamluk dynasty, see *idem*, "Saving Muslim Souls: The Khānqāh and the Sufi Duty in Mamluk Lands", *Mamlūk Studies Review* 3 (1999), pp. 59-83. Concerning "juridical Sufism", see Cornell, *Realm*, p. 67.

[7] Baḫǧat and Muḫlif, "Introduction", *Dīwān*, p. 21, and see the article in this volume by Thomas Bauer.

shortly after 751/1350, when he moved to Cairo and began to compose panegyric poems dedicated to high officials, including the sultan aṣ-Ṣāliḥ Ṣāliḥ (r. 752-55/1351-54).[8] When aṣ-Ṣāliḥ was deposed in 755/1354, Ibn Abī Ḥaǧalah appears to have made a seamless transition to lauding his successor Sultan Ḥasan (r. 748-52/1347-51; 755-62/1354-61) as he began a second reign as sultan.[9] Sultan Ḥasan was considered to be well-versed in Arabic language and literature, and the twenty year old sultan may have found the erudite Ibn Abī Ḥaǧalah, who was twenty-nine at the time, a like-minded companion. For the next six years, the two men would enjoy each other's company, as Sultan Ḥasan served as Ibn Abī Ḥaǧalah's patron.[10]

Ibn Abī Ḥaǧalah's presence in the royal court also may have facilitated his appointment to a religious position as well, that of a Sufi šayḫ at a ḫānqāh.[11] Similar to other Mamluk ḫānqāhs, this chantry was designed to contain the future tomb of its founder and other family members, and it was part of a larger complex of buildings, which, in this case, included a congregational mosque and a cistern, all built and paid for by a senior Mamluk amir, Manǧak al-Yūsufi (ca. 715-776/ca. 1315-1375). The complex was completed in 751/1350, when Manǧak served as Sultan Ḥasan's vizier and chief financial officer. But, Manǧak ran afoul of the sultan, and was dismissed from office, mulcted, and imprisoned for a time before he was allowed to return to royal service a few years later.[12] However, Manǧak's misfortunes did not detrimentally affect his mosque and chantry for which he had provided generous religious endowments. Though the original endowment deed for the complex is lost, the historian and topographer al-Maqrīzī (d. 845/1442) noted that ample endowments provided for a preacher at the congregational mosque on Fridays, and a number of paid positions for Sufis at the ḫānqāh. He noted further, that each day the Sufis were given their meals, including meat and bread, and that they received a monthly stipend, as well.[13]

---

8   Ibn Taġrībirdī, an-Nuǧūm, 11:131; Bahǧat and Muḫlif, "Introduction", Dīwān, pp. 14-15, and Ibn Abī Ḥaǧalah, Dīwān, pp. 67 (#8), 99 (#97), 101-103 (#103), 106-107 (#109), 181 (#223).

9   E.g. Ibn Abī Ḥaǧalah, Dīwān, pp. 73-74 (#25), 117-20 (#119), 187 (#239), 270-73 (#412). For studies of the political events of this period in Mamluk history, see Irwin, Robert, The Middle East in the Middle Ages: The Early Mamluk Sultanate, 1250-1382, Carbondale, IL 1986, pp. 125-51, and van Steenbergen, Jo, Order Out of Chaos: Patronage, Conflict, and Mamluk Socio-Political Culture, 1341-82, Leiden 2006.

10   Bahǧat and Muḫlif, "Introduction", Dīwān, pp. 16-17, and Gruendler, "Ibn Abī Ḥajalah", pp. 120-22.

11   Ibn Ḥaǧar al-ʿAsqalānī, Inbāʾ, 1:108, Ibn Taġrībirdī, al-Manhal, 2:259, and Bahǧat and Muḫlif, "Introduction", Dīwān, p. 15.

12   Al-Maqrīzī, al-Mawāʿiẓ wa-l-iʿtibār bi-ḏikr al-ḫiṭaṭ wa-l-āṯār, 2 vols., Cairo n.d., 2:320-24; Ibn Taġrībirdī, al-Manhal, 11:276-80; van Steenbergen, Order, p. 183, and Irwin, Middle East, pp. 134, 137-39.

13   Al-Maqrīzī, al-Mawāʿiẓ, 2:320. For a more recent description of the complex located below Cairo's citadel near the Bāb al-Wazīr cemetery, see Parker, Richard, et al., Islamic Monuments in Cairo: A Practical Guide, 2nd ed., Cairo 1985, pp. 89-90.

Unfortunately, al-Maqrīzī did not state how many Sufis served the chantry, nor did he give details regarding the šayḫ's particular duties and compensation. However, a review of endowment deeds that have survived for similar chantries can give us an idea of some of the benefits and responsibilities that Ibn Abī Ḥaǧalah may have had. Generally, the šayḫ and his family were provided with living quarters in a special section of the ḫānqāh; their meals were also provided, and the šayḫ received a substantial monthly income. In turn, the šayḫ was to be a respected religious scholar, knowledgeable about Sufism, pious, well-mannered and well-groomed, and, in the case of some ḫānqāhs, including Manǧak's chantry, the šayḫ must be of the Ḥanafī law school. Some ḫānqāh endowment deeds further stipulated that the šayḫ teach law, but none of the surviving biographical notices to Ibn Abī Ḥaǧalah report his undertaking that task.[14] Likewise, Ibn Abī Ḥaǧalah makes no mention of teaching law when he spoke of Manǧak's ḫānqāh and his place there:[15]

> The ḫānqāh [founded by Manǧak] is blessed with religious knowledge and activity due to the Sufi seekers, and it is as if [this ḫānqāh] has been secluded on a mountain top and occupied exclusively for God, Most High. Now, due to those living there, I fondly call it my home and family. I was given a position and salary there among the Sufis, and though I am their šayḫ, I am really their servant, a seeker, and their leader on the Sufi path. So no wonder when I speak about this path, I say:

أَرَى مِنَّةَ التَّوحيدِ أَعْظَمَ مِنَّةٍ   عَلَى غَيْظِ جُمَّالِ الوَرَى الثَنَوِيَّةِ

فَأَشْهَدُ أَنَّ اللهَ لا رَبَّ غَيْرَه   وَأَنَّ رَسُولَ اللهِ خَيْرُ البَرِيَّةِ

وَمِن مَذهَبي حُبُّ النَّبِيّ وآلهِ   وَأَصْحابِهِ والتَّابِعينَ الأَئِمَةِ

وَلَم أَخْشَ في أَثْناءِ قَولي دَسائِسًا   فَيا وَيلَ مَن أَمسى مِنَ الحَشَوِيَّةِ[16]

وَلَو كان هذا مَوضِعَ القَولِ أَظْهَرَتْ   بَدائِعُ نَظْمي عَنْهُمْ كُلَّ بِدعَةِ

وَبَيَّنْتُ قَولَ المُلْحِدينَ بِأَسْرِهِمْ   بِأَبْياتِ نَظْمٍ كالحُصُونِ المَنيعَةِ

تَرَى الهَمْزَ فيها مِثلَ وُرْقِ حَمائِمٍ   وقد أَعْرَبَتْ عَن أَلْسُنٍ أَعْجَمِيَّةِ

---

[14] Amin, Muḥammad Muḥammad, *al-Awqāf wa-l-ḥayāt al-iǧtimāʿiyyah fī Miṣr 648-923 AH/1250-1517 CE*, Cairo 1980, pp. 204-13; Fernandes, Leonor, *The Evolution of a Sufi Institution in Mamluk Egypt: The Khanqah*, Berlin 1988, pp. 1, 28-29, 34, 47-51, 68-95, and Homerin, "Souls", pp. 65-71.

[15] Ibn Abī Ḥaǧalah, *Sukkardān as-sulṭān*, ed. ʿAlī Muḥammad ʿUmar, Cairo 2001, pp. 59-60. Following the poem, Ibn Abī Ḥaǧalah noted the beauty of the ḫānqāh and praised Manǧak, its founder.

[16] The term ḥašawiyyah was originally used pejoratively by Muʿtazilī theologians to refer to traditionalists, especially those who accepted anthropomorphism; see Jon Hoover, "Hashwiyya", in: *EI Three*, consulted online on 13 October 2016, http://dx.doi.org/10.1163/1573-3912_ei3_COM_30377.

I see the gift of monotheism as the greatest grace
  against the ignorant dualists' rant and rave.
And I bear witness: "There is no lord save God,
  and His apostle is creation's best!"
Our way is love of the Prophet, his family,
  companions, and the leading followers.
So when I speak my belief, I fear no secret schemes,
  but woe to those idiots so full of it!
Was this poem a creed, my elegant verse
  would reveal their every heresy,
For I have exposed the doctrine of all deviants
  with poetic verses, like fortresses, strong,
So you see its smallest letter, like dusky doves,
  speaking clearly against those babbling tongues!

As šayḫ, Ibn Abī Ḥaǧalah may have chosen the Sufis who worked at the ḫānqāh, and, as is apparent from his poem, he was certainly careful to ensure that they were knowledgeable of proper doctrine, and Sufi etiquette and practice. Particularly important was the performance of a communal litany, which often involved ḏikr. Ḏikr is a corner stone of Sufi ritual, yet its practice can vary widely from silent prayers to boisterous religious celebrations with the chanting of verse, music, and dance.[17] Given Ibn Abī Ḥaǧalah's Ḥanbali inclinations and his comments above, congregational litanies and ḏikr recitals at Mangak's chantry were probably respectful, solemn affairs in line with the opinion of his teacher Ibn Qayyim al-Ǧawziyyah. Ibn Qayyim al-Ǧawziyyah recognized the benefits of ḏikr when properly performed, especially as a private recollection and invocation of God. However, he was quite uncomfortable when ḏikr led to public displays of weeping and ecstasy. Even worse were the chanting of verse and singing during ḏikr, which he forbade as it would only lead Muslims into sinful behavior.[18]

In a Mamluk ḫānqāh, the most important ḏikr would have occurred during the waẓīfat at-taṣawwuf, the "Sufi office." This was the daily ḥuḍūr, when Ibn Abī Ḥaǧalah, as šayḫ, led the Sufis gathered around him in recitations from the Qur'ān and communal prayers. The ḥuḍūr was held after one of the five daily canonical prayers, and all Sufis of the chantry were expected to attend, with any absences duly noted.[19] The sessions usually followed a set order, beginning with recitations from the Qur'ān including Sūrat al-Fātiḥah (1), the beginning and end of al-Baqarah (2) along with its Āyat al-Kursī or "Throne Verse" (2:256), then al-Iḫlāṣ (112), and the final two sūrahs known as the al-Muʿawwiḏatān (i.e., the two

---

17   Amin, al-Awqāf, pp. 204-13, and Trimingham, Spencer J., The Sufi Orders in Islam, London 1971, pp. 194-207.

18   Schallenbergh, Gino, "Intoxication and Ecstasy: Sufi Terminology in the Work of Ibn al-Qayyim al-Ǧawziya", in: Vermeulen, Urbain and Jo van Steenbergen (eds.), Egypt and Syria in the Fatimid, Ayyubid and Mamluk Eras IV, Leuven 2005, pp. 459-74. Also see Bell, Joseph Norment, Love Theory in Later Hanbalite Islam, Albany 1979, pp. 92-103.

19   Amin, al-Awqāf, pp. 208-10, Fernandes, Khanqah, pp. 54-58, and Homerin, "Souls", pp. 71.

requests for refuge with God = 113-114). Then Ibn Abī Ḥaǧalah would have presided over the *ḏikr*, which consisted of the repetition of prayers combining praise of God (*tamḥīd*) with declarations of His greatness (*takbīr*), glory (*tasbīḥ*), and oneness (*tahlīl*), followed by prayers for the prophet Muḥammad, and appeals for God's forgiveness (*istiǧfār*).[20]

There is nothing particularly mystical about the contents or ritual of the *ḥuḍūr* that would specifically require Sufi involvement. Yet in Mamluk domains, Sufis with their presumed piety and ascetical life styles were often viewed as conduits for God's blessings. This was vital to the *ḥuḍūr* of the *ḫānqāh*, which reflected the founder's desire to earn divine favor by supporting religious institutions and activities. But in addition to the blessings derived from charity, in general, the *ḥuḍūr* offered more regularized spiritual benefits. For the religious merit that accrued from the Sufis' daily Qurʾān readings and prayers was dedicated, first of all, to the *ḫānqāh*'s founder and his relatives both in this life and the next, and only, thereafter, to the members of the larger Muslim community.[21]

In addition to the daily *ḥuḍūr*, Ibn Abī Ḥaǧalah met outside of the *ḫānqāh* with other members of the religious establishment to say prayers in difficult times, including those of famine and plague, and on other, happier, special occasions. Thus in 756/1355, when the powerful Mamluk amir Šayḫū (or Šayḫūn; d. 757/1357), then commander of the army, dedicated his *ḫānqāh* complex, elite Mamluk amirs and important religious officials attended this gala event. The highlight of the occasion occurred after the evening prayer when Šayḫū personally unrolled the prayer rug for the Sufi šayḫ and Ḥanafī scholar of the new *ḫānqāh* complex, Akmaladdīn Muḥammad ibn Maḥmūd ar-Rūmī (d.786/1384), who then led the congregation in the *ḥuḍūr*. Šayḫū's *ḫānqāh* was substantial and lavish, supporting instruction in the four major law schools, Qurʾān chanting, and the study of hadith, while also sponsoring a large number of students, Sufis, and their Ḥanafī šayḫ. Several attendees publicly recited verses in honor of the *ḫānqāh* and its benefactor, including Ibn Abī Ḥaǧalah who said: [22]

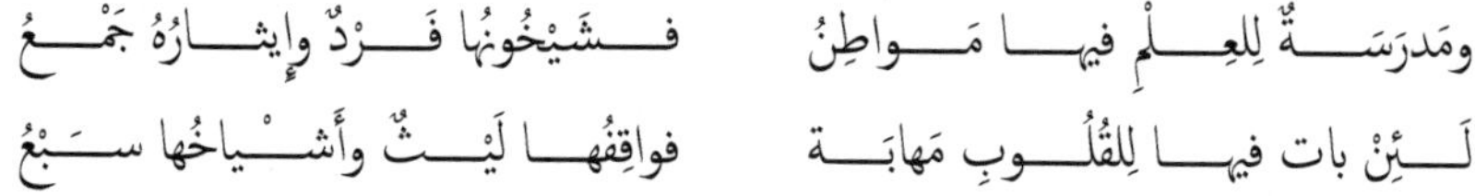

<hr>

[20] For descriptions of the *ḥuḍūr* in Arabic *waqf* texts, see Amīn, *al-Awqāf*, pp. 211-16, and *idem*, *Waṯāʾiq waqf as-Sulṭān an-Nāṣir Muḥammad ibn Qalāwūn*, Cairo 1982, pp. 75, 78-79, 110-11, and Fernandes, *Khanqah*, pp. 54-58. Also see Homerin, "Souls", pp. 71-73, and Trimingham, *Sufi Orders*, pp. 204-7.

[21] Homerin, "Souls", pp.72-83.

[22] Al-Maqrīzī, *Kitāb as-sulūk li-marʿifat duwal al-mulūk*, vol. 3, ed. S.A.F. ʿĀšūr, Cairo 1970, pt. 1, pp. 17-19; pt. 2, p. 527; *idem*, *al-Mawāʿiz*, 2:313-14, 421; Ibn Ḥaǧar al-ʿAsqalānī, *Inbāʾ*, 2:159-60, Fernandes, *Khanqah*, pp. 35-36, 106-108, and Parker, *Monuments*, pp. 71-74. Also see Ibn Abī Ḥaǧalah, *Sukkardān*, pp. 57-58, and *idem*, *Dīwān*, pp. 176 (#205); 222-23 (#324).

A school with many rooms for learning;
    Šayḫūn is but one man, yet how his impact multiplies!
Hearts hold his school in reverence,
    for its donor is a lion and its teachers, his pride![23]

A similar event occurred the next year in 757/1356, when another senior Mamluk amir, Sarġitmiš (d. 759/1358), dedicated his new madrasah and, once again, Ibn Abī Ḥaǧalah was among the honored guests who composed and recited verse for this special occasion.[24] Significantly, the madrasah of Sarġitmiš and the *ḫānqāhs* founded by Šayḫū and Manǧak were all in service to the Ḥanafi law school, its students, and scholars. This substantial support by these senior amirs may have been an attempt to make the Ḥanafi law school equal or even superior to the Šāfiʿī rite that had long been dominate in Egypt.[25] Ibn Abī Ḥaǧalah was clearly a beneficiary of this patronage, but the professional trajectory of one of his older colleagues better illustrates the attempts to increase Ḥanafi influence in Mamluk domains.

Like Ibn Abī Ḥaǧalah, Sirāǧaddīn ʿUmar ibn Isḥāq al-Hindī (704-773/1304-72) was not a native Egyptian, having been born and raised in India. After studying law, hadith, Sufism, and other religious subjects in Delhi, he went on the Hajj to Mecca, and then travelled to Cairo seeking employment around the year 740/1339.[26] He first clerked for the chief Ḥanafi judge of Egypt, Zaynaddīn al-Bisṭāmī (d. 771/1370), teaching law and composing legal opinions (*fatāwā*), and when al-Bisṭāmī stepped down as judge in 748/1347, al-Hindī clerked for the new chief Ḥanafi judge, ʿAlāʾaddīn at-Turkmānī (d. 750/1349), drawing up shares and contracts.[27] When ʿAlāʾaddīn at-Turkmānī died two years later, he was replaced as chief Ḥanafi judge by his son Ǧamāladdīn at-Turkmānī (d. 769/1368), and al-Hindī served him for the next eight years as his only deputy judge (*nāʾib qāḍī*), often adjudicating cases on his own.[28] Then, in 758/1357, the Ḥanafi judge of the army (*qāḍī l-ʿaskar*), ʿAlāʾaddīn Ibn al-Aṭrūš died, and al-Hindī asked the amir Šayḫū for the position. Šayḫū refused him, though he gave al-Hindī a handsome

---

[23] The Arabic term *sabʿu* is an instance of *tawriyah* or *double entendre* as it can mean "beasts of prey"/ "lions" as well as the number "seven", no doubt the number of teachers at the school.

[24] Al-Maqrīzī, *as-Sulūk*, 3:1:28-29; *idem, al-Mawāʿiẓ*, 2:403-05; Ibn Abī Ḥaǧalah, *Sukkardān*, pp. 54-55, and Parker, *Monuments*, pp. 59-60.

[25] Leonor Fernandes, "Mamluk Politics and Education: The Evidence from Two Fourteenth Century Waqfiyya", in: *Annales Islamologiques* 23 (1987), pp. 87-98, and Fernandes, *Khanqah*, pp. 1, 35, 37, 41, 48, 99, 102.

[26] Schacht, J. and Linda S. Northrup, "al-Shiblī, Sirādj al-Dīn", in: *EI²*, 9:433.

[27] Ibn Ḥaǧar al-ʿAsqalānī, *Inbāʾ*, 1:29-31; *idem, ad-Durar*, 3:230-31 (#2986); *idem, Rafʿ al-iṣr ʿan quḍāt Miṣr*, ed. ʿAlī Muḥammad ʿUmar, Cairo 1998, pp. 288-89; Ibn Taġrībirdī, *al-Manhal*, 8:273-76; *idem, an-Nuǧūm*, 11:120-21. Among Zaynaddīn al-Bisṭāmī's later positions was that of the Friday preacher at Manǧak's congregational mosque adjacent to the *ḫānqāh* where Ibn Abī Ḥaǧalah served as šayḫ of the Sufis; Ibn Ḥaǧar al-ʿAsqalānī, *ad-Durar* 3:240-41 (#3015), and 3:156-57 (#2809).

[28] Ibn Ḥaǧar al-ʿAsqalānī, *Inbāʾ*, 1:29; Ibn Taġrībirdī, *an-Nuǧūm*, 11:99.

additional salary (*iqṭāʿ*) as compensation. Not to be dissuaded, al-Hindi approached another senior Mamluk and Šayḫū's rival, Sarġitmiš about the vacant position. Sarġitmiš agreed, and al-Hindi was named Ḥanafī judge of the army. In this position, al-Hindi settled lawsuits brought to him involving Ḥanafī members of the army, and sources note that al-Hindi's Ḥanafī position was made equal to that of the Šāfiʿī military judge, which was unprecedented at that time.[29] Ibn Abī Ḥaǧalah congratulated Sirāǧaddīn al-Hindi for his new position with a poem:[30]

إذا مـــــا زادَ هَمِّـــيَ وَٱنْزِعـــاجِي   جَلَـــوتُ الـــرّاحَ في كَأْسِ الزُّجـــاجِ

مُـدامٌ قَـدْ غَـدَتْ مِـن نارِ قَلْبي   عَـلَى الثُّلُـثِ المُبـاحِ لَدَى المـزاجِ

فَحَيَّـــا اللهُ مَـــن أمـــسى نَـــديمي   عَلَيهـــا حـــينَ تُـــشرِقُ في الدَّياجِي

وحَيَّـــا بَـــلْدَةً فيهـــا مُحَيّـــا   سِراجُ الدّيـــنِ يَلْمَـــعُ كالـــسِّراجِ

إمـــامٌ في العُلُـــوم وفي القَـــضايا   فقَـوَّمَ أمْرَهـــا بعـــدَ ٱعْوِجـــاجِ

فَباتَـــتْ مِـــصْرُ في أمْـــنٍ وعَـــدْلٍ   وبات الـــشّامُ مُعْتَـــدِلَ المـــزاجِ

When my troubles and worries arise,
  I bring out a crystal cup with wine.
The wine was reduced by the fire in my heart,
  to be mixed as law allows.[31]
May God give long life to him who drank with me
  a wine aglow in darkest night,
May He give long life to the place
  where the face of Sirāǧaddīn shines like a lamp.
A leader in learning and in law,
  who set straight their crooked affairs.
Now, Egypt rests easy, safe in justice,
  while Damascus sleeps serene and sound!

Whatever the hyperbole in Ibn Abī Ḥaǧalah's verses, a number of sources praised al-Hindi's knowledge and dedication to the law, his honesty as a judge, his piety, and good character. Nevertheless, Šayḫū was vexed that he had been overruled by this appointment, yet before he could address the matter he was as-

---

[29] Ibn Ḥaǧar al-ʿAsqalānī, *Inbāʾ*, 1:30; Ibn Taġrībirdī, *al-Manhal*, 8:274; al-Maqrīzī, *as-Sulūk*, 3:1:38. Regarding the positions of deputy judge and judge of the army, see Petry, Carl F., *The Civilian Elite of Cairo in the Late Middle Ages*, Princeton 1981, pp. 228-29, 406, n. 15.

[30] Ibn Abī Ḥaǧalah, *Dīwān*, p. 94 (#88), and see the article in this volume by Thomas Bauer, pp. 59-60.

[31] Here, Ibn Abī Ḥaǧalah refers to *muṯallaṯ*, or a beverage reduced by two-thirds over heat. In the case of wine, this reduced the alcohol content so that, when mixed with water, it became a licit beverage. See Lane, E.W., *An Arabic English Lexicon*, London 1863, p. 394, and Wensinck A.J., "Ḫamr – 1. Juridical Aspects" in: *EI²* 4:994-997.

sassinated, and Sarġitmiš replaced him as commander of the army. Al-Hindī continued to be held in high regard by Sarġitmiš and Sultan Ḥasan, as both men vied for control of the Mamluk Empire. Then, in 759/1358, Sultan Ḥasan had Sarġitmiš seized and executed and, in the aftermath, others sought to extend their influence with the sultan, including another religious figure, Muḥammad ibn Maḥmūd ibn al-Hirmās (690-769/1291-1368), known as al-Hirmās.[32]

Unlike Ibn Abī Ḥaġalah and al-Hindī, al-Hirmās was not noted for his erudition or scholarship, and he was employed as a prayer leader at the congregational mosque of al-Ḥākim. He came to the attention of Sultan Ḥasan, however, because al-Hirmās was said to have the power of clairvoyance (*mukāšafah*). Some years earlier in 752/1351, Sultan Ḥasan had been deposed from his first reign, and replaced by his brother aṣ-Ṣāliḥ. During the latter's reign in 755/1354, the Hajj caravan set out from Cairo under the supervision of the Mamluk amir, ʿIzzaddīn Azdamur al-Aʿmā (d. 769/1368), and among the pilgrims was the chief Šāfiʿī judge of Egypt, ʿIzzaddīn Ibn Ğamāʿah (764/1363), and al-Hirmās. One day, Azdamur and Ibn Ğamāʿah were sitting near the Kaʿbah, when al-Hirmās joined them. Al-Hirmās bowed his head in silence for a while, then looked up and proclaimed: "There is no deity but God! Today the prince an-Nāṣir Ḥasan sits upon the throne of Egypt in place of the prince aṣ-Ṣāliḥ Ṣāliḥ, so take note!"[33] Azdamur noted the date of this prediction, and a few days later, news came that Sultan Ḥasan had indeed replaced aṣ-Ṣāliḥ on the very day of al-Hirmās' sudden pronouncement. Azdamur was very impressed with al-Hirmās and believed in his clairvoyance. When they returned to Cairo, Azdamur introduced al-Hirmās to Sultan Ḥasan, while recounting the miraculous occurrence. The sultan was delighted to have such a holy man near him, and he made al-Hirmās a member of his inner circle, such that al-Hirmās could approach Sultan Ḥasan without seeking prior permission.[34]

But al-Hirmās was jealous of other confidants of Sultan Ḥasan, including al-Hindī, and the Šāfiʿī legal scholar Muḥammad Ibn an-Naqqāš (720-63/1318-1361). Following the execution in 759/1358 of Sarġitmiš, who had supported al-Hindī, al-Hirmās went to Ğamāladdīn at-Turkmānī, the chief Ḥanafī judge of Egypt, with word that the sultan had ordered that al-Hindī be dismissed from office, which at-Turkmānī promptly did. Al-Hindī then left his judgeship and went to his home where, for the next year, he taught law and other subjects to a large number of students. Al-Hirmās then approached the chief Šāfiʿī judge of Egypt, ʿIzzaddīn Ibn Ğamāʿah and lodged a complaint that Ibn an-Naqqāš was not formulating legal opinions in accordance with the Šāfiʿī rite. Ibn Ğamāʿah held a public hearing on

---

[32] Ibn Ḥaġar al-ʿAsqalānī, *Rafʿ*, p. 288; idem, *Inbāʾ*, 1:30; Ibn Taġrībirdī, *al-Manhal*, 8:275-76, 11:120-22; Irwin, *Middle East*, pp. 142-43, and van Steenbergen, *Order*, pp. 156-58.

[33] Al-Maqrīzī, *as-Sulūk*, 3:1:10-11; 3:1:164, and Ibn Taġrībirdī, *al-Manhal*, 11:120-22.

[34] Al-Maqrīzī, *as-Sulūk*, 3:1:11; Ibn Ḥaġar al-ʿAsqalānī, *ad-Durar*, 5:21-22 (#4562); Ibn Taġrībirdī, *al-Manhal*, 11:120-22.

the matter, and concluded that Ibn an-Naqqāš should no longer be allowed to give legal opinions or hold office hours on legal matters; Ibn an-Naqqāš was humiliated.[35]

Soon thereafter, Azdamur, a most loyal supporter of al-Hirmās, was transferred to Damascus, while al-Hirmās chose to go on Hajj once again at the end of 760/1359. While al-Hirmās was away, Sultan Ḥasan renewed his friendship with both al-Hindī and Ibn an-Naqqāš, and the three men rode together on outings in and around Cairo. Al-Hindī and Ibn an-Naqqāš took this opportunity to protest the actions of al-Hirmās against them, and to inform the sultan of rumors circulating about al-Hirmās. Among them was that his miraculous prediction of Sultan Ḥasan's return to the throne, had actually occurred to a certain Šayḫ Abū Ṭarṭūr, and that al-Hirmās had overheard his prediction and then claimed it as his own when he spoke in front of Azdamur and Ibn Ǧamāʿah. Sultan Ḥasan became incensed with al-Hirmās, and when the Hajj caravan returned to Cairo at the beginning of 761/1360, al-Hirmās was barred from the sultan's presence. To celebrate the return of the Hajj caravan, the city of Cairo was decorated, and Sultan Ḥasan rode with his entourage down from the Citadel to the hospital and mosque complex founded by his grandfather, the sultan al-Qalāwūn (d. 689/1290). There, he visited the tomb of his grandfather and that of his father, the sultan an-Nāṣir Muḥammad (d. 741/1341). Sultan Ḥasan then went to the nearby madrasah attached to the complex, where he exchanged pleasantries and discussed religious matters with a number of senior scholars, including al-Hindī and Ibn an-Naqqāš. Finally, the sultan, accompanied by al-Hindī and Ibn an-Naqqāš, rode toward the mosque of al-Ḥākim, and on to the house that al-Hirmās had built nearby, no doubt with royal gifts. Sultan Ḥasan commanded that the house be torn down in front of al-Hirmās, who was subsequently stripped, flogged, and exiled to Syria.[36]

Sultan Ḥasan's severe corporal punishment of a religious official was unusual, but it may have resulted from the sultan's ire at being duped for years by a charlatan. In the aftermath of the scandal, Sultan Ḥasan reinstated al-Hindī to his judgeship and, along with Ibn an-Naqqāš, to the royal inner circle, which certainly included Ibn Abī Ḥaǧalah. By this time, Ibn Abī Ḥaǧalah had composed several notable works for the sultan including the *Sukkardān as-sulṭān* (*The Sultan's Sugar Box*, 757/1356) and the *Dīwān aṣ-ṣabābah* (*The Love Collection*, 760/1359).[37] Now, at

---

[35] Ibn Ḥaǧar al-ʿAsqalānī, *ad-Durar*, 5:21-22 (#4562); 4:190-92 (#4073); *idem, Raf*, p. 288; *idem, Inbāʾ*, 1:30; al-Maqrīzī, *as-Sulūk*, 3:1:47-48; Ibn Taġrībirdī, *al-Manhal*, 11:120-22.

[36] Al-Maqrīzī, *as-Sulūk*, 3:1:11, 47-48, 52-53; al-Maqrīzī, *al-Mawāʿiẓ*, 2:76-77; Ibn Taġrībirdī, *al-Manhal*, 11:120-22; Ibn Ḥaǧar al-ʿAsqalānī, *ad-Durar*, 5:22 (#4562); 4:190-92 (#4073); *idem, Raf*, p. 288; *idem, Inbāʾ*, 1:30. Also see Escovitz, Joseph H., "Patterns of Appointment to the Chief Judgeships of Cairo during the Baḥrī Mamlūk Period", in: *Arabica*, 30: 2 (1983), pp. 147-168, esp. 150, though Escovitz is mistaken on several details involving the dispute.

[37] Ibn Abī Ḥaǧalah, *Dīwān aṣ-ṣabābah*, Beirut 1980; *idem, Sukkardān*; Gruendler, "Ibn Abī Ḥajalah", p. 118.

the sultan's request, Ibn Abī Ḥaǧalah set about composing a collection of witty tales (*maqāmāt*) on various subjects including chess, but before Ibn Abī Ḥaǧalah could complete the work, Sultan Ḥasan was overthrown and killed in 762/1361, by one of his own Mamluks, Yalbuġā al-Ḥāṣṣakī (d. 767/1366).[38] Members of Sultan Ḥasan's circle of friends were shaken by his loss, and Ibn an-Naqqāš seems to have died a broken man the next year.[39] Al-Hindī fared better as he was able to retain his position as Ḥanafī judge of the army, though he had considerably less influence with Yalbuġā, who was, nevertheless, a strong partisan of the Ḥanafī law school.[40] As for Ibn Abī Ḥaǧalah, he remained šayḫ of the Sufis at Manǧak's chantry, and he continued to write works of prose, completing his collection of *maqāmāt*, entitled *Manṭiq aṭ-ṭayr* (*The Speech of the Birds*, c. 762/1361), and his *Salwat al-ḥazīn fī mawt al-banīn* (*Consolation for Mourning over the Death of Children*, c. 767/1366), a consolation manual for parents who, like him, had lost a child to the plague.[41]

Ibn Abī Ḥaǧalah also continued to compose poems for members of the ruling class, including the new sultan al-Manṣūr Muḥammad, and Yalbuġā, now commander of the army, thus pledging his allegiance to the new regime as he mourned the loss of Sultan Ḥasan.[42] Yalbuġā was an ambitious amir with dynastic aspirations of his own, marrying the lady Ṭūlūbāy, the former wife of Sultan Ḥasan, and for the next five years, he effectively ruled on behalf of the young sultans, al-Manṣūr Muḥammad (r. 762-764/1361-63) and al-Ašraf Šaʿbān (r. 764-78/1363-77). Yalbuġā was eventually overthrown and executed by a group of senior Mamluks and some of his own junior recruits in 768/1366, and over the next year, the sultan al-Ašraf Šaʿbān attempted to assert his own authority, albeit with the help of other senior Mamluks, including his father-in-law Ulǧāy an-Nāṣirī (d. 775/1373), who held a number of important positions over the next six years.[43] Perhaps from his service as Ḥanafī judge of the army, al-Hindī was on very good terms with Ulǧāy

---

[38] Ibn Ḥaǧar al-ʿAsqalānī, *Rafʿ*, 288; Ibn Ḥaǧar al-ʿAsqalānī, *Inbāʾ*, 1:30; Gruendler, "Ibn Abi Hajalah", pp. 118-25; Bahǧat and Muḫlif, "Introduction", *Dīwān*, pp. 36-37; Irwin, *Middle East*, pp. 142-43; van Steenbergen, *Order*, pp. 156-58.

[39] Ibn Ḥaǧar al-ʿAsqalānī, *ad-Durar*, 4:191 (#4073).

[40] Ibn Ḥaǧar al-ʿAsqalānī, *Rafʿ*, p. 288; *idem, Inbāʾ*, 1:30; van Steenbergen, Jo, "The Amir Yalbughā al-Khāṣṣakī, the Qalāwūnid Sultanate, and the Cultural Matrix of Mamlūk Society: A Reassessment of Mamlūk Politics in the 1360s", in: *Journal of the American Oriental Society* 131 (2011), pp. 423-43, esp. 440-41; Ibn Ḥaǧar, *ad-Durar*, 5:213-15 (#5079); Ibn Taġrībirdī, *al-Manhal*, 12:161-62.

[41] Gruendler, "Ibn Abi Hajalah", pp. 118, 123-25; Bahǧat and Muḫlif, "Introduction", *Dīwān*, pp. 30, 36-37; Robson, James, "A Chess *Maqāma* in the John Rylands Library", in: *Bulletin of the John Rylands Library* 36 (1953), pp. 111-27; Ibn Abī Ḥaǧalah, *Salwat al-ḥazīn fī mawt al-banīn*, ed. Muḥaymir Ṣāliḥ, Amman 1987.

[42] Ibn Abī Ḥaǧalah, *Dīwān*, pp. 85-87 (#65), 109-11 (#116), 288-90 (#429); van Steenbergen, Jo, "On the Brink of a New Era? Yalbughā al-Khāṣṣakī (d. 1366) and the Yalbughāwiyah", in: *Mamlūk Studies Review* 15 (2011), pp. 117-52.

[43] Ibn Ḥaǧar al-ʿAsqalānī, *Inbāʾ*, 1:73-74; al-Maqrīzī, *al-Mawāʿiẓ*, 2:399; Irwin, *Middle East*, pp. 144-49; van Steenbergen, *Order*, pp. 158-63, 187; *idem*, "Brink".

and several other powerful Mamluk amirs at this time, and so when Ǧamāladdin at-Turkmānī died in 769/1367, al-Hindī replaced him as the chief Ḥanafī judge of Egypt. Moreover, al-Hindī held rank and privileges comparable to his Šāfiʿī counterpart, setting a new precedent in the rise and prestige of the Ḥanafī law school in Mamluk domains.[44]

Though regarded as scholarly, affable, and humble, as the chief Ḥanafī judge of Egypt, al-Hindī was not afraid to stand up for the law and the rights of others, as Ulǧāy soon discovered. Among Ulǧāy's duties was to oversee the administration of religious bequests given to various institutions, and so he opened an investigation in to how these funds were spent at various law schools in order to pressure their beneficiaries into giving up a portion of their pay so he could spend it elsewhere. Al-Hindī was appalled by this, and he publicly confronted Ulǧāy on the matter, saying: "Your own revenues (*iqṭāʿ*) total one million dirhams a year, yet you will nickel and dime a poor legal scholar!" A surprised Ulǧāy responded defensively: "I am only taking these revenues for jihad, and to protect Muslims, and such things!" There were many scholars, judges, and other important officials in the room, and they sat in stunned silence, afraid to speak because of Ulǧāy's quick temper. But al-Hindī persisted: "For a hundred dirhams we could buy a Mamluk who could do this job instead of you! Where did you learn of jihad and Islam, except from us? If not for us, you would not even be a Muslim!" Al-Hindī was clearly riled, and he went on until Ulǧāy calmed him with an apology. Ulǧāy then cancelled his hearings on religious endowments, and left them as they were. The historian Ibn Taġrībirdī (d. 874/1470) noted that on that day, al-Hindī alone publicly opposed Ulǧāy when no one else dared speak a word, and he added: "Would that there be a judge like him in our evil times!"[45]

Professionally, Ibn Abī Ḥaǧalah also appears to have profited during the sultanate of al-Ašraf Šaʿbān, whom he praised in several odes, including a long poem celebrating the opening of a madrasah in 771/1369, which al-Ašraf Šaʿbān had built for his mother.[46] Ibn Abī Ḥaǧalah continued to laud other officials in his verse, and he composed an ode of congratulations to one of his benefactors, Manǧak, who al-Ašraf Šaʿbān had promoted to the important position of governor of Damascus.[47] Ibn Abī Ḥaǧalah also maintained his correspondence and literary exchange with the Andalusian scholar and courtier, Lisānaddin Ibn al-Ḫaṭīb (713-76/1313-75). Ibn Abī Ḥaǧalah had sent Ibn al-Ḫaṭīb a copy of the *Diwān aṣ-ṣabābah*, which Ibn al-Ḫaṭīb then read to Muḥammad V al-Ġāni bi-llāh (d. 793/1391), the Nasrid sultan of Granada. The sultan wondered why Ibn Abī

---

[44] Ibn Ḥaǧar al-ʿAsqalānī, *Inbāʾ*, 1:16, 30; al-Maqrīzī, *as-Sulūk*, 3:1:158, 196; Fernandes, "Mamluk Politics", p. 94; van Steenbergen, "Amir Yalbughā", p. 441.

[45] Ibn Taġrībirdī, *al-Manhal*, 8:276; Ibn Ḥaǧar al-ʿAsqalānī, *Inbāʾ*, 1:30-31; *idem*, *Rafʿ*, p. 288.

[46] Ibn Abī Ḥaǧalah, *Diwān*, pp. 198 (#277), 200-202 (#279); al-Maqrīzī *al-Mawāʿiẓ*, 2:399-400; Parker, *Monuments*, pp. 99-100.

[47] Ibn Abī Ḥaǧalah, *Diwān*, p. 96 (#95); Ibn Taġrībirdī, *al-Manhal*, 11: 278-79.

IBN ABĪ ḤAĞALAH AND SUFISM 25

Ḥağalah had focused only on carnal love, and so he challenged his courtiers to do better. This inspired Ibn al-Ḫaṭīb to write his own book, the *Rawḍat at-taʿrīf bi-l-ḥubb aš-šarīf* (*The Garden of Instruction on Noble Love*), which focused on the spiritual and mystical dimensions of love. Having finished this book, Ibn al-Ḫaṭīb sent copies to Cairo in 769/1368, including one for Ibn Abī Ḥağalah, and another as a bequest to the esteemed *ḫānqāh* Saʿīd as-Suʿadāʾ, where the Sufis eagerly read it.[48] Perhaps as a thank-you note, Ibn Abī Ḥağalah composed the following poem praising the *Rawḍat at-taʿrīf bi-l-ḥubb aš-šarīf*:[49]

أُصَافِي في المَوَدَّةِ كُلَّ صُوفِي   وآلَـفُ كُلَّ مَحْبُوبٍ أَلُوفِ

ولمْ أَعْرِفْ مَقَامَ الحُبِّ حَتَّى   أَتَى التَّعْرِيفُ بالحُبِّ الشَّرِيفِ

كتابٌ مِنْ بَعِيدِ الدّارِ أَمَسَتْ   بـهِ الأَوْراقُ دانِيَّةُ القُطُوفِ

حَدِيثُ ذَوي الهَوَى فيهِ قَدِيمٌ   يُقَوِّي الحُبَّ بالسَّنَدِ الضَّعِيفِ

وحارثُ أَرْضِهِ في كُلِّ فَضْلٍ   يَرَى زَرْعَ الصَّفا في كُلِّ صُوفِي

فكَمْ مَعْنى بـهِ يَحْويهِ بَيتٌ   أَحَبُّ إليَّ مِنْ قَصْرٍ مُنِيفِ

أَتَتْ أَذْكارُهُ وَقْفًا لِقَلْبِي   بمَا أَبْدَتْـهُ أَسْرارُ الحُرُوفِ

وزَهَّدَني تَصَوُّفُهُ إلى أَنْ   رأَيتُ الصُّوفَ مِن لِبْسِ العَفِيفِ

لَلُبْسُ عَباءةٍ وتَقَرَّ عَيني   أَحَبُّ إليَّ مِن لِبْسِ الشُّفُوفِ

I sincerely love every Sufi,
  and I'm attuned to every lover,
Yet I knew no station in love
  until *Instruction on Noble Love* arrived.
The book came from afar with pages
  full of fruit for the picking,
With talk of ancient lovers inspiring love,
  though who knows if it is true.
One gleaning each chapter will find
  a choice field on every Sufi kind.
How many subtleties are here in its house,
  dearer to me than a castle on high.[50]
Its sayings have stayed within my heart,
  with secrets revealed by its words.

---

48 Muḥammad al-Kattānī, "Introduction" to Ibn al-Ḫaṭīb, *Rawḍat at-taʿrīf bi-l-ḥubb aš-šarīf*, ed. Muḥammad al-Kattānī, 2 vols., Beirut 1970, 1:37-38.

49 Ibn Abī Ḥağalah, *Dīwān*, p. 188 (#245), and also see pp. 74-75 (#26).

50 There is a *tawriyah* here involving the words *bayt* ("house"/ "verse") and *qaṣr* ("castle"/ "concision"), thus the verse could also read: "How many subtleties are wrapped in its verse/dearer to me than concision sublime".

> Its Sufism drove me to abstinence,
>> till I saw wool as the robe of righteousness.
> Now the woolen wrap is pleasing to me,
>> dearer than a diaphanous gown!

As Ibn Abī Ḥaǧalah observed in this poem, the *Rawḍat at-taʿrīf* has chapters on many types of spiritual and mystical lovers, from the ancient Greek and Muslim philosophers, to Sufi theosophists, other Sufis who professed absolute oneness, and the saintly Sufis of the past. Ibn al-Ḫaṭīb carefully analyzed each group, and despite his misgivings with some individuals and their doctrines, he conceded that all of the lovers loved God in their own way.[51] He was especially careful not to condemn as heretics, Ibn al-ʿArabī and those associated with his mystical speculations, including Ibn al-Fāriḍ, and this omission may have been among the factors that led Ibn Abī Ḥaǧalah to compose a new work entitled *Ġayt al-ʿāriḍ fi muʿāraḍat Ibn al-Fāriḍ* (*The Sudden Downpour in Opposition to Ibn al-Fāriḍ*).[52] He began this work with a brief invocation to God and prayers upon the prophet Muḥammad, and then Ibn Abī Ḥaǧalah conceded the popularity of Ibn al-Fāriḍ's poetry:

> Ibn al-Fāriḍ's *Dīwān* is one of the most elegant collections of verse, with most precious pearls from land and sea. It is one of the quickest to wound hearts with lamentations over the empty encampments of the beloved, drawn from the outpourings of heartache from a forsaken lover with a heart broken by the fever of separation. People are fond of its rhymes and intensity. He has become so popular that few are those who have not seen his collected poems, or have not had his resounding odes ringing in their ears... But I did not see in his verse any explicit poems in praise of the Prophet (*al-madāʾiḥ an-nabawiyyah*).[53]

This last statement by Ibn Abī Ḥaǧalah is of interest since Ibn al-Fāriḍ did praise the prophet Muḥammad in his verse, yet not in the form of the poetic genre that came to be known as the *al-madīḥ an-nabawī*.[54] This genre was extremely popular in the Mamluk period, and Ibn Abī Ḥaǧalah composed five separate collections of verse praising the Prophet.[55] Yet, this genre was in its infancy when Ibn al-Fāriḍ died in the early 7th/13th century. Apparently, Ibn Abī Ḥaǧalah decided to

---

[51]　Ibn al-Ḫāṭib, *Rawḍat*, and Knysh, Alexander, *Ibn ʿArabi in the Later Islamic Tradition*, Albany 1999, pp. 172-84.

[52]　Ibn Abī Ḥaǧalah, *Ġayt al-ʿāriḍ fi muʿāraḍat Ibn al-Fāriḍ*, Cairo: Arab League Manuscript Institute, microfilm 319 (Taṣawwuf) of MS 31 (Adab), Sūhāǧ, Egypt: Maktabat Sūhāǧ (= *Ġayt-S*); Ibn Abī Ḥaǧalah, *Ġayt al-ʿāriḍ fi muʿāraḍat Ibn al-Fāriḍ*, MS 1846, Rabat: Bibliothèque Royale (= *Ġayt-R*). I am grateful to Dr. Ahmed Chaouqui Binebine, Director of the Roayl Library in Rabat, Nisrine Attar, and Oussama El Addouli for helping me to obtain a copy of the Rabat MS.

[53]　Ibn Abī Ḥaǧalah, *Ġayt-S*, p. 1; *Ġayt-R*, fol. 75a.

[54]　Th. Emil Homerin, *Passion Before, My Fate Behind: Ibn al-Fāriḍ and the Poetry of Recollection*, Albany 2011, pp. 77-102, 172-73, 236-39.

[55]　Ibn Abī Ḥaǧalah, *Dīwān*, and Bahǧat and Muḫlif, "Introduction", *Dīwān*, p. 24; ʿUmar Mūsā, *Adab ad-duwal al-mutatābiʿah*, Cairo 1967, pp. 458-63; an-Nabhānī, Yusūf, *al-Maǧmūʿah an-Nabhāniyyah fi al-madāʾiḥ an-nabawiyyah*, 2 vols., Beirut 1996.

exploit this perceived deficiency in Ibn al-Fāriḍ's verse in order to justify his use of the rhymes and meters of Ibn al-Fāriḍ's poems in order to compose panegyrics worthy of the Prophet. Further, Ibn Abī Ḥaǧalah noted that, following his poems, he would add a biographical notice on Ibn al-Fāriḍ, including what had been said for and against him and his ilk, who were regarded as controversial Sufis. In this way, Ibn Abī Ḥaǧalah hoped to expose the heresy hidden in this verse and so set straight those who foolishly admired Ibn al-Fāriḍ's poems. In the meantime, Ibn Abī Ḥaǧalah offered his reader a brief notice to Ibn al-Fāriḍ by Ǧaʿfar al-Udfuwī (d. 748/1347):[56]

> Ibn al-Fāriḍ has a collection of poetry, most of which follows the Sufi way. How fine is his ode rhyming in "F" that begins:

قَلْـــبِي يُحَـــدِّثُنِي بِأَنَّـــكَ مُثْلِفِـــي

> "My heart tells me that you are its destruction…"

> And his ode rhyming in "L" that begins:

هوَ الحُبُّ فَاسْلَمْ بِالحَشا ما الهَوَى سَهْلُ

> "It is love, so guard your heart, passion is not easy…"

> And his ode rhyming in "K" that begins:

تِـــهْ دَلَالاً فَأَنْـــتَ أَهْـــلٌ لِذالِـــكا

> "Be proud in coquetry, for you are worthy of that…"

> As for his poem the *Ode in T-Major* (*at-Tāʾiyyah al-kubrā*) in the opinion of religious scholars, it is unsatisfactory, intimating ruinous affairs. He was a passionate lover, loving absolute beauty, to the point that he loved a camel! Numerous stories like that are told about him, and other occurrences have been recorded. Concerning him, people are split between those who believe him to be sincere and those who believe him to be a heretic.

When citing from al-Udfuwī, Ibn Abī Ḥaǧalah appears to have altered the Arabic of the original to accommodate his rhymed prose, but what is more significant are portions of the original notice that Ibn Abī Ḥaǧalah left out. For instance, al-Udfuwī calls Ibn al-Fāriḍ "the outstanding Sufi" (*aṣ-ṣūfī al-fāḍil*), and though he may have had misgivings about the uninitiated reading the *Ode in T-Major*, al-Udfuwī clearly had a high opinion of Ibn al-Fāriḍ, ending his notice to him with a warning to those who oppose him: "The ignorant will be distinguished from those with vision on the day 'when inner hearts will be put to the test' (Q 86:9), may God be satisfied with him!"[57]

---

56   Ibn Abī Ḥaǧalah, *Ġayṯ-S*, pp. 1-4; *Ġayṯ-R*, fols. 75a-76b.
57   Ǧaʿfar al-Udfuwī, *al-Badr as-sāfir fī uns al-musāfir*, Cairo: Arab League Manuscript Institute, microfilm 81 (Taʾrīḫ) of MS 4201, Istanbul: Maktabat Fatḥi, fols. 42b-43a.

After this brief introduction, Ibn Abī Ḥaǧalah recorded his poems in praise of Muḥammad modelled on Ibn al-Fāriḍ's odes, citing the first verse of the target poem, followed by his imitation (*muʿāraḍah*).[58] An example of Ibn Abī Ḥaǧalah's method can be seen in his ode inspired by Ibn al-Fāriḍ's *al-Lāmiyyah*, which begins:[59]

هوَ الحُبُّ فَآسلَم بالحَشا ما الهَوَى سَهْلُ   فَـــما آختــارَهُ مُـــضْنًى بـــهِ ولَهُ عَقْـــلُ

It is love, so guard your heart, passion is not easy;
   wasted by it, would you choose it,
      if you had reason?

Ibn al-Fāriḍ's poem is a ghazal of sixty-two verses, opening with a warning to those who think love to be an easy affair, and this sets the tone and mood of the poem. The poetic persona is a wise and experienced teacher, who advises a younger man on the trials and tribulations of love. He tells of his own self-sacrifice that led to his annihilation in love, for true, mystical love demands the eradication of the lover's selfishness. This is a long and bitter process, yet when successfully endured, the resulting joy is sweet, since the beloved ever abides in one's heart. The martyrdom of love is the predominate theme of these verses, and it is underscored by Sufi allusions and references that establish a spiritual resonance throughout this love poem.[60] By contrast, Ibn Abī Ḥaǧalah's imitation takes the form of a wine-ode of thirty-eight verses, which he entitled *The Choice Wine of the Monastery* (*sulāfat ad-dayr*) (vv. 1-2):[61]

هيَ الـرّاحُ إنْ طابَـتْ ومَـصْرِفُها حِـلُّ   دَفَعـتُ بهـا الهَمَّ الذي شُغْلُهُ شُغْـلُ

مُــــدامٌ إذا مـــا كان فيهـــا مَـــرارةٌ   فَجُدْ لي بها وآختَرْ لِنَفسِكَ ما يَحْلو

It is wine!
   When its price is paid, and it brings delight,
      I drive away worries that trouble my mind!

---

[58] The Sūhāǧ manuscript is in poor condition due to extensive water damage, especially on the pages containing the poems. Further, prior to pagination, the manuscript was probably dropped, since pages containing part of the *al-Kāfiyyah*, all of the *al-Lāmiyyah*, and a portion of the *al-Mīmiyyah al-ḫamriyyah*, are out of place and found later in the manuscript (pp. 206-12). The Rabat manuscript is in better condition and contains all of the poems, but it is incomplete, ending in mid-sentence on fol. 108a. Concerning *muʿāraḍah*, or "imitation", see van Gelder, G.J.H., "*Muʿāraḍa*", in: Meisami, Julie Scott and Paul Starkey, (eds.), *Encyclopedia of Arabic Literature*, 2 vols., London 1998, 2:534.

[59] Ibn al-Fāriḍ, *Dīwān*, ed. Guiseppe Scattolin, Cairo 2004, pp. 181-86.

[60] Homerin, *Passion*, pp. 32-49.

[61] Ibn Abī Ḥaǧalah, *Ġayṯ-S*, pp. 207-209; *Ġayṯ-R*, fols. 77a-78a. Printed editions of this poem based on *Ġayth-S*, pp. 207-209 may be found in Ibn Abī Ḥaǧalah, *Dīwān*, 322-24 (#2), and idem, *Ṣarāʾiḥ an-naṣāʾiḥ wa-tamyiz aṣ-ṣāliḥ min aṭ-ṭāliḥ*, ed. Abū ʿAbd Allāh ʿIzzat ʿAbd ar-Raḥmān as-Salafi Mutaṭabbib, Beirut 2003, pp. 94-97.

An ancient vintage, and if it be bitter,
> give it to me anyway,
>> and choose for yourself what is sweet.

Ibn Abī Ḥaǧalah uses nearly half of Ibn al-Fāriḍ's end-rhyme words, and occasionally he reuses a whole phrase as we see here at the end of the second verse, which echoes the third verse of Ibn al-Fāriḍ's love poem (v. 3):

نَـــصَحْتُكَ عِلْمًـــا بالهَـــوَى والذي أَرَى   مُخـــالَفَتِي فَـــاخْتَرْ لِنَفْـسِكَ مَــا يَحْلــو

I have warned you,
> knowing passion and my enemy,
>> so choose for yourself what is sweet.

Over the next eight verses, Ibn Abī Ḥaǧalah lauds this pure drink, which turns out not to be that of the grape as found among Christians in their monastery. Rather, this elixir is none other than the holy water from the Zamzam well in the holy precincts of Mecca. No matter the cost, the poets' goal is to be there once again in the divine presence, and Ibn al-Fāriḍ's lover is willing to sacrifice himself for the beloved (v. 32):

حَـرامٌ شِـفا سُـقمي لَدَيْهَـا رَضِـيتُ مـا   بـهِ قَـسَمَتْ لي في الهَـوى ودَمي حِـلُّ

Though she forbid to cure my sickness,
> I am pleased with what she gave me of love,
>> so my blood may be shed!

Whereas, Ibn Abī Ḥaǧalah is ready to die to reach the Kaʿbah (v. 17):

لَـــئِنْ رَضِـــيَتْ مِـــني بُحُمْـــرِ مَـــدامِعي   رَضِـــيتُ بِمـا تَـرْضى ودَمّـي لهـا حِـلُّ

If this requires my bloody tears,
> I am pleased by what is sanctioned,
>> and my blood may be shed for that!

As in another poem by Ibn al-Fāriḍ, Ibn Abī Ḥaǧalah laments that his body is in Egypt, though his heart still resides in Mecca's holy land as he imagines the pilgrims, praying, fasting, and standing at ʿArafāt, while invoking blessings upon the prophet Muḥammad (vv. 18-24).[62] At the end of his love poem, Ibn al-Fāriḍ pledges his eternal love to the beloved (v. 58):

لَأَنْـتِ عَـلَى غَـيظِ النَّـوَى ورِضَى الهَـوَى   لَدَيَّ وقَلْـبي سَـــاعَةً مِنـــكِ مَا يَخْلــو

---

62 Cf., Ibn al-Fāriḍ, *Dīwān*, p. 157, and Homerin, *Passion*, pp. 137, 139.

> Whether in parting's anger or passion's acceptance,
>> you are with me,
>>> my heart holding you every hour!

Ibn Abī Ḥaǧalah, however, transitions from the pilgrims' prayers for Muḥammad to his own prayer, beginning his final fourteen verses with *ʿalayhi ṣalātu llāhi* ("God's blessings upon him"), a common feature of many panegyrics to the Prophet composed during the Mamluk period.[63]

Most of Ibn Abī Ḥaǧalah's imitations follow this general pattern of using the rhyme, meter, and selected vocabulary and phrases from Ibn al-Fāriḍ's verse to construct poems in praise of Muḥammad. However, in two important instances, Ibn Abī Ḥaǧalah parodies or directly criticizes Ibn al-Fāriḍ, and, not surprisingly this occurs with Ibn al-Fāriḍ's two most explicit Sufi poems, the *al-Mīmiyyah al-ḥamriyyah* (*The Wine Ode Rhyming in M*) and the *at-Tāʾiyyah al-kubrā* (*Ode in T-Major*). Ibn al-Fāriḍ's *Wine Ode* spans thirty-three verses and begins:[64]

شَرِبْنَـا عَـلَى ذِكْـرِ الحَبِيـبِ مُدامَـة   سَكِرْنا بهـا مِـن قَبْـلِ أنْ يُخْلَقَ الكَـرْمُ

> In memory of the beloved we drank a wine;
>> we were drunk with it before creation of the vine.

Clearly this is no earthly vintage, and as the poem progresses, it becomes apparent that the wine is a metaphor for the love of God and recollection of Him (*dikr*), which have intoxicated the poet and his companions. Ibn al-Fāriḍ describes aspects of the wine, including its bouquet and flavor, the wine cup and other accessories, and how the wine cleanses the senses and heals the body, mind, and spirit. He briefly describes the wine in allusive terms due to its spiritual character, and then he closes with mention of its lasting positive effects on those who seek it out in order to achieve spiritual intoxication and mystical union.[65]

Ibn Abī Ḥaǧalah also composed a wine ode in imitation, and his poem of thirty-seven verses is entitled *Daughter of the Vines* (*bint al-kurūm*) and begins (vv. 1-4):[66]

تَكَرَّمَ لِي مِـن قَبْـلِ أنْ يُعْـرَشَ الكَـرْمُ   بِـــشُرْبِ مُـــدامٍ لا يُمازِجُهــــا الإثْمُ

مُــدامٌ أَدَمْـتُ الـــشُرْبَ مِنْهـــا لأَنَّهـــا   لِقُـــوتِ قُلُـــوبِ العـارِفينَ بِهـــا أُدْمُ

تَجَـــلَّى لنـــا في عـــالَمِ الذَّرِّ كَأْسُـــها   وطافَـــتْ بِجَنّـــاتِ النَّعِـيمِ بِهـــا نُعْـمُ

---

[63] For more on Ibn Abī Ḥaǧalah's poetic style see Bahǧat and Muḫlif, "Introduction", *Dīwān*, pp. 39-58.

[64] Ibn al-Fāriḍ, *Dīwān*, pp. 158-61.

[65] Homerin, *Passion*, pp. 165-75.

[66] Ibn Abī Ḥaǧalah, *Ġayṭ-S*, pp. 4-5; *Ġayṭ-R*, fol. 76a-b.

وَأَحْيــــا مَـــواتَ الأرْضِ رَشْحُ إنائِهـا   وَأَقْلَـــعَ عَمَّـــنْ هَمَّ يَشْرَبُها الهَمُّ

Before the vine was trained on the trellis,
    he gave me a drink of wine unmixed with sin,
An ancient vintage whose drink nourished me
    since it is the daily nourishment of the gnostics' hearts.
Its cup appeared to us in the World of Atoms
    as Nuʿm circled round with it in the gardens of grace.
The drops on its jar revived the lifeless earth,
    and all worry was rooted out from a worrier who drank it.

In these opening verses, Ibn Abī Ḥaǧalah's wine appears to resemble that of Ibn al-Fāriḍ, and in the second verse, Ibn Abī Ḥaǧalah uses the phrase *qūt qulūb* ("nourishment of hearts"), alluding to the title of the famous Sufi manual by Abū Ṭālib al-Makkī (d. 386/996). In this work, al-Makkī often quoted from the Qurʾān and the traditions of Muḥammad to demonstrate Sufism's compatibility with Sunni Islam, and he left aside speculative mysticism to focus on morals, ethics, and practice, something Ibn Abī Ḥaǧalah would have appreciated.[67] Then in the third verse, Ibn Abī Ḥaǧalah invokes the name Nuʿm, a beloved in Ibn al-Fāriḍ's *Wine Ode*, as she brings the wine around to those in the World of the Atoms. This is yet another Sufi reference, and most likely one to Sahl at-Tustarī (d. 283/896) and his teachings concerning the Day of the Covenant (*yawm al-mīṯāq*). On this "day" outside of time in pre-eternity, the spirits of all humanity, in the form of atoms of light, bore witness to God's oneness. At-Tustarī and other Sufis believed that through the constant recollection of God, a mystic might return to this day and so, for a moment, stand again in the divine presence.[68] This primordial covenant and recollection are key elements in Ibn al-Fāriḍ's verse, especially in the *Wine Ode*.[69] Yet in Ibn Abī Ḥaǧalah's poem, it soon becomes apparent that this wine is not that of love or recollection, but something dangerous and deadly (vv. 5-6):[70]

وزالَ بهـــا وَهْمِـــي القَـــدِيمُ لأَنَّـــني   تَوَهَّمْتُهـا مِـــنْ قَبْلِ أَنْ يُخْلَقَ الـوَهْمُ

وجَلَّـــثْ لنــا في كُلّ عَـــصرٍ وتَرْكُهــا   عَلَينـــا حَـــرامٌ مِـــثلما جُـــرِمَ الإثْمُ

But means of it, my ancient illusion vanished,
    for I had surmised it before imagination's creation,
And it appeared to us in every pressing,
    and its abstention was forbidden us, like committing sin.

---

[67] Knysh, Alexander, *Islamic Mysticism: A Short Introduction*, Leiden 2000, pp. 121-22.

[68] Bowering, Gerhard, *The Mystical Vision of Existence in Classical Islam: The Qurʾānic Hermeneutics of the Ṣūfī Sahl al-Tustari (d. 283/896)*, Berlin 1980, pp. 145-49.

[69] Homerin, *Passion*, pp. 172-75.

[70] Ibn Abī Ḥaǧalah, *Ġayṯ-S*, p. 5; *Ġayṯ-R*, fol. 76b.

Ibn Abī Ḥaǧalah now begins to list some of the harmful effects of this wine, for which humans and jinn have gone mad and squandered fortunes. In fact, the controversial Sufi figure al-Ḥallāǧ (d. 309/910) drank it straight and so blurted out love's secret. He is said to have declared "I am the True Reality!" (*anā l-Ḥaqq*) thus revealing his beloved's true name and his union with God. Many believed that this outburst was a proclamation of heresy, whether of incarnation (*ḥulūl*) or monism (*ittiḥadiyyah*), thus justifying al-Ḥallāǧ's execution.[71] Perhaps alluding to the Christian Eucharist, Ibn Abī Ḥaǧalah then states that were a priest to drink a third of this wine, he would no longer believe in the trinity. Not surprisingly, Christian monks trek to their monasteries to drink this wine, though the Jews have lost sight of it, and gone astray. Moreover, were a baby to nurse on the breast of this wine, he would not cry if his own mother were to die, further underscoring the unnatural and harmful character of this drink (vv. 7-15). In context of these verses, the wine of Ibn Abī Ḥaǧalah's ode may be a metaphor for those experiences of spiritual revelation (*kašf*) that lead to states of intoxication, which were highly controversial among more conservative Muslims.[72] As Ibn Abī Ḥaǧalah's contemporary, Ibn Ḫaldūn had noted, such experiences have also occurred to Christians and ascetics of other religious traditions, and so they are no proof of sound doctrine or practice.[73]

But this was certainly not the opinion of Ibn al-Fāriḍ whose wine has miraculous healing powers (v. 14):

ولَـو جُلِيَـتْ سِرًّا عَـلَى أُكْمَـهٍ غَـدا   بَـصيرًا ومِـن راؤوقِهـا تَـسمَعُ الـصَّمُّ

Could it be unveiled in secret to the blind, he would see,
and from the strainer's sound, the deaf would hear.

However, Ibn Abī Ḥaǧalah counters that, whatever the wine's special properties, sin is sure to follow, and those who seek the wine are not gnostics, as in Ibn al-Fāriḍ's ode, but mindless addicts (vv. 17-18):[74]

وكَمْ ضَـلَّ قَـوْمٌ عَـنْ سَـناها لأنَّهُـمْ   إذا ظَهَـرَتْ عُمْـيٌ وإنْ ذُكِـرَتْ صُمُّ

وكَمْ دَنْـدَنَ النَّـدْمانُ مِـنْ حَـولِ دَنِّهـا   وغَـنَّى ولا زِيـرٌ هُنـــاكَ ولا بَمُّ

---

71 Kynsh, *Mysticism*, pp. 68-82.

72 Ibn Abī Ḥaǧalah, *Ġayṯ-S*, p. 5; *Ġayṯ-R*, fol. 76b, and see Homerin, "Ibn Taimiya", pp. 226-28.

73 Ibn Ḫaldūn, *al-Muqaddimah*, Beirut n.d., pp. 108-109, 467-73; tr. Franz Rosenthal, *The Muqaddimah*, Princeton 1968, 1:221-22; 3:76-103. Also see Morris, James Winston, "An Arab Machiavelli? Rhetoric, Philosophy and Politics in Ibn Khaldun's Critique of Sufism", in: *Harvard Middle Eastern and Islamic Review* 8 (2009), pp. 242–291, esp. 270-72, 289, no. 55; Knysh, *Ibn ʿArabi*, pp. 184-97.

74 Ibn Abī Ḥaǧalah, *Ġayṯ-S*, p. 206; *Ġayṯ-R*, fol. 76b. Printed editions of vv. 16-41 of this poem may be found in Ibn Abī Ḥaǧalah, *Dīwān*, pp. 324-26 (#3), and *idem*, *Ṣarāʾiḥ*, pp. 91-94.

How many a folk went astray from its gleam; when it appeared,
    they were blind, when it was mentioned, they were deaf.
And how many tavern mates have buzzed around its jar
    singing, though without lute or lyre.

When Ibn al-Fāriḍ is asked to describe the wine, he answers (v. 22):[75]

صَـــفَاءٌ ولا مَـــاءٌ ولُطْـــفٌ ولا هَـــوًا   ونُـــورٌ ولا نارٌ ورُوحٌ ولا جِـــسْمُ

Purity not water, subtlety not air,
    light but not fire, spirit without body.

Ibn Abī Ḥaǧalah, in turn, parodies this description as nonsense (vv. 20-22):[76]

ومِـــنْ وَصْفِها مَـــا بَـــينَ زَمْـــزَمَ والـــصَّفا   صَـــفَاءٌ ولا مَـــاءٌ وشُرْبٌ ولا إثْمُ

وسَـــاقٍ ولا كَأْسٌ وشُرْبٌ ولا طِـــلا   ومَعْـــنًى ولا لَفْـــظٌ ومَحْـــوٌ ولا رَسْمُ

ألا هكـــذا وَصْفُ المُـــدامِ الـــتي غَـــدا   لِواصِفِها ابـــنِ الفـــارِضِ الفَـــرْضُ والحُكْمُ

It has been described, somewhere between Zamzam and aṣ-Ṣafāʾ:
    "Purity not water, drink without sin,
"A cupbearer but no cup, a drink but no wine,
    meaning without words, annihilation without a trace."
Is that not the wine's description
    that became Ibn al-Fāriḍ's ritual and creed?

Toward the end of his poem, Ibn al-Fāriḍ calls his listeners to seek out this amazing drink in its tavern amid music and happiness (v. 30):

فمَـــا سَـــكَنَتْ والهَـــمَّ يَومًـــا بِمَوضِـــعٍ   كَـــذلِكَ لم يَـــسْكُنْ مَـــعَ الـــنَّغَمِ الغَـــمُّ

It never dwells with anxiety at any time or place,
    just as sorrow never lives with song.

For Ibn Abī Ḥaǧalah, however, this wine is deadly, and must be purged from the body (v. 25):[77]

فغَـــنِّ عَـــلَى الدِّرْياقِ مِنْهَـــا فإنَّهَـــا   بِـــلا نَغَـــمٍ غُمٌّ بِـــلا دَسَمٍ سَمُّ

So sing to me of its antidote, for it is sorrow without song,
    poison without sustenance!

After this verse, Ibn Abī Ḥaǧalah transitions away from the wine in order to mention his journey through the desert to reach the sacred precinct in Mecca

---

75   Ibn Abī Ḥaǧalah, *Ġayt-S*, p. 206; *Ġayt-R*, fol. 76b.
76   Ibn Abī Ḥaǧalah, *Ġayt-S*, p. 206; *Ġayt-R*, fol. 76b.
77   Ibn Abī Ḥaǧalah, *Ġayt-S*, p. 206; *Ġayt-R*, fol. 76b.

(vv. 26-34), and he then concludes his ode with praise and blessings upon the prophet Muḥammad (vv. 35-41).[78]

Ibn Abī Ḥaǧalah is even less subtle in his imitation of the *at-Tāʾiyyah al-kubrā* (*Ode in T-Major*). Ibn al-Fāriḍ's original, also known as the *Naẓm as-Sulūk* (*Poem of the Sufi Path*), is a long poem of 760 verses, which details a lover's mystical quest to be reunited with his divine beloved. In this mystical allegory, the lover is eventually freed of his selfish ways and attains union during the Hajj pilgrimage. Further, over the course of the poem, Ibn al-Fāriḍ touches upon a number of Sufi concepts and themes, including the vital role of love and recollection (*ḏikr*) to bring about a spiritual transformation in the seeker's heart, leading to a vision of the underlying oneness of reality.[79]

Ibn Abī Ḥaǧalah likewise begins his unnamed poem lamenting his separation from his beloved, who has left him heartbroken and in a dire emotional condition (vv. 1-85). But in time, he arrives in the holy land of Mecca and carries out the Hajj pilgrimage, which restores him to health (vv. 86-139). He then praises God and His prophet Muḥammad, the Prophet's wives, progeny, and his companions who fought against the infidels. He is thankful that the Prophet cares for his followers and will intercede on their behalf on the Judgment Day, when the poet will drink from the heavenly spring of Kawṯar (vv. 140-229).

Ibn Abī Ḥaǧalah then turns to more polemical matters as he contrasts his beautiful verses that praise the Prophet, to Ibn al-Fāriḍ's ode that is filled with the ugly heresies of incarnation (*ḥulūl*) and monism (*ittiḥādiyyah*) (vv. 230-35). Ibn Abī Ḥaǧalah's religious way is love of the Prophet, not the false beliefs of those who have gone astray (vv. 236-94). Besides Ibn al-Fāriḍ, Ibn Abī Ḥaǧalah denounces other heretics by name, including Ibn al-ʿArabī, Ibn Sabʿīn (d. 669/1269), Ibn Isrāʾīl (d. 677/1278), and ʿAfīfaddīn at-Tilimsānī (d. 690/1291). Ibn Abī Ḥaǧalah claims that their words are misleading lies, and so these heretics are bound for Hell. By contrast, true believers follow the *šarīʿah*, and they will enter Paradise accompanied by the Prophet. Ibn Abī Ḥaǧalah then concludes his ode with additional prayers and blessings for Muḥammad, God's greatest prophet (vv. 295-347).[80]

Most of Ibn Abī Ḥaǧalah's imitations of the odes by Ibn al-Fāriḍ are innocuous panegyrics to Muḥammad, though in the case of the *Yāʾiyyah*, Ibn Abī Ḥaǧalah composed a *maqāmah* in praise of the Prophet, which includes a short ode in the same letter of Y as Ibn al-Fāriḍ's poem.[81] However, his imitations of the *Wine Ode* and the *Ode in T-Major* are much more strident in tone, and this is also the case

---

[78] Ibn Abī Ḥaǧalah, *Ġayṯ-S*, pp. 206-207; *Ġayṯ-R*, fols. 76b- 77a; *idem, Dīwān*, pp. 324-26 (#3); *idem, Ṣarāʾiḥ*, pp. 91-94.

[79] Ibn al-Fāriḍ, *Dīwān*, pp. 66-143; Homerin, *Passion*, pp. 177-242.

[80] Ibn Abī Ḥaǧalah, *Ġayṯ-S*, pp. 33-56; *Ġayṯ-R*, fols. 87b-94a.

[81] Ibn Abī Ḥaǧalah, *Ġayṯ-S*, pp. 79-89; *Ġayṯ-R*, fols. 95b-97b, and see the article by Maurice Pomerantz in this volume, p. 181.

with the second and third sections of the *Ġayt al-ʿāriḍ*.[82] In section two of the work, Ibn Abī Ḥağalah relates opinions from religious scholars who had denounced Ibn al-Fāriḍ, Ibn al-ʿArabī, and other Sufis believed to have had monistic tendencies. Ibn Abī Ḥağalah offers these opinions as sound advice, so that others will not be fooled by Ibn al-Fāriḍ's honeyed words. Ibn Abī Ḥağalah supports his refutation by quoting two opinions from the Qurʾānic commentary, *al-Baḥr al-muḥīṭ* (*The Wide Ocean*) by the noted scholar Abū Ḥayyān al-Ġarnāṭī (d. 745/1344), who condemned Ibn al-Fāriḍ and others with monistic tendencies. Then Ibn Abī Ḥağalah quotes a long section from Ibn Taymiyyah's epistle *al-Furqān bayn awliyāʾ ar-Raḥmān wa-awliyāʾ aš-Šayṭān* (*The Distinction Between the Friends of the Merciful and the Friends of Satan*), in which Ibn Taymiyyah cites verses from the *Ode in T-Major* as proof of Ibn al-Fāriḍ's heresy. This is followed by the opinion of the noted Šāfiʿī jurist Taqīyaddīn as-Subkī (d. 756/1355), that Ibn al-ʿArabī and his ilk are Sufis in name only, as they are ignorant and astray from the right path of the Qurʾān, the traditions of the Prophet, and acceptable religious law.[83]

Ibn Abī Ḥağalah next cites eight legal opinions (*fatāwā*) that were given in 711/1311 during a dispute over Ibn al-ʿArabī's *Fuṣūṣ al-ḥikam* (*The Bezels of Wisdom*).[84] Nearly all of the opinions declare Ibn al-ʿArabī and those like him to be heretics and/or infidels, and some critics went so far to call on government authorities to seize and destroy the writings of these hypocrites, and to execute them and their followers, for even if they were to repent eventually, their repentance would be unacceptable.[85] Ibn Abī Ḥağalah then cites several passages from Ibn al-Ḥaṭīb's *Rawḍat at-taʿrīf*, noting proudly that he had received his copy of the work from the author, who had modelled it on a copy of the *Dīwān aṣ-ṣabābah*, which Ibn Abī Ḥağalah had sent him in Granada. In these passages, Ibn al-Ḥaṭīb calls into question the validity of a popular Sufi saying attributed to God, that prior to creation, He was "a hidden treasure", which some believed

---

82 The second and third sections of the *Ġayt al-ʿāriḍ* have been edited and published as Ibn Abī Ḥağalah, *Ṣarāʾiḥ an-naṣāʾiḥ wa-tamyīz aṣ-ṣāliḥ min aṭ-ṭāliḥ*, ed. Abū ʿAbd Allāh ʿIzzat ʿAbd ar-Raḥmān as-Salafī Mutaṭabbib, Beirut 2003.

83 Ibn Abī Ḥağalah, *Ṣarāʾiḥ*, pp. 9-25; Aḥmad Ibn Taymiyyah, *al-Furqān bayn awliyāʾ ar-Raḥmān wa-awliyāʾ aš-Šayṭān*, Damascus 1962, esp. pp. 106-07, and see Knysh, *Ibn al-ʿArabī*, pp. 96-111, 129-30, 168-69; Homerin, *Arab Poet*, pp. 31-32.

84 Ibn Abī Ḥağalah, *Ṣarāʾiḥ*, pp. 26-40. The legal opinions had originally been collected by ʿAbd al-Laṭīf ibn ʿAbd Allāh as-Suʿūdī (d. 736/1335) in his book *Bayān al-ḥukm mā fī l-Fuṣūṣ min al-iʿtiqādāt al-mafsūdah*. A legal opinion was given by ʿĪsā az-Zawāwī (d.743/1342), ʿUmar al-Kattānī (d. 738/1337), Badraddīn Ibn Ğamāʿah (d. 733/1332), Masʿūd ibn Aḥmad al-Ḥanbalī (d. 711/1311), Muḥammad ibn Yūsuf al-Ġazarī (d. 711/1311), ʿAlī al-Bakrī (d. 724/1324), Muḥammad ibn ʿAqīl (d. 729/1329), and Ibn Taymiyyah. Also see as-Saḥāwī, Muḥammad, *al-Qawl al-munbī ʿan tarğamat Ibn al-ʿArabī*, ed. Ḥālid Ibn al-ʿArabī Mudrik, Master's Thesis, Ğāmiʿat Umm al-Qurā, 2 vols., Saudi Arabia, 1422/2001, 2:182, 228-63.

85 Ibn Abī Ḥağalah, *Ṣarāʾiḥ*, pp. 28, 39-40. These legal opinions were also incorporated into a later polemical work by Muḥammad al-Fāsī (d. 832/1429), *al-ʿIqd aṯ-ṯamīn fī taʾrīḥ al-balad al-amīn*, vol. 2, ed. Fuʾād Sayyid, Cairo 1962, 2:160-99, and see Knysh, *Ibn al-ʿArabī*, pp. 120-26, who summarizes the various opinions as found in al-Fāsī's work.

supported a primordial oneness.[86] While Ibn al-ʿArabī and Ibn al-Fāriḍ seem to have accepted this saying as true, Ibn al-Ḫaṭīb does not condemn them, nor does he include Ibn al-ʿArabī or Ibn al-Fāriḍ among those extremist Sufis who believed in absolute oneness to the extent of rendering the laws of Islam null and void, something which could not be tolerated.[87]

Ibn Abī Ḥaǧalah ends this section of his work, with four additional entries. The first consists of a long letter, slightly abridged, which Ibn Taymiyyah wrote to the Sufi šayḫ Naṣr al-Manbiǧī (d. 719/1319), who was an admirer of Ibn al-ʿArabī, and sometimes served as a spiritual adviser to Mamluk amirs. In this letter, Ibn Taymiyyah once again calls into question spiritual states of intoxication, which have led to outlandish statements, including that of al-Ḥallāǧ regarding his identity with God. Further, Ibn Taymiyyah accuses the monists of deviating from the true faith by following the religion of Pharaoh, who thought himself divine. Ibn Taymiyyah asserts that Ibn al-ʿArabī's *Fuṣūṣ al-ḥikam* greatly abetted the monist movement, which included Ibn al-Fāriḍ and his *Ode in T-Major*, though the latter was by no means as explicit as the writings of later heretics, especially ʿAfīfaddīn at-Tilimsānī.[88] Following this letter is another, by ʿImādaddīn Aḥmad al-Wāsiṭī (d. 711/1311), an outspoken Damascene critic of monism, who specifically condemns Ibn al-ʿArabī's *Fuṣūṣ al-ḥikam*, and the intoxicated states of the heretic monists, who should not be considered Muslims.[89] Ibn Abī Ḥaǧalah then concludes this section with comments by two of his contemporaries, including his fellow courtier Ibn an-Naqqāš, who had condemned Ibn al-Fāriḍ, Ibn al-ʿArabī and other monists along the lines of Ibn Taymiyyah, and, finally, a short statement denouncing the *Fuṣūṣ al-ḥikam* by Ǧamāladdīn Ibn Hišām (d. 761/1360), who appears to have been among Ibn Abī Ḥaǧalah's teachers.[90]

In the third and final section of the *Ġayṯ al-ʿāriḍ*, Ibn Abī Ḥaǧalah gives a scathing denunciation of the "gang that has spread corruption in the world, and who will not make amends".[91] Ibn Abī Ḥaǧalah profiles the heretical doctrines and evil ways of prominent members of this gang, including Ibn Sabʿīn,[92] Ibn al-ʿArabī[93]

---

[86] Ibn Abī Ḥaǧalah, *Ṣarāʾiḥ*, pp. 41-42; Ibn al-Ḫaṭīb, *Rawḍat*, 2:583-84; Knysh, *Ibn al-ʿArabī*, p. 181.

[87] Ibn Abī Ḥaǧalah, *Ṣarāʾiḥ*, pp. 43-45; Ibn al-Ḫaṭīb, *Rawḍat*, 2:603-607; Knysh, *Ibn al-ʿArabī*, p. 183.

[88] Ibn Abī Ḥaǧalah, *Ṣarāʾiḥ*, pp. 46-55. The letter was composed in 704/1304; see Ibn Taymiyyah, *Kitāb Šayḫ al-Islām ilā l-ʿārif bi-llāh aš-šayḫ Naṣr al-Manbiǧī*, in: *Maǧmūʿāt ar-rasāʾil wa-l-masāʾil*, 5 vols. in 2, Beirut 1983, 1:169-90; Fernandes, *Khanqah*, p. 97; Knysh, *Ibn al-ʿArabī*, pp. 51, 92-93.

[89] Ibn Abī Ḥaǧalah, *Ṣarāʾiḥ*, pp. 56-59; as-Saḫāwī, *al-Qawl*, 2:176-81.

[90] Ibn Abī Ḥaǧalah, *Ṣarāʾiḥ*, pp. 60-65; as-Saḫāwī, *al-Qawl*, 2:316; Knysh, *Ibn al-ʿArabī*, pp. 218-20.

[91] *Rahṭun yufsidūna fī l-arḍ wa-lā yuṣliḥūna*; Ibn Abī Ḥaǧalah, *Ṣarāʾiḥ*, pp. 66-72; as-Saḫāwī, *al-Qawl*, 2:351-63. This third section is missing from the Rabat manuscript of the *Ġayṯ al-ʿāriḍ*.

[92] Ibn Abī Ḥaǧalah, *Ṣarāʾiḥ*, pp. 72-76.

[93] Ibn Abī Ḥaǧalah, *Ṣarāʾiḥ*, pp. 76-80.

and his son-in-law Ṣadraddīn al-Qūnawī (d. 673/1274),[94] ʿAfīfaddīn at-Tilimsānī,[95] Abū al-Ḥasan aš-Šuštarī (d. 668/1269),[96] Ibn Hūd (d. 699/1299),[97] ʿAlī al-Ḥarīrī (d. 638/1240),[98] and, finally, Ibn al-Fāriḍ.[99] Here, Ibn Abī Ḥaǧalah admits that Ibn al-Fāriḍ's fame has spread far and wide and that many visit his grave to pay their respects, yet, his verse is filled with obscenity and infidelity, which have led people astray. In fact, Satan inspired this poetry, and so Ibn al-Fāriḍ's followers are themselves devils. Ibn Abī Ḥaǧalah concedes that depraved lovers and even some people of taste have admired and recited Ibn al-Fāriḍ's verse, but due to their ignorance of his corrupt state, and he adds that this was particularly the case for Ibn al-Fāriḍ's admirers among the common folk and the Turks. Then, Ibn Abī Ḥaǧalah's rhetoric becomes even more shrill and provocative:[100]

> Some suppose that Ibn al-Fāriḍ was among the slaves of love, but that is completely ridiculous. As for one who outwardly professes Islam, yet is inwardly a hypocrite and so favorably interprets the infidelity in all of his verse, alas for him, alas for his Islam, and alas for the religion of Muḥammad! By God, this only multiplies abomination and brings the Last Hour closer; this perpetrates and spreads error, and hastens the appearance of the one-eyed Anti-Christ (*Daǧǧāl*)! By God, by God, O believers in God, to jihad, to jihad! The Garden is before you and Hell behind! Protect Islam and save your children!

As with his accounts of other members of the monism gang, Ibn Abī Ḥaǧalah cites opinions by earlier scholars on Ibn al-Fāriḍ, and Ibn Abī Ḥaǧalah begins with one of his teachers from Damascus, aḏ-Ḏahabī, quoting his entry on the poet in the *Mīzān al-iʿtidāl* (*The Scales of Equilibrium*):[101]

> ʿUmar ibn ʿAlī, known as Ibn al-Fāriḍ. He took hadith from al-Qāsim ibn al-ʿAsākir, while cawing with pure monism in his poetry, and this is a grave misfortune. So be circumspect about his verse and don't rush in—but think well of the Sufis. But this [poetry] is only the garb of the Sufis, general allusions, philosophical expressions, and machinations. So I have advised you, and God is the point of return.

Ibn Abī Ḥaǧalah next gives an abridged notice to Ibn al-Fāriḍ based on aḏ-Ḏahabī's *Taʾrīḫ al-Islām* (*The History of Islam*):[102]

> Ibn al-Fāriḍ was the master poet of the age. The collection of his poetry is famous, and it is of the utmost beauty, subtlety, and perfection, except that he mixed in pure and ac-

---

94 Ibn Abī Ḥaǧalah, *Ṣarāʾiḥ*, p. 80.
95 Ibn Abī Ḥaǧalah, *Ṣarāʾiḥ*, pp. 80-81.
96 Ibn Abī Ḥaǧalah, *Ṣarāʾiḥ*, pp. 82-83.
97 Ibn Abī Ḥaǧalah, *Ṣarāʾiḥ*, pp. 83-86.
98 Ibn Abī Ḥaǧalah, *Ṣarāʾiḥ*, pp. 86-91.
99 Ibn Abī Ḥaǧalah, *Ṣarāʾiḥ*, pp. 100-102.
100 Ibn Abī Ḥaǧalah, *Ṣarāʾiḥ*, p. 101.
101 Ibn Abī Ḥaǧalah, *Ṣarāʾiḥ*, p. 101; aḏ-Ḏahabī, *Mīzān al-iʿtidāl*, Cairo 1963, 3:214-15.
102 Ibn Abī Ḥaǧalah, *Ṣarāʾiḥ*, p. 101; aḏ-Ḏahabī, *Taʾrīḫ al-Islām*, Cairo: Arab League Manuscript Institute, microfilm 1033(Taʾrīḫ) of MS 2917, Istanbul: Maktabat Aḥmad aṯ-Ṯāliṯ, 17:59-60.

cursed monism, using the sweetest expressions and finest metaphors, like sweet pastries
laced with venom! Here, I will mention verses that will prove my assertion, for he said—
and God is far above that:

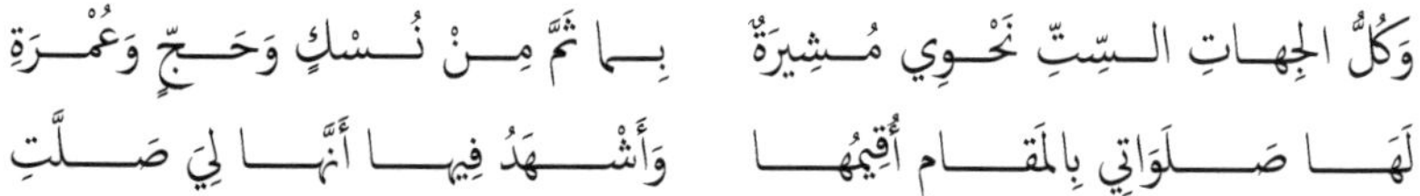

All six directions faced me with all there was
    of piety and pilgrimage, both great and small.
To her I prayed my prayers at Abraham's Station,
    and I witnessed in them her prayer to me.[103]

Ibn Abī Ḥaǧalah then quotes from the history *al-Bidāyah wa-n-nihāyah fī t-taʾrīḫ*
(*The Beginning and End in History*) by another of his teachers in Damascus, Ibn
Katīr:[104]

> Ibn al-Fāriḍ is the composer of the *Ode in T* on following the path of those so-called
> Sufis who ascribe to monism. More than one of our masters has criticized him for that
> poem...

Ibn Abī Ḥaǧalah then repeats several comments critical of Ibn al-Fāriḍ and his
fellow monists, cited earlier from al-Udfuwī, Abū Ḥayyān, and Ibn Taymiyyah,
after which, the Cairo manuscript ends. This abrupt ending, however, suggests
that something is missing from the manuscript, and this is verified by a later
scholar Muḥammad as-Saḫāwī (d. 902/1497). As-Saḫāwī drew extensively from
the *Ġayt al-ʿāriḍ* for his own work on Ibn al-ʿArabī and other controversial Sufis,
entitled *al-Qawl al-munbī ʿan tarǧamat Ibn al-ʿArabī* (*The Clear Statement on the Biography of Ibn al-ʿArabī*). Throughout this work, as-Saḫāwī quotes from Ibn Abī
Ḥaǧalah's *Ġayt al-ʿāriḍ*, and he gives a long separate notice to Ibn Abī Ḥaǧalah,
in which he describes the *Ġayt al-ʿāriḍ* in some detail. There, as-Saḫāwī quotes
Ibn Abī Ḥaǧalah's conclusion, which consists of Ibn Abī Ḥaǧalah's own legal
opinion condemning the harmful innovations and heresies contained in the
writings of this monist gang, including Ibn al-Fāriḍ's *Ode in T-Major*. Ibn Abī
Ḥaǧalah declares that the monists confirmed their apostasy with their own
words; they are heretics who, like maggots, infest and corrupt Islam.[105]

While quite favorable in his notice to Ibn Abī Ḥaǧalah and the *Ġayt al-ʿāriḍ*,
as-Saḫāwī offered a word of warning to the wise, namely, "to oppose Ibn al-Fāriḍ
among the Egyptians is always a grave affair of weighty significance".[106] As-
Saḫāwī and his mentor, the celebrated religious scholar Ibn Ḥaǧar al-ʿAsqalānī
(d. 852/1449), cautioned that Ibn Abī Ḥaǧalah was particularly extreme in his

---

¹⁰³ Ibn al-Fāriḍ, *Dīwān*, 82 (*at-Tāʾiyyah al-kubrā*, vv. 151-52).
¹⁰⁴ Ibn Abī Ḥaǧalah, *Ṣarāʾiḥ*, p. 102; Ibn Katīr, *al-Bidāyah wa-n-nihāyah fī t-taʾrīḫ*, ed. Fuʾād as-
Sayyid et al., Beirut 1985, 13:154.
¹⁰⁵ As-Saḫāwī, *al-Qawl*, 2:342-44.
¹⁰⁶ As-Saḫāwī, *al-Qawl*, 2:349.

views on Ibn al-Fāriḍ. Not only was he critical of the poet's *Ode in T-Major*, as were Ibn Ḥaǧar al-ʿAsqalānī and as-Saḫāwī, but he had gone so far as to declare Ibn al-Fāriḍ an infidel, while calling for the suppression of his writings, and death to his followers.[107] Though the death penalty was rarely imposed during the Mamluk period upon those accused of unbelief, heresy, and similar religious offenses, repercussions could still be severe, including jail time, flogging, and exile. Religious officials accused of such offenses might lose their jobs and face public humiliation.[108]

Therefore, Ibn Abī Ḥaǧalah's accusations against Ibn al-Fāriḍ and his supporters were not taken lightly. In fact, in the *Ġayt al-ʿāriḍ*, Ibn Abī Ḥaǧalah noted that his negative opinions of Ibn al-Fāriḍ had riled up an obstinate heretic, who became hostile toward him and slandered him.[109] While Ibn Abī Ḥaǧalah did not name this opponent, a number of individuals took issue with his outspoken and extremist views on Ibn al-Fāriḍ, including the head of the Ḥanafī law school in Mamluk domains, Sirāǧaddīn al-Hindī. Though both men appear to have had a collegial relationship during the reign of Sultan Ḥasan, the Ibn al-Fāriḍ issue drove a wedge between them. Al-Hindī was a highly respected legal scholar, who had also studied and written on Sufism, and he is reported to have been inclined toward monistic interpretations of God's oneness. Not surprisingly, he was a great admirer of Ibn al-Fāriḍ's verse, and he composed a favorable commentary on the poet's *Ode in T-Major*.[110] Of course, Ibn Abī Ḥaǧalah had explicitly denounced such commentaries when he declared:[111]

> As for one who outwardly professes Islam, yet is inwardly a hypocrite and so favorably interprets the infidelity in all of [Ibn al-Fāriḍ's] verse, alas for him, alas for his Islam, and alas for the religion of Muḥammad!

At the very least, Ibn Abī Ḥaǧalah had charged al-Hindī with guilt by association; at best al-Hindī was an ignoramus, but much more likely, Ibn Abī Ḥaǧalah was accusing him of being a dangerous heretic. As we saw earlier, al-Hindī was not one to back down from the bullying behavior of others, and so, as chief Ḥanafī judge of Egypt, he called a hearing to investigate Ibn Abī Ḥaǧalah's accusations against Ibn al-Fāriḍ and his supporters. The end result was that Ibn al-

---

[107] As-Saḫāwī, *al-Qawl*, 2:344-45; Ibn Ḥaǧar al-ʿAsqalānī, *Inbāʾ*, 1:108; *idem, ad-Durar*, 1:351, and see Homerin, *Arab Poet*, pp. 58-59, 121, n. 59.

[108] Petry, Carl, *The Criminal Underworld in a Medieval Islamic Society*, Chicago 2012, pp. 163-180, and note the example of al-Hirmās discussed earlier.

[109] Ibn Abī Ḥaǧalah, *Sarāʾiḥ*, p. 10.

[110] Ibn Ḥaǧar al-ʿAsqalānī, *Inbāʾ*, 1:29, 31; *idem, Rafʿ*, p. 288; *idem, ad-Durar*, 3:230-31 (#2986); Ibn Taġrībirdī, *al-Manhal*, 8:274. Ibrāhim al-Biqāʿī (d. 885/1480) noted that al-Hindī's commentary may not have contained the heresies found in earlier commentaries composed by followers of Ibn al-ʿArabī, though al-Biqāʿī denounced Ibn al-Fāriḍ's verse and any commentary on it; al-Biqāʿī, Ibrāhim, *Ṣawāb al-ǧawāb li-s-sāʾil al-murtāb al-muʿāriḍ al-muǧādil fī kufr Ibn al-Fāriḍ*, microfilm of MS 2040, Leiden Bibliotheek der Rijksuniversiteit, fols. 55b-57a.

[111] Ibn Abī Ḥaǧalah, *Sarāʾiḥ*, 101.

Fārid was exonerated from all charges against him, while Ibn Abī Ḥaǧalah was reprimanded for his extremist views. Ibn Abī Ḥaǧalah was further chastised in a number of poems composed on the case:[112]

يا آبْـــنَ أبي حَجَـــلَةٍ أَسَـــأْتَ مُـــذ عارَضْـــتَ لِلـشَّيْخِ الذي ما عارَضَـك

بعَـــارِضٍ أَشَـــنْتَ فيـــهِ عِرْضَـــهُ فَـــلا تَلُمْنـــا إنْ نَتَفْنـــا عارِضَـك

O Ibn Abī Ḥaǧalah, you did wrong when you opposed
  the master who never wronged you!
In the *ʿĀriḍ* you disgraced his honor,
  so don't blame us if we pluck out your beard!

Another couplet praised al-Hindī for defending Ibn al-Fāriḍ, while a third poem punned on the name Ibn Abī Ḥaǧalah to lampoon him as the plucked partridge.[113] But perhaps the most extraordinary composition on Ibn Abī Ḥaǧalah's reprimand was a poem of forty-six verses in the form of a letter to Ibn Abī Ḥaǧalah. The poet, who calls himself Sibṭ al-Imām al-Mawṣlī, opens with praise and glory to God, the creator, the first and the last, to whom all will return, the One who is beyond all human comprehension and speculation. The poet asks God to bless the prophet Muḥammad, his wives, their progeny, and his companions (vv.1-18), and then he directly addresses Ibn Abī Ḥaǧalah. He warns him that he is in over his head when he criticizes Ibn al-Fāriḍ and other great Sufis, for he lacks their selfless love and profound spiritual knowledge (vv. 19-29):[114]

أَمْ ذُقْتَ ما ذاقُوهُ مِن طِيبِ المَسَرَّةِ بالوِصالِ أَشَرِبْتَ ما شَرِبُوه مِن كَأْسِ المَحَبَّةِ والتّعـالَي

أَمْ كُنْتَ مُطَّلِعًا عَلَى ماذا أُجِيبُوا في السُّؤالِ أَمْ شاهَدَتْ عَيْناكَ ما شَهِدوهُ مِن سِرِّ الجَمالِ

هل جاءَكَ الوَحْيُ المُنَبِّي أَنّ ذاكَ مِنَ المُحالِ ولَئِمـا دَهَشوا بِمـا وَجَدُوهُ عـنْ سَـقطِ المَقـالِ

أَمْ قِيلَ إنْ لم تَفْعَلَنَّ فأَنْتَ مِنْ أَهْلِ الـشِّمالِ أَمْ قـالَ رَبُّكَ قُـمْ وقُـلْ فيهِم وبالِـغْ باحْتِفـالِ

Have you drunk as they did from the cup of love and loftiness,
  or tasted what they tasted of the pleasant joy of union?
Or did your eyes see what they saw of secret beauty,
  or were you told about the answers to their prayers?

---

[112] As-Saḫāwī, *al-Qawl*, 2:345. I have yet to find a detailed account of the hearing, which took place between 769-73/1368-1372, during al-Hindī's tenure as chief Ḥanafī judge of Egypt; Ibn Ḥaǧar al-ʿAsqalānī, *Rafʿ*, pp. 288-89. Al-Biqāʿī thought that al-Hindī had a hidden agenda and was biased toward Ibn al-Fāriḍ in his reprimand of Ibn Abī Ḥaǧalah, whose *Ġayt al-ʿāriḍ* was an important source for al-Biqāʿī's own refutations of Ibn al-ʿArabī and Ibn al-Fāriḍ; al-Biqāʿī, Ibrāhīm, *Maṣraʿ at-taṣawwuf*, ed. ʿAbd ar-Raḥmān al-Wakīl, Cairo 1953, esp. 55-56, 150-68; idem, *Ṣawāb al-ǧawāb*, fol. 55b.

[113] As-Saḫāwī, *al-Qawl*, 2:345.

[114] As-Saḫāwī, *al-Qawl*, 2:346-48, vv. 25-29.

> Perhaps they were in awe from what they found beyond all words,
>   or did inspiration come to you announcing that was all absurd?
> Or did your Lord tell you: "Rise and speak about them, overdo it as you will!"
>   or was it said to you: "If you don't do it, you will surely go to Hell!"

The poet reminds Ibn Abī Ḥağalah, that come the Judgment Day, he will be punished for the vile things he has said and done against these saintly folk who are close to God. He should, therefore, fear God and repent, especially of his false accusations that their writings are full of heresy. The poet asks Ibn Abī Ḥağalah if he thinks himself more knowledgeable than the great masters of the past; if so, he is badly mistaken. Rather than criticize others, Ibn Abī Ḥağalah should put his own affairs in order, beginning with his defective verse (vv. 30-39). The poet advises Ibn Abī Ḥağalah to refrain from slandering others, lest he prove to be a hypocrite, and so forfeit his own life. Instead, Ibn Abī Ḥağalah should return to God and seek His forgiveness. The poet then concludes his poem asking for God's blessings on the Judgment Day, and he prays to find a place in heaven near the prophets and great saints (vv. 40-46).

Though Ibn Abī Ḥağalah suffered a reprimand and was the target of public ridicule, he appears to have been spared any further grief, as was suffered by some other opponents of Ibn al-Fāriḍ.[115] No doubt, Ibn Abī Ḥağalah's long relationship with Manğak al-Yūsufī, then governor of Damascus and himself a guardian of public morals, was an asset at this troubled time, and Ibn Abī Ḥağalah retained his position as the šayḫ of the Sufis at Manğak's ḫānqāh. Sometime later, in 773/1372, al-Hindī died, followed in 775/1373 by his Mamluk patron Ulğāy, who had unsuccessfully revolted against the sultan. Soon thereafter, al-Ašraf Šaʿbān called Manğak al-Yūsufī back to Cairo to serve as viceroy of the empire and commander of the army, but whatever benefits Ibn Abī Ḥağalah might have gained from his patron's good fortune were short lived as both he and Manğak died the following year in 776/1375.[116] Significantly, Ibn Abī Ḥağalah held fast to his opinions against Ibn al-Fāriḍ and the monists, for shortly before his death, he willed that a copy of his Ġayṯ al-ʿāriḍ be buried with him, and so it was.[117]

Sufism was a major factor in Ibn Abī Ḥağalah's life, from his birth and early days in his great grandfather's Sufi lodge in Tlemcen, throughout his later studies as a young man in Damascus, and during his many years in Cairo, where he served as a Sufi šayḫ at a ḫānqāh until his death. Yet Ibn Abī Ḥağalah was not an otherworldly ascetic, and he was quite comfortable in the sultan's court with fellow courtiers and men of letters. A devotional streak is suggested by his many

---

[115] Little, Donald, "The Historical and Historiographical Significance of the Detention of Ibn Taymiyya", in: *International Journal of Middle Eastern Studies* 4 (1973), pp. 311-27; Homerin, *Arab Poet*, pp. 59-60; 62-75.

[116] Ibn Ḥağar al-ʿAsqalāni, *Rafʿ*, pp. 288-89; *idem, Inbāʾ*, 1:31, 73-74, 148; al-Maqrizi, *al-Mawāʿiẓ*, 2:323; *idem, as-Sulūk*, 3:1:212-14, 224-25, 243-44, 247; van Steenbergen, *Order*, pp. 183, 194.

[117] Ibn Ḥağar al-ʿAsqalāni, *Inbāʾ*, 1:107-108, 148; as-Saḫāwi, *al-Qawl*, 2:344.

panegyrics to the prophet Muḥammad, but he also composed numerous poems praising sultans, Mamluk amirs, religious officials, and other men of state. No doubt, his more worldly life was supported, at least in part, by his Sufi profession and the financial security it brought. In fact, Ibn Abī Ḥaǧalah fits securely into Ibn Taymiyyah's category of "funded Sufis," as he was supported by religious bequests and attached to a chantry. Ibn Abī Ḥaǧalah carried out his religious duties there, but clearly he did not renounce the more worldly aspects of his life as a litterateur. But neither was his position as a Sufi šayḫ a cynical ruse, and as evidenced in his *Ġayt al-ʿāriḍ fī muʿāraḍat Ibn al-Fāriḍ*, he was knowledgeable about Islamic mysticism in its various forms, some of which he vigorously denounced when they were at odds with his conservative juridical Sufism. Nevertheless, Ibn Abī Ḥaǧalah's vociferous rejection of Ibn al-Fāriḍ struck some of his contemporaries and later writers as intolerant and misguided. In fact, by the 8th/14th century, Ibn al-Fāriḍ's verse was enormously popular in Egypt, where his saintly reputation was on the rise, as Ibn Abī Ḥaǧalah begrudgingly had to admit. Ibn Abī Ḥaǧalah may have sought to rectify this situation with his *Ġayt al-ʿāriḍ* and its imitations and refutations, but he could not match Ibn al-Fāriḍ's saintly reputation or his elegant odes, which came to epitomize the best in Arabic Sufi poetry.

Bibliography

Primary Sources:

Amin, Muḥammad Muḥammad, *Waṯāʾiq waqf as-sulṭān an-Nāṣir Muḥammad ibn Qalāwūn*, Cairo 1982.

al-Biqāʿī, Ibrāhīm, *Maṣraʿ at-taṣawwuf*, ed. ʿAbd ar-Raḥmān al-Wakīl, Cairo 1953.

al-Biqāʿī, Ibrāhīm, *Ṣawāb al-ǧawāb li-s-sāʾil al-murtāb al-muʿāriḍ al-muǧādil fī kufr Ibn al-Fāriḍ*, microfilm of MS 2040, Leiden, Bibliotheek der Rijksuniversiteit.

aḏ-Ḏahabī, Muḥammad, *Mīzān al-iʿtidāl*, 4 vols., Cairo 1963.

aḏ-Ḏahabī, Muḥammad, *Taʾrīkh al-Islām*, Cairo, Arab League Manuscript Institute, microfilm 1033 (Taʾrīḫ), of MS 2917, Istanbul, Maktabat Aḥmad aṯ-Ṯāliṯ, vol. 17: 59-60.

al-Fāsī, Muḥammad, *al-ʿIqd aṯ-ṯamīn fī taʾrīḫ al-balad al-amīn*, vol. 2, ed. Fuʾād Sayyid, Cairo 1962.

Ibn Abī Ḥaǧalah, Aḥmad, *Dīwān Ibn Abī Ḥaǧalah*, ed. Muǧāhid Muṣṭafā Bahǧat and Aḥmad Ḥamīd Muḫlif, Amman 2010.

Ibn Abī Ḥaǧalah, Aḥmad, *Dīwān aṣ-ṣabābah*, Beirut 1980.

Ibn Abī Ḥaǧalah, Aḥmad, *Ġayt al-ʿāriḍ fī muʿāraḍat Ibn al-Fāriḍ*, Cairo, Arab League Manuscript Institute, microfilm 319 (Taṣawwuf) of MS 31 (Adab), Sūhāǧ, Egypt, Maktabat Sūhāǧ.

Ibn Abī Ḥaǧalah, Aḥmad, *Ġayṯ al-ʿāriḍ fī muʿāraḍat Ibn al-Fāriḍ*, MS 1846, Rabat, Bibliothèque Royale.

Ibn Abī Ḥaǧalah, Aḥmad, *Salwat al-ḥazīn fī mawt al-banīn*, ed. Muḥaymir Ṣāliḥ, Amman 1987.

Ibn Abī Ḥaǧalah, Aḥmad, *Ṣarāʾiḥ an-naṣāʾiḥ wa-tamyīz aṣ-ṣāliḥ min aṭ-ṭāliḥ*, ed. Abū ʿAbd Allāh ʿIzzat ʿAbd ar-Raḥmān as-Salafī Mutaṭabbib, Beirut 2003.

Ibn Abī Ḥaǧalah, Aḥmad, *Sukkardān as-sulṭān*, ed. ʿAlī Muḥammad ʿUmar, Cairo 2001.

Ibn al-Fāriḍ, ʿUmar, *Dīwān*, ed. Guiseppe Scattolin, Cairo 2004.

Ibn al-Ḫāṭib, Lisānaddīn, *Rawḍat at-taʿrīf bi-l-ḥubb aš-šarīf*, 2 vols., ed. Muḥammad al-Kattānī, Beirut 1970.

Ibn Ḥaǧar al-ʿAsqalānī, Aḥmad, *ad-Durar al-kāminah fī ʿayān al-miʾah aṯ-ṯāminah*, 5 vols., ed. Muḥammad Sayyid Ğād al-Ḥaqq, Cairo 1966.

Ibn Ḥaǧar al-ʿAsqalānī, Aḥmad, *Inbāʾ al-ġumr bi-anbāʾ al-ʿumr*, 9 vols. in 5, ed. Muḥammad ʿAbd al-Muʿīd Ḫān, Beirut 1986.

Ibn Ḥaǧar al-ʿAsqalānī, Aḥmad, *Rafʿ al-iṣr ʿan quḍāt Miṣr*, ed. ʿAlī Muḥammad ʿUmar, Cairo 1998.

Ibn Katīr, Ismāʿīl, *al-Bidāyah wa-n-nihāyah fī t-taʾrīkh*, 14 vols., ed. Fuʾād as-Sayyid et al., Beirut 1985.

Ibn Ḫaldūn, ʿAbd ar-Raḥmān, *al-Muqaddimah*, Beirut n.d. Tr. Franz Rosenthal, *The Muqaddimah*, 3 vols., Princeton 1968.

Ibn Taġrībirdī, Yūsuf, *al-Manhal aṣ-ṣafī wa-l-mustawfī baʿd al-Wāfī*, 13 vols., ed. Muḥammad Muḥammad Amīn, Cairo 1986-2005.

Ibn Taġrībirdī, Yūsuf, *an-Nuǧūm az-zāhirah fī mulūk Miṣr wa-l-Qāhirah*, 16 vols., Cairo 1963.

Ibn Taymiyyah, Aḥmad, *al-Furqān bayn awliyāʾ ar-Raḥmān wa-awliyāʾ aš-Šayṭān*, Damascus 1962.

Ibn Taymiyyah, Aḥmad, *Kitāb Šayḫ al-Islām ilā l-ʿārif bi-llāh aš-šayḫ Naṣr al-Manbiǧī*, in: Aḥmad Ibn Taymiyyah, *Maǧmūʿāt ar-rasāʾil wa-l-masāʾil*, 5 vols. in 2, Beirut 1983, 1:169-90.

al-Maqrīzī, Yūsuf, *Kitāb as-Sulūk li-marʿifat duwal al-mulūk*, vols. 3-4 in 6 pts., ed. S.A.F. ʿĀshūr, Cairo 1970.

al-Maqrīzī, Aḥmad, *al-Mawāʿiz wa-l-iʿtibār bi-dikr al-ḫiṭaṭ wa-l-āṯār*, 2 vols., Cairo n.d.

as-Saḫāwī, Muḥammad, *al-Qawl al-munbī ʿan tarǧamat Ibn al-ʿArabī*, ed. Ḫālid Ibn al-ʿArabī Mudrik, 2 vols., Master's Thesis, Ğāmiʿat Umm al-Qurā, Saudi Arabia 1422/2001.

al-Udfuwī, Ğaʿfar, *al-Badr al-sāfir fī uns al-musāfir*, Cairo, Arab League Manuscript Institute, microfilm 81 (Taʾrīḫ) of MS 4201, Istanbul, Maktabat Fatḥī.

Secondary Sources:

Amīn, Muḥammad Muḥammad, *al-Awqāf wa-l-ḥayāt al-iǧtimāʿiyyah fī Miṣr 648-923 AH/1250-1517 CE*, Cairo 1980.

Cornell, Vincent J., *Realm of the Saint: Power and Authority in Moroccan Islam*, Austin, Texas 1998.

Fernandes, Leonor, *The Evolution of a Sufi Institution in Mamluk Egypt: The Khanqah*, Berlin 1988.

Fernandes, Leonor, "Mamluk Politics and Education: The Evidence from Two Fourteenth Century Waqfiyya", in: *Annales Islamologiques* 23 (1987), pp. 87-98.

Gruendler, Beatrice, "Ibn Abī Ḥajalah (1325-75)", in: Lowry, Joseph E. and Devin J. Stewart (eds.), *Essays in Arabic Literary Biography: 1350-1850*, Wiesbaden 2009, pp. 118-26.

Homerin, Th. Emil, "Ibn Taimīya's *Al-Ṣūfiyyah wa-al-Fuqarā*", in: *Arabica* 32 (1985), pp. 219-44.

Homerin, Th. Emil, *Passion Before Me, My Fate Behind: Ibn al-Fāriḍ and the Poetry of Recollection*, Albany, New York 2011.

Homerin, Th. Emil, "Saving Muslim Souls: The Khānqāh and the Sufi Duty in Mamluk Lands", in: *Mamlūk Studies Review* 3 (1999), pp. 59-83.

Irwin, Robert, *The Middle East in the Middle Ages: The Early Mamluk Sultanate, 1250-1382*, Carbondale, Illinois 1986.

al-Kattānī, Muḥammad, "Introduction", in: Lisānaddīn Ibn al-Ḫāṭib, *Rawḍat at-taʿrīf bi-l-ḥubb aš-šarīf*, ed. Muḥammad al-Kattānī, Beirut 1970, 1:1-60.

Knysh, Alexander, *Ibn ʿArabī in the Later Islamic Tradition*, Albany, New York 1999.

Knysh, Alexander, *Islamic Mysticism: A Short Introduction*, Leiden 2000.

Parker, Richard, et al., *Islamic Monuments in Cairo: A Practical Guide*, 2nd ed., Cairo 1985.

Trimingham, J. Spencer, *The Sufi Orders in Islam*, London 1971.

van Steenbergen, Jo, "The Amir Yalbughā al-Khāṣṣakī, the Qalāwūnid Sultanate, and the Cultural Matrix of Mamlūk Society: A Reassessment of Mamlūk Politics in the 1360s", in: *Journal of the American Oriental Society* 131 (2011), pp. 423-43.

van Steenbergen, Jo, "On the Brink of a New Era? Yalbughā al-Khāṣṣakī (d. 1366) and the Yalbughāwiyah", in: *Mamlūk Studies Review* 15 (2011), pp. 117-52.

van Steenbergen, Jo, *Order Out of Chaos: Patronage, Conflict, and Mamluk Socio-Political Culture, 1341-82*, Leiden 2006.

The Micro-Qaṣīdah

A Formal Experiment from the 8th / 14th Century

Thomas Bauer

1 Ibn Abī Ḥaǧalah as a poet

Ibn Abī Ḥaǧalah is more famous for his anthologies than his poetry. This is not only true today, but was already the case in the Mamluk period. It is certainly no accident that his most famous anthology, the *Dīwān aṣ-ṣabābah*, has come down to us in a large number of manuscripts, whereas we only know of three manuscripts of the Dīwān of his own poetry.[1]

A remark by Ibn Ḥiǧǧah al-Ḥamawī (767-837/1336-1434) about Ibn Abī Ḥaǧalah is also helpful for an appraisal of Ibn Abī Ḥaǧalah's poetry. In his famous *badīʿiyyah*-cum-commentary-cum-anthology entitled *Ḫizānat al-adab*, Ibn Ḥiǧǧah mentions Ibn Abī Ḥaǧalah several times, mainly positively. He considers him one of those who had taken Ibn Nubātah (686-768/1287-1366) as their paragon and "walked under the Nubātian banner".[2] On the other hand, Ibn Ḥiǧǧah quotes conspicuously fewer poems by Ibn Abī Ḥaǧalah than by popular poet al-Miʿmār or by Ibn Abī Ḥaǧalah's contemporary al-Qīrāṭī (726-781/1326-1379), who was considered Ibn Nubātah's successor as the leading poet.[3] Ibn Ḥiǧǧah even expresses a slight doubt about the quality of Ibn Abī Ḥaǧalah's poetry, saying that for the sake of quantity, Ibn Abī Ḥaǧalah contented himself with "cheap" poetry (*kāna yarḍā li-aǧli l-katrati bi-r-raḫīṣ*).[4] Indeed, most readers will admit that in many of Ibn Abī Ḥaǧalah's poems one can find original, elegant and well-formulated verses side by side with clumsy and cumbersome lines. Nevertheless, even if Ibn Abī Ḥaǧalah's poetry is of uneven quality, it is still very interesting indeed.

For a first overlook of Ibn Abī Ḥaǧalah's Dīwān, the following chart displaying the length of the poems in the Dīwān may be useful:[5]

---

1 There are two editions of Ibn Abī Ḥaǧalah's *Dīwān* (see bibliography). I will quote the ed. by Bahǧat and Muḫlif as "ed. ʿAmmān", the ed. by Ḥulwah as "ed. Cairo". Both are based on the manuscript Dār al-Kutub al-Miṣriyyah 1525 *adab*, which I also use and quote as "ms.". The ed. Cairo uses also the manuscript 1127 *šiʿr Taymūr* and knows a third one, which the editor does not regard, all in the Dār al-Kutub.

2 Ibn Ḥiǧǧah al-Ḥamawī, *Ḫizānat al-adab wa-ġāyat al-arab*, ed. Kawkab Diyāb, 5 vols., Beirut 1421/2001, 3:366.

3 Ibn Ḥiǧǧah, *Ḫizānah* 3:366.

4 Ibn Ḥiǧǧah, *Ḫizānah* 3:444.

5 It is based on the ed. ʿAmmān, where similar statistics are given on p. 58. Note that poem no. 439, apparently a seven-liner, consists in fact of two poems, one in three, the other in four lines. The statistics have been adapted accordingly.

Number of lines	Σ
2	281
3	18
4	9
5	3
6	6
7	52
8	3
9	2
10-30	38
30-49	22
50 or more	15

During Ayyubid and Mamluk times, epigrams comprising two or three lines made an unprecedented career.[6] It is small wonder, then, that two- and three-liners (*al-maṯānī wa-l-maṯāliṯ*)[7] comprise exactly two-thirds of Ibn Abī Ḥaǧalah's entire Dīwān. The 75 poems of ten lines or more, mostly qaṣīdahs, amount to 17% of the Dīwān. This seems a comparatively small number, but a number of longer poems exist in sources outside the Dīwān.[8] Poems of four, five, six, eight or nine lines play a minor role, which is no surprise. Most striking, however, is the number of seven-liners in the Dīwān. There are 52 poems of seven lines, comprising 12% of all poems and 35% of all poems longer than three lines. The astonishing fact that more than one third of all non-epigrammatic poems in Ibn Abī Ḥaǧalah's Dīwān comprise exactly seven lines needs an explanation. In order to find one, let us have a closer look at three of them.

2 Three seven-liners

Let us start our examination of Ibn Abī Ḥaǧalah's seven-liners with a congratulatory poem (*tahniʾah* pl. *tahāniʾ*). Congratulatory poems are a subgenre of panegyric poetry (*madīḥ*) and constituted a very common means of communication for ʿulamāʾ and udabāʾ in the Mamluk period.[9] The addressee of the present poem,

---

[6] See Talib, Adam, *How Do You Say "Epigram" in Arabic?* (Leiden: Brill, forthcoming); Bauer, Thomas, "'*Ayna hādhā min al-Mutanabbī!*' *Toward an Aesthetics of Mamluk Literature*", in: *Mamlūk Studies Review* 17 (2013), pp. 5-22, here pp. 10-14.

[7] The title of a Dīwān of epigrams, all of them two- and three-liners, by Ṣafiyyaddīn al-Ḥillī (667-750/1278-1349 or 1350) is *Dīwān al-maṯāliṯ wa-l-maṯānī fī l-maʿālī wa-l-maʿānī*. The edition by Muḥammad Ṭāhir al-Ḥimṣī (Damaskus 1419/1998) is unsatisfactory and was undertaken without regarding the most important manuscript Paris 3341, fol. 1a-52b.

[8] See the contributions by Homerin, Masarwa and von Hees.

[9] See van Gelder, Geert Jan, "Congratulations, Arabic", in: *EI Three*, 2014-2, pp. 73-74.

however, is a certain Ṭaybuġā, a Turk and member of the military elite. While addressing members of the *aṣḥāb as-sayf* "bearers of the sword" with congratulatory poems is rather an exception, it is not so rare an occurrence with Ibn Abī Ḥaǧalah. Instead, the number of poems addressed to members of the military elite is conspicuously higher in the Dīwān of Ibn Abī Ḥaǧalah than in the Dīwāns of most other contemporary poets. This is in accordance with the general impression we get from his œuvre that his relation with the court played a considerably larger role for him than for his fellow-udabāʾ.

As the heading informs us, the occasion of the poem was Ṭaybuġā's safe return form the pilgrimage, which, however, does not play any role in the poem itself.[10] Remarkable is its rhyme in -aġā / -uġā, a very rare and difficult rhyme. Obviously, the poet chose it to rhyme with the addressee's name Ṭaybuġā (meter *ṭawīl*, rhyme *3ġā*[11]):[12]

وقال يُهَنِّئ الأمير طَيْبُغَا بالقدوم صُحْبَة الركاب الشريفة

صَغِيتُ لِداعي الحُبِّ فيه وما صَغَى   وظَبْيٍ غَـدا في قالَـبِ الحُـسْنِ مُفْرَغـا

تُـدِيرُ كُؤوسـاً مِـن مَلامِـكَ فُرَّغـا   فقُـلْ لِعَـذُولي فيـه يا صـاحِ كم كـذا

تَعَلَّمَ لِـينَ العَطْـفِ مِن رُمْـحِ طَيْبُغَا   لَواحِظُـهُ مثـلُ السُّيوفِ وقَـدُّهُ

يقُـولُ له بـدرُ السَّمـا أنتَ لي أغَـا   أبـو التُّرْكِ إلّا أنَّ نُـورَ جَبِينِـهِ

يُـدِيرُ كؤوسَ الحَتْـفِ فيهـا لِمَـنْ بَغَـا   أمِـيرٌ إذا دارتْ رَحَـا الحَـربِ لم يَـزَلْ

إذا انقـضَّ كالبـازِيِّ في حَوْمَـةِ الوَغَـا   تَحُـومُ طُيُـورُ النَـصْرِ فـوق لِوائِـهِ

بِـضَرْبَاتِه فـوق الدِمـاغِ مُـدَمَّغَا   فـلا زالَ في يـوم الهِيَـاجِ عَـدُوُّهُ

1   A gazelle appeared, cast in the mold of beauty. I gave ear to the call to love him, but he did not listen.

2   Tell the one who blames me for loving him: How many empty cups of rebuke will you pass around, friend?

3   His glances are like swords and Ṭaybuġā's lances taught his body how to bend tenderly.

---

[10] There are several umarāʾ called Ṭaybuġā at this time. This Ṭaybuġā could be ʿAlāʾaddīn Ṭaybuġā ad-Dawādār, who performed the pilgrimage with the Syrian caravan in 771/1370 and died in 779/1377, see *Taʾrīḫ Ibn Qāḍī Šuhbah*, vol. 3, ed. ʿAdnān Darwīš, Damascus 1994, p. 563.

[11] Abbreviations in noting the rhyme scheme: x = any consonant; 2 = ū or ī; 3 = a, i, u.

[12] Text: Ms. fol. 57b; ed. ʿAmmān no. 225; ed. Cairo p. 156. In line 5, the ل of يزَلْ is placed above the line, which led ed. Cairo to misread لم يزَلْ to لم يَزِدْ. Ed. Cairo uses modern standard orthography in the words رحى, بغى and الوغى, ed. ʿAmmān only in بغى. I follow the orthography of the manuscript even if it is considered "wrong".

4   You're father to the Turks, but the full moon in the heavens confesses to the bright-
    ness of your forehead that: You are my father / *lord* (*aġā*)!

5   When war breaks out, he shows himself to be a leader who hands out endless cups of
    death to the rebels.

6   When he pounces – falcon-like – on his enemies in the tumult of battle, the birds of
    victory hover over his banner.

7   May his enemies never cease, in days of strife, to be abased by his blows against their
    brains!

The poem starts with a *nasīb*, i.e. lines of love-poetry that introduce the typical
polythematic qaṣīdah. The genre is *ġazal*, love poetry in the "modern" form. The
beloved is probably a beautiful youth who does not yield to the lover's courting.
A censurer / blamer appears in line two, a well-known character in love poetry.
Three *kāf* plus a *qāf* provide for an interesting sound pattern echoing the blamer's
character.

Line three returns to the beloved, whose eyes are compared to swords. Since
the addressee is a "bearer of the sword", this military image leads nicely to the
first reference to the *mamdūḥ*, the person praised in the poem, i.e. Ṭaybuġā: "His
glances are like swords and Ṭaybuġā's lances taught his body how to bend tenderly". This is a perfect transition between *nasīb* and the praise of the *mamdūḥ*.
The technical term for such a transition is *taḫalluṣ*. Though the images are conventional, they are superbly intertwined: Whereas the beloved's glances are simply compared to swords – any swords –, his body is compared with particular
lances – those of Ṭaybuġā. Further, there is no simple comparison, but a dy-
namic relation: The beloved's body has learned how to bend elegantly from
Ṭaybuġā's lances, a surprising turn for the hearer, who might have expected another comparison parallel to the first one.

In line 4, the poet alludes to the Turkish descent of the Mamluk, which the
Turkish word *aġā* reflects. The "cups of death" in line 5 refer back to the empty
(!) "cups" of the censurer in line 2. Another belligerent line follows with a nice
ġinās (paronomasia) between *yaḫūmu* and *ḥawmah* and a parallelism between real
birds (probably vultures) and Ṭaybuġā's comparison with a falcon. The poem
ends in line 7 with a sort of "blessing", again a very belligerent one, and another
notable *ġinās* (*dimāġ – mudammaġ*).

The poem before us is not a *qiṭʿah* or *muqaṭṭaʿah*, i.e. a monothematic poem,
but a full-fledged qaṣīdah, a polythematic poem consisting of an introductory
nasīb, a transition (*taḫalluṣ*), and a concluding praise-section, the *madīḥ*. What is
special about this qaṣīdah is its length, or rather: its breath-taking brevity.

In order to get a clearer picture, let us examine another "micro-qaṣidah", as we might call it. It is a praise-poem for another emir, called Arūs an-Nāṣirī (meter *wāfir*, rhyme *2sū*):[13]

وقال يمدح الأمير أروس الناصري

ويُــــــذَلُ في وِصـــــالِكُمُ النفـــيسُ   برؤْيَــةِ حَــيِّكُمْ تَحْــــيى النفـــوسُ

فقَلـــــبي في مُحَبَّــــتِكُمْ حَبِــــيسُ   لــئن أطلقــتُ دمعــي في هـــواكُمْ

فــرأسُ الــــتُركِ في مـــصرٍ أروسُ   وإن أصــبحتُ في العُــشَّاقِ رأســـا

وتُطــرَقُ مِـــن مَهابَتِـــهِ الــرؤوسُ   أروسٌ تَختَـــشي الآسـادُ منـــه

وتُـــشرِقُ مِـــن مُحيَّــاهُ الــشموسُ   ويُخْجِـــلُ جــودُه السُحْبَ الغــوادي

كــما تُجــلى علــى الــشمعِ العَــروسُ   فــكَمْ جُلِيَـــتْ محاسِـنُهُ علينــا

ووجـــهُ عَـــدُوِّهِ منـــه عَبُـــوسُ   فــلا زالَ الزمــانُ بـــه ضَحــوكًا

1 Our souls revive at the sight of your tribe and everything precious is sacrificed to gain union with you.

2 In my passion for you, I let loose my tears, but my heart remains captive to my own love for you.

3 And though I may head up those who love passionately, the head of the Turks in Egypt is Arūs.

4 Lions fear Arūs and heads bow down, awe-struck.

5 His openhandedness shames the morning clouds and splendor rises from his face like the sun.

6 How many times have his excellent qualities been revealed before us like a bride revealed in candlelight!

7 May time never cease to smile through him and may his enemies never cease to frown.

The poem shares a number of characteristics with the first one. Again the poem addresses a 'bearer of the sword', and again the rhyme is chosen to match his name. The *nasīb* makes a more conservative impression. The beloved is addressed in a gender-neutral way (second person plural), and the word *ḥayy* calls forth associations with old Arabic bedouin-style *nasīb*. Line 2 is characterised by the sty-

---

13 Text: Ms. fol. 49a-b; ed. ʿAmmān no. 171; ed. Cairo pp. 134-135. Ed. ʿAmmān interprets the beginning of line 5 as ويخجلُ جودَهُ السحبُ الغوادي. I follow the interpretation of ed. Cairo. Different to both editions, I follow the orthography of the ms. in تحيى in line 1. – On Sayfaddīn Arūs an-Nāṣirī see the entry (in the year 775, the year in which he probably died) in *Taʾrīḫ Ibn Qāḍī Šuhbah*, vol. 3, ed. ʿAdnān Darwīš, Damascus 1994, p. 438.

listic device of *ṭibāq* "antithesis" by contrasting "letting loose" and "captivate". By bearing steadfastly his unrequitable love, the poet is the "head of lovers", an expression that calls to mind al-ʿAbbās ibn al-Aḥnaf's (c. 133-192/750-807) conception of himself as a lover.[14] By way of another *ṭibāq*, the "head of the lovers" is juxtaposed to the "head of the Turks", none other than the *mamdūḥ* Arūs an-Nāṣirī. As in the first poem, the *taḫalluṣ* comes again in the third line.

Three of the four remaining lines of the panegyric section are again characterised by antithesis (*ṭibāq*): Lions and men (line 4), clouds and the sun (line 5), smiling versus frowning (line 7). A *tašbīh* (comparison) interrupts this series in line 6. With the exception of line 6 and line 1, in which the most prominent stylistic device is *ǧinās* "paronomasia" (*ḥayy* – *taḥyā*, *nufūs* – *nafīs*), all lines are built around a *ṭibāq*. This form of contrast is therefore the most prominent characteristic of the poem besides its shortness. Both characteristics are even enforced by the meter. *Wāfir* verses are comparatively short. In this poem, each hemistich ranges from 11 to 13 syllables. The whole poem is no more than 167 syllables, indeed not much for a polythematic qaṣīdah. In addition, the last syllable of each hemistich is always shortened in the *wāfir* trimeter. This lends enormous prominence to the caesura between the first and the second hemistich of each line, and Ibn Abī Ḥaǧalah makes use of this caesura in each of the seven lines. In all lines of *ṭibāq*, each of the two hemistichs is dedicated to one part of the contrasting pair. In line 1, the caesura is enforced by the rhyme between hemistich 1 and 2; in line 6, the comparison starts exactly with the beginning of the second hemistich. Whereas poets used to avoid too parallel a structure in consecutive verses, in this poem the construction of utterances of exact hemistich length is a deliberate stylistic feature that evokes the impression of hastiness, which corresponds well to its shortness.

Before trying to trace the history of the micro-qaṣīdah, let us examine a third example. This time, a poem addressed to a member of the civilian elite (meter *ṭawīl*, rhyme *ānī*):[15]

وقال يمدح بعض الأدباء

أَتَعْذُلُني إنْ بانَ عَـنّي تَـصَبُّري   وقـد بانَ مَـن أهـوى بِـسَفْحِ أبانِ

ولم أنْـسَهُ إذْ قـالَ أيـنَ تُحِلُّـني   وقـد حَـلَّ مِـن قلبي أعـزَّ مـكانِ

لحـا اللهُ قلبي كُلَّـما طـارَ طـائرٌ   هَفَـا كَجَنـاحِ النَّـسْرِ في الخَفَقَـانِ

فيـا لَجَـمالٍ لا أزالُ بِقُرْبِـهِ   مُعـارَ جَنـاحٍ مُحْـسِنِ الطَّـيَرانِ

---

14 On ʿAbbās b. al-Aḥnaf see Enderwitz, Susanne, "al-ʿAbbās b. al-Aḥnaf", in: *EI Three*, 2009-1, pp. 2-4.

15 Text: Ms. fol. 96a; ed. ʿAmmān no. 421; ed. Cairo pp. 246-247.

له مِـن بَنَـاتِ الفِكْـرِ مـا لم أَزَلْ بِـهِ   صَرِيـعَ مَعـانٍ أو صَرِيـعَ غَـوانِ

فيـا لَيتَ شِعْري شِـعْرُهُ في آنتِـسابِهِ   بَـدِيعُ جَـمالٍ أم بَـدِيعُ زمـانِ

يَخِـفُّ عـلى سَمْـعِ المُحِـبِّ نَـشِيدُهُ   ولـو كانَ مِـن أعدائِـهِ الـثَّقَلانِ

1 How can you blame me for having given up my endurance after the one whom I love left me at Safḥ Abān / the foot of Abān mountain?

2 I'll never forget the moment he asked me: "Where do you place me? (= How much do I mean to you?)"—when he'd already taken up residence in the highest station of my heart.

3 May God scold this palpitating heart of mine that flutters like an eagle's wing each time a bird flies past!

4 Oh what a beauty! / *Oh Ğamāladdīn!* When I am close to him, I am given wings fit to fly.

5 His ideas, the 'daughters of his thought', are such that I am constantly being knocked down by ideas or by fair maidens / *Muslim ibn al-Walīd.*

6 I wish I knew whether his poetry is derived from the prodigy of beauty / *Ğamāl* or the prodigy of the age / *Badīʿ az-Zamān al-Hamaḏānī.*

7 Hearing it recited – and even if the 'two heavy ones' (man and jinn) were both its enemies – would still sound lightly in the ears of the one who loves.

The heading tells us that the addressee of the poem was an *adīb*. The praise of his *maʿānī* "ideas" (line 5) and his poetry (line 6) and the mentioning of two major littérateurs corroborate this. The first of them is Ṣarīʿ al-Ġawānī in line 5, a sobriquet for the early Abbasid poet Muslim ibn al-Walīd (d. 208/823).[16] The second is the famous pioneer of the *maqāmah* Badīʿ az-Zamān al-Hamaḏānī (358-398/968-1008) alluded to in line 6.[17] The *taḫalluṣ*, this time in line 4, and the expression *badīʿu ğamālin* in line 6 suggest that the name of the *mamdūḥ* was Ğamāladdīn. Since there are not too many notable poets known as Ğamāladdīn, it is probable that the *mamdūḥ* is none other than Ğamāladdīn Ibn Nubātah. One of his poems, which is in the same meter and rhyme as this seven-liner and shares several formulations with it, corroborates this.[18] Two hemistichs are (almost) identical. In line 3 of Ibn Nubātah's poem, which is a love poem, we learn that the beloved's beauty will overwhelm all enemies *wa-law kāna min aʿdāʾika l-qamarāni* "even if the two 'moons' (i.e. sun and moon) were both your enemies". In Ibn Abī Ḥağalah's poem, these words conclude the poem. The rhyme word is different, but the word *aṯ-ṯaqalāni* appears in Ibn Nubātah's poem in the following line. The second hemistich shared by both poems is the central passage in

---

16 See *EAL*, p. 557.
17 See *EAL*, pp. 123-134.
18 Ibn Nubātah al-Miṣrī, *Dīwān*, ed. Muḥammad al-Qalqīlī, Cairo 1312/1905, pp. 517-518.

Ibn Abī Ḥaǧalah's poem, *muʿāra ǧanāḥin muḥsini ṭ-ṭayarāni* "given wings fit to fly". In Ibn Nubātah's poem, the wings are given to the palpitating hearts of the lovers (line 8). One may also note the rhyme word *ġawānī*, which occurs in line 6 of Ibn Nubātah's poem, and the phrase *fī aʿazza makān* "in the highest place", which echoes the word *fī aḏalla makān* "in the most contemptible place" of Ibn Nubātah's line 9.

However, the intertextual relations are even more complex since Ibn Abī Ḥaǧalah's quotations are quotations of quotations. Their ultimate source is a poem in praise of Kāfūr written by al-Mutanabbī in 348/959.[19] The poem starts with a line about Kāfūr's enemies. We have already met its second hemistich twice: "All tongues will blame your enemy, even if sun and moon were both your enemies". In line 11, we learn that this enemy "did not know that death was above his head, having been given wings fit to fly". What were wings of death in al-Mutanabbī's poem became wings of lovers' hearts in Ibn Nubātah's *ġazal* and finally Ibn Abī Ḥaǧalah's own wings in the seven-liner. The phrase *fī aḏalla makān* is found in al-Mutanabbī's line 12, but he does not use the rhyme word *ġawānī*.

Ibn Nubātah transformed this heroic and bellicose poem into a love poem using some of its second hemistichs by way of a *tašṭīr*, but also quoting whole lines or only single phrases. In addition, he added two lines entirely of his own. Ibn Abī Ḥaǧalah in turn transformed Ibn Nubātah's recast into a seven-line qaṣīdah addressed to Ibn Nubātah. Consequently, Ibn Abī Ḥaǧalah used only those lines of al-Mutanabbī, which Ibn Nubātah had already used himself.

Stylistically, this seven-liner is quite different from the preceding two. Besides its intertextual references and the extensive use of *ǧinās*, upon which we will not comment further, its main stylistic trait is the use of a leitmotif. The leitmotif-technique was well established in Ayyubid and Mamluk poetry. Several studies show that Ibn Nubātah used it constantly and with great virtuosity.[20] It is remarkable that the use of leitmotifs works not only with longer texts, but even with a seven-liner like this one.

The leitmotif in the present poem is *movement*: upwards, downwards and away, sometimes associated with lightness versus heaviness. In the first line, endurance moved away (*bāna*), just as the beloved moved away (*bāna*) to the foot of a mountain, which may stand for "heaviness". In the second line, the question is about where the beloved is placed in relation to the lover (*tuḥilluni – ḥalla*). He is placed on the "highest place" (*aʿazza makān*). In line three, birds move lightly in the air. The mentioning of birds was a sort of identification tag for Ibn Abī

---

[19] al-Barqūqī, ʿAbdarraḥmān, *Šarḥ Dīwān al-Mutanabbī*, 4 vols., Beirut 1407/1986, 4:373-379.

[20] See for example Bauer, Thomas, "»Der Fürst ist tot, es lebe der Fürst!«: Ibn Nubātas Gedicht zur Inthronisation al-Afḍals von Ḥamāh (732/1332)", in: Marzolph, Ulrich (ed.), *Orientalistische Studien zu Sprache und Literatur. Festgabe zum 65. Geburtstag von Werner Diem*, Wiesbaden 2011, pp. 285-315.

Ḥaǧalah, the "son of the father of a partridge".[21] In line 4, it is "beauty" = the addressee Ibn Nubātah who gives wings to him. In a way, this line seems to continue the *nasīb*, but it is in fact the *taḫalluṣ* mentioning the name of the *mamdūḥ* – a fine, almost imperceptible transition and at the same time an intertextual signal pointing to both Ibn Nubātah and al-Mutanabbī.

On the one hand, "beauty" gives wings to him; on the other hand, the *mamdūḥ*'s ideas "knock him down" in line 5. Now the act of moving downwards counters the movements up and away. Line 6 does not take up the leitmotif but echoes line 5 instead with its parallel construction of the second hemistich. The last line suggests a last turn of the movement by suggesting a movement upwards again. *Ǧamāl*'s poetry is light in the ears of the speaker, who is the lover of *ǧamāl*. When it is recited, even the "two heavy ones" cannot prevent it from flying. It is quite surprising how many ideas seven lines can contain. It is also noticeable that this poem, which is addressed to one of the leading littérateurs of its time, is conspicuously more sophisticated than the two seven-liners addressed to Turkish emirs.

3 The history of the micro-qaṣīdah

We have examined three full-fledged qaṣīdahs comprising only seven lines, and there are about fifty more like this in Ibn Abī Ḥaǧalah's Dīwān. Normal qaṣīdahs were much longer, often exceeding fifty lines or more, and I wonder whether there were any qaṣīdahs of seven lines at all before the 8th/14th century. In the 14th century and onwards, qaṣīdahs continued to be of substantial length, the only exception being the conspicuous number of seven-liners in the Dīwāns of Ibn Abī Ḥaǧalah and several of his contemporaries (Ibn Nubātah and al-Qīrāṭī), most of which are fully developed polythematic qaṣīdahs.

In all these Dīwāns we find a number, albeit small, of madīḥ poems comprising six, eight or nine lines which are monothematic and clearly not qaṣīdahs. When there are *muqaṭṭaʿāt* of six and eight lines, it is hardly conceivable that there should not be *muqaṭṭaʿāt* of seven lines, and indeed there are. But their number is very small and the overwhelming majority of seven-liners in Ibn Nubātah's, al-Qīrāṭī's and Ibn Abī Ḥaǧalah's Dīwāns are qaṣīdahs. The only possible conclusion therefore is that in the 14th century, the qaṣīdah comprising seven lines was cultivated as a distinctive poetic form. Poets consciously composed qaṣīdahs of seven lines, demonstrating their skilful ability to condense a polythematic poem with extreme brevity, and their readers appreciated the very special aesthetics of what I call the micro-qaṣīdah. The most common Arabic designation is *al-qaṣīdah as-subāʿiyyah*.

---

[21] Homerin, Emil Th., "Ibn Abī Ḥaǧalah and Sufism", in this volume, p. 13

Readers of Ibn Abī Ḥaǧalah's poems might assume that the large number of *qaṣāʾid subāʿiyyah* might have to do with the anthology *Sukkardān as-sulṭān*, in which the number "seven" is the central topic. This is not the case, however. It was not the *Sukkardān* that inspired the seven-line qaṣīdah. If there was any influence in the opposite direction, it remains to be studied; all the same, there are several seven-line poems in the work. The origin of the micro-qaṣīdah does not lie with Ibn Abī Ḥaǧalah. Instead, it was Ǧamāladdīn Ibn Nubātah, the most respected and venerated poet and prose author of the 14th century, who played that crucial role.

The master-poet Ibn Nubātah, 38 solar years senior to Ibn Abī Ḥaǧalah, was his undisputed role model as a poet. Ibn Ḥiǧǧah al-Ḥamawī reckoned him among *al-ʿiṣābah allatī mašat taḥta l-ʿalam an-nubātī wa-taḥallat bi-qaṭr nabātihī* ... "the group (of poets) that walked under the Nubatian banner and took their sweetness from his sugar molasses / *the drops of his plant*".[22] Ibn Abī Ḥaǧalah addressed poems to Ibn Nubātah and he answered. At least four poems in the Dīwān of Ibn Nubātah, among them a seven-line qaṣīdah, are addressed to his younger colleague.[23]

Ibn Nubātah was also the model for Ibn Abī Ḥaǧalah's micro-qaṣīdah. It may be that Ibn Nubātah did not invent the qaṣīdah of seven lines outright, but he was the person who developed it and popularised it – and inspired Ibn Abī Ḥaǧalah and others to use this new poetic form.

But how was it that Ibn Nubātah arrived at the idea of the micro-qaṣīdah? The key scene took place in the sultan's palace in Ḥamāh sometime between 720 A.H., when Abū l-Fidāʾ was granted the title al-Malik al-Muʾayyyad and his death in 732/1331. On one occasion during these years, Ibn Nubātah composed his first full-fledged *qaṣīdah subāʿiyyah* in praise of al-Malik al-Muʾayyad, sultan of Ḥamāh. Its heading in the Dīwān – here one of the earliest manuscripts – says:[24]

وقال يَمدَحُهُ وقد قِيلَ أَنَّ جَدَّه الملك المنصور كان قد اَقترح على مُدَّاحِهِ أَنْ تكونَ القصيدةُ سبعة أبياتٍ

"With the following poem, (Ibn Nubātah) praised (al-Malik al-Muʾayyad), and it is told that (al-Muʾayyad's) ancestor al-Malik al-Manṣūr had suggested to his panegyrists that the qaṣīdah should have seven lines ..."

We do not know if it was Ibn Nubātah's idea to refer to a tradition current at the court of Ḥamāh to prove himself in a new challenge or if it was Abū l-Fidāʾs idea (hopefully not as a result of having been bored by listening to too many overlong qaṣīdahs). We do not even know at present if the tradition is true. Thus far I

---

[22] Ibn Ḥiǧǧah, *Ḫizānah* 3:366.
[23] Ibn Nubātah, *Dīwān*, pp. 227 (a *qaṣīdah subāʿiyyah*), 311 (a riddle), 318 (an epigram; on this and the preceding see Ibn Abī Ḥaǧalah, *Sukkardān*, p. 10-11), 522 (an epigram).
[24] *Dīwān Ibn Nubātah*, Ms. Berlin 7861, fol. 34b.

have not been able to find a single qaṣīdah of seven lines dedicated to al-Malik al-Manṣūr II, who reigned Ḥamāh between 642/1244 and 683/1284 and was Abū l-Fidāʾ's great-grandfather. Setting aside the issue of al-Malik al-Manṣūr's admonition, the story of the seven-line qaṣīdah is older than Ibn Nubātah and al-Malik al-Manṣūr. Its ultimate origin seems to be a short remark in the most famous and influential handbook of poetry *al-ʿUmdah* by Ibn Rašīq al-Qayrawānī (390-456/1000-1063). Here we read:[25]

وقيل إذا بلغت الأبيات سبعة فهي قصيدة ولهذا كان الإيطاء بعد سبعة أبيات غير عَيْب عند

أحد من الناس ، ومن الناس من لا يعد القصيدة إلا ما بلغ العشرة أو جاوزها...

"And it is said that if a poem reaches seven lines in length, it is a qaṣīdah and therefore *īṭāʾ* (i.e. the repetition of the rhyme word in identical sense) is not considered a fault. This is the opinion of a single person, whereas others do not reckon poems as qaṣīdahs unless they feature ten lines or more."

Obviously, this is not a definition of the qaṣīdah but a statement about two different things, the length of the qaṣīdah and the number of lines after which a poet may repeat a rhyme-word, and the number seven was brought in by a single person. Ironically, the statement has been taken much more seriously by Western scholars than it ever was by Arabic poets:[26]

"In medieval Arabic sources the term is applied to any poem of a certain length; according to Ibn Rashiq a *qaṣīda* must exceed seven (or ten) verses. In the Western tradition ... the application of the term has been limited to the polythematic form, as opposed to the *qiṭʿa*, the monothematic poem."

This is obviously not true, at least not for the Mamluk period. Being polythematic is the core idea of the micro-qaṣīdah in this time. As Ibn Abī Ḥaǧalah's six line qaṣīdahs, which will be examined in the next section, show, being polythematic was more important for being a qaṣīdah than the minimum of seven lines. There is another poem by Ibn Abī Ḥaǧalah, probably addressed to al-Qīrāṭī, which comprises nine lines but is clearly not a qaṣīdah.[27] All this corroborates the fact that Arabic poets of the middle period understood the qaṣīdah much the same as modern Arabists do.

Ibn Rašīq's report about one opinion according to which seven lines make a qaṣīdah had no immediate consequences for Arabic poets. It was only at the court of Ḥamāh where the idea was revisited two hundred years later. Even then it was only a marginal episode at first. Ibn Nubātah composed no more than two micro-qaṣīdahs for al-Malik al-Muʾayyad, and that was all. There are no other

---

[25] Ibn Rašīq al-Qayrawānī, *al-ʿUmdah fī ṣināʿat aš-šiʿr wa-naqdihī*, ed. Nabawi ʿAbdalwāḥid Šaʿlān, 2 vols., Cairo 1420/2000, 1:302. On Ibn Rašīq see *EAL*, p. 363.

[26] *EAL*, p. 630.

[27] *Dīwān Ibn Abī Ḥaǧalah*, ms. fol. 98b-99a, ed. ʿAmmān no. 408, ed. Cairo p. 254 (meter *ḫafīf*, rhyme *ānī*).

seven-liners in the oldest recension of Ibn Nubātah's Dīwān. A number of years passed until Ibn Nubātah took up the idea again, this time in a completely different dimension. During his last years in Damascus and the final period of his life in Cairo, Ibn Nubātah composed one seven-liner after the other. Micro-qaṣīdahs addressed to ʿAlāʾaddīn ibn Faḍlallāh, Sultan Ḥasan and others constitute a major part of his poetic output during these years. Finally, he collected his micro-qaṣīdahs in a special volume entitled *as-Sabʿah as-sayyārah* "the seven moving stars" = "the seven lines that circle widely". Like most works by Ibn Nubātah, it was a work in progress, and Ibn Nubātah added poems until the end.

Why has this story gone unnoticed so long? The reason for it lies in the fate of Ibn Nubātah's *as-Sabʿah as-sayyārah* and his Dīwān. So far, no manuscript of *as-Sabʿah as-sayyārah* has surfaced. The reason for this loss may have been the fact that al-Baštakī included all poems from *as-Sabʿah as-sayyārah* in his second recension of the Dīwān Ibn Nubātah (Baštakī β).[28] In Baštakī β we find about 170 *qaṣāʾid subāʿiyyah* that most probably formed part of *as-Sabʿah as-sayyārah*. In the manuscripts, sequences of micro-qaṣīdahs are introduced by headings such as *wa-qāla fī s-subāʿiyyāt* or *wa-qāla fī s-Sabʿah as-sayyārah* or just *wa-qāla 7* (the number "seven" written with a digit). After this headline, all *subāʿiyyāt* that pertain to the particular rhyme letter follow. So far, so good.

When in 1905 al-Qalqīlī produced his unsatisfactory edition of the *Dīwān Ibn Nubātah*, he had the whimsical ideal to separate all short poems that do not bear a heading of their own from all other poems and assemble them in a separate section at the end of each chapter. He gives these sections the headline *wa-min muqaṭṭaʿātihī* and arranges the poems according to their length. What is the consequence for the seven-liners? As we saw, in the manuscripts the first seven-liner bears the heading *min as-sabʿah as-sayyārah* and is followed by all the *subāʿiyyāt* with the same rhyme consonant. Al-Qalqīlī chose to leave the first *subāʿiyyah* in its proper place, since it came with a heading, but to transfer all the others to the final section. Obviously, al-Qalqīlī had not understood that the headline *min as-sabʿah as-sayyārah* (the meaning of which he obviously did not grasp) refers not only to the first seven-liner, but to the following seven-liners as well. Instead, they turn up in a section which, to top it off, is titled a section of *muqaṭṭaʿāt* thus obscuring Ibn Nubātah's central motivation: to compose qaṣīdahs, not *muqaṭṭaʿāt*. In this way, al-Qalqīlī's edition of Ibn Nubātah's Dīwān obscured the history of the *qaṣīdah subāʿiyyah*. Consequently, the editors of the Dīwān of Ibn Abī Ḥaǧalah, though realizing the high number of 53 seven-liners, could not contextualize it.

---

[28] On al-Baštakī (748-830/1347-1427) and his different versions of Ibn Nubātah's Dīwān and on al-Qalqīlī's 1905 edition see Bauer, Thomas, "Ibn Nubātah al-Miṣrī (686-768/1287-1366): Life and Works. Part 2: The Dīwān of Ibn Nubātah", in: *Mamlūk Studies Review* 12.2 (2008), pp. 25-69.

To sum up: To answer a fancy of the sultan of Ḥamāh, Ibn Nubātah composed two extremely short qaṣīdahs of seven lines. Years later, he took up the idea again and started to compose a large number of micro-qaṣīdahs. Many of them served to communicate with fellow udabā᾿ who answered with *qaṣā᾿id subāʿiyyah* of their own. In this way, micro-qaṣīdahs became a trend and a number of poets found pleasure in composing them. So far, all of them seem to belong to the group of "those who walked under the Nubātian banner", but we need further research to clarify the fate of the micro-qaṣīdah in later generations. Ibn Abī Ḥaǧalah was one of the most eager followers of Ibn Nubātah. This is also reflected in the number of his *qaṣā᾿id subāʿiyyāt*, which he directed to people from quite different social groups. Among those he addressed were the caliph, the sultan, members of the military elite, scholars, other littérateurs and a physician. Obviously, micro-qaṣīdahs found a broad public.

The charm of the micro-qaṣīdah lies in its concision. The poet assembles common, often conventional qaṣīdah themes and motifs in a minimal number of lines and takes the listener from one idea to the next in the shortest possible time. What the poet has to prove in the micro-qaṣīdah is the high art of transition, transitions from idea to idea without any opportunity to elaborate on a given one, and, of course, the most important transition of all is the *taḫalluṣ* between *nasīb* and *madīḥ*. In a *qaṣīdah subāʿiyyah*, the *taḫallūṣ* draws much more attention than in a longer qaṣīdah. It becomes the very core of the poem and its focus. After all, the *taḫalluṣ*-line comprises 14 percent of the whole. In Ibn Nubātah's micro-qaṣīdahs, the *taḫalluṣ* may even extend over two lines. Ibn Abī Ḥaǧalah did not emulate him in this respect. Instead, he placed his *taḫalluṣāt* comparatively late in the qaṣīdah. Whereas Ibn Nubātah preferred *taḫalluṣāt* in line 3 or stretching from line 3 to 4 (or even from line 1 to 2), more than 40% of Ibn Abī Ḥaǧalah's come in line 4. Two of them are even postponed to line 5. One can imagine how the *mamdūḥ* must have become rather nervous when the composer of a seven-line poem reached line 5 without yet mentioning him.[29]

4 Short and even shorter: Two qaṣīdahs in six lines

With more than 220 *qaṣā᾿id subāʿiyyāt*, Ibn Nubātah and Ibn Abī Ḥaǧalah alone amply demonstrate that it is very well possible to compose full-fledged, well-constructed, interesting and significant qaṣīdahs in the limited space of only seven lines. Whereas it is thus sufficiently clear that seven lines are enough for a qaṣīdah, the question remains if seven lines are even necessary for a qaṣīdah. Can we imagine a qaṣīdah of only six lines or fewer? Only rarely, however, did poets try this experiment. A seven-liner is short enough to provide the effect of unexpected brev-

---

[29] *Dīwān Ibn Abī Ḥaǧalah*, ms. fol. 7a-b, ed. ʿAmmān no. 26, ed. Cairo pp. 30-31 (meter *wāfir*, rhyme *2bā*); ms. fol. 106a-b, ed. ʿAmmān no. 434, ed. Cairo p. 272 (meter *wāfir*, rhyme *āwī*).

ity. A qaṣīdah of six or even five lines would only marginally add to this effect. Instead, it would lack space for the complexity expected in a qaṣīdah.

This does not mean that there are no qaṣīdahs of six lines. The following two poems by Ibn Abī Ḥaǧalah are polythematic qaṣīdahs of six lines, and nothing suggests that a line is missing. The first is again a congratulatory poem. As in the poem on Ṭaybuġā, the occasion is the *mamdūḥ*'s safe return from pilgrimage. This *mamdūḥ* belongs to a rather untypical category of people receiving panegyrics from littérateurs: he was a physician and "head of medicine", probably head of the physicians in Cairo (meter *wāfir*, rhyme *āṣū*).[30]

وقال يهنّئ القاضي علاء الدين الصغير رئيس الطبّ لمّا قدم صحبة الركاب السلطاني

وفي دينـارِهِ الذَهَــبُ الخِـــلاصُ   أمِــنْ خـدِّ الحبيــبِ لنــا خَــلاصُ

رَقيــــبي في محبَّتِــــهِ رَصـــاصُ   كَلِفتُ بــه خفيــفَ العطـفِ لكـنْ

تُـــشَدُّ لِـرَيِّسِ الطِــبّ القِلاصُ   حَبيــبٌ حَــلَّ في بَــلادٍ إليهــا

وفي قَــصِّ القُـرُوحِ له قِــصاصُ   له في الطــبّ والتَـــشريح شرحٌ

وزُيِّنَــتِ الـــشوارعُ والعِـــراصُ   أتَى مِـــصراً فــزالَ الــسُقْمُ عنهــا

ولي بِجَنَابِــهِ العــالي اختــصاصُ   فكيــفَ أخــافُ ضَــعْفَ الحــالِ فيهــا

1   How can we break away from the beloved so long as the dinar of his cheek is pure gold?

2   I fell in love with him, his body bends agilely, but the one overlooking my love for him is (as dense) as lead.

3   He is a beloved who repaired to a country toward which those who hope to meet the head of medicine saddle their camels.

4   He has many comments on issues of medicine and anatomy, and he takes vengeance on ulcers by cutting them out.

5   When he came to Egypt, illness abandoned it. The streets were adorned and the plazas.

6   Why then should I fear weakness there when I hold a distinguished position at his exalted side?

As in the first two sample poems, Ibn Abī Ḥaǧalah uses a rare rhyme consonant. This time, the choice was not made in response to the *mamdūḥ*'s name. Instead, *ṣād* is sort of a leitmotif in itself. In this short poem, the consonant *ṣād* occurs 12 times, which yields an average of two uses per line. The metals "gold" and "lead"

---

[30] Text: Ms. fol. 53b; ed. ʿAmmān no. 190; ed. Cairo p. 145. In line 4, the manuscript and both editions read الجروح. I would like to read القروح instead, which makes better sense and adds a third *qāf* to this very melodious line.

in the first two lines might already be an allusion to the scientific profession of the physician. The *taḫalluṣ* comes in line 3, in which the *mamdūḥ* is mentioned as *rayyis aṭ-ṭibb* (note the unclassical form) and not by name. Three lines remain for the *madīḥ*.

In Abbasid times, generosity and military prowess were expected to be the main subjects of a panegyric qaṣīdah. Since scholars could hardly be as generous as rulers or military leaders and because they are rather lacking in martial achievements worthy of praise, even poets like al-Mutanabbī found it challenging to praise one of their rank. By the Ayyubid and Mamluk period, poets had learned how to praise scholars and many if not most panegyrics were addressed to them. A physician was still an unusual object for poetic praise, however. Perhaps this accounts for the shortness of the poem. Another reason could be the overall lightness and easiness of the poem, which makes it a qaṣīdah in an epigrammatic mood, for which six lines may have been sufficient.

In at least one case, Ibn Abī Ḥağalah dedicated a *qaṣīdah sudāsiyyah*, as one might call it along the lines of *qaṣīdah subāʿiyyah* (though I have never come across such a designation in the sources) to a scholar, the *qāḍī l-ʿaskar* "judge of the army" Sirāğaddīn al-Hindī. The poem, which is again a congratulatory poem, demonstrates how alike epigram and qaṣīdah could be. The poem is also treated in Emil Homerin's contribution to this volume, in which he gives a detailed background of the person praised, the circumstances of the poem and a more beautiful translation than mine.[31] Here I shall limit myself to a few literary aspects of the qaṣīdah (meter *wāfir*, rhyme *āǧī*):[32]

قال يهنّئ قاضي العسكر الحنفي سراج الدين [عُمَر بن إسحاق الهندي]

إذا مــا زادَ هَمِّــي وآنزِعــاجي   جَلَــوتُ الــراحَ في كأسِ الزُّجَــاجِ

مُــدامٌ قــد غَــدَتْ مــن نار قلــبي   عــلى الثُلــثِ المُبَــاحِ لَدَى المِــزاجِ

فَحَيَّــا الله مَــن أمــسَى نَــدِيمي   عليهــا حــينَ تُــشرِقُ في الدَياجِي

وحَيَّــا بَــلْدَةً فيهــا مُحَيَّــا   سراجِ الديــن يلمَــعُ كالــسِّراج

إمــامٌ في العلــوم وفي القــضايا   فقــوَّمَ أمرهــا بعــد آعوجــاج

فباتَـــت مــصرُ في أمْــنٍ وعَــدْلٍ   وباتَ الــشامُ معتــدِلَ المــزاج

---

[31] See Homerin, Emil Th., "Ibn Abī Ḥağalah and Sufism", in this volume, p. 19ff.

[32] Text: Ms. fol. 15a; ed. ʿAmmān no. 88; ed. Cairo p. 52. In the beginning of line 4, ed. Cairo reads وحَيِّي بلدةً فيها محِبّا and corrects the last word to محبٌّ. The reading مُحيّا, however, is certain and makes excellent sense. For the sake of clearness, I follow ed. ʿAmmān and write the first words of lines 3 and 4 as فحيَا / وحيّا instead of فحيّي / وحيّى as in the manuscript.

1   When my sorrows and troubles grow, I let the wine shine in the goblet of glass.

2   An old wine that the fire of my heart boiled down to the permitted third when it was mixed.

3   May God preserve him who becomes my drinking companion when the wine sparkles in the dark,

4   And may he preserve a country in which the face of Sirāǧaddīn gleams like a lamp!

5   An imam in scholarship and in legal judgments: He straightens the matters when they were crooked.

6   Egypt can thus live in security and justice, and Syria enjoys a well-tempered condition ("mixture").

The parameters of the poem are determined by the name of the *mamdūḥ* and his profession as judge (*qāḍī l-ʿaskar* "judge of the army"). The name Sirāǧaddīn provides for the rhyme in *āǧī* and the leitmotif "lamp, light, sparkling, gleaming". The profession as judge, who has to act with *ʿadl* "fairness", adds a second leitmotif, the "right mixture".

As in many poems from the period, the slot of the *nasīb* is filled by a wine-song, which gives ample occasion to develop the "right mixture" motif as well as the "light" motif. Line 1 starts with the drinker's complaint about his sorrows and troubles, against which he seeks help in the wine, which is "unveiled, made clear" in a glass, the first occurrence of the "light" motif.

The second line brings together both leitmotifs, the *mizāǧ* "mixture" and the "fire of the heart", which causes the wine to boil until two-thirds of its original quantity are evaporated. Such a wine is called *ṭilāʾ* or *muṯallaṯ* and considered lawful according to most legal scholars.[33] The right mixture therefore consists of water and legally permitted wine. Line 3 welcomes a drinking companion who may or may not be the judge himself. The wine again provides the motif "light". Line 4, a relative late *taḫalluṣ* in a six-liner, is linked to line 3. It starts with the same verb and bids a welcome (*ḥayyā*) to the face (*muḥayyā*) of the *mamdūḥ* Sirāǧaddīn. Not only does his name mean "lamp of religion", his face also gleams lamp-like (*sirāǧ*). Now it is no longer the wine but the judge who provides the "light". In line 5 he is praised for making crooked things straight—an easily recognizable variant of the "right mixture" motif, which is again transferred from the wine to the judge. In the last line, security and justice replace the sorrows and troubles with which the poem began. The poem ends with an invocation of the "right mixture". The shortness of the poem allows the poet to intertwine two leitmotifs as tightly as one can imagine.

---

[33] See Wensinck, A.J., "Khamr – 1. Juridical Aspects" in: *EI²* 4:994-997, esp. 995b and 996b.

5 The micro-qaṣīdah as a means of communication

Its brevity renders the *qaṣīdah subāʿiyyah* especially suitable as a means of communication. It is longer than an epigram, which can only convey a single idea and has to be pointed; it is shorter and more informal than a full-length qaṣīdah. Hence, the micro-qaṣīdah functions like a greeting card today. Typically, a considerable number of micro-qaṣīdahs are *tahānīʾ* "congratualtions". Often poets answered a micro-qaṣīdah with another one, keeping the same rhyme and meter. Unfortunately, poets used to include only their part of the conversation in their Dīwāns and to skip the text of their dialogue partner. Sometimes, however, we are able to reconstruct a poetic exchange, as in the following case.

Ibn Abī Ḥaǧalah's sparring partner is Burhānaddīn al-Qīrāṭī, probably the most important of those poets who "walked under the Nubatian banner".[34] The conversation was initiated by al-Qīrāṭī, who included the poem in his Dīwān (but not Ibn Abī Ḥaǧalah's answer). Ibn Abī Ḥaǧalah instead included his poem in his own Dīwān, again without al-Qīrāṭī's poem, but he provides both texts in his chapter on al-Qīrāṭī in his *Maǧnāṭīs ad-durr an-nafīs*,[35] and this enables us to detect a veritable surprise.

This is al-Qīrāṭī's poem in the version of the *Maǧnāṭīs* (meter *basīṭ*, rhyme *āʾū*):[36]

وكتب إلى الأديب شهاب الدين بن أبي حجلة

يا ناعِسَ الطَرْفِ مـا لِلعَـين إغْفـاءُ	فَـلا لِأُذْنِـكَ إنْ نادَيْـتُ إصْـغـاءُ
بِنُـونَ أُقْـسِمُ مـا في واوِ صُدْغِكَ لي	كالـواوِ عَـينٌ ولا طـاءٌ ولا فـاءُ
نَعَمْ ولا في شهاب الدِين حـين أضـا	سَـناه قـافٌ ولا دالٌ ولا حـاءُ
أفدِيـه مِـن حجـلِيٍّ طـائرٍ لمـداً	سـير الـيمانيّ فيـه عنـه إبطـاءُ
لا غَـرْوَ إنْ رَكِبَ الشهبا على نفـرٍ	في الـنظم قـد دَهَمَتهُم منـه دهمـاءُ
يا فاضـل العصر إنّ المغـرب آبتـهجت	مـذ لاحَ مـن صُبْحِكَ الوضَّاح لألاءُ
[...] مـن نظمـك النامي فأحرف مـا	نظمتـه عنـده الـوأواء فأفـاءُ

---

[34] On al-Qīrāṭī and his relation to Ibn Nubātah see Bauer, Thomas, "»Extremely Beautiful and Extremely Long«: Al-Qīrāṭī's Exuberant Letter from the Year 761/1360", in: Lowry, Joseph E. & Shawkat M. Toorawa, *Arabic Humanities, Islamic Thought: Essays in Honor of Everett K. Rowson*, Leiden 2017, pp. 338-360.

[35] On *Maǧnāṭīs ad-durr* see the contribution by Nefeli Papoutsakis in this volume.

[36] Text: Ms. Riyāḍ p. 16, ms. Yale fol. 10b. In line 5, ms. Yale reads الشهاب instead of الشهبا. At the beginning of the last line, three syllables are missing in both manuscripts.

1 O you of the languid glance: You don't allow the eye to slumber, nor does your ear listen when I call.

2 I swear by (sūrat) Nūn: In the *wāw* of your sidelocks there is neither *ʿayn* nor *ṭāʾ* nor *fāʾ* like this *wāw* for me! (= *ʿaṭf* "inclination").

3 Yes, and when Šihābaddin's splendor sheds light, there is neither *qāf* nor *dāl* nor *ḥāʾ* in him. (= *qadḥ* "blemish").

4 I pay homage to him as a man who flies like a partridge such that the flight of a dove seems slow in comparison.

5 Small wonder then that when he mounts the white horse to vie with other people in poetry, disaster / *a black horse* overwhelms them.

6 O solitaire of the epoch: the West is delighted that light has dawned from your bright morning.

7 […] of your flourishing poetry / *an-Nāmī*, so that compared to your arranging letters in poetry, al-Waʾwāʾ suffers a speech defect.

This poem is obviously a *qaṣīdah subāʿiyyah* that starts with a *nasīb* in which the poet complains about being neglected by his beloved. After a rather unspectacular *taḫalluṣ* in line 3, the remaining lines are in praise of the addressee with special reference to his poetry. Besides a number of words of the pattern *faʿlāʾ*, the stylistic feature that sticks out are the many words that are also the names of letters of the alphabet. The word *ʿayn* in line one means "eye", but it is also the name of a letter, although the reader may not be aware of this double meaning yet. Only after learning the importance of letter names, might he go back and catch the reference to a letter-name already in line 1. In line 2, the reference is to surah 68 of the Quran, known by the name of the letter *nūn*. The *wāw* in the same line is a common object of comparison to the sidelock. The letter-names that follow together spell the words *ʿaṭf* and *qadḥ* (line 3). The word *aḥruf* "letters" occurs in the last line together with the name of the poet al-Waʾwāʾ, which sounds like the name of a letter, but is not. At first, the reader might doubt whether this play on letter-names is a good idea. It is too easy to solve to count as a riddle. And it seems a bit too silly to come across as a serious communication. Taken as an independent poem in praise of a poet, it seems not entirely convincing.

However, the poem is not an autonomous praise poem. Rather it conveys a barely concealed message to its addressee. A careful reading of this poem and the reply to it leaves no doubt that the poem was written to criticise Ibn Abī Ḥaǧalah for not writing to him and not answering his letters. To reprimand people for not communicating or to excuse one's self for not having responded in time was always a major subject of human communication, and so it remains in the present day. No one has studied the many Arabic letters and poems on this subject so far, but there are many, and this poem is one.

Read as reprimand in the guise of praise, most of the lines assume a second meaning. In line 1, the notion of the beloved whose glance is full of sleep whereas the lover is sleepless, can easily be transferred to the relation between al-Qirāṭī, the sleepless lover, and Ibn Abī Ḥaǧalah, the drowsy friend who does not react. The second hemistich expresses in clear words the writer's concern: "Your ear does not listen when I call". What is missing is your "inclination", as line 2 says. This "inclination" is spelled letter-by-letter demonstrating the way the addressee could show his inclination: Letters! Do write me letters! I am waiting for your ʿayn, your ṭāʾ, your fāʾ and all the other letters of the alphabet. This is obviously what is behind the obsession with letter names in this poem.

After this reprimand, the poet continues with a conciliatory line 3: "Yes" (meaning: "Yes, so is the state of affairs, but …"), if Šihābaddīn would answer finally, there would be no qadḥ "blemish". In a normal madīḥ poem, this line would be odd. No one would reasonably assume that a mamdūḥ who "lets his splendour shine" would deserve rebuke. As an offer to pardon him for his negligence, it makes perfect sense.

Formally, the poem consists of nasīb, taḫalluṣ and madīḥ. As regards content, all three parts form a whole and treat a single subject, the addressee's neglect, as line three makes sufficiently clear. Nevertheless, al-Qirāṭī changes his line of argument in line 4. In this line, al-Qirāṭī picks up Ibn Abī Ḥaǧalah's self-identification with the partridge. As such, he can fly more quickly than a dove, the bird with which al-Qirāṭī identifies. In line 5, Ibn Abī Ḥaǧalah is again portrayed as running away from other poets (such as al-Qirāṭī), much to their detriment. This is a perfect case of rebuke in the guise of praise (aḍ-ḍamm fī maʿraḍ al-madḥ), as a theorist of rhetoric would say. On the one hand, the fellow poet is praised for outstripping his fellows. At the same time, he is rebuked for not caring about them and their friendship to him. The last two lines are an appeal to answer this poem with his poetry. Line 5 contains an allusion to Ibn Abī Ḥaǧalah's western origin. Line 7 contains the name of two poets, the first in the form of a tawriyah. The word nāmin "flourishing" is also the name of the Syrian poet an-Nāmī (399/1008)[37]. His contemporary al-Waʾwāʾ ad-Dimašqī (4th/10th century)[38] was chosen for the sound-effect of his name rather than his poetry.

Burhānaddīn al-Qirāṭī himself included the poem in his own Dīwān entitled *Maṭlaʿ an-nayyirayn*. This version, however, is surprisingly different from the version in *Maġnāṭīs ad-durr*. Here is the full text of the *Maṭlaʿ an-nayyirayn* version (meter *basīṭ*, rhyme *āʾū*):[39]

يا ناعِــسَ الطَّــرْفِ مــا لِلعَــين إغْفــاءُ   فَهَـــلْ لِأُذْنِـــكَ إنْ نادَيْـــتُ إصْـــغاءُ

بِـصادَ أقْـسِمُ مــا في واوِ صُــدْغِكَ لي   كالـــواوِ عَــينٌ ولا طــاءٌ ولا فــاءُ

---

[37] See *EAL*, p. 577.
[38] See *EAL*, p. 808.
[39] Text: *Maṭlaʿ an-nayyirayn*, ms. Istanbul Fatiḥ 3861 fol. 102a, ms. British Museum OR. 2913 fol. 200a.

نَعَمْ وما في شهاب الدِّيـن منـذ بَـدَا سَـــناه قـــافٌ ولا دالٌ ولا حـــاءُ

أفدِيـــه مِـــن حجـــليٍّ طـــائرٍ لمـــدىً مــا أَعْنَقَـتْ فيـه قبـلَ اليَـوْمِ عَنْقـاءُ

سَـــبّاقُ غـــاياتِ آدابٍ مَطالِعُـــهُ لـــشُهْبِها في مَجَـرِّ الأُفْـق إجـراءُ

إنْ ذكّـر الوَصْـفَ تَـشْبِيبًا وأنَّثَـهُ سَـبَا الـوَرَى حَـسَنٌ منـه وحَـسْناءُ

أغْـزالُهُ في كِلا النَـوْعَينِ مـا بَرِحَـتْ لهـا محبّـــانِ لُـــوطيٌّ وزَنّاءُ

1 O you of the languid glance: You don't allow the eye to slumber, but will your ear listen when I call?

2 I swear by (sūrat) Ṣād: In the *wāw* of your sidelocks, there is neither *ʿayn* nor *ṭāʾ* nor *fāʾ* that is like this *wāw* for me! (= *ʿaṭf* "inclination").

3 Yes, and since Šihābaddīn's splendor has appeared, there is neither *qāf* nor *dāl* nor *ḥāʾ* in him (= *qadḥ* "blemish").

4 I pay homage to him as a man who flies like a partridge to a point that not even a griffon has hastened to before.

5 He is the winner in the race to reach the goals of literature; the white horses / *shooting stars* of the initial parts (of his poems) keep running at the trail of the horizon.

6 Whenever he portrays a male or female in his amorous poetry, the whole world is captivated by a beautiful youth or a beautiful girl.

7 His love poems are of both natures and so will never be without "two kinds of lovers: the sodomite and the fornicator".

The variants in the first three lines are inconspicuous. In line 1 we have *fa-hal* instead of *fa-lā* and in line 3 *mundu badā sanāhu* instead of the rather synonymous *ḥīna aḍā sanāhu*. In line 2, the surah whose name is also the name of a letter is *Ṣād* (surah 38) instead of *Nūn*. I cannot detect any reason for this change.

The differences between both versions increase considerably in line 4, where the entire second hemistich changes. Now it is not the peaceful dove that cannot keep up with the partridge, it is the legendary griffon who is left behind. Other than in case of the dove, al-Qīrāṭī certainly did not identify with the griffon. The hyperbole is much stronger and the reproach seems to be more violent. The addressee is not content to compete with normal birds, but vies with supernatural creatures instead. How could he care about a normal man like him?

Both versions of line 5 have nothing more in common than the addressee's taking part in a race for the best literature, in which a white horse (*ašhab*, alluding to the addressee's name Šihābaddīn) takes part. Just as the griffon is a supernatural creature, the race takes place in the celestial spheres in the *Maṭlaʿ an-nayyirayn* version, whereas the competition takes place down on earth in the *Maǧnāṭīs* version.

The last two lines differ completely in both versions. The only thing they have in common is references to poets. In the last line of the *Maġnāṭīs* version, two poets of average prominence are mentioned. In the last line of the *Maṭlaʿ an-nayyirayn* instead, no poet is mentioned by name, but one of the most prominent poets in the history of Arabic literature is quoted, Abū Nuwās. The last hemistich of the poem is a verbatim quote from what was probably Abū Nuwās's most famous poem. It is his *ḫamriyyah* no. 1, which starts with Abū Nuwās's most often quoted verse: *daʿ ʿanka lawmī fa-inna l-lawma iġrāʾū*.[40]

The third line of the poem, hardly less famous than the first line, describes a *ġulāmiyyah* who pours the wine. She is a girl "with a pussy" dressed as a boy "with a penis" and is desired by both "the sodomite and the fornicator".[41] Quoting this frivolous verse is obviously harsher than the version of the *Maġnāṭīs*. It seems as if al-Qīrāṭī wanted to say in lines 4 and 5 that, on the one hand, his friend moved into other spheres and does not deal any longer with his true friends and colleagues. Line 6 and 7 tell us that, on the other hand, he still addresses even people with dubious reputation. In this "rebuke in the guise of praise", the praise seems rather dubious and the rebuke is all too clear.

Which of the two version is the original one? Several interpretations are possible but all have to take the following observations into account:

(1) The *Maṭlaʿ an-nayyirayn* version is more spiteful than the *Maġnāṭīs* version. When Ibn Abī Ḥaǧalah wrote his *Maġnāṭīs*, both poets must have been reconciled again. Not only did Ibn Abī Ḥaǧalah dedicate a large entry in his *Maġnāṭīs* to al-Qīrāṭī, he also gave space to this exchange of micro-qaṣīdahs. It is hardly conceivable that al-Qīrāṭī produced a nastier version of his qaṣīdah after their reconciliation.

(2) The main clue is the role of Abū Nuwās. In strophic poems, in almost all epigrams and in many other poems, the key line of the poem is the last one. The rest of the poem is often modelled on it. In the *Maṭlaʿ an-nayyirayn* version, Abū Nuwās's poem is the starting point. The last line, or rather the last hemistich with its Abū Nuwās quotation, is a key sentence of the poem. It also provides for rhyme and meter of the poem. A closer look turns up another quotation from the same poem in the first hemistich. The phrase *li-l-ʿayni iġfāʾū* occurs (in the form *bi-l-ʿayni iġfāʾū*) at the end of line 5 of Abū Nuwās's *ḫamriyyah*.[42] Inconspicuous as it is, only those who notice the Abū Nuwās quotation in the last line may have realized this. Most readers of the *Maġnāṭīs* version, if they noticed the

---

[40] Ewald Wagner lists 31 complete translations of the poem and cites a large number of translations of its first and its third line, see his *Abū Nuwās in Übersetzung. Eine Stellensammlung zu Abū Nuwās-Übersetzungen vornehmlich in europäische Sprachen*, Wiesbaden 2012, pp. 14, 62-64, 207-215.

[41] The text of the poem is given in *Der Dīwān des Abū Nuwās. Teil III*, ed. Ewald Wagner, Wiesbaden, Stuttgart 1988, pp. 2-4.

[42] *Dīwān des Abū Nuwās III*, p. 3.

parallel at all, would have likely considered it a coincidence. It can almost be ruled out that al-Qīrāṭī would transform a poem starting with an imperceptible Abū Nuwās-quotation and mentioning the poets an-Nāmī and al-Waʾwāʾ into one that concludes with a famous hemistich by Abū Nuwās. In fact, only a transformation in the other direction is conceivable.

(3) Ibn Abī Ḥaǧalah's reply, which we will examine next, is ambivalent. On the one hand, there could be a reference to the "dove" of the *Maġnāṭīs* version of al-Qīrāṭī's poem. On the other hand, a woman called *Asmāʾ* provides the rhyme word at the end of the first line. Examined against the backdrop of the *Maġnāṭīs* version of al-Qīrāṭī's poem, there is no subtext to the name. The *Maṭlaʿ an-nayyirayn* version, however, gives an interesting clue, again through the poem by Abū Nuwās. In line 9 – a sort of an "anti-*nasīb*"– Abū Nuwās says that the tavern in which he and his companions drink wine served by the *ġulāmiyyah* is the place over which he weeps when he has to leave it. Instead, he does not weep over the places that the old Arab poets bemoaned in the *nasīb*-sections of their poems, the places *tuḥillu bihā Hindun wa-Asmāʾū* "where Hind and Asmāʾ alight".[43] The deeper meaning of the phrase could have been: I am not like the *ġulāmiyyah* but rather like Asmāʾ, her counterpart. This understanding presupposes the reader's understanding of the Abū Nuwās connection, which is hardly possible without knowing the last hemistich of the *Maṭlaʿ an-nayyirayn* version of al-Qīrāṭī's poem.

To reconcile these points, I would suggest the following sequence of events:

1. Burhānaddīn al-Qīrāṭī was upset with the behavior of his friend Ibn Abī Ḥaǧalah, who maintained close contact with many people who were not very involved in literature, but he did not respond when his colleague got in touch with him. As a result, he composed a *qaṣīdah subāʿiyyah* (a form much more popular with Ibn Abī Ḥaǧalah than with al-Qīrāṭī himself), which on the surface maintained decorum and masqueraded as a poem praising the addressee, but which contained a bitter undertone.

2. Ibn Abī Ḥaǧalah responded with a qaṣīdah in the same form, which may have been an earlier version of the qaṣīdah we have now. The reference to Asmāʾ must have already been there.

3. Both poets reconciled; al-Qīrāṭī included his own poem in his Dīwān *Maṭlaʿ an-nayyirayn*.

4. Ibn Abī Ḥaǧalah devised his large anthology *Muǧtabā l-udabā* and, in order to get more contributions, wrote his *Maġnāṭīs ad-durr an-nafīs*, a sampler of already existing entries plus a "call for papers". One of the entries already present was the one on al-Qīrāṭī. As a document of his relationship with him, he wanted to include their exchange of *subāʿiyyah*s, but found al-Qīrāṭī's text too

---

⁴³ *Dīwān des Abū Nuwās III*, p. 3.

harsh. Therefore, he asked al-Qīrāṭī to produce a milder version. Another possibility is that al-Qīrāṭī, asked to proofread the entry about him, decided to produce the second version of the poem. Whatever the case may have been, he crossed out the frivolous Abū Nuwās quotation, replaced Abū Nuwās by two lesser known poets, and moved the racecourse down to earth.

5. Ibn Abī Ḥaǧalah adapted his own poem to this new version and included both poems in their revised form in his *Maġnāṭīs ad-durr*.

Finally, let us look at Ibn Abī Ḥaǧalah's response to al-Qīrāṭī's poem. The text in the *Maġnāṭīs ad-durr* is identical to the text in the Dīwān. The poem, in which he admits his guilt, confirms our interpretation of al-Qīrāṭī's *qaṣīdah subāʿiyyah* as a sophisticated poem, combining reprimand, praise and an offer of reconciliation. Here is Ibn Abī Ḥaǧalah's response (meter *basīṭ*, rhyme *āʾū*):[44]

غَنَّتْ عـلـى الْعُـودِ في الأوراقِ ورقـاءُ   ووافقـت جنكهـا في الفِعـلِ أسـمـاءُ

فكيفَ لا يبعثُ التشبيبُ مَيْتَ هـوىً   أمـسَى لهُ في نَـسِيمِ الحـيّ أهـواءُ

وكيـفَ تَخْفَـى لإبـراهيمَ نارُ قِـرىً   بهـا الـثُّريّا لهـا في الـشُّهبِ إثـراءُ

يَجـودُ حـتَّى بـنـَظمٍ كُلُّـهُ دُرَرٌ   عنـدَ الدَّراري له كالبـدر لألاءُ

بقـافَ أُقسِمُ عـينُ الشمسِ لـيسَ لها   لـولاه شـينٌ ولا راءٌ ولا فـاءُ

إنْ دَكَّـني نظُمُـهُ العـالي فـلا عجـبٌ   إذا خَفيـتُ فـكمْ لـلدكِّ إخفـاءُ

ما طـابَ لي بعدَ خيرِ الرُّسلِ في أحدٍ   سـواهُ مـيمٌ ولا دالٌ ولا حـاءُ

1 A dove sang on the bough amidst the leaves and Asmāʾ harmonized with its harp in what she did.

2 How could amorous poetry fail to awake a victim of love when passions reach him via breezes wafting from (the beloved's) tribe?

3 And how could Ibrāhīm's fire of hospitality be hidden, where the Pleiades shine to enrich (the brightness of) shooting stars?

4 He grants generously, even poetry all of which is pearls that shine like the full moon when the bright stars glisten.

5 I swear by (sūrat) Qāf: If it were not for him, even the disc of the sun / *the quarter ʿAyn Šams* would lack *šīn* and *rāʾ* and *fāʾ* (= *šaraf* "glory").

---

44 Text: *Dīwān Ibn Abī Ḥaǧalah*, Ms. fol. 3a; ed. ʿAmmān no. 2; ed. Cairo pp. 18-19; *Maġnāṭīs ad-durr*, Ms. Riyāḍ p. 16-17, ms. Yale fol. 10b-11a. – Variant readings: Line 1: Ms., ed. Cairo, ms. Riyāḍ, ms. Yale: جنكها, ed. ʿAmmān: حبكها. – Line 3: Ms., ed. ʿAmmān, ed. Cairo: تخفى, ms. Riyāḍ, ms. Yale: يخفى. – Line 4: Ms., ed. ʿAmmān, ms. Riyāḍ, ms. Yale: حتى, ed. Cairo: حبّي. – Ms., ed. ʿAmmān, ed. Cairo: كالدرّ, ms. Riyāḍ, ms. Yale: كالبدر. – Line 6: Ms., ed. ʿAmmān, ms. Riyāḍ, ms. Yale: دكني, ed. Cairo: دلّني. – Ms., ed. ʿAmmān, ms. Riyāḍ, ms. Yale: للدكّ, ed. Cairo: للتُرك.

6 No wonder that I disappeared as his exalted poetry crushed me (*dakka*). How often has crushing caused things to disappear!

7 Besides the best prophet of all, no one else deserves to receive a *mīm*, a *dāl* and a *ḥā'* from me more than he (= *madḥ* "praise").

Ibn Abī Ḥaǧalah's answer to al-Qirāṭī is again a *qaṣīdah subāʿiyyah* with two lines of *nasīb* and a *taḫalluṣ* in line 3. As in al-Qirāṭī's poem, the structure does not determine the content and the *nasīb* is already part of the message. Here it is a message of peace and harmony. In the *nasīb*-sections of countless poems, doves complain about a loss. In this poem, the dove is not complaining. Instead, it is in complete harmony with a harp player who accompanies its singing. One can imagine that insiders could take the dove as the one that could not catch up with the partridge and Asmā' as Ibn Abī Ḥaǧalah's denial to be identified with Abū Nuwās's *ġulāmiyyah*. This interpretation presupposes knowledge of both versions of al-Qirāṭī's poem, while those who read only the *Maǧnāṭīs* may have still grasped the identity of both doves.

The pigeon is sitting on a *ʿūd* "bough", a word that could also mean "lute". This meaning, which is not the intended one, is suggested by mention of the "harp". We have the stylistic device of a *tawriyah muhayya'ah* before us. One might also detect the stylistic device *tawǧīh*. Three words in this line correspond to terms from the fields of writing and grammar: *awrāq* "leaves (of paper)", *fiʿl* "verb" and *asmā'* "nouns". The message seems to be: Now that I am writing, harmony is re-established.

The "awakening" in line two seems to correspond to the "sleepiness" in al-Qirāṭī's *nasīb*. In the language of love-poetry, the poet conveys the message that his friend's poetry, in which sleepy eyes were mentioned, has awakened in him. As in al-Qirāṭī's poem, the *taḫalluṣ* is so smooth a transition that the reader does not get the impression that the *nasīb* treats a subject different from the *madīḥ*.

Two lines about Ibrāhīm (al-Qirāṭī)'s generosity, which certainly includes forgiveness, follow, and all conceivable celestial bodies are united in lines 3 to 5. Line 6 responds to the oath on the Quran in line 2 of al-Qirāṭī's poem. This time it is surah 50 called surat *Qāf*, another surah named for a letter. Having begun with the name of a letter, Ibn Abī Ḥaǧalah spells out the word *šaraf* "glory" in the way al-Qirāṭī spelled out the words "(no) inclination" and "blemish".

Before coming to the end, Ibn Abī Ḥaǧalah finds an excuse for not writing to his colleague earlier through use of a stylistic form called *ḥusn at-taʿlīl* "phantastic etiology". He admits that he "disappeared" (*ḫafītu*), but it was only his friend's "exalted poetry" that "crushed" him and made him disappear. In the last line, the word *qadḥ* of al-Qirāṭī's reproach is transformed into the word *madḥ* "praise", and harmony and friendship are restored.

6 Conclusion

An inconspicuous marginal note in a handbook of poetry from the 11th century gave rise to the idea that seven lines are enough to make a qaṣidah. The idea was revived at the court in Ḥamāh in the third decade of the 8th/14th century and came to the fore when Ibn Nubātah composed a large number of *qaṣāʾid subāʿiyyah* later in life and assembled them in a Dīwān called *as-Sabʿah as-sayyārah*. This happened at a time when all walks of society cultivated poetry, which was used as a means of communication both to address people of higher rank as well as to communicate with peers or even with those of a lower segment. These circumstances paved the way for the epigram's unprecedented career, but it also provided fertile ground for the micro-qaṣidah. A number of poets composed poems in this new form, which proved to be flexible for a number of purposes, less demanding than a long qaṣidah (for both the poet and the audience), but with a high level of complexity and sophistication as well. Its *nasīb* offered the opportunity to reshape traditional themes of love and wine poetry in a playful manner, often in accordance with the main subject of the qaṣidah, and the transition between the *nasīb* and the final part, mostly *madīḥ*, gained especial importance. The attention that the *taḥalluṣ* necessarily catches in so short a poem as in a *qaṣidah subāʿiyyah* gives the impression that many micro-qaṣidahs are in fact tripartite qaṣidahs with the *taḥalluṣ* as a section in its own right.

With his more than fifty *subāʿiyyāt*, Ibn Abī Ḥaǧalah was perhaps the most zealous poet to emulate his revered model Ibn Nubātah in the production of seven-liners. He used them to address people from very different layers of society. Among his addressees are the Abbasid caliph, the Mamluk sultan an-Nāṣir Ḥasan, who had already received a number of *qaṣāʾid subāʿiyyāt* from Ibn Nubātah, and the Marinid sultan of Fez. Wazīrs, dawādārs and umarāʾ of different ranks followed. Poems for fellow udabāʾ such as Ibn Nubātah, al-Qīrāṭi and, again from the west, Lisānaddīn Ibn al-Ḥaṭīb played an important role. More important still were the scholars, especially scholars of law and judges, but even the doctor ʿAlāʾaddīn aṣ-Ṣaǧīr got a *qaṣidah subāʿiyyah* of his own. Micro-qaṣidahs were used as a means of exchange instead of or in addition to letters and epigrams. They proved an ideal instrument in order to congratulate or welcome people but also to reproach friends in a mild and elegant way. The composers of micro-qaṣidahs could show their mastery of a traditional and complex form with the utmost brevity.

Finally, *qaṣāʾid subāʿiyyah* are interesting also for literary history. They demonstrate that Arabic poets, at least in the 7th-8th/13th-14th century (but most probably also earlier) did not consider length the main criterion of a qaṣidah. The existence of *muqaṭṭaʿāt* that are longer than *qaṣāʾid subāʿiyyah* shows that being polythematic, i.e. consisting of *nasīb* and a final part, most often *madīḥ*, was paramount.

Despite the undeniable fascination of the micro-qaṣīdah, its career, initiated by Ibn Nubātah, seems to have been rather short. As far as one can tell at the present state of our knowledge, micro-qaṣīdahs did not play any role further in the Ottoman period.

Bibliography

Primary Sources

Abū Nuwās, *Der Dīwān des Abū Nuwās. Teil III*, ed. Ewald Wagner, Wiesbaden, Stuttgart 1988.
Ibn Abī Ḥaǧalah, *Dīwān*, Ms Cairo 1525 adab (copied 1028/1619).
Ibn Abī Ḥaǧalah, *Dīwān*, ed. Muǧāhid Muṣṭafā Bahǧat & Aḥmad Ḥumayd Muḫlif, ʿAmmān 1431/2010.
Ibn Abī Ḥaǧalah, *Dīwān*, ed. Aḥmad Ḥilmī Ḥulwah, Kairo 1435/2014.
Ibn Abī Ḥaǧalah, *Maǧnāṭīs ad-durr an-nafīs*, Ms Riyadh King Saud University Library, 2932 zāy (copied 1274/1857).
Ibn Abī Ḥaǧalah, *Maǧnāṭīs ad-durr an-nafīs*, Ms Yale Landberg MSS 69 (copied 1302/1885).
Ibn Abī Ḥaǧalah, *Sukkardān as-Sulṭān*, ed. ʿAlī Muḥammad ʿUmar, Cairo 1421/2001.
Ibn Ḥiǧǧah al-Ḥamawī, *Ḫizānat al-adab wa-ġāyat al-arab*, ed. Kawkab Diyāb, 5 vols., Beirut 1421/2001.
Ibn Nubātah al-Miṣrī, *Dīwān*, ed. Muḥammad al-Qalqīlī, Cairo 1312/1905.
al-Qīrāṭī, Burhānaddīn Ibrāhīm: *Maṭlaʿ an-nayyirayn*, Ms. Istanbul Fatih 3861 (copied 782/1380).
al-Qīrāṭī, Burhānaddīn Ibrāhīm: *Maṭlaʿ an-nayyirayn*, Ms. British Museum OR. 2913 (copied 823/1420).

Secondary Sources

EAL = Meisami, Julie Scott & Paul Starkey, *Encyclopedia of Arabic Literature*, 2 vols., London, New York 1998.

Literary Sweets

Interlacing Motifs in the *Sukkardān as-Sulṭān* of Ibn Abī Ḥaǧalah (1325-1375)

Beatrice Gruendler

> BLUE IS A mysterious color, hue of illness and nobility, the rarest color in nature. It is the color of ambiguous depth, of the heavens and of the abyss at once; blue is the color of the shadow side, the tint of the marvelous and the inexplicable, of desire, of knowledge, of the blue movie, of blue talk, or raw meat and rare steak, of melancholy and the unexpected (once in a blue moon, out of the blue). It is the color of anode plates, royalty at Rome, smoke, distant hills, postmarks, Georgian silver, thin milk, and hardened steel; of veins seen through skin and notices of dismissal in the American railroad business. Brimstone burns blue, and a blue candle flame is said to indicate the presence of ghosts. The blue-black sky of Vincent van Gogh's 1890 *Crows Flying over a Cornfield* seems to express the painter's doom. But, according to Grace Mirabella, editor of *Mirabella*, a blue cover used on a magazine always guarantees increased sales at a newsstand. "It is America's favorite color," she says.
> Paradoxically, it is the only one of all the colors which can be legitimately seen as essentially symbolic of, dark and light both, oddly black in the night and almost white at the horizon by day...
>
> Alexander Theroux, *The Primary Colors*, pp. 1-2.

Alexander Theroux travels along a seemingly endless string of associations across spheres of nature, culture, and language with no other unifying element than the motif of the color blue. His line of association is at once puzzling and beguiling, surprising and logical, as are his imaginary journeys through ever new contexts in which some shade of blue appears. He recalls in us situations we never thought of in terms of color, situations we are nonetheless familiar with and recognize through the connection he establishes. But it takes letting go of familiar ways of order and following his particular thread of thought, something the reader of modern literature is not accustomed to.[1]

The above epigraph is the beginning of the first chapter, and Theroux continues in this vein for sixty-seven pages, followed by similar chapters on yellow and red. (He also wrote a book on orange). The color motif is an unusual choice. But it works – if one allows oneself to be guided by Theroux's sheerly inexhaustible repertoire of associations, ranging from the daily to the recondite and from the trivial to the recherché.

---

[1]   I am indebted to David Brennan, Isabel Toral-Niehoff, and Ghassan El Masri for their valuable comments and suggestions on an earlier version of the present article.

To the readers and writers of the Mamluk age, Theroux's method would not have appeared as outlandish as it does to us. They were living in the later centuries of a long and continuous textual tradition, which they felt obliged to be conversant in, and they often did so by excerpting and compiling what had come about in the many preceding centuries. The only difference would have been their greater reliance on texts, past and present, rather than on surrounding real life. Otherwise, an educated Mamluk reader would not have been fazed by Theroux's firework of successive contexts connected only by one common element.

Ibn Abī Ḥaǧalah played in many registers of literature; he composed panegyrics, lamentations, *maqāmah*s, thematic anthologies on love, death, epidemics, and cemeteries, and a handbook on chess.[2] The book under discussion *Sukkardān as-sulṭān* (The Sultan's Sugar Bowl) takes the seventh regnal year of the highly educated al-Ḥasan b. Qalāwūn (1356, counting both rules 1347-51 and 1354-61), who was esteemed by contemporary intellectuals, as an occasion for a literary gift.[3] Its overall plan is the number seven, which recurs in the sultan's vita (he is the seventh sibling to rule), the creation, Islam, and the cosmology of Egypt, and Ibn Abī Ḥaǧalah mirrors this with the book's two sets of seven chapters. Yet the book's architecture is more complex than this and contains various further structuring principles.[4] Its larger topics are historical accounts of the Qalāwūnid rulers, their Egyptian predecessors, and the geography and legends of Egypt and Cairo. These are briefly covered in the first series of seven chapters.

For instance, in the Cairo chapter, the author tells of Ibn Ṭūlūn's expedition to explore the great pyramid. He recounts how robbers drag away treasures during the subsequent raids and lose one of their group who goes mad and vanishes inside the tomb. Ibn Abī Ḥaǧalah also writes about other religious groups of his own time and their sometimes peculiar customs, such as the Coptic sacrifices to the Nile. The book's main part, however, is an expanded second series of seven more detailed chapters, treating for example rulers from before the Mamluk era, from the Qurʾānic Moses and Joseph to the maligned Fatimid al-Ḥākim (r. 386-411/996-1021).

Each chapter of the second set is followed by a digressive flight of seven sections strung along one aspect of the foregoing chapter and exceeding it in length.

---

[2]   On Ibn Abī Ḥaǧalah, see, Robson, James & Umberto Rizzitano, "Ibn Abī Ḥajala", in: *EI²* 3 (1968), p. 686; Gruendler, Beatrice, "Ibn Abi Ḥajalah", in: Lowry, Joseph & Devin Stewart (eds.), *Essays in Arabic Literary Biography 1350-1850*, Wiesbaden 2009, pp. 118-126; and Seidensticker, Tilman, "Ibn Abī Ḥajala (725-76/1325-75)", in: Meisami, Julie S. & Paul Starkey (eds.), *Encyclopedia of Arabic Literature*, 2 vols., London and New York 1998, 1:305.

[3]   On this work, see Salim, Maḥmūd Rizq, *ʿAṣr salāṭīn al-mamālīk wa-nitāǧuhu l-ʿilmī wa-l-adabī*, 8 vols., Cairo 1955-65, vol. 5 (part 3.1.), p. 329, Sallām, Muḥammad Zaġlūl, *al-Adab fī l-ʿaṣr al-mamlūkī*, 4 vols., reprint Alexandria 1996-99, 2:216-37, and al-Musawi, Muhsin, "Premodern Belletristic Prose", in: Allen, Roger & D. S. Richards (eds.), *Arabic Literature in the Post-Classical Period*, Cambridge UK 2006, pp. 101-33, esp. 117.

[4]   On the structure of the chapters, see Appendix A to this article.

In this article I focus on this part of the book. The appendices have no unifying subject; their cohesion is provided by a mesh of variegated motifs that strings together the widest possible array of historical, geographic, religious, legendary, literary, and medical tidbits. The author does not introduce these appendices other than with the subtitle "The cooing of [the chapter's] sweet bird." What really connects them is the motifs by which he groups the various elements together. But he does not limit himself to one motif at a time, nor does he in many cases spell out the motif. He uses several motifs at once, combining or alternating between them, like the different registers in a piece of music, following now this now that motif, and keeping the reader guessing in each new selection which thread will be picked up and which one dropped. For the author, the pleasure here lies in collecting, and for the erudite reader in uncovering snippets from the entirety of Arabic written heritage up to Ibn Abī Ḥaǧalah's own time. The logic of motifs is the sole structural device of this literary bouquet, or kaleidoscope, unfettered by subject matter.

It is in the chapters' conclusions that Ibn Abī Ḥaǧalah comes into his own, in the display of his repertoire, taste, and acumen as a compiler, abandoning the orders of time and place followed in the preceding chapters, and guided solely by the logic of the literary motif. In keeping with the book's overall structure, there are seven items per appendix. Beyond this they differ dramatically.

He begins an appendix with an account, then adds another that stays with the same motif, then shifts to another motif contained in either of the previous accounts and connects further accounts to the second motif, and so on. Not satisfied with strings of tales on one motif, like Theroux with the color blue, Ibn Abī Ḥaǧalah selects accounts that reunite multiple motifs and then switches between different threads of association in a given section, creating a layered web of crisscrossing connections. He further includes accounts that echo motifs from the other appendices, linking these together across the second half of the book. He focuses on these motifs; literary form and style differ from case to case. Poetry alternates with prose, legend with historical fact, anecdote with miracle story or prophetic tale. The period covered ranges from the pre-Islamic *Ǧāhiliyyah* to Ibn Abī Ḥaǧalah's own time, the geography from Spain in the west, via Cyprus and Egypt to the Caucasus, Transoxania, Tibet, and China in the east. The appendices are of course best enjoyed when they are read in full in the original.[5] Yet to show their unique composition, I provide a commented digest of two of them here.

The Appendix to the second chapter will serve as a first example. The chapter's topic is Moses (like Joseph, a ruler in Egypt, according to the Qurʾān), and the appended selections display three motifs: the **ambiguous answer**, the **self-delivered death sentence** (identical with the Biblical motif of Uriah's letter[6]), and the **eloquent repartee**. Added to these are submotifs, which constitute re-

---

[5]   A synopsis of the motifs is given in Appendix B to this article.
[6]   See Frenzel, Elisabeth, *Motive der Weltliteratur*, Stuttgart 1999, p. 583.

curring minor aspects of the selections, namely the **self-harming schemer,** the **dream,** and the **number series.**

The first section of the appendix ties back in with the chapter's topic, Moses. It belongs to the genre of exegetical tales about prophets *(qiṣaṣ al-anbiyā᾽)* which flesh out allusive Qurʾānic verses with narratives derived from Rabbinic lore *(Isrāʾīliyyāt).* The first motif is that of the **ambiguous answer.** The protagonist is Pharaoh's uncle, a secret believer in God and supporter of Moses. Two men from Pharaoh's entourage claim that the uncle venerates Moses as his god. Pharaoh has the two accusers bring the suspect before him to verify the charge. Before questioning him, Pharaoh asks the two men which god they themselves serve. "You" they answer, correctly, according to the Qurʾānic understanding of ancient Egyptian religion. Satisfied with their answer, Pharaoh then repeats the question to his uncle, who responds ambiguously, "My Lord is their Lord." Brevity and compactness makes this statement also an **eloquent repartee.** Pharaoh understands this to mean himself and is reassured of the uncle's proper Egyptian faith, whereas the uncle had actually intended the monotheistic god of the Abrahamic tradition who is, according to his own belief, the god of all humankind. However, Pharaoh, based on his interpretation, believes he has unmasked the two men as liars and has them crucified. The accused is saved.

The story ends with the moral that **schemers fall victim to their own plots,** a submotif which is used to connect the second section with a tale lacking any proper names or geographic specifics. A vizier salutes his king at every appearance with the phrase, "The doer of good will be rewarded by his own deed and be safe from the evildoer, whose actions will harm only himself." Once, a jealous courtier accused the vizier of having spread lies about the king. The courtier then invited the unsuspecting vizier to eat a meal full of garlic, and when the vizier saw the king on the following day, he covered his mouth. The king interpreted this to be a confirmation of the courtier's charge and wrote with his own hand the vizier's death sentence. In the letter he identified its carrier as the one to be executed, and gave it to the vizier to deliver. Usually the only documents the king wrote himself were letters of reward. Believing this to be the letter's content, the vizier shared this knowledge with the courtier who intercepted him on the way and offered to deliver it himself — only to suffer the deadly fate intended for the vizier. The next day the vizier appeared before the surprised king; the scheme came to light, and the king declared the vizier's greeting formula to be true.

The story contains a new motif, the **self-delivered death sentence,** which Ibn Abī Ḥaǧalah uses to add a further tale in the same section, a legend from the *Ǧāhiliyyah.* The poets al-Mutalammis and Ṭarafah had satirized the Lakhmid king ᶜAmr b. Hind, but thereafter praised him again. The king then dispatched them to al-Ḥīrah (or al-Baḥrayn)[7] with letters they believed to stipulate rewards

---

7   According to the narrative's beginning, Baḥrayn, given as a variant, is the more logical destination, since the men were presumably dispatched from the capital al-Ḥīrah. However,

for their praise, but which were in truth death sentences for their carriers by the vengeful king. A clairvoyant man they encountered on the way warned them, and al-Mutalammis had his letter opened and read by a local youth of al-Ḥirah and the presage was confirmed. He fled. But Ṭarafah refused to believe that his case was the same and he thereupon faced execution in al-Ḥirah. Ibn Abī Ḥaǧalah completes the tale with the incipit of Ṭarafah's *Muʿallaqah* as well as two of its verses that seem to foretell the young poet's untimely death. He also shows his own reuse of the *Muʿallaqah*'s second verse, slightly adapted, in a couplet within his own *Maqāmah* on the pyramids.

In the third section, Ibn Abī Ḥaǧalah carries on both the motif of the **self-delivered death sentence** and the submotif of the **self-harming schemer**, presenting a historical tale about Aḥmad b. Ṭūlūn (r. 254-70/868-84). As a youth he took pity on the needy petitioners waiting outside the gate of his father, who was governor, and proposed to his father that he decree some aid for them in writing. The governor accepted. Fetching an inkwell in the hallway outside, Aḥmad surprised his father's favorite with a servant. She feared that he would divulge their affair to the governor, and hurried to reach him before Aḥmad, claiming that it was he who had accosted her. Believing her, the governor wrote a letter decreeing death to its carrier and handed it to his son for delivery. The favorite intercepted the son and inquired about the letter's content, which Aḥmad believed to be an important gubernatorial decree. To enrage father against son even more, she took the document and gave it to the servant to deliver. He was executed. When the servant's head was then presented as proof to the puzzled governor, he asked his son for an explanation, learnt the true course of events, and had the favorite killed.

Ibn Abī Ḥaǧalah rounds out the story with historical information about Ibn Ṭūlūn's rise to power, his laudable character traits, especially his generosity to scholars and the indigent, his enormous wealth, but also his bloodthirstiness. All this is expressed through a **series of numbers** in which the exact figures are somewhat fantastic: 120,000 dinars spent on the construction of the sultan's Friday mosque (which still stands today), 18,000 people killed under his rule, and a yearly income of 400 million dinars. The number series is interrupted by two stories involving **dreams**, one by Ibn Ṭūlūn himself and another about him, both of which stress a ruler's duty to protect the weak and heed the Qurʾān. The dream recurs as a motif throughout the appendices. Its placement here in the midst of a series of numbers seems to imply that numbers and dreams impart different kinds of truths that can stand alongside, and up to, each other.[8]

---

the fact that Arabic writing is associated with al-Ḥirah in the Arabic tradition makes al-Ḥirah a more appropriate place for the story's end; see Toral, Isabel, *Al-Ḥira. Eine arabische Kulturmetropole im spätantiken Kontext*, Leiden und Boston 2014, pp. 114-18.

[8] Ibn Abī Ḥaǧalah was not unique in this respect. For a broader study devoted to the issue of coexisting alternate or conflicting discourses in premodern Islam, see Bauer, Thomas, *Die Kultur der Ambiguität. Eine andere Geschichte des Islams*, Berlin 2011, pp. 42-45.

In the fourth section Ibn Abī Ḥaǧalah returns to the initial motif of the **ambiguous answer** with a historical anecdote. In a period of debate between Sunnite and Shiite factions in Baghdad about the relative merits of Abū Bakr and ʿAlī, a man put the preacher Ibn al-Ǧawzī (d. 597/1201) on the spot, as he was presiding over a gathering, by asking his opinion on the topic. Ibn al-Ǧawzī retorted with presence of mind, "The better of the two is the one for whom is true: 'His daughter is his wife.'" This satisfied both parties. The Sunnites understood Abū Bakr, whose daughter was married to the Prophet, to be meant, while the Shiites, held ʿAlī, who had married the Prophet's daughter, for the one intended. Ibn al-Ǧawzī swiftly left the premises to shirk further questions on the subject.

Ibn Abī Ḥaǧalah praises the answer also as an **eloquent repartee** *(luṭf al-aǧwibah)* and one moreover promptly delivered, though it would have been as excellent if given upon long reflection. The remaining sections continue the third motif of the **eloquent repartee**, one being about jars (fifth section), and another about a retort to a man who jokingly challenged Ibn al-Ǧawzī when boasting in a couplet about his own subtle wit (sixth section). In the seventh section, Ibn al-Ǧawzī explains that for each good leader in the world God created an evil match, citing as examples Adam and the devil, Abraham and Nimrod, Moses and Pharaoh. "So who is your match?" someone piped up and was shut up by Ibn al-Ǧawzī with the words, "Nothing is my match *(laysa bi-šayʾ)*". In his commentary Ibn Abī Ḥaǧalah vaunts the preacher's quickness *(surʿa)* and appositeness *(iṣābah)*.

As with Ibn Ṭūlūn above, he rounds off the anecdote with two curious tales *(ʿaǧāʾib)* about Ibn al-Ǧawzī. First, the shavings of his collected reed pens, with which he copied hadith, sufficed as fuel wood to heat the water for the washing of his corpse. The second connects to the book's main theme of the number seven: upon counting the copious notebooks Ibn al-Ǧawzī had written over the course of his life and breaking them down by the days, they numbered exactly seven for each day. The appendix thus weaves together legend and history from Egypt and Iraq from the time before Islam to the twelfth century.

In the appendix to the fifth chapter on "Events That Happened in Egypt", Ibn Abī Ḥaǧalah uses the four motifs of **natural catastrophe, human strife, miracle**, and **foreign lands**, and the three submotifs of **letter, legal attestation**, and **number series** (the last of which already appears in the appendix to the second chapter).

In the first section, he takes the famine mentioned in chapter five as a transition to the two motifs of **natural catastrophe** and **human strife**. Both phenomena occurred during the reign of the Ayyubid al-Malik al-ʿĀdil (r. 596-615/1200-18) in Egypt. The author begins with a survey of the casualties: 220,000 (or 300,000) foreigners alone starved to death, and the king paid for their shrouds. Then follow sensational tidbits: people ate dogs, corpses, their own children, and each other. One widespread trick was to lure doctors to houses and then to snatch and cook them. This is illustrated by the anecdote of a doctor who suspects a man who comes to fetch him of such an intention, but who is reassured by his pious talk and almsgiving along the way. However, as they arrive at the man's dilapidated home and the man's companion, expecting them, complains about the delay of the "prey," the doctor wises up and succeeds in escaping following a hard struggle.

Ibn Abī Ḥaǧalah follows this up with a famous tale from the reign of the Fatimid caliph al-Mustanṣir al-ʿAlawī (r. 427-87/1036-94). A vizier's mule was taken from him, slaughtered, and eaten at the moment he arrived in front of the caliphal palace. He had the thieves crucified on the spot, and on the following morning, only their stripped bones hanging off the crosses remained. The section concludes with a **list of numbers**. During the siege of Mayyāfāriqīn by Hülegü,[9] food prices reached fantastic amounts: 600 dirhams were paid for a pound of bread or meat, 53 dirhams for an onion, and 60 dirhams for a dog's head. A cow was sold for 70,000 dirhams to a certain Naǧmaddīn Muḫtār, who passed on its head and knuckles[10] for 6,500 dirhams to al-Malik al-Ašraf.[11] Again Ibn Abī Ḥaǧalah dresses up extraordinary facts with precise numbers, fully exploiting the sensational topic.

The second section continues both motifs of **natural catastrophe** and **human strife** and adds **miracles** as a third. In Hama in 741H., hail descended in the shape of humans and animals; in Mosul in 524H. it rained fire, and in Yemen two decades later, blood. For this, proof or **legal attestation** is provided. The blood that had rained down was visible on people's garments, and the zoomorphic hail was attested to in a court session before the local judge, the record of which was forwarded by **letter** to the judge of Hama. The same applies to the most fantastic precipitation: giants, high as the sky, crashed into the earth in Bukhara, leaving behind a smoking, bottomless crater. The judge of Bukhara had this confirmed by forty witnesses and produced a report which was conveyed by letter from the Iraqi governor Ibn Hubayrah to the caliph Sulaymān b. ʿAbdalmalik (r. 96-99/715-17).

The third section continues with **natural catastrophes** and **miracles**. An earthquake in 552H. claimed lives in Damascus, Shiraz, Antakia, and Tripoli. Again, anecdotes bring the events down to human scale: in Hama a school teacher returned to his class to find all his pupils crushed to death. In Shiraz, a women and her servant were the sole survivors. The flood caused by the quake

---

9   The region of Diyār Bakr (including Mayyāfāriqīn) was definitely conquered by the Mongols under Hülegü in 648/1260, and Ibn Abī Ḥaǧalah mentions his killing of the local Ayyubid ruler al-Malik al-Kāmil [r. 642-58/1244-60]; see Bosworth, C.E., *The New Islamic Dynasties. A Chronological and Genealogical Manual*, Edinburgh 1996, p. 72, and Barthold, W., "Mayyāfāriqīn" in: *EI*[2] 3 (1967), p. 569.

10   For this meaning of *kawāriʿ*, pl. of *kāriʿ* (and *kurāʿ*), and the meal prepared from this, see Dozy, Reinhart, *Supplément aux dictionnaires arabes*, 2 vols., Leiden 1881, reprint Beirut 1991, 2:465.

11   Based on the event's date, he cannot be identical either with the first Ayyubid ruler of Diyār Bakr with this honorific name (r. 607-17/1210-20) or the second (r. 828-36/1425-33), see Bosworth, *New Islamic Dynasties*, p. 72f.

ravaged the Levantine coastal cities and the sea withdrew as far as Cyprus, leaving ships beached on the shores.

A plague which spread between Hijaz and Yemen in the same year supplies a curious fact: whilst eighteen out of twenty towns were wiped out and became uninhabitable, because everyone entering them died instantly, two towns remained completely unaffected.[12]

The fourth section adds further **miracles,** this time reported from **foreign lands,** and picks up once again the submotif of the **letter.** In 638H. (1240-41)[13] a messenger from the Khan of the Mongols delivers a letter to the Muslim rulers ordering them to surrender and dismantle the walls of their cities. The messenger, an educated Muslim from Isfahan, then recounts miracles from the Mongol lands, such as of humans with their eyes on their shoulders and their mouths in their chests, sheep growing from grain and unable to procreate. The most fantastic of these is a minaret-sized wooden object that surfaces in a spring in Māzandarān once every thirty years and sinks back into it at sunset. Even iron chains cannot hold it back, as one king discovered. Remnants of the broken chains, as Ibn Abī Ḥaǧalah remarks, are still dangling off the object as it periodically reappears.

The fifth section continues the motif of **foreign lands** and the submotif of the **letter** and brings back the motif of **human strife** and the submotif of the **number series.** The Ghaznavid sultan Maḥmūd b. Sebüktigin (r. 388-421/998-1030) reports to the caliph about his campaign in India in a letter which is partially quoted. The letter relates how in India in 412H. Maḥmūd destroyed an old idol which people believed to be alive and came to consult, and to which they brought offerings. The idol's significance is illustrated with figures: 300 barbers alone were needed to shave the hair and beards of the visiting pilgrims, 500 women sang and danced at the shrine's gates and so forth. Maḥmūd specifies that he departed on the campaign with 30,000 horsemen and, in the course of it, killed 500,000 Indians.

Another letter is sent upon the conquest of a further Indian city which contains one thousand palaces and temples, each housing an idol covered in gold which weighed 98,000 *miṯqāl*.[14] Maḥmūd had the city burned to the ground, and the fifth part of the booty he took as a leader amounted alone to 55,000 slaves and 350 elephants.

The sixth section continues only the motif of **human strife.** A pretended descendant of the Fatimids, who claimed to be of Qarmatian persuasion, imposed

---

[12] Though described as an epidemic *(wabāʾ)* and not specifically as a plague *(ṭāʿūn)*, it was probably a local outbreak of the latter kind; Dols, Michael W., *The Black Death in the Middle East,* Princeton 1977, p. 33. Ibn Abī Ḥaǧalah was the first to produce a full enumeration of plagues and other epidemics in his *Dafʿ an-niqmah fī ṣ-ṣalāh ʿalā nabī ar-raḥmah,* in which he also cites numerous older works; ibid., pp. 19-20nn19-20.

[13] See Barthold, "Mayyāfāriqīn", p. 931a.

[14] As a monetary value, one *miṯqāl (dīnār)* was equivalent to 4.231 grams of gold, as a merchandise weight, 4.46 grams; Hinz, W., *Islamische Maße und Gewichte umgerechnet ins metrische System,* Leiden 1955, pp. 4, 12.

a brutal rule in Yemen, performing mass killings, butchering children, and disemboweling pregnant women. His son and successor outdid him in bloodthirstiness and lecherousness and, moreover, erected a sumptuous mausoleum to his father, which he forced people to circumambulate under threat of death, banning them from performing the pilgrimage to Mecca. This went on until his subjects appealed to the Ayyubid sultan Salāḥaddīn (Saladin, r. 564-89/1169-93) for help. The sultan dispatched his brother, who dethroned and killed the tyrant and exhumed and burnt the remains of the tyrant's father.

Ibn Abī Ḥağalah reserves the seventh and last section for a **natural catastrophe** at the heart of the Islamic lands in Medina and reunites all three submotifs used so far, **letter, attestation,** and **number series,** to authenticate the description of the events.

In 654H. an earthquake struck in the valley between Medina and Mt. Uḥud, causing a stream of lava to erupt. The author gives the precise date of when the first ominous rumblings were heard, five days prior to the actual quake, and the exact dimensions of the lava stream filling the valley, to wit, four parasangs long, four miles wide, and with a depth of one and a half times a man's height. Its sparks "devoured the stones" and its molten rock flowed at a camel's pace until it solidified into pitch-black blocks. This information is taken from Abū Šāmah (d. 665/1267), whom Ibn Abī Ḥağalah acclaims here as an authority on hadith-transmission and historiography, and who himself relied on confirmation by multiple letters *(kutub mutawātirah)* sent from Medinan eyewitnesses. The lava glowed so brightly that one could write at night with its light, and was so strong as to be visible from Mecca.[15]

A further source is Ibn Katir's (d. 774/1373) *History*, which relies in turn on the chief judge Ṣadraddīn ʿAlī at-Tamīmī al-Ḥanafī. He reports from his father, teacher at the *madrasah* in Bosra, that the Bedouins from the surrounding desert told him that the glow coming from Hijaz illuminated the necks of their camels at night.[16] Returning to Abū Šāmah, the author depicts the human scene in Medina. People flocked in panic to the Prophet's mosque, repented their sins at his tomb, freed their slaves, and lavished alms on the poor. He closes with an anonymous quatrain that throws the crisis into full relief, and alludes to the Qurʾānic description of hell:

---

15 Abū Šāmah, who was contemporary to the event, gives a detailed description in his *Ḏayl*; see on this and other sources, Abraseys, Nicholas N., Charles P. Melville & Robin D. Adams, *The Seismicity of Egypt, Arabia and the Red Sea. A historical review*, Cambridge UK 1994, p. 40.

16 Ibn Katir reproduces four of the eyewitnesses' letters cited by Abū Šāmah (see previous paragraph) in which the quake is interpreted as an earthly manifestation of the Qurʾānic description of hellfire (see next note); Ibn Katir, *al-Bidāyah wa-n-nihāyah*, ed. ʿAbdallāh b. ʿAbdalmuḥsin al-Turkī, Riyadh 1419/1998, vol. 17, pp. 329-33. Ibn Abī Ḥağalah reworks the content of the letters into a shortened and synthesized narrative.

A sea of fire, upon it float ships of plateaus
that cast their anchor into the earth.

We see stray sparks huge like castles,[17]
as if it were a downpour from a heavy cloud

Their smoke thickens the air
till the sun turns dark.

What a sign among the miracles of God's Prophet,
a sign which the intelligent understand.

A prophetic hadith stating that volcanic fire illuminating the necks of camels in
Bosra is a sign of Judgment Day[18] concludes the appendix. Supplying a graphic
illustration of the preceding events, the poem and the hadith continue in the
vein of Ibn Abī Ḥaǧalah, yoking together astounding facts with rational perception, yet they elevate the miracle to a new level as a sign (*āyah*) whose meaning
only the intelligent can decipher. They instruct their reader how to compute
miracle and truth. Again, seemingly different modes of telling are placed parallel
to one another and treated as complementary. Ibn Abū Ḥaǧalah thinks on several levels and expects his reader to do the same.

This appendix also shows particularly well how Ibn Abī Ḥaǧalah weaves together two layers of motifs. The main motifs supply the subject matter, to wit,
catastrophes of vast proportions, while the various submotifs circulating through
these add undertones of authenticity.

Ibn Abī Ḥaǧalah cites his sources here and there, and points out where he himself has added an item with the phrase "I say" (*aqūlu*), irrespective of whether this
is transmitted material, an account of something he witnessed, or his own original poetry or prose. As for his chosen manner of composition, Ibn Abī Ḥaǧalah
points to the literary motif as his guiding principle. In two appendices he restates
a topic from the preceding chapter which he selects to focus on. Leading on
from chapter IV on the Fatimid caliph al-Ḥākim's misdeeds and violations of religious law, he begins the appendix with "Among the scholars al-Ḥākim killed
was...". The motif of the caliph's causing the violent death of various persons
then supplies the first three selections. After chapter V, which covers events that
happened in Egypt, the author opens the appendix with "I say: the rise of prices
in the days of [the Mamluk sultan al-Malik] al-ʿĀdil Zaynaddīn Kitbuǧā [al-
Manṣūrī, r. 694-96/1294-96] has been mentioned above.[19] It so happens that the

---

[17] The verse's beginning *narā lahā šararan ka-l-qaṣri* is an allusion to the hyperbolic descrip-
      tion of hellfire *innahā tarmī bi-šararin ka-l-qaṣri / ka-annahū ǧimālātun ṣufrun* (Q. Mur-
      salāt/77:32-33), an early Meccan sura. The Qurʾānic image reuses the comparison of build-
      ings with camels from early Arabic poetry and applies both to describe the flying debris of
      a huge blaze; Neuwirth, Angelika, *Der Koran. Band 1: Frühmekkanische Suren*, Berlin 2001,
      pp. 503, 510-11.
[18] The hadith is likewise quoted by Ibn Kaṯīr, *Bidāyah*, vol. 17, p. 329.
[19] Ibn Abī Ḥaǧalah, *Sukkardān*, p. 180.

same occurred in the days of the great [Ayyubid sultan al-Malik] al-ʿĀdil [r. 596-615/1200-18] in the year 597H." The appendix then assembles natural catastrophes (famine, earthquakes, and epidemics) as one of its motifs.

On a few occasions Ibn Abī Ḥaǧalah states that he will follow up a motif with a further item. He does not, however, use very precise terminology. Only rarely does he define the continued motif explicitly; one such example is that of the self-harming schemer, described with the words "similar to the mention of the rebuked vizier and the demise of the one who badmouthed him" (*ʿalā ḏikri ma-lāmati l-waziri wa-halāki llaḏī wašā ʿalayhi*, II.3).[20] Likewise, he introduces a follow up on the motif of the ambiguous answer with the phrase "like the preceding an-swer of the believer from Pharaoh's family" (*miṯla ǧawābi muʾmini Āli Firʿawna l-mutaqaddimi ḏikruhū*, II.4). In a sequence on the poetic conceit of red and yellow flowers which are compared to the complexions of a lover and his/her beloved, he merely states that he will add more "on the conceit of the cited couplet" (*wa-fī maʿnā l-baytayni l-maḏkūrayni*, VII.3.c). The suite to a dream motif is announced by the phrase "Similar to the mention of this dream is a report from Abū Ḥanīfah" (*ʿalā ḏikri hāḏā l-manāmi ruwiya ʿan Abī Ḥanīfah*, IV.4). On one occasion he points out the repetition of a paired motif: "similar to the dream and the nar-cissus" (*ʿalā ḏikri l-manāmi wa-n-narǧisi*, VII.3.b).

More often, however, the author merely notes an iteration of the previous motif with the phrase "on the motif of this tale" (*fī maʿnā hāḏihī l-ḥikāyah*, II.2), or by simply implying similarity: "similar to the mention of this addendum" (*ʿalā ḏikri hāḏihī ṣ-ṣilah*, II.2), or again with adverbs, such as "like this" (*miṯlu hāḏā*, I.4), "he also wrote" (*kataba ayḍan*, III.4), or "this also occurred" (*waqaʿa ayḍan*, V.1). Nonetheless the few occasions of explicit connection suffice for the Mam-luk reader to understand Ibn Abī Ḥaǧalah's logic, whose purpose is not a sys-tematic definition of motifs, but variegated renditions of one and the same motif in texts from different times and places.

Common literary genres, such as the eloquent repartee (*luṭf al-aǧwibah*, II.4), are rarely specified, but a general predilection for the strange and exotic is per-ceivable. Curious events are repeatedly defined as such. The curious fact of two men from the Islamic east and west carrying the exact same name is commented upon as a "strange coincidence" (*min ǧarībi l-ittifāq*, I.7) as is a thousand-petaled rose seen in Nihāvand (*min ǧarībi mā samiʿtu*, VII.6). The many motifs of foreign lands and monarchs and their customs (*min ʿādat al-ʿaǧam*, III.1) belong to the exotic. Several motifs pertaining to the genre of marvels or *mirabilia* (*aǧāʾib*)[21] are described in the same way, and the instances in which Ibn Abī Ḥaǧalah applies

---

[20] The reference numbers to the respective sections are the same as those in the alphabetical list of motifs in Appendix C to this article.

[21] See Dubler, C. E., "ʿAdjāʾib", in: *EI²* 1 (1960), 203-4 and Richter-Bernburg, Lutz, "ʿAǧāʾib literature", in: *Encyclopedia of Arabic Literature*, 2 vols., edited by Julie S. Meisami and Paul Starkey, London and New York 1998, 1: 65-66.

the phrase *min al-ʿağāʾib* usually concern foreign lands. Among these are depictions in the secret compartment of a table predicting the Arab conquest of Spain (VI.1),[22] a magical storm brought on by a people in the Caucasus (VI.3), a bronze statue of a duck spewing huge amounts of water (VI.5), or starlings feeding the monks in a Christian cloister (VI.6). But at least one marvel is local: Ibn al-Ğawzī's achievement of filling seven notebooks for each day of his life (II.6). Overall, the author provides minimal guidance in his linking comments, but it is just enough to take his reader by the hand on a journey through a mosaic of Arabic literature, and to teach him or her to discover the implicit connections between the pieces. As with Paul Theroux, the reader is expected to "get the drift and enjoy the ride."

The above can only be a first and provisional attempt to chart Ibn Abī Ḥağalah's procedure. For instance, the boundary between motif and submotif is at times difficult to draw, and some motifs switch between being a main motif in one appendix and a submotif in another. Not all aspects of the selections could be taken account of, and the artful assemblage contains more intriguing facets than can be presented here. Many allusions evident to a contemporary of Ibn Abī Ḥağalah must elude the present writer. An intellectually voracious and investigative mind such as Ibn Abī Ḥağalah's cannot be grasped with bounded precision. The present essay has merely attempted to depict one aspect of his anthology writing that eludes regular classification, and to show the existence of an internal order where all outward order seems to have been discarded.

Appendix

A. The Structure of Chapters

[*First set of seven chapters*]

I The Nobility of Seven
II The Dedicatee Sultan Ḥasan's Relationship to It
III The Definition of Egypt, the Seventh Clime
IV The Dedicatee as the Seventh Sibling to Rule
V Biographic Pieces on the Dedicatee and His Family
VI Coincidences and Marvels that Occurred to the Dedicatee and his Family
VII Explanation of Cited Hadith

---

[22] On this motif, referred to as Solomon's table, in Muslim historiography, see Clarke, Nicola, *The Muslim Conquest of Iberia. Medieval Arabic narratives*, London and New York 2012, pp. 92-99.

Transition

Further Facts about Seven

[Second set of seven chapters]

I The Story of Joseph
II The Story of Moses
III Select Tales about Ancient Kings of Egypt
IV The Vita of al-Ḥākim, His Crimes and Violations of the *Šarīʿah*
V Events That Happened in Egypt
VI Events That Happened in Cairo and around the Pyramids
VII Prose and Verse on Seven Flowers Growing in Upper Egypt

B. Digest of the Appendices to the Second Set of Chapters

I The Story of Joseph, Appendix

(*Sukkardān*, Cairo 1421/2001, pp. 130-33)

Motifs

1. Speaking animal |×|×|×|×|×|–|×|
2. Animal fable |–|–|–|–|×|–|×|
3. Curiosities about animals |–|–|–|–|–|×|–|

Submotif

a. Eloquent repartee |×|×|–|×|×|–|×|
b. Proof of prophecy |×|–|×|×|–|–|–|
c. Attestation[23] |×|×|×|–|–|–|–|

1. A wolf, presented by Joseph's brothers to their father as Joseph's killer, is given speech by God and declares his innocence to Jacob, explaining that the meat of prophets is forbidden *(ḥarām)* to wolves (aṯ-Ṯaʿālibī and other exegetes; Q. Yūsuf/ 12:18).

2. A speaking wolf challenges a shepherd over a sheep he took, arguing that it would be his on Judgment Day anyway; a speaking cow complains about being misused for carrying loads instead of ploughing fields. The Prophet, Abū Bakr,

---

[23] This concerns facts being verified and attested to by human and non-human characters within the selections beyond a regular *isnād*. It likewise differs from the citations of sources by Ibn Abī Ḥaǧalah. These are given in parentheses, retaining his formulation.

and ʿUmar believed that these events happened (Abū Hurayrah according to Muslim, *Ṣaḥīḥ* and al-Buḫārī, *Ṣaḥīḥ*).[24]

3. A speaking wolf claims a sheep from a shepherd as God-given food and sends the shepherd to the Prophet, who confirms the wolf's words and explains the speech of animals as proof of "the hour" (at-Tirmiḏī, *Ṣaḥīḥ*, transmitter: Abū Saʿīd al-Ḫudri and at-Tirmiḏī, *al-Ǧāmiʿ fī l-ḥadīṯ*, transmitter: Sufyān b. ar-Rabīʿ — his father — al-Qāsim b. al-Faḍl; the second hadith is qualified as sound).

Addendum by Ibn Abī Ḥaǧalah: in another version of this hadith, the wolf describes the prophet's mission in detail and offers to herd the sheep so that the shepherd may go to Muhammad and convert to the new faith. This is how it occurs. Thereafter the Prophet sends the shepherd back to his herd and when the shepherd finds it intact, he slaughters a sheep for the honest wolf (al-Qāḍī ʿIyāḍ, *aš-Šifāʾ bi-taʿrīf ḥuqūq al-Muṣṭafā*, transmitter: Abū Hurayrah).

4. Abū Sufyān b. Ḥarb and Ṣafwān b. Umayya observe a wolf track a gazelle but let her go when she escapes into the sacred precinct in Mecca. As they marvel at the wolf's piety, he tops their amazement by informing them of the Prophet's mission, of his being called to paradise, and by marveling at people's preference for hell instead (al-Qāḍī ʿIyāḍ, *Šifāʾ* and *Ibn Wahb*).

Addendum by Ibn Abī Ḥaǧalah: verses by himself and an anonymous poet on God's signs *(āyāt)*.

5. A lion, wolf, and fox hunt together, capturing an onager, a gazelle and a rabbit. The lion asks the wolf to distribute the booty, but is dissatisfied by the even outcome and kills him. Then he asks the fox to do the same, and the fox apportions everything to the lion. Asked where he learnt to perform such excellent distribution, the fox answers "from the verdict served upon the wolf" (aš-Šaʿbī).[25]

6. On wolves sleeping with only one eye shut at a time and rabbits sleeping with their eyes open (verses by Ḥumayd b. Hilāl[26] and al-Mutanabbī).

7. A wolf and a fox serve as the entourage at a lion's court. The lion falls sick and the wolf uses the absence of the fox to badmouth him. Upon his return, the fox excuses his absence by explaining that he has been investigating a remedy for the

---

[24] Sources are cited as given in the text by Ibn Abī Ḥaǧalah.

[25] On the motif of the fox as a smart distributor *(der Fuchs als kluger Teiler)* and its Aesopian provenance, see Brockelmann, Carl (1926), "Fabel und Tiermärchen in der älteren arabischen Literatur", *Der Islam* 2 (1926), pp. 96- 109, esp. p. 99f. This motif and the one cited in n. 27 below appear also in Ibn al-Jawzī's (d. 597/1200) *Kitāb al-Adhkiyāʾ* and al-Ibshihī's (d. ca. 850/1446) *Mustaṭraf* from either of which Ibn Abī Ḥaǧalah may have taken it.

[26] Ḥumayd b. Ṭawr al-Hilālī (d. ca. 90/709?) was renowned for his animal descriptions. The verse is cited with a different rhyming word *(hāǧiʿu* instead of *nāʾimu)* by al-Ǧāḥiẓ, *al-Ḥayawān*, ed. ʿAbdassalām Muḥammad Hārūn, 7 vols., Beirut 1357, reprint 1388/1969, 6:467 (section on the sleep of wolves) and al-ʿAskarī, Abū Hilāl, *Dīwān al-maʿānī*, ed. Aḥmad Salīm Ġānim, 2 vols., Beirut 1424/2003, 2:903-4 (section on descriptions of wild animals where al-Aṣmaʿī calls this the best description of a wolf).

lion, which, it turns out, is a wolf's testicles. The lion bites off the wolf's testicles, and as the bleeding wolf exits the audience, the fox warns him to be careful when mentioning the retinue in the king's presence (Abū l-Farağ al-Muʿāfā b. Zakariyyāʾ al-Nahrawānī [d. 390/1000]).[27]

Addendum by Ibn Abī Ḥağalah: When on pilgrimage, the narrator of the previous tale, Muʿāfā, heard his name called in the crowd, at first only the *kunya*, then again with more and more parts of his name until the entire name was called, and he believed he was the one meant and responded. But to his great surprise, the caller explained that there was an Eastern (Iraqi) and a Western Nahrawān, which Muʿafā did not know, and a man with an identical name from the latter town had been intended (Abū ʿAbdallāh al-Ḥumaydī [d. 488/1095]).[28]

II The Story of Moses, Appendix[29]

(*Sukkardān*, Cairo 1421/2001, pp. 145-50)

Motifs

1. Eloquent repartee |×|–|–|×|×|×|×|
2. Ambiguous answer |×|–|–|×|–|–|–|
3. Self-delivered death sentence |–|×|×|–|–|–|–|

Submotifs

a. Self-harming schemer |×|×|×|–|–|–|–|
b. Number series |–|–|×|–|–|–|×|
c. Dream |–|–|×|–|–|–|–|

1. An ambiguous answer saves Pharaoh's relative, who is a believer, and his calumniators are crucified.

2. Ibn Abī Ḥağalah: on the same *maʿnā*: a vizier is badmouthed by a rival and sentenced to death, but the rival delivers the death sentence intended for the vizier himself and is executed.

---

27 He was a religious scholar, polymath, and adherent of aṭ-Ṭabarī's legal school; GAS 1:522-23. On the motif of the fox as physician of the lion *(der Fuchs als Arzt des Löwen)* and its Aesopian provenance, see Brockelmann, Carl (1926), "Fabel und Tiermärchen in der älteren arabischen Literatur", *Der Islam* 2 (1926), pp. 96-109, esp. p. 100f. (see also note 25).

28 The account is reproduced in Yāqūt, *Muʿğam al-buldān*, ed. M. ʿAbdarraḥmān al-Marʿašlī, 8 pts. in 4 vols., Beirut, n.d., 4:419-20 (s.v. Nahrawān).

29 The synopses of the second and fifth appendices are kept brief as these have been discussed in detail in the article.

Ibn Abī Ḥaǧalah adds the parallel of the self-delivered death sentences of al-Mutalammis and Ṭarafah by the Lakhmid king ʿAmr b. Hind of al-Ḥirah [r. 554-70 AD]. Verses of Ṭarafah's *Muʿallaqah*. Verses by Ibn Abī Ḥaǧalah from his Pyramid *maqāmah*.

3. The young Ibn Ṭūlūn is falsely accused by his father's favorite and sentenced to death, but she mistakenly hands her lover the death sentence and he is executed.

Addenda by Ibn Abī Ḥaǧalah: Ibn Ṭūlūn's [r. 254-70/868-84] piety, education, and bloodthirstiness; an old man's dream about him at his tomb; his offspring and wealth.

4. Ibn al-Ǧawzī's [d. 597/1201] ambiguous answer on the relative merits of Abū Bakr and ʿAlī, delivered in a moment of Sunnite-Shiite tensions in Bagdad.

5. A quick-witted answer by Ibn al-Ǧawzī on jars.

6. Verses by Ibn al-Ǧawzī praising his own subtlety and his retort to someone who mocked him.

7. Ibn al-Ǧawzī's quick-witted answer on the question of who would be his match.

Addendum by Ibn Abī Ḥaǧalah: the curious fact that Ibn al-Ǧawzī's total number of notebooks written during his life, if broken down by days, totals seven for each day.

III Select Tales about Ancient Kings of Egypt, Appendix

(*Sukkardān*, Cairo 1421/2001, pp. 159-66)

Motifs

1. Foreign royal customs and gifts	|×|×|×|×|×|–|–|
2. Foreign royal letters	|–|–|×|×|×|–|–|
3. Fantasy creatures	|–|–|–|–|×|×|×|

Submotifs

a. Eloquent repartee	|–|–|–|–|×|×|–|
b. Number series	|–|–|–|×|×|–|×|
c. Attestation	|–|–|–|–|–|×|×|
d. Ambiguous answer	|–|–|–|–|×|–|–|

1. Anointment and attire of Persian kings on the occasion of their festival. Description of the tray of foods and flowers offered them on this day by the high priest (containing etrog, a sugar cone, lotus fruit, quince, apple, white grapes,

and bunches of myrtle). Similar trays offered to them by other people in descending order of rank.

Addendum by Ibn Abī Ḥaǧalah: Seven foods eaten by Persians on New Year's Day.

2. Ardašīr's and Anūširwān's gifts of garments to people according to their rank on the Nawrūz and Mihraǧān festivals. They motivated this by discarding their garbs worn in the previous season (winter or summer) and enabling their subjects to do the same.

3. A letter from the king of India to Anūširwān, containing all their honorific titles, with Anūširwān being addressed, e.g., as "King of the most moderate one among the seven climes". A list of the sumptuous gifts accompanying the letter, among them soluble wood, a drinking bowl of ruby rimmed with pearls, camphor of the size of pistachios, a snakeskin bed, a tall beautiful slave with eyelashes so long as to touch her cheeks etc.

4. A letter by the king of China, called Faġfūr, containing all his honorific titles, including the description of his palace, servants (1,000 princesses), and animals (1,000 white elephants) and the gift sent along with the letter, a statue of a horseman encrusted with jewels and pearls and wearing a garb of gold and lapis threads with an embroidered image of the Chinese king in full ornate, surrounded by his attendants.

5. Story about the gifts of Queen Bilqīs to Solomon intended to test his prophethood. According to one exegete these were 500 gold and silver bricks, each weighing 100 *ratl*, a crown, musk and amber, a box containing a pearl and an onyx bead with curved boring, and 500 cross-dressed female slaves and as many cross-dressed male slaves. Her letter, co-written by the astute Munḏir b. ʿAmr, asked Solomon to guess the slaves' gender, guess the contents of the box and pierce the pearl without the aid of a man or jinn. Solomon solved all riddles with the help of the hoopoe, Gabriel, and a worm (Q. Naml/27:35).

Informed of this, Bilqīs accepted Solomon's prophethood and announced her visit. To anticipate her, he asks for her throne, which she had locked inside seven castles, to be brought to him before her arrival. At first the miracle is denied him. Then he addresses the request to his retinue, and a jinn (Saḫr or Āṣif b. Barḫiyā) or, in a variant, Gabriel, brings the throne. Asked whether it is indeed hers, Bilqīs answers ambiguously, neither denying nor confirming the transported throne's identity with her real one. Upon entering his palace, she believes the glass floor to be water and lifts her dress, revealing beautiful but hairy legs.

Later she converted, and Solomon desired to marry her, but before that he had a jinn create a depilatory paste which Bilqīs was the first one to use. He loved her much, built her three castles in Yemen and visited her once a month

(Q. Naml/27:38-40, 42, 44 [verses integrated into the narrative, as is typical in the exegetical tales of prophets (*qiṣaṣ al-anbiyāʾ*)]; al-Kawāši, *Tafsir*[30]).

6. From the same sura: three descriptions of the miraculous animal which God brings out of the earth to speak to humankind about his revelation. In the first version it has a bull's head, pig's eyes, elephant's ears, a leopard's coat, a lion's breast, a cat's waist, a roebuck's tail, a billy goat's horns, and a cow's legs. In the second version it is a bird with a human face, and in the third, a winged creature as high as the heavens (Q. Naml/27:82; al-Kawāši, *Tafsir*).

Description of a mysterious creature that will appear at Jesus' circumambulation of the Kaaba. It is covered with hair and feathers, moves at great speed, and carries Moses' staff and Solomon's ring (Prophetic hadith). This creature will brand the unbelievers' noses with the ring and brighten the believers' faces with the staff in order to distinguish them from each other (hadith, transmitter Ibn ʿUmar); in a variant it brands the words "unbeliever" and "believer" upon people's foreheads (Prophetic hadith).

7. Gog and Magog are described as giants of three sizes, ranging from the height of a cedar tree, to a height of 120 cubits, and a further one with large sprawling ears. They devoured every animal they came across, even elephants, as well as the carrion of their own species, and drank entire rivers and lakes (al-Kawāši, *Tafsir*).

Gog and Magog were twelve species of beings (Ibn ʿAbbās).

Gog and Magog were two peoples, each of them comprising 400 tribes. If one member of these died, a thousand men in full armor grew out of his back. They came into being when Jesus killed the Antichrist, and he fortified the cities of Mecca, Medina, and Jerusalem to keep these men at bay. Finally, God sent worms to devour them, birds to scatter their remains, and rain to wash these away (Ḥudayfah b. al-Yamān [alive first/seventh century]).

The Turks split from Gog and Magog and left them for the desert, then Ḏū l-Qarnayn built a wall to keep them out.

Gog and Magog were twenty-two tribes which Ḏū l-Qarnayn kept at bay with his wall, except for one which he left [Arabic *taraka*] inside; thence derives their name, Turk. They commit the same crimes as the people of Lot, or, it is said, cannibalism. The wall had enormous dimensions, 50 cubits wide, 200 cubits high and one parasang long (Qatādah[31]).

---

[30] Abū l-ʿAbbās Aḥmad b. Yūsuf al-Kawāši al-Mawṣili, d. 680/1281; the work might be either his *Tabṣirat al-mutaḏakkir wa-taḏkirat al-mutadabbir*, abbreviated as *at-Tabṣirah fi t-tafsir*, or his shorter *Talḫiṣ fi t-tafsir*, one of the main sources of *Tafsir al-Ǧalālayn*; GAL 1:416, GALS 1:737 and Ḥaǧǧi Ḥalifah, *Kašf aẓ-ẓunūn* with appended *Īḍāḥ al-maknūn* [author index] by Ismāʿil Bāša al-Baġdādi, ed. Muḥammad ʿAbdalqādir ʿAṭā, Beirut 2008, 1:367, no. 2830, 1:485, no. 4065, and (on the author) 6:90, no. 679.

[31] Qatādah b. Diʿāmah, d. 117/735, was a Successor, blind from birth and gifted with a prodigious memory and a broad knowledge of language, exegesis, and history.

A man claiming to have seen the wall describes it to the Prophet as being made up of alternating black and red rows of stones, and the Prophet confirms this (Prophetic hadith).

The caliph al-Wāṯiq [r. 227-32/842-47] dreamt that invaders had breached the wall and sent Salmān al-Tarğumān from Samarra to inspect it. Salmān did so and returned with a true and entertaining tale (cross reference by Ibn Abī Ḥaǧalah to his *Ġarāʾib al-ʿaǧāʾib wa-ʿaǧāʾib al-ġarāʾib*, where the tale is reproduced).

IV The Vita of al-Ḥākim, His Crimes and Violations of the Šarīʿah, Appendix

(*Sukkardān*, Cairo 1421/2001, pp. 174-78)

Motifs

1. Dreams about deceased people	|–|–|×|–|×|×|×|
2. People whose death al-Ḥākim caused	|×|×|×|–|–|–|–|

Submotifs

a. Eloquent repartee	|×|–|×|–|–|–|–|
b. Helpful dreams	|–|–|×|×|–|–|×|
c. Fatal dreams	|–|–|–|–|×|×|–|

1. One of the scholars killed by al-Ḥākim [r. 411-27/1021-36] was Ǧunādah al-Luġawī al-Harawī.[32]

Ǧunādah once tried to gain entrance to the vizier aṣ-Ṣāḥib b. ʿAbbād but was denied it due to his poor and shabby appearance. However, he demurred and sneaked in behind the chamberlain's back and sat down near an inkwell. When aṣ-Ṣāḥib had finished his letters, he noticed the intruder and shouted "Get up, you dog!", but Ǧunādah retorted, "A dog is he who does not know 300 words for dog," and aṣ-Ṣāḥib took him by the hand and led him to the seat of honor (al-Musabbiḥī [d. 420/1030], *Taʾrīḫ Miṣr*[33]).

2. A man from Siǧilmāsah left a thousand dinars in trust with a merchant before departing for pilgrimage. Upon his return, the merchant denied knowing him and sent him away. The pilgrim appealed to al-Ḥākim, who proposed to meet

---

[32] Abū Usāmah Ǧunādah b. Muḥammad al-Luġawī al-Azdī al-Harawī (d. 399/1009), a student of al-Azharī, was the most famous lexicographer of his time; GAS 9:210-11, Ibn Ḥallikān, *Wafayāt al-aʿyān*, ed. Iḥsān ʿAbbās, 8 vols., Beirut n.d., 1:372, no. 143.

[33] This work, which only survives in later quotations, had the original long title *Aḫbār faḍāʾil Miṣr wa-ʿaǧāʾibihā wa-ṭawāʾifihā wa-ġarāʾibihā wa-mā bihā mina l-biqāʿ wa-l-āṯār wa-siyar man ḥallahā wa-ḥalla ġayrahā min al-wulāh wa-l-quḍāh wa-l-aʾimmah wa-l-ḫulafāʾ*; Bianquis, Thierry, "Al-Musabbiḥī", in: *EI²* 7 (1992), pp. 650-52.

the pilgrim in front of the merchant's shop and publicly honor him. The scheme worked; the merchant returned the money and apologized, and after the pilgrim informed al-Ḥākim of this, he had the merchant executed and hung upside down in front of his shop.

3. In al-Ḥākim's audience, a noble recites a Qur'ān verse that calls for obedience to the Prophet as an arbiter and commander (Q. Nisāʾ/4:65) and gestures at the caliph, implying that he is meant. Another noble counters this implication by reciting a verse saying that those who believe in anything other than God "will not create a fly" (Q. Ḥaǧǧ/22:73). Al-Ḥākim rewards only the second reciter, but he is warned of the caliph's vengefulness. He decides to go on pilgrimage but drowns in a shipwreck. He thereupon appears in a friend's dream, declaring: "The failure of the ship's captain anchored me at the gate of paradise."

4. Abū Ḥanīfah dreams of God ninety-nine times and decides, should he dream of Him again, to ask how one can be saved on Judgment Day. He has indeed a hundredth dream and asks God the question, and God gives him an invocation of His unicity (which is cited) to perform every morning and evening.

5. A man of letters by the name of Abū l-ʿAlāʾ b. ʿAbdarraḥmān is loved by a beautiful slave girl but does not reveal his own feelings for her until she dies of a broken heart and he regrets his own coldness. Thereafter she appears to him in a dream and he weeps, but she recites verses calling his weeping meaningless as long as he is alive. When he awakens, his guilt has ceased, he lets out a cry, and passes away.

6. The caliph al-Hādī [r. 169-70/785-6] had bought a beautiful slave by the name of Ġādir, whom he loved ardently. Fearing his brother Hārūn's desire to marry her after his own death, he forces him and the slave to swear that they will not marry. He dies within a month. Hārūn [ar-Rašīd] violates this oath, marries the slave and loves her even more than his brother had done. One day the girl falls asleep in Hārūn's arms and dreams of al-Hādī, who recites verses calling her a traitress, true to her name, and wishes death upon her. She wakes up and expires in Hārūn's arms (ʿAbd al-Ḥaqq, al-ʿĀqibah[34]).

Addendum by Ibn Abī Ḥaǧalah referring to similar stories in his own *Dīwān aṣ-ṣabābah*.

7. Dulaf b. Abī Dulaf dreams of being summoned by a commander, and finds his father sitting naked and dejected in the upper room of a burnt-out, ruined house. He recites two couplets warning that everyone is asked about his deeds on Judgment Day. The son wakes up depressed (Ibn Ḥallikān and others).

---

[34] Abū Muḥammad ʿAbdalḥaqq b. ʿAbdarraḥmān b. ʿAlī al-Azdī al-Išbīlī Ibn al-Ḥarrāṭ (d. 581/1185), was an Andalusian traditionist, orator, and imam; his *ʿĀqibah fī l-baḥt [fī aḥwāl al-āḥirah]* is an anthology about death; GAL 1:371.

Addendum by Ibn Abī Ḥaǧalah: Dulaf's father was a famous Abbasid general, patron, and man of letters.

When fighting Kurdish waylayers, Abū Dulaf impaled two of them on one lance. This is followed by a couplet by Bakr b. an-Naṭṭāḥ [d. 222/837] on this event and another couplet by the same poet elevating Abū Dulaf's generosity over Jesus' alchemy in an inverted comparison, for which he the poet received 10,000 dinars. Reformulation of the motif in a couplet by Abū Bakr b. Hāšim: the *mamdūḥ* transforms papyrus inscribed with panegyrics into bags containing pure gold coins.

V. Events That Happened in Egypt, Appendix

(*Sukkardān*, Cairo 1421/2001, pp. 186-202 / Cairo 1317H., *in margine* pp. 209-19)

Motifs

1. Natural catastrophes	|×|×|×|−|−|−|×|
2. Strife between humans	|×|×|−|−|×|×|−|
3. Miracles	|−|×|×|×|−|−|−|
4. Foreign lands	|−|−|−|×|×|−|−|

Submotifs

a. Letters	|−|×|−|×|−|−|×|
b. Number series	|×|−|−|−|×|−|×|
c. Attestations	|−|×|−|−|×|−|×|

1. In 597H. [1201] during the reign of the Ayyubid ruler al-Malik al-ʿĀdil[35], famine and cannibalism occurred in Egypt. The king paid for thousands of shrouds for foreigners who perished (Abū Šāmah, *aḏ-Ḏayl* [ʿalā r-Rawḍatayn]). Doctors were called to houses, snatched, and eaten. Anecdote on this topic.

Addendum by Ibn Abī Ḥaǧalah: Cannibalism also occurred during a famine which struck at the time of the Fatimid al-Mustanṣir al-ʿAlawī [r. 427-87/1036-94]. A vizier's mule was taken and eaten in front of the caliph's palace.

List of exorbitant prices for food in Mayyāfariqīn after Hülegü's long siege of it.

---

35 Probably the first ruler of this name, Ṣalāḥaddīn's brother and successor Muḥammad b. Ayyūb (r. 596-615/1200-18), not Muḥammad's grandson al-Malik al-ʿĀdil II, Abū Bakr Sayfaddīn b. al-Malik al-Kāmil (r. 635-37/1238-40), Bosworth, C.E., *New Islamic Dynasties*, p. 70, and H. A. R. Gibb, "al-ʿĀdil", in: *EI²* 1 (1960), pp. 197-98.

2. In 741H. hail in the shapes of animals and humans fell in Hama. Attestation of this before the local judge is forwarded to the judge of Hama (ʿAlamaddīn al-Birzālī [d. 739/1339], *Taʾrīḫ*).[36]

Addendum by Ibn Abī Ḥaǧalah: In the days of the Umayyad caliph Sulaymān b. ʿAbdalmalik [r. 96-99/715-17] a letter from the Iraqi governor [ʿUmar] b. Hubayrah[37] reported that in Bukhara the skies opened and giants fell from them, leaving smoldering craters in the earth. Attestation by local judge and witnesses.

In 524H. rain of fire fell in Mosul and flying scorpions killed many people.

In 544H. rain of blood fell in Yemen.

Addendum by Ibn Abī Ḥaǧalah: in the same year Bedouins robbed the pilgrimage caravan including Ḫātūn, the sister of Seljuq ruler Masʿūd [r. 510-51/1116-56], and left the travelers behind to perish of thirst.

3. In 552H. an earthquake claimed lives in Damascus, Shiraz, Antakia, and Tripoli. Students were crushed while in class. In Tell Hawran and Latakia the earth cleft to reveal ancient buildings, sarcophagi, and an idol. Destruction of the Lebanese coastal cities and all Frankish fortresses. The sea receded to Cyprus.

1.1 million casualties (author of *al-Mirʾāt*[38]).

In the same year a plague in Hijaz and Yemen annihilated eighteen out of twenty towns, but two towns were left completely unscathed (Q. Yā Sīn/36:83).

4. In 638H. a messenger from the Mongol ruler Toluy b. Čingiz Khān[39] delivered a letter to the Muslim rulers, beginning with Šihābaddīn Ġāzī b. al-ʿĀdil, demanding their surrender; the educated Isfahani messenger tells of miracles in the Mongol lands, such as people, on the border of Sind, with eyes on their shoulders, grain that brings forth sheep, a source in Māzandarān [southeastern shore of the Caspian sea] that spouts a wooden object once every thirty years and which then disappears in a day (Ibn Katīr, *al-Bidāyah wa-n-nihāyah*).

5. In 412H. the Ghaznavid sultan Maḥmūd b. Sebüktigin [r. 388-421/998-1030] sends the caliph a letter describing his conquests in India, among them the destruction of a great golden idol with a rich treasury and many temple servants. Maḥmūd describes the dangerous journey there and the great number of Indians killed.

---

[36] On this historian and hadith scholar, whose *History* (actually titled al-*Muqtafā*) was much quoted by later scholars, see Rosenthal, F. "al-Birzālī, ʿAlam al-Dīn", in: *EI*[2] 1(1960), pp. 1238-39.

[37] Based on the date of the event, it was the father, ʿUmar, not the son, Yūsuf b. ʿUmar, who later served as governor of Iraq (129-32/741-49); Vadet, J.C., "Ibn Hubayra", in: *EI*[2] 3 (1968), p. 802.

[38] The *Mirʾāt az-zamān* by the Ayyubid historian Sibṭ b. al-Ǧawzī (d. 654/1256) is meant here.

[39] The actual ruler was Toluy's brother Ödegey [r. 626-39/1229-41]; Toluy [d. 629/1232] himself never ruled, but two of his sons became great Khans (Möngke and Qubilay) and another son founded the Īlḫānid dynasty (Hülegü); Amitai, R., "Toluy", in: *EI*[2] 10 (1999), p. 564, and Bosworth, C.E., *New Islamic Dynasties*, pp. 246-47, 250-51.

Further details about the site surrounded by other silver idols. A further letter by Maḥmūd b. Sebüktigin recounting that he discovered a city filled with golden palaces and idols, one of them supposedly 300,000 years old, which he burnt to the ground, and that he captured numerous slaves and elephants (aḏ-Ḏahabī, *Taʾrīḫ*).

6. A Kharijite by the name of ʿAbd an-Nabī b. al-Mahdī, allegedly related to the Fatimids and claiming to be a Qarmatian, set up a brutal rule in Yemen which was continued by his son who built a shrine for his father and forced people to circumambulate this instead of the Kaaba. People implored Ṣalāḥaddīn [r. 564-89/1169-93] for help, and he sent his brother Šamsaddawla who killed the tyrant.[40]

7. In 654H. an earthquake in Medina tore open a huge crater, and its glow shone as far as Mekka (Abū Šāmah, *Taʾrīḫ*); according to the chief judge Ṣadraddīn ʿAlī at-Tamīmī, the Bedouins of Bosra could see the necks of their camels by night in the earthquake's glow (Ibn Kaṯīr, *Taʾrīḫ*); the people of Medina flocked to the prophet's mosque and repented their sins at that time (anon. quatrain describing the earthquake as a sign *(āyah)* from God).

Prophetic hadith: Judgment Day will not arrive before "fire comes out of the earth in Medina and lights up the necks of camels in Bosra" (al-Buḫārī, *Ṣaḥīḥ*, transmitter Abū Hurayrah).

VI Events That Happened in Cairo and around the Pyramids, Appendix

(*Sukkardān*, Cairo 1421/2001, pp. 203-6)

Motifs

1. Miracles	|×|×|×|×|×|×|×|
2. Foreign lands	|×|–|×|–|–|–|×|
3. Strange customs	|–|–|×|×|–|–|–|

Submotifs

a. Mountains	|–|×|×|×|–|×|–|
b. Miraculous mass feedings	|–|–|–|–|×|×|×|

1. At the conquest of al-Andalus, twenty-four crowns inscribed with the names and regnal years of Spanish kings and the table of Solomon[41] were discovered in its "Royal City" *(madīnat al-mulūk)* (Several historians).

---

[40]   The event is dated to 569H. by aḏ-Ḏahabī, see Ibn Abī Ḥaǧalah, *Sukkardān*, p. 190n4.
[41]   See note 22 above.

Solomon's table was brought to al-Walīd b. ʿAbdalmalik [r. 86-96/705-15], who discovered a locked compartment. The last Christian king, Ludrīq,[42] had insisted on opening it against the advice of his bishops and priests, and it revealed images of armed Arabs on horses. That same year Spain was conquered by the Arabs (*Mirʾāt az-zamān*[43]).

2. In a mountain in Kūrat Rustam[44] a cave with a man-sized hole revealed a tangle of fifteen strands of unknown material. When their knot was untied, no one was able to retie it again in the same way, and whenever the bundle was removed, another one appeared in the same place (al-Qāḍī Abū Yusr ʿAṭāʾ b. Nabhān).

3. Near Derbend[45] stands a tall mountain with a town at the bottom named Zirih Karān,[46] which means "armor-making." All its inhabitants, including women and children, only produced weapons and cuirasses, which people came from everywhere to buy. They gave their deceased males to men living in underground dwellings, and these stripped the flesh off the corpses and fed it to black ravens. Women's corpses were given to the earth-dwellers' women and their flesh was fed to kites. The town's inhabitants followed no ruler or religion. Once, Sayfaddīn Muḥammad, the caliph's son (variant: the later caliph Sayfaddawla) besieged them. Seeing themselves surrounded by the army, they gestured towards the mountain, conferring in a foreign tongue, and vanished beneath the earth. A heavy snowstorm arose, the army panicked and fled, with the horsemen crushing each other to death. Then, the storm ceased immediately. This was their magic.

4. Mount Fath, the world's tallest mountain, is inhabited by seventy-two peoples, each with its own language and king. It contains the city of Bāb al-Abwāb, which was built by Kisrā as a fortress against the Khazars and Turks and includes a wall extending from the Caspian Sea across the mountain all the way to Tabaristan.[47] It was 40 parasangs long and had a gate every three miles, where Kisrā settled people as guards. In the mountains there lived a type of monkey, which kings trained to smell poison in their food ([Sibṭ b. al-Ǧawzī], *Mirʾāt az-zamān*).

5. There stood between China and India a duck on top of a pillar, both made of copper. Once a year, on the day of ʿĀšūrāʾ, the duck would stretch her neck down to the river beneath and drink and then spout enough water to satisfy the

---

[42] The name is a corruption of Roderic, Spain's last Visigothic king, defeated by Ṭāriq b. Ziyād in 92/711.

[43] See note 38.

[44] Two towns named after Rustam (Rustamābād, Rustamkūyah) near Qazwīn on the southwestern shore of the Caspian Sea are mentioned by Yāqūt, *Muʿǧam al-buldān*, 2:402.

[45] Also called Bāb al-Abwāb, it is located in ancient Dagestan.

[46] Pl. of Persian *zirihgar*, a maker of coats of mail. Zirihgarān is both the name of a mountain range in the north of Dagestan and a people (today's Kubačis) famous for their coats of mail in Timurid times; Barthold, W., and Bennigsen, A., "Dāghistān", in: *EI*² 2 (1965), pp. 85-89, esp. p. 86.

[47] Probably a corruption of Tabarsaran, the region south of Derbend.

needs of the people and livestock of the region for the entire year ([Sibṭ] Ibn al-Ǧawzī, [*Mirʾāt az-zamān*], transmitter ʿAbdallāh b. ʿAmr b. al-ʿĀṣ).

6. Near Mosul stands a mountain with a cloister, called Dayr al-Ḥanāfis ["Cloister of the Scarabs"][48], with a yearly nocturnal festival. On this day all scarabs of the region crawl up to the mountain in such numbers that people step on them all night long. By morning the scarabs have vanished (Sibṭ b. al-Ǧawzī [*Mirʾāt az-zamān*], based on people from Mosul).

Addendum by Ibn Abī Ḥaǧalah: another cloister, called Dayr al-Zarāzīr ["Cloister of the Starlings"] has a similar story. On a specific day all the earth's starlings would assemble there, each carrying three olives, one in its beak and two with in its claws, and drop these in the cloister. These olives would supply the priests with lamp oil and condiments for an entire year. The cloister is located in Rūmiyah.[49]

7. Tubbat[50] is a city founded by and named after Tubbaʿ; its name was changed by the Turks. It is famous for its musk, and whoever enters it becomes cheerful and laughs until he leaves (az-Zamaḫšarī, *Rabīʿ al-abrār*).

Addendum by Ibn Abī Ḥaǧalah: China is known for fine craftsmanship and amazing paintings that depict even the facial expressions of human figures.

VII 7 Prose and Verse on Flowers that Grow in Upper Egypt, Appendix

(*Sukkardān*, Cairo 1421/2001, pp. 218-25)

Motifs

1. Rose	|×|×|−|×|×|×|×|
2. Narcissus	|−|−|×|−|×|−|×|
3. Color combinations	|−|−|×|−|−|×|×|
4. Comparison	|×|×|×|×|−|−|−|

Submotifs

a. Love passion	|×|×|×|−|−|−|×|
b. Opposites	|−|×|×|−|−|−|−|

---

48 See Yāqūt, *Muʿǧam al-buldān*, 2:341 s.v. Dayr al-Ḥanāfis, who mentions the periodic appearance of scarabs but not the festival.

49 The Arabic name for the city of Rome; cf. Traini, R. "Rūmiya", in: *EI²* 8 (1994), pp. 612-13, and Yāqūt, *Muʿǧam al-buldān*, 2:445-48.

50 The Arabic name of Tibet; see Barthold, W., "Tubbat", in: *EI²* 10 (1999), pp. 576-78 with the alternate spellings Tibbat and Tibat. Yāqūt, *Muʿǧam al-buldān*, 1:428-30, also gives the vocalizations Tubbit and Tabbut and records the inhabitants' natural cheerfulness as well as the Arabic foundation legend in greater detail.

c. Dreams |–|–|×|–|–|–|–|
d. Number series |–|–|×|–|–|–|–|
e. Foreign royal customs |–|–|–|×|–|–|–|
f. Prophetic miracle |–|–|–|–|×|–|–|
g. Attestation |–|–|–|–|–|×|–|

1. The courtier al-Faḍl [b. Yaḥyā] recounts how he once found the caliph ar-Rašīd in the company of an accomplished slave girl with a rose on a tray, and the caliph asked him for a poetic comparison for the flower. The courtier compared the rose's red color to the blushing cheek of a kissed girl. The slave girl then extemporized a verse comparing the rose to her own cheek flushed from intercourse with the caliph. Aroused, the caliph asked al-Faḍl to leave; the latter hastily closed the curtains on the pair and left (al-Masʿūdī, *Šarḥ Maqāmāt* [*al-Ḥarīrī*],[51] according to a book by Abū l-ʿIzz Aḥmad b. ʿAbdallāh al-ʿUkbarī,[52] transmitter: Ayyūb al-Wazzān).

2.a. A comparison serves to clarify something for the hearer; in order to praise, one compares the lofty with the low; in order to lampoon, one compares the low with the lofty (Ibn Rašīq, *ʿUmda*).

b. Addendum by Ibn Abī Ḥağalah: comparison of the rose to a mule's anus (couplet by Ibn ar-Rūmī).

c. Further addendum: though technically correct, Ibn ar-Rūmī overshoots in his comparison. He did not like the fragrance of roses and in this respect he was "like a dung beetle" *(ğuʿalī)* because dung beetles die from the fragrance of roses and revive at the stench of rubbish.

d. The rose causes coughing in dry-brained people but cures excessive yellow bile and headaches arising from hot blood. The rose is the only simple medication with two contrasting effects, namely decongestant and congestive (medical books).

e. Wormwood *(afsintīn)*, which is cold and dry, likewise has two effects: when kneaded with honey, it cures cold fever and reduces phlegm in the stomach. When kneaded with sugar, it does not have the same effect (Galen).

f. Ibn ar-Rūmī praised the ugly and lampooned the beautiful (verses by Ibn ar-Rūmī on speech which changes the truth and on comparing honey both to bees' saliva and wasps' vomit as an example of the magic of eloquence, which makes darkness shine).

---

[51] The hadith scholar Abū ʿAlī or Abū s-Saʿīd Muḥammad b. Abī as-Saʿādāt ʿAbdarraḥmān b. Masʿūd (al-Masʿūdī) al-Panğdahī (also al-Fanğdahī, al-Banğdahī, al-Bandahī), d. 584/1188, hailing from Panğdih in Khorasan, composed the earliest *Šarḥ Maqāmāt al-Ḥarīrī* of those which Brockelmann lists, as well as another work, *Mağānī l-muqāmāt fī maʿānī l-maqāmāt*; both are unedited. He also tutored Ṣalāḥaddin's son al-Malik al-Afḍal; GAL 1:277 and 356, S1:487 and 604, S2:910.

[52] Not to be confused with the philologist and *faqīh* ʿAbdallāh b. al-Ḥusayn al-ʿUkbarī (d. 566/1219), to whom a commentary of al-Mutanabbī's *Dīwān* is attributed.

g. Ibn al-Muʿtazz's retort to Ibn ar-Rūmī comparing the rose to the cheek of a conquered beloved, whose waistband is loosened after his earlier anger has subsided (quatrain by Ibn al-Muʿtazz).

3. a. Abū Nuwās appears in a man's dream and is asked how he fared in his afterlife. He answers that he was pardoned and admitted to Paradise on account of his verses on the narcissus, which included an etiology of the narcissus' declaration of God's unicity and Muḥammad's prophethood and mission (quatrain by Abū Nuwās).

b. Addendum by Ibn Abī Ḥağalah: the lexicographer Ibn Durayd [d. 312/933] saw in a dream a thin-bearded and pallid man who identified himself as Ibn Nāğiyah from Syria and claimed to outdo Abū Nuwās in wine poetry. In a couplet he compared the color change of mixed wine, from red to yellow, to a narcissus and a red anemone, which represent the rosy cheek of a glowing beloved and the pallid cheek of a lovesick lover, respectively. Ibn Durayd criticized the metaphors' inverted color sequence from red to yellow, and Ibn an-Nāğiyah was appalled by such interfering editing *(taḥrīr)* and nitpicking *(istiqṣāʾ)*. Ibn Durayd awoke amazed (al-Marzubānī).

c. Addendum by Ibn Abī Ḥağalah (couplet): description of an apple, colored half like the lily of the valley and half like pomegranate blossom and red anemone, as if passion had reunited the cheeks of the beloved and the lover after their separation.

d. Addendum by Ibn Abī Ḥağalah of a number riddle: how does one bring an apple to cure a sick man in a city with seven walls, when at each gate half of one's load is taken away? Answer: one starts with 128 $(=2^7)$ apples [128 > 64 > 32 > 16 > 8 > 4 > 2 > 1] *(adab* collections).

4.a. The caliph al-Mutawakkil [r. 232-47/847-61] likened himself as the king of humans to the rose as the king of flowers.

b. The Persian kings removed sweets from their tables in the season of dates, saltwort *(ušnān)* in the season of melons, and fragrant herbs in the season of roses.

c. Ardašir[53] b. Bābak described the rose as white pearls and ruby, seated on emerald, filled with shards of gold and as having the delicacy of wine and the fragrance of perfume.

d. Kisrā Anūširwān once picked up a rose dropped on his path and stopped at that place to drink for seven nights (az-Zamaḫšarī, *Rabīʿ al-abrār*).

5.a. When Abraham's people tried to burn him they ceased all activities to gather firewood and to light a gigantic fire which burnt for seven days. Because it was too hot to go near and even scorched the birds flying over it, Iblis taught the people to use a catapult to fling Abraham inside. He, in turn, cared about noth-

---

53 Emendation of Azdašir in Ibn Abī Ḥağalah, *Sukkardān*, 221.

ing but invoking God's unicity. Heaven and earth revolted and asked God to permit them to help Abraham. God agreed in the case that Abraham should ask them. The lords of wind and water then offered their help to cease the fire, but Abraham rejected their aid, trusting solely in God (al-Kawāšī, *Tafsīr* of Q. An-biyāʾ/21:68).

b. Another version of Abraham's invocation and his rejection of Gabriel's help and of a direct supplication to God, relying on His knowledge of all things (Ibn ʿAbbās).

c. All animals tried to extinguish the fire, except the gecko, which blew on the fire. But the fire only devoured Abraham's fetters. Then the angels lifted Abraham by his arms and set him down near a stream of sweet water in the midst of a garden of red roses and fresh narcissus, where he stayed for seven days.

6. In Nihāvand, Muḥammad b. ʿAlī al-Anṣārī saw a type of yellow rose with one thousand petals and counted the petals of one rose to confirm this (Šihābaddīn Ibn Faḍlallāh al-ʿUmarī [d. 749/1349]).

Al-ʿUmarī himself saw a sheet of paper divided into one bright red and one pure white half, and another sheet divided by strokes into sections (Ibn Faḍlallāh al-ʿUmarī).

7.a. Whenever he saw the first rose, a teacher in Baghdad gave himself up to debauchery for the full season of roses (quatrain by him).

b. Addendum by Ibn Abī Ḥağalah in ornate prose: the roses' beauties are manifold. The roses' season serves as an incitement and excuse for the profligates. Disgusted by people's sinning in this season Ibrāhīm al-Ḥawāṣṣ asked God to be rescued. The most fragrant flowers are the Bengal (Ğūr) rose, the Kufan violet, the narcissus of Jurjan, and the Baghdadi gillyflower.

c. A couplet by Muğīraddīn b. Tamīm on the gillyflower *(manṯūr)*. Feeling observed, the gillyflower warns the narcissus to avert its glance lest it stick its fingers[54] into the narcissus' eye (couplet).

Anonymous couplet, in which the speaker prefers the rose to the gillyflower, which turns yellow with rage and points its fingers at him.

A further couplet by Muğīraddīn b. Tamīm, in which he warns of the fingers of those whom one mistreats, such as the rose thrown into turmoil by the praying fingers of the gillyflower.

d. Addendum by Ibn Abī Ḥağalah in prosimetron: a panegyric epigram on his previous patron, the sultan al-Nāṣir [b. Qalāwūn, r. 693-741/1293-1341 with two interruptions], beginning with etiologies of the narcissus, rose, and moringa tree. The epigram is framed by ornate prose, concluding with a prayer for God's support and the *ḥamdalah*.

---

[54] The dentellated petals of the gillyflower, or carnation, are reinterpreted as fingers in this fantastic etiology.

C. Motifs in Alphabetical Order

(Roman numbers stand for the chapter in whose appendix the motif (M) or submotif (SM) appears; Arabic numbers stand for the section within the appendix.)

Animals
    curiosities about ~ I.6 (M)
    ~ fable I.5, 7 (M)
    speaking ~ I.1-5, 7 (M)
Attestation I.1-3 (SM); III.6-7 (SM), V.2, 5, 7 (SM); VII.6 (SM)
Ambiguous answer II.1, 4 (M); III.5 (SM)
Color combinations VII.3, 6-7 (M)
Comparison *(tašbīh)* VII.1-4 (M)
Customs
    strange ~ VI.3-4 (M)
    foreign royal ~ III.1-5 (M); VII.4 (SM)
Dream II.3 (SM); VII.3 (SM)
    ~ about deceased people IV.3, 5-7 (M)
    fatal ~ IV.5-6 (SM)
    helpful ~ IV.3-4, 7 (SM)
Eloquent repartee I.1-2, 4-5, 7 (SM); II.1, 4-7 (M); III.5-6 (SM); IV.1, 3 (SM)
Fantasy creatures III.5-7 (M)
Foreign lands V.4-5 (M); VI.1-5, 7 (M)
Foreign: see also customs
Letters V.2, 4-5, 7 (SM)
    foreign royal ~ III.3-5 (M)
Love passion VII.1-3, 7 (SM)
Miracles V.2-4 (M), VI.1-7 (M)
    prophetic ~ VII.5 (SM)
Miraculous mass feedings VI.5-7 (SM)
Mountains VI.2-4, 6 (SM)
Narcissus VII.3, 5, 7 (M)
Natural catastrophes V.1-3, 7 (M)
Number series II.3, 7 (SM); III.4-5, 7 (SM); V.1, 5, 7 (SM); VII.3 (SM)
Opposites VII.2-3
People whose death was caused by al-Ḥākim IV.1-3 (M)
Proof of prophecy I.1, 3-4 (SM)
Rose VII.1-2, 4-7 (M)
Self-delivered death sentence II.2-3 (M)
Self-harming schemer II.1-3 (SM)
Strife between humans V.1-2, 5-6 (M)

Bibliography

Primary Sources

Ibn Abī Ḥaǧalah, *Sukkardān as-sulṭān*, ed. ʿAlī Muḥammad ʿUmar, Cairo 1421/2001 [based on MS Baghdad University 24, dated 879/1474-75].

Ibn Abī Ḥaǧalah, *Sukkardān as-sulṭān, in margine* of al-ʿĀmilī, Muḥammad b. Ḥusayn *al-Miḫlāh* with his appended *Asrār al-balāġah*], Cairo: Muṣṭafā al-Bābī al-Ḥalabī 1317 [1888; not to be confused with the similarly titled edition of *al-Miḫlāh* and *Sukkardān*, Cairo: al-Ḥānǧī al-Kutubī 1317, which has a different pagination].

Yāqūt, *Muʿǧam al-buldān*, ed. M. ʿAbdarraḥmān al-Marʿašlī, 8 pts. in 4 vols., Beirut, n.d.

Secondary Literature:

Bosworth, Clifford E., *The New Islamic Dynasties. A Chronological and Genealogical Manual*, Edinburgh 1996.

Dols, Michael W., *The Black Death in the Middle East*, Princeton 1977.

EI² = *Encyclopaedia of Islam*, new [second] edition, 11 vols., and supplement, Leiden 1950-2004.

GAL, GALS = Brockelmann, Carl, *Geschichte der arabischen Litteratur*, 2 vols. and three supplements., reprint Leiden 1996.

GAS = Sezgin, Fuat, *Geschichte des arabischen Schrifttums*, 17 vols. to date, Leiden and Frankfurt 1967-

Theroux, Alexander, *The Primary Colors. Three Essays*, New York 1994.

Urban Architecture and Poetry:
Two Medieval Arabic Anthologies as Manuals
of Mapping Urban Space

Alev Masarwa

Introduction[*]

Looking through the prism of texts that focus on cities, we obtain important clues about the relation of living in and writing about a city. Both spheres generate their specific textual representations as well as their narrative shapes, motifs and imagery. Corresponding to their actual cultural significance these patterns have undergone some changes over the course of time. The poetic perception of urban space to some extent records actual events of everyday life in cities. However, to a greater extent it records and canonizes imagery and a vision of urban culture through the rules of poetic speech.

This paper will portray how poets perceived their domestic environment and how they organized the urban space according to the rules of poetic speech, especially in 14ᵗʰ/early 15ᵗʰ-century Damascus and Cairo. For this purpose, two exceptional Arabic anthologies, which were written in immediate sequence and served as manuals on how to write about a city, will be compared: Ibn Abī Ḥaǧalah's (1325-1375) *Sulūk as-sanan fī waṣf as-sakan* (The Right Path in the Description of Dwellings) and al-Ġuzūlī's (d. 1411 or 1412) *Maṭāliʿ al-budūr fī manāzil as-surūr* (Book of the Rising of the Full Moons on the Dwellings of Joy).

On the one hand, by examining the criteria of selection, the formal structure of the works as well as the (in-)frequency of topics, we will gain insight into processes of canonization of the required urban topics. On the other hand, we will observe a poetic map of urban space, one not necessarily corresponding to the 'topographical' perception of a city. Moreover, this pattern appears as a system of arrangement and promotion of the literary scene while the anthologists' own pieces of poetry secure a spot for themselves in the contemporary discourse. The comparison will reveal their contents and some of their own compositional features and it will be shown that besides common and classical city imagery, newer topics also entered the poetical sphere and that the content and form of these works had different agendas; in their entirety, they might give us clues to the works' cosmological concepts.

---

[*] A slightly revised version of a paper presented on the panel "Reinterpreting cities" at the 13ᵗʰ International Conference on Urban History of the European Association for Urban History in Helsinki; August 24-27, 2016. I am grateful to Ronald Mayer-Opificius, Samir Mubayd and Nefeli Papoutsakis for their proofreading and their helpful suggestions.

There are two basic assumptions which concern the topic of the so-called Islamic city and which fall short in describing the complexities of urban life in premodern times. Firstly, poetic speech is more or less regarded as irrelevant for historical data, as it was seemingly preoccupied with frozen traditional imagery and not reflecting the supposed 'historical reality'. The second assumption is – and this concerns the debate on the inwardness of the 'Islamic/Oriental' city in contrast to the western more 'public' type – that the characteristics of urban structure were formed to "maintain the quiet, safe and private life of the family"[1] – in other words to favour the private over the public.

It is not my intention to question these differences in general, as I am more concerned with the further consequences of these assumptions, which lead – especially among certain urban historians – to some narrow understandings of city perception in premodern times. Taking the contradictory requirement for representation and privacy as an integral part of the human condition, and considering the cultural, religious and of course climatic realities, there have always been opportunities to compensate for the part that is considered to be lacking, be it representation or privacy. This is true, for example, of the curtained beds or concealed doors in palaces of estates-based societies in western culture[2] and this is also true for a Muslim governor, who assembled the most learned men in his court in order to create a 'public' audience. What I want to say is that 'Islamic' cities had their public areas and lives and that poetry has its significance for historical reflection. For nowhere else could this 'publicness of the private' be better expressed than in poetical works.

The two anthologies presented in this paper may provide evidence for the aforementioned objections. These works by authors living in Mamluk Cairo and Damascus are particularly concerned with the motifs of urban morphology. Despite constant military threats this was a period[3] of flourishing trade between East and West and the heyday of monumental architectural buildings as a means of communication of wealth and power.[4] To no lesser degree it was also a highly productive era of literary and scholarly output.

---

[1]   See Masashi Haneda and Toru Miura, *Islamic Urban Studies: Historical Review and Perspectives*, Abington 2010, p. 22, quoting L. Torrès Balbas, "Les villes musulmanes d'Espagne" (1942) and linking to R. Brunshwig, "Urbanisme medieval" (1947) on the Islamic law regulating various facets of urban life, such as roads, walls, drainage and relations between neighbours.

[2]   Eugen Wirth, „Zur Konzeption der islamischen Stadt: Privatheit im islamischen Orient versus Öffentlichkeit in Antike und Okzident", in: *Die Welt des Islams* 31 (1991), pp. 50-92, esp. p. 72, and Lewis Mumford, *The Culture of Cities*, New York 1970 [1938], p. 41.

[3]   The last decades of the Baḥri Mamluks (1250-1390) and the first decades of the Burǧi Mamluks (1390-1517).

[4]   Beatrice Gruendler, "Ibn Abī Ḥajalah (1325-1375)", in: *Essays in Arabic Literary Biography; 1350-1850* (subsequently *EALB*), ed. by Joseph E. Lowry and Dewin Stewart, Wiesbaden 2009, pp. 118-126 (quotation p. 119).

Anthology I
Ibn Abī Ḥaǧalah (1325-1375):
(ms.) Sulūk as-sanan ilā [fī] waṣf as-sakan
(The Right Path to the Description of Dwellings)

The first work is an anthology by Ibn Abī Ḥaǧalah (1325-1375), whose name is connected to more than 70 works with a wide range of topics (e.g. on love poetry, warfare and the art of archery, on chess playing, medicine and epidemics), and mostly to nonconventional arrangements of *sujets*, including historical accounts and poetry. One of these exceptional and unconventional compositions is his *Sulūk as-sanan ilā waṣf as-sakan*, of which I recently discovered a copy in the Istanbul University library (İÜ: 877).[5] As this is still a work in progress I will only roughly outline its form and contents and some of its special features. Until now the work was only known by its title in bibliographical accounts but not by its content. Ibn Abī Ḥaǧalah, who frequently records many of his writings either in his poems or in his works of prose, gives only a few references to the *Sulūk*.[6] But these brief references help us to determine the *Sulūk*'s completion period; as his *Dīwān aṣ-Ṣabābah* was completed in 760/1359,[7] *Sulūk* must have been written prior to that year.

Sulūk is a collection of city poetry combined with prose sections arranged by topics of urban motifs and is the first of its kind as the author emphasises in his introduction. In most of its chapters Ibn Abī Ḥaǧalah begins in the manner of a lexicographer and gives brief information about the correct pronunciation of the word presented or some lexical variants, before citing older sayings about the topic (e.g. *dihlīz*: vestibule, entrance hall)[8] and quotes from poetry from older as well as contemporary poets, mostly introducing them with an appraising phrase (e.g. *"among*

---

5   İstanbul Üniversitesi Kütüphanesi (subsequently *Ms. Sulūk*) no: 877: 54 folios, 25 lines, written from one hand, clear *nasḫī*, rubrications and poems headings mostly in red ink, barely vocalised, scattered marginal comments, with a likely copy date of about 1207/1792 – this is the date given in a possession note on the frontispiece, when the copy became library property. A second copy at the *Dār al-Kutub* in Cairo turned out to be a photographical reproduction of the ms. Istanbul.

6   Reference is made in two instances in his *Dīwān aṣ-ṣabābah* [Istanbul, lithograph Šaʿrānī 1279/1863], p. 90: *"wa-qad ʿaqadtu li-n-nasīmi bāban mustaqillan fī kitābī Sulūku s-sanan fī [sic!] waṣfi s-sakan, wa-ḏakartu fīhi ašyāʾan taliqu bi-hāḏā l-bāb"* and p. 92: *"wa-qad ḏakartu fī n-nasīmi ašyāʾan malīhatan fī kitābī Sulūku s-sanani l-maḏkūr"*. See Umberto Rizzitano, "Il Dīwān aṣ-Ṣabābah dello Scrittore Maghrebino Ibn Abī Ḥaǧalah", in: *Rivista degli Studi Orientali* 28 (1953), pp. 35-70, here p. 39 and note 3 and Gruendler, "Ibn Abī Hajalah", p. 118. In his *Ǧiwār al-aḫyār Ibn Abī Ḥaǧalah* also refers to the *Sulūk* in the context of neighbourhood (Ibn Abī Ḥaǧalah, *Ǧiwār al-aḫyār fī dār al-qarār*, Ms. Yeni Cami 701, fol. 37b). – I thank Syrinx von Hees for pointing me to this passage.

7   On the completion date of *Dīwān aṣ-ṣabābah* in 760/1359, see Rizzitano, "Il Dīwān aṣ-Ṣabābah", p. 53.

8   *dihlīz*: a corridor or vestibule, see Muḥammad Muḥammad Amīn and Laylā ʿAlī Ibrāhīm, *al-Muṣṭalaḥāt al-miʿmāriyyah fī waṯāʾiq al-mamlūkiyyah*, Cairo 1990, p. 49.

104 ALEV MASARWA

the best verse I heard on it, is: …").[9] Many of his fellow poets seem to have sent him dedicated verses which signals both the popularity of the author and the popularity of these poetic themes. Ibn Abī Ḥaǧalah introduces them with the phrase: *"and he wrote me … / he sent me …"*. He inserts his own poems by writing: *"and what I said on this topic is …"*, or concludes using some literary and historical narratives connected to the topic.

Starting with a brief introduction in rhymed prose, the work offers 33 relatively short chapters[10] combining different genres of ornate speech in prose and poetry and containing amusing stories and puns. We can subsume those in units with more general headings (see also the contents section): Ibn Abī Ḥaǧalah starts with the entrance hall (ch. 1: *dihlīz: waǧh ad-dār, manzil aḍ-ḍayf,* i.e. the vestibule), which is situated between the entrance door and the house. It is, so to speak, the sphere of transition, entering the realm of privacy from the outer sphere, where the rules and ceremonies of 'entering' are performed. Then Ibn Abī Ḥaǧalah progresses to the door (ch. 2: *al-bāb*) and the doorkeeper (ch. 3). This is also to artfully show that there were borders and limits for entering the private sphere. In the following chapters Ibn Abī Ḥaǧalah elaborates on more general topics like building sites, representative decoration/furnishing, religious and social demands for construction and housing, the outer (physical) architecture of the city (chs. 4-11),[11] wind/cooling systems (chs. 12-14), water supply (chs. 15-17), urban fauna (chs. 18-20), courtly social activities (chs. 21-22), lighting types (chs. 23-26), food, cooking and hosting (chs. 27-33). The presented topics match many of the main principles of modern urban planning (with some restrictions in the last units of the chs. 27-33), as it is seen *"as a technical and political process […] concerned with the welfare of people, control of the use of land, design of the urban environment including transportation and*

---

9   E.g. *Ms. Sulūk,* fol. 1b:

”الدِّهْلِيزُ“ ـ بِكَسْرِ الدَّالِ ـ فَارِسِيٌّ مُعَرَّبُ، وَالجَمْعُ: ”الدَّهَالِيزُ“، وَهُوَ: مَا بَيْنَ البَابِ وَالدَّارِ. وَمِنْ أَحْسَنِ مَا سَمِعْتُ فِيهِ: / ب/2 ...

10   Considering that Ibn Abī Ḥaǧalah had a special sense for symmetry in his works, I could not see a clear subdivision into eleven chapters of the *Sulūk,* but many of the sequences follow a three-part order, where the topic of the last chapter gives a contextual transition to the next three chapters.

11   These chapters (esp. chs. 4-10) follow common topics of the legal literature on the religious principles of building, housing and social behaviour. A special compilation of these topics can be found in the work of the Andalusian Ibn al-Imām at-Tuṭīlī (d. 386/996): *Kitāb al-qaḍāʾ wa-nafy ḍ-ḍarar ʿan al-afniyah wa-ṭ-ṭuruq wa-l-ǧudur wa-l-mabānī wa-ṣ-ṣāḥāt wa-š-šaǧar wa-l-ǧamīʿ* (The book of jurisdiction and the elimination of harm regarding houses, streets, walls, buildings, public squares, trees, etc.) and also in the work of the Tunisian Ibn ar-Rāmī (d. 734/1334): *Kitāb al-iʿlān bi-aḥkām al-bunyān* (The book of pronouncing judgements in [matters of] building). For a substantial discussion of both authors, see Simon O'Meara, "A Legal Aesthetic of Medieval and Pre-Modern Arab-Muslim Urban Architectural Space", in: *Journal of Arabic and Islamic Studies* 9 (2009), pp. 1-17 (with further literature). For the connection of ruin-poetry and legal building principles provided by Ibn ar-Rāmī, see María Dolores Rodríguez Gómez, "Describing the Ruin: Writings of Arabic Notaries in the Last Period of al-Andalus", in: *Studia Orientalia* 112 (2012), pp. 71-101.

communication networks, and protection and enhancement of the natural environment".[12] The chapters are not very cohesive, but Ibn Abi Ḥaǧalah's introduction unambiguously reveals the purpose of his composition:

الحمد لله الَّذي خصَّنا مِن وَصف السَّكن بما يسكن إليه، وجعل كتابنا هذا في وصف العمارة أصل ما يُبنى عليه. أحمدُه حمد من فاز بالمكان والإمكان، وأسَّس بنيانه على تقوى من الله ورضوان.

> "All praise be to God, who singled us out to describe the habitations (resting places) reliably,[13] and also for making this book of ours (mine) about the description of the buildings/edifices a foundation which can be built upon. And I praise Him with the praise of one who has gained a place and ability and built his house on fearing and pleasing God".[14]

In his – also literally speaking ground-breaking – work, Ibn Abi Ḥaǧalah has admittedly not very artfully but roughly outlined a poetic raising up of a house, its important architectural segments and functional interiors. Further on, the author provides the reader with a summary of the functions and relevance of buildings among the inhabitants and the cityscape and likewise its functions within the poetic space. We can assume, that the closing chapter (*al-wakīrah*) was not chosen randomly, for it bears significance for both fields (i.e. for literature and architecture): the celebration of the house's completion emphasises the social component of architecture and it is also connected to the celebration of the completion of the literary work. This type of literature can be seen as an important expression of how architecture and space were perceived by the inhabitants, while it provides an important source for what Simon O'Meara rightly laments in his concluding remarks on the body of *fiqh al-bunyān* texts, when he states: *"Rarely, for example, is it satisfying to know only the outward, formal aspects of an architectural space – the history, appearance, and intended meaning of the madrasas, mosques, and mausoleums comprising a medina, say. One would also like to know the inner workings of this space; for in this space commingle what these monuments are in historical time and selectively frame out of time with the lives and beliefs of those subject to them. And from this space arise a society's representations of the world and the inhabitants' place in it, which in turn re-inform the space"*.[15]

---

12 McGill University (2016), School of Urban Planning: https://www.mcgill.ca/urbanplanning/planning.

13 Quranic reference: (7: 189,1): هُوَ الَّذِي خَلَقَكُم مِّن نَّفْسٍ وَاحِدَةٍ وَجَعَلَ مِنْهَا زَوْجَهَا لِيَسْكُنَ إِلَيْهَا *"He it is Who did create you from a single soul, and therefrom did make his mate that he might take rest in her [...]"* (tr. Pickthall).

14 *Ms. Sulūk*, fol. 1 a.

15 Simon O'Meara, "A Legal Aesthetic of Medieval and Pre-Modern Arab-Muslim Urban Architectural Space", p. 17.

Content of as-Sulūk

Chapter	Title	General heading milieu: high and learned society; court officials
(1)	On entrances/vestibules البَابُ الأَوَّلُ: فِي الدِّهْلِيزِ [1/ب]	entrance, vestibule vs. barriers for entering
(2)	On doors البَابُ الثَّانِي: فِي البَابِ [2/ب]	
(3)	On door-keepers and what visitors and gate-keepers were criticised for البَابُ الثَّالِثُ: فِي البَوَّابِ مَا وَرَدَ فِي ذَمِّ القُصَّادِ وَالحُجَّابِ [4/أ]	
(4)	On the spaciousness of houses and what has been said on this in the reports of the Islamic tradition البَابُ الرَّابِعُ: فِي سَعَةِ الدُّورِ وَمَا وَرَدَ فِيهَا مِن الآثَارِ الوَارِدَةِ [6/أ]	sites as a means of representation
(5)	On the site to be chosen for building a mansion البَابُ الخَامِسُ: فِي المَكَانِ المُخْتَارِ لِبِنَاءِ السَّكَنِ [6/ب]	religious and social demands for building and housing
(6)	On the rules/provisions for the construction of a building and on maintaining the builder's honour and memory البَابُ السَّادِسُ فِي أَحْكَامِ البِنَاءِ وَكَيْفِيَّتِهِ، وَبَقَاءِ الذِّكْرِ وَالشَّرَفِ بِبَقَائِهِ [7/أ]	*cf. Vitruvius: de architectura; Aristotle: Politica, on siting*[16]
(7)	On the willingness to build a house البَابُ السَّابِعُ: فِي الرَّغْبَةِ فِي البِنَاءِ [7/ب]	

---

[16] The chapter titles and ideas behind them echo passages of the theoretical works of Aristotle's (d. 322 B.C.) *Politics*, al-Fārābī's (d. 339/950) *Perfect State*, and Vitruvius (wrote ca. 30 B.C.), *De architectura* (book I: chs. 4-7, IV: ch. 6, V: ch. 10, VI: chs.1-5; VIII: chs.1-6). See esp. Vitruv, *Zehn Bücher über Architektur. De architectura libri decem*, übers. und d. Anm. erläutert von Franz Reber, 3rd ed., Wiesbaden 2015; see also the study of Wim Boerefijn, *The foundation, planning and building of new towns in the 13th and 14th centuries in Europe: an architectural-historical research into urban form and its creation*, UvA-DARE (Digital Academic Repository) 2010, who points to the work of the Aragonese cleric Francesc Eiximenis (1340-1409), a younger contemporary of Ibn Abī Ḥaǧalah. Contrary to the topic-oriented and more theoretical works of the former authors, Eiximenis' *El Crestia* (The Christian), "*has become the most explicit and therefore the most important European source on town planning theory*" (*ibid*, p. 310). However, our texts are neither theoretical nor normative handbooks on architecture and siting, moreover they deal with the perception of the built environment through poetry.

Chapter	Title	General heading
		milieu: high and learned society; court officials
(8)	On longing for a house and on homesickness (homelands) البَابُ الثَّامِنُ: في حُبِّ السَّكَنِ وَالحَنِينِ إِلَى الوَطَنِ [7/ب]	
(9)	On seeking information about the neighbour and being patient with him and on respecting the neighbourhood, and on the saying: *"The neighbour before the house and the companion before the road"* البَابُ التَّاسِعُ: في اخْتِبَارِ الجَارِ، وَالصَّبْرِ عَلَى أَذَاهُ، وَحُرْمَةِ الجِوَارِ، وَأَخْذِ الجَارِ بِالجَارِ قَبْلَ الدَّارِ وَالرَّفِيقِ قَبْلَ الطَّرِيقِ [9/ب]	
(10)	On selling and buying a house; and on the saying: *"renting is better than buying"* البَابُ العَاشِرُ: في بَيْعِ الدَّارِ، وَابْتِيَاعِهَا، وَكَوْنِ الكَرْيِ خَيْرًا [1] مِنَ الشَّرْيِ [11/أ]	
(11)	On the description of palaces and fortresses and what has been said about it in prose and poetry البَابُ الحَادِي عَشَرَ: في وَصْفِ الحُصُونِ وَالقُصُورِ، وَمَا قِيلَ فِيهَا مِنْ مَنْظُومٍ وَمَنْثُورٍ [11/ب]	cityscape
(12)	**On wind towers** البَابُ الثَّانِي عَشَرَ: في الباذهينج [sic!][14/أ]	wind / cooling systems
(13)	On winds and the different directions and their mildness البَابُ الثَّالِثَ عَشَرَ: في النَّسِيمِ عَلَى اخْتِلاَفِ ضُرُوبِهِ وَلَطَافَةِ هُبُوبِهِ [16/أ]	
(14)	On fans البَابُ الرَّابِعَ عَشَرَ: في المِرْوَحَةِ [19/ب]	
(15)	On pools, pitches, *shadirvāns* and water wheels البَابُ الخَامِسَ عَشَرَ: في البِرْكَةِ، وَالنَّوَّارِ، والشَّادِرْزَوَان، وَدُولاَبِ السَّاقِيَةِ [21/أ]	water-/supply
(16)	On bathhouses البَابُ السَّادِسَ عَشَرَ: في الحَمَّامِ [23/أ]	

Chapter	Title	General heading milieu: high and learned society; court officials
(17)	On lavatories/privies البَابُ السَّابِعَ عَشَرَ: فِي بَيْتِ الخَلَاءِ [26/أ]	
(18)	On the places infested with mosquitoes, bugs, fleas and other insects البَابُ الخَامِسَ عَشَرَ: فِي ذِكْرِ مَا تَعُمُّ بِهِ البَلْوَى مِن النَّامُوسِ وَالبَقِّ وَالبَرَاغِيثِ وَسَائِرِ الحَشَرَاتِ [26/ب]	urban fauna
(19)	On doves/pigeons البَابُ التَّاسِعَ عَشَرَ: فِي الحَمَامِ [30/ب]	
(20)	On parrots, peafowls, quails and cages البَابُ العِشْرُونَ: فِي الدرة، وَالطَّاؤُوسِ، وَالسُّمَّانِيّ، وَالقَفَص [31/أ]	
(21)	On chess البَابُ الحَادِي وَالعِشْرُونَ: فِي الشِّطْرَنْج [33/أ]	social and court activities
(22)	On maids playing music instruments and the description of their instruments. And what is said in praise and criticism of singing البَابُ الثَّانِي وَالعِشْرُونَ: فِي ذِكْرِ نُبْذَةٍ مِنْ أَحْوَالِ الجَوَارِي المُطْرِبَاتِ، وَوَصْفِ آلَاتِهِنَّ، وَمَا جَاءَ فِي مَدْحِ الغِنَاءِ وَذَمِّهِ، وَنُبْذَةٍ مِنْ أَحْوَالِهِ [35/أ]	
(23)	On candles البَابُ الثَّالِثُ وَالعِشْرُونَ: فِي الشَّمْعَةِ [37/أ]	lighting types
(24)	On (round) lanterns and (metal) lamps البَابُ الرَّابِعُ وَالعِشْرُونَ: فِي فَانُوسِ الأَكْرَة وَالقِنْدِيلِ [38/أ]	
(25)	On (decorative) lamps and lamp stands البَابُ الخَامِسُ وَالعِشْرُونَ: فِي السِّرَاجِ وَالمَسْرَجَةِ [38/ب]	
(26)	On fire البَابُ السَّادِسُ وَالعِشْرُونَ: فِي النَّارِ [40/ب]	
(27)	On the cook and kettles and on some dinner ware البَابُ السَّابِعُ وَالعِشْرُونَ: فِي الطَّبَّاخِ، وَالقُدُورِ، وَنُبْذَةٍ مِنْ حَوَائِجِ الطَّعَام [42/ب]	cooking, food and beverage

Chapter	Title	General heading milieu: high and learned society; court officials
(28)	On the differences between table and dining table الْبَابُ الثَّامِنُ وَالْعِشْرُونَ: فِي الْفَرْقِ بَيْنَ الْخِوَانِ وَالْمَائِدَةِ [44/أ]	
(29)	On the description of the dining table, bread and various kinds of vegetables الْبَابُ التَّاسِعُ وَالْعِشْرُونَ: فِي وَصْفِ السُّفْرَةِ وَالْخُبْزِ وَأَنْوَاعِ الْبُقُولِ [45/أ]	
(30)	On vegetables الْبَابُ الثَّلَاثُونَ: فِي الْبُقُولِ [46/ب]	
(31)	On various kinds of food and some narratives on the harm and good of them الْبَابُ الْحَادِي وَالثَّلَاثُونَ: فِي أَنْوَاعِ الْأَطْعِمَةِ، وَنُبْذَةٍ مِنْ ذِكْرِ مَنَافِعِهَا وَمَضَارِّهَا [47/ب]	
(32)	On sweets and beverages الْبَابُ الثَّانِي وَالثَّلَاثُونَ: فِي الْحَلْوَى وَالْمَشْرُوبِ [49/أ]	
(33)	On the festivity of the completion of a house / housewarming party (al-wakīrah) and on banquets and the etiquette of visiting and hosting الْبَابُ الثَّالِثُ وَالثَّلَاثُونَ: فِي الْوَكِيرَةِ، وَنُبْذَةٍ مِنْ أَوْصَافِ الْوَلَائِمِ وَآدَابِ الزَّائِرِ وَالْمَزُورِ [51/أ - 54/أ]	hosting

Anthology II
ʿAlāʾaddīn al-Ġuzūlī (d. 1411 or 1412):
Maṭāliʿ al-budūr fī manāzil as-surūr
(Book of the Rising of the Full Moons on the Dwellings of Joy)

The second work which presents a parallel *sujet* of planning and building a house, is that of a freed Turkish slave and poet ʿAlāʾaddīn al-Ġuzūlī. His book is entitled *Maṭāliʿ al-budūr fī manāzil as-surūr (Book of the Rising of the Full Moons on the Dwellings of Joy)*.[17] It contains 50 chapters and presents a more elaborate com-

---

[17] ʿAlāʾaddīn al-Bahāʾī al-Ġuzūlī, *Maṭāliʿ al-budūr fī manāzil as-surūr*, edition Port Said 1419/2000, p. 7, first published 1882 in Cairo, see Michael Cooperson, "ʿAlāʾ al-Dīn al-Ghuzūlī (died 1411 or 1412)", in: *EALB*, pp. 106-117 (esp. p. 116). For the many copies of

position technique than the work of Ibn Abī Ḥaǧalah.[18] As this important work is edited and to some extent known to modern scholarship, I will just outline some of the parallels. What was not known, of course, is that the *Maṭāliʿ* is completely based on and imitates the *Sulūk* of Ibn Abī Ḥaǧalah. Most of the passages in common (see contents) are copied verbatim and only extended by using more recent examples.[19] However, this strategy is significant for the relationship of these texts: it allows us to compare many of the passages of the Maṭāliʿ and *Sulūk* verbatim, and to correct a lot of al-Ġuzūlī's quotations, as the editions of the Maṭāliʿ are entirely deficient.

Al-Ġuzūlī himself is presented by his biographers as a talented but minor poet. One of the purposes of composing such a book is clearly to canonize himself and the quoted scholars in the literary field. This is carried out not only by a mere collection of poetry, but also by presenting the most important verses that include special rhetorical devices. The work reveals the author's learnedness through his quoting of a huge repertory of pre-Islamic and Islamic sayings, texts and scholarly documents which gain him a place within contemporary local scholarship. He obviously tries to convince his audience in Damascus of his literary abilities.[20] But he somehow pretends to be unaware of the preceding work of Ibn Abī Ḥaǧalah, although he quotes his poetry frequently and follows his work regarding form and content.

The chapters of the *Maṭāliʿ* provide the reader with motifs of urban poetry mostly in chronological order and poets' contemporary discourse on city imagery. Al-Ġuzūlī writes that his book is unprecedented in its composition style and proceeds to boast about his work. He says that if great scholars like aḏ-Ḏahabī (d. 1348), whose father was a goldsmith, read his book they would choose to copy it in golden ink (obviously only to present a pun on this name).[21] Describing his composition style, al-Ġuzūlī also presents similar connections to the topic in focus and the most famous scholar associated with it, e.g. in the

---

the manuscript, see Franz Rosenthal, "Poetry and Architecture: The Bādhanj", in: *Journal of Arabic Literature* 8 (1977), pp. 1-19, here p. 2 note 5 and p. 3 note 8.

[18] Al-Ibšīhī's *al-Mustaṭraf fī kull fann mustaẓraf* (The Exquisite Elements from Every Art Considered Elegant) can be seen in the same line of anthologies as those by Ibn Abī Ḥaǧalah and al-Ġuzūlī, sharing with them several topics, though the basis of the "building" paradigm is relinquished for a more and general *adab*-compilation style. On the *al-Mustaṭraf*, see Kelly Tuttle, "al-Ibshihi (1388 - ca. 1446)", in: *EALB*, pp. 236-242.

[19] I was able to examine the manuscripts at the Topkapı Museum (A. 2291 and E.H. 1506) in Istanbul and the ms. Wien (Cod. N.F. 77), which differ among each other and much more from the editions. There are more recent (partial) editions as master's thesis' at the University of Muʾtah in Jordan, and I am most grateful to Iyad Shraim who provided me with copies. The first thesis provides an edition of the first ten chapters by Samīr b. ʿAbd ar-Raḥmān aḍ-Ḍamir submitted in 2002 and the second offers an edition of the following ten chapters by Ḥaǧǧāǧ b. Riḍwān al-Ḥarbī, submitted in the same year.

[20] Cf. Cooperson, "ʿAlāʾ al-Dīn al-Ghuzūlī", p. 109.

[21] Cf. Cooperson, "ʿAlāʾ al-Dīn al-Ghuzūlī", p. 111.

chapter on slaves: "were Ibn Nubātah (d. 1366) to hear them, he would himself be led to the auction block", and be "enslaved by al-Ġuzūlī's eloquence".[22]

The author guides the reader in associated chapters from the outer spheres gradually into the inner spheres of a house which corresponds to phases of building and furnishing the household, even including the privy.[23] This topic is, of course, known in the Islamic tradition and there are also scattered references in poetry, but again Ibn Abī Ḥaǧalah was the first to include a chapter on privies in a literary work. However, al-Ġuzūlī is innovative, because he extends the range of poetic urban imagery and his model *as-Sulūk*. After some digressions on religious ordinances, the social (neighbourhood) and natural environment (climate and topographical conditions) he goes outside the buildings, jumping from one urban spot to another, passing impressive palaces, gardens, bathhouses, assemblies of court officials, encountering urban joys and sorrows (e.g. with the insects [ḥašarāt], giving some instructions on how to repel them, end of ch. 49) until, in the last chapter, he reaches a point of longing for the pleasures of paradise (ch. 50). In many of the digressions, the inner and formal composition style of his work corresponds to the chronological stages of planning, building and furnishing a house, then living in a city as an earthly place of transience, until he eventually elevates it into the gardens of paradise, – as man's most desired and permanent residence. It is, as Shaun Marmon rightly suggests, "a poetic map of domestic space".[24]

Content of the Maṭāliʿ

chapter		corresponding ch. in Sulūk	general heading (milieu: high and learned society; court officials)
في تخير المكان المتخذ للبنيان (1) building site	5	planning
في أحكام وضعه وسعة بنائه وبقاء الشرف والذكر ببقائه (2) building principles, spaciousness, honour	4; 5; 6	considering building principles
في اختيار الجار والصبر على أذاه وحسن الجوار (3) neighbour	9	social environment

---

22 Cf. Cooperson, "ʿAlāʾ al-Dīn al-Ghuzūlī", p. 111, who points out that al-Ġuzūlī is alluding to Ibn Nubātah's (1287-1366) *Sūq ar-raqīq* (The Slave Market = The Market of Elegance), which is a collection of love poetry. For more on him and his works, see Thomas Bauer, "Jamāl al-Dīn Ibn Nubātah", in: *EALB*, pp. 184-202, esp. p. 199.

23 The sequences of entering a house, starting with the chapter on the door, followed by the *dihlīz*, may indicate that both authors had different types of representative buildings in mind.

24 Shaun Marmon, *Eunuchs and Sacred Boundaries in Islamic Society*, New York 1995, p. 3. I thank Syrinx von Hees for pointing me to this work.

chapter		corresponding ch. in Sulūk	general heading (milieu: high and learned society; court officials)
(4) في الباب	door, gate	2	entering the house
(5) في ذم الحجاب	gate-keeper	3	
(6) في الخادم والدهليز	servant and vestibule	(3); 1	
(7) في البركة والفوارة والدواليب وما فيهن من كلام وجيز	pool, water wheel	15	supplying natural resources
(8) في الباذهنج وترتيبه	**wind tower**	12	
(9) في النسيم ولطافة هبوبه	wind	13	
(10) في الفرش والمساند والأرائك	furniture and cushions (+ cloth)	14?	interior – eye – sense of vision
(11) في الأراييح الطيبة والمروحة وما شاكل ذلك	perfume, incense, fan	14	fragrances – nose – sense of olfaction
(12) في الطيور المسمعة	singing birds	19	domestic animals – ear – acoustic sense
(13) في الشطرنج والنرد وما فيها من محاسن مجموعة	chess, board games, (back-gammon)	21 (-)	social amusements
(14) في الشمعة والفانوس والسراج	candle, light, lamp	23; 24; 25	joys of light
(15) في الخضروات والرياحين	vegetables, sweet-smelling herbs	30?	dishes – sense of taste
(16) في الروضات والبساتين	gardens, meadows	-	pleasures of nature
(17) في آنية الراح	(wine-) jugs	27?	enjoyment of wine/drinking
(18) فيما يستجلب بها الأفراح	what brings pleasure (drinking wine)	-	
(19) في الصاحب والنديم	friend and (drinking) companion	-	

chapter		corresponding ch. in Sulūk	general heading (milieu: high and learned society; court officials)
(20) في مسامرة أهل النعيم	evening entertainment (spending the night) among the affluent	-	social - noble circle
(21) في الشعراء المجيدين	poets	-	intellectual circle
(22) في الحذاق المطربين	singer	22	entertainment - sounds
(23) في الغلمان	slaves	22	
(24) في الجوارى ذات الألحان	singing girls	22	
(25) في الباه	sex	-	joy - health
(26) في الحمام وما غزى مغزاه	bathroom, bathhouses	16	body hygiene
(27) في النار والطباخ والقدور	fire, cooking	26	heating
(28) في الأسماك واللحوم والجزور	fish and meats	29-32	dishes
(29) فيما تحتاج إليه الأطعمة من البقول في السفرة	vegetables	29-32	
(30) في الخوان والمائدة وما فيها من كلام مقبول	table, dining table	28	banquet
(31) في الوكيرة والأطعمة المشتهاة	feasts (house-warming party and wedding) and tasty foods	30	feast
(32) في الماء وما جرى مجراه	water	15	drinking
(33) في المشروب والحلواء	beverage, sweets	32	
(34) في بيت الخلاء المطلوب	**privies**	17	privy
(35) في نبلاء الأطباء	on noble physicians	-	professions (medical)
(36) في الحساب والوزراء	book-keeping, vizier	-	(administrative) (armoury) (intellectual)
(37) في كتاب الإنشاء	chancellery	-	

chapter		corresponding ch. in Sulūk	general heading (milieu: high and learned society; court officials)
(38) في الهدايا والتحف النفيسة الأثمان	accepting gifts	-	
(39) في خواصّ الأحجار وكيانها في المعادن	stone cutter, mines	-	
(40) في خزائن السلاح والكنائن	armoury	-	
(41) في الكتب وجمعها وفضل اتخاذها ونفعها	books and li-braries	-	
(42) في الخيل والدوابّ ونفعها	riding ani-mals	-	animals
(43) في مصائد الملوك وما فيها من نظم السلوك	hunting	-	
(44) في خطائر الوحوش الجليلة المقدار	zoo animals	-	
(45) في الأسد النبل والزرافة والفيل	lions, giraffes and ele-phants	-	
(46) في الحمام وما في وصفها من بديع النظام	pigeons, doves	19	
(47) في الحصون والقصور والآثار وما قيل فيها من رائق الأشعار	fortification, royal resi-dences, and edifices	11	broader cityscape - main urban buildings
(48) في الحنين إلى الأوطان وتذكر من بها من القطّان	longing for the home-land, re-membering its dwellers	8	leaving, looking back to the city
(49) في دار سكنت كثيرة الحشرات قليلة الخير عديمة النبات	insects, ro-dents	18	lowest creatures
(50) في وصف الجنان وما فيها من حور وولدان	gardens of paradise	-	heavenly pleasures

Wind tower (bādhang̊)-poetry

Among the topics common to both works I have selected some poems on wind towers (*bādhang̊*)[25] as examples for poetic descriptions of architecture and how poetry reveals what is considered private or not public.[26] This could perhaps be all the more evident in the chapters on privies (chs. 17 and 34) or bathhouses (chs. 16 and 26). What happened in privies, for example, is normally not the subject of narration. Privies are private places shielded from the gaze/curiosity of outsiders, even of family members, but once they here become an object of poetry, the poet allows his voyeurism and creative mind free rein and he exhibits all that happens or can happen there.[27] However, an analysis of them would exceed the scope of this article and I will restrict myself pragmatically to one significant topic.

As visible architectural constructions, the wind towers were used in hot and dry climates to achieve cool air circulation in houses. In the cityscape, they must have looked like a "forest of television antennas extending to the sky"[28] like in modern cities, as Rosenthal states. He also suggests that they were invented in Iran and in use in late Fatimid, Ayyubid and most evidently in Mamluk times in Egypt and Syria. This is also the period when the wind towers entered the literary field. As an already secondary motif of poetry, the wind towers rarely appear as a *Leitthema* of a long poem, more often we have two-liners or three-liners.[29] But much aesthetic effort was displayed to present them with wit and rhetorical skill, because wind towers were, at least until the 19th century, an everyday architec-

---

25 The Persian word *bādhang̊* or *badgīr* (Arabicized: *bādhang̊*, *bādahang̊*, more common *bādahang̊*, occasionally syn. to *malqaf*, i.e. catcher) for "drawer of the wind", see Rosenthal, "Poetry and Architecture: The Bādhanj", p. 2. For more concise information about the functional aspects and constructional elements of wind towers, see David A. King, "Architecture and Astronomy: The Ventilators of Medieval Cairo and Their Secrets", in: *Journal of the American Oriental Society* 104 (1984), pp. 97-133; for a Geniza document on some expenses on a wind tower, see Moshe Gil, *Documents of the Jewish Pious Foundations from the Cairo Geniza*, Leiden 1976, p. 188 (with further references).

26 An edition of ch. 12 of Ibn Abī Ḥaǧalah's *Sulūk* is provided in the appendix.

27 Ibn Abī Ḥaǧalah quotes (Ms. Sulūk, fol. 26a) an anonymous poet who discusses this discrepancy between the outer "representative" sphere of the house in contrast to the inner "disclosed" place of the privy. While the former is diplomatic and reluctant in his answer to the stranger, the latter lays bare what goes on in the private sphere: (meter: *kāmil*)

فَتَبَـــسَّمَتْ عَجَبًـــا وَلَـــمْ تُبْـــدِ   وَلَقَدْ سَـأَلْتُ الـدَّارَ عَـنْ أَخْبَـارِهِمْ

أَمْـــوَالُهُم وَنَـــوَالُهُمْ عِنْـــدِي   حَتَّى مَرَرْتُ عَلَى الكَنِيفِ فَقَالَ لِي

"When I asked the house how they are / it smiled with amazement and said nothing. // Until I went to the toilet, which told me: / "(I have all their possessions and gifts) All their longings and belongings are in me.""

28 Rosenthal, "Poetry and Architecture: The Bādhanj", p. 1.

29 For an early mention of a *bādhāng̊* in a longer poem, see Ibn Munīr aṭ-Ṭarābulusī (473-548/1080-1153), *Dīwān*, ed. ʿUmar ʿAbd as-Salām Tadmurī, Beirut 1940, p. 146-149, verse 40.

tural feature.[30] However, the tradition of composing lines about wind towers ends in Arabic literature, presumably by the early 15th century, while in the Persian tradition it seems to have been continued.[31]

The chart (see appendix) reveals the analogous sequence of poetry quotations of both works. Ibn Abī Ḥaǧalah contributes to this chapter with twelve of his own poems, whereas al-Ġuzūlī has none of his own but quotes ten poems by Ibn Abī Ḥaǧalah. Both authors provide a well-balanced selection of praise poems, lampoons and special figures of speech (e.g. *tawriyah* in no: 3; 16; 28), among which the *taḍmīn* (cento, intertextual quotation, reference)[32] is the one most favoured. With this figure, new topics of poetry seemed to be easily chained to a classical verse. Furthermore, this figure shows that new topics entered the aesthetic scene only in a classic setting. Thus, as a canonizing instance this device nourishes two fields of discourse; one, (re-)canonizing the already canonized and the other, canonizing the new topic. The tradition of using a *taḍmīn* had great appeal for the poets, and evolved into a kind of artistic race, in which they repeatedly elaborate on the same verse with differing contextual settings.

As Rosenthal states, the earliest literary mention of a *bāḏhanǧ* in Arabic is attributed to a certain Ibn aṭ-Ṭūbī (first half of the 5th/11th century).[33] The poem occurs under the heading of poetry on coldness, which is a very prominent topos in adab literature and especially in the city panegyrics.[34] Here the poem provides a comparison of the *bāḏhanǧ* with a frigid (dull) youth, by offering the antithesis of a hot summer day (i.e. being passionate in love) and a cold refusal (i.e. cold air of the *bāḏhanǧ*): (meter: *wāfir*)

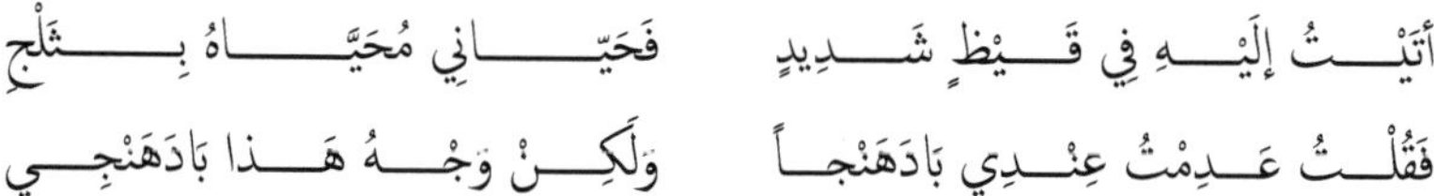

I came to him on a hot summer day, / and he gave me a frosty welcome. // I said: "I do not have a bāḏahanǧ in my house, / but the face of that fellow is my bāḏahanǧ." [35]

---

[30] Rosenthal, "Poetry and Architecture: The Bādhanj", p. 7.

[31] Quotations from earlier periods in Persian are given in Mehdi Bahadori and Alireza Deghani-Saniyy, *Wind Towers. Architecture, Climate and Sustainability*, Heidelberg 2014, p. 42-45. The earliest mention seems to be the couplet by Roudaki-e Samarghand (d. 908).

[32] On the tradition of using a *taḍmīn* in poetry, see Ewald Wagner, "Abū Nūwās-Verse als Taḍmīn", in: *Asiatische Studien* 3 (2010), p. 707-726.

[33] A Siculo-Arabic writer, whose full name is Abū ʿAbdallāh Muḥammad Ibn al-Ḥasan al-Kātib aṭ-Ṭūbī. On him and his brother ʿAlī, also a well-known poet, see Francesca M. Corrao, "al-Ṭūbī", in: *Encyclopedia of Arabic Literature*, ed. by J. Scott Meisami and P. Starkey, 2 vols., London 1998, II: p. 782. The couplet presented is neither known to Ibn Abī Ḥaǧalah nor to al-Ġuzūlī, and is cited with several other examples of his poems in al-Isfahānī (519-579/1125-1201), *Ḫarīdat al-qaṣr*, ed. al-Marzūqī et. al., Tūnis 1966, vol. I (Western poets), p. 64.

[34] See Hussein Bayyud, *Die Stadt in der arabischen Poesie, bis 1258 n. Chr.*, Berlin 1988.

[35] Transl. Rosenthal "Poetry and Architecture: The Bādhanj", p. 3 and p. 8.

The poems in our chapters offer similar contrasts connected to wind towers. They were praised for transforming the outdoor summer into an indoor winter, or blamed for dysfunctions.[36] Further popular topics related to wind towers are that they provided welcome hideaways from persecutors,[37] – even the Mamluk Sultan Ašraf Šaʿbān was found hiding there – or that it was tempting to sleep in the *bāḏhang̱*. However, the air was not considered healthy (e.g. no: 28). The poems also inform us that the wind towers were covered by a grating and were making noise and that their openings were – at least in Cairo – directed towards Mecca, as David King revealed by comparing medieval astronomical works with poetry.[38] Most common among the topics include those also used in erotic and wine-poetry: the act of trapping air was compared with the thirst of the lover; drinking/breathing air was like drinking wine concerning its consumption and its effects (like enjoyment, addiction, intoxication, etc.). In case of dysfunctions, the wind tower was blamed for allowing the thirsty lover to suffer, thus the *bāḏhang̱* defends himself and complains about being an object of blame, as pictured in the following two poems[39] by Ibn Abī Ḥag̱alah, which include a *taḍmīn*: (meter: *basīṭ*)

19 وَمُضَمِّنًا قُلْتُ فِيهِ أَيْضًا

يَا بَاذَهنجـي أَمَـا تَـرْثي لِذي حُـرَقٍ   يُبْـدِي لَهِيـبَ الجَـوَى مُـذْ بَاتَ يُخْفِيهَـا

عَوَّدْتَنَـا صَدَقَاتٍ مِـنْ لَطِيـفِ هَـوًى   ‹فَـامْنُنْ عَلَيْنَـا بِـرِيحٍ مِنْـكَ تُجْرِيهَـا›

A cento:

O my bādhang̱, why don't you take pity on the one burning? / Who bares the flame of violent passion which he had earlier always kept concealed! // You have accustomed us to alms of subtle passion (air). / "Thus bestow upon us a wind coming from you, and let it run (flow)".[40]

---

36   Cf. Rosenthal, "Poetry and Architecture: The Bādhanj", p. 6.

37   For more on the case of Sultan Malik al-Ašraf, who was found by the Mamluks hiding in a *bāḏhang̱* in female clothes, then dressed in military clothing by them before he was led away, see Ibn Taġrībirdī, *an-Nug̱ūm az-zāhira fī mulūk Miṣr wa-l-Qāhirah*, ed. Maḥmūd Ḥusayn Šamsaddin, Beirut 1992, 11: p. 61 [account of the year 778 H.].

38   King, "Architecture and Astronomy", pp. 97-133. On the building practice in Mamluk Cairo and the sets of buildings directed towards the astronomical or the geographical *qibla*, see also Nasser Rabbat, *Staging the City: Or How Mamluk Architecture Coopted the Streets of Cairo* (Ulrich Haarmann Memorial Lecture; 9), Berlin 2014, esp. pp. 22-36 with further literature.

39   The numbering follows the chapter in *Ms. Sulūk*, see appendix.

40   Slightly emended transl. of Rosenthal's (see "Poetry and Architecture: The Bādhanj", p. 11-12, no: 8 (g), see also his commentary on the variants). The *cento* (سفينة الفقر في بحر الرّجا وقفتْ … فامنُنْ عليَّ بريح منك تُجْريها) is attributed to the Andalusian scholar and poet Abū Isḥāq Ibrāhīm b. Muḥammad an-Nafzī (d. 659/1260) and is quoted in Ibn Farḥūn al-Mālikī (d. 799/1397), *ad-Dībāg̱ al-muḏahhab fī maʿrifat aʿyān ʿulamāʾ al-maḏhab*, ed. Muḥammad al-

28 وَقُلْتُ أَيْضًا فِيهِ: [مضمننا[41] (الوَافِرُ)]

هَجَـــا الـــشُّعَرَاءُ جَهْـــلًا بَاذَهَنْجِـــي   بِـــأَنَّ نَـــسِيمَهُ أَبَـــدًا عَلِيـــلُ

فَقَـــالَ البَـــاذَهَنْجُ وَقَـــدْ هَجَـــوْهُ   إِذَا صَحَّ الهَـــوَى دَعْهُـــمْ يَقُولُـــوا

A cento:

In their ignorance, the poets have satirized my bāḏhanǧ, / Because its zephyr is always sickly (a tawriyah with ʿalil: sick/unhealthy and mild/pleasant). // But when they satirized it, the bāḏhanǧ said: "When there is true love (tawriyah with "air"), let them talk!"[42]

Alternatively, elaborate similes were used to contrast the trapped air with killing a person (here the wind), for whom the community weeps during his funeral with tears (of sweat).

25 (مَجْزُوءُ الكَامل)

لَكَ بَاذَهَـــنْجٌ كَالكَئِيـــبِ لَهُ   نَفَـــسٌ يُـــصَاعِدُ لَوْعَـــةَ الحَـــرَقِ

مَـــاتَ النَّـــسِيمُ بِـــهِ فَأَجْمَعُنَـــا   نَـــبْكِي عَلَيـــهِ بِـــأَدْمُعِ العَـــرَقِ

You have a bāḏhanǧ like a sad mourner, which has a breath / that increases the grief of the burning one. // In it the wind has died, and we are all weeping with tears of sweat.[43]

A personified *bāḏhanǧ* full of sounds, fragrances and praise, which turns out to be self-praise, is described by the famous poet Burhānaddin al-Qīrāṭī (726-781/1326-1379):

13 وَأَنْشَدَنِي لِنَفْسِهِ أَيْضًا: (مَجْزُوءُ الكَامِلِ)

أَنَا بَاذَهَـــنْجٌ مِلْـــؤُهُ   طَـــرَبٌ وَطِيـــبٌ وَانْـــشِرَاحْ

غَنَّـــتْ بِـــأَعْلَايَ الحَمَـــا   مُ وشَـــبَّبَتْ فِيَّ الـــرِّيَاحْ[44]

Aḥmadī Abū n-Nūrī, 2 vols., Cairo, I: p. 277. This is the second hemistich of a four-liner, itself including a cento of a famous mocking verse by Abū Šamaqmaq (d. 180/769).

[41] The *taḍmīn* is indicated in al-Ġuzūlī's quotation (no: 17).

[42] Transl. differs slightly from Rosenthal's, "Poetry and Architecture: The Bādhanj", p. 13, no: 8 (j).

[43] Transl. differs slightly from Rosenthal's, "Poetry and Architecture: The Bādhanj", p. 8, no: 2. I could not find out which verse al-Qīrāṭī is referring to in his cento exactly, but it could be a poetic insertion of the phrase: *wa-l-aǧsādu qad bakat ʿalā mayyiti n-nasimi l-ʿalīli bi-admuʿi al-ʿaraq"* used by Ibn Nubātah in his *Saǧʿ al-mutawwaq* (Ms. Aya Sofya 4045, fol. 56b). – I thank Andreas Herdt for pointing out this passage to me.

[44] For the variants in *Ms. Sulūk* and al-Qīrāṭī's *Maṭlaʿ*, see appendix.

I am a bāḏhanǧ all filled / With emotion, fragrant pleasantness, and happiness. // High on top of me, the pigeons sing. / Inside me, the winds recite love poems.[45]

And to give an example of wine-poetry:

3 وَقَالَ أَبُو الحَسَنِ عَبْدُ الكَرِيمِ الأَنْصَارِيُّ: (من الوَافِر)

وَجَـــــدْتُ لِرَوْحِهَـــــا بَـــــرْدَ النَّعِـــــيمِ   وَنَفْحَـــــةٍ بَاذهــــنجٍ أَسْـــــكَرَتْنَا

تَـــــرَاهُ مِثْـــــلَ رَاووقِ النَّـــــدِيمِ   أَتَتْنَـــــا مِــــن أَنِيـــــقِ الـــــشَّكْلِ شَمْـــــحٍ

فَـــــسَمَّيْنَاهُ رَاووقَ النَّـــــسِيمِ   صَـــــفَا وَجَـــــرَى الهَـــــوَا فِيـــــهِ رَقِيقًـــــا

The blast (blow) of a wind tower has made us drunken / In her breath I found a refreshing / smooth cold. //

It came to us from a well-shaped form from the height (tower)[46] / Which you could compare to the wine-strainer of a cup companion. //

The air is clean and runs through it gently,[47] / So that we called it the strainer of the gentle breeze. [48]

In the next two poems, Ibn Abī Ḥaǧalah discusses the height of wind towers: The first was probably written when a wind tower collapsed due to its height and was blamed for being too high up in the air, reaching the clouds.

17 وَقُلْتُ أَيْضًا فِيهِ: (مِنَ الكَامِلِ)

تَعْلُـــــو عَـــــلَى بَانِ الحِمَـــــى   يَـــــا بَاذهنجِـــــي كَمْ كَـــــذَا

وَرَفَعْـــــتَ رَأَسَـــــكَ لِلـــــسَّمَا   أَبْـــــدَيْتَ حُمْقًـــــا زَائِـــــدًا

O bāḏahanǧ, how much taller you are / Than the willow tree of the tribal pasture! // You have shown excessive foolishness, / and raised your head toward heaven. [49]

The second delivers a subtle ironic comparison with the legendary castle of the pre-Islamic warrior as-Samaw'al, which was built on top of a hill. The poet inte-

---

45 Transl. differs slightly from Rosenthal's, "Poetry and Architecture: The Bādhanj", p. 14; verses are only included in *Ms. Sulūk*, fol. 15a. See for these verses also al-Qirāṭi's *Maṭlaᶜ an-nayyirayn*, ms. Br. Mus. Or. 2913, fol. 11b, for some other of al-Qirāṭi's *bāḏhanǧ*-poetry, see fol. 73a, 92b, 199b, 215a-216a in the same manuscript. See also Šamsaddin an-Nawāǧi, *Šifā' fi badīᶜ al-iktifā'*, ed. Maḥmūd Ḥusayn Abū Nāǧi, Beirut 1403/1980, p. 80.

46 *Ms. Sulūk* has *šamḥ* for *šāmiḥ* "lofty", however the variant reading with *samḥ* for "generous, magnanimous" is also possible, metrically and contextually.

47 A *tawriyah* between the two meanings of *raqīq*, "gentle" and "wine".

48 *Ms. Sulūk*, fol. 26, no: 3, see al-Ġuzūli, *Maṭāliᶜ al-budūr*, edition Port Said 1419/2000, p. 55, no: 3.

49 *Ms. Sulūk*, fol. 28, no: 17; transl. by Rosenthal, "Poetry and Architecture: The Bādhanj", p. 11, no: 8 (c), see also *Maṭāliᶜ al-budūr*, Port Said 1419/2000, pp. 55-56, no: 8. The cento might be derived from the proverb: *ra'su fi s-samā' wa-stu fi-l-mā'* (The head in the heavens, the hinder parts in water).

grates Samaw'al's own verse in a cento in the last line to justify such a comparison out of the mouth of the house, praising his wind tower. This technique also
shows an example of a simile used to bridge dissimilar elements, while simulta-
neously emphasising their inequality.

18 وَقُلْتُ فِيهِ أَيْضًا: (مِنَ الطَّوِيلِ)

وَدَارٍ حَكَتْ دَارَ السَّمَوْأَلِ فَاغْتَدَتْ   تُبَاهِي بِبُنْيَانٍ لَهَا وَتَقُولُ

أَرَى بَاذهنجِي فِي الهَوَاءِ ارْتِفَاعُهُ   ‹يَعِزُّ عَلَى مَنْ رَامَهُ وَيَطُولُ›[50]

A cento:

A house resembling as-Samaw'al's castle[51] has come to brag / About one of its architec-
tonical features, saying: // I see my bāḏhang rise up high in the air, / "Being mightier
and taller than those who go after it." [52]

It is obvious that the amount of poetry about the *bāḏhang* is not sufficient to reconstruct the mechanics and buildings' components,[53] but it does inform us about
"the meaning that the objects he [the poet] takes notice of hold for him and his
society"[54] and the awareness of a man-made environment. An aesthetic description
can hardly deliver an all-encompassing reproduction of a rigid cityscape. Its focus
and instruments are directed at the flexible functionality, utility and even comfort-
ing aspects of the city (-buildings) for the inhabitants and the poets themselves.
Considering the presented communicative aspects of wind towers, the frozen and
fixed architecture has become flexible and noisy, it is given a language as if it is
speaking as a beloved or lamented one, – and just like a human it has desires and
acts in moral categories and participates as a subject within urban society. We can

---

[50] This cento is the second hemistich of a poem attributed to Samaw'al describing his castle
(*ḥuṣn al-ablaq*) near Taymā:

هُوَ الأَبْلَقُ الفَرْدُ الَّذِي شَاعَ ذِكْرُهُ   يَعِزُّ عَلَى مَنْ رامَهُ وَيَطُولُ

For the poet and warrior as-Samaw'al bin ʿĀdiyāʾ, see Thomas Bauer, "al-Samaw'al b.
ʿĀdiyāʾ", in: *EI²*, vol. 8, Leiden 1995, pp. 1041-1042.

[51] Read *qaṣr as-Samaw'al instead of dār as-Samaw'al*, cf. variants.

[52] *Ms. Sulūk*, fol. 28, no: 18; tranl. by Rosenthal, "Poetry and Architecture: The Bādhanj", p.
11, 8 (d), see al-Ġuzūlī, *Maṭāliʿ al-budūr*, Port Said 1419/2000, p. 56, no: 9.

[53] Even a view from within, e.g. the treatise on architecture (*risāle-i miʿmāriyye*) composed by
the Ottoman architect Ǧaʿfer Efendi (d. 1614) does not encompass all expected features of
urban morphology. Like our anthologies, and also similar to legal works on building, it offers only some selected topics due to formal textual strategies and the motivation of the
narrative. As it is grouped under the genre of *taḏkirah*s (biographical memories) it delivers
a small but highly impressive amount of material in prose and poetry concerning the ethics and aesthetics of building, architects, their tools and materials and a glossary of architectural terminology in Arabic, Persian and Turkic. See Aydın Yüksel, (ed.) *Risale-i
Miʿmâriyye: Caʿfer Efendi 1023/1614*, İstanbul 2005 and Howard Crane, *Caʿfer Efendi:
Risāle-i Miʿmāriyye. An early seventeenth-century Ottoman treatise on architecture*, Facs. with
transl. and notes by Howard Crane, Leiden 1987, esp. pp. 6-7.

[54] Rosenthal, "Poetry and Architecture: The Bādhanj", p. 6-7.

conclude, that literature communicates architecture using its own language and tradition while at the same time forming a (verbal) language for the nonverbal communication of architecture and the built environment.[55]

Résumé

To summarise our initial results regarding both works, there are two fields of discourse that each are connected to: literature and architecture.[56] Both authors constantly elevate their artistic buildings with the use of ornate speech in their anthologies, that corresponds to the enveloping city. It is not a holistic approach. The texts provide selected themes with no central focus. As an anthology cannot encompass all the relevant topics in the same depth and degree, several main topics that urban historians would certainly apply to urban morphology are definitely missing in these works.[57] They are not generally omitted in literature; other authors in other times would probably have selected different topics and genres.

The cities our authors describe seem to have no centre, no mosques-chapter and within the poetic urban morphology the many religious institutions do not seem to matter at all as structuring units, though there are, of course, several references within the chapters. As there are no chapters on religious buildings, there are also no chapters on secondary religious buildings (*saqāyah; awqāf*). We have no chapters on schools, prisons, professions (except the few mentioned by al-Ġuzūlī), hospitals, cemeteries, market buildings or squares (*ḫāns, karavanserays*),[58] and most importantly there seem to be no axes and no streets. This is not to say, that they did not exist or did not have any function,[59] but in poetic speech the poet does not need streets and axes to move forward, for his motion is non-linear and not bound to the borders of the physical world. The notion of streets and motion is vaguely connected with the structuring of the texts' chapters that correspond to a parkour through the envisioned city. Though there is a vast legal literature on the regula-

---

55 On verbal and non-verbal communication of architecture and poetry, see Alev Masarwa, "Performing the Occasion: The Chronograms of Māmayya ar-Rūmī (930–985 or 987/1534–1577 or 1579)", in: Stephan Conerman und Gül Şen (eds.), *The Mamluk-Ottoman Transition: Continuity and Change in Egypt and Bilād aš-Šām in the Sixteenth Century*, Bonn 2016, pp. 177-206. For this approach see the in-depth study by Amos Rapoport, *The Meaning of the Built Environment: A nonverbal Communication Approach*, Beverly Hills 1990 [repr. 1982].

56 Further research will reveal more about the agendas and the social and cultural dimensions of these works on a more profound level, when the texts are sufficiently edited and indexed.

57 On the substantial discussion revealing an orientalists' notion of city perceptions and what was considered typical for the Muslim city, see chapters II and VI in Nezar Alsayyad, *Cities and Caliphs: on the genesis of Arab Muslim Urbanism*, New York 1991.

58 For more on many of these main buildings in the cityscape of Mamluk Cairo, see Howaydah al-Harithy, "The Concept of Space in Mamluk Architecture", in: *Muqarnas* 18 (2001), pp. 73-93.

59 On 'streetscapes' as representational spaces in Mamluk Cairo see al-Harithy, "The Concept of Space in Mamluk Architecture", pp. 84-86.

tion of streets and buildings they were not included in the repertoire of poetic imagery. The last point supports the assertion of Eugen Wirth, who comments on streets and axes in Oriental cities as non-organized[60] public places: *"Streets and squares are to a certain extent 'negative spaces' - the result of a spatial exclusion from the private sphere and not the result of the fencing in of publicly and communally usable open urban space. The bordering walls are the protective barrier of a private inner sphere and not the frame, facade, scenery and background for a communal public civic life".*[61] What poetry offers in these anthologies is in fact a gaze into these private spaces by constantly crossing the boundaries and limits of the physical architecture. The city's shape of 'an inconsistent and inorganic assembly of quarters'[62] seems to correspond to the general composition style of our anthologies. The chapters correspond to several buildings or topoi and the decorations and furnishings correspond to the specific construction of verses and ornate speech. The inspiration from *adab* themes is perfectly evident. A verse is called *bayt* (house) in Arabic and the main prosodic nomenclature is borrowed from tent-building, while Arabic poems have a specific modular architecture. In addition to that, the works' composition styles and their motivation are based on the general structure of a building (a chapter is called *bāb* = door) and the city. Therefore, we are presented with the link between the architecture of poetry and the architecture of a literary anthology that both provide the language of the architecture of cities. Both works present the tensions between the language of the built environment and the architecture of poetry. This can be understood as an *invasion* of urban space through poetic speech by communicating the predominant aspects in city imagery. In other words, poetry matters, because poets sought to establish themselves and ensure their rank as integral parts of urban space, by composing works on cities in the shape of cities.

---

[60]   There was not always a negative perception of the non-linear and non-squared city-shape, as it caters very well to climatic necessities (see *Vitruvius*, I: ch. IV: "The distribution and situation of buildings within the walls" on healthy and unhealthy winds) and to those of security: "Aristotle does emphasise the importance of a beautiful appearance of the city, and he states that a regular plan is attractive and that it is particularly appropriate for a democracy, but that it should be combined with irregularity, with streets '[...] *following the contours of old footpaths* [...]' in order to confuse intruding enemies, so that '[...] *beauty and security will be combined'."* (Boerefijn, *The foundation, planning and building of new towns*, p. 310, note 58 according to Aristotle, *Politica* II, 5,1; IV, 5, 4; VII, 10 &16,4).

[61]   Wirth, "Zur Konzeption der islamischen Stadt: Privatheit im islamischen Orient versus Öffentlichkeit in Antike und Okzident", p. 68: *„Straßen und Plätze sind gewissermaßen „Negativraum" – das Ergebnis eines räumlichen Ausgrenzens aus dem privaten Bereich, nicht eines räumlichen Eingrenzens von öffentlich und gemeinsam zu nutzenden städtischen Freiflächen. Die randlichen Mauern und Wände sind also nur Schutzwall eines privaten Innenbereichs, nicht hingegen Rahmen, Fassade, Kulisse und Hintergrund für gemeinschaftliches öffentliches städtisches Leben."*

[62]   J. Sauvaget (Alep, 247-48) quoted in Andre Raymond, "Islamic City, Arab City: Orientalist Myths and Recent Views", in: *British Journal of Middle Eastern Studies* 21 (1994), pp. 3-18 (quotation p. 7).

Appendix:
Edition ch. 12: *bāḏhanǧ*

Sigla

(س)   *Ms. Sulūk* (İÜ 877), fol. 14a-16a.

(م)   *Maṭāliʿ*, ed. Samīr b. ʿAbd ar-Raḥmān aḍ-Ḍamīr, pp. 161-168.

(ب)   *Maṭāliʿ*, ed. [Port Said] 1419/2000, pp. 55-59.

(ن)   Maṭāliʿ, *Ms. Wien* (Cod. N.F. 77), fol. 22a-23a.

(د)   *Dīwān Ibn Abī Ḥaǧalah*, ed. Muǧāhid Muṣṭafā Bahǧat, Amman 2010 [poems numbered].[63]

(ح)   Ibn Ḥiǧǧah al-Ḥamawī, *Ḫizānat al-adab*, ed. ʿIṣām Šaʿaytū, vol. II., Beirut, 1987.

(ش)   Šihābaddīn al-Ḥafāǧī, *Šifāʾ al-ġalīl fī-mā fī kalām al-ʿarab min ad-daḫīl*, ed. Muḥammad Kaššāš, Beirut 1997, p. 90.

(ق)   Burhānaddīn al-Qīrāṭī, *Maṭlaʿ an-nayyirayn*, ms. Br. Mus. Or. 2913.

Variants: only in the poems

‏**1** : في (ن) / (م) / (ب) : [أَنا] ، وفي الأصل (س) : إنما ؛ [أَنْعَشُ] وفي (م) : أُنْعِشُ ؛ ينقص البيت الثاني في : (م) / (ب) / (ن) ؛

‏**2** : في (م) / (ب) / (ن) :[عَلا عَلاءَ] وفي الأصل (س) : على عُلاءٍ، ولعل الصواب ما أثبتنا ؛ [هَوَى] وفي (ن) : هَوَا ؛

‏**3** : [شمخ] كذا وفي (س) / (ن) ؛ في (م) / (ب) : سمح ؛

‏**6** : [لِريَّاهَا] في (ب) : لرباها ؛ [بِهَبَّاتِ] وفي (ب) / (م) : بتهباب ؛ [القوم يحسبني جلدا] هذا زيادة من (ب) / (ن) ، وفي (س) :القَومِ ودّا ، وفي (ب) : القوم يحسبني . (انتهى). لم أجد لهما معنى ، لعل الصواب ما أثبتنا من المصادر: (ب) / (ن) ؛

‏**10** : [تَجْرِي عَلَى] كذا وفي (س) وفي (ق) : يَجْري على ، وفي (ش) : يَجْري على غيرِ ؛

‏**11** : [تَنفيسُ] كذا في (ق) ، في (س) : يتنفس وهذا استلزم نحو(مَغْنَا طَيِّسُ) . والصواب كما ورد في (ق) ؛

---

63   For other *bāḏhanǧ*-poems of Ibn Abī Ḥaǧalah, not included in his *bāḏhanǧ*-chapter in *Sulūk*, see *Dīwan Ibn Abī Ḥaǧalah*, no: 236 and no: 106.

13 : [أنا باذهنجٌ] كذا في (ق) ، وفي (س) : يا باذهنج والصواب كما ورد في (ق) ؛ [بِأَعْلَايَ] كذا في (ق) وفي (س) : بعلاءٍ ؛

15 : [حُسْنِهِ] كذا وفي (س) وفي (م) / (ب)/ (ن) : أنسهِ ، في (د) : حسه ؛

16 : [مَنْظَرُهُ] وفي (ب) : منظر؛ [مَنْظَرَةٍ تَبْدُو] في (ح) : مخبره يبدو ؛ [سكني] في (ن) : سكن ؛

17 : [بَانِ الحِمَى] كذا في (م) / (ب) وفي (س) : الحِمَا ، في (د) : باقي الحِما ؛

18 : [حَكَّثُ دَارَ] لعل الصواب كما ورد في (م) / (ب) / (ن) / (د) : حكت قصر ؛ [زَامَهُ] في (م) / (ب) : راحه ؛

19 : [تَرَنِّي لِذِي] كذا في (م) / (ب) / (ن) ، وفي الأصل : ترني لدى ، والصواب ما أثبتنا ؛ [مُذْ بَاتَ يُخْفِيهَا] في (ن) : من بات يجفها ؛ [عَلَينَا] في (م) / (ب) : على ؛ [فَامْنُنْ عَلَينَا بِرِيحٍ مِنْكَ تُجْرِيهَا] في (ن) : وامنن على بريح منك يجلبها ؛ [تُجْرِيهَا] في (ب) : يجريها، (م) : يجريها ؛

20 : [مُدِلِّهَا] في (م)/ (ب) / (ن) / (ح) : مولها ،] بِحُبِّكَ لَمْ تَزَل] في (م) / (ب) : بحبك دائما ، [خُلِقَتْ ... خُلِقَت] في (ح) : خلعت ... خلعت ؛

22 : [وَبَاذهنج] في (ن) : يا بادهنج ؛

24 : [أَضْعَافُ مَا في] في (ن) : كمثل ما ، [شَرْعٍ] في (ن) : سرع ؛

25 : [كَالكَثِيبِ] في (ن) : كالكثيب ، في (م) / (ب) : قلب صبّ ، [يُصَاعِدُ] في (م) / (ب) : تصاعد ، [فأجمعنا] ورد في (س) / (م) / (ب) / (ن) / (ش) : فَاجْتَمَعْنَا ، والصواب كما أثبتنا من (ن) ، [الغَرَقِ] في (م) / (ن) / (ش) : الغرق ؛

26 : [دَوَا] في (م) / (ب) : دوى ، [يَأْمَنُ] في (م) / (ن) تأمن ؛

27 : [يُضْرِمُ] في (م) / (ب) : تضرم ؛

28 : [هَجَا الشُّعَرَاءُ ... بِأَنَّ نَسِيمَهُ] ورد الشطران معكوسا في (م) ، [بِأَنَّ نسيمه] في (م) / (ن) : أنه نسيمه ، وفي (د) : لأنّ نسيمه.

Bāḏhang-poetry in *Ms. Sulūk* with text witnesses in the *Maṭāliʿ*

Sulūk	*Maṭāliʿ*	also quoted in	poet
(1)	no: (1) 2 verses		Ibn ʿAbd aẓ-Ẓāhir
(2)	no: (2)		Ibn Sanāʾ al-Mulk
(3)	no: (3)	Šifāʾ, p. 90	ʿAbd al-Karim al-Anṣārī
(4)	-		ʿAbd al-Karim al-Anṣārī
(5)	-		anon.
(6)	no: (4)		anon. (baʿḍ al-ʿarab)
(7)	-		al-Munawī
(8)	-		Ṣadraddin Sulaymān ʿAbd al-Ḥaqq al-Ḥanafī
(9)	-		Ṣadraddin Sulaymān ʿAbd al-Ḥaqq al-Ḥanafī
(10)	-	Maṭlaʿ an-nayyirayn, fol. 215a-215b	Burhānaddin al-Qīrāṭī
(11)	no: (5)	Maṭlaʿ an-nayyirayn, fol. 216b	Burhānaddin al-Qīrāṭī
(12)	-	Maṭlaʿ an-nayyirayn, fol. 216b	Burhānaddin al-Qīrāṭī
(13)	-	Maṭlaʿ an-nayyirayn, fol. 11b	Burhānaddin al-Qīrāṭī
(14)	-		Saʿdaddin al-Ḥāʾiri
(15)	no: (6)	Diwān, no: 157; aṭ-Ṭabaqāt as-saniyyah II: 126, no: 419[64]	IAH = Ibn Abī Ḥaǧalah
(16)	no: (7)	Diwān, no: 398 [cf. no:106?]; Ḫizānat al-adab, II: 197	IAH
(17)	no: (8)	Diwān, no: 17; Ḫizānat al-adab, II: 197	IAH
(18)	no: (9)	Diwān, no: 312	IAH
(19)	no: (10)		IAH

---

[64] Taqiyyaddin at-Tamīmī ad-Dārī, *aṭ-Ṭabaqāt as-saniyyah fī tarāǧim al-ḥanafiyyah*, ed. ʿAbd al-Fattāḥ Muḥammad al-Ḥulw, 4 vols., Cairo 1390/1970-1410/1989.

Sulūk	Maṭāliʿ	also quoted in	poet
(20)	no: (11)	Ḫizānat al-adab, II: 197; aṭ-Ṭabaqāt as-saniyyah, II: 126	IAḤ
(21)	-		IAḤ
(22)	no: (12)	Dīwān, no: 107	IAḤ
(23)	-	Dīwān, no: 63	IAḤ
(24)	no: (13)		IAḤ
(25)	no: (14)	Šifāʾ, p. 90	Abū l-Fatḥ [Ibn] Qādūs
(26)	no: (15)		Ṣadraddīn Sulaymān ʿAbd al-Ḥaqq al-Ḥanafī
(27)	no: (16)	Dīwān, no: 435, with 3 verses	IAḤ
(28)	no: (17) different maṭlaʿ	Dīwān, no: 313; Ḫizānat al-adab, II: 197, 334; aṭ-Ṭabaqāt as-saniyyah, II: 126	IAḤ
(29)	no: (19) with a longer quotation from aṣ-Ṣafadī		prose section: al-Qāḍī al-Fāḍil
-	no: (18) poem, 2 verses		Šihābaddīn as-Sunbulī or Šihābaddīn as-Subkī
-	no: (20) poem, 44 verses; 88 verses in [W]		Burhānaddīn al-Qīrāṭī[65]

---

[65] Translation is provided by Rosenthal, "Poetry and Architecture: The Bādhanj", p. 15-18; some of these verses are also cited in Ibn Ḥiǧǧah al-Ḥamawī, *Ḫizānat al-adab*, II: p. 343 in the chapter *alġāz* (riddles).

/14/أ/ ... البَابُ الثَّانِي عَشَرَ فِي البَاذَهِينج

[1] نَقَلْتُ مِن خَطِّ القَاضِي مُحْيِي الدِّينِ بْنِ عَبْدِ الظَّاهِرِ رَحِمَهُ اللهُ تَعَالَى قَوْلَهُ مِمَّا يُكْتَبُ: (مَجْزُوءُ الخَفِيفِ)

أنا نُعْمَــى مَـــنِ ابْـــتَهَجْ **·** أُنْعِـــشُ الـــرُّوحَ والمُهَــجْ

طَيِّــبُ العَــرْفِ والشَّذَا **·** عَــاطِرُ النَّــشْرِ والأَرَجْ

فَعَــنِ البَحْــرِ يَا نَــسِيــــــمُ **·** تَحَــدَّثْ وَلاَ حَــرَجْ

[2] وَقَالَ ابْنُ سَنَاءِ المُلْكِ: (مُخَلَّعُ البَسِيطِ)

وَبَاذَهِــــنْجٍ عَــلاَ عَـــلاَءَ **·** لَكِنَّــهُ قَــدْ هَــوَى هَـــوَاءَ

دَامَ عَلِيــلُ النَّــسِيمِ فِيـــهِ **·** كَأَنَّــهُ يَطْلُــبُ الشِّفَاءَ

[3] وَقَالَ أَبُو الحَسَنِ عَبْدُالكَرِيمِ الأَنْصَارِيُّ: (مِنَ الوَافِرِ)

وَنَفْحَــــةِ بَاذَهِــــنْجٍ أَسْــكَرَتْنَا **·** وَجَــدْتُ لِرَوْحِهَا بَــرْدَ النَّعِيمِ

أَتَتْنَا مِنْ أَنِيقِ الشَّكْلِ شَمخٍ **·** تَــرَاهُ مِثْــلَ رَاووقِ النَّدِيمِ

صَفَا وَجَــرَى الهَـوَا فِيـهِ رَقِيقًا **·** فَسَمَّيْنَاهُ رَاوُوقَ النَّسِيمِ /14/ب/

[4] وَقَالَ أَيْضًا: (الكَامِل)

مَــا تَعْجَبُــوا مِــنْ بَاذَهِــنْجٍ أَقْبَلَــتْ **·** مِــنْ طَيِّــهِ بِدَعُ الحُلَى تَــشُوُوقا

رَقَّ النَّــسِيمُ بِــهِ وَرَاقَ فَخِلْــتُ مَـا **·** أَبْصَرْتُهُ مِــنْ شَــكْلِهِ رَاووقا

[5] وَقَالَ آخَرُ: (الطَّوِيل)

وَلِي بَاذَهِنْجٍ رَقَّ فِيهِ هَوًى هَــوَى **·** وَرَاقَ فَــأَضْحَى فِي المَلاَحَــةِ وَاحِدَا

غَــدَا قِبْلَةً يَــسْعَى النَّــسِيمُ لِحَجِّهَا **·** إِذَا جَاءَهَا مِــنْ أُفْقِــهِ خَرَّ سَـاجِدَا

[6] وَمِمَّا يَحْسُنُ أَنْ يُنْشَدَ عَلَى لِسَانِ البَاذَهنج قَوْلُ بَعْضِ العَرَبِ حَيْثُ يَقُولُ: (الطَّويل)

إِذَا الرِّيحُ مِنْ نَحْوِ الحَبِيبِ تَنَسَّمَتْ وَجَدْتُ لِرَيَّاهَا عَلَى كَبِدِي بَرْدا

وَإِنِّي بِهَبَّاتِ الـرِّيَاحِ مُـوَكَّلٌ طَرُوبٌ وَبَعْضُ القَومِ [يحسبني جِلْدَا]

[7] وَقَالَ آخَر مُضَمِّنًا قَوْلَ المُنَاوِي: (الوَافِر)

يَـصُدُّ الـشَّـمْسَ أَنَّى وَاجَهَتْنَا فَيَحْجِبُهَـا وَيَـأْذَنُ لِلنَّـسِيمِ

[8] وَقَالَ مِنْ لَفْظِهِ لِنَفْسِهِ الشَّيخُ صَدْرُ الدِّينِ سُلَيْمَانُ بْنُ عَبْدِالحَقِّ الحَنَفِيّ مُوَقِّعُ الدَّسْتِ الشَّرِيف وَنَاظِرُ الأَحْبَاسِ المَبْرُورَةِ: (مَجْزُوءُ الوَافِرِ)

عَـصَتْ مِـنْ بَاذَهنْجِي عَـنْ حُـلُـولِ الحَـرِّ قَلْعَتُـهُ

أَلاَ يَا حُـسْـنَهُ لَمَّـا تَـرُدُّ الـشَّـمْسَ طَلْعَتُـهُ

[9] وَأَنْشَدَنِي لِنَفْسِهِ أَيْضًا: (مَجْزُوءُ الرَّجَز)

وَبَاذَهـنْجٍ كَاهِـنٍ يَنْطِـقُ فِيـهِ بِالهَـوَى

أَطَـلَّ قَوْمًـا وَأَتَى لَـيْلًا بِأَخْبَـارِ الـسَّمَا

[10] وَأَنْشَدَنِي مِنْ لَفْظِهِ لِنَفْسِهِ بُرْهَانُ الدِّينِ القِيرَاطِيُّ رَحِمَهُ اللهُ مِمَّا قَالَهُ في الدَّارِ البَدْرِيَّةِ مُضَمِّنًا: (مِنَ البَسِيط)

وَبَاذَهـنْجٍ هَوَاءُ الخَـافِقَيْنِ بِـهِ تَجْـرِي عَلَى خَـيْرِ مِنْهَاجٍ وَأُسْـلُوبِ

إِذَا أَتَتْـهُ رِيَاحُ الجَـوِّ شَـارِدَة فَمَـا تَهُـبُّ بِـهِ إِلاَّ بِتَرْتِيـبِ

[11] وَأَنْشَدَنِي لِنَفْسِهِ أَيْضًا: (الكَامِل)

يَا طِيبَ نَفْحَةٍ بَاذَهـنْجٍ لَـمْ يَزَلْ بِهَوَائِـهِ لِنُفُوسِـنَا تَنفِيسُ

مُغْرًى بِجَـذْبِ الـرِّيحِ مِـنْ آفَاقِهَا فَكَأَنَّـهُ لِلـرِّيحِ مَغْنَـاطِيسُ

[12] وَأَنْشَدَنِي لِنَفْسِهِ أَيْضًا: (السَّرِيع)

وَبَاذهنجٍ قَالَ فَضْلِي الَّذِي لَا يَخْتَفِي عَنْكَ وَلَا يُكْتَمُ /15أ/

يَصْبُو لِأَنْفَاسِي نَسِيمُ الصَّبَا وَيَلْثِمُ لِلْأَرْضِ لِيَ المَلْثَمُ

[13] وَأَنْشَدَنِي لِنَفْسِهِ أَيْضًا: (مَجْزُوءُ الْكَامِلِ)

أَنَا بَاذهنج مِلؤُهُ طَرَبٌ يُرِيحُ وَانْشِرَاحْ

غَنَّتْ بِأَعْلَايَ الحَمَا مُ وَشَبَّبَتْ فِيَّ الرِّيَاحْ

[14] وَأَنْشَدَنِي مِنْ لَفْظِهِ لِنَفْسِهِ السَّيِّدُ سَعْدُ الدِّين الحَائِرِيُّ مِمَّا قَالَهُ في الدَّارِ البَدْرِيَّةِ: (البَسِيط)

وَبَاذهنج إِذَا مَرَّ النَّسِيمُ بِهِ في الصَّيْفِ أَدْنَى وَإِنْ جَاءَ الشِّتَا طُرِّدَا

كَأَنَّهُ عَاشِقٌ حَالَاتُهُ اخْتَلَفَتْ فَلَمْ يَكُنْ فَوْزُهُ في القُرْبِ مُطَّرِدَا

[15] وَقُلْتُ أَنَا في بَاذهنج الدَّارِ البَدْرِيَّةِ عَمَّرَهَا اللهُ بِبَقَاءِ مَالِكِهَا: (مِنَ الرَّجَز)

وَبَاذهنج لَا خَلَتْ دِيَارُنَا مِنْ حُسْنِهِ

كَأَنَّهُ مُتَيَّمٌ يَلْقَى الهَوَى بِنَفْسِهِ

[16] وَقُلْتُ أَيْضًا وَفِيهِ تَوْرِيَةٌ: (مِنَ البَسِيط)

وَبَاذهنج غَدَا في الجَوِّ مَنْظَرُهُ مِنْ فَوْقِ مَنْظَرَةٍ تَبْدُو عَلَى سَنَنِ

فَانْظُرْ فَدَيْتُكَ يَا مَحْبُوبُ رِفْعَتَهُ وَاسْتَنْشِقِ الرِّيحَ مِنْ تلقَاهُ يَا سَكَنِي

[17] وَقُلْتُ أَيْضًا فِيهِ: (مَجْزُوءُ الْكَامِل)

يَا بَاذَهَنْجِي كَمْ كَذَا تَعْلُو عَلَى بَانِ الحَمَى

أَبْدَيْتَ حُمْقًا زَائِدًا وَرَفَعْتَ رَأْسَكَ لِلسَّمَا

[18] وَقُلْتُ فِيهِ أَيْضًا: (من الطويل)

وَدَارٍ حَكَتْ دَارَ السَّمَوْأَل فَاغْتَدَتْ   تُبَاهِي بِبُنْيَانٍ لَهَا وَتَقُولُ

أَرَى بَاذَهَنْجِي فِي الهَوَاءِ ارْتِفَاعُهُ   يَعِزُّ عَلَى مَنْ رَامَهُ وَيَطُولُ

[19] وَقُلْتُ فِيهِ أَيْضًا مُضَمِّنًا: (البَسِيط)

يَا بَاذَهَنْجِي أَمَا تَرْثِي لِذِي حُرَقٍ   يُبْدِي لَهِيبَ الجَوَى مُذْ بَاتَ يُخْفِيهَا

عَوَّدْتَنَا صَدَقَاتٍ مِنْ لَطِيفِ هَوًى   فَامْنُنْ عَلَيْنَا بِرِيحٍ مِنْكَ تُجْرِيهَا

[20] وَقُلْتُ فِيهِ أَيْضًا: (الكَامِل)

يَا بَاذَهَنْجِي لَا بَرَحْتَ مِنَ الهَوَى   مِثْلِي عَلَى حُبِّ الدِّيَارِ مُدَلَّهَا

دَارِي بِحُبِّكَ لَمْ تَزَل مَشْغُوفَةً   خُلِقَتْ هَوَاكَ كَمَا خُلِقْتَ هَوًى لَهَا

[21] /15ب/ وَقُلْتُ فِيهِ أَيْضًا مُضَمِّنًا: (البَسِيط)

انْظُرْ إِلَى بَاذَهَنْجٍ بِتُّ أَعْشَقُهُ   يُطْفِي النَّسِيمُ بِهِ نِيرَانَ تَبْرِيحِي

أَسْتَنْشِقُ الرِّيحَ مِنْ أَرْجَائِهِ سَحَرًا   إِنِّي قَنِعْتُ مِنَ المَعْشُوقِ بِالرِّيح

[22] وَقُلْتُ فِيهِ أَيْضًا: (مِنَ المُجْتَثّ)

وَبَاذَهَنْج تَرَاهُ   كَغُصْنِ بَانٍ تَرَنَّح

يَهْتَزُّ عِنْدَ العَطَايَا   لِأَنَّهُ يَتَرَيَّح

[23] وَقُلْتُ فِيهِ أَيْضًا: (مَجْزُوءُ الرَّجَز)

وَبَاذَهَنْج تَحْتَهُ   مُجْتَمَعُ الأَحْبَابِ

فَلَيْسَ يَخْلُو مِنْ هَوًى   كَقَلْبِيَ المُذَابِ

سَمَّاهُ رَاووقُ الهَوَى   بَعْضُ أُولِي الأَحْبَابِ

فَاجْزِمْ بِطِيبِ عَيْشِ مَنْ   يُخْتَصُّ بِالطِّيَابِ

[24] وَقُلْتُ أَيْضًا مُلْغِزًا فِيهِ: (مَجْزُوءُ الرَّجَزِ)

وَذِي جَنَـــاحٍ طُـــولُهُ   أَضْـــعَافُ مَـــا فِي العَـــرْضِ

مَـــا جَـــارَ فِي شَرْعِ الهَـــوَى   فِي حُكْمِـــهِ إِذْ يَقْـــضِي

وَلَـــمْ يَطِـــرْ مَـــعْ كَوْنِـــهِ   بَـــيْنَ الـــسَّمَا والأَرْضِ

[25] قَالَ أَبُو الفَتْحِ قَادُوسُ يَهْجُوهُ وَأَحْسَنَ مَا شَادَ: (مِنَ الكَامِلِ)

لَكَ بَاذَهَنْج كَالكَئِيـــبِ لَهُ   نَفَـــسٌ يُصَاعِدُ لَوْعَـــةَ الحَـــرَقِ

مَـــاتَ النَّـــسِيمُ بِـــهِ فَاجْمَعْنَـــا   نَـــبْكِي عَلَيـــهِ بَـــأَدْمُعِ العَـــرَقِ

[26] وَأَنْشَدَنِي لِنَفْسِهِ الشَّيْخُ سُلَيْمَانُ بْنُ عَبْدِ الحَقِّ يَهْجُوهُ: (مَجْزُوءُ الرَّجَزِ)

فِي البَـــاذَهَنْجِ لاَ تَـــــنَمْ   فَمَـــا لِمَرْضَـــاهُ دَوَا

لاَ يَـــأَمَنُ الـــشَّخْصُ الَّذِي   يَسْرِقُ فِي اللَّيْـــلِ الهَـــوَى

[27] وَقُلْتُ أَنَا أَيْضًا فِيهِ: (مِنَ الرَّجَزِ)

وَبَاذَهِـــــنْجٍ رِيحُـــــهُ   يُضْرِمُ نِـــيرَانَ الجَـــوَى

مَدَحْتُـــــهُ جَهْـــــلًا بِـــهِ   فَـــرَاحَ مَدْحِي فِي الهَـــوَى

[28] وَقُلْتُ أَيْضًا فِيهِ: /16أ/ (مِنَ الوافر)

هَجَـــا الشُّـــعَرَاءُ جَهْـــلًا بَاذهنجِي   بِـــأَنَّ نَـــسِيمَهُ أَبَـــدًا عَلِيـــلُ

فَقَـــالَ البَـــاذَهَنْجُ وَقَـــدْ هَجَـــوْهُ   إِذَا صَحَّ الهَـــوَى دَعْهُـــمْ يَقُولُـــوا

[29] وَأَكْثَرُ النَّاسِ وُلُوعًا بِالبَاذهنج القَاضِي الفَاضِلُ رَحِمَهُ اللهُ تَعَالَى فَإِنَّهُ قَالَ - مِنْ رِسَالَةٍ:

[اِبى مِـن مدرجه ستين وَمَا قَارَبَهَا وَهِيَ المُدَّةُ مِنْ تَارِيخِهَا، ورخ بِهَجْرِهِ وَكري، وَعُلُوِّ سِعْرِ شِعْرِي، قَدْ نَظَمْتُ مِائَتَيْنِ وَخَمْسِينَ أَلْفَ بَيْتٍ مِنَ الشِّعْرِ بِشَهَادَةِ عَيَانِهَا وَحُضُورِ دِيوَانِهَا مِثْلُ قَوْلِي فِي صِفَةِ بَاذهنج شَدِيدِ الحَرِّ مَا يُنَاهِزُ أَلْفَ بَيْتٍ، وَمِثْلُ قَوْلِي فِي رَجُلٍ طَوِيلِ الآذَانِ كَأَنَّهُمَا فِي رَأْسِهِ خُفَّانِ أَوْ قَدْ عُجِّلَ لَهُ مِنْهُمَا نَعْلاَنِ مَا يُقَارِبُ أَلْفَ بَيْتٍ، وَمِثْلُ قَوْلِي فِي رِثَاءِ الوَطَنِ الَّذِي دَرَجْتُ

عَنْ وَكْرِهِ وَخَرَجْتُ فَلَمْ أَخْرُجْ عَنْ ذِكْرِهِ مَا يُنَاهِزُ عَشَرَةَ آلَافٍ، وَمِثْلُ قَوْلِي فِي
مَـدَائِحَ مَنْـصُوصَةٍ وَأَهَـاجِيّ مَخْـصُوصَةٍ، وَمِثْـلُ قَـوَافٍ لَـمْ أُسْـبَقْ إِلَيْـهَـا.]

Bibliography

Boerefijn, Wim, *The foundation, planning and building of new towns in the 13th and 14th centuries in Europe: an architectural-historical research into urban form and its creation*, UvA-DARE (Digital Academic Repository) 2010.

Cooperson, Michael, "ʿAlāʾ al-Din al-Ghuzūli (died 1411 or 1412)", in: *Essays in Arabic Literary Biography; 1350-1850*, ed. by Joseph E. Lowry and Dewin Stewart, Wiesbaden 2009, pp. 106-117.

Gruendler, Beatrice, "Ibn Abī Ḥajalah (1325-1375)", in: *Essays in Arabic Literary Biography; 1350-1850*, ed. by Joseph E. Lowry and Dewin Stewart, Wiesbaden 2009, pp. 118-126.

al-Ġuzūli, ʿAlāʾaddin al-Bahāʾi, *Maṭāliʿ al-budūr fi manāzil as-surūr*, edition Port Said 1419/2000.

al-Ġuzūli, ʿAlāʾaddin al-Bahāʾi, *Maṭāliʿ al-budūr fi manāzil as-surūr*, ed. Samir b. ʿAbd ar-Raḥmān aḍ-Ḍamir, University of Muʾtah 2002.

al-Ġuzūli, ʿAlāʾaddin al-Bahāʾi, *Maṭāliʿ al-budūr fi manāzil as-surūr*, [Ms. Wien, Cod. N.F. 77].

al-Ḥafāǧi, Šihābaddin, *Šifāʾ al-ġalil fi-mā fi kalām al-ʿarab min ad-daḫil*, ed. Muḥammad Kaššāš, Beirut 1997.

Ibn Abī Ḥaǧalah, *Dīwān Ibn Abī Ḥaǧalah*, ed. Muǧāhid Muṣṭafā Bahǧat, Amman 2010.

Ibn Abī Ḥaǧalah, *Ms. Sulūk*, İstanbul Üniversitesi Kütüphanesi, no: 877.

Ibn Ḥiǧǧah al-Ḥamawi, *Ḫizānat al-adab*, ed. ʿIṣām Šaʿaytū, vol. II., Beirut, 1987.

King, David A., "Architecture and Astronomy: The Ventilators of Medieval Cairo and Their Secrets", in: *Journal of the American Oriental Society* 104 (1984), pp. 97-133.

O'Meara, Simon, "A Legal Aesthetic of Medieval and Pre-Modern Arab-Muslim Urban Architectural Space", in: *Journal of Arabic and Islamic Studies* 9 (2009), pp. 1-17.

al-Qirāṭi, Burhānaddin, *Maṭlaʿ an-nayyirayn*, ms. Br. Mus. Or. 2913.

Rizzitano, Umberto, "Il Dīwān aṣ-Ṣabābah dello Scrittore Maghrebino Ibn Abī Ḥaǧalah", in: *Rivista degli Studi Orientali* 28 (1953), pp. 35-70.

Rosenthal, Franz, "Poetry and Architecture: The Bādhanj", in: *Journal of Arabic Literature* 8 (1977), pp. 1-19.

at-Tamimi ad-Dāri, Taqiyyaddin, *aṭ-Ṭabaqāt as-saniyyah fi tarāǧim al-ḥanafiyyah*, ed. ʿAbd al-Fattāḥ Muḥammad al-Ḥulw, 4 vols., Cairo 1390/1970-1410/1989.

Vitruv, *Zehn Bücher über Architektur. De architectura libri decem*, übers. und d. Anm. erläutert von Franz Reber, 3rd ed., Wiesbaden 2015.

Wirth, Eugen, „Zur Konzeption der islamischen Stadt: Privatheit im islamischen Orient versus Öffentlichkeit in Antike und Okzident", in: *Die Welt des Islams* 31 (1991), pp. 50-92.

Friedrich Rückerts Übersetzungen aus
Ibn Abī Ḥaǧalahs *Dīwān aṣ-Ṣabābah*

Anke Osigus

Der Dichter und Sprachgelehrte Friedrich Rückert (1788-1866) ist als virtuoser Übersetzer orientalischer Dichtung bekannt. Die Arabistik verbindet mit seinem Namen vor allem die Makamen von al-Ḥarīrī, den Dīwān von Imra'alqays, die *Ḥamāsah* von Abū Tammām oder den Koran, die er kongenial ins Deutsche übersetzte. Ob in seinen eigenen Werken oder in seinen Übertragungen aus dem Indischen, Persischen und Arabischen, meist hat sich Rückert der Poesie zugewandt. Dass er auch ein guter Prosaist war, der lebendig und pointiert formulieren konnte, zeigen seine Briefe, die er Freunden, Kollegen und seiner Familie schrieb.[1] Sie sind nicht nur zeitgeschichtlich interessant, sondern vermitteln auch einen Eindruck von Rückerts Persönlichkeit. Häufig nimmt er in ihnen kein Blatt vor den Mund und lässt sich gegenüber Vertrauten offen über Widrigkeiten des Alltags, Enttäuschungen und Krankheiten aus.

Ein Brief, der hierfür ein schönes Zeugnis liefert, ist der lange Brief, den er 1828 seiner Ehefrau Luise von seinem ersten Besuch der Herzoglichen Bibliothek in Gotha schrieb.[2] Rückert, seit zwei Jahren Professor für morgenländische Sprachen in Erlangen, erfüllte sich mit dieser „literarischen Reise" einen lange gehegten Wunsch. Schon Jahre zuvor hatte er angekündigt, den in Gotha aufbewahrten Bestand orientalischer Handschriften ansehen und eine Auswahl davon mit nach Hause nehmen zu wollen.[3] Im August 1828 beendet Rückert seine „Collegien" einen Monat früher[4] und macht sich – versehen mit den nötigen Empfehlungen – auf den Weg in die rund 190 km entfernte Residenzstadt Gotha. Wie viele seiner Reiseberichte liest sich auch dieser mitunter wie eine Leidensgeschichte, die schon mit einer Klage beginnt: „[I]ch wollte, [die Reise] wäre vorbey, u[nd] ich wieder in Neuses. Ich bin ganz aus dem sonst so gewohnten Gleise des Reisens durch das lange Hocken hinaus gekommen, und es ist nicht der Mühe Werth wieder hinein-

---

[1] Vgl. Friedrich Rückert, *Briefe*. Hg. Rüdiger Rückert, 2 Bde., Schweinfurt 1977; Bd. 3: *Spezial-Register und Nachtrag*, Schweinfurt 1982.

[2] Rückert, *Briefe*, Bd. 1, Nr. 310, S. 455-458, vom Herausgeber datiert auf den 8. August 1828.

[3] Bereits 1823 fragt Rückert seinen Dichterfreund August Graf von Platen (1796-1835), ob dieser ihn im Sommer nach Gotha begleiten will (*Briefe*, Bd. 1, Nr. 201, S. 284 vom 31. Mai sowie Nr. 219, S. 307 vom 19. Oktober 1823, in dem Rückert zurückschreibt, dass er noch nicht nach Gotha gereist ist). Von Reiseplänen berichtet Rückert auch in Briefen an Joseph von Hammer(-Purgstall) und den Gothaer Buchhändler Friedrich Perthes (*Briefe*, Bd. 1, Nr. 253, S. 368 vom 4. März 1825; Nr. 299, S. 437 vom 4. November 1827).

[4] Rückert, *Briefe*, Bd. 1, Nr. 309, S. 454, datiert vom 2. August 1828, an seinen Vetter Emil Rückert.

kommen zu wollen". Neuses bei Coburg, der Familienwohnsitz in der bayerischen Provinz, war Rückerts Refugium und „kleine Freudenfrohburg",[5] in die er sich immer wieder zum Dichten und Arbeiten zurückzog.[6]

Ausführlich schildert Rückert seiner Frau „das Geschick der Reise" und lässt dabei kein Ärgernis aus: Das Wetter ist abscheulich, die Landschaft unschön, die Kutsche – „ein niederträchtiger Stoßkarren" – zu kurz für sein Fußgestell, der Kaffee ist schlecht, das Essen wird zu spät serviert. In Gotha angekommen, widerfährt Rückert im Gasthof das Missgeschick, einen Gast gleich zweimal für einen Kellner zu halten und mit ihm anschließend am Tisch zu sitzen. Auf dem Weg zur Bibliothek gerät er schließlich in einen Regenschauer und bricht völlig durchnässt die erste Begegnung mit dem Direktor Johann Heinrich Möller ab. Was sich hier so unglücklich anlässt, ist der Beginn einer intensiven Arbeitsbeziehung mit der Herzoglichen Bibliothek.[7] Auch wenn Rückert in den folgenden Jahren nicht mehr nach Gotha fahren wird, lässt er sich immer wieder Handschriften und Drucke zuschicken oder erteilt reisenden Freunden und Verwandten den „eigennützigen Rat", einmal in Gotha vorbeizuschauen und ihm Orientalia mitzubringen.[8]

Seine erste Reise beendet Rückert nach nur wenigen Tagen und macht sich mit den gewünschten Handschriften auf den Heimweg. Schauen wir uns einen Teil dieser „gesuchten Beute" etwas genauer an! Da sind zunächst die Handschriften, die Rückert für Übersetzungen mit heranzog, die er noch zu Lebzeiten veröffentlichte: Hierzu gehört der berühmte *Dīwān al-ašʿār as-sittah* (Ms. orient. A 2191), den Rückert für ausgewählte Übersetzungen aus dem Dīwān von Imraʾalqays nutzte, die 1843 unter dem Titel *Amrilkais, der Dichter und König* erschienen. Auf dieser Handschrift fußen auch die Übertragungen der *Muʿallaqāt* von Zuhayr und ʿAntarah.[9] Aus Gotha stammt ferner die Textvorlage für das Volksepos *Sīrat ʿAntar*, das Rückert in Auszügen übersetzte und 1848 in der *Zeitschrift der Morgen-*

[5]   Friedrich Rückert, *Gesammelte poetische Werke*, Bd. 2, Frankfurt/M. 1868, S. 259.

[6]   Vgl. Jürgen Erdmann (Hg.), *200 Jahre Friedrich Rückert. 1788-1866. Dichter und Gelehrter. Katalog der Ausstellung*, Coburg 1988, S. 55-68.

[7]   Vgl. hierzu auch Hartmut Bobzin, „Friedrich Rückert als Benutzer Gothaischer Handschriften", in: *Ulrich Jasper Seetzen (1767-1811). Leben und Werk. Die arabischen Länder und die Nahostforschung im napoleonischen Zeitalter. Vorträge des Kolloquiums vom 23. und 24. September 1994 in der Forschungs- und Landesbibliothek Gotha, Schloß Friedenstein*, hg. von der Forschungs- und Landesbibliothek, Gotha 1995, S. 103-112.

[8]   Vgl. z.B. Rückert, *Briefe*, Bd. 2, Nr. 876, S. 1141f., geschrieben um den 15. Dezember 1849 an seinen Sohn Heinrich, den Rückert bittet, etwas aus den „dortigen persischen Vorräthen" für seine Arbeit an Saʿdis *Bustān* auszuleihen. Einige Monate später meint er jedoch, seiner „Unbeweglichkeit einen Stoß geben [zu] müssen", um selbst im Sommer nach Gotha zu fahren (*Briefe*, Bd. 2, Nr. 881, S. 1148 vom 21. Mai 1850).

[9]   Rückert nahm die beiden *Muʿallaqāt* als Zugaben in seine Übertagung der *Ḥamāsah* mit auf; vgl. Friedrich Rückert, *Hamâsa oder die ältesten arabischen Volkslieder - Gesammelt von Abu Temmâm*, übersetzt und erläutert von F.R., bearbeitet von Wolfdietrich Fischer, 2 Bde., Göttingen 2004, Bd. 1, Nr. 223 (Zuhayr ohne den „müßigen Eingang von 15 Versen") und Bd. 2, Nr. 941 (ʿAntarah).

ländischen Gesellschaft abdrucken ließ.[10] Der Kreis wird größer, wenn man Rückerts nachgelassene Schriften mit einbezieht und sich darunter nur einmal die Gothaer Manuskripte ansieht, die zur Grundlage der vier umfangreichsten Übersetzungsarbeiten wurden:

Ṣafiyyaddīn al-Ḥillī, *Dīwān*

>   ULB Münster, Nachlass Rückert 5, 025[11]
>
>   Reinschrift: 66 Übersetzungen, die 1988 von Hartmut Bobzin publiziert wurden[12]
>
>   Vorlagen: Mss. Gotha orient. A 2300 – 2301

Ibn Abī Ḥaǧalah, Anthologie *Dīwān aṣ-Ṣabābah*

>   ULB Münster, Nachlass Rückert 5, 035 – 5, 036[13]
>
>   2 Reinschriften: 59 Übersetzungen
>
>   Vorlage: Ms. Gotha orient. A 2306

Ibn Ḥiǧǧah al-Ḥamawī, Anthologie *Taʾhīl al-ġarīb*

>   ULB Münster, Nachlass Rückert 5, 037 – 5, 040[14]
>
>   3 Arbeits-Manuskripte, 1 Reinschrift: 226 Übersetzungen
>
>   Vorlage: Ms. Gotha orient. A 2156

Anonyme titellose Anthologie (*Maǧmūʿ*), die noch nicht identifiziert ist und vermutlich aus der frühen Osmanenzeit stammt

>   ULB Münster, Nachlass Rückert 5, 041 – 5, 042[15]
>
>   1 Arbeits-Manuskript, 1 Reinschrift: 96 Übersetzungen
>
>   Vorlage: unbekanntes Gothaer Ms.

Die drei letzten Übersetzungsmanuskripte sind bislang unpubliziert, bei den beiden letzten kommt erschwerend hinzu, dass die arabischen Texte, soweit mir be-

---

[10]   Friedrich Rückert, „Auswahl von Gedichten und Gesängen aus dem arabischen Volksheldenroman Siret Antarat Ilbattal, d.i. Leben und Thaten Antara's des Kämpfers. Aus den Gotha'schen Handschriften". In: *ZDMG* 2 (1848), S. 188-204. Wahrscheinlich hat Rückert das Konvolut Ms. Gotha orient. A 2435-2475 benutzt (Wilhelm Pertsch, *Die orientalischen Handschriften der Herzoglichen Bibliothek zu Gotha.* [...]. Teil 3: *Die arabischen Handschriften der Herzoglichen Bibliothek zu Gotha*, Bd. 4, Gotha 1883, S. 363-367; zu weiteren möglichen Vorlagen aus Gotha vgl. Pertsch, ibid., S. 366-372).

[11]   Anke Osigus, *Der orientalistische Nachlass Friedrich Rückerts in der Universitäts- und Landesbibliothek Münster. Katalog der Äthiopica, Arabica, Turcica, Hebraica und Persica*, Erlangen 2008, S. 116.

[12]   Friedrich Rückert, *Safi Eddin von Hilla. Arabische Dichtung aus dem Nachlass*, hg. und eingeleitet von Hartmut Bobzin, Wiesbaden 1988.

[13]   Osigus, *Katalog*, S. 186-195.

[14]   Osigus, *Katalog*, S. 196-235.

[15]   Osigus, *Katalog*, S. 236-256. Die Verfasserin arbeitet an einer Edition der genannten Übersetzungs-Manuskripte.

kannt, noch nicht in einer kritischen Edition vorliegen. Auch unter den weiteren kleineren Übersetzungen nach Gothaer Handschriften finden sich Anthologien aus der Mamlukenzeit.[16] Es würde zu weit führen, Rückert ein besonderes Interesse an diesen späteren Jahrhunderten der arabischen Vormoderne zu unterstellen; vielmehr scheint es so, dass ihn die Epoche, aus der ein Werk stammte, wenig gekümmert hat, wenn es nur Gedichte enthielt. Deshalb war ihm jede Anthologie als Fundgrube für Gedichte willkommen, so auch die *Ḥamāsah* von Abū Tammām, mit der er sich vermutlich wenige Jahre vor der ersten Gotha-Reise zu beschäftigen begann.[17]

Rückerts Übersetzungen sind Teil seines orientalistischen Nachlasses, der 1922 auf Initiative des Bibliothekars und Orientalisten Herman Kreyenborg in die Münsteraner Universitätsbibliothek gelangte und dort bis heute aufbewahrt wird. Wie beim Vielschreiber Rückert nicht anders zu erwarten, ist der Nachlass schon quantitativ beachtlich: Auf rund 23.500 eigenhändig beschriebenen Seiten vereint er Rückerts orientalistische Gelehrsamkeit zur indischen, arabischen, persischen, hebräischen, türkischen und äthiopischen Sprache und Literatur.[18] Allein die Übersetzungen indischer und arabischer Poesie, zum Großteil unveröffentlicht, sind so reichhaltig, dass ihre Edition Jahre in Anspruch nehmen wird. Die Bibliothek besitzt damit einen einzigartigen Textschatz, der in interdisziplinärer Zusammenarbeit noch gehoben werden will.

Doch zurück zu Rückerts Übersetzungen nach Gothaer Handschriften: Die Arbeits-Manuskripte aus diesem Korpus sind alle undatiert. Mit der gebotenen Vorsicht lässt sich vermuten, dass sich Rückert unmittelbar nach seiner ersten Gotha-Reise die mitgebrachten Schätze vorgenommen und mit unermüdlichem Eifer eine Handschrift nach der anderen exzerpiert und übersetzt hat.[19] Es entspricht Rückerts sprunghafter Arbeitsweise, dass er die entstandenen Manuskripte für Jahre zur Seite legt und sich anderen Projekten widmet. Erst 15 Jahre später, im April 1843, wendet er sich diesen Texten wieder zu. Es entstehen mehrere Reinschriften, offenbar in der Absicht, die Übersetzungen für eine Veröffentlichung vorzubereiten. Rückert hatte inzwischen eine gut besoldete „Winter-Professur" in Berlin angetreten. Der anfangs wie eine Verbesserung erscheinende Wechsel von Erlangen nach Berlin stellte sich schon bald als Enttäuschung heraus, die er wiederholt offen zum Ausdruck bringt. So schreibt er am 14. April an den befreundeten Gymnasiallehrer Karl Bayer (1806-1883): „[I]ch habe von meiner Stellung dort

---

[16] Vgl. z.B. ULB Münster, Nachlass Rückert 5, 046 (Osigus, *Katalog*, S. 267-269).

[17] Vgl. die Einleitung von Wolfdietrich Fischer in Rückert, *Hamâsa*, Bd. 1, S. 7-45.

[18] Zum indologischen Teil des Nachlasses vgl. Volker M. Tschannerl, *Der orientalistische Nachlass Friedrich Rückerts in der Universitäts- und Landesbibliothek Münster. Katalog der Indica*, Erlangen 2008.

[19] Einen Hinweis auf diesen frühen Entstehungszeitpunkt liefert das Arbeits-Manuskript 5, 038 mit Exzerpten und Übersetzungen aus Ibn Ḥiǧǧah al-Ḥamawī, *Taʾhīl al-ġarīb*, das auf einer Blattrückseite einen Brief an Rückert, datiert vom 6. August 1828, enthält; vgl. dazu Osigus, *Katalog*, S. 209.

nichts als den wesentlichen Vortheil, von Erlangen befreit zu seyn; sonst ist Berlin mir nichts, u[nd] ich ihm auch nichts, doch einige Wintermonate kann ich dort leidlich für mich in der Stille zubringen. Meine Kenntniß der dortigen Verhältnisse ist höchst mangelhaft, u[nd] mein Einfluß ziemlich gar keiner".[20] Die „verwünschte[…] Residenz"[21] wurde zu Rückerts „Wintergefängnis",[22] dem er so oft wie möglich zu entfliehen suchte. Deshalb begegnen wir auf dem Deckblatt einiger dieser Reinschriften dem kleinen Ort Neuses wieder, wo diese Arbeiten in „behaglicher Stille"[23] entstanden sind.

Hierzu gehören nun die beiden Manuskripte zum *Dīwān aṣ-Ṣabābah*, der wie auf Rückert zugeschnitten war: Eine gut lesbare Handschrift mit Poesie verschiedener Autoren aus verschiedenen Epochen, die dazu einlädt, nach Belieben einzelne Blüten zu pflücken und zu einem neuen Strauß zusammenzustellen. Die Liebesdichtung nahm auch in Rückerts eigener Dichtung, gerade in jüngeren Jahren, einen festen Platz ein.[24] Das zugehörige Arbeits-Manuskript ist – wie bei den Übersetzungen von Ṣafiyyaddin al-Ḥilli – offenbar verloren gegangen. Dies ist bedauerlich, weil die *erhaltenen* Arbeits-Manuskripte nicht nur wesentlich mehr Exzerpte und Übersetzungen enthalten, sondern auch Notizen und Kommentare, die einen Einblick in Rückerts Arbeitsweise erlauben und belegen, wie intensiv er sich mit Text, Inhalt und Metrik auseinandergesetzt hat.

Auf dem Umschlagblatt der zweiten Reinschrift (Nachlass Rückert 5, 036) hat Rückert die Informationen, die ihm zu seiner Vorlage zur Verfügung standen, festgehalten: Zunächst in arabischer Schrift den Titel der Gothaer Handschrift, darunter mit Bleistift Ort und Datum von Rückerts Niederschrift „Neuseß April [18]43". Die lateinschriftliche Angabe „Kahira 1809 Nᵒ 1528 Seetzen", die sich auch auf dem Titelblatt der arabischen Handschrift findet, nimmt Bezug auf Ulrich Jasper Seetzen (1767-1811), der die Handschrift offenbar 1809 in Kairo erstanden hat. Sie gehört damit zu den rund 2.700 – zumeist arabischen – Handschriften, die der norddeutsche Naturwissenschaftler Seetzen im Auftrag der Herzöge von Sachsen-Gotha-Altenburg auf einer mehrjährigen Forschungsreise im Orient erworben und an den Hof des thüringischen Herzogtums verschickt hatte.[25] Rückerts weitere Angabe „Möller Catal[ogus]. N. 583" bezieht sich auf den schon erwähnten Direktor der Gothaer Bibliothek Johann Heinrich Möller

---

20 Rückert, *Briefe*, Bd. 2, Nr. 670, S. 899 vom 14. April 1843.

21 Rückert, *Briefe*, Bd. 2, Nr. 618, S. 841 an Johann David Sauerländer vom 27. Januar 1842.

22 Vgl. Rückert, *Briefe*, Bd. 2, Nr. 690, S. 918 an Robert Froriep vom 28. Oktober 1843.

23 Rückert, *Briefe*, Bd. 2, Nr. 625, S. 848 an Rudolf Hirsch vom 15. März 1842, ohne sich ausdrücklich auf die Arbeit an den Gothaer Mss. zu beziehen.

24 Erwähnt seien hier nur der 1812 geschriebene Sonettzyklus *Amaryllis* (Druck Frankfurt/M. 1825) und der 1821 entstandene umfangreiche Zyklus *Liebesfrühling*, der nahezu vollständig 1836 in der ersten Rückert-Gesamtausgabe (*Gesammelte Gedichte*, Bd. 1, Erlangen 1836, S. 209-476) und 1844 in einer Separatausgabe (Frankfurt/M.) erschien.

25 Vgl. hierzu Hans Stein, Norbert Nebes, „Ulrich Jasper Seetzen und Gotha", in: *Orientalische Buchkunst in Gotha. Ausstellung zum 350jährigen Jubiläum der Forschungs- und Landesbibliothek Gotha. Spiegelsaal 11. September 1997 bis 14. Dezember 1997*, Gotha 1997, S. 17-46.

كتاب

ديوان الصبابة تاليف الشيخ

الامام الفاضل الاديب العلامة

شهاب الدين ابى العباس

احمد بن ابى حجلة

Müller
April 43

Kahira 1809. № 1528

Seetzen

Müller Catal. N. 583.

نقل الكرام فى مدح المقام

(1792-1867) und dessen ersten (unvollständigen) Katalog, dem Rückert seine genaue Kenntnis dieser Sammlung verdankt.[26] Möller rubriziert das Werk als „collectio carminum amatorium", übersetzt die Titel der ersten zwei Kapitel des Buches, nennt Ibn Abī Ḥaǧalahs Todesjahr („774 H./1372 Chr."), weist auf eine weitere Handschrift in der Pariser Bibliothek hin und beschreibt Schrift – „bene exaratus" – und Umfang des Codex, der laut Möller im Jahre 1019/1610 vollendet wurde.[27]

Unten auf dem Titelblatt notiert Rückert schließlich: „Der Sammler", gemeint ist Ibn Abī Ḥaǧalah, „gibt sich gelegentlich kund als Verfasser mehrerer ähnlicher Sammlungen, wovon eine سكردان Zuckernapf, eine andere نقل الكرام في مدح المقام". Die Angabe der beiden Werktitel, die Rückert der Gothaer Handschrift entnommen hat,[28] zeigt, dass er den Text recht gründlich gelesen hat und auch an dem Anthologisten und seinem Werk interessiert war.

Rein äußerlich stimmen die beiden Manuskripte mit den übrigen Reinschriften aus dieser Arbeitsperiode überein: Sie bestehen aus kleinformatigen Doppelblättern, die 15 bzw. 101 beschriebene Seiten enthalten. Der Beschreibstoff ist Industriepapier von noch guter Qualität. Auf der linken Blattseite findet sich die äußerst sorgfältige Abschrift der arabischen Vorlage, wobei die Vokale von Rückert ergänzt sind, da die arabische Handschrift nahezu vokallos ist. Gegenüberliegend steht die Übersetzung in ebenso sorgfältiger, gut lesbarer Schrift. Einzelne Dubletten und Korrekturen zeigen, dass Rückert während der Niederschrift hier und da noch an seinen Übersetzungen gefeilt hat. Unter einigen Übersetzungen stehen textkritische Anmerkungen, die mit Bleistift geschrieben und wahrscheinlich nicht für eine Publikation bestimmt waren. In den meisten Fällen sind die arabischen Langverse und ihre Übersetzungen auf jeweils zwei Zeilen verteilt, vermutlich nicht nur aus Platzgründen, sondern auch weil diese Aufteilung im Deutschen vertrauter ist. Was gänzlich fehlt, sind Kommentare zu den Gedichten, beispielsweise zur arabischen Metaphorik, einzelnen Autoren oder zur Kompilation des *Dīwāns*. Die 30 Kapitelüberschriften, in der arabischen Handschrift groß und rot abgesetzt, erwähnt Rückert an keiner Stelle. Die sonst üblichen Ausflüge in andere Disziplinen

---

[26] Johann Heinrich Möller, *Verzeichniss der für die orientalische Sammlung zu Gotha zu Damask, Jerusalem usw. angekauften orientalischen Manuscripte und gedruckten Werke, Kunst und Naturprodukte usw.*, Leipzig 1810; id., *Catalogus librorum tam manuscriptorum quam impressorum, qui iussu Divi Augusti Saxo-Gothani a beato Seetzenio in oriente emti in Bibliotheca Gothana asservantur*, Teil 1 (Codices arabici) [...], Gotha 1826. Dieser Katalog gehörte zu Rückerts Bibliothek.

[27] Möller, *Catalogus*, S. 235. Vgl. auch die Beschreibung im neueren Katalog von Wilhelm Pertsch, einem Schüler Rückerts, *Die orientalischen Handschriften der Herzoglichen Bibliothek zu Gotha*, Bd. 4, S. 301, der das Ms. unter der bis heute gültigen Nummer 2306 verzeichnet.

[28] Zu der Anthologie *Sukkardān as-sulṭān al-Malik an-Nāṣir*, erwähnt in Ibn Abī Ḥaǧalah, *Dīwān aṣ-Ṣabābah*, Ms. Gotha orient. A 2306, fol. 39b, 60a u.ö. (Ibn Abī Ḥaǧalah, *Dīwān aṣ-Ṣabābah*, ed. Muḥammad Zaġlūl Sallām. Alexandria 1987, S. 72, 106), s. GAL G II 13, S II 16, zu *Naql al-kirām fī madḥ al-maqām*, erwähnt auf fol. 39a und 42a, s. GAL G II 13.

halten sich in Grenzen: Nur zu einem Wort, arabisch *ǧannah* „Garten des Heils", findet sich ein Verweis auf den Propheten Hesekiel im Alten Testament.[29]

Die beiden Reinschriften lassen nicht erkennen, ob Rückert die Absicht hatte, den Übersetzungen eine Einleitung voranzustellen. Oft war er abgeneigt, erläuternde Vorreden zu verfassen und damit seinen Lesern den Zugang zu den übersetzten Werken zu erleichtern. Auch seine *Hamāsah*-Übersetzung wurde allen Bitten seines Verlegers zum Trotz 1846 ohne Einleitung gedruckt. Allgemein hat sich Rückert schwer damit getan, seine Arbeiten redaktionell zu überarbeiten und fertigzustellen.[30] Hierin ist wohl mit ein Grund für die ausgebliebene Veröffentlichung zu sehen. In einem Brief von 1852 klagt er: „Meine eigne Production ist im größten Misverhältnis zum literarischen Markt. Ich mache Buch auf Buch fertig, kann aber nicht dazu kommen, eins druckfertig zu machen. Der ganz fertige Saadi verstaubt nun [...]".[31]

Denkbar ist auch, dass die genannten Arbeiten aus fachlichen Gründen zurückgehalten wurden, etwa weil für alle Übersetzungen jeweils nur eine handschriftliche Textvorlage zur Verfügung stand und die Angaben, die Rückert zu Autor und Werk vorlagen, zu dürftig waren. Die Gothaer *Sabābah*-Handschrift enthält etliche Schreib- und Überlieferungsfehler, die Rückert nicht entgangen sind und für die er teilweise Konjekturen anbietet. Dass er Schwierigkeiten dieser Art mit Kollegen erörtert und er ihnen Proben seiner Übersetzungen zu lesen gegeben hat, ist für den *Dīwān aṣ-Sabābah* ebenso wenig bekannt wie für die anderen Anthologien nach Gothaer Handschriften. Der Mangel an Austausch und Zuspruch hat Rückerts Schaffensfreude nicht bremsen können, hat aber vielleicht dazu beigetragen, dass so viele Arbeiten nicht in den Druck gegeben wurden: „Lobt niemand mich, lob ich mich selber / und leg es schweigend in den Kasten", schrieb er im Alter mit selbstironischem Trotz, als er in einer Ghasele auf die Arbeit an der *Hamâsa* zurückblickte.[32]

Unter den 30 Kapiteln des *Dīwān aṣ-Sabābah* wird Rückert in 17 fündig und wählt daraus 59 Gedichte aus, die ihn ansprechen und die er versteht. Besonders ausgiebig bedient er sich in Kapitel 27:[33]

---

[29] ULB Münster, Nachlass Rückert 5, 036, Bl. 11b-12a zu einem anonym überlieferten Gedicht nach einem Bericht von al-Aṣmaʿi Verweis auf „Ez[echiel] 34, 29".

[30] Vgl. hierzu die Einleitung von Fischer in Rückert, *Hamâsa*, Bd. 2, S. 21f.

[31] Rückert, *Briefe*, Bd. 2, Nr. 915, S. 1182 an Paul de Lagarde vom 30. April 1852. „Der ganz fertige Saadi" erschien erst sechzehn Jahre nach Rückerts Tod (*Saadi's Bostan. Aus dem Persischen übers. von Friedrich Rückert* [Aus dem Nachlaß hg. von Wilhelm Pertsch], Leipzig 1882.

[32] Friedrich Rückert, *Poetisches Tagebuch 1850-1866*, hg. von Marie Rückert. Frankfurt 1888, S. 305.

[33] Ibn Abī Haǧalah, *Sabābah*, Ms. Gotha orient. A 2306, fol. 156a-161b; Ibn Abī Haǧalah, *Sabābah*, ed. Sallām, S. 267-275.

في ذكر طرف يسير من المقاطيع الفايقه • والأغزال الرايقه • مما اشتمل على[34] ورد الخدود •
ورمان النهود • وغير ذلك

„Über Glanzstücke unter vortrefflichen Epigrammen und schönen Liebes-
gedichten, welche die Rosen der Wangen und die Granatäpfel der Brüste und
dergleichen mehr enthalten". Obwohl der *Dīwān aṣ-Ṣabābah* auch eine ganze
Reihe von längeren Gedichten enthält, hat Rückert vor allem die kürzeren Stücke
ausgesucht. Insbesondere die zahlreichen Epigramme, die bekannte Themen
kunstvoll variieren und oft in einer geistreichen Zuspitzung enden, haben ihn –
ebenso wie in den anderen Gothaer Anthologien – angesprochen, weisen sie
doch einen Zug auf, den man auch seiner eigenen Dichtung bisweilen nachsagte.
Über den 1822-1824 erstmals in Auszügen erschienenen *Liebesfrühling* urteilte
Willibald Alexis (1798-1871):

> „Wo das Lied nicht aus dem übervollen Gemüte geboren wird, da geht die Lyrik leicht in
> einen gewissen Epigrammatismus über, und auf diesen verläßt sich unser Dichter zu oft.
> Wir glauben dabei zu sein und zu sehen, wie ein Lied, das seiner Seele entquoll und ihn
> selbst überraschte, ihn dahin führt, nach andern verwandten Liebesklängen zu suchen;
> wie er diese dann hin und her anstimmt, und im Notfalle immer gewiß ist, in seinem
> kecken, lebensreichen Geiste einen Einfall, eine Spitze zu finden, die dem kleinen Werke
> einen flüchtigen Reiz beimischt und es stets verhindert, ohne Genius zu erscheinen.
> [...]".[35]

Anders als bei der Übersetzung der *Ḥamāsah*, die Rückert durch zahlreiche Gedichte aus anderen Quellen bereichert hat, hält er sich beim *Dīwān aṣ-Ṣabābah* an
den textlichen Rahmen der Vorlage. Meist übernimmt er die Reihenfolge der
Gedichte und ordnet nur einige neu an. In einem Fall lässt er zwei Verse aus
(s.u.), in einem anderen stellt er einen Vers um. Aus den Prosapartien übersetzt
er, wenn überhaupt, nur einzelne Sätze, um den Kontext, aus dem ein Gedicht
stammt, zu skizzieren.

Von den ausgewählten Gedichten sind gut ein Drittel anonym überliefert, die
Autoren der übrigen decken das zeitliche Spektrum der Vorlage ab: frühislamische
und abbasidische Dichter (Maǧnūn, Abu Tammām) sind ebenso vertreten wie
Dichter der Mamlukenzeit (Ibn Abī l-Ḥadīd st. 655-656/1257-1258, Nūraddin al-
Isʿirdī st. 656/1258, Ibn an-Naqīb st. 745/1344). Vor allem für die zeitliche Einordnung dieser späteren Autoren, die Rückert überwiegend unbekannt gewesen sein
dürften, war er ganz auf sein philologisches Gespür angewiesen.

Obwohl Rückert noch 1823 gegenüber Joseph von Hammer(-Purgstall) be-
merkte, dass „es eine unlohnende Mühe [ist], arabische Verse mit Beibehaltung
des Reims u[nd] Versmaaßes zu übersetzen",[36] hat er sich, soweit möglich, um
eine teilweise formale Entsprechung bemüht. So ahmen alle Übersetzungen die

---

34 Zu Beginn von Kapitel 27 auf fol. 156a علی, im Inhaltsverzeichnis auf fol. 7b علیه.
35 Zit. nach Erdmann (Hg.), *200 Jahre Friedrich Rückert*, S. 216.
36 Rückert, *Briefe*, Bd. 1, Nr. 224 vom 23. Dezember 1823, S. 315.

strenge Form des arabischen Monoreims nach, was dafür spricht, dass sie unmittelbar nach der ersten Reise nach Gotha entstanden sind, da Rückert in späteren Jahren vermehrt zum deutschen Paarreim übergegangen ist. In der *Hamâsa*[37], mit der er sich nahezu zwei Jahrzehnte immer wieder beschäftigt hat, stammen vermutlich die Übersetzungen mit Monoreim aus einer früheren Arbeitsperiode, während die paarig gereimten überwiegend später entstanden sind.[38] Auch in der 1843 publizierten Übersetzung aus dem Dīwān von Imra'alqays (*Amrilkais*) haben die weitaus meisten Gedichte ein paariges Reimschema, was auch daran liegen mag, dass die übersetzten Qaṣīden-Auszüge erheblich mehr Verse enthalten als die aus dem *Dīwān aṣ-Ṣabābah* ausgewählten Gedichte, die überwiegend zwei, seltener drei bis vier und nur zweimal fünf Verse umfassen. Bei diesen kurzen Stücken wird es Rückert leicht gefallen sein, einen einheitlichen Endreim zu finden, der nur vereinzelt an den arabischen Reim lautlich anklingt. Rückert war bei der Suche nach Reimwörtern sehr erfinderisch, nur in wenigen Gedichten muss er ein Reimwort wiederholen, häufiger begnügt er sich mit dem Stilmittel der Assonanz, das er regelmäßig in der Übertragung des Korans eingesetzt hat. Beispiele aus den vorliegenden Manuskripten sind „betrachten – wachen", „erglühte – wüthet", „geglättet – hätte" und – weniger deutlich und ungewöhnlich – „Namen – begraben", wo ihm offensichtlich das lange *a* als vokalische Assonanz ausreichte. Selten gerät Rückert einmal in Verlegenheit und greift zu Notlösungen, die den Lesefluss stören. So wirkt es etwas unglücklich, wenn in Versen von Ibn Zaydūn (st. 463/1070) die ferne Geliebte angeredet wird[39]

وقال ابن زيدون [40] [من الكامل]

يا ليتــني أصــبحتُ بعــض مُنـاكِ   أمّــا مُــنَى قلــبي فأنــتِ جميعُها

وَهْمٌ أُكاذِبُـــهُ أُقَبِّــــلُ فـــاكِ [41]   يُـدْنِي مـزارَكِ حـين شَـطَّ بـه النَّـوَى

und Rückert im jambischen Rhythmus nachdichtet:

---

[37] Im Folgenden verweist die Schreibung *Ḥamāsah* auf das arabische Original, *Hamâsa* jedoch auf Rückerts Übersetzung.

[38] Vgl. dazu Fischer in Rückert, *Hamâsa*, Bd. 2, S. 20.

[39] ULB Münster, Rückert Nachlass 5, 036, Bl. 66b-67a; Ibn Abī Ḥaǧalah, *Ṣabābah*, Ms. Gotha orient. A 2303, fol. 140b; Ibn Abī Ḥaǧalah, *Ṣabābah*, ed. Sallām, S. 239. Die arabischen Exzerpte und Übersetzungen Rückerts werden in Orthographie, Vokalisierung und Interpunktion zeichengenau zitiert. Lediglich einzelne Zeichen (*hamzah, alif otiosum*) werden in den arabischen Texten um einer besseren Lesbarkeit willen ergänzt und offensichtliche Schreibfehler korrigiert. Die arabischen Verse, die Rückert meist in zwei Zeilen schreibt, werden in eine Zeile gesetzt.

[40] Die Edition von Sallām (ibid.) schreibt das Gedicht Abū Bakr al-Ḥātimī, d.i. Ibn ʿArabī (st. 638/1240) zu. Das vollständige Gedicht ist im Dīwān von Ibn Zaydūn enthalten (Ibn Zaydūn, *Dīwān*. Hg. Yūsuf Farḥāt, Beirut ²1994, S. 210-213).

[41] Vers 2 entspricht in Rückerts Abschrift dem Text der Gothaer Handschrift. Die Edition von Sallām (ibid.) hat die Lesung: يدني مزارك حين شطر [!] به النوى * وهمّ أكاذُ به أقبّل فاكِ. V. 1a passt metrisch nicht.

Du aller meiner Herzenswünsche Inbegriff,
Wär' ich von deinen Wünschen auch ein Theilchen!

Wenn den Besuch die Ferne hemmt, bringt ihn mir nah
Ein Wahn, mich täuschend, als küss' ich dein Mäulchen.

Zurückhaltender ist Rückert bei der Übertragung der arabischen Versmaße. In einzelnen Übersetzungen bildet er die Vorlage metrisch nach, so wie er es auch in anderen Arbeiten getan hat, recht häufig etwa in der *Hamâsa* sowie in Übersetzungen nach der (wahrscheinlich gleichfalls in Gotha entliehenen) *Anthologie arabe* von Grangeret de Lagrange (1828)[42].

Für Rückerts Übersetzerprinzipien aufschlussreich ist eine Stelle aus einem Brief an den Sanskritisten Franz Bopp (1791-1867) vom 1. November 1828: „Diesen Herbst habe ich angefangen in Gotha aus den dortigen Schätzen einer arab[ischen] poet[ischen] Blumenlese zu excerpiren. Ich habe schon eine gute Menge, u[nd] alles auch deutsch übersetzt, nicht nachgebildet [Auszeichnung von F.R.], wie beim Hariri [...]"[43]. Welche „Blumenlese" damit gemeint ist, bleibt unklar, man kann aber sicher davon ausgehen, dass Rückert die Gothaer Anthologien in der gleichen Weise übersetzt hat und diese Einschätzung deshalb auch für den *Dīwān aṣ-Ṣabābah* zutrifft. Hatte Rückert bei den Makamen seiner überschäumenden Lust am Spiel mit Wort und Reim freien Lauf gelassen, hält er hier sein dichterisches Temperament meist im Zaum und weicht nur dann von der Vorlage ab, wenn ihn Reim und Metrum dazu zwingen.

Zunächst ein Beispiel für eine Übersetzung, die in Wortlaut und Inhalt eng an das Original anschließt. Aus dem ersten Kapitel über Schönheit und Anmut (*fī ḏikri l-ḥusni wa-l-ǧamāl*) stammt folgendes Epigramm von einem ungenannten Dichter:[44]

قال بعضهم [من الخفيف]

حلقــو[ا]45 رأسَـــه لِـــيَزْداد قُبْحًـــا   غَـــيْرَةً مـــنهُم عليــه وشَحّــا

كان صُـــبْحًا عليـــه ليـــلٌ بَهـــيمٌ   فمحَـــوْ[ا] ليلَه وأَبْقَـــوْهُ صُـــبْحَ

Rückert ergänzt den alliterierenden Titel „Der geschorene Schöne" und übersetzt nahezu wörtlich:

---

42   Vgl. Osigus, *Katalog*, S. 289-301; Edition dieser Übersetzungen in Magda Gohar-Chrobog, „Friedrich Rückerts Auswahl arabischer Dichtung in deutscher Übersetzung nach ‚Anthologie arabe' von Grangeret de Lagrange". In: *Rückert-Studien. Jahrbuch der Rückert-Gesellschaft e.V.* 10 (1996), S. 47-118.

43   Rückert, *Briefe*, Bd. 1, Nr. 312, S. 460.

44   ULB Münster, Nachlass Rückert 5, 035, Bl. 8b-9a; Ibn Abī Ḥaġalah, *Ṣabābah*, Ms. Gotha orient. A 2306, fol. 33b; Ibn Abī Ḥaġalah, *Ṣabābah*, ed. Sallām, S. 63. In dem biographischen Lexikon von Ibn Ḥallikān wird als Dichter al-Wazīr Abū l-Qāsim al-Maġribī (st. 418/1027) angeführt (*Wafayāt al-aʿyān wa-anbāʾ abnāʾ az-zamān*, Kairo 1948, Bd. 1, S. 430).

45   In den vorliegenden Beispielen schreibt Rückert auslautendes -ū ohne, die Gothaer Handschrift mit *alif otiosum*.

Sie schoren ihm das Haar, ihn zu entstellen,
Aus Eifersucht sie thaten ihm die Schmach.

Er war ein Tag, von dunkler Nacht umfangen;
Sie nahmen ihm die Nacht, u[nd] er blieb Tag.

Im Unterschied zum Original wechselt in Vers 2b das Subjekt – „er blieb" anstelle „sie ließen ihn bleiben" –; eine Änderung, die schon aus metrischen Gründen erforderlich ist und die Wirkung der Antithese (*ṭibāq*) verstärkt. Der Geschorene wird zum Subjekt und bleibt unversehrt, weil der Haarverlust der Schönheit seines taghellen Gesichts nichts anhaben kann. Das Klangbild der in fünfhebigen Jamben gehaltenen Übersetzung wird bestimmt durch den dunklen Vokal *a* und entspricht dem ernsten Thema der entblößenden Liebesstrafe. Die Reimwörter „Schmach" und „Tag" zeigen überdies, dass Rückerts Verständnis der deutschen Phonetik dialektal geprägt war und er sich von der fränkischen Aussprache, in der auslautendes *g* zumeist wie *ch* gesprochen wird, hat leiten lassen. Fast hat man den Eindruck, als habe Rückert hier doch einmal versucht, den arabischen Reim *-xā* im Deutschen lautlich nachzuahmen.

In den nächsten zwei Beispielen ergänzt Rückert einzelne Wörter, die im Arabischen keine Entsprechung haben. Aus Kapitel 27 hat er zunächst ein wieder anonym überliefertes Epigramm ausgewählt:[46]

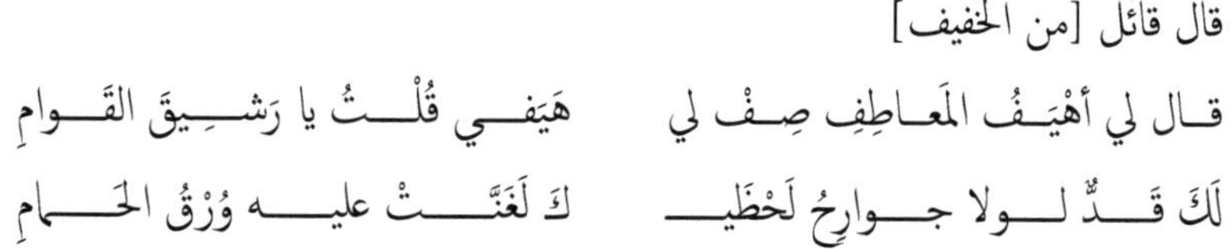

Mein Schlanker sprach: Beschreibe meine Schlankheit!
Ich sprach: o zarter Sproß aus Edens Lauben!

Dein Wuchs ist so, daß, wären deine Blicke
Stoßvögel nicht, gern sängen drauf die Tauben.

Der Zusatz „aus Edens Lauben" im ersten Vers ist in mehrfacher Hinsicht von Nutzen: Der Halbvers erreicht die erforderliche Anzahl von elf Silben, er erhält ein zu „Tauben" in Vers 2 passendes Reimwort und wird um ein poetisches Bild bereichert, das die Schlankheit des Geliebten überirdisch erhöht. Die Anrede „o zarter Sproß aus Edens Lauben" für arabisch *yā rašīqa l-qawāmī* harmoniert überdies mit den aus der Tierwelt entlehnten Metaphern „Stoßvögel" und „Tauben" im zweiten Vers. Ähnlich verfährt Rückert bei der Übersetzung des anschließenden Gedichts von Nūraddīn al-Isʿirdī (st. 652/1254):[47]

---

46 ULB Münster, Nachlass Rückert 5, 036, Bl. 75b–76a; Ibn Abī Ḥaǧalah, *Ṣabābah*, Ms. Gotha orient. A 2306, fol. 158a; Ibn Abī Ḥaǧalah, *Ṣabābah*, ed. Sallām, S. 269.

47 ULB Münster, Nachlass Rückert 5, 036, Bl. 73b–74a; Ibn Abī Ḥaǧalah, *Ṣabābah*, Ms. Gotha orient. A 2306, fol. 158a; Ibn Abī Ḥaǧalah, *Ṣabābah*, ed. Sallām, S. 270.

وقال نور الدين الإسعردي [من الخفيف]

قـــد قَنَعْنـــا بالخَمْـرِ والمـــاءِ والخُـــضْـ   رَةٍ والأَهْيَــــفِ الرشــــيقِ القَـــوامِ

وَتَـــرَكْنا مَناصِـــبَ النّـــاسِ زَهْـــدًا   فلِـــماذا يُؤْذُونَنــــا بالــــكَلامِ

Mir genügt Wein und fließend Wasser u[nd] Grüne
Und ein schlank zartgewachsner Sprößling aus Eden.

Dafür lass' ich den Menschen gern ihre Würden;
Warum stets denn verfolgen sie mich mit Reden?

Wieder dient im ersten Vers die Ergänzung „aus Eden" dazu, eine einheitliche Anzahl von zwölf Silben und einen passenden Endreim zu erhalten. Während die erste Übersetzung einem fünfhebigen Jambus folgt, hat Rückert im zweiten Gedicht offenbar das Metrum der Vorlage nachgeahmt, indem er die arabischen Längen und Kürzen durch deutsche betonte und unbetonte Silben ersetzt. Bis auf die jeweils unbetonte Silbe am Versende entspricht das metrische Schema dem Versmaß *ḫafīf*.

Größer sind die Freiheiten, die sich Rückert in seiner Übersetzung eines Gedichtes aus Kapitel 2 über edle Liebende unter Königen und Kalifen (*fī ḏikri l-muḥibbīna ẓ-ẓurafāʾ min mulūki wa-l-ḫulafāʾ*) erlaubt. Es wird dem andalusischen Umayyadenkalifen al-Mustaʿīn bi-llāh ibn al-Ḥakam (reg. 400, 403-407/1009-1010, 1013-1016) zugeschrieben und lautet:[48]

وقال المستعين بالله بن الحكم الأمويّ أحد خلفاء المغرب [من الكامل]

عجبـــا يَهـــابُ الليـــثُ حَــدَّ سِـــنانَ   وأَهـــابُ لحــــظَ فَـــواتِرِ الأجفـــانِ

وأُقـــارِعُ الأبطـــــالَ لا متهيِّبـــــا   منهـــا سِـــوَى الإعْـــراضِ والهجـــرانِ

فَـــأَبُحْنَ مـــن قلـــبي الحِمَـــى وتـــركنني   في عـــزِّ مُلـــكي كالأســـيرِ العـــانِي

لا تعـــذلو[ا] مَلِـــكًا تَـــذَلَّل للهـــوى   ذلُّ الهـــوى عـــزٌّ ومُـــلكٌ ثانِي

مـــا ضَرَّ أنّي عبـــدهنَّ صـــبابةً   وبنـــو الزمـــانِ وهُـــنَّ مـــن عبـــداني

al-Mustaʾin Billah Ben Hakam, ein umeijischer Chalif in Spanien

Leun zittern vor dem Sper in meiner Rechten,
Und ich vor Fraun, die ihre Locken flechten.

Am Tag des Kampfes schlag' ich Helden nieder,
Und bebe vor versagten Liebesnächten.

Geplündert haben sie mein Herz, und halten
Gefangen mich in meinen Königsmächten.

---

48 ULB Münster, Nachlass Rückert 5, 036, Bl. 29b-31a; Ibn Abī Ḥaǧalah, *Ṣabābah*, Ms. Gotha orient. A 2306, fol. 38a; Ibn Abī Ḥaǧalah, *Ṣabābah*, ed. Sallām, S. 70.

> Wer schilt den König, der sich unterworfen?
> Die Unterwerfung hilft ihm Sieg erfechten.
>
> Was schadt' es, daß ich bin ein Knecht der Frauen?
> Sie und die Männer hab' ich doch zu Knechten.

Wie er in der Anmerkung notiert, hat Rückert „nach B[eit] 2 zwei Beits aus-gelassen, die nur schlechte Nachahmung des vorhergehenden Gedichts sind".[49] Der übersetzte Ausschnitt weist eine klare Dreiteilung auf. Verse 1 und 2 stellen die Kampfesstärke des Königs antithetisch seiner Abhängigkeit von Frauen ge-genüber. Als das Resultat dieser Schwäche schildert Vers 3 den Sieg der Frauen über den königlichen Willen. Verse 4 und 5 bringen die Auflösung dieser Situa-tion: Der König ermannt sich und versichert sich seiner Alleinherrschaft. In der Übersetzung fällt vor allem Vers 1 ins Auge, der wörtlich übersetzt lautet: „O Wunder! Der Löwe fürchtet die Spitze meines Speers / Und ich fürchte den Blick matter Augenlider". Während Rückert den ersten Halbvers lediglich etwas freier übersetzt, tauscht er im zweiten den verführerisch „matten" Blick durch die (fe-minine) Geste des Haareflechtens aus. Die Umdichtung, die sicher auch ein Zu-geständnis an ein deutsches Lesepublikum ist, verhilft zu einem Endreim, der leicht über sechs Verse – entsprechend arabischer Konvention auch im ersten Halbvers – durchgehalten werden kann. Im zweiten Vers, der den ersten variiert, interpretiert Rückert arabisch *(a)l-iʿrāḍi wa-l-hiǧrāni* „Abkehr und Trennung" sexu-ell direkter als „versagte[...] Liebesnächte". Die antithetische Struktur des Verses wird betont, indem die Tapferkeit im Kampf dem Tag, die Angst vor weiblicher Abweisung der Nacht zugeordnet wird. In beiden Eingangsversen dominiert die 1. Person Singular und der König hat das Heft noch in der Hand. In Vers 3 wird dagegen das Kollektiv der Frauen zum handelnden Subjekt, das den Herrscher wie einen unterwürfigen Gefangenen (*ka-l-asīri l-ʿāni*) emotional fesselt. Das schwer zu fassende *fa-abaḥna min qalbī l-ḥimā* ersetzt Rückert durch das inversive „Geplündert haben sie mein Herz" (*ḥimā* übersetzt Rückert sonst gern mit „Hag"). Dieser Versanfang und die Fortführung „halten / Gefangen mich ..." ahmen den Parallelismus in arabisch *fa-abaḥna ... wa-taraknanī* ... nach und ge-winnen jeweils durch weitere Alliterationen auf *h* („haben", „Herz", „halten") und *m* („mich", „meinen", „-mächten") an klanglicher Eingängigkeit. Die frei übersetzten „versagten Liebesnächte" in Vers 2 und die wortgetreuen „Königs-mächte" in Vers 3 bilden ein formal harmonierendes Reimpaar, das für den Kon-flikt des lyrischen Ichs steht. Während der König sich im Mittelteil noch als machtloses Opfer weiblicher Anziehung beschreibt, zeigen die Verse 4 und 5 eine geänderte Sichtweise an, die das verschobene Kräfteverhältnis zurechtrückt. In der Übersetzung werden die Verse parallel durch eine rhetorische Frage ein-geleitet. Die selbstgerechten Antworten „belegen", dass aus der vermeintlichen

---

49 Damit gemeint ist ein gleichfalls exzerpierter und übersetzter Dreizeiler von Hārūn ar-Rašīd (ULB Münster, Nachlass Rückert 5, 036, Bl. 27b-28a; Ibn Abī Ḥaǧalah, *Ṣabābah*, Ms. Gotha orient. A 2306, fol. 38a; Ibn Abī Ḥaǧalah, *Ṣabābah*, ed. Sallām, S. 69f.).

Schwäche auch Stärke erwachsen kann und die Herrschaft des Regenten ungefährdet ist. Die Abhängigkeit von Frauen, die anfangs als unvereinbar mit der königlichen Souveränität angesehen wurde, integriert das lyrische Ich in das Selbstbild eines allmächtigen Herrschers.

Wieder aus Kapitel 27 hat Rückert ein Gedicht von as-Salāmī (st. 393/1003) ausgewählt:[50]

وقال السلامي [من المنسرح]

بَـــدائِعُ الحُـــسنِ فيهِ مُفْتَرَقَـــهْ   وَأَعْـــيُنُ النــاسِ غَـــيرُ مُتَّفِقَـــهْ

سِـــهامُ ألحاظِـــهِ مُفَوَّقَـــةٌ   فَـــكُلُّ مَـــن رامَ لَحْظَـــهُ رَشـــقَهْ

قـــد كَتَـــبَ الحُـــسْنُ فَـــوْقَ وَجْنَتِـــهِ   هـــذا مَلِـــيحٌ وَحَـــقٍّ مِـــن خَلَقَـــهْ

Mannigfaltig sind seine Reize beschaffen,
Daß die Augen verschiedentlich sich vergaffen.

Wohlversehn sind der Blicke Pfeil' ihm mit Spitzen;
Wund daran wird, wer rühren will an die Waffen.

Sieh, die Schönheit hat auf die Wang' ihm geschrieben:
Schön ist dieser, bei Jenem der ihn geschaffen!

Die Übersetzung korrespondiert inhaltlich recht gut mit der Vorlage. Der erste Vers enthält mit „sich vergaffen" ein Reimwort, über das der (heutige) Leser stolpert, weil es stilistisch aus dem Rahmen fällt und wie eine dem Reim geschuldete Entgleisung erscheint. Wörtlich könnte man den Vers so übersetzen: „Die Reize sind in ihm so mannigfaltig, dass die Augen der Leute sich nicht einig (über ihn) werden". Rückerts Version hat dagegen eine vulgär-verächtliche Nuance,[51] die der arabische Wortlaut nicht hergibt. Das Verb „sich vergaffen" ist der in Rückerts unterfränkischem Heimatdialekt übliche Ausdruck für „sich verlieben, sich vergucken",[52] den er auch in seiner eigenen Dichtung bisweilen verwendet.[53] Auch wenn Ham-

---

50   ULB Münster, Nachlass Rückert 5, 036, Bl. 89b-90a; Ibn Abī Ḥaǧalah, *Ṣabābah*, Ms. Gotha orient. A 2306, fol. 160a; Ibn Abī Ḥaǧalah, *Ṣabābah*, ed. Sallām, S. 273.

51   Vgl. Jacob und Wilhelm Grimm, *Deutsches Wörterbuch*, 16 Bde. in 32 Teilbänden, Leipzig 1854-1961, Quellenverzeichnis Leipzig 1971, Bd. 25, Sp. 370 s.v. „vergaffen".

52   Vgl. Alois Joseph Ruckert, *Unterfränkische Mundart. Beiträge zu einer Sammlung von Ausdrücken, Redensarten und Sprichwörtern in unterfränkischer Mundart*, Würzburg 1901, S. 189 s.v. „vergaff".

53   Vgl. z.B. die Ballade *Erscheinung der Schnitterengel*, in der das Reimpaar „erschaffen – vergaffen" gleich zweimal vorkommt: „Sie tanzen wie sie Gott erschaffen, / Es wird sich niemand hier vergaffen; [...].Wir tanzen wie uns Gott erschaffen, / Er ist zu alt sich zu vergaffen, [...]." (Friedrich Rückert, *Gesammelte Gedichte*, Bd. 4, Erlangen 1837, S. 324). In seinen Übersetzungen (aus dem Arabischen) scheint das Wort hingegen eher selten aufzutauchen; weder in den Makamen von al-Ḥarīrī, der Dichtung von Imraʾalqays noch in der *Hamāsa* von Abū Tammām findet sich ein Beleg dafür (vgl. Friedrich Rückert, *Die Verwandlungen des Abu Seid von Serug oder die Makamen des Hariri in freier Nachbildung von F.R.* [...], 2 Bde. in einem,

mer-Purgstall an der *Hamâsa* (überkritisch) die Verwendung von Dialektwörtern bemängelt hat,[54] greift Rückert in Übersetzungen nur dann auf dialektale Ausdrücke zurück, wenn er, wie im vorliegenden Fall, in Formulierungsnöte gerät und ihm kein adäquates hochsprachliches Wort zur Verfügung steht.

Nachdem Vers 1b den Blick der Liebenden auf den Geliebten thematisiert, geht es im zweiten Vers um den Blick des Geliebten auf die Liebenden. Die verletzende Wirkung dieses Blicks beschreibt das beliebte Bild der Pfeile, die mit Kerben, „mit Spitzen" (*mufawwaqah*) versehen sind und deshalb empfindlich verwunden können. Die recht freie Nachbildung des zweiten Halbverses „Wund daran wird, wer rühren will an die Waffen" knüpft harmonisch an das Pfeilmotiv an und ist zudem klanglich sehr eingängig. Ausgiebig setzt Rückert hier das Stilmittel der Alliteration ein, das den Vers durch die Wiederholung des Buchstabens *w* in sechs Wörtern bindet. So wie sich der arabische Text durch lautliche Intensität auszeichnet,[55] so versucht auch Rückert, die deutsche Version klanglich bewusst zu gestalten und eine vergleichbare Wirkung zu erzielen. Eine Art Rahmen erhält das Gedicht durch die fast identischen Reimwörter des ersten und letzten Halbverses „beschaffen" – „geschaffen", die sich nur durch ihre Vorsilben unterscheiden.

Die folgende in sich geschlossene Übersetzung beruht auf einem Gedicht von Abū Tammām (st. 231/845), das Ibn Abī Ḥaǧalah in Kapitel 6 über die Eifersucht (*fī ḏikri l-ġayrah*) anführt:[56]

قال أبو تمام [من الوافر]

وأَحْـــسِـدُ مُقْلَـــتِي نظــرًا إلَيْــهِ   بنفـسِي مَـــن أَغـــارُ عليهِ مِـــنّي

عيــونَ النـــاسِ مــن حَـــذَري عَلَيْـهِ   ولـــو أَنّي قـــدرتُ طمـــستُ عنـــه

وأَمْـــسَكَ مُهْجَـــتِي رَهْنًـــا لَدَيْــهِ[57]   حبيـــبٌ بَـــتَّ في قَلْـــبِي هـــواه

بـــلا روحٍ وقلـــبِي في يَدَيْـــهِ   فـــروحي عنـــده والجـــسمُ خـــالٍ

Sein bin ich, um den ich mich selbst beneide;
Den Blick beneid' ich, den ich ihm gesandt.

Und wenn ich könnte, längst aus Eifersucht hätt'
Ich ihn der Menschen Augen abgewandt.

Stuttgart/Tübingen ²1837; id., *Amrilkais, der Dichter und König. Sein Leben dargestellt in seinen Liedern.* Aus dem Arabischen übertragen von F.R., Stuttgart/Tübingen 1843; id., *Hamâsa*).
[54] Vgl. dazu Fischer in Rückert, *Hamâsa*, Bd. 1, S. 43.
[55] Man beachte die Reihung der Stilmittel *ǧinās* und *ištiqāq* (Wurzelentsprechung, figura etymologica): *muftariqah – muttafiqah – mufawwaqatun – fawqa.*
[56] ULB Münster, Nachlass Rückert 5, 036, Bl. 34b-35a; Ibn Abī Ḥaǧalah, *Ṣabābah*, Ms. Gotha orient. A 2306, fol. 65a; Ibn Abī Ḥaǧalah, *Ṣabābah*, ed. Sallām, S. 115.
[57] In der Anmerkung schlägt Rückert zu Vers 3 zwei Lesarten vor: „b[eit] 3, a بَتَّ؟ oder بِتُّ i.e. وهواه في قلبي بِتُّ". Die Druckedition von Sallām, ibid. überliefert mit بث die erste Lesart.

Ein Liebster, dessen Liebe mir im Herzen,
Dafür mein Leben ist bei ihm zum Pfand.

Mit ihm ist meine Seel', und ledig ohne
Seele mein Leib, mein Herz in seiner Hand.

Bei größtmöglicher Nähe zum arabischen Wortlaut gelingt es Rückert, dem Thema der hingebungsvollen Liebe einen innigen, fast beschwörenden Ausdruck zu verleihen. Wirkungsvoll formuliert der Eingangsvers „Sein bin ich, um den ich mich selbst beneide" die Seelenlage des lyrischen Ichs, das sich monomanisch dem Geliebten verschrieben hat. Diese Zeile ist im ersten und letzten Wort durch die Wiederholung des Diphtongs *ei*, der an den arabischen Reim *-ayhī* anklingt, besonders einprägsam und spiegelt das um eine Person kreisende Gefühl auch auf lautlicher Ebene wider. Während in der Vorlage die Reimwörter *ilayhī*, *ʿalayhī*, *ladayhī* und *yadayhī* den Blick auf diesen Einen lenken, erreicht dies Rückert, indem er das Possessivpronomen „Sein" markant an den Gedichtanfang setzt und die Personalpronomen „ihm"/„ihn" in allen vier Versen an Stellen, auf die das jambische Versmaß den Akzent legt. Nachdem in Vers 1 der Blick zunächst introspektiv auf die eigene Person gerichtet war, sind es in Vers 2 „der Menschen Augen", vor denen der Geliebte abgeschirmt werden soll. Ob dieser die Gefühle erwidert, ist unsicher, da ausschließlich der Liebende von und für sich spricht. Dennoch kommt es in Vers 3 zu einer „Verbindung": Das lyrische Ich trägt im Herzen die Liebe zum Geliebten, dieser erhält „dafür" das „Leben" des Liebenden (*muhğatī*) „zum Pfand". Am Ende wird die Hingabe zur Selbstaufgabe, das lyrische Ich verliert Seele und Herz an den Geliebten und bleibt „ledig ohne Seele" zurück. Klanglich dominieren in der Übersetzung helle Vokale, von denen sich der dunkel vokalisierte männliche Reim auf *-and(t)* hörbar abhebt.

Ein seltenes Beispiel für eine weibliche Stimme wird in Ibn Abī Ḥağalahs Anthologie im Schlusskapitel, der *ḫātimah*, angeführt. Die zwei anonym überlieferten Verse lauten:[58]

قالت امرأة [من الخفيف]

كُلَّ يَـــــوْمٍ قطيعـــــةٌ وعِتـــــابُ   يَنقَـــضِي دَهْـــرُنَا ونَحْـــنُ غِـــضابُ

لَيْـتَ شِـعْرِي فَهَـلْ خُصِـصْتُ بِهـذا   دُونَ ذا الخَلْـقِ أم كـذا الأَحْبـابُ

Ein Weib sang

An jedem Tag ein Zank oder Zwist,
In Groll vergeht unsers Lebens Frist.

Wüßt' ich, ob mir's nur allein so geht,
Oder die Liebe nicht anders ist!

---

58 ULB Münster, Nachlass Rückert 5, 036, Bl. 99b-100a; Ibn Abī Ḥağalah, *Ṣabābah*, Ms. Gotha orient. A 2306, fol. 189a; Ibn Abī Ḥağalah, *Ṣabābah*, ed. Sallām, S. 310 (V. 2a أنا statt فهل).

Geschickt fängt die Übersetzung in ihrem prosaischen Duktus den verdrossenen Ton der Vorlage ein. Der am Anfang monotone, fast leiernde Rhythmus in Vers 1 passt sich dem Lamento des lyrischen Ichs an. Im zweiten Vers richtet sich der Blick nach außen und der Ton wird lebhafter. Der Wunsch zu wissen, ob es anderen genau so geht, ist verbunden mit der Hoffnung, Trost zu erfahren und sich leichter ins Unvermeidliche zu schicken. Nach dem Vorbild des Originals enthält auch die deutsche Übersetzung ausschließlich kurze Wörter von 1-2 Silben, die dem Text etwas Unmittelbares geben und seiner lakonischen Einfachheit entsprechen. Die Verse wirken wie ein Kommentar, der dem Gefühlsüberschwang vieler Gedichte in dieser Sammlung den frustrierenden Alltag einer Liebesbeziehung entgegenhält. Die Aufnahme des Gedichts in eine Reinschrift zeigt, dass der Übersetzer auch dem Alltäglich-Banalen etwas abzugewinnen wusste. Auf diese Eigenart hat mit Blick auf Rückerts eigene Dichtung vielleicht Clemens Brentano (1778-1842) angespielt, der während einer gemeinsamen Rheinfahrt 1829 bemerkt haben soll: „Aus dem, was andere aus der Stube kehren, weiß dieser Rückert etwas zu machen, daß man sich wundern muß; aber seine Gedichte gehen nicht in's Volk".[59]

Wie anders das Gedicht in einer Prosa-Fassung wirkt, zeigt die recht freie Übertragung von Dieter Bellmann nach dem *Kitāb al-Muwaššā* von Ibn al-Waššāʾ (st. 325/936), wo sie al-Ǧāḥiẓ (st. 255/868) einer Lautenspielerin in den Mund legt. Vers 2 ist deutlich abweichend interpretiert:[60]

> Jeder Tag endet mit einem Bruch der Liebe,
>   und der Tadel folgt gleich auf die Tat.
>
> So verzehrt sich unser Dasein,
>   wundert's, daß wir zornig sind?
>
> O wenn ich doch nur einem zugetan,
>   einem einz'gen nur!
>
> Und wenn er noch so ungehobelt
>   oder aber liebenswürdig wär!

Fast ein Zeitgenosse Ibn Abī Ḥaǧalahs ist der Verfasser des folgenden Gedichts. Das reizvolle Epigramm des etwas älteren Ibn an-Naqīb (st. 745/1344) wird überliefert im zehnten Kapitel über das Erhaschen des Traumbildes (*fī ḏikri l-iḥtiyāl ʿalā ṭayfi l-ḫayāl*). Das lyrische Ich versucht, die Augenlider als Fangnetz für das Traumbild des Geliebten zu nutzen. Diese Hoffnung wird spielerisch hinterfragt: Wie kann das gelingen, wo doch das Wild nur mit einer geöffneten Schlinge, der

---

[59] Zit. nach Helmut Prang, *Friedrich Rückert. Geist und Form der Sprache*, Schweinfurt/ Wiesbaden 1963, S. 134.

[60] Abū ṭ-Ṭayyib Ibn al-Waššāʾ, *Das Buch des buntbestickten Kleides*, aus dem Arabischen übers. und hg. von Dieter Bellmann, 3 Bde., Leipzig und Weimar 1984 (Lizenzausgabe Bremen), Bd. 1, S. 110; Ibn al-Waššāʾ, *Kitāb al-Muwaššā*, ed. from the manuscript of Leyden by Rudolph E. Brünnow, Leiden 1886, S. 62 (V. 2a اذا statt فهل).

Geliebte nur mit geöffneten Augen, d.h. im wachen Zustand gefangen werden kann?[61]

قال ابن النقيب [من الطويل]

لَعَـلَّ خيــالًا في الكَرَى منــه يَسْنَحُ[62]   نَــصَبْتُ جُفُــوني للخيــــال حَبـــائلًا

ومِــن عــادةِ الأشراكِ[64] لِلـصَّيدِ تُفْـتَحُ   وكيـــــف اذا أغْمَـــــضْتُهُنّ[63] أصِـــــيدُهُ

Rückert übersetzt im jambischen Rhythmus:

Als Netz gestellt hab' ich die Augenlider,
Ob etwa käm' im Traum von ihr ein Bild.

Sie sind geschlossen; wie da soll ichs fangen?
Man fängt ja nur im offnen Garn ein Wild.

Ungewöhnlich für Rückert ist, dass er das maskuline Personalpronomen *minhu* in Vers 1 als Femininum übersetzt („von ihr"). Möglicherweise handelt es sich um eine Verschreibung, die unterlaufen ist, weil der Übersetzer schon in Gedanken bei dem folgenden Gedicht von al-Buḥturī war, wo eindeutig das Traumbild einer weiblichen Person heraufbeschworen wird und Rückert entsprechend übersetzt „Sie sandt' ihr Traumbild mir auf eine Strecke …".

Was in Rückerts Manuskript am Anfang steht, soll in dieser kleinen Auswahl am Schluss stehen: zwei Verse aus einem Gedicht von Abū Tammām, die zu den beliebtesten der arabischen Ġazaldichtung zählen und fast sprichwörtlich geworden sind.[65]

قال حبيب [من الكامل]

مَـــــا الحُــــبُّ إلَّا للحبيــــبِ الأوَّلِ   نَقِّلْ فُؤادَكَ حَيْثُ شِئْتَ من الهَوَى

وحَنينُــــهُ أَبَـــــدًا[ا] لأوَّلِ مَــــنْزِلِ   كَمْ مَــــنْزِلٍ في الأرض يَألُفُــــهُ الفَــتَى

Über den Vorzug der ersten Liebe

1.

Wohin du wenden magst dein Herz in Liebe,
Die erste Liebe hat allein Bestand:

---

61 ULB Münster, Nachlass Rückert 5, 036, Bl. 48b-49a; Ibn Abī Ḥaĝalah, *Ṣabābah*, Ms. Gotha orient. A 2306, fol. 81b; Ibn Abī Ḥaĝalah, *Ṣabābah*, ed. Sallām, S. 143.

62 Rückert weist in einer Fußnote darauf hin, dass er diese Lesart aus يسبح im Gothaer Manuskript konjiziert hat.

63 Rückert schreibt أغْمَصْتُهُنّ.

64 Rückert schreibt الأسراك.

65 ULB Münster, Nachlass Rückert 5, 035, Bl. 0b-1a, 3b; Ibn Abī Ḥaĝalah, *Ṣabābah*, Ms. Gotha orient. A 2306, fol. 2b; Ibn Abī Ḥaĝalah, *Ṣabābah*, ed. Sallām, S. 15; Gedicht vollständig in Ḥabīb ibn Aws aṭ-Ṭā'ī Abū Tammām, *Dīwān Abī Tammām bi-šarḥ al-Ḫaṭīb at-Tibrīzī*, Hg. Muḥammad ʿAbduh ʿAzzām, Kairo ³1983, Bd. 4, S. 253, Nr. 303.

In welchem Land ein Mann auch heimisch werde,
Stets seufzt er nach dem ersten Heimatland.

Das Manuskript enthält noch eine Variante, die Rückert durchgestrichen hat:

Streitfrage über den Vorzug der ersten Liebe

Habib:

Wohin du wenden magst dein Herz in Liebe,
Der ersten Liebe bleibt es zugewandt.

Woimmer heimisch werd' ein Mann im Lande,
Er seufzt nach seinem ersten Heimatland.

Im *Dīwān aṣ-Ṣabābah* entspinnt sich daraus ein Wortgefecht zwischen Abū Tammām und Dīk al-Ǧinn al-Ḥimṣī (st. 235/850) mit weiteren Epigrammen „über den Vorzug der ersten Liebe". Rückert exzerpiert auch diese Verse, übersetzt aber nur ein Gegengedicht (*muʿāraḍah*) von Dīk al-Ǧinn und vermittelnde Schlussverse von einem gewissen Abū l-Barq. Nach dem Vorbild der arabischen Originale stimmen beide in Reim und Versmaß (jambische Fünfheber) mit den Übersetzungen der Verse von Abū Tammām überein:[66]

فقال ديك الجنّ الحمصيّ يردّ على حبيبٍ قولَهُ [من الكامل]

كَـذبَ الذيـن تَحَـدَّثُوا[١] أنّ الهــوى   لا شَـــكَّ فيـــه للحبيـــب الأَوَّلِ

مـــا لي أحَـــنُّ الى خـــرابٍ مُقْفـــرٍ   درسَـــتْ مَعالِمُـــهُ كأنَّ لَـــمْ يُؤْهَـــلِ

2.

Sie lügen, die von erster Liebe sagen,
Sie sei allein der Sehnsucht Gegenstand:

Sollt' ich nach der verlassnen Wohnung seufzen,
Wann ihre Spuren sind verweht im Sand?

وقال أبو البرق [من الكامل]

وسلكَ بينها جادّةَ الإنصاف وبقوله يَجِبُ الإعتراف

زادوا[١] عــلى المعــنى وكلٌّ مُحْـــسِنٌ   والحَـــقُّ فيـــه مَقالةٌ لَـــمْ تُجْهَـــلِ

الحُـــبُّ للمحبـــوب ســـاعَةَ وَصْـــلِهِ   مـــا الحُـــبُّ فيـــه لآخِـــرٍ ولِأَوَّلِ

3.

Sie reden hin u[nd] her, u[nd] schön spricht jeder,
Allein die Wahrheit hat allein Bestand:

---

66 ULB Münster, Nachlass Rückert 5, 035, Bl. 0b-1a, 3b (wörtlich übereinstimmende Dublette); Ibn Abī Ḥaǧalah, *Ṣabābah*, Ms. Gotha orient. A 2306, fol. 3a; Ibn Abī Ḥaǧalah, *Ṣabābah*, ed. Sallām, S. 15.

Die Liebe liebt im Augenblick der Wonne,
In welchem Gegenwart u[nd] Zukunft schwand.

Einmal mehr sind Rückert hier ansprechende poetische Übersetzungen gelungen, die sich flüssig lesen und die Vorlage sinngetreu nachbilden, ohne sich unnötig weit vom arabischen Wortlaut zu entfernen.

Auch wenn dieser Eindruck für die meisten Übersetzungen der vorliegenden Manuskripte zutrifft, trägt Rückerts *Ṣabābah*-Auswahl doch unverkennbar die Handschrift des Dichtergelehrten, der gar nicht die Absicht hatte, einem Wissenschaftsanspruch zu genügen. Für Rückert war es deshalb unproblematisch, neben mehr oder weniger präzisen Übersetzungen manches „Zwittergebild"[67] mit willentlichen Abweichungen zu stellen und darauf nicht eigens hinzuweisen. Seinen Lesern macht er es damit nicht leicht, wenn sie entscheiden wollen, ob eine freie Übersetzung auf das Konto des Poeten oder des Philologen geht, der allein schon wegen fehlender Hilfsmittel und ungenügender Textgrundlagen schnell zu einer anderen Deutung kommen kann. „Wer Philolog und Poet ist in einer Person wie ich Armer, / kann nichts anderes tun, als übersetzen wie ich. / [...] Was philologisch gefehlt, vergibst du poetischer Freiheit, / und die poetische Schuld vergibst du der Philologie", dichtete er nach Abschluss der Makamen-Nachbildung.[68]

So sehr Rückert von seiner philologisch-poetischen Doppelbegabung profitiert hat, so ungünstig hat sich der Mischcharakter seiner Texte auf ihre Rezeption ausgewirkt und erschwert sie bis heute. Die aus philologischer Sicht befremdliche Inkonsequenz lässt sich leichter verstehen, hält man sich vor Augen, dass es Rückert auch darum ging, die orientalische Poesie der deutschen anzuverwandeln und so die deutsche Literatur zu bereichern. Um ein Publikum über die engen akademischen Grenzen hinaus zu erreichen, war es notwendig, sich an den Lesegewohnheiten des gebildeten Bürgertums seiner Zeit zu orientieren und Unverständliches durch vertraute Formen und Bilder zu ersetzen. Die fremde Poesie durch „schmeichelnde Gewöhnung"[69] nahezubringen war Rückerts erklärtes Ziel, für das er sich zunächst der Mittel der deutschen Sprache und Poesie bediente. Die Alternative, die Übersetzungen wortgetreuer zu gestalten und ihnen einen Kommentar zur Seite zu stellen, hat Rückert wenig behagt, auch wenn er das philologische Rüstzeug dazu hatte, wie u.a. seine eingestreuten Notizen in Arbeits-Manuskripten belegen. Für ein solches Vorgehen war Rückert zu sehr Sprachkünstler und Dichter, der die

---

[67] Friedrich Rückert, *Harīrī. Die Verwandlungen des Abu Seid von Serug. 24 Makamen*, aus dem Arabischen übertragen von F.R., hg. von Annemarie Schimmel, Stuttgart 1966, S. 3.

[68] Rückert, *Harīrī*, S. 3.

[69] Friedrich Rückert, *Schi-King. Chinesisches Liederbuch, gesammelt von Confucius*, dem Deutschen angeeignet von F.R., Altona 1833, S. 6 („Die Geister der Lieder, Vorspiel"). Der Vers lautet dort „Mög' euch die schmeichelnde Gewöhnung / Befremden [Befreunden!] auch mit fremder Tönung, / Daß ihr erkennt: Weltpoesie / Allein ist Weltversöhnung". Eine kritische Auseinandersetzung mit diesem Vorgehen in Peter Bachmann, „Rückert als Übersetzer arabischer Dichtung in Johannes Scherrs *Bildersaal der Weltliteratur*", in: Harald Kittel (Hg.), *International anthologies of literature in translation*, Berlin 1995, S. 189-198.

arabischen Texte eher als Literatur denn als wissenschaftlich interessante Texte verstand, wie es viele Fachkollegen ab der zweiten Hälfte des 19. Jahrhunderts vermehrt taten.[70]

Dass es sich lohnt, Rückerts Übersetzungen im Hinblick auf ihr Verhältnis zu den Originalen noch genauer zu untersuchen, zeigt der *Dīwān aṣ-Ṣabābah* eindrücklich. Eine Anthologie arabischer Liebesdichtung in poetischer Übersetzung, die 150 Jahre nach Rückerts Tod noch darauf wartet, kritisch ediert und kommentiert zu werden. Rückert wäre über ein solches Vorhaben nicht verwundert, hat er doch gegen Ende seines Lebens in weiser Voraussicht gedichtet:

> Beseitigt glaubt ihr mich und abgetan,
> Und was ich schuf geh' euch nicht weiter an;
> Gott sei euch gnädig, wenn mit ihren Lasten
> Sich öffnen meine Nachlaßversekasten,
> Dann geht von vorn für euch die Arbeit an.[71]

Bibliographie

Primärquellen

Ibn Abī Ḥaǧalah, Šihābaddīn Aḥmad at-Tilimsānī, *Dīwān aṣ-Ṣabābah*, Ms. Gotha orient. A 2306.

Ibn Abī Ḥaǧalah, Šihābaddīn Aḥmad at-Tilimsānī, *Dīwān aṣ-Ṣabābah*, ed. Muḥammad Zaġlūl Sallām, Alexandria 1987.

Rückert, Friedrich, Mss. Universitäts- und Landesbibliothek Münster, Nachlass Rückert Kapsel 5, 035 und 5, 036.

Rückert, Friedrich, *Hamâsa oder die ältesten arabischen Volkslieder – Gesammelt von Abu Temmâm*, übersetzt und erläutert von F.R., bearbeitet von Wolfdietrich Fischer, 2 Bde., Göttingen 2004 (Erstausgabe Stuttgart 1846).

Rückert, Friedrich, *Briefe*, hg. von Rüdiger Rückert, 2 Bde., Schweinfurt 1977, Bd. 3: *Spezial-Register und Nachtrag*, Schweinfurt 1982.

Rückert, Friedrich, *Die Verwandlungen des Abu Seid von Serug oder die Makamen des Hariri in freier Nachbildung von F.R.* [...], 2 Bde. in einem, Stuttgart/Tübingen ²1837.

Rückert, Friedrich, *Harīrī. Die Verwandlungen des Abu Seid von Serug. 24 Makamen*, aus dem Arabischen übertragen von F.R., hg. von Annemarie Schimmel, Stuttgart 1966.

---

[70] Vgl. dazu auch Wolfdietrich Fischer in Rückert, *Hamâsa*, Bd. 1, S. 37-44.

[71] Stadtarchiv Schweinfurt, Sammlung Schweinfurt, A II 71h-88 [1863]. Für diesen und weitere Hinweise bedanke ich mich herzlich bei Rudolf Kreutner (Schweinfurt).

Sekundärquellen

Erdmann, Jürgen (Hg.), *200 Jahre Friedrich Rückert. 1788-1866. Dichter und Gelehrter. Katalog der Ausstellung*, Coburg 1988.

Möller, Johann Heinrich, *Catalogus librorum tam manuscriptorum quam impressorum, qui iussu Divi Augusti Saxo-Gothani a beato Seetzenio in oriente emti in Bibliotheca Gothana asservantur*, Teil 1 (Codices arabici) [...], Gotha 1826.

Osigus, Anke, *Der orientalistische Nachlass Friedrich Rückerts in der Universitäts- und Landesbibliothek Münster. Katalog der Äthiopica, Arabica, Turcica, Hebraica und Persica*, Erlangen 2008.

Pertsch, Wilhelm, *Die orientalischen Handschriften der Herzoglichen Bibliothek zu Gotha.* [...]. Teil 3: *Die arabischen Handschriften der Herzoglichen Bibliothek zu Gotha*, Bd. 4, Gotha 1883.

A Courtier's Chess Book:
Ibn Abī Ḥaǧalah's *Unmūḏaǧ al-qitāl fī naql al-ʿawāl*[1]

Remke Kruk

Unmūḏaǧ al-qitāl fī naql al-ʿawāl is one of Ibn Abī Ḥaǧalah's better known works. It has been known and extensively studied by scholars since the middle of the 19th century. Not surprisingly, the attention of these scholars was specifically focused on the chess aspects of the book. Bland's article "Persian Chess"[2] was the first publication to devote attention to the *Unmūḏaǧ* and it gave an extensive summary of its contents. It was especially H.J.R. Murray, the great chess historian, who made extensive use of the *Unmūḏaǧ* in his monumental *A History of Chess*[3] and analyzed its importance for our knowledge of chess in Islamic culture. His work was continued and expanded by Reinhard Wieber in his study of chess in Arabic culture,[4] which contains a thorough study of the *Unmūḏaǧ* as well as numerous references to it.[5]

The *Unmūḏaǧ* has been edited twice: in 1980 in Baghdad, by Zuhayr al-Qaysī[6], on the basis of a 20th-century MS that originally belonged to Father Anastase Marie the Carmelite, who, as al-Qaysī mentions in his introduction, also possessed other chess MSS; and in 2012 by Muʿǧib al-ʿAdwānī[7], on the basis of two MSS, a Manchester MS dating from the 15th century (John Rylands Library 767) and a British Library MS dating from the 19th century (BL Or. 15517). I recently

---

[1] Since my knowledge of chess and mathematics is limited, I have gratefully relied on Prof. Frans Oort (Utrecht) for advice in writing this article.

[2] Bland, Nathaniel, "Persian Chess", in: *Journal of the Royal Asiatic Society* 13 (1852), pp. 1-70.

[3] Murray, Harold James Ruthven, *A History of Chess*, Oxford 1913.

[4] Wieber, Reinhard, *Das Schachspiel in der arabischen Literatur von den Anfängen bis zur zweiten Hälfte des 16. Jahrhunderts*, Walldorf-Hessen 1972.

[5] Tracing information relevant to the *Unmūḏaǧ* in Murray and Wieber is not altogether easy. Murray's index only provides a limited number of references, while Wieber's book has no indexes at all. For the benefit of other researchers, I give here my own, undoubtedly also incomplete, lists of the page numbers where Murray and Wieber refer to the *Unmūḏaǧ*, indicated as "Man." (for Manchester) by Murray and as "H" (for Ḥaǧalah) by Wieber. Murray's references are found on the following pages: 175, 176-77, 183, 185, 192, 210, 212, 221-22, 224 n. 1, 225 n. 8, 227, 232, 234, 235, 235 n. 3, 236, 237, 243, 245-46, 271, 277, 279, 280, 281, 304, 318, 324, 327. As to Wieber, the page numbers are: 29-32, 124, 125, 126, 148, 149, 150, 173 n. 6, 178 n. 3-5, 181 n. 7, 183 n. 4, 185 n. 1-2, 186 n. 2, n.6, 187 n. 4, n. 9, 191 n. 3, 192 n. 1, 193 n. 2, n.4, n.5, 194 n. 4, 197 n. 5, 198 n. 1,199 n.5, 203 n., n.8, 204 n. 4, 205 n. 6, n.8, 206 n. 8, 207 n. 6, 208 n. 1, 211 n, n. 3, 236 n.9, 237 n.5, 242 n. 4 H, n. 7, 243 notes 1, 2, 4, 5, 8, 9, 11, 20, 21, 25, 27, 29, 33, 244 n. 3, 245 n., 246 n. 1, n.5, 251 n. 1, 252 n. 1, 254 n. 13, n. 18, n. 21, 255 n. 6.

[6] Ibn Abī Ḥaǧalah, *Unmūḏaǧ al-qitāl fī naql al-ʿawāl*, ed. Zuhayr Aḥmad al-Qaysī, Baghdad 1401/1980.

[7] Ibn Abī Ḥaǧalah, *Unmūḏaǧ al-qitāl fī naql al- ʿawāl*, ed. Muʿǧib al-ʿAdwānī, Beirut 2012.

found that another MS, originating from the Maghreb and dated 1093/1682-83, was auctioned in London at Christie's in 1993.[8] I do not know the current whereabouts of this MS.

There is some dispute about the title of the work, and, curiously enough, even about Ibn Abī Ḥaǧalah's authorship. As regards the title: the problem lies in the meaning of ʿawāl, interpreted by some scholars as "players of the highest class, grand masters".[9] Another possible meaning is suggested by ʿAdwānī: ʿawāl, al-qaṭʿ al-muʿaddiya ilā l-ġalb (or: ġalab), "the move that leads to winning".[10] Beatrice Gruendler, in her article on Ibn Abī Ḥaǧalah in *Essays in Arabic literary biography*,[11] translates the title as: *The Model Combat, on Moving Pawns*.

There is some additional evidence regarding this question from the text itself, namely in the story told about a chess player who reached a complicated sort of draw.[12] It is difficult to make sense of the text as its stands in the edition; therefore, I propose two emendations: firstly, to read *manaʿahā* instead of *minhā*, and, secondly, instead of *manʿ al-ʿawāl*, to read *manʿ al-ʿawālī*, grandmasters (unless we accept Wieber's reading of the title and read ʿuwāl). This would yield the meaning: "he reached a *māniʿ*-type of draw in the manner of the grandmasters".[13]

Doubt about Ibn Abī Ḥaǧalah's authorship was expressed by Wieber,[14] based on the fact that Ibn Abī Ḥaǧalah[15] cites Abū Zakariyyā Yaḥyā b. Ibrāhīm al-Ḥakīm al-Adīb al-Kātib's *Kitāb al-manṣūbāt* (Book of chess problems; a work otherwise unknown). Wieber assumes that this Abū Zakariyyā Yaḥyā al-Ḥakīm is the same as the author of another chess book, *Nuzhat arbāb al-ʿuqūl fī š-šaṭranǧ al-manqūl*, in which he cites Ibn Sūdūn (d. 864/1464). This places the author Abū

---

[8]   http://www.christies.com/LotFinder/lot_details.aspx?from=salesummary&intObjectID=1039293 . Retrieved January 13th, 2016.

[9]   Wieber, *Das Schachspiel*, p. 30 gives the title as: *K. unmūḏaǧ al-qitāl fī naql al-ʿuwāl* (note: so *GAL*, S II: 6; in the MS: ʿawāl) *mā ṣunnifa miṯluhū li-baʿḍi s-salafi* ("Das Buch vom Modell für die Schlacht in der Überlieferung der erstklassigen Schachspieler. Von einem Vorfahren wurde nichts dergleichen verfasst"). Wieber evidently interprets ʿuwāl as synonymous with ʿāliya, pl. ʿawālī, the highest class of players. Cf. Rosenthal, F., "Shaṭranǧ", in: *Encyclopaedia of Islam*, New edition, vol. IX, Leiden 1997, p. 367.

[10] *Unmūḏaǧ*, ed. al-ʿAdwānī, p. 4 n. 1. ʿAdwānī unconvincingly bases himself on the meaning which az-Zabīdī gives to the verb ʿāla – yaʿūlu – ʿawl: ʿāla šayʾan iḏā ġalabahu wa-ṯaqula ʿalayhi wa-ahammahu (az-Zabīdī, *Tāǧ al-ʿarūs*, 15 vols., ed. ʿAlī Šīrī, Beirut 1994, XV: 528, lemma [ʿw l]).

[11] Gruendler, Beatrice, "Ibn Abī Ḥajalah (1325-1375)", in: Lowry, Joseph E. and Devin J. Stewart (eds.), *Essays in Arabic Literary Biography 1350-1850*, Wiesbaden 2009.

[12] *Unmūḏaǧ*, ed. al-ʿAdwānī, p. 39.

[13] On this type of draw, see Wieber, *Das Schachspiel*, pp. 261-2, d: "Das Spiel ist beendet durch Unentschieden, wenn eine Partei noch eine weitere Figur neben dem König hat und nicht auf die unter a) ["Steht eine Partei patt, hat der Gegner gewonnen"], b) ["Hat ein König keine weitere Figur mehr neben sich, hat der Gegener gewonnen"], e) ["Das Matt ist dasselbe wie im modernen Schachspiel"] angegebene Arten besiegt werden kann ("māniʿ", eine Abart des Rémis ("qāʾima")).

[14] Wieber, *Das Schachspiel*, pp. 34-35.

[15] *Unmūḏaǧ*, ed. al-ʿAdwānī, p. 76.

Zakariyyā al-Ḥakīm much too late to be cited by Ibn Abī Ḥaǧalah, who died in 776/1375 and thus cannot be the author of the *Unmūḏaǧ*.[16] The *Nuzhah* was edited by Muʿǧib al-ʿAdwānī in 2012,[17] just like the *Unmūḏaǧ*. I have not been able to locate the reference to Ibn Sūdūn in the printed edition of the *Nuzhah*.

In any case, there can be no doubt about the authorship of the *Unmūḏaǧ*: in the text, Ibn Abī Ḥaǧalah refers to several of his own works, among them his well-known *Sukkardān aṣ-ṣulṭān*.[18] Furthermore, in his study Wieber is not consistent in his doubt about Ibn Abī Ḥaǧalah's authorship, for elsewhere he mentions him as the author of the *Unmūḏaǧ* without further comment. "Ḥ" (for Ḥaǧalah) is also the sign he uses throughout to refer to the Manchester MS of the *Unmūḏaǧ*.

Some remarks on chess in the Islamic world

First some notes about chess in the Islamic world, necessary for a proper understanding of the *Unmūḏaǧ*. Chess, imported from Iranian culture, was a popular game in the Islamic world from the seventh century on. It was not, however, played according to the same rules as in modern times: pre-modern chess was a very different game from how it is played today. The most basic differences were the following: the queen, then called *firzān* (vizier)[19], could only move diagonally, one square at a time. The bishop (in Arabic: *fīl*, elephant) was only allowed to move two squares diagonally, but was allowed to jump over another piece if this was in the way. Pawns, unlike today, were not allowed to move two squares when setting out. A pawn, upon reaching the other side of the board, could only promote to queen. Castling did not exist. The starting positions of king and queen could vary. The rules for declaring a game as won or drawn also varied. It was only some centuries after the game moved to Europe that the rules were changed dramatically, with the result that the game became much faster. This development took place in Europe in the 15th century. Castling was introduced later still, namely at the end of the 16th century.[20]

For a proper understanding of Arabic chess literature it is also useful to know that the chess pieces were red and black instead of white and black, and that the

---

16   Wieber, *Das Schachspiel*, pp. 32-36.
17   Al-Ḥakīm, Abū Zakariyyā Yaḥyā, *Nuzhat arbāb al-ʿuqūl fī š-šaṭranǧ al-manqūl*, ed. Muʿǧib al-ʿAdwānī, Beirut 2012.
18   *Unmūḏaǧ*, ed. al-ʿAdwānī, p. 58. Other works by him that are referred to are: an *urǧūza* called *Šaqāʾiq an-nuʿmān fī l-fiqh* (p. 8); at-tadmīn aṯ-ṯamīn (p. 23); *Radd al-hazl ilā l-ǧidd* (p. 51); some verses from his panegyric poem for al-Malik an-Nāṣir Ḥasan (p. 91).
19   Ibn Ǧinnī, quoted in the *Unmūḏaǧ*, ed. al-ʿAdwānī: 20, said that the common people generally said *firz* or *firza*, just as they often said *šāt* for *šāh*. The change from *al-firzān* to "queen" occurred via the Spanish *alferza*, which in Latin became *ferce* and *virgo*, and subsequently "dame, lady, queen". See Murray, *A History of Chess*, pp. 426-28.
20   Murray, *A History of Chess*, pp. 830-33; Wieber, *Das Schachspiel*, pp. 257-270.

chess board (except in some rare cases) was not made of wood, but of cloth or leather,[21] with the pattern embroidered or engraved on it without any difference in colour between the squares. The board was thus not chequered, which had important consequences for the evaluation of the chessmen's positions, a circumstance which is reflected in the chess terminology.[22] It was only in the later Middle Ages that this started to change in some locations. When exactly this took place is not clear. Medieval European miniatures, such as in the *Libro de los Ajedres*, show a chequered and apparently wooden board. Wooden, chequered boards were also used at the Nasrid court in Granada,[23] and chequered boards sometimes appear in miniatures with the Persian *Shahnameh*, such as in the Bayasanghori *Shahnameh*, dated 1430. In Egypt, however, wooden boards were still not common in the 18th century: Carsten Niebuhr, describing the popularity of chess in 18th-century Cairo, says that the board was an embroidered piece of cloth.[24] This, however, is not the place for a full discussion of this complicated topic. Extensive analysis of chess references from a variety of sources is needed to further elucidate this matter. References to the black and white chequered pattern of the chessboard, in any case, are not at all rare in Persian and Arabic literature, in poetry as well as in prose.[25]

Chess manuals

The popularity of chess in Arabic (and in general Islamic) culture is demonstrated by the existence of an extensive literature about chess. Much of it is still extant in manuscripts, but only a few texts have been published. Ibn Abī Ḥaǧalah's *Unmūḏaǧ* is one of them. In order to understand what kind of chess book the *Unmūḏaǧ* is, we have to see how its contents relate to that of other, especially older, chess books. Do these older books just contain technical information about the game, such as explanations of the rules and discussions of problems, or other information as well? Do *adab* aspects, prominent in the *Unmūḏaǧ*, play a part in them?

---

[21] See for instance Ibn Ḥaǧalah's comparison of a patched garment with an old chessboard, *Unmūḏaǧ*, ed. al-ʿAdwānī, p. 129.

[22] Murray, *A History of Chess*, pp. 230-310.

[23] Museo de la Alhambra. No VII/28: Tablero de juego, Nasrid, XIV-XV century.

[24] Niebuhr, Carsten, *Beschryving van Arabie*, vol. I, Amsterdam 1776.

[25] Some examples: Edward Fitzgerald's translation of the line from the *Rubaiyat* by ʿUmar Ḥayyām (d. 517/1123), no. 49, is sufficiently well known: "'Tis all a Chequer-board of Nights and Days/ Where Destiny with Men for Pieces plays". See also, for instance, Ibn Ḥazm, *Ṭawq al-ḥamāmah*, ed. D. K. Pétrof, St. Petersburg-Leiden 1914, p. 93, where the alternating pattern of light and shadow in the foliage is compared to a chessboard; and, from a very different type of source: Scheper, Karin, *The Technique of Islamic Bookbinding*, Leiden 2014, pp. 155-56: al-Išbili's 13th-century description of the "chessboard-like pattern" of end bands. A sample of such an end band shown to me by Dr. Scheper had differently coloured squares.

In order to get a clearer view of these matters I shall give a, necessarily very sketchy, account of the contents of the major older chess manuals, basing myself primarily on the information provided by Murray[26] and Wieber,[27] who give extensive surveys of the contents of the MSS they used. No printed editions of these texts were available to them. This situation has now changed, given that, apart from the *Unmūḏaǧ* and the work by Abū Zakariyyā al-Ḥakīm mentioned above, the oldest known Arabic chess book, too, is available in print, albeit in a facsimile edition. The book in question, *Kitāb aš-šaṭranǧ mimmā allafahu l-ʿAdlī wa-ṣ-Ṣūlī wa-ġayruhumā*, is an anonymous compilation of material originating from famous Arab chess players, whose own works have not survived. The most important of these chess players are al-ʿAdlī (a 9th-century chess player about whom very little is known) and aṣ-Ṣūlī (10th century; he was a well-known courtier and man of letters who died in 335/946). At the end of the MS there is another text, a four-page text by aṣ-Ṣūlī's pupil al-Laǧlāǧ, also a famous authority on chess. Some *qaṣīdah*s about chess conclude the MS.

This compilation is extant in two MSS, the oldest of which was edited in facsimile by Fuat Sezgin.[28] It contains extensive discussions of chess rules, tactics and discussions of problems, *manṣubāt*, usually referring to endgames. As opposed to many later chess MSS, it has very good diagrams, showing both parties, the one in red (= white), the other in black. In later MSS, often only one party is represented.

Obviously, it is a book primarily intended as a chess manual. To quote Wieber: "it is the oldest, largest and most elaborate account of Arabic chess, and many parts of it are taken over in later chess works (or at least agree with them)".[29] Besides technical discussions, the book devotes attention to various matters related to chess, knowledge of which was apparently considered basic in connection with the game. These matters are: the legends about the origins of chess, which all say that it was invented for an Indian king; reports about early Islamic chess players in *ḥadīth* form, relevant to the discussions about the legal acceptance of the game; the classes of players (five); the value of the pieces; other varieties of chess (circular chess, chess on a board of ten by ten squares).

Wieber mentions two other anonymous chess manuals, both similar to the compilation described above. One is MS Atif Efendi (formerly Vefa) 2234, completed in 618/1221, which has no title and features many correspondences with MS Lale 560, mentioned above. It is also a compilation of materials from the works of al-ʿAdlī and aṣ-Ṣūlī. It contains some legends about the origins of chess as well as some anecdotes and *ḥadīṯ*s, taking up just a few pages. Otherwise the

---

26 Murray, *A History of Chess*, Chapter X.

27 Wieber, *Das Schachspiel*, pp. 12-37.

28 Sezgin, Fuat (ed.), *Kitāb aš-šaṭranǧ mimmā allafahu l-ʿAdlī wa-ṣ-Ṣūlī wa-ġayruhumā* (Book on Chess: Kitāb aš-Šaṭranǧ. Seleted (sic) texts from al-ʿAdlī, Abū Bakr aṣ-Ṣūlī and others), Frankfurt a.M. 1986, MS Lale Ismail Efendi 560, formerly ʿAbdalḥamīd 56, dated 535/1141.

29 Wieber, *Das Schachspiel*, p. 16.

text deals exclusively with core information about chess.[30] The other is a British Library MS, Arab Add. 7515, completed in 655/1257. This is a compilation similar to the other one, but contains still fewer anecdotes and legends. It includes, however, a discussion about the question of whether chess and backgammon are permitted, and one page of chess poems. All the rest is information on chess directly relevant to the playing of the game.[31]

These examples may serve to show that basic chess manuals generally (but not always) contain technical information as well as some additional chess-related material, such as arithmetic exercises and mathematical puzzles (later called *maḫāriq*) involving chessboard and chessmen, and especially legends about the origin of the game and *ḥadīṯ*s that are relevant for the question of the legal acceptability of chess. Additional information of a wider *adab* nature is only present to a limited extent.

This is quite different in the other two texts that Wieber adds to his collection of basic chess books, namely the *Unmūḏaǧ* and the slightly later *Nuzhah* by al-Ḥakīm. Both of these have since been edited.[32] In these texts, *adab* and poetry are much more emphatically present, especially in the *Nuzhah*, where at least 44 of the 153 pages are taken up by chess poems. In Arabic literature, chess crops up in a variety of ways: in historical anecdotes, in poetry and proverbs, and even in the medical context, where the question of how one's temperamental constitution relates to chess-playing is asked, and what, in connection to temperament, is the best season, weather, and time of day to play chess. Chess is also said to be beneficial as a cure for, for instance, diarrhoea. Such material may find its way into chess books, giving them the character of *adab* books, as is the case with the *Unmūḏaǧ* and the *Nuzhah*. Here, I will focus specifically on the *Unmūḏaǧ*. As we will see, not only the contents of the *Unmūḏaǧ* but also the manner of presentation indicate the *adab* character of the book.

Unmūḏaǧ

I should like to start with some general remarks about the *Unmūḏaǧ*. Like the majority of chess books, it is a compilation, both regarding the chess material and the other information provided. While this implies that it contains little original material, it also means that, like most compilations, it has preserved material otherwise lost. Furthermore, the choice of the compiler is interesting, because it demonstrates his interests as well as his literary taste and that of his contemporaries. It also tells us something about the purpose of the book. As in most compilations, the author has also included information about himself and his works,

---

[30] Wieber, *Das Schachspiel*, p. 20.

[31] Wieber, *Das Schachspiel*, p. 25.

[32] My thanks go to Dr. P.M. Kurpershoek for providing me with a copy of this edition of the *Nuzhah*.

and about contemporary persons and events. This latter material, however, has to be approached with some caution: a story presented by Ibn Abī Ḥaǧalah as a personal communication from aṣ-Ṣafadī is in fact a literal quotation from the latter's *al-Ġayt al-musaǧǧam* and thus offers a nice example of fictitious orality.

All this applies to the chess material as well as to the other parts of his work. It is not my intention here to trace the material used by Ibn Abī Ḥaǧalah back to its sources, except in a selected number of cases. Ibn Abī Ḥaǧalah frequently, but by no means always, mentions his sources, as is demonstrated by the way he handles his references to aṣ-Ṣafadī's *al-Ġayt al-musaǧǧam fī šarḥ Lāmiyyat al-ʿaǧam*. The section of this work devoted to chess[33] was exhaustively used by Ibn Abī Ḥaǧalah, but not always acknowledged.

Contents[34]

To give an idea of how the *Unmūḏaǧ* relates to other chess works, I shall briefly sketch its contents, dealing with the material in an eclectic manner, and trying to point out which elements it has in common with the basic chess manuals mentioned above.

The book starts with the *basmalah*, followed by praise of the game, an explanation of the title and a brief outline of the way in which the book is conceived and the subject of each chapter. It is divided into an introduction and eight chapters, in accordance with the number of squares on a row of the chessboard. Each chapter is concluded by five chess problems, *manṣūbāt*: the first is an opening; the second, a problem where red wins; the third, a problem where black wins; the fourth, a "light" (*ḫafīfa*) draw; the fifth, an undisputable draw (*qāʾima lā ġayr* or *bilā ḫilāf*). As Ibn Abī Ḥaǧalah says: "I have not put the problems in a separate chapter because I was afraid that it would be boring".[35] Clearly, this statement is crucial for our understanding of the *Unmūḏaǧ*: it may be a book about chess, but first of all it intends to offer enjoyable reading.

The introduction (*muqaddimah*) deals with two topics: the legal position of the game and linguistic views on the word *šaṭranǧ*. In connection with the question of whether chess is permitted by Muslim law, stories (*ḥadīṯ*) about early Muslim players are brought up (all well-known anecdotes), and the views of the different law schools are given. Ibn Abī Ḥaǧalah refers to one of his own works, an *urǧūza* titled *Šaqāʾiq an-nuʿmān fī l-fiqh*, a work of which no known copy exists. Interestingly, although he was a Ḥanafī with Ḥanbalī inclinations and he makes it clear that Ḥanafīs, Ḥanbalīs and Mālikīs all unconditionally forbid it, he seems in this

---

[33] Aṣ-Ṣafadī, *al-Ġayt al-musaǧǧam fī šarḥ Lāmiyyat al-ʿaǧam*, 2 vols., Cairo 1305/1888, II, pp. 50-56.

[34] For a summary of the contents see also Bland, "Persian Chess", pp. 27-32; Murray, *A History of Chess*, pp. 176-77; Wieber, *Das Schachspiel*, pp. 92-32.

[35] *Unmūḏaǧ*, ed. al-ʿAdwānī, p. 7.

respect to follow aš-Šafiʿī, the only one to allow it within strict regulations about the conditions in which it is played. It is not to be played on the street, no betting should be involved, no foolish conversation should accompany it, and it must not keep people from prayer.[36]

The linguistic remarks in the introduction concern matters such as the correct spelling of *šaṭranǧ*, namely *šiṭranǧ*, and various etymologies of the word. On the latter, for instance, aṣ-Ṣafadī's *Šarḥ Lāmiyyat al-ʿaǧam,* which cites a number of sources on this matter, is quoted.[37] The type of information provided in this introduction is also found in the older chess manuals listed above.

Chapter 1: legends about the invention of chess, all well known from older sources. The inventor of chess was an Indian sage called Ṣiṣṣa b. Dāhir al-Hindī.[38] The legends cited usually centre around chess being invented for Indian kings as a replacement of actual warfare, but in one case its invention serves to demonstrate human free will, as opposed to the game of *nard* (backgammon) which is presented as exemplary of a fatalistic course of events.[39] It was also for this reason that Ibn Taymiyyah preferred *nard* over chess: in chess, as opposed to *nard,* the player is master of the game and does not depend on chance.[40] In this last story, the well-known reward demanded by the inventor of chess (whose name is omitted here) is also mentioned: the sage involved asks for grains of wheat to be put on the chessboard, starting with one grain and doubling the number on each subsequent square, resulting in 2^{64} -1 grains, a quantity much bigger than can be provided.[41] Ibn Abī Ḥaǧalah subsequently gives methods for computing this number and visualizing the resulting quantity, for instance, by computing the size of a pyramid containing the resulting quantity of grain,[42] or putting the grains into standard volume measures counting up to the number of cities needed to contain them. The latter visualization is used by Ibn Ḥallikān, the first of the authors quoted.[43] What is noteworthy here is that Ibn Abī Ḥaǧalah seemingly fails to realize that Ibn Ḥallikān does not actually compute the quantity of grain resulting from the story above, namely the sum total of the grains on each individual square (2^{64} -1), but only the number of grains on the last square, namely 2^{63}, a quantity half as large as that in the story. This, Ibn Ḥallikān says, is equivalent to what can be contained in 16,384 cities, the maxi-

---

[36] Cf. Lois Giffen, quoted in Gruendler, "Ibn Abī Ḥajalah", p. 123: "a hard to define man, who dodged a clear religious stance".

[37] *Unmūḏaǧ,* ed. al-ʿAdwānī, p. 17-19.

[38] *Unmūḏaǧ,* ed. al-ʿAdwānī, p. 26.

[39] *Unmūḏaǧ,* ed. al-ʿAdwānī, pp. 26-29, cf. Wieber, *Das Schachspiel,* p. 90, no. 2.

[40] *Unmūḏaǧ,* ed. al-ʿAdwānī, p. 29.

[41] *Unmūḏaǧ,* ed. al-ʿAdwānī, p. 29.

[42] *Unmūḏaǧ,* ed. al-ʿAdwān, p. 34, the method of al-Akfānī. See Wieber, *Das Schachspiel,* p. 116, 242.1.

[43] *Unmūḏaǧ,* ed. al-ʿAdwānī, p. 30; Ibn Abī Ḥaǧalah's source is Ibn Ḥallikān *Wafāyāt al-aʿyān,* 8 vols., ed. Iḥsān ʿAbbās, Beirut 1977-78, 4:358-59.

mum number of cities that the habitable part of the globe (roughly a quarter) can contain, given the earth's circumference.[44]

The matter is confused further by the diagram (eight by five squares) which is placed in the text after Ibn Ḥallikān's computation, either by Ibn Abī Ḥaǧalah himself or by the copyist.[45] The diagram gives the total sum of grains demanded by the sage (not Ibn Ḥallikān's end result), namely 2^{64}-1, written out in full, the numbers written as words, to be read from right to left.[46]

In addition, Ibn Abī Ḥaǧalah shows four (three, in fact, for he combines numbers two and three) other computation methods for dealing with the problem.[47] Such legends about the origin of chess are a standard element of all chess manuals.

Chapter 2 deals with the classes of players, mentioning six classes instead of the usual five, just like in al-Ḥakīm's *Nuzhah*.[48] The relative strength of these players is determined by the odds given to a player of a lower class. Al-ʿAdlī and aṣ-Ṣūlī are quoted on this matter; for the next subject, too, the value of the pieces, an extensive quotation by aṣ-Ṣūlī is given in which he defines these values in dirhams. These values, he says, are only valid at the outset of the game, since during the game their weight may shift.[49] A paragraph on the symbolism of the game concludes the chapter: the šāh is the king, the vizier stands next to him and protects him, etc.[50] This kind of material is a regular feature of chess manuals. Note the number of classes: older manuals usually mention five classes of players instead of six.[51]

Chapter 3 starts with a long extract from aṣ-Ṣūlī, giving maxims and advice on tactics for chess players, mixed with statements about warfare and politics. The passage is not known otherwise but does not provide much new information because

---

[44] The full computation is given by Wieber, *Das Schachspiel*, pp. 106-108, 241.3a; 117-18, 242.3, who, however, also seems to be confused about the end result: in Wieber, *Das Schachspiel*, p. 117, 242.3, he deducts one grain from the final number, apparently supposing that Ibn Ḥallikān computed 2^{64}-1 instead of 2^{63}.

[45] *Unmūḏaǧ*, ed. al-ʿAdwānī: 31; Wieber, *Das Schachspiel*, p. 121; 243.3.

[46] Both the diagram as it appears in ʿAdwānī's edition of the *Unmūḏaǧ* and that in Wieber's study contain mistakes: in ʿAdwānī's diagram, the number on the second square from the left, second row from above, should be 700 instead of 1000; in Wieber's diagram, the number on the second square from the left on the last row should be 10 instead of 15, and that on square 8 of the same row, 100 instead of 1000. Cf. Al-Ḥakīm, Abū Zakariyyā Yaḥyā, *Nuzhat arbāb al-ʿuqūl fī š-šaṭranǧ al-manqūl*, ed. Muʿǧib al-ʿAdwānī, Beirut 2012, pp. 9-10, which is free of mistakes. Written according to our system, the total number amounts to 18,946,744,073,707,551,615.

[47] Cf. Wieber, *Das Schachspiel*, pp. 111-112, 241.4; 112, 241.5, the latter referring specifically to *Unmūḏaǧ*; 116, 242.1.

[48] al-Ḥakīm, *Nuzhat*, p. 41.

[49] On the value of the pieces in relation to each other see Wieber, *Das Schachspiel*, p. 263: 70, where the dirham-system is not used.

[50] The passage was translated by Murray, *A History of Chess*, p. 221.

[51] Cf. Wieber, *Das Schachspiel*, pp. 236-39.

the contents are very similar to a small text ascribed to aṣ-Ṣūlī's pupil Laǧlāǧ included at the end of the anonymous *K. aš-šaṭranǧ*, edited by Sezgin.[52]

The passage by aṣ-Ṣūlī clearly illustrates what is also a leading motif in the legends about the origins of chess: the game was seen as symbolic warfare, a replacement for actual war or training in tactics for battle. In connection with this, Ibn Abī Ḥaǧalah adds a section showing how aṣ-Ṣūlī's maxims apply to actual warfare, giving historical examples. *Ṯabāt*, standing firm against seemingly unbeatable odds, is a central motif. It is quite interesting that among these examples Ibn Abī Ḥaǧalah includes a long account of the battle between Mangū-Timur and Qalāwūn, which was won by the latter against tremendous odds in 680/1281. Again, *ṯabāt* is the leading motif: nothing else about the relation between the tactics explained by aṣ-Ṣūlī and the actual course of the battle is made explicit. The choice of this particular battle is, of course, noteworthy: Qalāwūn was the ancestor of several of Ibn Abī Ḥaǧalah's dedicatees, including aṣ-Ṣāliḥ Ṣalāḥaddin Ṣāliḥ, governor of Mardin, the dedicatee of his chess maqāmah, who was a grandson of Qalāwūn. As Ibn Abī Ḥaǧalah announces in the title of this chapter, these stories were taken from another work of his, one that we no longer possess, *Radd al-hazl ilā al-ǧidd fī kalām al-lāʿib ʿalā siyāsat al-malik wa-tadbīrihi, wa-mā yaǧibu ʿalā l-malik wa-waẓirihi wa-ǧayr ḏālika*.

The connection between chess and warfare is a standard element in chess manuals, but, unlike in the *Unmūḏaǧ*, it is not illustrated with actual examples from recent history.

Chapter 4 treats matters such as the right time and the etiquette of playing. The player should have an untroubled mind. One should not play against people of higher status, or against despicable people of lower status. Then there are the views of physicians on the relation between chess and temperament. They say: the king stands for yellow bile, the *firzān* for black bile, the *fīl* (bishop) for blood, and the rook for phlegm. The best season for playing is autumn, and the best day is Saturday. Examples are given, such as Ibn Māsawayh saying to the caliph Hārūn at the time of the plague that chess chases off illnesses, and, played at the right time, it counteracts overbalance in the constitution.[53] This sort of material is not usually found in chess manuals and hence the *Unmūḏaǧ* is cited as a source for it by, for instance, Wieber.

Chapter 5 deals with the praise and dispraise of chess, quoting a variety of authors. It starts with a statement by Ibn Abī Ḥaǧalah himself: three excellent things have come from India, things by which the people of India have taken a lead on other people, namely the book of Kalilah wa Dimnah, the game of

---

[52] Sezgin, Fuat (ed.), *Kitāb aš-šaṭranǧ*, pp. 266-69. For a summarized translation see Murray, *A History of Chess*, pp. 245-46.
[53] The three medical stories given here were translated by Wieber, *Das Schachspiel*, p. 149.

chess, and the nine numbers 111, 222, etc. until 999 which, as Ibn Abī Ḥaǧalah says, bring together various types of computing.

Ibn Abī Ḥaǧalah then continues with various statements pro and contra the game of chess, taken from various sources and obviously chosen less for their moral and juridical value than for their literary qualities and wittiness. They include the passage from Abū Zakariyyā al-Ḥakīm's *K. al-manṣūbāt*, discussed above, in which the many virtues of chess are summed up, followed by Ibn al-Muʿtazz' well-known verse about chess.[54] Among the subsequent quotations is a long a quotation from aṯ-Ṯaʿālibī's *Yatīmat ad-dahr*, explaining, for instance, word games about the pawn, the vizier and the rook. A small or insignificant person may be referred to as a "pawn", and if such a person gains importance he has "queened" (*tafarzana*). The chapter concludes with some paragraphs on linguistic nonsense (*haḏāyāt wa-falatāt al-lisān*) involving chess.

The approach taken in this chapter is typically that of *adab*, focusing on amusement, wittiness and literary elegance rather than on providing real information about the game of chess. The discussions pro and contra chess included in this chapter, too, are along these lines, reminding us of al-Ǧāḥiẓ. The chapter shows where Ibn Abī Ḥaǧalah's attention lies in the *Unmūḏaǧ*: while little snippets of this kind of material occasionally occur in the older, more basic chess manuals, they never amount to substantial chapters.

Chapter 6 deals with varieties of chess, a familiar subject in chess manuals. Ibn Abī Ḥaǧalah gives only two examples (no need to give more, he says): chess on a ten by ten board (with two extra pieces) and "elongated chess", with a four by thirteen board and the usual number of chessmen.

Of greater interest is the other subject treated in this chapter, namely the *maḫārīq*, puzzles figured out on or with the help of a chessboard. These are not chess problems, but mathematical exercises involving the chessmen and their moves. There are various types: some involve chessmen on the board making their usual moves, while others are just logical or arithmetical puzzles which may be illustrated by using chessmen, but where there is no special reason to do so.

To quote Murray: "Of less interest in themselves, they are of considerable importance historically as illustrating the extent of the indebtedness of the earlier European players to Muslim sources". This is demonstrated by the fact that a number of these problems are also found in European texts of the 14th to the 16th century.[55]

Such puzzles also occur in earlier chess books, but, according to Murray, Ibn Abī Ḥaǧalah was the first to give them a special name, *maḫārīq* (Murray spells it as *miḫārīq*) and to treat them under a separate heading.[56] Accordingly, Murray

---

[54] For a translation by Bland, see Murray, *A History of Chess*, p. 185, where the whole passage is traced back to aṯ-Ṯaʿālibī's *K. al-laṭāʾif wa-ẓ-ẓarāʾif fī madḥ al-ašyāʾ wa aḍdādihā* and to his *K. al-yawāqīt fī baʿḍ al-mawāqīt*.
[55] Murray, *A History of Chess*, p. 337 and n. 53.
[56] Murray, *A History of Chess*, p. 217.

uses the *Unmūḏaǧ* as a major source for this subject and explains most of the *maḫāriq* included there.[57]

A well-known *miḫrāq* is the knight's tour, in which the knight has to visit every square in only 63 moves. Ibn Abī Ḥaǧalah does not include this *miḫrāq*, but presents a number of others, among them the four knights problem, in which two black and two white knights have to change places on a board of three by three squares in 16 (8x2) moves, starting from the corner squares. It may serve here to illustrate a familiar problem encountered in these chess texts, namely the defective transmission of diagrams. Both editions of the *Unmūḏaǧ* give wrong diagrams for the four knights problem, while both their texts are correct.[58] The diagrams are shown below, followed by the solution. For practical reasons the knights are indicated by K instead of the usual Kt.

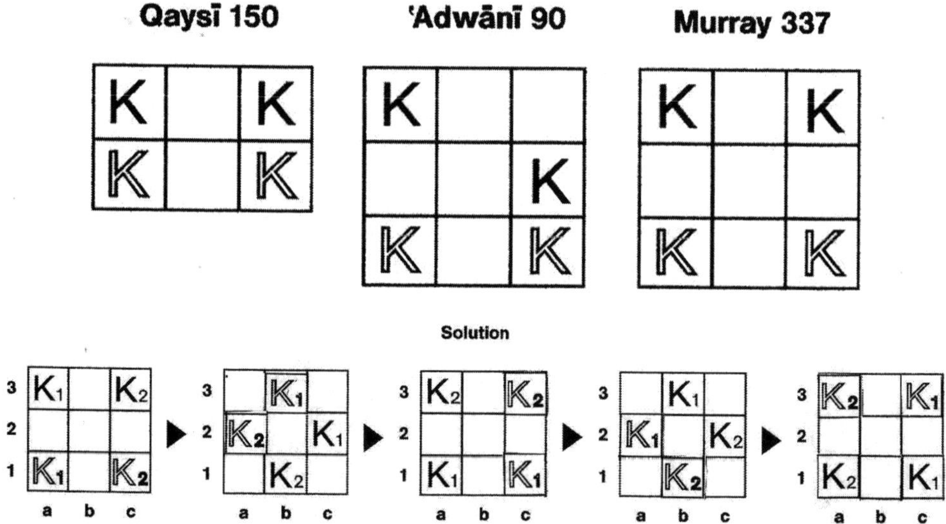

It was not unusual to hide the key to the solution of a *miḫrāq* in a poem. Murray gives the example of a poem by Ṭāhir al-Baṣrī.[59] Ibn Abī Ḥaǧalah also used this means, hiding the solution of one of the problems in verses from his ode to Sultan al-Malik an-Nāṣir Ḥasan.[60] Infuriatingly enough there is no diagram for this particular problem in the extant texts, let alone two diagrams, as the text suggests, and the problem is not easy to understand without them.

---

[57] Murray, *A History of Chess*, pp. 337-38; Wieber, *Das Schachspiel*, pp. 479-82.

[58] *Unmūḏaǧ*, ed. al-ʿAdwāni, p. 90; *Unmūḏaǧ*, ed. al-Qaysi, p.150. The latter presents the problem in such a way that it cannot be solved, namely on a board of two by three squares. For the solution in abbreviated form see Murray, *A History of Chess*, p. 337; Wieber, *Das Schachspiel*, p. 481.

[59] Murray, *A History of Chess*, p. 337, n. 337; Wieber, *Das Schachspiel*, p. 49.

[60] *Unmūḏaǧ*, ed. al-ʿAdwāni, pp. 91-92.

The text runs as follows:

"There is another of those problems. The way you go about this problem is that you take the chessmen and put them on the half of the board that is closest to you. Then you take them all with the knight that is on the square of the rook. The way to do this is to follow the numbers drawn on those squares, starting with the knight from the right square of the rook. If you also want to take with the knight everything that is on the whole board, you must also follow the words of these verses that I will draw (*arsumuhā*) for you on this following problem (*fī hāḏā al-miḫrāq al-ātī*)". Could this mean "in this following problem", "problem" meaning a problem represented in a diagram?

How the poem might be used to solve the *miḫrāq* also baffled me. I appealed for help to Professor Geert Jan van Gelder (Oxford), a poetry specialist as well as a chess enthusiast, who indeed came up with useful ideas. He noted that the verses cited contained a total of 64 words, a fact that can hardly be meaningless in this context. He suggested that Ibn Abī Ḥaǧalah's words imply that he wrote the 64 words of the poem on the squares of a chessboard diagram in such a way that the problem could be solved by following the word order of the verses which he subsequently mentions. Since the diagram is missing, this is of no great help to us.

Prof. van Gelder also translated the verses, suggesting several emendations to the text of the edition. Here follow his provisional translation and comments:

> The figure of the one I love is like a pliant spear,
>> sweet when he sways like a willow twig.
> I shackled my heart in love to his cheek down
>> when it appeared like chains of sweet basil,
> If a critic [reading *ʿaḏūl*, not *ʿuḏūl*] should blame me, ignorantly,
>> I would complain about him to al-Nāṣir, the Sultan,
> A King whose Bishop's assault is feared by the Rook:
>> he has never seen such great might.
> [interpreting *lammā yarā* as a poetic variant for *lammā yara*]
> If he sets in ranks, like noble steeds, (his) pawns
>> they reach every lofty position.
> Kings submit in awe of him, for
>> his vizier/Queen is made of the same stuff ...(?)
>> [The meaning of *min nafsi ʿ.ẓmi l-ʿānī* is unclear to me. *ʿAẓīm*, in the edition, is unmetrical. Al-Qaysī's edition (1980: 152) has *ʿaẓm*. *ʿĀnī* is 'humble' or 'captive', but I do not see how this fits here.]
> The earth said, 'My board /patch is well-protected
>> now that the sheep grazes freely on me with the wolf.'
>> [reading *aš-šātu* instead of *aš-šāhu*, as in al-Qaysī's edition]

The section on *maḫārīq* in this chapter concludes with a series of amusing anecdotes and riddles involving arithmetic exercises, sometimes illustrated with chess pieces. Verses frequently offer the key to the solution. Several of the puzzles present Muslims, Christians and the occasional Jew. One such anecdote, taken from aṣ-Ṣafadī's *Al-Ġayt al-musaǧǧam*[61] became fairly well known in Europe through its inclusion in Thomas Hyde's *Mandragorias seu Historia Shahiludii*, the earliest scholarly study on the history of chess.[62] The problem is how to arrange thirty passengers, 15 Christians and 15 Muslims, on a ship in such a way that if in an emergency every ninth passenger has to be thrown overboard, only Muslims remain. Chess pieces can be used to demonstrate the problem. Aṣ-Ṣafadī's text contains a circle diagram to explain the solution. The diagram is announced in the text of the *Unmūḏaǧ*, but not included in ʿAdwānī's edition,[63] as opposed to that of al-Qaysī.[64] Ibn Abī Ḥaǧalah adds two variants of this puzzle, plus a number of other riddles to be solved by arithmetic or with the key offered by the verses.

The emphasis in this chapter clearly lies on providing amusement to the reader. None of the older chess manuals offers similar material on the scale of the *Unmūḏaǧ*.

Chapter 7 starts with extensive praise of aṣ-Ṣūlī. It describes his wide erudition, his excellent relations with a series of successive caliphs (*addaba ar-Rāḍī, ṯumma taʾaddaba wa-nādama al-Muktafī, wa-nādama al-Muqtadir*), his many famous writings on a wide variety of subjects, and how he became proverbial as a chess player. One cannot fail to notice that the points highlighted here may also apply to Ibn Abī Ḥaǧalah himself, and may have been included specifically for that reason. Among the earlier authors quoted are Ibn Ḥallikān, who included a biography of aṣ-Ṣūlī in his *Wafāyāt al-aʿyān*.[65] Al-Masʿūdī's *Murūǧ aḏ-ḏahab* is also quoted with several anecdotes about aṣ-Ṣūlī and other chess players.

Several other anecdotes about chess players are provided. In one of these, chess puns are made about a man called Baydaq (soldier, the name used for the pawn in chess)[66] and a story about a *ṭufaylī* (gate-crasher) whose various capacities are tested. Another deals with people being beaten with chess pieces. Finally, there is an explicitly pointless story.

Some of the anecdotes concern contemporary chess players. One of these stories, according to Ibn Abī Ḥaǧalah as told to him by aṣ-Ṣafadī, is about an exceptionally good, blind chess player (a man who was really blind, not a player of

---

[61] aṣ-Ṣafadī, *Al-Ġayt al-musaǧǧam*, 2:54-55.

[62] Hyde, Thomas, *Mandragorias seu Historia Šahiludii*, Oxford 1694, II, p. 23.

[63] *Unmūḏaǧ*, ed. al-ʿAdwānī, p. 95.

[64] *Unmūḏaǧ*, ed. al-Qaysī, p. 156.

[65] Ibn Ḥallikān, *Wafāyāt al-aʿyān*, 4:356-60.

[66] Murray, *A History of Chess*, p. 183 n. 13 especially refers to this part of the *Unmūḏaǧ* for references to chess in poetry. Favourite themes are the strength of the rook in attack and the promotion of the pawn.

blind chess), whom aṣ-Ṣafadī knew in Egypt. This chess player sat with them, talking, reciting poetry and telling stories, then briefly went outside and when he returned he had missed nothing of what had gone on in the meantime. This story is an obvious case of fictitious orality: the story is actually taken from the chess section of aṣ-Ṣafadī's *al-Ġayṯ al-musaǧǧam fī šarḥ Lāmiyyat al-ʿaǧam*, cited above.

As in the previous chapter, the emphasis in this chapter clearly lies on providing amusing reading of a kind that is not found in the older chess manuals.

8. Chapter 8 contains chess poems, four by Ibn Abī Ḥaǧalah himself (these are not the only poems of his in the *Unmūḏaǧ*) and six by other poets (al-Qāḍi al-Fāḍil; al-Qāḍi Abū l-Faḍl at-Tamīmī; Ibn Qalāqis; Ibn al-Habbāriyyah; Ibn Šaraf al-Qayrawānī; Nāṣiraddīn Ibn an-Naqīb).[67] Again, this is a chapter which provides elegant and amusing reading for literates, material of the kind that is not, or only very sparingly, included in the older chess manuals.

The book ends with a *ḫātimah* consisting of a *maqāmah* about chess, dedicated to al-Malik aṣ-Ṣāliḥ Ṣāliḥ, the governor of Mardin. Its protagonist is called Abū r-Riyāš. The *maqāmah* also contains a number of verses. James Robson has devoted an article to this, in which he also provides a translation.[68]

Summarizing, we see that chapters 6, 7, 8 and the *ḫātima*, and partly also chapter 3 of the *Unmūḏaǧ*, consist exclusively of *adab* material – material with a chess angle, but intended to amuse rather than to instruct. A further point of note is that in chapter 3 Ibn Abī Ḥaǧalah illustrates aṣ-Ṣūlī's account of tactics with examples from history, possibly chosen specifically to appeal to the rulers whose courts he frequented. It all contributes to what is clearly the nature of the *Unmūḏaǧ*: rather than being a chess manual, it is a courtier's book on chess. In the following we will see whether the extensive amount of chess material that it contains confirms this picture.

The chess problems

Next to all the chess material of general interest and amusement and the long quotation from aṣ-Ṣūlī's lost work on chess in Chapter 3, the *Unmūḏaǧ* contains a large number of chess problems. As I mentioned above, each of the eight chapters concludes with five problems: the first is an opening game; the second a game where red wins; the third a game where black wins; the fourth is a "light" (*ḫafīfah*) draw; the fifth an undisputable draw (*qāʾima lā ġayr* or *bilā ḫilāf*). In addition to this, the *maqāmah* serving as *ḫātimah* contains two opening games pre-

---

[67] On chess poets, see Wieber, *Das Schachspiel*, pp. 122-37.

[68] Robson, James, "A Chess *Maqāma* in the John Rylands Library", in: *Bulletin of the John Rylands Library* 53 (1953-54), pp. 111-127.

sented in one diagram, the one of the *muġannaḥ* ("winged") type and the other of the *sayyāl* ("torrential") type.[69] The *ḫātimah* contains many puns on birds and feathers, starting with the name of its protagonist, Abū r-Riyāš (Father of the Feathers). The choice of a *muġannaḥ* opening fits well with this.

The chess problems in the *Unmūḏaǧ* are illustrated by diagrams, showing both parties in ʿAdwānī's edition, based on the Manchester MS, and only one party in al-Qaysī's edition, based on a Baghdad MS possibly related to the British Library MS of the *Unmūḏaǧ*, which also shows only one party in the diagrams. The diagrams, even when they show both parties, are not as easy to interpret as it may seem: in the case of the openings, the situation given in the diagram shows the end position of the opening game, to be memorized by players. There is no explanation about the way this position is reached. This differs in the end games where all the moves are usually described in the adjoining text, starting from the position given in the diagram. It takes some effort to grasp the terminology, but the lists given by Murray[70] and especially Wieber, who provides a full vocabulary of chess terms with source references based on an extensive number of Arabic texts and European publications,[71] are most helpful.

For an evaluation of the importance of this material to modern chess historians I rely on the works of Murray and Wieber, already frequently cited. While their works contains a wide range of information on chess, their main interest of course lies with the chess problems and what they have to offer in the way of new information about the game. The crucial question in this respect is whether the *Unmūḏaǧ* contains chess material not known from other sources. Murray's pioneering research gives us a clear idea about this.

Since not everybody may be familiar with Murray's monumental *A History of Chess*, it might be useful to explain what he did and how his research brings this particular aspect of the *Unmūḏaǧ* into focus. His book is a worldwide history of chess in historical perspective, covering all relevant cultures, including the Islamic world. In order to understand medieval *šaṭranǧ*, he studied all the Arabic, Persian and Ottoman chess MSS (no editions existed at the time) available to him. This situation, incidentally, had not significantly changed by 1972, when Wieber wrote his book.

One of the things Murray did was to make an inventory of the *manṣūbāt*, in this case meaning endgames, treated in these texts. They roughly amounted to

---

[69] *Unmūḏaǧ*, ed. al-ʿAdwānī, p. 133. The Manchester MS used for the edition does not usually present two problems in one diagram. See Murray, *A History of Chess*, p. 235 for the way in which openings are described and noted in the MSS. "In Man., however, the different developments are given on half-boards (n. 4: with the single exception of the muġannaḥ and sayyāl, f85a [of the Manchester MS; this is the diagram referred to], given on one board as in the older MSS". The diagram is not included in al-Qaysī's edition, whose text presents a number of variations in the text of the *maqāmah*.

[70] Murray, *A History of Chess*, pp. 224-29.

[71] Wieber, *Das Schachspiel*, pp. 270-344.

1,600. Eliminating the doubles, he ended up with a list of 553. "The labour of collation has been no light one", as he remarks.[72] This is a massive understatement. He then proceeded to describe and analyse the 553 *manṣūbāt*, including diagrams to explain the games.[73]

Murray's list demonstrates how much, or rather how little, of the chess material in the *Unmūḏaǧ* is not known from other sources. This was already clear with the opening games, which could be traced back to al-ʿAdlī and aṣ-Ṣūlī. As for the endgames: only eight of the 553 endgames which Murray collected come from the 33 found in the *Unmūḏaǧ*.[74] To compare: almost a hundred come from a single other source, an anonymous Persian chess manual. The question of course arises of whether there are any indications that these eight problems were an original contribution by Ibn Abī Ḥaǧalah, but there is nothing to confirm this. The only instance in which Ibn Abī Ḥaǧalah possibly expresses his personal view in a discussion of the game is in problem 24 (Murray's and Wieber's numbering)[75] where the text runs as follows: "Aṣ-Ṣūlī said: This is a draw, and there is no *tarǧama* ('explanatory comment'). I said: It is obvious how you reach a draw, and the picture is as you see". Most likely the "I" in this case is Ibn Abī Ḥaǧalah. In the comment[76] on one of the opening games, however, where at first sight it may also seem that Ibn Abī Ḥaǧalah is providing his own view, the "I" is actually aṣ-Ṣūlī.[77]

What else is there in Ibn Abī Ḥaǧalah's chess material that is of interest for the development of the game in the Islamic world? In Murray's view, an important new aspect is the way in which openings (*taʿbiyāt*, of which there are a number of varieties) are dealt with, particularly in the diagrams: in the Manchester MS of the *Unmūḏaǧ*, which contains ten openings, the chess problems are put on half-boards, thus eliminating much of the confusion found in older MSS which put two games on one full board. Murray deals extensively with the openings in Chapter XIV of his book, analyzing the sixteen oldest opening games that he managed to collect by careful collation of MSS and putting them into diagrams. For this, he says, he relied mainly on the *Unmūḏaǧ*. He specifically points out the importance of the ten *taʿbiyāt* which it contains. As Ibn Abī Ḥaǧalah's frequent references show, these are based on the work of aṣ-Ṣūlī.[78]

Another important aspect of the chess problems in the *Unmūḏaǧ* pointed out by Murray is that the endgames are phrased conditionally, saying that mate has

---

72 Murray, *A History of Chess*, p. 270.
73 Murray, *A History of Chess*, pp. 270-335.
74 Murray, *A History of Chess*, p. 280; 327, VII. In *Unmūḏaǧ*, ed. al-ʿAdwānī these eight are found on the following pages: no. 408, p. 37; 409, p. 46; 410, p. 62 (2); 411, p. 63; 412, p. 64; 413, p. 116; 414, p. 123 (2); 415, p. 126.
75 *Unmūḏaǧ*, ed. al-ʿAdwānī, p. 85.
76 *Unmūḏaǧ*, ed. al-ʿAdwānī, p. 69.
77 The text of this passage is corrupt in both editions, but that of al-Qaysī (p. 119) makes the issue clear.
78 Murray, *A History of Chess*, pp. 235-38.

to be reached in a specified number of moves, neither more nor less. This is one of the later developments, with the first instance dating from 1257.[79]

To conclude, we will discuss a chess problem from the *Unmūḏaǧ* that serves well to demonstrate various difficulties encountered in the study of Arabic chess texts, and especially the *Unmūḏaǧ*.[80] The problem in question is how to reach a draw with two bishops against a rook and a pawn. As it is presented in the Manchester MS and in both editions, the problem is incomprehensible. Murray corrected it on the basis of its occurrence in another text.[81]

The following story is attached by Ibn Abī Ḥaǧalah to this problem:

"Five. A problem ending in an undisputable draw. This problem is very strange. Our friend [reading *ṣāḥibunā* instead of *ṣāḥibuhā*] Šihābaddīn Aḥmad al-Mutarǧim told it to me as follows: 'When Niẓām al-ʿAǧamī[82] came to Damascus, he claimed that he could reach a *māniʿ*-draw (see note 7) with two bishops against a rook and a pawn. We asked him about it and he said: "I am not going to play or sketch it unless you give me two hundred dirhams.' Nāṣiraddīn told this straightaway to aṣ-Ṣāḥib Šamsaddīn, who ordered to bring the amount and gave him two hundred dirhams. He [i.e. Niẓām al-ʿAǧamī] then played it and reached a *māniʿ*-draw [reading *manaʿahā* instead of *minhā*] in the manner of the grandmasters [*manʿ al-ʿawāl*; the meaning is not certain. See also the discussion about the meaning of the title at the beginning of this article]. When I told this in Egypt to Badraddīn ibn aṣ-Ṣāḥib he was very surprised and said: 'This is impossible!' When I drew it for him, he found it very beautiful and memorized it. The party who chooses to do so makes the first move".[83]

Several difficulties are illustrated by this story. First, there are the problems with the transmission of diagrams, already referred to earlier. In this case, too, the diagrams in the editions which are based on different MSS and differ from each other do not properly illustrate the problem. The diagram in the edition by al-Qaysī only gives the red (=white) party, while the diagram in ʿAdwānī's edition shows two rooks and is placed with the wrong problem.[84] Here follow the diagrams as they appear in the editions and in Murray's corrected version.[85] For easier understanding I have adapted all diagrams to Murray's notation. K=king; B=bishop; R=rook; P=pawn.

---

[79] Murray, *A History of Chess*, p. 277.

[80] *Unmūḏaǧ*, ed. al-ʿAdwānī, pp. 38-39.

[81] Murray, *A History of Chess*, p. 299, diagram no. 339; "Problems from AE", solution given on p. 324.

[82] A famous Persian chess player. Wieber, *Das Schachspiel*, p. 82: aṣ-Ṣafadī frequently saw him in Damascus in 731/1229.

[83] Murray's rendering of what Ibn Abī Ḥaǧalah says about the problem (*A History of Chess*, p. 324) suggests that Niẓām had won money with this game, but this is not quite correct.

[84] *Unmūḏaǧ*, ed. al-Qaysī, p. 74; *Unmūḏaǧ*, ed. al-ʿAdwānī, p. 38.

[85] Murray, *A History of Chess*, p. 299, no. 339.

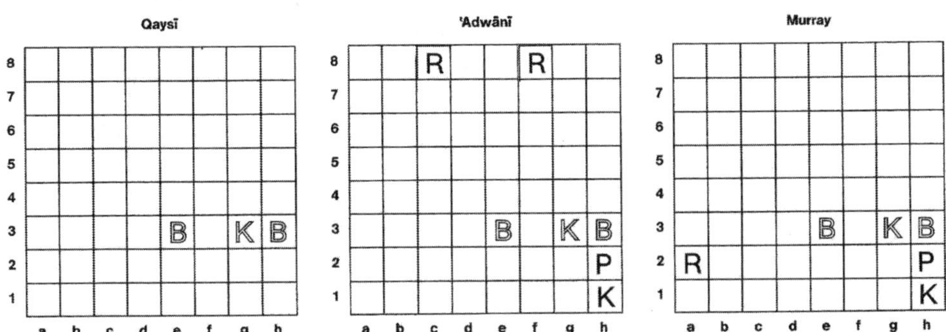

Solution of the problem in Murray[86]: Red (=white) begins.1 Kf3, Ra7; 2 Kg3, Rg7+; 3 Kf2, Rf7+; 4 Kg3, Rf8; 5 Bc5, Kg1; 6 Be3+, Kh1. Drawn.

Murray's solution, however, leaves us with several problems. First, there is the fact that it is quite straightforward, and it is hard to see why it should have been so surprising to the people in the story. Then there is the point that the solution given does not result in a *māniᶜ*- type of draw, in which the king is left with one other piece, but in a different kind of draw altogether. This leaves us puzzled. Was the meaning of *māniᶜ* possibly more general than modern chess historians suggest? Was the *manᶜ al-ᶜawāl* perhaps a special kind of draw? Or was the solution, and maybe even the setup, of Niẓām's game different from what the sources assume? We do not know. In any case, Ibn Abī Ḥaǧalah seems content with reproducing the amusing story without bothering himself about the solution and its puzzling aspects.

Concluding remarks

While, as Murray and Wieber say, the *Unmūḏaǧ* has valuable information to offer chess historians, it is also clear that it is not primarily a chess manual. There is no explanation of the rules, and discussions about the game itself do not have the central position that they have in the manuals mentioned above. It is clear from the beginning what Ibn Abī Ḥaǧalah had in mind. He states that he will not devote whole chapters to chess problems, but include just five with each chapter so as not to make it too boring. Then he sets forth to talk about chess, providing amusing anecdotes and sayings chosen more for their wittiness and verbal elegance than for their information on chess itself. A substantial number of poems about chess is included. Extensive attention is paid to amusing puzzles which use chessboards and chessmen, but otherwise have no relation to the game. In several cases Ibn Abī Ḥaǧalah does not bother to give the solutions. The same applies to a number of the actual chess problems. He concludes with a witty and elegant *maqāmah*. All this demonstrates the nature of the *Unmūḏaǧ*: it deals with chess, but it is a book

---

86 Murray, *A History of Chess*, p. 324, no. 339.

intended to amuse the cultured circles in which Ibn Abī Ḥaǧalah moved rather than to offer new views on the game. It is a courtier's chess book.

Bibliography

Bland, Nathaniel, "Persian Chess", in: *Journal of the Royal Asiatic Society* 13 (1852), pp. 1-70.

Gruendler, Beatrice, "Ibn Abī Ḥajalah (1325-1375)", in: Lowry, Joseph E. and Devin J. Stewart (eds.), *Essays in Arabic Literary Biography 1350-1850*, Wiesbaden 2009, pp. 118-126.

Al-Ḥakīm, Abū Zakariyyā Yaḥyā, *Nuzhat arbāb al-ʿuqūl fī š-šaṭranǧ al-manqūl*, ed. Muʿǧib al-ʿAdwānī, Beirut 2012.

Hyde, Thomas, *Mandragorias seu Historia Šahiludii*, Oxford 1694.

Ibn Abī Ḥaǧalah, *Unmūḏaǧ al-qitāl fī naql al-ʿawāl*, ed. Zuhayr Aḥmad al-Qaysī, Baghdad 1401/1980.

Ibn Abī Ḥaǧalah, *Unmūḏaǧ al-qitāl fī naql al- ʿawāl*, ed. Muʿǧib al-ʿAdwānī, Beirut 2012.

Ibn Ḥazm, *Tawq al-ḥamāmah*, . ed. D. K. Pétrof, St. Petersburg-Leiden 1914.

Ibn Ḥallikān, *Wafāyāt al-aʿyān*, 8 vols., ed. Iḥsān ʿAbbās, Beirut 1977-78.

Murray, Harold James Ruthven, *A History of Chess*. Reprint of the classic Oxford edition of Oxford University Press, 1913. Northampton, Massachusets: Benjamin Press. N.d.

Niebuhr, Carsten, *Beschryving van Arabie*, vol. I, Amsterdam 1776.

Robson, James, "A Chess *Maqāma* in the John Rylands Library", in: *Bulletin of the John Rylands Library* 53 (1953-54), pp. 111-127.

Rosenthal, F., "Shaṭrandj", in: *Encyclopaedia of Islam*, New edition, vol. IX, Leiden 1997, pp. 366-8.

Aṣ-Ṣafadī, *al-Ġayt al-musaǧǧam fī šarḥ Lāmiyyat al-ʿaǧam*, 2 vols., Cairo 1305/1888.

Scheper, Karin, *The Technique of Islamic Bookbinding*, Leiden 2014.

Sezgin, Fuat (ed.), *Kitāb aš-šaṭranǧ mimmā allafahu l-ʿAdlī wa-ṣ-Ṣūlī wa-ġayruhumā* (Book on Chess: Kitāb aš-Šaṭranǧ. Seleted (sic) texts from al-ʿAdlī, Abū Bakr aṣ-Ṣūlī and others), Frankfurt a.M. 1986.

de Somogyi, Joseph, "The Arabic chess manuscripts in the John Rylands Library", in: *Bulletin of the John Rylands Library* 41 (1959), pp. 430-45.

Wieber, Reinhard, *Das Schachspiel in der arabischen Literatur von den Anfängen bis zur zweiten Hälfte des 16. Jahrhunderts*, Walldorf-Hessen 1972.

Az-Zabidī, *Tāǧ al-ʿarūs*, 15 vols., ed. ʿAli Širī, Beirut 1994.

A *Maqāmah* on the Book Market of Cairo in the 8th/14th Century: The "Return of the Stranger" of Ibn Abī Ḥaǧalah (d. 776/1375)[1]

Maurice A. Pomerantz

1. The Maqāmah *in the Mamluk Period: Between Elite and Popular Form*

For historians of Arabic literature and culture the Mamluk period is of particular interest for the apparent expansion in both the volume of texts and the number of readers. It consequently witnessed a widening of the reading public as tradesmen and craftspeople participated in scholarly and literary gatherings. Moreover, readers publicly performed *sīrah* literature from written texts such as the *Sīrat Banī Hilāl* and *Sīrat ʿAntar b. Šaddād* in markets and street-corner locales. As Konrad Hirschler has noted, the Mamluk period marked an important moment of change in reading culture, identifying changes to "the nature of the texts read out", "the setting where the reading took place", and the "social composition of the group of readers".[2]

Long the guardians of the transmission of written knowledge, *ʿulamāʾ* looked upon the profusion of new circles of readers and texts with anxiety. Ibn Taymiyyah (d. 728/1328) issued a *fatwā* in which he criticized the falsehoods of *Sīrat ʿAntar*, while the fourteenth-century jurist, Ibn al-Ḥaǧǧ (d. 737/1336) urged merchants not to trade with those transmitting popular epics.[3] For scholars of the eighth/fourteenth century the reading of popular epics was a source of moral and religious corruption. How could the spread of these texts and their heterodox contents be curtailed?

Scholars, however, were not a uniform group, and many were not immune from the charms of popular literature and freely borrowed from its rich stock of characters and subjects. The boundaries between elite and popular literature were porous in ways that often defy modern scholars' attempts to classify them.[4] Mamluk-era

---

1 This article has been greatly improved by the numerous corrections and additions made to the translation and edition by Nefeli Papoutsakis as well as by Thomas Bauer. I am extremely grateful for their assistance. Similarly, I wish to thank Bilal Orfali who encouraged me with this edition at an earlier stage.

2 Hirschler, Konrad, *The Written Word in the Medieval Arabic Lands: A Social and Cultural History of Reading Practices*, Edinburgh 2011, p. 164.

3 *Ibid*, p. 169.

4 Heath, Peter, *The Thirsty Sword:* Sirat ʿAntar *and the Arabic Popular Epic*, Salt Lake City 1996, pp. xvi-xvii.

authors surely fashioned their works to meet the demands of new literary audiences. The emergence of new reading communities doubtless had an effect on the literary production of elites.

The genre of *maqāmah* offers a particularly interesting viewpoint from which to consider these changes in literary culture during the Mamluk period. Although scholars often associate the *maqāmah* only with the "Classical" models of genre represented by al-Hamadānī (d. 398/1008) and al-Ḥarīrī (d. 516/1122), the *maqāmah* was an extremely vibrant literary form during the Mamluk period. More than one-third of the *maqāmāt* works recorded by Jaakko Hämeen-Anttila are from the period 7th-9th/13th-15th centuries.[5] Moreover, there was a great interest in the genre during the Mamluk period, more than half of the poets and *udabā'* identified by Thomas Bauer composed *maqāmāt*.[6]

The *maqāmāt* of the Mamluk period reflect the complexities of the literary culture mentioned above. In previous work, I discussed the fourteenth-century administrator and poe, Ibn ar-Rayyān (d. 770/1369), who composed a *maqāmah* that included characters drawn from the *Sīrat ʿAntar*.[7] Similarly, al-Ḥasan b. Abī Muḥammad aṣ-Ṣafadī al-Barīdī (fl. 1st quarter of the 7th/14th c. C.E.) explored topics of popular literature such as dream interpretation, vernacular poetry, and tales drawn from folklore in a series of thirty *maqāmāt*.[8] In the hands of the *literati* of seventh/fourteenth century, the *maqāmah* form was a malleable substance which authors crafted to meet their audience's changing expectations.

In this article, I consider the *Maqāmah kutubiyyah* of Ibn Abī Ḥaǧalah, which discusses the book market of 7th/14th-century Cairo. I argue that Ibn Abī Ḥaǧalah's *maqāmah*, in its portrayal of the decline and subsequent restoration of the book market provides evidence for elite reactions to the rise of popular literary forms and their circulation in the book market of Cairo. I also claim that Ibn Abī Ḥaǧalah's *maqāmah* mobilizes fears about popular literature in order to denigrate the beliefs of the author's ideological opponents. Ibn Abī Ḥaǧalah's learned allusions to elite literary works in this *maqāmah* assures his status as a belletrist and scholar, while at the same time, the characters of the narrator and the trickster provide him with two masks that allow him to address the conflicts and complexities of the literary culture of his time.

---

[5] Hämeen-Anttila, Jaakko, *Maqama: A History of a Genre*, Wiesbaden 2002, p. 368 and following.

[6] Bauer, Thomas, "Mamluk Literature: Misunderstandings and New Approaches", in: *Mamlūk Studies Review* 9 (2005), pp. 131-132.

[7] Pomerantz, Maurice A., "An Epic Hero in the *Maqāmāt*? Popular and Elite Literature in the 8th/14th Century", in: *Annales Islamologiques* 49 (2016), pp. 1-16.

[8] Pomerantz, Maurice A., "A *Maqāma* Collection by a *Mamlūk* Historian: *Al-Maqāmāt Al-Ǧalāliyya by Al-Ḥasan b. Abī Muḥammad Al-Ṣafadī* (fl. First Quarter of the 8th/14th c.)", in: *Arabica* 61 (2014), pp. 631–663; *idem*, "The Play of Genres: A *Maqāma* of 'Ease After Hardship' from the 8th/14th Century and Its Literary Context", in: Pomerantz, Maurice A. and Aram Shahin (eds.), *The Heritage of Arabo-Islamic Learning: Studies in Honor of Wadad Kadi*, Leiden 2016, pp. 461-482.

2. Ibn Abī Ḥaǧalah and the Maqāmah *Form*

Ibn Abī Ḥaǧalah was an important belletrist (*adīb*) who was close to the circles of power. A poet, anthologist, and prose writer, he traversed across the wide range of possible genres available to the belletrist during the 7th/14th century. Ibn Abī Ḥaǧalah's *maqāmah*s demonstrating innovations in form and content are surely no exception to the author's inventiveness. The largest extant collection of his *maqāmāt* is found in his work of auto-anthology, the *Manṭiq aṭ-ṭayr*.[9]

Ibn Abī Ḥaǧalah refers to his *maqāmāt* as ten feathers (*rīš*) in the *Manṭiq aṭ-ṭayr*. There seems to be some indication that he had gathered these *maqāmāt* together in some form prior to their inclusion. He introduces the ten *maqāmāt* thusly,

> These are "The feathers" which I atrributed in my *māqāmāt* to Abū r-Riyāš the trickster (*ṣāḥib kayd*) who stands in for Abū Zayd [as-Sarūǧi]. And as-Sāǧiʿ b. Ḥamām who stands in the place of al-Ḥāriṯ b. Hammmām.[10]

Ibn Abī Ḥaǧalah states that he had spent much time reading the *Maqāmāt* of al-Ḥarīrī, and had discussed them in the presence of Sultan Ḥasan. The Sultan had commanded Ibn Abī Ḥaǧalah to write a similar work to the *Maqāmāt* of al-Ḥarīrī knowing that only one skilled in the weaving of words could work upon the same loom as that master. Ibn Abī Ḥaǧalah states that he wrote some of these texts during Sultan Ḥasan's life, and then gathered them together at the request of a certain "Badr at-Tammām",[11] following the Sultan's death.

Table 1: A List of Maqāmāt of Ibn Abī Ḥaǧalah in the Kitāb Manṭiq aṭ-ṭayr

References are to MS Berlin Wetzstein 1803 and MS Rabat 1901.

1. *al-Maqāmah ar-rafiʿah fī mawlid ḫayr al-bariyyah* (excerpt). This *maqāmah* is written in praise of the Prophet's birth. MS Berlin Wetzstein 103r-103v; MS Rabat 73r-73v.
2. *al-Maqāmah al-ǧiziyyah* (excerpt). MS Berlin Wetzstein 104r-104v; MS Rabat 73v-74r.
3. *al-Maqāmah al-qāhiriyyah* (excerpt). MS Berlin Wetzstein 104v-105r; MS Rabat 74v-75r.

---

[9] I had available to me three manuscripts of the *Manṭiq aṭ-ṭayr* during the writing of this article: Berlin Wetzstein MS I 1803, Wetzstein II 221 and Rabat MS 1901. I would like to thank Aḥmad Mašhadānī for generously sharing pages from his preliminary edition of this work based on the Rabat MS. I am extremely grateful to Dr. Paul Heck of Georgetown University for introducing me to Dr. Mašhadānī. I would also like to thank Th. Emil Homerin for obtaining a copy of the Rabat MS, and graciously sending me copies of this work.

[10] MS Berlin Wetzstein 1803, 102v.; MS Rabat 73r.

[11] I have not been able to identify this individual.

4. *al-Maqāmah al-mārdāniyyah* (excerpt). A *maqāmah* on chess. MS Berlin Wetzstein 105r-106r; MS Rabat 75r-76r.[12]

5. *al-Maqāmah az-zurzūriyyah*. MS Berlin Wetzstein 106r–106v; MS Rabat 76r–76v.

6. *Maqāmat al-ḫaymah*. MS Berlin Wetzstein 106v–107v; MS Rabat 76v-78r.

7. *al-Maqāmah al-ḥarāmiyyah fī ziyādat an-nīl*. MS Berlin Wetzstein 107v-109r; MS Rabat 78r-79v.

8. *al-Maqāmah al-mawsūmah bi-l-wāqiʿat al-wāqiʿah fī l-miʾḏanat as-sulṭaniyyah lammā waqaʿat*. MS Berlin Wetzstein 109r-109v; MS Rabat 79v-80r.

9. *al-Maqāmah al-kutubiyyah al-mawsūmah bi-ʿawd al-ġarīb*. MS Berlin Wetzstein 109v-112r; MS Rabat 80r-82v.

10. *al-Maqāmah az-zaʿfarāniyyah*. MS Berlin Wetzstein 112r-114v; MS Rabat 83r–85v.

11. *Maqāmat al-ġirbān*. MS Berlin Wetzstein 124v-125r; MS Rabat 105v-106.

3. *The* Maqāmah Kutubiyyah *or "Return of the Stranger"*

The subject of this article, the *Maqāmah kutubiyyah* (herein referred to as *MK*) is one of the more elaborate of Ibn Abī Ḥaǧalah's *maqāmah*s. He likely composed it in the years following the death of Sultan Ḥasan in 761/1361.[13] Judging from the titles of his own works that he mentions in the *MK*, he seems to have composed this *maqāmah* in 762/1362-3.[14]

Like many authors of *maqāmah*s, Ibn Abī Ḥaǧalah invents the names of his protagonists to signal his indebtedness to al-Ḥarīrī. Ibn Abī Ḥaǧalah also uses the names to signal his own authorial persona. Punning on his avian family connection, he names his narrator, al-Sāǧiʿ b. Hamām, "Cooer son of the Dove". To his trickster figure, he gives the name, Abū r-Riyāš, "the one having many feathers" perhaps evoking thereby the variability of the trickster.[15] These two characters of the *maqāmah* provide the author with two authorial "masks" through which he can address the complexities of the literary market of his time. The *maqāmah* is divided into three main sections. Sections one and two feature the two protagonists: as-Sāǧiʿ b. Hamām and Abū r-Riyāš, while the third section provides a conclusion.

---

[12] See Robson, James, "A Chess *Māqama* in the John Rylands Library", in: *Bulletin of the John Rylands Library* 36 (1953), pp. 111-127.

[13] See Homerin, pp. 22-23 of his contribution to this volume.

[14] Ibn Abī Ḥaǧalah cites his own *Dīwān aṣ-ṣabābah* of 759/1359 in the *MK*, but not his later *Salwat al-ḥazīn* of 766/1366. Moreover, the last contemporary work of any author he cites is the *Kunāsat ad-Dukkān* of Lisānaddīn Ibn al-Ḫaṭīb (d. 775/1375), see Robinson, Cynthia, "Lisān al-Dīn Ibn al-Khaṭīb (1313-1374 or 1375)", in: Lowry, Joseph E., and Devin J. Stewart (eds.), *Essays in Arabic Literary Biography: 1350-1850*, Wiesbaden 2009, pp. 159-174.

[15] Since Ibn Abī Ḥaǧalah terms each of his *maqāmah*s "feathers" (*rīš*) the title may also reference the author's multiple works.

The Structure of the MK

In the first section of the *MK* (ll. 1-54), the narrator, as-Sāǧiʿ b. Hamām recounts the demise and restoration of the book market. The narrator begins by playing upon the meanings of the titles of books, a device that will persist through the remainder of the *maqāmah*. This section of the *maqāmah* begins with lamentation for the fate of the book market of Cairo evoking the conventional scene of a poet's "mourning by the ruins of the abandoned campsite" (*al-wuqūf ʿalā l-aṭlāl*). The section concludes, however, with a glorious celebration and marriage of the books.

The second section (ll. 54-85) of the *MK* comes with the arrival of Abū r-Riyāš. He warns the audience in the book market, to beware of certain genres and titles of works. The list of these prohibited books is quite diverse: *ars erotica* (*kutub al-bāh*), magic (*siḥr*), astrological works, and popular *sīrah*s, such as *Sīrat ʿAntar*, and *al-Baṭṭāl*. These works, however, are not Abū r-Riyāš's main target. Rather he is interested in the works of the so-called monist Sufis (*ittiḥādiyyah*) whose members he attacks specifically in ll. 71-83.

In the third and final section of the *MK* (ll. 84-102), Abū r-Riyāš counsels the copyists of the book market to pay greater attention to what they copy and to not propagate errors. Copyists' mistakes (*taṣḥīf*) are equated with errors of doctrine. At the finale of the *maqāmah,* Abū r-Riyāš leaves a copy of his speech concerning the prohibited books with the market inspector (*muḥtasib*), encouraging him thereby to limit the circulation of such illicit materials. The implicit aim of this section is to criticize copyists and booksellers for aiding in the circulation of the falsehood and error in the form of illicit books.

Section 1: as-Sāǧiʿ b. Hamām Mourns and Rejoices in the Book Market of Cairo

Ibn Abī Haǧalah's *MK* opens with a lament of the book market for the loss of works of elite learning. The elegiac mode echoes the opening of a *qaṣīdah* in which the lover laments the departure of the beloved. The titles of books throughout the *maqāmah* have a double signification. For instance, we read in the opening lines,

> The market has given up hope for finding *The Salvation* and is in despair for the loss of *The Healing*, as well as seeking *The Sufficiency of the Intelligent.*[16]

In each phrase the author plays upon the well-known titles of the works of Ibn Sīnā (d. 427/1037), Qāḍī ʿIyāḍ (d. 554/1149) and the Mamluk medical compendium of Ibn al-Akfānī (d. 749/1348). This poetic device of employing technical terms (such as book titles) in their non-technical sense is known as *tawǧīh* and is the fundamental organizing trope of this *maqāmah*.[17]

---

[16] Ibn Abī Haǧalah, *MK*, ll. 1-3.

[17] Bauer, Thomas, "Ambiguität in der klassischen arabischen Rhetoriktheorie", in: Auge, Oliver and Christiane Witthöft (eds.), *Ambiguität im Mittelalter: Formen zeitgenössischer Reflexion und interdisziplinärer Rezeption*, Berlin/Boston 2016, pp. 21-47, esp. 40-44.

A poetic citation from the *Ḥamāsah* of Abū Tammām offers a subtler example of the way that this opening play upon the meaning of books' titles represents the lost physical presence of books in the market. The following lines of the poet Kuthayyir ʿAzzah (d. 105/723), in which he was addressing his beloved named ʿAzzah al-Ḥāǧibiyyah of the Banū al-Ḥāǧib, portray wondering about whether or not the beloved truly loves him:

> I wish – even though wishes do not avail –
> I knew what is in the heart of the *Ḥāǧibiyyah*[18]

The name *Ḥāǧibiyyah* however conceals reference to the famed *al-Kāfiyah al-ḥāǧibiyyah* of the grammarian Ibn al-Ḥāǧib (d. 646/1249). Like a distant lover, a book too can be an object that is lost and knowledge of its contents can be mourned.

In other poetic citations, Ibn Abī Ḥaǧalah employs the device of *taḍmīn* which allows the narrator to embody the words of previous poets. For instance, as-Sāǧiʿ b. Ḥamām intones lines that reference the famed opening (*nasīb*) of the *Muʿallaqah* of Imruʾ al-Qays,

> I walked by the book market and it was no longer functioning,
> so the tears of my eyes soaked my sword belt
> My book said, when I passed by its gate (*bāb*),[19]
> Let us two cry over the mention of the beloved and the abandoned campsite![20]

He then recites a poem in his own voice again from Imruʾ al-Qays:

> Greetings to you, oh barren traces!
> And its once flourishing home, in an empty campsite.
> Who will greet you, but a fortunate man of long life
> whose worries are few and sleeps the night without fear?[21]

Intoning the words of the ancient poem, the narrator fashions himself as the lover of the Arabic literary tradition.[22] Later on, he describes the book market as a place of desolation recalling thereby the desert wastes of the *qaṣīdah* through which the poet-hero must traverse:

> The books were transported to the place of destruction, and the market of dust. The *Eastern Wind* became a "[stubble] which the winds scatter" (Q 18:45). *The Lamp's Glow* and the *Lantern* were both extinguished. May the book market perish! What a Book Market whose books are all worm-eaten, and their meters are all shortened. Oh how many times was the string of its *Necklace* broken! The *Revival* expired in its own leather skin, while the *Luminous Pearl* became the *Orphan of Time*. The *Rubies* shed tears on the

---

[18] Ibn Abī Ḥaǧalah, *MK*, l. 7.

[19] This is also a play on *bāb* as meaning both gate and chapter.

[20] Ibn Abī Ḥaǧalah, *MK*, ll. 13-14

[21] Ibn Abī Ḥaǧalah, *MK*, ll. 15-16.

[22] Perhaps one can understand the subtitle of this *maqāmah* "The Return of the Stranger" (*ʿawd al-ġarīb*) as not only a reference to Abū r-Riyāš's return to Cairo, but also signaling the restoration of the book market.

Rocks like the tears of the poetess al-Ḥansāʾ for her brother Ṣaḫr (lit. the stone). *The Garden* was violated and water washed over the *Walls* and drowned the *Orchard*.[23]

The end of the first section of the *MK* discusses the return of the market to its former glory. The narrator mentions the works of the contemporaries of Ibn Abī Ḥaǧalah, such as Ibn Nubātah (d. 768/1366), Bahāʾaddīn as-Subkī (d. 773/1372), and Ṣalāḥaddīn aṣ-Ṣafadī (d. 764/1363). The prominence of these works in the *MK*, suggests the pivotal role that Ibn Abī Ḥaǧalah believed authors of his generation had played in the restoration of the book market. In the final scenes of this opening section (ll. 50-55) the once desolate marketplace has returned to its former glory. The opening lament has turned into a joyous celebration of marriage,

> The *Marvelous One*, the *Dancer and Singer* all attended, and the *Bride of Happiness* was unveiled, like *Dolls*. From the *Found Pearls*, the *Precious* were strewn. The daughters of thought were conducted to their husbands to the melodies of the *Book of Songs*. Those sweetest of meaning of the sons of elegant expression (/the *badīʿ* style) mated with them. And so none of the noble sons remained who was not glad and did not scatter the *Flecks of Gold* like they were the *Scattering of Pearls*.[24]

The scenes of loss and desolation that opened the *maqāmah* are replaced by a joyful marriage celebration in which works of refined knowledge beget further refined knowledge and the market itself is alive with the energy and excitement of a celebration of marriage.

Section 2: Abū r-Riyāš Enters the Market with a Warning

The section begins with the appearance of, he is described as,

> a *šayḫ* as if he were a partridge hen, and upon him was a mark of the Ḥiǧāz.

This trickster, Abū r-Riyāš imitates in the opening of his speech the language of a popular preacher. He condemns works of *ars erotica* (*kutub al-bāh*) and specifically targets books containing images.[25] The preacher then turns his attention to books of magic (*siḥr*), talismans, astrology and augury.[26]

Abū r-Riyāš then aims at popular literature, he counsels his listeners to,

> Augury is but the *ḥadīṯ* of Ḫurāfah, and the *Sīrat ʿAntar* is made of impossibilities. [Beware of] wasting of your life in the empty exploits of the *Baṭṭāl* and the *Conquest of Syria*, and the *Expeditions of the Prophet*, and the *Weapon of the Believer* and the *Victory of the Rebel* in every place. Beware of the *Seeker of Subjects* and the Alchemy which is not correct, like most natural magic.

---

23 Ibn Abī Ḥaǧalah, *MK*, ll. 17-21. See the translation (Appendix 1) for an explanation of the titles of the particular books, here and elsewhere.
24 Ibn Abī Ḥaǧalah, *MK*, ll. 50-55.
25 This reference to illustrated manuals of *ars erotica* is the first indication that they existed in Arabic.
26 Ibn Abī Ḥaǧalah, *MK*, ll. 60-62.

The trickster's warnings then turn to the explicitly "popular" literature of the Mamlūk period the *Sīrat ʿAntar* and *al-Baṭṭāl*.[27] Abū r-Riyāš then cautions against popular religious works, such as the *Conquest of Syria* (*Futūḥ aš-Šām*), and the *Weapon of the Believer* (*Silāḥ al-muʾmin*) and the *Conquest of the Avenger* (*Nuṣrat aṭ-ṭāʾir*), and the *Seeker of Subjects* (*Ṭālib al-maṭālib*). Although these titles are not readily identifiable, they are similar in form to the popular religious works ascribed to the shadowy figure known as al-Bakrī.[28]

4. Ibn Abī Ḥaǧalah and the Polemics of Literature

The aim of the trickster Abū r-Riyāš is not popular literature. Rather Ibn Abī Ḥaǧalah through using the mask of Abū r-Riyāš targets those persons he terms as the "monists" (*ittiḥādiyyah*). He then associates these monists' works with other texts of ill-repute, superstition, and ignorance that he sees as corrupting the world of books and ideas. Challenging their ideas about Sufism and claiming that they are unscholarly and harmful to the larger population seems to be the central goal of Ibn Abī Ḥaǧala's *MK*.

Abū r-Riyāš's long poem is a vitriolic attack on the key authors and books of the monist Sufis.[29] In this poem, he alludes to the names of: Ibn ʿArabī (638/1240), ʿAbd al-Ḥaqq Ibn Sabʿīn (d. 669/1271), Ṣadraddīn al-Qūnawī (d. 673/1274), Ibn al-Aḥlā (d. 645/1247), Ibn Isrāʾīl (d. 677/1278), ʿAfīfaddīn at-Tilimsānī (d. 690/1291). Abū r-Riyāš also plays upon the titles of these authors' books, such as *The Bezels of Wisdom* and *The Meccan Openings* (*Futūḥāt al-makkiyyah*) of Ibn ʿArabī, *The Encompassing Book* (*Kitāb al-Iḥāṭah*) of Ibn Sabʿīn, and *The Key to the Unknown* (*Miftāḥ al-ġayb*) of Ṣadraddīn al-Qūnawī.

The story of the deviant and dangerous works of the *monists* which Ibn Abī Ḥaǧalah places in the mouth of his trickster Abū r-Riyāš already had a long lineage prior to its use in the *MK*. Rather, as Alexander Knysh has shown, such attacks on monistic Sufism frequently linked Ibn ʿArabī to the monistic Sufis and others. Knysh states that the trend begins at the end of the 7th/13th century with the *faqīh* Quṭbaddīn al-Qasṭallānī (d. 686/1287) and persists and expands in the works of Abū Ḥayyān al-Ġarnāṭī (d. 745/1344).[30] Al-Ġarnāṭī left the Muslim West for Egypt. Moreover he expands his field of blame to al-Ḥallāǧ (d. 309/922), aš-Šūḏī (d. ca.

---

27 Hirschler, *The Written Word*, p. 169 and following.

28 For a list of works ascribed to al-Bakrī see Shoshan, Boaz, *Popular Culture in Medieval Cairo*, Cambridge 1993, pp. 97-99, where several titles are *futūḥ* of various regions. I have not been able to locate the remaining three titles, but they may also relate to works of a similar genre. Given the context of popular literature, it seems unlikely that the title *Nuṣrat aṭ-ṭāʾir* refers to the work of Ṣalāḥaddīn aṣ-Ṣafadī (d. 764/1363) *Nuṣrat aṭ-ṭāʾir ʿalā l-Maṯal as-sāʾir*.

29 Ibn Abī Ḥaǧalah, *MK*, ll. 70-83.

30 Knysh, Alexander D., *Ibn ʿArabi in the Later Islamic Tradition: The Making of a Polemical Image in Medieval Islam*, Albany 1999, p. 44.

600/1203), Ibn Aḥlā (d. 645/1271) and the poet ʿUmar Ibn al-Fāriḍ (d. 632/1235).[31]

Like al-Ġarnāṭī, Ibn Abī Ḥaǧalah was a migrant from the Muslim West in Cairo, and like him, he also was a virulent opponent of the works of the monists, and in particular the poet ʿUmar Ibn al-Fāriḍ. Ibn Abī Ḥaǧalah wrote an independent treatise about the errors of his poetry, the *Ġayṯ al-ʿāriḍ fī muʿāraḍat Ibn al-Fāriḍ*. In it, Ibn Abī Ḥaǧalah imitates poems from the *Dīwān* in the same meter and rhyme, thereby attempting to "correct" Ibn al-Fāriḍ's errors in doctrine. Ibn Abī Ḥaǧalah was eventually brought before the Ḥanafī chief judge in Cairo Sirāǧaddīn al-Hindī for the virulence of the attack that he had leveled at the popular poet Ibn al-Fāriḍ. Ibn Abī Ḥaǧalah would later request to be buried with the text of his book of poetry, the *Ġayṯ al-ʿāriḍ*.[32]

Ibn Abī Ḥaǧalah does not mention the poetry of Ibn al-Fāriḍ in the *MK*. Does this mean that he had yet to write the *Ġayṯ* and to envision this poetry as a danger? It is difficult to know. The main target of this *maqāmah* is the circulation of texts in the marketplace. Books of doctrine, not poetry, are the main concern of Abū r-Riyāš and Ibn Abī Ḥaǧalah. What was the reason he later turned his attention to poetry?

In the conclusion to the *MK*, Ibn Abī Ḥaǧalah admonishes copyists to be more careful and avoid errors in transcription (*taṣḥīf*). Such a concern might seem far from the doctrinal issues at the center of the *MK*. But in some ways, the concern with scribal errors, too, relates to fears about the loss of scholarly authority at the hands of copyists. If authoritative versions of texts were not being produced, then this would impact the foundations of right religion.

5. Conclusion: Words in the World

The conclusion of the *MK* is a powerful statement that books and the book market are central to the maintenance of society. The poetic devices of the *maqāmah* such as the play on the titles of the books, do not simply offer an entertaining frame. Rather, the extended recourse to the latent possible meanings of books' titles evokes the unseen power of books as a meaningful presence in the world.

The finale of the *MK* in which the trickster leaves the text of his speech to be for the market inspector (*muḥtasib*) merits our final consideration.[33] Through this act, the trickster figure Abū r-Riyāš authorizes the text of the *maqāmah* to have a real work in the world. The act suggests the way that the author hoped the words of his fictional *maqāmah* might have real consequences.

---

[31] *Ibid*, p. 168.
[32] Homerin, Th. Emil, *From Arab Poet to Muslim Saint: Ibn Al-Farid, His Verse, and His Shrine*, Columbia SC 1994, p. 58. See also his contribution to the present volume.
[33] Ibn Abī Ḥaǧalah, *MK*, l. 101.

APPENDIX, Translation

The Ninth Feather from the *Maqāmah of the Books* Which is Entitled "The Return of the Stranger"

The Cooer, Son of the Dove said:

> When that which was written on the book market's brow finally happened, it suffered! Fate raised its sharp swords and rained down catastrophes. The book market despaired of ever finding the *Salvation*.[34] It cried for the loss of the *Healing*.[35] It was in dire need of the *Sufficiency of the Intelligent*[36] and it made the *Tear of the Wretched*[37] flow:

> Although he is free from care, he is nevertheless unhappy.
> Although he is healthy, he is unwell.

The *Occupant of Every Market Stall*[38] is gone. Its grammar books were all in the past tense. The *Book that Brings Grammar Near*[39] and those similar to it, had gone far away. The *Secrets of Arabic*[40] disclosed its sorrows:

> I wish – even though wishes do not avail –
> I knew what is in the heart of the *Ḥāǧibiyyah*

And *belles-lettres* escaped it (=the market) and the *Sipping of Pure Honey*[41] became difficult.

> Do you keep your sweet water from me while you give it to the wall!?

It made the *Choice Questions*[42] [lit. sources of watercourses] flow, and was devoid of the *Book of Firsts*.[43] The book market's people left, and ignorance came after knowledge. It was sale of sputum, a refuge of refuse!

> I passed by the book market and it was out of business.
> Tears soaked my sword belt.

---

[34] *Kitāb an-Naǧāh*, *The Salvation*, by Ibn Sīnā (d. 427/1037).

[35] *Kitāb aš-Šifāʾ*, *The Healing*, by Ibn Sīnā (d. 427/1037), or alternatively the *Kitāb aš-Šifāʾ li-taʿrīf ḥuqūq al-Muṣṭafā* by Qāḍi ʿIyāḍ (d. 554/1149).

[36] *Kitāb Ġunyat al-labīb fīmā yustaʿmalu ʿinda ġaybat aṭ-ṭabīb*, *The Sufficiency of the Intelligent in that which is used when the Doctor is Absent*, by Ibn al-Akfāni (d. 749/1348), *GAL* 2:137.

[37] The reference should be to the *Kitāb ʿIbrat al-labīb li-ʿaṯrat al-kaʾib*, *Warning the Intelligent Concerning the Stumbling of the Wretched*, by Ṣalāḥaddin aṣ-Ṣafadi (d. 764/1363), but Ibn Abī Ḥaǧalah condensed the title and turned ʿibrah (admonition, warning) into ʿabrah (tear).

[38] *Kunāsat ad-dukkān baʿd intiqāl as-sukkān*, *The Sweepings of the Market Stall after the Dwellers have Gone Home*, by Lisānaddin Ibn al-Ḫaṭib (d. 776/1375), *GAL* Suppl. 1:546.

[39] *Al-Muqarrib fī n-naḥw*, *The Book that Brings Grammar Near*, by Ibn ʿUṣfūr al-Išbīli (d. 669/1270).

[40] *Asrār al-ʿarabiyya*, *The Secrets of Arabic*, by ʿAbd ar-Raḥmān al-Anbāri (d. 577/1181).

[41] *Irtišāf aḍ-ḍarab ʿalā lisān al-ʿarab*, *The Sipping of Pure Honey in reference to the Arab Tongue*, by al-Ġarnāṭi (d. 745/1344).

[42] *ʿUyūn al-masāʾil*, *The Choice Questions*, is a title of multiple works by various authors.

[43] Possibly referring *Kitāb al-Awāʾil*, *The Book of Firsts*, by Abū Hilāl al-ʿAskari (d. post 395/1005) or of Abū Bakr al-Baṭalyawsi (d. 494/1100).

My book said to me, when I wandered near its gate [chapter],
"Halt you two! Let us cry over the memory of the beloved and the former abode".

So I halted and, I stopped, I summoned tears and intoned:

Morning greetings, you empty ruins,
and the once flourishing place is now an abandoned campsite.
Who greets (the ruins) except for an ever fortunate man,
without worry who sleeps soundly at night.

The books were transported to the place of destruction, and the market of dust. The *Eastern Wind*[44] became a "[stubble] which the winds scatter" (Q 18:45). The *Lamp's Glow*[45] and the *Lantern*[46] were both extinguished. May the book market perish! Woe to the book market where the books are all worm-eaten, and their meters are all shortened. How often has the string of pearls of its *Necklace*[47] been dispersed!

The *Revival*[48] died in its own skin (lit. binding), while the *Luminous Pearl*[49] became the *Orphan of Time*.[50] The *Rubies*[51] shed tears on the *Rocks*[52] like those of the poetess al-Ḥansāʾ for her brother Ṣaḫr (lit. the stone). The *Garden*[53] was violated, and water washed over the *Walls*[54] and drowned the *Orchard*.[55]

The *Thicket and Branches*[56] complained by means of the *Leaves*[57] and the *Entranceway*[58] bore witness to this, from the Gate to the Arch.[59] Ibn Baṭṭah[60] affirms that the roof argues for the point of "The Truth Has Come Forth" (Q 12:54) and a knock has come upon its door. So it received the legal punishment, and was received with rejection on account of its great putrefaction. It was thus sentenced

---

44 *Nasīm aṣ-ṣabā, The Eastern Wind,* by Ibn Ḥabīb al-Ḥalabī (d. 779/1377).

45 *Lumʿat as-sirāǧ, The Lamp's Glow,* by Ṣalāḥaddīn aṣ-Ṣafadī (d. 764/1363).

46 *Al-Miṣbāḥ al-munīr fī ġarīb šarḥ al-kabīr, The Shining Lantern Illuminating the Rare Terms in the Great Commentary,* by Aḥmad b. Muḥammad al-Fayyūmī ar-Rāfiʿī (d. 769/1368).

47 *Al-ʿIqd al-farīd, The Unique Necklace,* by Ibn ʿAbdrabbih (d. 328/940).

48 *Iḥyāʾ ʿulūm ad-dīn, The Revival of the Religious Sciences,* by Abū Ḥāmid al-Ġazālī (d. 505/1111).

49 *Ad-Durrah al-fāḫirah, The Luminous Pearl,* by Abū Ḥāmid al-Ġazālī (d. 505/1111).

50 *Yatīmat al-dahr, The Orphan of Time,* by Abū Manṣūr aṯ-Ṯaʿālibī (d. 429/1039).

51 Possibly in reference to the book, *al-Yawāqīt fī aḥkām al-mawāqīt, The Rubies Concerning the Rulings on the Timings,* by Šihābaddīn al-Qarāfī (d. 684/1285) or *al-Yawāqīt fī baʿḍ al-mawāqīt, The Rubies (to be used) at Certain Times,* by aṯ-Ṯaʿālibī (d. 429/1039).

52 In possible reference to the book, *Kitāb al-Aḥǧār ʿalā raʾy Balīnās, The Book of Stones According to the Opinion of Balīnās,* attributed to Ǧābir b. Ḥayyān.

53 *Ǧinān al-ǧinās, The Garden of Paronomasia,* by Ṣalāḥaddīn aṣ-Ṣafadī (d. 764/1363).

54 *Al-Ḥīṭān, The Walls,* by Muraǧǧā aṯ-Ṯaqafī (fl. 4th/10th century?)

55 *Bustān al-ʿārifīn The Orchard of the Gnostics,* by Imām an-Nawawī (d. 676/1275).

56 *Al-Ayk wa-l-ġuṣūn, The Thicket and Branches,* by Abū l-ʿAlāʾ al-Maʿarrī (d. 449/1057).

57 *Al-Awrāq, The Leaves,* by Abū Bakr aṣ-Ṣūlī (d. 335/946).

58 *Al-Madḫal, The Entryway.* The title is too common to attribute to a single work, although it may refer to the work of Ibn al-Ḥāǧǧ (d. 737/1336) by this name.

59 This could be a reference to the Bāb aṭ-Ṭāq in Baghdad.

60 Ibn Baṭṭah refers to the Ḥanbalī jurist (d. 387/997). The meaning of this phrase is not entirely clear.

for depravity, and were it not for Ibn al-Ḥāǧib,[61] it would have been executed by hanging.

The original book market took advantage of the situation, and made on the *Pages*[62] a formal complaint and submitted it to the ruler. Justice finally was made in its favor, so the *Book of Happiness*[63] returned to it:

If you consider the various regions, you would find that they suffer,
like men do, but then they find happiness.

[The book market] appointed the *Dīwān of the Puller*[64] for its rebuilding *and the Foundations*[65] were erected, and the *Floors of the Ascendant.*[66] And it received a lift from Ibn Rifʿa[67] and it increased in brilliance like the *Flashes*[68] thanks to the *Lamp of Kings*[69], and the minarets shone thanks to the *Omnibus on Jurisprudence* (lit. in all Friday mosques),[70] and *Desires*[71] beamed from the *Dawn of the Lights*[72] and it [= the market] lit the *Minaret*[73] of the *Great Mosque.*[74] Every stall became an *Apothecary's Shop*,[75] so it was like a *Paradise*[76] which had a sweet scent. And all came together in a *Delight*[77], as quick as a *Glance.*[78] And it returned to its previous state.

The book market's wind tower became more agreeable, and the book market made all flourish with its dawning, and it stood up on its legs. There was no one

---

[61] Ibn al-Ḥāǧib refers to the grammarian (d. 646/1249).

[62] *Al-Waraqāt fī uṣūl al-fiqh, The Pages on Jurisprudence*, by ʿAbd al-Malik al-Ǧuwaynī (d. 478/1085).

[63] *Safar as-saʿāda wa-safīr al-ifāda, Book of Happiness and the Ambassador of Aid*, by ʿAlī b. Muḥammad as-Saḥāwī (d. 642/1244).

[64] *Dīwān Ibn Qizil al-Mušidd, Dīwān of the Puller* by Ibn Qizil al-Mušidd (d. 656/1258).

[65] Possibly a reference to *al-Qawāʿid, The Foundations*, by Abū ʿAbdallāh al-Maqqarī (d. 758/1357). There are several other works bearing this title.

[66] Apparently a reference to *Ṭabaqāt al-umam, The Classes of the Nations*, by Abū Qāsim Ṣāʿid (d. 462/1070) (Ṣāʿid means 'ascendant'; in this word play Ibn Abī Ḥaǧalah combines the title with the author's name).

[67] Ibn Rifʿah (d. 710/1310).

[68] Possibly a reference to *al-Lumaʿ fī l-ʿArabiyyah, Flashes of Arabic*, by Ibn Ǧinnī (d. 391/1002). There are several other works bearing similar titles.

[69] *Sirāǧ al-mulūk, The Lamp of Kings*, by Abū Bakr aṭ-Ṭurṭūši (d. 520/1126).

[70] *Ǧamʿ al-ǧawāmiʿ fī uṣūl al-fiqh, The Omnibus on Jurisprudence*, by Tāǧaddin as-Subki (d. 771/1370).

[71] This may refer to the *qaṣīdah* entitled, *Ġurūr al-maṭāmiʿ, The Deceptions of Desires*, by Abū al-ʿAtāhiyah (d. 211/826).

[72] *Mašāriq al-anwār ʿalā ṣiḥāḥ al-āṯār, The Dawn of the Lights on the Correct Traditions of the Prophet*, by Qāḍī ʿIyāḍ (d. 554/1159).

[73] *Al-Manār al-munīf fī ṣ-ṣaḥīḥ wa-ḍ-daʿīf, The Lofty Minaret concerning the Correct and Doubtful Traditions*, by Ibn Qayyim al-Ǧawziyyah (d. 751/1350).

[74] *Al-Ǧāmiʿ al-kabīr, The Great Compendium*, by aš-Šaybānī (d. 189/805).

[75] *Ḥānūt al-ʿaṭṭār, An Apothecary's Shop*, attributed to al-Ǧāḥiẓ (d. 255/868-9).

[76] *Firdaws al-ḥikmah, The Paradise of Wisdom*, by ʿAlī b. Sahl aṭ-Ṭabarī (d. middle of the 3rd/9th c.).

[77] *Mulḥat al-iʿrāb, The Delight of Clear Expression*, by Abū l-Qāsim al-Ḥarīrī (d. 516/1122).

[78] *Al-Lamḥah al-badriyyah fī ʿilm al-ʿarabiyyah, The Glimpse of the Moon Concerning the Arabic Language*, by Abū Ḥayyān al-Ġarnāṭī (d. 745/1344).

who did not fall in love with it (/roam in it) and who did not say spontaneously:

> I think I fell deeply in love with the book market
> So that my heart melts whenever I abandon that place!
> If the [market's] wind tower is not visible on the horizon,
> my life in his love (wind) has no delight!

So [the book market] started to visit judges frequently and gave religious opinions on every question with the speech of an imam, so that it obtained a cure from the inkwells of people of religion. And thus the market's edifice became protected by God. The market as a whole remained in a good condition, while its wind tower stood erect [/in the nominative case], propped up [/put in the accusative case] in ease [/oblique case].

The *Good Tidings of the Wise*[79] came to the book market with the *Return of the Stranger*[80] and the *Mention of the Beloved*[81]. It opened its door with the *Key of Happinesses*[82] and the *First Signs of Dawn*.[83] So it offered *Sustenance for the Wayfarer*[84] like the *Traveling Proverb*[85] and the *Dove's Neckring*[86] like the *Flying Eagle*[87] and the *Spectre of the Imagination*[88] came to its door, and the *Best Portion*[89] of the *Sugar Dish*[90] did not delay, and the *Connections of the Disconnected*[91] entertained like a reed flute.

The ache of passion said in the Dīwān of Ardent Love:[92]

> They said, "You vanquished the one you had desired!"
> So I said to them, "My ardent desire is now prolonged!"

He brought together the scattered things in the *Sentences*[93] of sound plurals, and thanks to the *Eye/ʿAyn*[94] he saw what Zarqāʾ al-Yamāma could not. So his speech

---

79 *Bušrā l-labīb, The Good Tidings of the Wise*, by Ibn Sayyid an-Nās (d. 734/1334).

80 The reference is to this work, the *Maqāmah Kutubiyyah* which is entitled, ʿ*Awd al-ġarīb*, "the Return of the Stranger".

81 *Ḏikrā Ḥabīb, The Mention of Ḥabīb/the Beloved*, by Abū l-ʿAlāʾ al-Maʿarrī (d. 449/1057).

82 *Miftāḥ al-afrāḥ fī mtidāḥ ar-rāḥ, The Key of Happinesses in the Praise of Wine*, by ʿAbd al-Muḥsin at-Tanūḫī (d. 643/1245).

83 I have not been able to identify this work.

84 *Zād al-musāfir, Sustenance for the Wayfarer*, by Aḥmad b. al-Ġazzār al-Qayrawānī (d. 369/979) or possibly by Ṣafwān b. Idrīs (d. 598/1201).

85 *Al-Maṯal as-sāʾir wa-adab al-kātib wa-š-šāʿir, The Traveling Proverb and the Education of the Scribe and Poet*, by Ḍiyāʾaddīn Ibn al-Aṯīr (d. 637/1239).

86 *Ṭawq al-ḥamāmah, The Dove's Neckring*, by Ibn Ḥazm al-Andalusī (d. 456/1056).

87 *An-Nasr aṭ-ṭāʾir, The Flying Eagle*, by Ibn Abī Ḥaǧalah (d. 776/1375).

88 *Ṭayf al-ḫayāl, Spectre of the Imagination*, by aš-Šarīf al-Murtaḍā (d. 436/1044).

89 *Lubāb al-Išārāt wa-t-tanbīhāt, The Best Part of Indications and Warnings*, by Faḫraddīn ar-Rāzī (d. 606/1209).

90 *Sukkardān as-sulṭān, The Sultan's Sugar Dish*, by Ibn Abī Ḥaǧalah (d. 776/1375).

91 *Mawāṣil al-maqāṭiʿ, Connections of the Disconnected*, by Ibn Abī Ḥaǧalah (d. 776/1375).

92 *Dīwān aṣ-ṣabābah, Dīwān of Ardent Love*, by Ibn Abī Ḥaǧalah (d. 776/1375).

93 *Kitāb al-ǧumal fī n-naḥw, The Sentences Concerning Grammar*, by al-Ḫalīl b. Aḥmad (d. 170/786).

192   MAURICE A. POMERANTZ

was sweetened with the sweetest of sweets and the *Downpour of Eloquence*,[95] which is like the *Dripping of Sugar*.[96] The book market was married to the *Doll of the Palace*[97] in the region known as "the Space between the Two Castles (*bayn al-qaṣrayn*)". And the *Eye*[98] of the books of language settled therein [/became refreshed thereby]:

> She cast away her walking stick, and ended her journey.
> Such as when the eye of the traveler delights upon return home.

It was ordered to be adorned, so it was stitched with the *Embroidery of the Court*[99] and the *Ornament of the Innocents*.[100] And the *Jewel*[101] was strewn with *Necklaces of Pure Gold*[102] and clothed with the *Embroidery of the Court*[103] which was adorned with that made *Silken* (/*Refined*):

> When he was clothed like this, it was as if he had never been nude;
> And when given such wealth, it was as if he had never been poor.

The *Marvelous One*,[104] the *Dancer and Singer*,[105] all attended, and the *Bride of Happiness*[106] was unveiled, like *Dolls*.[107] From the *Found Pearls*,[108] the *Precious*[109] were strewn. The daughters of thought were conducted to their husbands to the melodies of the *Book of Songs*.[110] Those sweetest of meaning of the sons of elegant expression (/the *badīʿ* style) mated with them. And so none of the noble

---

[94]   *Al-ʿAyn* by al-Ḥalil b. Aḥmad (d. 170/786).

[95]   *Ġayt al-adab alladī nsaġama fī šarḥ Lāmiyyat al-ʿaǧam*, *The Downpouring of Erudition which flowed forth in the explication of the* Lāmiyyat al-ʿaǧam, by Ṣalāhaddin aṣ-Ṣafadi (d. 764/1362).

[96]   *Al-Qaṭr an-nubāti*, *The Dripping of Sugar*, by Ibn Nubātah (d. 768/1366).

[97]   *Dumyat al-qaṣr*, *The Doll of the Palace*, by al-Bāḫarzi (d. 467/1074).

[98]   *Al-ʿAyn* by al-Ḥalil b. Aḥmad (d. 170/786).

[99]   *Dār aṭ-ṭirāz fī ʿamal al-muwaššaḥāt*, *The House of Embroidery for the Manufacture of poetic brocades*, Ibn Sanāʾ al-Mulk (d. 608/1211).

[100]   *Ḥilyat al-abrār*, *The Ornament of the Innocents*, by an-Nawawi (d. 676/1277).

[101]   *Dār aṭ-ṭirāz fī ʿamal al-muwaššaḥāt*, *The House of Embroidery for the Manufacture of poetic brocades*, Ibn Sanāʾ al-Mulk (d. 608/1211).

[102]   *Qalāʾid al-ʿiqyān*, *The Necklaces of Pure Gold*, by al-Fatḥ Ibn Ḥāqān (d. 247/861).

[103]   *Al-Muḥarrar fī ʿilm al-ḥadīt*, *The Clarifier in the Science of Ḥadīt*, by Ibn ʿAbd al-Hādi (d. 744/1343). Perhaps there is a pun on *taḥrīr* meaning to be made "silken".

[104]   *Al-Bayān al-muġrib fī mulūk al-Andalus wa-l-Maġrib*, *The Wondrous Revelation about the Rulers of al-Andalus and Maghreb*, by Ibn al-ʿIdāri (d. 712/1312-1313). Or possibly *al-Muġrib fī ḥulā al-Maġrib*, *The Wondrous Book Concerning the Ornaments of the Maghreb*, by Ibn Saʿid al-Andalusi (d. 685/1286).

[105]   *Al-Muraqqiṣ wa-l-muṭrib*, *The Dancer and the Singer*, by Ibn Saʿid al-Andalusi (d. 685/1286).

[106]   *ʿArūs al-afrāḥ fī šarḥ Talḫīṣ al-Miftāḥ*, *The Bride of Happiness in Commentary on the Summary of the* Key, by Bahāʾaddin as-Subki (d. 773/1372).

[107]   *ʿArāʾis al-maǧālis*, *The Dolls of the Gatherings*, by aṯ-Ṯaʿlabi (d. 427/1035).

[108]   *Ad-Durr al-laqīt min al-baḥr al-muḥīṭ*, *The Found Pearl from the Great Ocean*, by Aḥmad b. ʿAbd al-Qādir al-Qaysi an-Naḥwi (d. 749/1348).

[109]   *Nafāʾis al-uṣūl fī šarḥ al-maḥṣūl*, *The Precious Principles in Commentary on the Gathering*, by al-Qarāfi (d. 684/1285).

[110]   *Kitāb al-Aġāni*, *The Book of Songs*, by Abū l-Faraǧ al-Iṣfahāni (d. 360/971).

sons remained who was not glad and did not scatter the *Flecks of Gold*[111] like they were the *Scattering of Pearls*.[112] The *Abodes of Lovers*[113] became inhabited once again, and rhapsodizing about Zaynab and Rabāb delighted all those present.

While people put on sweet perfume and rested, the market became lively. Lo, there appeared a *šayḫ* as if he were a partridge hen, and upon him was a mark of the Ḥiǧāz, with feathers like those of flies (*ḫāzbāz*), barer than a locust, more illuminating a brain than a flint, grinning more than lightening, crying more than the rain. He spoke like Abū Zayd, and was skipping like a prisoner of war bound by a chain. He stretched out his neck like a stork, and he brought the ḥadīt of ʿAmr to the market, and awoke the sleeping from slumber. He inscribed for the one who agreed with him seventy thousand merits. Then he made his speech elegant and resounding, clucking like a chicken and cooed like a dove, chirped, squawked, hoo-hooed and then said:

Oh you servants of God, fear God and avoid images! Especially the books concerning sex, for images are prohibited and angels will not enter a house which has an image in it. Beware of the books of magic and sinful amulets. Beware, beware of Abū Maʿšar's[114] group:

> Those who cast stones and augur from birds do not know
> what God is about to do.

Augury is but the *ḥadīt* of Ḫurāfah, and the *Sīrat ʿAntar* is made of impossibilities. [Beware of] wasting of your life in the empty exploits of *Baṭṭāl* and the *Conquest of Syria*, and the *Expeditions of the Prophet*, and *The Weapon of the Believer* and the *Victory of the Rebel* in every place. Beware of the *Seeker of Subjects*[115] and the Alchemy that is not correct, like most natural magic.

Oh her home in al-Ḫayf! It is not too far to visit, but beneath it are fears.

As to the books of divine presence in human nature (*ḥulūl*),[116] what is bound in them, is loosed. The explicit command of God has been violated in them, and a bezel from the *Bezels* has blinded his eye,

He thinks he is an expert in this, but he is (like) a blind man who has lost his cane.[117]

---

[111] *Šuḏūr aḏ-ḏahab, The Flecks of Gold,* by Ibn Hišām al-Anṣāri (d. 761/1359).

[112] *Natr ad-durr, A Scattering of Pearls,* by Abū Saʿd al-Ābi (d. 421/1030).

[113] *Manāzil al-aḥbāb wa-manāzih al-albāb, The Abodes of Lovers and the Gardens of the Wise,* by Šihābaddin Maḥmūd b. Sulaymān (d. 725/1325).

[114] Abū Maʿšar al-Balḫi (d. 272/886).

[115] I have not been able to identify this work.

[116] Massignon, Louis, *Essay on the Origins of the Technical Language of Islamic Mysticism,* trans. B. Clark, Notre Dame, Ind. 1997, p. 29, defines *ḥulūl* as a "term with Christian resonance, condemned by Muʿtazilite theologians and Bāqillāni (against Fāris the Ḥallajian), for whom speaking of a "place", a point of impact for immaterial realities, was to materialize them"; p. 292 n. 75 identifies the later usage of the term *ḥulūl* by Ibn Taymiyyah.

[117] The verse is by al-Mutanabbī, see *Dīwān Abī t-Ṭayyib al-Mutanabbī, Šarḥ al-Wāḥidi,* ed. Dieterici, Berlin 1861, p. 309.

Avoid the filth of the idols and of the unifiers, who are the brothers of Satan!
What they are can be recognized/seen by their signs, as is true of criminals.

> Curse the people who have formed in their souls
> the image of the indwelling of the Lord of the Throne in every image!

> Curse those who have become polytheistic in monism!
> Wrong belief has made them fall into the wrong.

> Woe for the people of unity!
> They have led others astray and wandered in luminous nights.

> Had they not given proof of (their) blindness/error in the *Bezels*,[118]
> they would not have fallen into every abyss.
> You will see them tomorrow in the *Gathering*.[119]
> They have fallen into a real trap.

> The *Key to the Unknown Unity* is a feminine plural (/effeminate group?)
> And among them slept the dog of the Byzantines.[120]

> And in some of the doors/chapters of the *Openings* there has been disclosed[121] what the
> people of the šariʿah have shut their ears.

> In the *Escape*[122] Ibn Sabʿin's idols have become apparent,
> they are more than seventy if they are counted.

> And the saying of Ibn Aḥlā[123] which is bitter in taste and repeats bitterness on every oc-
> casion.

> And the saying of Ibn Isrāʾil[124] in some of his verse,
> "You are not different from the universe" is the greatest lie.

> "He decreed that I be and created me, then became absent (from me), as He wished" –
> Who has ever seen such a thing?

> How many hateful things did ʿAfifaddin at-Tilimsāni[125] do?
> In them he was bereft of all shame and modesty!

> They supported with their ʿAbd al-Ḥaqq[126] a manifest untruth. With their Balyāni[127]
> they went down in a disaster.

---

[118] Referring to the *Fuṣuṣ al-ḥikam, Bezels of Wisdom*, by Ibn ʿArabi (d. 638/1240).

[119] *Al-Iḥātah, The Encompassing Work*, by ʿAbd al-Ḥaqq Ibn Sabʿin (d. 669/1271).

[120] *Kitāb Miftāḥ ġayb al-ǧamʿ wa-l-ǧūd, The Key of the Unknown Unity and Generosity*, by Ṣadraddin
al-Qūnawi (d. 673/1274). Perhaps *bāta* here refers to the dog of the *Ahl al-Kahf* in Q 18.

[121] *Al-Futūḥāt al-makkiyyah, The Meccan Openings*, by Ibn ʿArabi (d. 638/1240).

[122] *Budd al-ʿārif, The Escape of the Gnostic*, by ʿAbd al-Ḥaqq Ibn Sabʿin (d. 669/1271).

[123] Ibn al-Aḥlā (d. 645/1247).

[124] Ibn Isrāʾil (d. 677/1278).

[125] ʿAfifaddin at-Tilimsāni (d. 690/1291).

[126] ʿAbd al-Ḥaqq Ibn Sabʿin (d. 669/1271).

[127] A reference to Awḥadaddin al-Balyāni (d. 686/1288), who was a follower of Ibn Sabʿin. See
Chodkiewicz, Michel, *Awḥad al-Din Balyāni. Epître sur l'unicité absolue*, Paris 1982. Thanks
to Nefeli Papoutsakis for this reference and for much other illuminating and helpful advice on this poem and throughout the *maqāmah*.

Sāǧiʿ b. Ḥamām said:

Then he turned to the copyist corrupter (*an-nāsiḫ al-māsiḫ*).

He said, "Clarify the *sīn* lengthen the *yāʾ* of *Yāsīn*! Beware of the slips of the pen's tongue and the writing of faults of nations:

> Do not write anything with your hand
> apart from what would gladden you to see it on Judgment Day.

Do not be one who destroys the traces of the past, and mistakes "the pebbles of stoning" (*ḥaṣā ǧimār*) for a "donkey's testicles" (*ḫuṣā l-ḥimār*), so that you write differently than you read, and you read differently than you write.

And you Illuminator in Gold (*muḏahhib*), if you work properly, illuminating (books) will be sufficient for you, so delight eyes with gold! Inscribe this in your soul, "Every picture maker is in Hell":

> If you drew yourself, you would not increase that which is within you of noble nature.

There remained none of the bookbinders who did not scratch the ear of his laborer, like the scratching of leather. And walked along from his ruler along the straight rule and feared God, and sharpened his blade, until it stood upright like it was a spear.

> How many books were made tightly bound! And its pages were like a well-ordered string of pearls! Whenever it complains of its drawings, they say: "Do not be sad, be well bound!"[128]

Then he said to every merchant and agent in the market, "Avoid the prohibited things, oh you good men! Fear the day, 'wherein shall be neither bargaining and nor befriending' (Q. 14:31). The undutiful son never behaves righteously, and the upright merchant never is impoverished. Speak truth among the people. Distinguish between what is endowed and what is to be freely disposed. Make clear the weaknesses and the wet spots.

Do not lie about that which is unacceptable. Flee from sin! And know that granting from a generous heart is profit!".

Sāǧiʿ b. Ḥamām said, "After he had shown himself to be the bees' harvest and ʿAlqama [lit. bitterness] the stallion poet, and distinguished between *Ṣarr baʿr* and *Ṣarr durr*,[129] and cooed like a pigeon.[130] We then realized that it was Abū r-Riyāš, a literary notebook. Oh what a notebook! So we thanked him for his efforts, and

---

[128] This is a pun on the word *taǧalladī*, "be patient and endure" which is the overt meaning of the verse. However, given the context of book binding, the word can mean "be well bound".

[129] The poet ʿAlī b. al-Ḥasan Ṣarr Durr (lit. "purse of pearls") had originally been named Ibn Ṣarr Baʿr (lit. "son of a bucket of dung"). Allegedly it was the great Seljuk vizier Niẓām al-Mulk who gave him the more flattering nickname.

[130] The phrase *kašafa ʿan sāq ḥurr* plays on Q 68:42, *yawma yukšafu ʿan sāqin*, as a description of Judgment Day. Here however the trickster reveals his *sāq ḥurr* which is the sound of a male dove/pigeon. See *Lisān al-ʿArab*, Beirut 2000, 7: 306.

we carried out his commands and prohibitions. His opinion struck the mark, and did not fail. After he sat down, we did the right thing (i.e. threw coins at him), and he stretched himself like a tall palm tree to collect (the coins). And he left a copy of what he had commissioned us, with the inspector of the market. Then he left the city, and after Monday no one saw him again.

Bibliography

Hämeen-Anttila, Jaakko, *Maqama: A History of a Genre*, Wiesbaden 2002.

Hirschler, Konrad, *The Written Word in the Medieval Arabic Lands: A Social and Cultural History of Reading Practices*, Edinburgh 2011.

Knysh, Alexander D., *Ibn ʿArabi in the Later Islamic Tradition: The Making of a Polemical Image in Medieval Islam*, Albany 1999.

Note on the Arabic Text

I have edited the Arabic text of this *maqāmah* to modern Standard Arabic spelling conventions and added the vocalization. I have also indicated the rhymed units (*qarāʾin*) using asterisks, and the book titles using quotation marks, as an aid to the modern reader. While the notes identify most of the book titles, in some cases the references could be to the titles of multiple books, and it is difficult to know which the author intends. Textual variants are given at the end of the Arabic text.

الرّيشةُ التّاسعةُ مِنَ المَقامةِ الكُتُبيّةِ الموسومة بـ«عَوْدِ الغَريب»

حكى السّاجِعُ بن حمام:

لَمّا جرى ما كاتِب على جَبِينٍ[1] سُوقِ الكُتُب * فنُكِبَ وجُرِّدتْ له مِن اللّيَالي والأيّام[2] الدُّهْمُ والقُضُب * فأيِسَ مِن «النّجاة»[1] * وقال لفقْدِ «الشِّفاء»[2] آه * فافْتقر إلى «غُنيةِ اللّبيب»[3] * وأجرى «عَبْرة الكَئيب»[4] *

فَـتَـراهُ وَهـوَ الخَـلِـيُّ شَـجِـيّـاً   وَتَـراهُ وَهـوَ الـصَّـحيحُ سَـقِـيما[5]

فخلا به مِنْ «السُّكّان كلُّ دُكّان»[6] * ودخلتْ كُتُبُ نحْوِه في خبرِ كان * فبعُد عنْه «المُقرّب»[7] ونحْوُه * وظهر من «أسْرارِ العربيّةِ»[8] شجْوُه *

وَدَدْتُ وَمـا تُغْنِـي الـوَدادةُ أَنَّـنـي   بِــمـا في ضَمِـيـرِ الحاجِبيـةِ عـالِـمُ[9]

ففاتَهُ[3] مِنْ كَلامِ العَرب الأدَب * وتَعَذَّرَ عليه «ارْتِشافُ الضَّرَب»[10]

أَتَمْنَـعُ ريقَـكَ المَغْـسـولَ عَـنِّي   وَأَنْـتَ عَـلى الجِدارِ بِـهِ تَجـودُ[11]

---

¹ يشير إلى كتاب «النَّجاة» لأبي علي ابن سينا المتوفى 427/1037.

² يشير إلى كتاب «الشِّفاء» لأبي علي ابن سينا. وقد يكون كتاب «الشفاء لتعريف حقوق المصطفى» للقاضي عياض المتوفى 554/1149.

³ يشير إلى كتاب «غنية اللبيب عند غَيبة الطبيب لابن الأكفاني المتوفى 749/1348. انظر GAL 2:137.

⁴ يشير إلى كتاب «عِبْرة اللبيب لعَثْرة الكَئِيب» لصلاح الدِّين الصّفدي المتوفى 764/1363.

⁵ الخطيب التبريزي، «شرح ديوان أبي تمّام» تحقيق ر. الأسمر، بيروت، 1994، 2:113، ويقول في شرح هذا البيت: ترى طالب المجد متقسّم القلب في طلبه من وجوه.

⁶ يشير إلى «كُناسة الدُّكّان بعد أنْتقال السُّكّان» للسان الدِّين ابن الخطيب المتوفى 776/1375. انظر GAL Supp. 1:546.

⁷ يشير إلى كتاب «المُقرّب في النحو» لابن عصفور الإشبيلي المتوفى 669/1270.

⁸ يشير إلى كتاب «أسْرار العربية» لعبد الرّحمن بن محمّد بن عبيد الله الأنباري المتوفى 577/1181. انظر GAL 1:282.

⁹ نسب الخطيب التبريزي هذا البيت إلى كُثيِّر عَزّة، انظر الخطيب التبريزي، «شرح ديوان الحماسة» لأبي تمّام، تحقيق م. محيي الدين عبد الحميد، القاهرة، بدون تأريخ النشر، 3:250 يقول: تمنيت أني عالم بما ينطوي عليه قلب هذه المرأة لي.

¹⁰ يشير إلى كتاب «ارْتِشاف الضَّرَب على لسان العرب» للغرناطي المتوفى 745/1344.

فأجرى «عُيون المسائِل» [12] * وأقفرَ [4] مِنْ «كِتابِ الأوائِل» [13] * فبان عنهُ أهلُهُ * ونظم عليهِ بعدَ العلم [5]

جُمْلُهُ * فأصبح عَرْض النُّخامة * ومأْوى القُمامة *

مَـرَرْتُ بِسُـوقِ الكُتْـبِ وَهـوَ مُعَطَّـلٌ   فَبَلَّـتْ عُيُـوني مِـنْ دُمـوعي مِحْمَـلي

وَقَـــالَ كِتـــابي حِــينَ جُـزْتُ بِبابِــهِ   قِفـا نَبْكِ مِن ذِكْرى حَبيبٍ وَمَـنْزِلِ [14]

فوقفْتُ واستوْقفْتُ وبكيْتُ واستبْكيْتُ وقُلْتُ:

أَلا عِمْ صَـباحاً أيُّهـا الطَّلَـلُ البـالي [6]   وَربعُــهُ المعمـورُ في المَـنْزِلِ الخـالي

وَهَـــلْ يَعِمَـــنْ إلا سَـعيدٌ مُخَـلَّدٌ   قليـلُ الهُمـومِ مـا يَبِيـتُ بأوْجالِ [15]

فنُقِلتْ كُتْبُهُ إلى دارِ البَوار * وسُوقِ الغُبار * فأصبح «نسيمُ الصبا» [16] ﴿تذروه الرِّياح﴾ [17] * وطُفِئتْ

«لُمعةُ السّراج» [18] كـ«المِصباح» [19] * فتبًّا له من السُّوق أيِّ سُوق كُتْبُهُ مأروضة * وفاصلةُ عروضه مقْبوضة

* كم أنْفرط سِلْكُ «عِقْدِه» [20] * ومات به «الإحْياءُ» [21] في جِلْدِه * فأصبحتْ «الدُّرَّةُ الفاخِرةُ» [22] «يَتيمَةَ

<hr>

[11]   نُسِبَ هـذا البيـت إلى أبي الوليـد محمّـد بـن يحيى بـن حزم، انظر الشّـنتريني، الذخيرة في محاسـن أهل الجزيرة، بيروت، ١٩٩٧، ٢:٦٠٩. وهناك رواية أخرى لهذا البيت: وأنت على التُّراب به تجود.

[12]   هناك عدد كبير من الكتب بهذا العنوان لعلماء كبار مثل الفارابي، أبي القاسم البلخي، النووي وغيرهم.

[13]   قد يشير الكاتب إلى كتاب ألّفه أبو هلال العسكري المتوفى بعد 395/1005 بهذا العنوان أو إلى كتاب لأبي بكر البطليوسي المتوفى 521/1127. انظر إلى GAL Supp. 1:543.

[14]   يشير إلى مطلع معلّقة امرئ القيس، ديوان امرئ القيس، تحقيق ع. المصطاوي، بيروت، ٢٠٠٤، ٢٢.

[15]   يشير إلى مطلع قصيدة لامرئ القيس، انظر ديوان امرئ القيس، ١٣٥. وهناك رواية أخرى لصدر البيت الأوّل:
وهل يَعِمنْ من كان في العُصُرِ الخالي.

[16]   يشير إلى كتاب «نسيمُ الصبا» لبدر الدين بن الحلبي المتوفى 779/1377 بهذا العنوان.

[17]   سورة الكهف ٤٥.

[18]   يشير إلى كتاب «اللُّمَع في التصوّف» لأبي نصر السرّاج المتوفى 378/988.

[19]   يشير إلى كتاب «المصباح المُنير في غريب الشرح الكبير» لأحمد بن محمّد الفيومي الرافعي المتوفى 769/1368.

[20]   يشير إلى «العقد الفريد» لابن عبد ربه المتوفى 328/940.

[21]   يشير إلى الكتاب «إحياء علوم الدين» لأبي حامد محمد بن محمد الغزالي المتوفى 505/1111.

[22]   يشير هذا العنوان إلى عدد كبير من الكتب منها «الدُّرَّة الفاخرة في كشف علوم الآخرة» لابي حامد محمد بن محمد الغزالي.

الدَهْر» * وبكتْ «اليواقيتُ» [23] على «الأَحْجار» [24] بُكاء الخَنْساء [25] على صَخْر * وحتّى علا على [26]

«الجِنان» [27] وغَرِق «البُسْتان» [28] مِن «الحِيطان» [29] * فشكاهُ «الأَيْكُ والغُصون» [30] بـ«الأَوْراق» [31] *

وشَهِدَ عليه «المَدْخَلُ» [32] مِن الباب للطّاق [7] * فثبت عند ابن بطّة [33] أنّ سقْفهُ [8] يقول بالنُّقطة

فِ﴿حَصْحَص الحَقّ﴾ [34] * وقيل لِبابِه طَقْ * فضرب الحَدّ * وقُوبل لِكثرةِ صديدِه بالصَّدّ * فُحِكِم بِفِسْقِه *

ولولا ابن الحاجِب [35] أُمِر بِشنْقِه * فَاَنْتهز السَّوقُ الأَوّلُ الفُرْصة * ورفع فيه مِن «الورقات» [36] قصة *

فُحِكِم لهُ وأُعيد «سِفْرُ السّعادةِ» [37] إليه

وإذا تَأَمَّلْــــتَ البِقـــاعَ وَجَـــدْتَها　تَشْقى كَمَا تَشْقى الرِّجالُ [9] وَتَسْعَدُ [38]

---

[23]　يشير إلى «يتيمة الدهر في محاسن أهل العصر» لأبي منصور الثعالبي المتوفى 429/1029.

[24]　لعله يشير إلى كتاب «اليواقيت في أحكام المواقيت» لشهاب الدين أحمد بن إدريس القرافي المتوفى 684/1285 أو «اليواقيت في بعض المواقيت» لأبي منصور الثعالبي المتوفى 429/1029.

[25]　لعله يشير إلى كتاب «الأحْجار على رأي بالينِاس» نسب إلى جابر بن حيان، انظر إلى GAS 4:253.

[26]　يشير إلى الرثاء المشهور لتماضر بنت عمرو السلمية المعروفة بالخنساء.

[27]　يشير إلى كتاب «جنان الجِناس» لخليل بن أيبك الصفدي.

[28]　يشير إلى «بستان العارفين» للإمام النووي 676/1275.

[29]　«كتاب الحِيطان» للمرجى الثقفي الذي من رجال القرن الرابع الهجري.

[30]　يشير إلى كتاب «الأيك والغصون في الأدب» لأبي العلاء المعرّي المتوفى 449/1057.

[31]　يشير إلى كتاب «الأوراق» لأبي بكر الصولي المتوفى 335/946.

[32]　لعله يشير إلى كتاب «المدخل» لأبي عبد الله محمّد بن محمّد بن محمّد العبدري الفاسي المالكي الشهير بابن الحاج المتوفى 737/1336.

[33]　يشيرإلى ابن بطّة العكبري المتوفى 387/997.

[34]　سورة يوسف ٥١.

[35]　أبو عمرو عثمان بن عمر بن أبي بكر بن يونس الدويني الأسنائي الشهير بـابن الحاجب، الفقيه المالكي والأصولي النحوي المقرئ المتوفى 646/1249.

[36]　يشير إلى «الورقات في أصول الفقه» لإمام الحرمين عبد الملك الجويني المتوفى 478/1085.

[37]　يشير إلى كتاب «سِفْرُ السّعادة وسفير الإفادة» للإمام أبي الحسن علي بن محمّد السخاوي 642/1244.

[38]　هذا البيت لأبي تمّام عند خروج المعتصم إلى أرض مصر: وإذا تأملت البقاع وجدتها تشقى كما تشقى الرجال وتنعمُ، انظر ابن خلكان، وفايات الأعيان، تحقيق إ. عباس، بيروت، دار صادر، ١٩٧٨، 1:442.

وندب لِعِمارتِهِ «ديوان المُنشِدّ»[39] فرُفِعتْ «القواعِد»[40] و«طبقات صاعِد»[41] ونال بابنِ[10] الرِّفعةِ رِفْعة [42][11] وازْداد بـ«سِراجِ المُلوكِ» كـ«اللمع»[43] لمعة ولاحتْ بـ«جَمْعِ الجوامِعِ»[44] «الصّوامِعِ»[45] وأشرقتْ من «مشارِقِ الأنْوار»[46] «المطامِع»[47][12] فأنار من «الجامِعِ الكبير»[48] «المنار»[49] وأصبح في كلِّ دكّانٍ «حانوت العطّار»[50] فأصبح كـ«الفِرْدَوس»[51] طيّب النَّفْحة وٱجتمع شمْلهُ بـ«المُلْحة»[52] في أقلِّ من «اللمْحة»[53] فعاد إلى سيرتِهِ الأولى وازْداد باذهنْجُهُ قَبُولا فعمُر بشُرُوقِه وٱسْتوى على سُوقِه فلَمْ يبقَ إلّا منْ هام فيه وقال على البديه:

أراني بِسُوقِ الكُتْبِ أَمْسَيتُ مُغْرَماً   وقَلْبي إذا ما غِبْتُ عَنْهُ يَـذوبُ

ولـــو لم يلُـــحْ لي البـاذَهَنْجُ بأُفْقِـهِ   لَـمـا كانَ عَيْـشي في هـواهُ يَطيبُ

فجاور السَّادةَ الحكّام وأفْتى في كلِّ مسألةٍ بقولِ إمام فحَصَلَ بدوى العلماء دواه وأصبح هيْكلُهُ في حِرْزِ الله فبـات حَسَنَ المَجْموع منْصوباً بخَفْضِ العَيْشِ باذهنْجُهُ المَرْفُوع فقَدِمَ إليه «بُشْرى

---

39   يشير إلى «ديوان المُنشِدّ» لابن قزل المُنشِدّ المتوفى 656/1258.

40   لعله يشير إلى «القواعد» لأبي عبد الله المقَّري المتوفى 758/1357.

41   يشير إلى «طبقات الأُمم» لأبي القاسم صاعد بن أحمد الأندلسي القُرطبي المتوفى 462/1070.

42   يشير إلى «سِراج الملوك» لأبي بكر مُحمَّد بن مُحمَّد بن الوليد الفهري الطرطوشي المالكي المتوفى 520/1126.

43   يشير إلى كتاب «اللمع في العربية» لابن جنّي المتوفى 392/1002.

44   يشير إلى كتاب «جمع الجوامع في أصول الفقه» لتاج الدين عبد الوهاب بن علي السُّبكي المتوفى 771/1369.

45   لم أقدر على عثور كتاب بهذا العنوان. لعله يشير إلى أنّ كلمة «صومعة» تعني مناراً في المغرب.

46   يشير إلى كتاب «مَشارِق الأنْوار على صحاح الآثار» للقاضي عياض بن موسى بن عياض اليحصبي السبتي المالكي المتوفى 554/1159.

47   قد يشير إلى قصيدة «غرور المطامع» لأبي العتاهية المتوفى 211/826.

48   يشير إلى «الجامع الكبير» لمحمد بن حسن الشيباني المتوفى 189/805.

49   يشير إلى «المنار المنيف في الصحيح والضعيف» لابن قيم الجوزية المتوفى 751/1350.

50   «حانوت العطّار» عنوان كتاب منسوب إلى عمرو بن بحر الجاحظ. انظر GAL Supp.1:245.

51   يشير إلى كتاب «فردوس الحكمة في الطبّ» لعلي بن سهل الطبري المتوفى 3/9 ق.

52   يشير إلى كتاب «ملحة الإعراب» لأبي القاسم الحريري المتوفى 516/1122.

53   يشير إلى كتاب «اللمحة البدرية في علم العربية» لأبي حيان الغرناطي المتوفى 745/1344.

اللبيب» * بـ«عودِ الغريب» * و«ذِكرى حبيب» * ففتح بابه بـ«مِفْتاح الأفراح» * و«تباشير الصباح» * فَقَدَّمَ «زاد المُسافر» * كـ«المثل السائر» * و«طوق الحمامة» * كـ«النسر الطائر» * وخرج إليه «طيفُ الخيال» * في بابه * ولَمْ يتأخَّرْ مِن «السُّكَرْدانِ» * «لُبابه» * وأطربتْ «مواصيلُ المقاطيعِ» * كالشِّبّابة * وقالت حُرْقةُ الصبِّ بـ«ديوانِ الصّبابة» * :

قـالوا ظَفِـرْتَ بِمَـنْ تَهْـوَى فَقُلـتُ لهـم   الآن أطْـوَلُ مـا كانـتْ صَبـاباتي

وجمع شَمْلهُ بـ«الجُمل» * جَمعَ السّلامة * ورأى بناظِرِ «العين» * ما لَمْ ترهُ زرقاءُ اليمامة * فطاب حديثُهُ بأطْيبِ الطيِّبات * و«غيثِ الأدب» * الذي هو كـ«قَطْر النّبات» * وزُقّتْ إليه «دُميةُ القصر» * بين القصرين * وقرّتْ به مِنْ كُتُبِ اللُّغة «العَين» *

---

54   يشير إلى «بشرى اللبيب بذكرى الحبيب» لابن سيّد الناس اليعمري 734/1334.

55   يشير إلى هذه المقامة التي اسمها الكامل هو «المقامة الكُتُبيّة الموسومة بعود الغريب».

56   قد يشير إلى «ذكرى الحبيب» لأبي العلاء المعرّي المتوفى 449/1057.

57   يشير إلى كتاب «مِفْتاح الأفْراح بامْتِداح الرّاح» لعبد المحسن بن حمود التّنوخي 643/1245.

58   لم أقدر على وجود كتاب بهذا العنوان.

59   يشير إلى كِتاب «زاد المسافر» لأحمد بن الجزّار القَيرواني المتوفى 369/979 أو «زاد المسافر» لصفوان بن إدريس المتوفى 598/1201.

60   يشير إلى كتاب «المثل السائر وأدب الكاتب والشاعر» لضياء الدين ابن الأثير المتوفى 637/1239.

61   يشير إلى كتاب «طوق الحمامة» لابن حزم الاندلسي المتوفى 456/1056.

62   يشير إلى كتاب «النسر الطائر» لابن أبي حجلة المتوفى 776/1375.

63   يشير إلى كتاب «طَيف الخيال» للشريف المرتضى 436/1044.

64   يشير إلى «سُكَرْدان السُّلطان» لابن أبي حجلة المتوفى 776/1375.

65   يشير إلى كتاب «مواصيل المقاطيع» لابن أبي حجلة المتوفى 776/1375.

66   يشير إلى كتاب «ديوان الصبابة» لابن أبي حجلة المتوفى 776/1375.

67   انظر راغب الاصفهاني، محاضرات الأدباء ومحاورات الشعراء والبلغاء ، ت. ع. الطبّاع ، بيروت، 1999، 2: 97.

68   يشير إلى كتاب «الجُمَل في النحو» للخليل بن احمد الفراهيدي المتوفى 175/791 وقد يشير إلى «الجمل في النحو» لأبي القاسم الزجّاجي المتوفى 340/951.

69   يشير إلى كتاب «العين» للخليل بن أحمد.

70   يشير إلى كتاب «غيث الأدب الذي انْسجم في شرح لامية العجم» لصلاح الدين الصفدي المتوفى 764/1363.

فَأَلْقَتْ عَـصاها واسْـتَقَرَّ بِهـا النَّـوَى   كَـما قَـرَّ عَيْنـاً بالإيابِ الْـمُـسافِرُ [74]

وأُمِـرَ بِتَزيينِهِ[14] فطُـرِّزَ[15] بِـ«طِـرازِ الدّارِ» * و«حِليةِ الأبـرارِ» [75] * وقُـلِّدَ مِنْ «قلائـدِ العِقيـانِ» [76]

«الجوهر» [77] * وكُسِي من «دارِ الطِّرازِ» [78] «المُحَرّر» [79] *

كَأنَّ الفَـتى لَمْ يَعْـرَ يَوْمـاً إذا اكْتَـسَى   وَلَـمْ يَـكُ صُـعْلوكاً إذا مـا تَمَـوَّلا [80]

وحضر «المُغرِبُ» [81] * و«المُرَقِّصِ والمُطرِبِ» [82][16] * فجُلِيت «عروسُ الأفراحِ» [83] كـ«العرائِسِ» [84] *

وَنُثِرَتْ مِنْ «دُرِّ اللقيطِ» [85] «النفائس» [86] * وزُفَّتْ بَناتُ الأفكار بأصواتِ «الأغاني» [87] * ودخل بها من

---

[71] يشير إلى «القطر النباتي» لجمال الدين ابن نُباتة المتوفى 768/1366.

[72] يشير إلى كتاب «دُمية القصر وعُصرة أهل العصر» لعلي بن الحسن بن علي بن أبي الطيِّب الباخَرزي المتوفى 467/1074.

[73] يشير إلى كتاب «العين» للخليل بن أحمد.

[74] المُضَرِّس الأسدي، انظر إلى الجاحظ، كتاب البيان والتبيين، بيروت، 1993، 2:731. وينسب ابن منظور هذا البيت إلى مُعَقِّر بن أوس البارقي، انظر ابن منظور، لسان العرب، 14: 394.

[75] يشير إلى كتاب محيي الدين أبي زكرياء يحيى بن شرف النَّوَوي المتوفى 676/1277.

[76] يشير إلى كتاب «قلائد العقيان» للفتح بن محمد بن عبيد الله بن خاقان المتوفى بين 528/1134 و555/1160.

[77] قد يشير إلى كتاب «الجوهر النقي على سنن بيهقي» لأبي الحسن علي بن عثمان المارديني الشهير بابن التركماني المتوفى 750/1349.

[78] يشير إلى كتاب «دارالطِّراز في عَمَل المُوَشَّحات» لابن سناء الملك المتوفى 608/1211.

[79] يشير إلى كتاب «المحرّر في الحديث» لمحمد بن أحمد الجماعيلي الصالحي الشهير بابن عبد الهادي المتوفى 744/1343.

[80] التبريزي، شرح ديوان الحماسة، ت Freytag، 102.

[81] قد يشير إلى كتاب «البيان المغرب في ملوك الأندلس والمغرب» لابن العذاري المتوفى 713/1312.

[82] يشير إلى كتاب «المُرَقِّص والمُطرِب في أخبار أهل المغرب» لابن سعيد الأندلسي المتوفى 685/1286.

[83] يشير إلى كتاب «عروس الأفراح في شرح تلخيص المفتاح» لبهاء الدين السُّبْكي المتوفى 773/1372.

[84] يشير إلى كتاب «عرائس المجالس» لأحمد بن محمد الثعلبي المتوفى 427/1035.

[85] يشير إلى كتاب «الدرّ اللقيط من البحر المحيط» لأحمد بن عبد القادر بن أحمد بن مكتوم بن أحمد بن محمد بن سليم القيسي النحوي المتوفى 749/1348.

[86] يشير إلى كتاب «نفائس الأصول في شرح المحصول» لأبي العباس أحمد بن إدريس بن عبد الرحمن الصنهاجي المصري المشهور بالقرافي المتوفى 684/1285.

[87] يشير الكتاب المشهور لأبي فرج الإصفهاني المتوفى 360/971.

أبناءِ البديع كُلُّ أطيبِ[17] المعاني * فلمْ يبق مِنْ نُجباء الأبناءِ إلّا مِنْ سُرَّ * وَنَثَرَ «شُذُورَ الذّهبِ»[88] و«نثر الدرّ»[89] * فعَمَرَتْ «منازِلُ الأحباب»[90] * وأطْرَبَ التّشبيبُ بزيْنب والرّباب *[91]

فبيْنما الناسُ قد ضمخوا بالخلوق * وقعدوا حين قامت السُّوق * وإذا بشيخٍ كأنّه زعْقوق[92] * عليه سِيما الحِجاز * ورياش الخازباز * أجْرَدَ من الجراد * وأقْدحَ ذِهْناً من أبي الزِّناد[93] * أُضْحكَ مِن بَرْق * وأبْكى مِن وَدْق * يُبدي قول أبي زيد * يُحَجِّلُ كالأسيرِ في القيْد * فمَدّ عُنْقاً كالغُزْنوق * وساق حديث عمرو[18] في السُّوق[94] * فأيْقظ إيقاظ الوسْنانِ من السِّنة * وكتب لمنْ وافقهُ سبْعين ألْف حَسَنَة * ثُمّ رقّ ودقّ وصقع وسجع وزرْزر وقرْقر وهدْهد وهدّد ثُمّ قال:

عِبادَ الله اتّقوا الله وتجنّبُوا المصوَّر ولا سِيّما مِنْ كُتُبِ الباه * فالتصاويرُ محْظُورة * والملائكةُ لا تدخُلُ بيتاً فيه صُورة[95] * وإيّكم وكُتُب السحرة * وطلاسِم الفَجَرة * والحَذَر الحَذَر * مِنْ عشيرِ أبي مَعْشَر *[96]

فــوالله مــا تَــدري الــضَّوارِبُ بالحَــصَى   ولا زاجِــراتُ الطَّــيرِ مــا الله صَــانِعُ[97]

---

[88] يشير إلى كتاب «شرح شذور الذهب» لابن هشام الأنصاري المتوفى 761/1359.

[89] يشير إلى كتاب «نَثْر الدُرّ» لأبي سعيد الآبي المتوفى 421/1030.

[90] يشير إلى كتاب «منازِل الأحباب ومنازه الألْباب» لشهاب الدين محمود بن سليمان بن فهد المتوفى 725/1325.

[91] يشير إلى مطلع قصيدة لابن شُهيد، هذه دار زَينَب والرّباب انظر «ديوان ابن شُهيد الأندلسي» تحقيق يعقوب زكي (القاهرة: دار الكاتب العربي للطباعة والنشر، بدون تأريخ الإصدار)، 85.

[92] الزعقوق: نوع من قبج أو كروان أو حِجل، انظر إلى Lane 2:1232.

[93] لعله يشير إلى عبد الله بن ذكوان القرشي المدني الشهير بأبي زناد المتوفى 31/651.

[94] قد يشير إلى حديث روى عن عمرو بن دينار «من دخل السوق فقال: لا إله إلا الله وحده لا شريك له، وله الحمد، يحيى ويميت وهو حيّ لا يموت بيده الخير وهو على كل شيء قدير، كتب الله له ألف ألف حسنة ومحا عنه ألف ألف سيئة ورفع له ألف ألف درجة» انظر إلى ابن قيم الجوزية، المنار المنيف في الصحيح والضعيف، ت ي. الثالي، مكة، 2011، 12.

[95] يشير إلى الحديث «الملائكة لا تدخل بيتاً فيه صور» انظر البخاري، صحيح البخاري، (بيروت: دار ابن الكثير، 2001)، 1496،(باب من كره القعود على الصور).

[96] أبو معشر البلخي المتوفى 272/886.

[97] البيت للبيد بن ربيعة العامري، انظر ديوان لبيد بن ربيعة بيروت، بدون تأريخ الإصدار)، 88، حيث ورد مطلع البيت «لَعَمْرُكَ ما تَدري».

فالعيافة * حديث خرافة * «وسِيْرة عنتر» [98] من المُحال * وإضاعة العُمرِ في الفراغِ «للبطّال» * [99] وفي «فُتُوحِ الشام» * و«غزواتِ النّبيّ عليه السّلام» * «سِلاحِ المؤمِن» * و«نُصْرةِ الثّائِر» * [100] في كلِّ المَوْطِن * واحْذروا «طالِب المطالِب» * [101] والكيمياء التي لا تصحُّ كالسيمياء في الغالِب *

فَيَـــا دارَهـا بالخَيـــفِ إنّ مزارَهـــا   قَريـــبٌ وَلكِـــنْ دونَ ذلك أهْـوالُ [102]

وكُتُبُ الحُلول * المَربوطُ بها محُلول * قدْ خالف فيها النّصّ * وطلع على عيْنِهِ من «الفُصوص» * فصٌّ * [103]

وَيَـــرى أنَّـــهُ البَصـــيرُ بِهـــذا   وَهْـــوَ في العُمـــي ضائعُ العُكّاز [104]

فاجْتنبوا الرّجس من الأوْثان * والاتّحادية إخوانُ الشيطان * وهم ما هم * يعرفون كما تعرف المُجرِمون بسيماهم *

فَتَبًّـــا لِقَـــوْمٍ صَـــوَّروا في نُفُوسِـــهِم   حُلـــولَ إلهِ العَـــرْشِ في كلِّ صُـــوْرَةِ

وتَبًّـــا لِقَـــوْمٍ أشْرَكـــوا باتّحـــادِهِم   وأوْقَعَهُـــم في السـوءِ سُـــوءُ العَقيـدةِ

فَيَـــا وَيْـــلُ أهْـــلِ الاتّحـــادِ فَـإنّهُـم   أضَـــلّوا وَضَـــلّوا في اللّيَـــالي المُـــضيئةِ

وَلـو لَمْ يبينـوا بـ«الفُصوصِ» على عمًى [105]   لَـــما وَقَعـــوا باللَّهْـــوِ في كلِّ هُـــوَّةِ

وَسَـــوف تَـــراهُم بـــ«الإحاطـــةِ» في غَـدِ [106]   وَقَـــدْ وَقَعـــوا في حَوْطـــةٍ أيِّ حَوْطـــةِ

---

98   يشير إلى «سيرة عَنْتَر بن شَدّاد».

99   يشير إلى «سيرة ذات الهِمّة».

100   لعله يشير إلى «نصرة الثائر على مثل السائر» لصلاح الدين الصفدي المتوفى 764/1363.

101   لم أقدر على وجود كتاب بهذا العنوان.

102   البيت لأبي العلاء المعرّي، سقط الزند، بيروت، ١٩٥٧، ٢٢٩: يا دارها بالحزن إن مزارها قريبٌ ولكنْ دون دلك أهوال.

103   يشير إلى كتاب «فُصوص الحِكَم» لابن العربي المتوفى 638/1240.

104   البيت للمتنبّي الواحدي، شرح ديوان المتنبّي، (ed. Dieterici)، برلن، ١٨٦١، ٣٠٩.

105   يشير إلى كتاب «فصوص الحِكَم» لابن العربي المتوفى 638/1240.

106   يشير إلى كتاب «الإحاطة» لابن سَبْعين المتوفى 669/1269.

«مِفْتـاحُ غَيْبِ الجَمْعِ» [107]   جَمْعٌ مُؤَنَّث   بِهِ بَاتَ كَلْبُ الرُّومِ مِنْ أَهْلِ رُومَتِ

وفي بَعْضِ أَبْوابِ «الفُتُوحاتِ» [108]   فَتْحُ ما   تُسَدُّ لَهُ آذانُ أَهْلِ الــشَّريعةِ

وفي «البُدِّ» [109]   أَصْنامُ ابْنِ سَبْعِينَ قَدْ بَدَتْ   تَزيدُ على الــسَّبْعِين إنْ هِيَ عُدَّتِ

وقَـوْلُ ابْـنِ أَحْلـى [110]   المُـرُّ في الذوقِ عَلْقَمْ   تَكَـرَّرَ مِنْــهُ المُـرُّ في كُلِّ مَــرَّةِ

«قَــضاني فَأَبْــداني وَغـابَ بِــما قَـضَى»   فَمَــنْ ذا رَأَى يوماً كَهـذِي القَضِيَّةِ [19]

وَقَـوْلُ ابْـنِ إسْرائيـلَ [111]   في بَعْضِ نَظْمِهِ   «وَما أَنْتَ غَيْرُ الكَوْنِ» أَعْظَمُ فِرْيةِ

وَكَمْ لِلعَفيـفِ التِلِمْـسـانِي [112]   قَـبـائِحَ   بِهـا بـاتَ عـارٍ مِـنْ حِياءٍ وعِفَّـةِ

أَقـاموا بِعَبْـدِ الحَـقِّ باطِـلَ قَـوْلِهِم   وأَمْــسوا بِبَلْيانِـهِمْ [113]   في بَلِيَّــةِ

قال السّاجِعُ بن حَمام: ثم ٱلتفت إلى الناسِخ * الماسِخ *

وقال: بَيِّنْ السِّينِ * ومدّ الياء مِن يس [20] * إِيّاك وفلتاتِ لِسانِ القَلَمِ * وكِتابة مساوئ [21] الأُمَمِ *

فَـلا تكْتُـبْ بكَفِّـكَ [22] غَيـر شيءٍ   يَسُـرُّكَ في القِيامَـةِ أَنْ تَـراهُ [114]

ولا تكُ مِمَّن يُعفّي الآثارَ * ويُصحِّف حصى الجِمارِ بحُصى الحِمارِ * فتكتب غَيرما تقرأ وتقرأ غَيرما تكتب [23]

وأَنْت أَيُّها المُذَهِّبُ إذا حَسَنْتَ الخَرْش * قعد لك النَّقْش * فأرض النُّظّار بالنُّضارِ [24] * وصوِّر في نَفْسِك كُلَّ مُصوِّرٍ في النّارِ *

107   يشير إلى كتاب «مفتاح غيب الجمع والوجود» لصدر الدين القونوي المتوفى 673/1274.

108   يشير إلى كتاب «الفتوحات المكّية» لابن العربي المتوفى 638/1240.

109   يشير إلى كتاب «بدّ العارف» لابن سَبْعين المتوفى 669/1269.

110   يشير إلى ابن أحلى المتوفى 645/1247.

111   يشير إلى ابن إسرائيل الحريري المتوفى 677/1278. أخذ ابن أبي حجلة من شعر ابن إسرائيل، انظر: ديوان ابن إسرائيل، ت. محمد الجادر، دمشق، 2009، 269. أشكر د. نفلي بابوتساكس لهذا.

112   يشير إلى عفيف الدين التِلِمْساني المتوفى 690/1291.

113   يشير إلى أوحد الدين البلياني المتوفى 686/1288.

114   ابن عبد ربّه، العقد الفريد، بيروت، 1983، 2: 78.

وَلَـــوْ صَــوَّرْتَ نَفْـسَكَ لم تَرِدْهـا   على ما فيك مِـن كرم[25] الطّبـاع[115]

فلم يبْق مِن المُجلِّدِين إلا مَنْ عرك أُذَنَ أجيرِه عزْك الأديم * ومشى من مسطرتِهِ على قانونٍ مستقيم * فحشِي ربّهُ وأرْهف شَفْرته * حتَّى قعدتْ كأنّها حرْبة *

وَكَمْ مِـنْ كِتـابٍ بات بالحُبّكِ عِنـدَهُمْ   وأوراقُــهُ في سِــلْكِ دُرٍّ مُنَـضِّدِ

إذا مـا اشْـتَكَى مِـن نَقْـشِهِم حُرْقَـةَ الأسى   يَقُولُـــونَ لا تَهْـــلِكْ أسى وَتَجَـــلَّـــدِ[116]

ثُمَّ قال لِكُلِّ تاجِرٍ ودلّال * تجنّبوا الحرام يا أوْلاد الحلال * واتّقوا يوماً ﴿لا بِيْعَ فيهِ ولا خِلال﴾[117] * فما بَرّ عَقُوق * (ولا أمْلق تاجِرٌ صدوق)[118] * فقُولوا الحقّ بين الخلْق * وميّزوا الوقْف مِن الطِلْق * وبيّنوا الخلل ومواضِع البَلَل ولا تقُولوا عمّا لم[26] يُقابِل بِما ليْس بهِ قِبل* فاجْنحوا[27] عن الجُناح * واعلمـوا أنّ (السَّماح رباح)[119] *

قال السّاجِعُ بن حمام فلمّا ضاهى جنى النحْل * وعلْقمة الفحْل * وميّز صُرّ بعْرٍ * من صُرّ دُرّ * وكَشَف عنْ ساقٍ حُرّ[121] * علِمْنا أنّه أبو الرِّياش * وكُنّاش أدب أيُّ كُنّاش * فشكرْنا سعْيه * وامْتثلْنا[28] أمرهُ ونهيه * فأصاب ظنّهُ ولمْ يخِب * وقُمْنا عند قعوده بِما يجِب * فَتَطاوَلَ إلى أخْذِهِ كالنخْلةِ السّحوُق * وترك بما عَهِدَ إلينا نسْخة عِنْد مُحْتسِبِ السُّوْق * ثُمَّ فارقَ البلد * ولمْ يرهُ[29] مِنْ يوم الاثْنينِ أحد *

---

[115] الخطيب التبريزي، شرح ديوان أبي تمام، ت. ر. الأسمر، بيروت ١٩٩٤، ١: ٤٠٨.

[116] يشير إلى البيت الثاني من معلّقة طرفة بن العبد، انظر الزوزني، شرح المعلّقات السّبع، دمشق، ١٩٧٢، ٦٤.

[117] سورة ابراهيم ٣١.

[118] يشير إلى المثل «ما أملق تاجر صدوق»، انظر الثعالبي، التمثيل والمحاضرة، ت. ع. الحلو، رياض، ١٩٨٣، ٢٧.

[119] يشير إلى الحديث «السماح رباح والعسر شؤم»، انظر القاضي القضاعي، مسند الشهاب، ت. ح. السلفي بيروت، ١٩٨٥، ٤٨.

[120] يشير إلى أبي منصور علي بن الحسن بن علي بن الفضل البغدادي المعروف بصر بعر المتوفى 465/1072. وهناك قصة تقول أن نظام الملك كان يقول له: أنت صر در لا صر بعر. انظر الذهبي، سِير أعلام النبلاء، ت. ح. عبد المنان، رياض ٢٠٠٤، ٢٧٥٨.

[121] ساق حرّ صوت القَمَاري، انظر ابن منظور، لسان العرب، بيروت، ٢٠٠٠، ج. ٧، ٣٠٦: ساق حرّ الذكر من القَمَاريّ سمي بصوته.

Variants
MS Berlin Wetzstein 1803 (= ب *) MS Rabat 1901 (=* ر *)*

١. ب: ما كتب على سوق الكتب ٢. ر: الأيام والليالي ٣. ب: فعانه ٤. ر و ب: أفقر من ٥. ر: ظهر عليه ٦. ر: البيت فقال طلله البالي ٧. ب: من الباب إلى الطاق ٨. ر: شقفه ٩. ر: تشقى كما الرجال وتسعد ١٠. ر: نال بان؟ بابن رفعة ١١. ر: بسروج الملوك ١٢. ب: المطالع ١٣. ر: ذكر حبيب ١٤. ر: بزينته ١٥. ر: فزين ١٦. وقلد من «قلائد العقيان» الجوهر ... المرقص والمطرب، سقط من ب. ١٧. ب: ألطف ١٨. ر: عمر ١٩. ب: سقط هذا البيت ٢٠. ر: ياسين ٢١. ر: ما ساوي ٢٢. ب: بخطك ٢٣. ر: فيكتب غير ما يقرأ ويقرأ غير ما يكتب ٢٤. ر و ب: النظار ٢٥. ر: حسن ٢٦. ب: عالم ٢٧. ب: احتجوا ٢٨. ب: أمثلنا ٢٩. ر: لم تره لم تره

Ibn Abī Ḥaǧalah und sein Traktat „Das Feien gegen jedwede Widerwärtigkeit[1] mittels des Bittgebets[2] für den Propheten der Gnade (*Dafʿ an-niqmah bi-ṣ-ṣalāh ʿalā nabī ar-raḥmah*)[3]

Andreas Herdt

Wenn man Ibn Abī Ḥaǧalah[4] ausgehend von seiner literarischen Produktion besser als Autor kennen lernen möchte, so stellt man bei der Recherche fest, dass unter seinen wenigen bisher gedruckten Werken die beiden folgenden, nämlich *Dīwān aṣ-ṣabābah* und *Sukkardān as-sulṭān*, eine herausragende Stellung einnehmen. Diese zwei prägen maßgeblich unser Bild von dem, was IAḤ als Autor war, nämlich ein literarisch gebildeter und feinsinniger Kompilator von Anthologien. Doch das Wirken dieses Autors erschöpft sich keineswegs in den heute im Druck vorliegenden Werken und somit ist auch die Einschätzung und Würdigung der

---

1 Das arabische Wort *niqmah* wurde häufig als das genaue Gegenteil von *niʿmah* verwendet. *Niʿmah* hat heute zwei allgemeine Grundbedeutungen: „Wohltat, Gunsterweis" sowie „Wohlleben, Wohlergehen". Im vormodernen Sprachgebrauch war *niʿmah* ein Oberbegriff für jeglichen Erweis göttlicher bzw. herrscherlicher Gunst, der für in dessen Genuss kommenden Empfänger unterschiedliche konkrete Formen annehmen konnte. Hierunter konnten je nach Kontext u.a. Vergebung verübter Missetat, Verleihung des militärischen Sieges, Ehrenerweisung sowie auch nicht zuletzt Betrauung mit einem Amtsposten gemeint und verstanden werden. Aufschlussreich ist in diesem Zusammenhang die Verwendung des Begriffs im Titel des Werks *Muʿīd an-niʿam wa-mubīd an-niqam*, sinngemäß etwa: „die Wiederherstellung des Gunsterweises und die Überwindung des Gunstentzugs", aus der Feder Tāǧaddin as-Subkīs (gest. 1370), eines Zeitgenossen Ibn Abī Ḥaǧalahs mithin. Im Grunde geht es in diesem Werk darum, Amtsinhabern in den unterschiedlichsten Funktionen innerhalb des mamlukischen Verwaltungsapparates vor Augen zu führen, was das von ihnen im Hinblick auf die Ausübung ihres jeweiligen Amtes erwartete und zu leistende Äquivalent zu der Gunst war, welche ihnen durch ihre Einsetzung erwiesen wurde. *Niqmah* als das genaue Gegenteil zu *niʿmah*, sozusagen als Zustand der „*Niʿmah*-losigkeit" bzw. des „*Niʿmah*-Entzugs", kann somit auch weit aufgefasst werden und je nach Kontext unterschiedlichste konkrete Formen für den Betroffenen annehmen. Eine sehr aufschlussreiche weitere Bedeutung von *niqmah* findet sich ferner in *as-Sīrah an-nabawiyyah* von Ibn Hišām (Ibn Hišām, ʿAbd al-Malik, *as-Sīrah an-nabawiyyah*, 2 Bde., hrsg. von Muṣṭafā as-Saqqā, Ibrāhim al-Abyārī & ʿAbd al-Ḥafiẓ Šalabī, Kairo 1936, Bd. 1, S. 300) bei der Schilderung von Ermahnungsreden, die Mohammed in Mekka an die Zuhörer hielt und in welchen er die Mekkaner „vor der Strafe Gottes" (*niqmat Allāh*) warnte, welche frühere Gemeinschaften ereilt hatte.

2 Der das Bittgebet ausmachende Wortlaut variiert nach mehrheitlichem islamischem Verständnis je nachdem, wer dieses Bittgebet verrichtet. Drei Subjekte kommen hierbei in Frage: Gott, die Engel und die Muslime. Siehe hierzu die zweite Einführung, Teilaspekt 7.

3 Diese Titelfassung kommt jeweils auf dem Titelblatt der beiden benutzten Handschriften vor; im Vorwort zu den beiden wird der Titel allerdings in geringfügig abgewandelter Form angegeben: *Dafʿ an-niqmah fī ṣ-ṣalāh ʿalā nabī ar-raḥmah*.

4 Im Folgenden wird auf ihn mit dem Kürzel IAḤ verwiesen.

schriftstellerischen Leistungen IAḤs noch weit davon entfernt, umfassend oder gar endgültig zu sein. Für die Einseitigkeit der geläufigen Einschätzung ausgehend von dem wenigen, was wir aus der Feder dieses Autors gegenwärtig in gedruckter Form vorliegen haben, spricht auch die Tatsache, dass die Zeitgenossen IAḤs ihm bis zu 60 Werke zuschrieben.[5] Im vorliegenden Beitrag soll ein weiterer Aspekt des Wirkens IAḤs beleuchtet werden. Dies soll auf der Grundlage einer bisher noch nicht edierten Schrift dieses Autors *Dafʿ an-niqmah bi-ṣ-ṣalāḥ ʿalā nabī ar-raḥmah*[6] – im späteren Verlauf nur verkürzt *Dafʿ an-niqmah* genannt – geschehen. Dieses Werk war mir in zwei Handschriften zugänglich und umfasst jeweils 83 bzw. 87 Textfolien.[7] Laut Dols ist *Dafʿ an-niqmah* eines der drei Werke, die IAḤ unter dem Schock des erneuten Pestausbruchs in Kairo im Jahr 1363 daselbst verfasst hat;[8] die anderen zwei seien *Ǧiwār al-aḫyār fī dār al-qarār* und *Kitāb aṭ-ṭibb al-masnūn fī dafʿ aṭ-ṭāʿūn*, wobei das zuletzt genannte Werk eine Zusammenfassung von *Dafʿ an-niqmah* sei.[9] Es ist in diesem Zusammenhang erwähnenswert, dass diesem genannten Pestausbruch ein Sohn IAḤs zum Opfer gefallen ist, sodass IAḤ nicht nur Augenzeuge des ungeheuren von dieser Krankheit ausgelösten Massensterbens war, sondern auch unmittelbar davon in der wohl denkbar schmerzlichsten Weise getroffen wurde. Im Folgenden werden die das Werk ausmachenden Kapitel kurz vorgestellt und im Hinblick auf einige charakteristische Merkmale beschrieben. Den Abschluss dieses Artikels bilden einige zusammenfassende Gedanken und – sofern es in diesem knappen Rahmen möglich ist – der Versuch, *Dafʿ an-niqmah* literaturgeschichtlich einzuordnen.

Der Inhalt des Traktats Dafʿ an-niqmah

IAḤ gibt seinen Lesern im Vorwort bereitwillig Aufschluss darüber, was ihn zur Verfassung von *Dafʿ an-niqmah* veranlasst hat: aufgrund der Tatsache, dass das Bittgebet zugunsten Mohammeds die Wirkkraft besitze, Sünden zu tilgen und vor den Schrecknissen am Tage des Jüngsten Gerichts zu schützen, sowie angesichts des unbeschreiblichen durch die Pest verursachten Leidens bestehe das einzige Heilmittel im erwähnten Bittgebet, das gegen dieses Unheil schützen, die

---

[5] Gruendler, Beatrice, "Ibn Abī Ḥajalah (1325-75)", in: Lowry, Joseph E., and Devin J. Stewart (eds.,), *Essays in Arabic Literary Biography: 1350-1850*, Wiesbaden 2009, S. 118-26, 120.

[6] Dieses Werk ist meines Wissens von zwei Autoren bisher besprochen worden: Dols, Michael W., *The Black Death in the Middle East*, Princeton 1977, S. 326 ff., sowie Conrad, Lawrence I., "Arabic plague chronologies and treatises: social and historical factors in the formation of a literary genre", in: *Studia Islamica* 54 (1981), S. 51-94.

[7] Für den vorliegenden Beitrag wurden zwei Manuskripte benutzt: N 1772 der Biblioteca del Escorial und Istanbul Laleli 1361. Bei der Angabe der Folien des Manuskripts folge ich der Istanbuler Handschrift.

[8] Die im Kapitel Nr. 7 von *Dafʿ an-niqmah* gegebene Auflistung aller Pestfälle in der islamischen Geschichte endet mit diesem genannten Pestausbruch.

[9] Dols, *Black Death*, S. 326 f.

herrscherliche Gunst erwirken und den Zorn Gottes beschwichtigen könne. Die Gliederung des Werks wird im Vorwort wie folgt beschrieben: es enthält zwei Einleitungen, vierzig Ḥadīṯe, einen abschließenden Nachtrag, Kapitel eins bis sieben durchgehend und den Abschluss.

Erste Einleitung[10] – Erste Einleitung über den Anlass für die Verfassung dieser reichlichen Lohn einbringenden Schrift sowie über die Untermauerung der Aussage eines der frommen Männer, dass die Häufigkeit des an Gott gerichteten Bittgebets für Mohammed – sofern es Gottes Willen entspricht – tatsächlich gegen die Pest feit.

Darin berichtet IAḤ darüber, dass in der Zeit, als die Pest in Kairo grassierte, bei einer Unterhaltung zwischen ihm und einem bekannten Gelehrten die Pest und ihre Ursachen thematisiert wurden. Der Letztere habe ihm davon berichtet, von einem frommen Mann gehört zu haben, dass das häufig wiederholte Bittgebet zugunsten Mohammeds gegen die Pest feie. Dies habe die Zustimmung IAḤs gefunden und er habe die entsprechende Bittgebetsformel bei jeder Gelegenheit aufgesagt und darüber hinaus auch seinen Gefährten davon berichtet. Später jedoch bei einer Diskussion mit einem Rechtsgelehrten darüber, als IAḤ für das erwähnte Bittgebet zugunsten Mohammeds argumentiert habe, habe ihn sein Kontrahent aufgefordert, hierfür einen stichhaltigen Beweis anzuführen. IAḤ räumt zwar ein, zu seiner Verteidigung sich weder auf ein explizites Zitat aus dem Koran oder der Sunna berufen zu können, verweist aber gleichzeitig darauf, dass hierfür trotzdem mittelbar gute Argumente aus der islamischen Überlieferung abgeleitet werden könnten. Hieran schließen sich entsprechende indirekte Belege, die vornehmlich aus Ḥadīṯen bestehen.

Zweite Einleitung[11] – Zweite Einleitung über das koranische Versfragment, dass Gott und seine Engel den Segen über den Propheten sprechen,[12] was von der großen Obsorge um den Propheten zeugt.

Die Einleitung ist unterteilt in zwanzig Teilaspekte (waǧh), in welchen IAḤ den in die Kapitelüberschrift eingeflochtenen Koranvers aus unterschiedlichen Perspektiven nach formalen sowie inhaltlichen Gesichtspunkten analysiert. Teilaspekt Nr. 4 ist der Untermauerung der Behauptung gewidmet, die dem Mohammed zuteil gewordene Ehrung durch Gott und seine Engel sei noch größer als die Ehrung Adams durch die Engel, welche vor ihm laut dem Koran kniefällig wurden. Der Teilaspekt Nr. 5, in dem IAḤ auf die besondere Wertachtung Gottes gegenüber Mohammed eingeht, die aus dem angeführten Koranvers hervorgehe, wird seinerseits in zehn weitere Unteraspekte unterteilt. Teilaspekt Nr. 8 hat die Betrachtung des Wortes *aṣ-ṣalāh* aus philologischer Perspektive zum Gegenstand;

---

[10] Fol. 3a-5a.
[11] Fol. 5a-14b.
[12] Sure 33, Vers 56. Hier und bei allen nachfolgenden Koranzitaten folge ich der Paretschen Koranübersetzung.

im Mittelpunkt des Teilaspektes Nr. 9 stehen die Engel: ihre Lichtbeschaffenheit, ihre Zahl und die ihnen zugeteilten Funktionen werden beleuchtet. Teilaspekte 12 bis 15 sind der Auseinandersetzung mit den Einwänden und Feststellungen Faḫraddīn ar-Rāzīs (gest. 1210) bezüglich des angeführten Koranverses gewidmet. Teilaspekt Nr. 16 geht der Frage nach, ob das Bittgebet zu Gunsten anderer Propheten sowie zu Gunsten derjenigen, die weder Propheten noch Engel sind, zulässig sei. Teilaspekt Nr. 17 enthält Zitate jeweils Abū Muḥammad al-Ǧuwaynīs (gest. 1047) bezüglich der Bittgebetsformel *ʿalayhi s-salām*, welche ausschließlich den Propheten vorbehalten sei, sowie ʿImādaddīn Ibn Kaṯīrs (1300-1372) bezüglich des Inhalts der Bittgebetsformeln zugunsten ʿAlī Ibn Abī Ṭālibs als auch anderer Prophetengenossen. Teilaspekt Nr. 20 enthält ein Zitat Muḥyiddīn an-Nawawīs (1233-1277) darüber, dass der Wortlaut des Bittgebets[13] zugunsten Mohammeds unbedingt zweierlei umfassen solle: *aṣ-ṣalāh*, d.h.: *ṣallā llāhu ʿalayhi*, und *taslīm*, d.h.: *wa-sallama*. An diesen letzten zwanzigsten Teilaspekt schließt sich ein Abschnitt (*faṣl*) an über das gebührende Wann und Wo der Verrichtung des Bittgebets zugunsten Mohammeds (*fī ḏikr al-mawāṭin allatī tataʿayyan aṣ-ṣalāh fīhā ʿalā n-nabī*).

Es sei an dieser Stelle etwas näher auf den siebenten Teilaspekt eingegangen, in dem es darum geht, welche drei konkreten Formen das im koranischen Vers 56 der Sure 33 – durch *yuṣallūna* bzw. *ṣallū* – angesprochene Bittgebet *aṣ-ṣalāh* zugunsten des Propheten annehmen kann, und zwar je nachdem, wer – Gott, Engel oder Menschen – dieses Bittgebet verrichtet. IAḤ trägt diesbezügliche Aussagen einiger namhafter Autoren – u.a. namentlich von al-Buḫārī (gest. 870) und Abū ʿĪsā at-Tirmiḏī (gest. 892) – zusammen und fasst diese dann dahingehend zusammen, dass das von Gott verrichtete Bittgebet als Loben Mohammeds [vor der Schar der Engel] (*aṯ-ṯanāʾ*), als Segnungsakt Mohammeds (*at-tabrīk*) sowie als Barmherzigkeit ihm gegenüber (*ar-raḥmah*) aufzufassen sei; das Bittgebet der Engel sei die Anrufung Gottes zu Mohammeds Gunsten (*ad-duʿāʾ*) und das Herabflehen göttlicher Vergebung für ihn (*al-istiġfār*); was das Bittgebet der Menschen betreffe, so bestehe es in der Anrufung Gottes zu seinen Gunsten (*ad-duʿāʾ*) und zwar des Inhalts, dass Gott ihm im Diesseits dadurch Größe verleihen möge, dass Er Mohammed Herrlichkeit verleiht (*iʿẓāmihī*), den islamischen Geltungsanspruch durchsetzt (*iẓhār daʿwatihī*) und die durch Mohammed gestiftete Scharia bestehen lässt (*ibqāʾ šarīʿatihī*); im Jenseits solle diese Größe verliehen werden durch das Privileg der Fürsprache für die Muslime, durch das Doppelte bzw. das Mehrfache des Lohns und des Entgelts Mohammeds.[14]

---

[13] Dieser Wortlaut ist: *ṣallā llāhu ʿalayhi wa-sallama*.

[14] Die gesamte Passage der Istanbuler Handschrift (Fol. 7b), die den Inhalt des Bittgebets der Menschen beschreibt, ist an dieser Stelle für mich nicht ganz klar, durch Heranziehung der Handschrift Escorial (Fol. 8b) glaube ich an dieser Stelle folgenden Text zu erkennen: *ʿaẓẓimhu fī d-dunyā bi-iʿẓāmihī wa-iẓhār daʿwatihī wa-ibqāʾ šarīʿatihī wa-fī l-āḫirati bi-š-šafāʿati wa-bi-ḍiʿf aǧrihī wa-maṯūbatihī.*

Es sei hier auf ein aufschlussreiches Detail im Verständnis des Koranverses „*inna llāha wa-malāʾikatahū yuṣallūna ʿalā n-nabī. Yā ayyuhā alladīna āmanū ṣallū ʿalayhi wasallimū taslīman*" (Sure 33, Vers 56) hingewiesen, welcher der zweiten Einleitung zu Grunde liegt. In der Übersetzung Rudi Parets heißt es an dieser Stelle: „Gott und seine Engel sprechen den Segen über den Propheten. Ihr Gläubigen! Sprecht (auch ihr) den Segen über ihn und grüßt (ihn), wie es sich gehört!". *Yuṣallūna* bzw. *ṣallū* wird auch in der Übersetzung Hartmut Bobzins[15] gleicherweise mit „den Segen sprechen" übersetzt. Alan Jones[16] übersetzt diesen Vers mit: „God and His angels bless the prophet. O you who believe, bless him and salute him". Wie man aus den angeführten Beispielen ersieht, wird darin das eine Verb *yuṣallūna* bzw. *ṣallū* einheitlich übersetzt, unabhängig davon, wer als Subjekt der mit *ṣallā* angezeigten Handlung auftritt. Dies kontrastiert mit den von IAḤ zusammengetragenen Auffassungen muslimischer Theologen, die bereits sehr früh dazu tendierten, dem einen Verb *ṣallā* dieses Verses je nach einem der drei genannten Subjekte – Gott, die Engel oder die Gläubigen – drei unterschiedliche Bedeutungen zu Grunde zu legen. Eine weitere Bedeutung dieses Verbs mit der Präposition *ʿalā* kann ferner eine allgemeine Bedeutung „j-m zugewandt das Gebet verrichten" haben, wie es eindeutig aus folgendem von IAḤ angeführtem Ḥadīt hervorgeht: „Es überlieferte Abū Masʿūd al-Anṣārī – möge er Gottes Wohlgefallen finden – Folgendes: ,Einmal kam ein Mann herzu und setzte sich vor dem Gesandten Gottes – Gott möge ihn segnen und ihm Heil spenden – nieder, als wir bei ihm versammelt waren. Dann sagte er: ,Oh Gesandter Gottes, wie wir dich grüßen, das wissen wir inzwischen, aber wie sollen wir das Bittgebet zu deinen Gunsten verrichten, wenn wir Gott zugewandt beten?'[17] Da schwieg der Gesandte Gottes – Gott segne ihn und spende ihm Heil – so lange, dass wir uns wünschten, dieser Mann hätte ihn das nicht gefragt. Danach sagte er: ,Wenn ihr euer Bittgebet zu meinen Gunsten verrichtet, so sprecht: Oh Gott, sprich deinen Segen über Mohammed, den des Lesens und Schreibens unkundigen Propheten, und über seine Familie wie du einst deinen Segen sprachst über Abraham und seine Familie, und segne Mohammed und seine Familie wie du einst Abraham und seine Familie segnetest; daran schließt ihr dann die Grußformel an, so wie ihr sie kennt".[18]

Vierzig Ḥadīte[19] – Über die vierzig Ḥadīte, welche vom Vorzugsstatus[20] des erwähnten Bittgebets sowie vom hierfür festgesetzten Entgelt handeln, ferner von

---

[15] Bobzin, Hartmut, *Der Koran*, München 2010.

[16] Jones, Alan, *The Qurʾān*, Exeter 2007.

[17] *Fa-kayfa nuṣallī ʿalayka idā naḥnu ṣallaynā fī ṣalātinā ʿalā llāhi ʿalayk?*

[18] Fol. 20a.

[19] Fol. 14b-29b.
    Die beiden Handschriften weichen voneinander erheblich ab beim Ḥadīt Nr. 21: während in der Istanbuler Handschrift (Fol. 20b f.) dieser Prophetenausspruch auf die Autorität von Ğābir Ibn ʿAbdallāh überliefert wird, worauf sieben weitere Ḥadīte folgen und die Zählung dann mit dem Ḥadīt Nr. 24 fortgesetzt wird, ist die Zählung in der Handschrift Escorial (Fol. 21b f.) ununterbrochen und der in der Istanbuler Handschrift unter Nr. 21 angeführte

der Zeit und dem Ort für die Verrichtung dieses Bittgebets, von der für dessen Verrichtung festgesetzten Belohnung und von der aus dessen Unterlassung folgenden Bestrafung sowie auch von den nutzenbringenden Aufschlüssen u. ä.

Es sind genau genommen mehr als vierzig Ḥadīṯe und das Bestreben des Autors, unbedingt auf diese Zahl zu kommen, ist unverkennbar. Die Zahl vierzig kommt häufig in den Titeln arabischer Werke vor. So verweist z.B. Yaḥyā Ibn Šaraf an-Nawawī im Vorwort zu seiner Sammlung der vierzig Ḥadīṯe *Kitāb al-arbaʿīn* darauf, dass viele islamische Gelehrte vor ihm bereits auf unterschiedlichen Gebieten der islamischen Gelehrsamkeit Werke verfasst haben, deren Titel den Bestandteil „vierzig" enthielten.[21] Auch der wie folgt überlieferte Prophetenausspruch weist in diese Richtung: „Wer an meine muslimische Gemeinde vierzig Aussprüche betreffs der rechten [islamischen] Glaubenspraxis intakt weiterreicht, den wird Gott am Jüngsten Tage als Mitglied der Gemeinschaft der Rechtsgelehrten und der Islamgelehrten auferwecken".[22]

Das Erreichen der heilsmäßigen Zahl 40 geschieht u.a. dadurch, dass unter dem Ḥadīṯ Nr. 40 viele weitere Ḥadīṯe zusammengefasst werden, die streng genommen eine eigene Numerierung erfordert hätten. Dies ist wohl damit zu erklären, dass IAḤ dabei genau den eben zitierten Prophetenausspruch vor Augen hatte.

Formal gesehen folgt IAḤ – von einigen wenigen Ausnahmen abgesehen[23] – einem einheitlichen Muster beim Zitieren der Ḥadīṯe: nach der Angabe der Per-

---

Prophetenausspruch wird hier unter Nr. 23 auf die Autorität von ʿAlī Ibn Abī Ṭālib überliefert.

[20] Mit *Fī faḍl aṣ-ṣalāh* an dieser Stelle ist auch mitgemeint, wie sehr Verdienst bringend, heilsmäßig ergiebig das genannte Bittgebet ist.

[21] Ibn Daqīq al-ʿĪd, *Šarḥ al-arbaʿīn ḥadīṯan an-nawawiyyah li-l-imām Yaḥyā Ibn Šarafaddīn an-Nawawī*, Mekka [o.J.], S. 5.

[22] *Man ḥafiẓa ʿalā ummatī arbaʿīna ḥadīṯan min amri dīnihā baʿaṯahū llāhu yawma l-qiyāmati fī zumrati l-fuqahāʾi wa-l-ʿulamāʾ* (Ibn Daqīq al-ʿĪd, *Šarḥ al-arbaʿīn ḥadīṯan an-nawawiyyah*, S. 4). Das hier gebrauchte Wort *ḥadīṯ* muss in diesem Zusammenhang nicht unbedingt Ḥadīṯ im engen Sinn bedeuten. In *as-Sīrah an-nabawiyyah* von Ibn Hišām (Bd. 1, S. 300) meinte *ḥadīṯ* u.a. Erzählungen profanen, unterhaltsamen Charakters. Eine genauere Beschreibung dessen, was eigentlich unter *dīn* verstanden wurde, findet sich in einer berühmten Überlieferung darüber, dass einst ein Mann Mohammed vor seinen Genossen nach verschiedenen Aspekten der islamischen Offenbarung befragt habe, nämlich nach *al-islām, al-īmān, al-iḥsān, as-sāʿah, amārāt [as-sāʿah]*. Nachdem Mohammed zu jeder Frage die richtige Antwort gegeben habe und der erwähnte Mann weggegangen sei, habe der Prophet die Befragung mit den Worten zusammengefasst: „Dies war [der Erzengel] Gabriel, der euch über euren *dīn* (hier sinngemäß: die Eckpunkte eures islamischen Glaubens) belehrt hat" (Ibn Šaraf an-Nawawī, Abū Zakariyā Yaḥyā, *Riyāḍ aṣ-ṣāliḥīn min kalām sayyid al-mursalīn*, ed. Riḍwān Muḥammad Riḍwān, Beirut [ca. 1970], S. 41 f.). Die Wahl der Zahl vierzig gepaart mit der Tatsache, dass IAḤ die Kenntnis des eben zitierten Prophetenausspruchs bei seinen zeitgenössischen Lesern zweifelsohne als bekannt voraussetzen konnte, dürfte somit einiges sowohl über den Anspruch IAḤ mit seiner Abhandlung *Dafʿ an-niqmah* als auch über seine Selbsteinschätzung aussagen.

[23] So z.B. ist beim Ḥadīṯ Nr. 30 die Quelle nicht angegeben und bei den dem Prophetenausspruch Nr. 40 zugeordneten und in einem eigenen Abschnitt (*faṣl*) zusammengefassten Ḥadīṯen ist in den meisten Fällen weder der Überlieferer noch die Quelle angegeben.

son, auf deren letztliche Autorität ein Ḥadīṯ überliefert ist, d.h. die Isnad-Kette ist bis auf den Gewährsmann direkt vor Mohammed[24] verkürzt, folgt der Wortlaut des jeweiligen Ḥadīṯs, woran sich ein Hinweis darauf anschließt, welche Autoren diesen Ausspruch in ihre jeweilige Ḥadīṯ-Sammlung aufgenommen haben. Der Ḥadīṯ Nr. 40 enthält mehrere leicht voneinander abweichende Fassungen des Bittgebets für Mohammed; diesem Gegenstand sind auch die Ḥadīṯe Nr. 20 und 39 gewidmet.

Abschließender Nachtrag[25] – Nachtrag, welcher handelt von den großen göttlichen Gunsterweisen, die im Jenseits einigen frommen Muslimen aufgrund der Verrichtung des Bittgebets zugunsten des Propheten zuteil geworden sind.

Hierin sind insgesamt fünfzehn Träume (al-manām) enthalten, welche die unterschiedlichen Formen jenseitiger wie diesseitiger göttlicher Gunst gegenüber namentlich genannten Personen beschreiben. Im als Traumbericht Nr. 8 bezeichneten Abschnitt wird kein Traum überliefert. In den allermeisten Fällen folgen die Traumberichte einem einheitlichen Aufbauschema und enthalten in der Regel durchgehend zwei formale Elemente, die geringfügig voneinander abweichen können: eine meistens namentlich genannte Person berichtet, eine andere kürzlich verstorbene Person im Traum gesehen zu haben und dieser als erstes die Frage danach, welches jenseitige Schicksal Gott dieser Person zugeteilt habe, gestellt zu haben.[26] Nach der Auskunft der befragten Person über die ihr zugeteilten jenseitigen Gunsterweise folgt die zweite Frage danach, wodurch sich diese verstorbene Person die göttlichen Gunsterweise erarbeitet habe.[27] Die Antwort besteht dann immer im Hinweis auf die Häufigkeit des Bittgebets für Mohammed. Für die betreffenden Personen habe die erwiesene Gunst unterschiedliche Formen angenommen. Sie habe jeweils darin bestanden, im Himmel zusammen mit den Engeln das Bittgebet verrichten zu dürfen (Traumbericht Nr. 1), Vergebung der Sünden und die höheren Paradiesstufen erlangt zu haben (Traumbericht Nr. 2), von der Gerichtsverhandlung am Tage des Jüngsten Gerichts ausgenommen worden zu sein (Traumbericht Nr. 3),[28] das Privileg zu haben, zusammen mit den Engeln im Himmel Gott zu preisen (Traumbericht Nr. 9), sowie das Vorrecht zu haben, sich bei Gott für die Erledigung der Anliegen von noch lebenden Menschen einzusetzen (Traumbericht Nr. 12). In einem Fall (Traumbericht Nr. 13) habe ein lebender Frommer den Lohn, der ihm eigentlich für das Bittgebet für Mohammed zugestanden hätte, an die Toten verschenkt und sie damit von der Pein im Grab

---

24 Hierbei folge ich der Logik der Ḥadīṯ-Wissenschaft, der zufolge die Gewährsmännerreihenfolge bis hin zu ihrem Ausgangspunkt (al-muntahā), dem eigentlichen Aussprecher des jeweiligen Ḥadīṯs, nach oben verläuft.

25 Fol. 29b-33b.

26 Überwiegendes Formulierungsmuster: mā faʿala llāhu bika?

27 Überwiegendes Formulierungsmuster: bimā balaǧta ḏālik?

28 Mit Ausnahme der beiden Traumberichte Nr. 5 und Nr. 8 enthalten die nachfolgenden Traumberichte Nr. 4, 6 und 7 ebenfalls mindestens als einen der jenseitigen Gunsterweise die Vergebung der Sünden.

befreit. Im Traumbericht Nr. 15 werde ein Mann wegen eines früheren Vergehens damit bestraft, dass bei dessen Tod sein Gesicht wie das Maul eines Esels aussehe; letztlich jedoch werde es doch durch ein leuchtendes Antlitz ersetzt, und zwar als Entgelt für die zu seinen Lebzeiten praktizierte Gewohnheit, vor dem Schlaf hundert Mal das Bittgebet für Mohammed zu verrichten. Im Bericht Nr. 14 dient ein im Traum einer Person mitgeteiltes Bittgebet für Muhammed dazu, das im Sturm unterzugehen drohende Schiff samt allen Menschen an Bord zu retten. Im Traumbericht Nr. 10 dient das jeden Freitagabend von einem Vezier tausend Mal verrichtete Bittgebet für Mohammed als Kennwort, das Mohammed einem frommen, aber verarmten Mann im Traum mitteilte und das den Letzteren als einen glaubwürdigen Überbringer der prophetischen Anordnung an den Vezier ausweisen soll, ihm hundert Dinar auszuzahlen.

Kapitel Nr. 1[29] – Das erste Kapitel darüber, was Gott für einen Pestkranken an jenseitiger Wonne und am Status eines Blutzeugen bereithält, sowie darüber, dass demjenigen, der [die Pest] standhaft und mit Fassung erträgt, dafür der einem Blutzeugen vorbehaltene Lohn zusteht, auch dann, wenn er [diese Pestkrankheit] überlebt.

Zur Untermauerung dieser Kapitelüberschrift führt IAH entsprechende Ḥadīṯe an. Hierbei erscheinen besonders zwei Ḥadīṯe interessant, da IAH auf die in ihnen angesprochenen Themen auch im weiteren Verlauf seiner Schrift immer wieder zurückkommt und weil in ihnen zwei wichtige Aspekte der Pest thematisiert werden. Zum einen geht es um die Feststellung, welche Funktion die Pest in der Beziehung zwischen Gott und den Menschen erfüllt; zum anderen geht es um die Symptomatik der Pest. Was den ersten, theologischen Aspekt betrifft, führt IAH einen auf die Autorität von ʿĀʾišah in „Ṣaḥīḥ al-Buḫārī" überlieferten Prophetenausspruch an, dass die Pest [ehemals] eine von Gott nach seinem Ratschluss gegen seine Knechte eingesetzte Strafe gewesen sei, dann aber von ihm in einen Gnadenakt gegenüber den Gläubigen verwandelt worden sei; jeder Muslim, der in einer von der Pest heimgesuchten Ortschaft sei und dort ausharre, diese Ortschaft nicht verlasse, sondern standhaft und mit Fassung [diese Heimsuchung] ertrage, wissend, dass ihn nur das treffen könne, was ihm zuvor von Gott vorherbestimmt worden sei, werde einen dem Lohn eines Blutzeugen gleichwertigen Lohn erhalten.[30] In einem weiteren ebenfalls auf die Autorität von ʿĀʾišah überlieferten Ḥadīṯ sagt Mohammed, seine Gemeinde werde durch zweierlei untergehen, nämlich durch Lanzenstiche (ṭaʿn) und die Pest (ṭāʿūn).[31] Als

---

[29] Fol. 33b-35b.

[30] Fol. 34a.

[31] In *Lisān al-ʿarab* wird *ṭāʿūn* als eine Massenkrankheit bzw. Epidemie definiert, die zum Miasma führt, welches seinerseits das Missverhältnis der [vier] Körpersäfte und körperliches Leiden zur Folge hat. IAH geht im Kapitel Nr. 4 detailliert auf die beiden Begriffe *ṭāʿūn* und *wabaʾ* ein und setzt sie gegeneinander ab, indem er einschlägige Aussagen anderer Autoren hierzu anführt.

ʿĀʾišah nach der genauen Bedeutung von *ṭāʿūn* sich erkundigt, antwortet Mohammed, dass die Pest ein Wulst (*ġuddah*) sei, der dem Wulst bei den Kamelen ähnlich sei und an den Ellenbögen und in den Achselhöhlen auftrete; wer daran gestorben sei, sei den Tod eines Blutzeugen gestorben.[32] Ein im Anschluss daran sehr ähnlicher, wenn auch auf einem anderen Wege überlieferter Prophetenausspruch enthält dieselbe Ankündigung, allerdings wird dort die Erkundigung danach, was *ṭāʿūn* sei, damit beantwortet, *ṭāʿūn* seien die Stiche eurer, d.h. der Muslime, Feinde, nämlich der Dschinnen. Darüber hinaus widmet IAḤ dieses Kapitel der sprachlichen Erklärung des Wortes „Blutzeuge" sowie den verschiedenen Typen von Blutzeugen.

Kapitel Nr. 2[33] – Das zweite Kapitel über einige Prophetengenossen, die sich den Pesttod herbeigewünscht haben,[34] sowie über derer solche, die die Flucht davor für richtig hielten.

Die Einleitung hierzu bildet der Bericht über den Pestausbruch von ʿAmwās, der bei der Vorstellung des 3. Kapitels etwas ausführlicher besprochen wird. Vorausgreifend sei nur soviel gesagt, dass die Schilderung des besagten Pestausbruchs bei Ibn al-Aṯīr sich aus zwei Teilen zusammensetzt, die zueinander nicht zu passen scheinen, wie es im Folgenden noch zu sehen sein wird. In *Dafʿ an-niqmah* werden nun diese beiden Teile voneinander getrennt und auf die Kapitel 2 und 3 verteilt. Hierbei wird die Abfolge der beiden Teile bei Ibn al-Aṯīr von IAḤ beibehalten, d.h. der bei diesem Autor zuerst angeführte Bericht kommt in *Dafʿ an-niqmah* im 2. Kapitel, und der nächste entsprechend im 3. Kapitel vor. Wie bereits in der Kapitelüberschrift angedeutet, geht es um die unterschiedlichen Sichtweisen der Prophetegenossen darauf, wie man sich angesichts der Pest verhalten solle. Ihre Reihe wird mit dem Prophetegenossen Abū ʿUbaydah Ibn al-Ǧarrāḥ (gest. 639) eröffnet, der sich geweigert habe, das von der Pest heimgesuchte Gebiet zu verlassen, und hiermit den Aufruf ʿUmar Ibn al-Ḫaṭṭābs (gest. 644), dies um der eigenen Unversehrtheit willen zu tun, ignoriert habe. Im Zusammenhang mit dem Pestausbruch von ʿAmwās wird ein weiterer Bericht von Aḥmad Ibn Ḥanbal (gest. 855) angeführt, der aufgrund der Tatsache, einen für die Pest-Thematik relevanten Ḥadīṯ zu enthalten, hier etwas ausführlicher wiedergegeben sei. Dem zufolge habe sich Abū ʿUbaydah Ibn al-Ǧarrāḥ dann, als die Pest in ʿAmwās heftig grassiert habe, an die Menschen mit den Worten gewandt: „Dieses Leiden (*al-waǧaʿ*)[35] verkörpert einen Gnadenakt Gottes [euch gegenüber],

---

[32] Fol. 35a.

[33] Fol. 35b-38b.

[34] Hierin ist ein Ausspruch Mohammeds enthalten, der mit „Es soll sich niemand unter euch den eigenen Tod herbeiwünschen" (*lā yatamannayna aḥadukumū l-mawta*) anfängt und danach in teilweise sehr unterschiedlicher Fortsetzung überliefert wird. Dieser Ḥadīṯ findet im Verlaufe des Kapitels einige Male Erwähnung und wird erörtert.

[35] Wohlgemerkt, ist das semantische Umfeld von „Schmerz" im Arabischen etwas weiter aufgefasst: zum einen kommen die beiden arab. Wörter mit dem Wortsinn „körperlicher Schmerz", nämlich *al-alam* und *al-waǧaʿ*, häufig auch in der allgemeinen Bedeutung „Krank-

das Bittgebet eures Propheten [für euch] und den Tod von frommen Männern, die vor euch gelebt haben (*hāḏā l-waǧʿu raḥmatu rabbikum wa-daʿwatu nabīyikum wa-mawtu ṣ-ṣāliḥīn qablakum*). Ich, Abū ʿUbaydah, bitte Gott darum, mir auch meinen Anteil daran zu geben". Daraufhin sei auch er an der Pest erkrankt und infolgedessen gestorben. Sein Nachfolger, der Prophetengenosse Muʿāḏ Ibn Ǧabal (gest. 639) habe sich mit dem gleichen Prophetenausspruch an die Menschen gewandt und die Pest auf sich und seine Familienangehörigen herabgefleht; das gleiche Schicksal habe zuerst seinen Sohn und dann auch ihn ereilt. Erst ʿAmr Ibn al-ʿĀṣ (592-682), der berühmte Eroberer Ägyptens und in diesem Kontext Nachfolger Muʿāḏ Ibn Ǧabals, habe angesichts der hohen Zahl der Dahingerafften die Menschen dazu aufgerufen, sich Schutz suchend auf die Berge zurückzuziehen. Dies sei auch ʿUmar Ibn al-Ḫaṭṭāb gemeldet worden, und dieser habe dieses Vorgehen nicht missbilligt. Der auf den ersten Blick etwas befremdlich wirkende Ausspruch, die Pest sei Folge des prophetischen Bittgebets, wird auf der übernächsten Seite erklärt. Dort allerdings ist der geringfügig abgeänderte Wortlaut[36] dieses Ḥadīṯs im Anschluss an eine Ansprache von ʿAmr Ibn al-ʿĀṣ, in welcher er die zerstörerische Wirkung der Pest beschreibt, in Gestalt eines Einwandes einem weiteren Prophetengenossen namens Šuraḥbīl Ibn Ḥasanah (gest. 639) in den Mund gelegt. Diesen Ausspruch Šuraḥbīl Ibn Ḥasanahs erklärt IAḤ mit einem – weiteren – prophetischen Ausspruch: „Gott! Lass meine Glaubensgemeinschaft im Kampf für deine Sache durch zweierlei untergehen: durch Tod entweder durch Lanzenstiche oder Pest [bzw. Stiche der Dschinnen]!"[37] Auffallend ist

---

heit, Leiden, Unpässlichkeit" vor; diese Verwendung ist z.B. für beide genannten Wörter in den Briefauszügen belegt, die in *Ṣubḥ al-aʿšā fī ṣināʿat al-inšāʾ* al-Qalqašandīs im Kapitel „Beglückwünschung zur Genesung von Krankheit und zum Gesundwerden vom Leiden" (*at-Tahniʾah bi-l-iblāl min al-maraḍ wa-l-ʿāfiyah min as-saqam*) zusammengetragen sind, wobei *al-alam* quantitativ eindeutig überwiegt (al-Qalqašandī, Aḥmad Ibn ʿAlī, *Ṣubḥ al-aʿšā fī ṣināʿat al-inšāʾ*, hrsg. von Muḥammad Ḥusayn Šamsaddīn, 15 Bde., Beirut 1988, Bd. 9, S. 64, 66, 67, 68, 69 und 70). Gewichtiger hier ist allerdings die Verwendung von *al-waǧʿ* auch in der Bedeutung „Pest", was aus einer im Zusammenhang mit dem Pestausbruch von ʿAmwās stehenden Überlieferung hervorgeht, die mit den Worten anfängt: Abū ʿUbaydah [Ibn al-Ǧarrāḥ] und seine Familienangehörigen waren von der Pest [viell. genauer: vom Pest-Leiden] in ʿAmwās [vorerst] verschont geblieben (*inna waǧʿa ʿAmwāsa kāna muʿāfan minhu Abū ʿUbaydata wa-ahluh*). Danach habe er allerdings von Gott seinen eigenen und seiner Familienangehörigen Anteil an der Pest herabgefleht (Fol. 37a). Diesen Sinnaspekt von „Schmerz" sollte man auch bei den übrigen Nennungen von *al-alam* und *al-waǧʿ* in *Dafʿ an-niqmah* mitbedenken.

[36] Der Unterschied besteht im Wort *qabḍ* (Dahinraffen), das anstelle von *mawt* (Tod) bei der Erwähnung der frommen Männer im letzten Teil gebraucht wird.

[37] *Allāhumma ǧʿal fanāʾa ummatī qatlan fī sabīlika bi-ṭ-ṭaʿni wa-ṭ-ṭāʿūn*. Dieser zuletzt angegebene Sinn von *aṭ-ṭāʿūn* ist bereits im Kapitel Nr. 1 im Zusammenhang mit einem inhaltlich sehr ähnlichen Ausspruch Mohammeds (35a) erwähnt worden, der dort allerdings die Form einer Ankündigung hatte; diese beiden Ḥadīṯe werden auch in *Fatḥ al-bārī* erwähnt und dabei wird *aṭ-ṭāʿūn* die Bedeutung „Stiche der Dschinnen" zu Grunde gelegt (Ibn Ḥaǧar al-ʿAsqalānī, *Fatḥ al-bārī bi-šarḥ Ṣaḥīḥ al-imām Abī ʿAbdallāh Muḥammad Ibn Ismāʿīl al-Buḫārī*, 13 Bde., hrsg. von Muḥibbaddīn al-Ḫaṭīb, 1379 h/[1959], Bd. 10, S. 181). Vgl. auch den Kommentar hierzu bei Ibn al-Aṯīr, der dieses Bittgebet Mohammeds in einen gänzlich an-

in diesem Kapitel, dass die beiden Prophetengenossen Abū ʿUbaydah Ibn al-Ǧarrāḥ und Muʿāḏ Ibn Ǧabal öfter als andere vorkommen, und der Letztere dabei im Hinblick auf die Häufigkeit der Berichte, in welchen er in Erscheinung tritt, heraussticht. Wenn man das Verhältnis zwischen den Berichten betrachtet, die zur Untermauerung einer der beiden in der Kapitelüberschrift angesprochenen Handlungsweisen angesichts der Pest angeführt werden, so bilden solche Überlieferungen, in welchen die erwähnten Prophetengenossen sich bewusst der Pest ausgesetzt bzw. diese herbeigesehnt oder sogar auf sich herabgefleht haben, eindeutig die Mehrheit. IAḤ schließt dieses Kapitel mit dem Befund, welchem zufolge beides, nämlich sowohl das bewusste Sichaussetzen der Pest als auch die Flucht davor, verboten seien. Diesen scheint er aus dem Kommentar an-Nawawīs zu „Ṣaḥīḥ Muslim" übernommen zu haben.[38]

Kapitel Nr. 3[39] – Das dritte Kapitel über das Verbot, sich absichtlich der Pest auszusetzen, indem man sich in Gebiete begibt, welche die Pest heimgesucht hat und dort grassiert, sowie über das Verbot, aus Angst um sein Leben vor der Pestheimsuchung zu fliehen.

Dieses Kapitel wird mit folgendem Prophetenausspruch zur Pest eingeleitet: „Dieser [körperliche] Schmerz bzw. diese Krankheit ist eine Strafe (*riǧz*), welche an einigen Glaubensgemeinschaften vor euch vollstreckt wurde. Danach ist diese auf Erden geblieben, verschwindet für eine Zeitlang und kommt wieder. Jeder, der hört, dass ein Landstrich von ihr [d.h. Pest] heimgesucht ist, soll diesen Landstrich bloß meiden! Und jeder, den es in einen Landstrich verschlägt, der gerade von der Pest heimgesucht ist, soll nicht in der Flucht vor der Pest sein Heil suchend diesen Landstrich verlassen!"[40] Hieran schließt sich ein Bericht über den ersten Pestausbruch in der islamischen Geschichte an, nämlich über die Pest von ʿAmwās. Diese soll sich im Jahr 639 ereignet haben, und bereits im Bericht darüber sind die wichtigsten Elemente enthalten, die wiederkehrend bei jedem weiteren Pestausbruch erörtert werden. Es ist bemerkenswert, dass IAḤ an mehreren Stellen in *Dafʿ an-niqmah* auf diesen ersten Pestausbruch zu sprechen kommt, um daraus die mit den jeweiligen Kapiteln korrespondierenden Schlussfolgerungen zu gewinnen. Der Bericht über die mit diesem Pestausbruch im Zusammenhang stehenden Ereignisse setzt mehr oder minder unvermittelt nach dem erwähnten Prophetenausspruch ein. Demzufolge brach ʿUmar Ibn al-Ḫaṭṭāb (gest. 644) nach Syrien auf. In Sarǧ[41] angelangt, sei er auf das syrische Kontingent getroffen, beste-

---

deren Sinnzusammenhang einordnet und es abweichend überliefert (Ibn al-Aṯir, Muḥammad Ibn Muḥammad aš-Šaybānī, *al-Kāmil fi t-tariḫ*, 10 Bde., Beirut 1965, Bd. 2, S. 560).

38 *Ṣaḥīḥ Muslim bi-šarh an-Nawawī*, 18 Bde., Kairo 1929-1930, Bd. 14, S. 207.

39 Fol. 38b-39b.

40 Ein ähnlicher Ausspruch wird auch am Anfang des nachfolgenden Kapitels etwas abgewandelt und stark verkürzt zitiert; beide Aussprüche werden vom Prophetengenossen Usāmah Ibn Zayd (gest. 674) verbürgt.

41 Yāqūt Ibn ʿAbdallāh al-Ḥamawī ar-Rūmī, *Kitāb muʿǧam al-buldān*, hrsg. von Ferdinand Wüstenfeld, 6 Bde., Leipzig 1866-1877, Bd. 3,1, S. 77.

hend aus Abū ʿUbaydah Ibn al-Ǧarrāḥ (gest. 639) und seinem Trupp, die ihn über den Pestausbruch in Syrien in Kenntnis gesetzt hätten. ʿUmar, unschlüssig über das weitere Vorgehen, habe daraufhin zunächst die mit ihm ziehenden Auswanderer der ersten Stunde (al-muhāǧirīn al-awwalīn) eingeladen und sie um Rat gefragt. Diese hätten zwei widersprüchliche Meinungen vertreten: die einen hätten gemeint, ʿUmar solle die Reise fortsetzen, die anderen seien der Ansicht gewesen, er solle umkehren und die wenigen noch lebenden Prophetengenossen nicht der Epidemie aussetzen. ʿUmar habe daraufhin bei der von ihm einberufenen nächsten Versammlung, welche diesmal nur die Helfer (al-anṣār) umfasst hätte, die gleiche Frage gestellt. Die Helfer hätten genau wie die Auswanderer zuvor die beiden Meinungen vertreten. Erst die Mitglieder der dritten von ʿUmar einberufenen Versammlung, nämlich die quraišitischen Šayḫs, welche die Auswanderung erst nach der Eroberung Mekkas durch Mohammed vollzogen hatten (mašyaḫat Qurayš min muhāǧirat al-fatḥ)[42], hätten sich einhellig für die Rückkehr ausgesprochen. Nach der Ankündigung ʿUmars, am nächsten Tag umkehren zu wollen, habe sich Abū ʿUbaydah Ibn al-Ǧarrāḥ mit dem Einwand zu Wort gemeldet: „Fliehst du etwa vor dem Ratschluss Gottes?" Die Antwort ʿUmars darauf habe gelautet: „Ja, wir fliehen vor dem Ratschluss Gottes hin zum Ratschluss Gottes. Was meinst du, wenn du eine Kamelherde hättest und es hätte dich in ein Tal mit zwei unterschiedlichen Talseiten verschlagen; die eine Talseite wäre fruchtbar und die andere dürr. Hättest du nicht, wenn du deine Kamele auf der fruchtbaren Seite hättest grasen lassen, dies gemäß dem Ratschluss Gottes getan? Und wenn du deine Kamele auf der dürren Talseite hättest grasen lassen, hättest du dies nicht auch gemäß dem Ratschluss Gottes getan?" In diesem Moment sei ʿAbd ar-Raḥmān Ibn ʿAwf (gest. 652) dazu gestoßen und habe die Position ʿUmars mit dem Prophetenausspruch gestärkt: „Jeder, der hört, dass ein Landstrich von ihr [d.h. Pest] heimgesucht ist, soll diesen Landstrich meiden! Und jeder, den es in einen Landstrich verschlägt, der gerade von der Pest heimgesucht ist, soll nicht in der Flucht vor der Pest sein Heil suchend diesen Landstrich verlassen!"

Die Tragweite dieses Ereignisses besteht darin, dass alle drei genannten Personen, nämlich ʿUmar Ibn al-Ḫaṭṭāb, Abū ʿUbaydah Ibn al-Ǧarrāḥ und ʿAbd ar-Raḥmān Ibn ʿAwf als Anhänger der ersten Stunde zu Mohammed noch in seiner mekkanischen Wirkungszeit gestoßen waren[43] und dadurch ein denkbar großes Ansehen in der islamischen Geschichte genossen. Sie waren nicht nur als Überlieferer prophetischer Traditionen bekannt, sondern gehörten darüber hinaus zu je-

---

42 Nach landläufiger Auffassung können mit der Bezeichnung *mašyaḫat Qurayš min muhāǧirat al-fatḥ* zwei unterschiedliche Gruppen gemeint sein: zum einen diejenigen, die kurz vor der Einnahme [Mekkas durch Mohammed] den Islam angenommen haben, und zum anderen diejenigen – und dieser Zuordnung wird mehr Gewicht beigemessen – , die erst nach der Einnahme [Mekkas den Islam angenommen haben und] zu Mohammed ausgewandert sind (*Ṣaḥīḥ Muslim bi-šarḥ an-Nawawī*, Bd. 14, S. 209).

43 Ibn Hišām, *as-Sīrah an-nabawiyyah*, Bd. 1, S. 251 zu ʿAbd ar-Raḥmān Ibn ʿAwf, S. 252 zu Abū ʿUbaydah Ibn al-Ǧarrāḥ und S. 348 ff. zu ʿUmar Ibn al-Ḫaṭṭāb.

nen zehn Personen, denen Mohammed zu seinen Lebzeiten den Eintritt ins Paradies zugesichert hatte (*al-ʿašarah al-mubaššarūna bi-l-ğannah*).[44] Mit anderen Worten, die Aussagen aller drei dieser Personen waren gewichtig und gleich schwer, sodass der offensichtliche Widerspruch zwischen den beiden Haltungen, jeweils durch ʿUmar Ibn al-Ḫaṭṭāb und ʿAbd ar-Raḥmān Ibn ʿAwf einerseits und Abū ʿUbaydah Ibn al-Ğarrāḥ andererseits vertreten, nicht ohne weiteres abgetan werden konnte. Wenn man diesen Bericht IAḤ mit der Schilderung Ibn al-Aṯirs im Kapitel „Über die Pest von ʿAmwās" (*Ḏikr ṭāʿūn ʿAmwās*) vergleicht, so sticht als erstes ins Auge, dass Ibn al-Aṯir zu diesen Ereignissen zwei separate Berichte anführt. Dem ersten Bericht zufolge, der hier nur sehr verkürzt wiedergegeben sei, habe ʿUmar Ibn al-Ḫaṭṭāb nach dem Ausbruch der Pest in Syrien an Abū ʿUbaydah Ibn al-Ğarrāḥ einen Brief geschrieben und darin den Letzteren inständig darum gebeten, wegen einer nicht weiter konkretisierten, aber sehr dringenden Angelegenheit sofort nach Medina zu kommen. Abū ʿUbaydah Ibn al-Ğarrāḥ habe die wahre Absicht ʿUmars durchschaut, ihn nämlich unter diesem Vorwand vor dem Pesttod retten zu wollen, und sich geweigert, der Bitte ʿUmars nachzukommen. Daraufhin habe ʿUmar einen zweiten Brief an ihn gerichtet, diesmal mit der Bitte, die Muslime aus den betroffenen Gebieten hinaus auf die Anhöhen zu führen. Kurz nach dem Aufbruch sei Abū ʿUbaydah Ibn al-Ğarrāḥ an der Pest gestorben. Dieser erste Bericht endet damit, dass ʿAmr b. al-ʿĀṣ letztlich die Leitung übernommen und sich mit den übrigen Menschen in die Berge zurückgezogen habe. Der zweite sich daran direkt anschließende Bericht, der mit „Es wurde auch überliefert" (*wa-qad qīla*) eingeleitet wird, stimmt weitestgehend mit der erwähnten Schilderung IAḤs überein und ist laut Ibn al-Aṯir glaubwürdiger.[45] Nun, wenn beide Berichte tatsächlich auf den gleichen Pestausbruch Bezug nehmen,[46] dann kann die gezeichnete Chronologie aus offensichtlichen Gründen nicht stimmen; vielmehr müssten dann die Geschehnisse des zweiten Berichts von Ibn al-Aṯir und dessen Wiedergabe durch IAḤ zuerst stattgefunden haben und erst danach diejenigen des bei Ibn al-Aṯir zuerst angeführten Berichts.

Kapitel Nr. 4[47] – Das vierte Kapitel über das Wesen der Pest und der Epidemie samt einer Beschreibung der beiden, über die diesen beiden gemeinsame Ursa-

---

[44] In einem bekannten, auf die Autorität von ʿAbd ar-Raḥmān Ibn ʿAwf überlieferten Ausspruch, spricht Mohammed ihnen sowie sieben weiteren Prophetengenossen das Paradies zu (at-Tirmiḏī, Muḥammad Ibn ʿĪsā, *Ṣaḥīḥ sunan at-Tirmiḏī*, 3 Bde., hrsg. von Muḥammad Nāṣiraddīn al-Albānī, Riyad 2000, Bd. 3, S. 529). Vgl. ferner aḏ-Ḏahabī, Šamsaddīn Muḥammad Ibn Aḥmad, *Siyar aʿlām an-nubalāʾ*, hrsg. von Ṣalāḥaddīn al-Munağğid, Ibrāhīm al-Abyārī und Muḥammad Asʿad Ṭalas, 3 Bde., Kairo 1956-1962, Bd. 1, S. 3 zu Abū ʿUbaydah Ibn al-Ğarrāḥ und S. 46 zu ʿAbd ar-Raḥmān Ibn ʿAwf.

[45] Ibn al-Aṯir, *al-Kāmil fī t-tarʾīḫ*, Bd. 2, S. 558 ff.

[46] Für den Pestausbruch in ʿAmwās werden zwei Hiğra-Daten überliefert, 638 und 639, sodass es zumindest theoretisch möglich erscheint, dass das erste Datum sich auf den ersten Pestausbruch und das zweite sich auf das erneute Auftreten der Pest jeweils beziehen könnte (Dols, *Black Death*, S. 21).

[47] Fol. 39b-41a.

che, darüber, ob Pest und Epidemie identisch oder verschieden sind, und über der beiden medizinischen Grund, welcher ist das Miasma u. ä.

Dieses Kapitel wird mit einem in „Ṣaḥīḥ al-Buḫārī" überlieferten Prophetenausspruch eingeleitet, in dem es heißt, dass die Pest (*ṭāʿūn*) eine Strafe (*riǧz*) sei, welche Gott gegen eine Gruppe der Kinder Israels niedergesandt habe. IAH räumt ein, dass die Pest zwar auch unspezifisch verwendet und die Bedeutung Massenkrankheit (*al-maraḍ al-ʿāmm*), Züchtigung (*ar-riǧz*),[48] Strafe (*al-ʿaḏāb*), körperlicher Schmerz bzw. Unpässlichkeit (*al-alam*) sowie Sünde (*aḏ-ḏanb*) haben kann, stellt aber fest, dass mit *riǧz* im angeführten Ausspruch der Sinn „Strafe" intendiert sei. Hieran schließen sich Zitate einiger arabischer Lexikographen zu *ṭāʿūn* und *wabaʾ*. Darauf lässt IAH weitere Zitate folgen, mit welchen der pathologische Aspekt der Pest aus medizinischer Sicht erläutert wird. Allen hierunter zusammengefassten Definitionen ist gemeinsam, dass die Pest darin als eine spezifische Erkrankung geschildert wird, nämlich als eine krankhafte Schwellung,[49] die an verschiedenen Körperteilen[50] auftritt und für die Betroffenen tödlich endet. Zu *wabaʾ* führt IAH ebenfalls unterschiedliche einschlägige Aussagen an und stellt – an-Nawawī in seinem Kommentar zu „Ṣaḥīḥ Muslim" folgend – fest, dass die richtige Definition diejenige sei, welche *wabaʾ* als eine unspezifische Massenkrankheit beschreibt, die nur eine bestimmte Gegend der Erde heimsuche, sich im Hinblick auf ihren großen Verbreitungsgrad u. ä. von den üblichen Krankheiten unterscheide und durch ein bestimmtes einheitliches Krankheitsbild (*wa-yakūnu maraḍuhum nawʿan wāḥidan*) gekennzeichnet ist; dies im Unterschied zu anderen Zeiten, in welchen ja unterschiedliche Krankheiten auftreten können.[51] Die gezogene Abgrenzung zwischen den beiden Begriffen festigt IAH mit dem überlieferten Zitat „Jede Pest ist eine Epidemie, aber nicht jede Epidemie ist eine Pest". Was den medizinischen Grund für das Auftreten der Pest anbetrifft, so gibt IAH wie bereits explizit in der Kapitelüberschrift konstatiert hierfür das Miasma an, das in der Vormoderne sowohl im Orient als auch im Okzident das durch Galen maßgeblich beeinflusste ätiologische Verständnis der Pest dominiert hat.[52]

---

[48] *Ar-riǧz* kann laut *Lisān al-ʿarab* je nach Kontext göttliche Strafe, Götzendienst oder Polytheismus bedeuten.

[49] *Waram radī* in „al-Aḥkām an-nabawiyyah fī ṣ-ṣināʿah aṭ-ṭibbiyyah", Abszess (*al-ḫurrāǧ*) bei Ibn Sīnā, Pustel und Schwellung (*baṭr wa-waram*) bei an-Nawawī, welcher an einer anderen Stelle in seinem Werk von Geschwüren (*qurūḥ*) spricht.

[50] Achselhöhle (*al-ibṭ*), Bereich hinter den Ohren (*ḫalfa al-uḏn*) und Leistengegend (*al-arnabah*) in „al-Aḥkām an-nabawiyyah fī ṣ-ṣināʿah aṭ-ṭibbiyyah"; Körperfalten (*al-maǧābin*), Bereich hinter den Ohren (*ḫalfa al-uḏn*) und Leistengegend (*al-arnaba*) bei Ibn Sīnā und Ellenbögen (*al-marāfiq*), Achselhöhlen (*al-ābāṭ*), Finger (*al-aṣābiʿ*), Hände (*al-aydī*) sowie der übrige Körper (*sāʾir al-badan*) bei an-Nawawī.

[51] Fol. 40a f.

[52] Dols geht auf die damals vorherrschende miasmatische Erklärung detailliert ein (Dols, *Black Death*, S. 84 ff.).

Kapitel Nr. 5[53] - Das fünfte Kapitel über den schariatischen Grund für den Ausbruch der Pest, welcher ist die zum vorzeitigen Tod führende Hurerei sowie auch u.a. Alkoholgenuss und Verübung von Freveltaten; [dieses Kapitel handelt des weiteren] vom Anspornen zur Abkehr [vom Verwerflichen] sowie zur nach dem allgemeinen Konsens gültigen Buße, ferner vom Verbot, nach der Erfüllung der für den Vollzug der Buße vorgesehenen Auflagen sich der Verzweiflung hinzugeben, und von der Zuversicht, dass Gottes Barmherzigkeit am Ende überwiegen wird.

Dieses Kapitel wird mit einer Auflistung von Ḥadiṯen eingeleitet, in welchen das Thema der göttlichen Bestrafung für menschliche Vergehen und Frevel eine zentrale Rolle spielt. Als solche werden z.B. Hurerei, Wucherzins, betrügerisches Tricksen beim Abmessen und Abwiegen (*taṭfīf al-kayl, baḫs al-mīzān*),[54] widernatürliche sexuelle Praktiken (*aʿmāl qawm Lūṭ*), die Weigerung, die Läuterungsabgabe abzuführen (*manʿ az-zakāt*), Übergriffe auf die Schutzbefohlenen (*at-taʿaddī ʿalā ahl aḏ-ḏimmah*) sowie Sünden allgemein benannt; als hierfür mögliche Strafen können fungieren Dürre (*manʿ al-qaṭr*), Massensterben (*al-mawt*), Geisteskrankheiten (*al-ǧunūn*), Übermacht der Feinde (*tasliṭ al-ʿaduww*), vorzeitiger Tod (*taʿǧīl al-halāk*) usw. Bezeichnenderweise kommt in allen hier angeführten Ḥadiṯen nur ein einziges Mal *ṭāʿūn* vor. Dieser betreffende Ḥadiṯ sei auch nachfolgend übersetzt, da er ausführlich bestimmten menschlichen Verstößen die dafür von Gott vorgesehenen Strafen zuordnet. ʿUmar b. al-Ḫaṭṭāb hörte den Propheten Folgendes sagen: „Ihr Auswanderer, Gott bewahre euch davor, fünf folgende Dinge zu erleben: Wenn schwere Sünden sich unter den Menschen ausbreiten, dann suchen sie Pest und Krankheiten heim, welche unter den Vorfahren dieser Menschen nie da gewesen waren; wenn Menschen beim Abmessen oder Abwiegen tricksen, dann werden sie von Missjahren, Lebensmittelknappheit und tyrannischer Willkür ihres Herrschers heimgesucht; wenn Menschen die Abführung der Läuterungsgabe verweigern, wird ihnen der Regen vorenthalten, und wäre es nicht der Tiere wegen, dann würde überhaupt kein Regen je niedergehen; wenn Menschen vertragliche Vereinbarungen brechen, dann gibt sie Gott der Gewalt der äußeren Feinde anheim, sodass die Letzteren ihnen einen Teil ihres Besitzes entringen; immer dann, wenn die Imame[55] nicht danach handeln, was Gott – erhaben und mächtig ist er – in seinem Buch geoffenbart hat, dann richtet er die Kampfeswut der Mitglieder einer Gemeinschaft widereinander".[56] Eine auffallende Gemeinsamkeit dieser Ḥadiṯe besteht ferner darin, dass das sündhafte Verhalten häufig[57] von einer Gruppe verant

---

[53] Fol. 41a-53a.

[54] Die entsprechenden arabischen Bezeichnungen werden in den jeweiligen Ḥadiṯen auch verbal ausgedrückt und sie wurden hier der Einheitlichkeit und der Einfachheit des Zitierens halber substantiviert, d.h. aus *mā ṭaffafa qawm kaylan* ist somit *taṭfīf kayl* geworden.

[55] Damit sind hier eher die Oberhäupter der Muslime gemeint, mit höchster weltlicher und religiöser Macht ausgestattet.

[56] Fol. 41b.

[57] Laut einer Überlieferung habe der Prophet David nach Begehung einer Missetat Gott um Vergebung gebeten. Diese habe der Letztere ihm zwar gewährt, doch gleichzeitig die [zu

wortet wird und dass die Ahndung hierfür immer die explizit definierte Gemeinschaft als Ganzes trifft. Die sittlichen bzw. religiösen Missstände führen dieser Logik nach immer zur Bestrafung der ganzen Gemeinschaft, d.h. der Übeltäter selbst sowie der diese Missstände stillschweigend hinnehmenden, teilnahmslos zuschauenden Mehrheit.[58] Nicht alle hier zitierten Ḥadīte beinhalten indes die aufgrund der Kapitelüberschrift zu erwartende Wiederholung des kausalen Zusammenhangs zwischen dem menschlichen Fehlverhalten und der angemessenen Bestrafung dafür; einige Ḥadīte warnen vielmehr vor der heranrückenden Stunde des Jüngsten Gerichts und vor den diesem vorausgehenden Missständen, welche ganz allgemein als Auflösung der gestifteten islamischen Ordnung sich beschreiben lassen können. An dieser Stelle endet der erste thematische Teil, und auf ihn folgt der zweite, der innerhalb des Kapitels den größten Platz einnimmt und seinerseits zwei aus der Einsicht, sich sündhaft verhalten zu haben, resultierenden Aspekten gewidmet ist: erstens der Reue bzw. deren ordnungsgemäßem Vollzug, zweitens der Zuversicht, dass die Barmherzigkeit Gottes gegenüber Sündern größer sei als sein Zorn, bzw. dem Verbot, diese Zuversicht aufzugeben. Dieser Teil ist ferner in drei Unterkapitel (faṣl) gegliedert, die sich inhaltlich überschneiden, und setzt sich größtenteils aus einschlägigen Koranzitaten und Prophetenaussprüchen zusammen. Interessant sind die im Zusammenhang mit Abū Nuwās (757-814) überlieferten Geschichten, dessen Weingedichte ihm den Beinamen „der Weindichter" (šāʿir al-ḫamrah) eingebracht haben. Der einen Geschichte zufolge soll der bereits moribunde Abū Nuwās Besuch empfangen haben. Der Besucher, der Jugendsünden Abū Nuwās' bewusst und angesichts der Tatsache, dass der Letztere bereits mit einem Fuß im Grabe stehe, habe ihn zur reuigen Umkehr aufgefordert. Darauf habe Abū Nuwās den Ḥadīt „Jeder Prophet besitzt das Privileg der Fürsprache; meine Fürsprache hebe ich für die Schwerstsünder meiner Gemeinde am Tage des Jüngsten Gerichts auf" aufgesagt und mit der Frage gekontert, ob der Besucher denn nicht meine, dass er, d.h. Abū Nuwās, zur genannten Gruppe gehöre. Laut einer weiteren Geschichte soll jemand Abū Nuwās bereits nach seinem Tod im Traum gesehen und ihn danach gefragt haben, welches jenseitige Los Gott ihm zugeteilt habe.[59] Der Dichter antwortet, von Gott Vergebung seiner Sünden durch einen unter seinem Kissen versteckten Vierzeiler[60] empfangen zu haben. Der allgemeine Tenor dieses

---

ertragende] Schmach für diese Untat den Kindern Israels aufgebürdet (*alzamtu ʿārahā* [d.h. *ʿār al-ḫaṭīyah*] *banī Isrāʾīl*). Als sich David gegen solch eine offensichtliche Ungerechtigkeit verwahrt habe, habe Gott sein Urteil damit begründet, dass bei der Begehung der Missetat niemand diese verurteilt hätte (Fol. 42b).

58 Wohlgemerkt weist IAH darauf hin (Fol. 48a), dass der berühmte Pestausbruch in ʿAmwās durch eine Gruppe von Muslimen verursacht worden sei, die zuvor Wein getrunken hätten.

59 Die hier vorkommende Frage *mā faʿala llāhu bika?* ist auch oft im abschließenden Nachtrag zu den vierzig Ḥadīten vorgekommen.

60 „Oh mein Gott, auch wenn meine Sünden zahlreich sind, so weiß ich, dass deine Gnade größer ist; ich rufe dich, mein Gott, so wie du befohlen hast voller Demut an, und wenn du mich zurückweist, wer soll sich dann [meiner] erbarmen? Wenn nur diejenigen dich an-

Teils lässt sich dahingehend zusammenfassen, dass es außer der Sünde der Vielgötterei keine andere Sünde gibt, die bei echter aufrichtiger Umkehr zu Gott von ihm nicht vergeben werden könnte.

Auch bei den zitierten Ḥadīṯen dieses Kapitels gilt, dass der Isnad entweder sehr stark verkürzt ist oder gänzlich ausgelassen ist. Es gibt allerdings eine Ausnahme in Gestalt eines Ḥadīṯs,[61] auf dessen besonderen Stellenwert IAḤ ausdrücklich hinweist und dies durch die eben genannte formale Besonderheit, in der vollständigen Überliefererkette bestehend, auch implizit bekräftigt. Den Rahmen dieses Ḥadīṯs bildet eine Art Vorsprache des Teufels bei Gott, bei welcher er auf die Rolle Adams bei seiner Vertreibung aus dem Paradies verweist sowie darauf, dass er Adam nur mit Gottes Ermächtigung habe überwältigen können. Diese Ermächtigung sowie weitere Zugeständnisse, die diesem Zweck förderlich sind, werden ihm auf Nachfrage von Gott erteilt. Dann tritt Adam mit dem Einwand auf den Plan, der Macht des Teufels ausgeliefert zu sein und keine sonstige Handhabe gegen ihn zu haben als allein die, sich Schutz suchend an Gott zu wenden. Daraufhin werden auch ihm Zugeständnisse gemacht, zwei hiervon des Inhalts, dass die Möglichkeit der reuigen Umkehr zu Gott bestehe, solange der Geist im Körper sei, sowie dass Gott sämtliche Sünden vergeben könne.[62]

Kapitel Nr. 6[63] – Das sechste Kapitel über die Heilmittel, welche im wohl gefügten geoffenbarten Gesetz gegen die Pest vorgesehen sind, sowie über die Aussagen von klugen Ärzten, welche Nahrung dafür empfohlen ist usw.

Dieses Kapitel ist in zwei Teile gegliedert. Der erste besteht zum großen Teil aus Ḥadīṯen und greift den bereits im Vorwort formulierten Hinweis auf, dass das häufig zugunsten Mohammeds verrichtete Bittgebet gegen die Pest feie. Der Inhalt dieses ersten Teils ist im Geiste der Überlegungen gehalten, durch welche frommen Handlungen bzw. Bittgebete ein Muslim von sich aus nicht nur der Pest, sondern auch jeder beliebigen Widerwärtigkeit oder Not abhelfen könnte. Der zweite erheblich kürzere Teil nähert sich dieser Problematik aus medizinischer Sicht. Am Anfang des ersten Teils wird ferner die Passage eines bereits im Kapitel Nr. 3 erwähnten und von ʿAbd ar-Raḥmān Ibn ʿAwf verbürgten Prophetenausspruchs aufgegriffen und für weiterführende theologische sowie medizinische Überlegungen genutzt. Allerdings erweisen sich diese bei näherem Hinsehen als eine direkte Übernahme der Ausführungen Ibn Qayyim al-Ğawziyyahs (gest. 1350)[64] aus dem Kapitel „Seine [d.h. Mohammeds] Rechtleitung bei der

---

riefen, die recht handeln, wen sollten dann die Übeltäter anrufen? Ich kann [um deine Gnade zu erwirken] auf nichts anderes verweisen als auf meine Hoffnung, auf deine Barmherzigkeit und auf die Tatsache, dass ich Muslim bin" (Fol. 46b f.).

61 Fol. 49b.
62 Dieses letzte Zugeständnis ist ein Koranzitat, Sure 39, Vers 53.
63 Fol. 53a-57a.
64 Ibn Qayyim al-Ğawziyyah, Šamsaddin Muḥammad Ibn Abī Bakr, *Zād al-maʿād fī hady ḫayr al-ʿibād*, hrsg. von Muṣṭafā ʿAbd al-Qādir ʿAṭā, 6 Bde., Beirut 1998, Bd. 4, S. 98 ff.

Pest, bei deren Behandlung und bei Vorsichtsmaßnahmen gegen sie". Insbesondere der ca. ein Folio betragende Umfang des plagiierten Materials[65] überrascht, denn üblicherweise benennt IAH die von ihm zitierten Autoren bzw. ihre Werke. Hieran schließt sich die Erörterung der im genannten Ḥadīt formulierten Handlungsanweisungen angesichts der Pest in Form von rhetorischen Fragen und Antworten darauf. Ein abgesehen vom Bittgebet für Mohammed weiteres Heilmittel sieht IAH im Bittgebet allgemein (*ad-duʿāʾ*) und bekräftigt dies mit einer Geschichte, die sich zur Zeit eines erneuten Pestausbruchs im Jahre 1363 zugetragen habe. Angesichts des durch die Pest verursachten Massensterbens habe ein frommer Muslim dem Propheten im Traum die Not seiner Mitmenschen geklagt. Dieser habe ihm daraufhin mit dem Finger ein apotropäisches Bittgebet (*ad-duʿāʾ*) auf die Handfläche gezeichnet, dessen Wortlaut IAH zitiert.[66] Der nächste darauf folgende thematische Abschnitt des ersten Teils ist der Wirksamkeit des allgemeinen Bittgebets gewidmet, die so weit reiche, dass es die bereits auf ihrem Weg nach unten hin zu den Menschen befindlichen Heimsuchungen aufzuhalten und bis zum Tage des Jüngsten Gerichts aufzuschieben vermag.[67] Das allgemeine Bittgebet, insbesondere dann, wenn es auf Mohammed zurückgehende Heilungsformeln enthalte, sei – so IAH weiter – den üblichen medizinischen Heilmitteln weit überlegen. Hierauf folgen mehrere diesbezügliche Überlieferungen, die sowohl den Wortlaut der jeweils vom Propheten verwendeten Formel als auch den Namen der damit behandelten Person beinhalten. Ausgehend von einem Ḥadīt, dass Gott jedem Muslim helfe, der bei Kummer den „Thron-Vers"[68] sowie den letzten Teil der Sure „die Kuh" rezitiere, plädiert IAH dafür, die genannten Koranteile auch bei der Pestheimsuchung intensiv zu rezitieren, da die Pest ja der größte denkbare Kummer sei, sowie sich mit einem Bittgebet an Gott zu wenden. Das nächste Heilmittel gegen die Pest bestehe ferner im rituellen Gebet (*aṣ-ṣalāh*), zu dem auch der Prophet selbst bei Traurigkeit seine Zuflucht genommen habe. Wenn also ein Muslim den durch die Pest oder auch durch andere Krankheit verursachten Schmerz spüre und im Gebet zu Gott Zuflucht suche, in welchem er sein Herz dem Allmächtigen ausschütte und mit größtmöglicher Hingabe an Gott sein Gebet verrichte (*wa-ǧamaʿa himmatahū ʿalā llāhi fī*

---

[65] Fol. 53a-b.

[66] Fol. 54a. Das Bittgebet beginnt mit den Anrufungen Gottes darum, vor Lanzenstichen, der Pest sowie vor nicht wieder gut zu machenden Verlusten an Eigentum, Leben, Familienangehörigen und Kindern zu bewahren; das Bittgebet für Mohammed ist ebenfalls Teil dieses Bittgebets. Die Parallele zur im Kapitel „abschließender Nachtrag" unter Nr. 14 (Fol. 33a) geschilderten Begebenheit ist offenkundig. Dort sei einem frommen Muslim, der sich auf einem gegen heftigsten Seesturm ankämpfenden Schiff befunden habe, im Traum der Prophet erschienen und habe ihm ein Bittgebet zu seinen, d.h. Mohammeds, Gunsten beigebracht. Dieses hätten alle Passagiere tausend Mal aufsagen sollen, doch bereits beim dreihundertsten Mal habe Gott die Seenot aufgelöst.

[67] Fol. 54b.

[68] Vers 255, genannt „*āyat al-kursī*", der 2. Sure „die Kuh".

ṣalātihī), dann werde er von diesem Schmerzen befreit oder dieser werde zumindest gelindert.

Zusammenfassend kann man sagen, dass IAḤ in diesem Kapitel zusätzlich zum bereits erwähnten Bittgebet für Mohammed drei weitere Heilmittel gegen jede Notlage einführt und seinen Lesern somit weitere Handhaben dagegen gibt: das allgemeine Bittgebet (*ad-duʿāʾ*), welches die größte Wirksamkeit entfalte, wenn es von Mohammed her überlieferte Heilungsformeln umfasse, bestimmte koranische Abschnitte sowie das rituelle Gebet (*aṣ-ṣalāh*).

Der zweite Teil dieses Kapitels ist der Erörterung oder eher der Zitierung von medizinischen Behandlungsratschlägen gewidmet. Dieser Teil ist – wie bereits eingangs angemerkt – erheblich kürzer als der erste und besteht im Wesentlichen aus einschlägigen Zitaten von al-Akfānī (gest. 1348), Ibn Sīnā (980-1037) und Ibn an-Nafīs (1210-1288).[69] Bemerkenswert ist die sich hieran anschließende Passage, eine Art erklärender Nachtrag (*at-tanbīh*), in welchem IAḤ erneut auf das Thema der Ansteckung beim Pestausbruch zu sprechen kommt. Hierbei zitiert er eine Passage des bereits erwähnten Ibn Qayyim al-Ğawziyyahs, diesmal allerdings aus einem anderen Kapitel seines Werks.[70] Darin führt Ibn Qayyim al-Ğawziyyah aus, dass der Prophet aus seiner umfassenden Sorge um das Wohl der Muslime heraus es ihnen verboten habe, sich absichtlich all jenen Dingen auszusetzen, durch welche sie Schaden an Körper oder Geist nehmen könnten. Ferner bestehe kein Zweifel darüber, dass mancher Körper eine größere Anfälligkeit für diese Krankheit – siehe weiter unten – habe; ferner könnte eventuell die Angst zu erkranken und die entsprechende Vorstellung eher zu diesem Leiden führen. Manchmal gelange der Atem des Kranken zu einem gesunden Menschen und dieser erkranke dann daran. Diese Überlegungen entwickelt Ibn Qayyim al-Ğawziyyah allerdings im Zusammenhang mit Lepra. IAḤ übernimmt die eben zusammengefasste Passage und fügt an einer Stelle das Wort „Pest" ein, sodass die Ausführungen Ibn Qayyim al-Ğawziyyahs durch diesen Kunstgriff auf einen ganz anderen Sachverhalt bezogen werden und dadurch einen anderen, ursprünglich nicht intendierten Sinn bekommen.[71]

Das Kapitel Nr. 7[72] – Das siebente Kapitel enthält die Auflistung der meisten Pestheimsuchungen, von der Entstehung des Islam bis zu diesem Jahr, und handelt

---

69 Die Werke, aus welchen zitiert wird, sind nach der Ordnung, in welcher diese Autoren genannt wurden, jeweils folgende: *Ġunyat al-labīb ʿinda ġaybat aṭ-ṭabīb*, *al-Qānūn* und *Mūğaz al-Qānūn*.

70 Ibn Qayyim al-Ğawziyyah, *Zād al-maʿād*, Bd. 4, S. 167.

71 Die betreffende Stelle lautet: *wa-qad taṣilu rāʾiḥatu l-ʿalīli ilā ṣ-ṣaḥīḥi fa-tusqimahū* (Ibn Qayyim al-Ğawziyyah, *Zād al-maʿād*, Bd. 4, S. 167); daraus wird bei IAḤ (Fol. 57a): *wa-qad taṣilu rāʾiḥatu al-ʿalīli bi-ṭ-ṭāʿūni wa-ġayrihī ilā ṣ-ṣaḥīḥi fa-tusqimahū*. Wohlgemerkt benutzt Ibn Qayyim al-Ğawziyyah in diesem Kapitel mehrfach das Substantiv *al-ʿadwā*, doch es hat bei ihm einen nicht üblicherweise heute darunter verstandenen Sinn „Ansteckung" (daselbst, S. 169).

72 Fol. 57a-73a.

davon, welche Hiebe die Tyrannen versetzt haben, welche schlimmer sind als die Pest selbst, insbesondere die ruchlosen Mongolen im Jahr des Hülegü; dies mit dem Zweck, den Dahingerafften nachzuweinen und dem Vergangenen nachzutrauern.

In diesem umfangreichsten Kapitel seiner Abhandlung listet IAH insgesamt dreiunddreißig Pestheimsuchungen chronologisch aufsteigend auf,[73] von welchen er zwei in der vorislamischen Zeit verortet.[74] Dabei geht er jeweils von den beiden Koranzitaten aus, „Da sandten wir die Flut über sie"[75] sowie „Hast du nicht jene gesehen, die in Todesfurcht zu Tausenden aus ihren Wohnungen auszogen? Gott sagte zu ihnen: Sterbet!",[76] die im Sinne des ersten und des zweiten Pestausbruchs in der vorislamischen Zeit gedeutet werden. Den Pestheimsuchungen der islamischen Zeit sind die Vorfälle ab der Nummer drei bis dreiunddreißig gewidmet. Die diesbezüglichen Angaben schöpft IAH nach eigener Aussage hauptsächlich aus *al-Mudhiš* von Abū l-Faraǧ Ibn al-Ǧawzī (gest. 1201), *al-Aḏkār* und *Šarḥ Muslim* an-Nawawīs (gest. 1277) als auch aus maßgebenden Korankommentaren und Geschichtswerken sowie aus anderen Quellen.[77]

Laut Dols war IAH der erste arabische Autor, der eine vollständige Auflistung der Epidemien, einschließlich der Pest, vorgenommen habe.[78] Im Kapitel Nr. 4 verfolgte IAH den Zweck, dem unpräzisen Gebrauch seiner Zeitgenossen entgegenzusteuern und diese beiden Begriffe, Pest und Epidemie, jeweils klar zu definieren und voneinander abzusetzen. Vor diesem Hintergrund dürfte das siebente Kapitel streng genommen schon allein um der Kohärenz der Abhandlung willen nur solche Heimsuchungen enthalten, die der im Kapitel Nr. 4 gegebenen Definition von „Pest" folgen. Beim bloßen Überfliegen des Inhalts des 7. Kapitels stellt man allerdings fest, dass dies nicht der Fall ist und dass IAH die Definition der Pest nicht nur auf Naturkatastrophen ausweitet, sondern auch wie in einem besonders bemerkenswerten Fall auf den Mongolensturm des 13. Jahrhunderts. IAH behauptet ferner, dass Ibn al-Ǧawzī in seinem Werk *al-Mudhiš* ein Kapitel der Pest gewidmet habe, und dieses sei recht überschaubar und umfasse lediglich nur ein Folio (*waraqa*).[79] In *al-Mudhiš* selbst gibt es nur zwei Kapitel, auf welche diese Beschreibung zutreffen könnte. Es ist zum einen das Kapitel „Über Dürrezeiten und Mas-

---

[73] Es gibt hierbei allerdings eine Unregelmäßigkeit, die IAH nicht weiter kommentiert: den Pestausbruch Nr. 17 datiert IAH auf das Jahr 346 h., springt dann zeitlich beim Pestfall Nr. 18 zurück in das Jahr 204 h. und fasst in diesem Abschnitt auch die Pestheimsuchungen der Jahre 245 h., 257 h. und 258 h. zusammen. Die Pest Nr. 19 wird dann mit dem Jahr 423 h. fortgesetzt und alle nachfolgenden Pestberichte sind dann wieder chronologisch aufsteigend.

[74] Conrad hat in seinem Artikel „Arabic plague chronologies and treatises", S. [51]-93, dieses siebente Kapitel einer genauen Betrachtung unterzogen.

[75] Sure 7, Vers 133.

[76] Sure 2, Vers 243.

[77] Fol. 57b f.

[78] Dols, *Black Death*, S. 19.

[79] Fol. 57b.

sensterben" (*Fī l-ğudūb wa-ʿumūm al-mawt*)[80] und „Über Erdbeben und Wunderdinge" (*Fī z-zalāzil wa-l-āyāt*).[81] Das zuerst genannte hiervon umfasst tatsächlich in der gedruckten Ausgabe des Werks etwa anderthalb Seiten und benennt ausdrücklich vier Pest- und drei Epidemiefälle u.a.; das andere ist etwa vier Seiten groß. Der Vergleich der im siebten Kapitel unter der Nr. 10 aufgeführten Pest mit der entsprechenden Beschreibung bei Ibn al-Ğawzī, auf welchen IAḤ explizit als Quelle hinweist, ergibt eine deckungsgleiche Übereistimmung im Wortlaut der beiden Passagen, sodass kein Zweifel darüber besteht, dass IAḤ für seine Auflistung das bei Ibn al-Ğawzī im Kapitel „Über Dürrezeiten und Massensterben" zusammengetragene Material verwendet. Diese Feststellung sagt einiges darüber aus, welchen unterschiedlichen Denkkategorien jeweils Ibn al-Ğawzī und IAḤ dieselben von ihnen geschilderten Heimsuchungen und Naturkatastrophen jeweils zuordneten. Interessanter mit Bezug auf die Denkweise IAḤs ist allerdings ein weiterer Pestausbruch, den IAḤ unter der Nummer 18[82] anführt. Hierunter berichtet er, dass im Jahr 204 h. ein Wind, von Zentralasien kommend, über Ḫurasān, Rayy, Hamaḏān, Ḥulwān und den Iraq nacheinander hinweggefegt sei, sodass viele der Menschen, infolge dessen an Husten (*suʿāl*) und Schnupfen (*zukām*) erkrankt, gestorben seien. Ibn al-Ğawzī berichtet in *al-Mudhiš*[83] in weitestgehend gleichen Worten – wenn auch mit leicht differierender Wortstellung – über diese Begebenheit, obgleich er diese im Jahr 240 h. verortet und bei der Angabe der vom Wind betroffenen Orte von IAḤ in Merw und Nischapur abweicht, der statt dieser beiden Ḫurasān angibt. Wenn man jedoch bedenkt, dass Ḫurasān in der Abbasidenzeit neben Herat und Balkh auch Merw und Nischapur mit einbezog,[84] so spricht dies umso mehr für eine Abhängigkeit der beiden Berichte voneinander, oder genauer: für die Abhängigkeit IAḤs von Ibn al-Ğawzī.[85] Diese Begebenheit ist allerdings in *al-Mudhiš* im Kapitel „Über Erdbeben und Wunderdinge" enthalten, in dem im Gegensatz zum vorausgegangenen Kapitel das Wort „Pest" kein einziges Mal fällt. Wenn also diese Windepisode für Ibn al-Ğawzī nicht als Pest zu klassifizieren war, so mag man sich fragen, was IAḤ dazu veranlasste? Eine mögliche Antwort könnte in der Nennung des Windes liegen, womit die gesamte Episode in die assoziative Nähe zur Luftverschmutzung rückt, welche in der vormodernen Zeit als Hauptursache für die Pestheimsuchung galt. Interessanterweise subsumiert IAḤ unter dem Pestausbruch Nr.

---

[80] Ibn al-Ğawzī, Abū l-Farağ ʿAbd ar-Raḥmān, *al-Mudhiš*, hrsg. von Marwān al-Qabbānī, Beirut [1981], S. 70-71.

[81] Ibn al-Ğawzī, *al-Mudhiš*, S. 71-75.

[82] Fol. 62b f.

[83] Ibn al-Ğawzī, *al-Mudhiš*, S. 72; wortgleicher Bericht darüber findet sich bei diesem Autor auch in seinem Geschichtswerk (Ibn al-Ğawzī, Abū l-Farağ ʿAbd ar-Raḥmān, *al-Muntaẓam fī taʾrīḫ al-mulūk wa-l-umam*, 19 Bde., hrsg. von Muḥammad ʿAbd al-Qādir ʿAṭā und Muṣṭafā ʿAbd al-Qādir ʿAṭā, Beirut 1992-1993, Bd. 11, S. 270).

[84] Yāqūt al-Ḥamawī, *Muʿğam al-buldān*, Bd. 2,1, S. 409.

[85] Diese Windepisode, diesmal auf 240 h. datiert, überliefert IAḤ mit dem gleichen Wortlaut ein weiteres Mal (Fol. 67a) im Zusammenhang mit den Katastrophen, die sich beim Pestfall Nr. 26 ereignet haben.

18 darüber hinaus noch weitere Vorfälle, die jeweils in den Jahren 245 h., 257 h. und 258 h. sich zugetragen haben. Drei von IAḤ im Jahr 245 h. erwähnte Katastrophen fanden jeweils in Tinnis und Kairo, Latakia und Antiochien statt und scheinen den wörtlichen Übereistimmungen nach zu urteilen verkürzte Übernahmen aus aṭ-Ṭabaris Einträgen für dieses Jahr zu sein.[86] Wohlgemerkt sind bei aṭ-Ṭabarī im betreffenden Jahr auch weitere ähnliche Naturphänomene wie Erdbeben verzeichnet, die allerdings im Vergleich zu solchen, die IAḤ übernommen hat, einen geringeren Zerstörungsgrad gehabt zu haben scheinen.[87] Ferner fällt auf, dass bei allen Übernahmen IAḤs an dieser Stelle Erdbeben sowie Winde eine zentrale Rolle spielen. Was die restlichen pesthaften Vorfälle anbelangt, die IAḤ erwähnt, so war es mir auf Anhieb nicht möglich, diese ihrem ersten Überlieferer zuzuordnen. Doch auch vor diesem zugegebenermaßen skizzenhaft erhellten Hintergrund lässt sich zumindest ein Teilaspekt der Vorgehensweise IAḤs erkennen, der Berichte früherer Autoren über stattgefundene besonders destruktive Naturphänomene nicht nur abweichend von der eigenen Definition von Pest, sondern auch entgegen dem Verständnis der Bezugsautoren selbst zusammenfügt.

Der Abschluss[88] – Der Abschluss, welcher enthält die von mir verfasste Pestmaqāme, genannt „Schlaflos angesichts derjenigen, die in der Erde ruhen",[89] ferner Fragmente und besonders gelungene Gedichte wie beispielsweise u.a. „die Nachricht über die Epidemie" (*an-Naba' fī l-wabā'*) von Zaynaddīn Ibn al-Wardī sowie des Weiteren das Gedicht auf den Tod des Propheten.[90]

Mit diesem letzten Kapitel verleiht IAḤ seiner Abhandlung abschließend doch noch den Anflug einer Anthologie. Man beachte ferner, dass dieses Kapitel eines der umfangreichsten in *Daf' an-niqmah* ist, nämlich nach dem 7. Kapitel (16 Folien) und dem Abschnitt mit den vierzig Ḥadīṯen (15 Folien) das drittgrößte. Bei Zaynaddīn Ibn al-Wardī handelt es sich um den berühmten šāfiʿitischen Rechtsgelehrten, Literaten und Geschichtsschreiber Zaynaddīn ʿUmar Ibn al-Muẓaffar Ibn al-Wardī (1290-1349). Gegenstand des Schreibens[91] *an-Naba' fī l-wabā'* ist die in Eu-

---

[86] aṭ-Ṭabarī, Muḥammad Ibn Ǧarīr, *Taʾrīḫ ar-rusul wa-l-mulūk*, 10 Bde., hrsg. von Muḥammad Abū l-Faḍl Ibrāhīm, Kairo 1960-1969, Bd. 9, S. 213.

[87] Darauf deutet z.B. hin, dass aṭ-Ṭabarī bei den besonders schlimmen Naturphänomenen immer den Grad der Zerstörung bzw. die Zahl der dadurch verunglückten Menschen andeutet.

[88] Fol. 73a-82b.

[89] Der arabische Titel „*Al-ʿayn as-sāhirah fī man ḥalla bi-s-sāhirah*" ist wohl angelehnt an Sure 79, Vers 14.

[90] Wohlgemerkt weicht diese Fassung der Überschrift, welche im einleitenden Teil bei der Schilderung des Gesamtaufbaus der Abhandlung genannt wird (Fol. 2b), etwas von der Überschrift ab, die dieses Kapitel einleitet (Fol. 73a).

[91] Die Zuordnung zu einem bestimmten Genre der arabischen Literatur ist nicht ganz klar: der Autor selbst – sowie auch IAḤ (Fol. 78b) – bezeichnete *an-Naba' ʿan l-wabā'* als eine *risālah*; spätere Autoren sahen darin eine *maqāmah* (Rāʾid ʿAbd ar-Raḥīm, „Risālat „an-Naba' ʿan al-wabā'" li-Zaynaddīn Ibn al-Wardī t 749 h – dirāsah naqdiyyah", in: *Maǧallat Ǧāmiʿat an-Naǧāḥ li-l-abḥāṯ (al-ʿulūm as-siyāsiyyah)*, 24,5 (2010), S. 1495-1530, S. 1499). Dieses in Reimprosa gehaltene kurze Schreiben, das ungefähr zur Hälfte aus Versen besteht,

ropa unter dem Namen „Schwarzer Tod" bekannte Pandemie[92], welcher der Autor selbst in Aleppo zum Opfer gefallen ist.[93] Das erwähnte Gedicht auf den Tod des Propheten, mit welchem das Kapitel eingeleitet wird, ist eine Elegie aus der Feder IAḤs. Dieser folgen recht knappe Verse einiger namhafter Literaten und Zeitgenossen IAḤs wie Ibrāhīm al-Miʿmār (gest. 1349), Ğamāladdīn Ibn Nubātah (1287-1366) und Ṣalāḥaddīn aṣ-Ṣafadī (1296-1363) über die Pest des Jahres 1349. Von diesem Letzteren wird zum gleichen Thema ein Briefauszug zitiert. Hieran schließt sich direkt das erwähnte Prosastück Zaynaddīn Ibn al-Wardīs. Den Abschluss des Kapitels bilden die genannte Maqāmah IAḤs sowie seine Gedichte bzw. Fragmente daraus.

Abschließende Bemerkungen

Das hier besprochene Werk IAḤs sticht vor dem Hintergrund des literarischen Horizonts seiner Zeit zweifelsohne hervor, und zwar dadurch, dass dieser Autor die erste vollständige Aufzählung der Pestheimsuchungen in der islamischen Geschichte bis zum Jahr 1362 bietet.[94] Das dieser Auflistung gewidmete siebente Kapitel hat zwar den größten Umfang unter allen Kapiteln, es spielt jedoch in *Dafʿ an-niqmah* keine zentrale Rolle. Denn die diesem Werk zu Grunde liegende und ihm thematische Stoßrichtung gebende Idee, zumindest so, wie sie im Titel und in der ersten Einleitung formuliert ist, bestand ja darin, jedem von der Pest heimgesuchten Muslim ein wirksames Heilmittel dagegen an die Hand zu geben. Somit rückt der also formulierte Zweck diese Abhandlung in den religiös-ethischen Bereich. Das Kapitel Nr. 7 mit der erwähnten Auflistung sollte eher dem Zweck dienen, den Zeitgenossen IAḤ vor Augen zu führen, dass auch frühere Generationen der Muslime von derselben Krankheit heimgesucht worden seien, und sie somit durch ihre Eingliederung in die Reihe wiederholt vorkommender Pestausbrüche über ihre eigene Heimsuchung hinwegzutrösten und ihnen zu helfen, diese zu verwinden. Mit der explizit artikulierten religiös-ethischen Stoßrichtung seiner Abhandlung dürfte IAḤ ein Gebiet betreten ha-

---

handelt von der Ausbreitung und der Auswirkung der Pest im Nahen Osten; trotz seiner Kürze ist es in vielerlei Hinsicht gehaltvoll (Rāʾid ʿAbd ar-Raḥīm, „Risālat „an-Nabaʾ ʿan al-wabaʾ" li-Zaynaddīn Ibn al-Wardī", S. 1500 ff.).

92   Diese beschreibt IAḤ als Pestausbruch Nr. 31 (Fol. 71a-72a).

93   Bemerkenswerterweise bezeichnet Ibn al-Wardī diese Pandemie als den 6. Pestausbruch in der islamischen Geschichte (*Dīwān Ibn al-Wardī ʿUmar Ibn al-Muẓaffar*, hrsg. von Aḥmad Fawzī al-Hayb, Kuwait 1986, S. 90 f.) – für IAḤ ist es hingegen bereits der Pestfall Nr. 31 (Fol. 71a).

94   Dols spricht davon, dass „The first full enumeration of epidemics, including plague, was written by Ibn Abi Hajalah in 764/1362 [...]" (Dols, *Black Death*, S. 19). Streng genommen listet IAḤ jedoch nur Pestheimsuchungen auf, denn ein jeder Abschnitt zu einem Pestvorfall im Kapitel 7 wird ausnahmslos mit „Pest [Nr.] XY" eingeleitet, obgleich er die eigene im Kapitel Nr. 4 definierte Unterscheidung zwischen der Pest und der Epidemie nicht konsequent einhält. Siehe hierzu die Zusammenfassung des Kapitels Nr. 7.

ben, das bisher in den Darstellungen seines Wirkens ausgespart geblieben ist;[95] wie bereits eingangs angemerkt wurde, ist IAH vor allem als Dichter und Anthologist bekannt. Es ist bemerkenswert, wie auffallend zurückhaltend und vorsichtig IAH im von ihm betretenen Bereich sich zu bewegen bemüht ist. Dies äußert sich vor allem darin, dass er sich in den allermeisten Fällen darauf beschränkt, gemäß der jedes Kapitel einleitenden Überschrift Hadite, historische Überlieferungen sowie wo nötig medizinische Ausführungen aneinanderzureihen und sich kaum auf eine Erörterung dieses Materials einlässt; hierbei sind die Übergänge zwischen den einzelnen Kapitelbausteinen oft einsilbig und kurz. Wenn man Ibn Qayyim al-Ǧawziyyah, einen Zeitgenossen IAHs, als Beispiel nimmt, so sticht der Unterschied zwischen diesen beiden Autoren deutlich ins Auge. Denn Ibn Qayyim al-Ǧawziyyah – um nur ein einschlägiges Beispiel zu nennen – lässt es nicht dabei bewenden, zum Thema Pest lediglich Prophetensprüche und -handlungen zu erwähnen, die sich auf den ersten Blick ausschließen bzw. ihm zufolge sich nur auszuschließen scheinen, sondern er versucht auch, diese sodann gegeneinander abzuwägen, zu analysieren und letztlich doch miteinander in Einklang zu bringen. Dabei lässt er auch die tatsächliche oder die imaginäre Gegenseite zu Wort kommen, die in den genannten Worten und Taten Mohammeds unauflösbare Widersprüche anspricht, um sie sodann zu entkräften. Ibn Qayyim al-Ǧawziyyah stellt also nicht bloß verschiedene, für ihn nur scheinbar widersprüchliche prophetische Überlieferungen nebeneinander, sondern versucht, diese durch eigenen analytischen Aufwand zu einem in sich schlüssigen und konsistenten Ganzen zusammenzuführen.[96] Wenn man nun sich das dritte Kapitel bei IAH anschaut, in dem es um das Verbot geht, sich absichtlich der Pest auszusetzen, indem man sich in die von der Pest heimgesuchten Gebiete begibt, sowie über das Verbot, aus Angst um sein Leben das von der Pest gerade heimgesuchte Gebiet zu verlassen, so stellt man fest, dass dieses recht kurze Kapitel aus relevanten Überlieferungen sowie Aussagen anderer Autoren darüber besteht. Während der Prophetenausspruch, der diesem Kapitel zu Grunde liegt und der für einige Muslime einen offensichtlichen Widerspruch enthielt, Ibn Qayyim al-Ǧawziyyah zu seinen harmonisierenden Ausführungen veranlasste, in deren Zuge er auch weitere für ihn nur auf den ersten Blick widersprüchliche Hadite anführt und miteinander zu vereinbaren versucht, beschränkt sich IAH darauf, das im Umlauf befindliche Material bloß wiederzugeben. Es ist diese auffallende Scheu IAHs vor jeglicher tiefer gehenden Erörterung sowie davor,

---

[95] Im Kapitel Nr. 5 der hier besprochenen Handschrift (Fol. 41a) über den schariatischen Grund für den Ausbruch der Pest – vor allem durch Hurerei verursacht – verweist IAH auf ein anderes Buch von ihm, *at-Taʿrīf bi-āyāt at-taḫwīf*, in welchem er den Grund für die Heimsuchung durch die Pest sowie durch andere Schrecknisse, Krankheiten, Tod der Kinder und durch Massensterben, welches zuerst Kinder und dann Erwachsene treffe, ausführlich behandelt habe. Der nachstehende Inhalt des Kapitels bilde einen Auszug aus dem genannten Buch.

[96] Siehe z.B. Ibn Qayyim al-Ǧawziyyah, *Zād al-maʿād*, Bd. 4, S. 165 ff.

sich auf eine echte Auseinandersetzung auch mit kontrastierenden Urteilen ein-
zulassen, die das gesamte hier vorgestellte Werk prägt. Nicht ausgeschlossen, dass
diese Zurückhaltung IAHs bei der Behandlung des von ihm zitierten Materials
dem Umstand geschuldet ist, dass er sich der Tatsache wohl bewusst war, mit seiner Abhandlung ein für ihn eigentlich fremdes Terrain betreten zu haben.

Formale Charakteristika der Abhandlung bestehen darin, dass die Überliefererkette der zitierten Ḥadīte sehr häufig bis auf das erste Isnad-Glied von der
Ḥadīṯquelle her abgekürzt ist.⁹⁷ Diese Praxis wurde immer dann angewandt,
wenn es darum ging, einen Ausspruch nicht zu überladen und das Auswendig-
lernen des so gebrachten Materials zu erleichtern.⁹⁸ Sehr häufig gibt IAH auch
die Textquelle an, aus der er den jeweiligen Ḥadīt zitiert, im Gegensatz zu as-
Saḥāwī allerdings versieht er das von ihm gebrachte Ḥadīt-Material nie mit einer
der in der Ḥadīt-Wissenschaft üblichen Bewertungen.

Es ist also nicht ganz einfach, die Frage nach dem Sitz im Leben der vorliegenden, genremäßig doch recht heterogenen⁹⁹ Abhandlung eindeutig zu beant-
worten. Denn es besteht eine Diskrepanz zwischen der Einordnung des Werks
durch IAH selbst, durch as-Saḥāwī sowie durch die spätere Forschung, vor allem
durch L. I. Conrad vertreten. Was die Einordnung des Werks durch den Autor
selbst betrifft, so hat er diese an mindestens zwei Stellen formuliert: zum einen
durch den Titel selbst sowie explizit in der Einleitung, wo es heißt, dass er angesichts des Ausmaßes des durch die Pest verursachten Massensterbens kein anderes Heilmittel gegen dieses hereingebrochene Unheil als das Bittgebet für den
Propheten Mohammed gesehen habe, welches das Mittel zum Heil sei und den
größtmöglichen Stellenwert und Ansehen besitze, ferner das Verderben abwehre
und den Zorn Gottes beschwichtige; aus diesem Grunde habe er dieses Buch
über den Vorzugsstatus des Bittgebets für Mohammed verfasst.¹⁰⁰ So gesehen,
gehört *Daf⁽ an-niqmah* auch der religiös-ethischen Gattung, in welcher der Vorzugsstatus des Bittgebets für Mohammed mit allen daraus resultierenden und
damit zusammenhängenden Aspekten im weiteren Sinne – wie z.B. dem aus
dem Aufsagen des Bittgebets resultierenden Lohn für jeden Muslim, Wortlaut
des Bittgebets, Zeit und Ort für dessen Verrichtung usw. – behandelt wird. Inter-

---

⁹⁷ Mindestens eine Ausnahme bildet allerdings der im Kapitel Nr. 5 angeführte Ḥadīt über
   die dem Teufel von Gott gewährte Vollmacht, Adam und seine Nachkommen zu versuchen.
⁹⁸ Vgl. hierzu eine ähnliche Praxis bei as-Saḥāwī (as-Saḥāwī, Muḥammad Ibn ʿAbd ar-
   Raḥmān, *al-Qawl al-badīʿ fī ṣ-ṣalāh ʿalā l-ḥabīb aš-šafīʿ*, hrsg. von Bašīr Muḥammad ʿUyūn,
   Taif, Damaskus [1988], (S. 4)), der allerdings immer den Ḥadīṯkompilator angibt, in dessen
   Sammlung der jeweilige Ḥadīt enthalten ist, und häufig die zitierten Prophetenaussprüche
   durch einen der in der Ḥadīt-Wissenschaft üblichen Bewertungstermini - ṣaḥīḥ, ḥasan oder
   daʿif – gewichtet.
⁹⁹ Man beachte das abschließende Kapitel, in welchem IAH Beispiele seines eigenen literarischen Outputs sowie desjenigen seiner Zeitgenossen anführt, womit die ganze Abhandlung
   in die Nähe einer Anthologie gerückt wird.
¹⁰⁰ *Daf⁽ an-niqmah*, Fol. 1b f.

essanterweise reiht as-Saḫāwī *Dafʿ an-niqmah* in die Reihe der Schriften eben dieser Thematik ein. In dessen Schrift *al-Qawl al-badīʿ fī ṣ-ṣalāh ʿalā al-ḥabīb aš-šafīʿ*, in welcher er sich mit größter Ausführlichkeit dem Themenkomplex des Bittgebets für Mohammed widmet, wird bei der Auflistung der Werke, die den Vorzugsstatus des Bittgebets für Mohammed behandeln, auch *Dafʿ an-niqmah* IAHs genannt: in der Reihe der einschlägigen Werke kommt es nämlich an neunter Stelle vor, also zwischen at-Tuǧībīs (gest. 1155) *Anwār al-āṯār al-muḫtaṣṣah bi-faḍl aṣ-ṣalāh ʿalā an-nabī al-muḫtār*[101] und Fīrūzābādīs (gest. 1418) *aṣ-Ṣilāt wa-l-bišar fī ṣ-ṣalāh ʿalā sayyid al-bašar*.[102] Auch wenn as-Saḫāwī etwas weiter dann einräumt, dass die das Bittgebet für Mohammed betreffenden Passagen nur rund ein Drittel von *Dafʿ an-niqmah* ausmachten und dass der Grund für die Abfassung dieser Abhandlung der Ausbruch der Pest gewesen sei,[103] so ist es doch bemerkenswert, dass ausgerechnet dieses Drittel für die literaturgeschichtliche Einordnung des Gesamtwerks als ausschlaggebend betrachtet wurde. Im krassen Gegensatz hierzu sieht Lawrence I. Conrad in *Dafʿ an-niqmah* vor allem die früheste bekannte nahöstliche arabischsprachige Pestschrift[104] und misst dabei dem Kapitel Nr. 7 mit der erwähnten Auflistung der bekannten Pestfälle in der islamischen Geschichte eine ausschlaggebende Rolle bei.[105] Auch dieses Urteil tut *Dafʿ an-niqmah* nicht Unrecht, auch wenn es nur von einem Kapitel ausgeht und dabei die Anlage des Gesamtwerkes außer Acht lässt. Wenn man jedoch die Abhandlung *Dafʿ an-niqmah* in ihrer Ganzheit betrachtet, so ist sie mehr als lediglich eine weitere Schrift zum Vorzug des Bittgebets für Mohammed oder die erste bekannte nahöstliche Pestschrift. Sie ist vor allem der Versuch eines von der Pest direkt getroffenen literarisch gebildeten Muslims, das über ihn unvermittelt hereingebrochene unsägliche Unheil in Worte zu fassen und darauf nach Maßgabe der Ausdrucksmittel, die ihm in seiner Religion und Kultur zur Verfügung stehen, eine ganz persönliche Antwort zu finden und seinen Zeitgenossen mitzuteilen. *Dafʿ an-niqmah* ist nicht zuletzt Augenzeugenbericht eines der vielen stummen

---

[101] Auch unter dem Namen bekannt: al-Uqlīšī, Aḥmad Ibn Maʿadd Ibn ʿĪsā Ibn Wakīl at-Tuǧībī al-Andalusī.

[102] as-Saḫāwī, *al-Qawl al-badīʿ*, S. 368.

[103] as-Saḫāwī, *al-Qawl al-badīʿ*, S. 369.

[104] Es gibt allerdings eine weitere Pestschrift mit dem Titel *Fī aḫbār aṭ-ṭāʿūn* aus der gleichen Zeit, welche ein Jurist der ḥanbalitischen Rechtsschule, Muḥammad al-Manbiǧī (gest. 1383), verfasst hat. Diese Schrift hat M. Dols eingesehen und beschrieben (Dols, Michael, "Al-Manbijī's *Report of the Plague*: A Treatise on the Plague of 764-65/1362-64 in the Middle East", in: Williman, Daniel (Hrsg.), *The Black Death: The Impact of the Fourteenth Ccentury Plague; Papers of the Eleventh Annual Conference of the Center for Medieval and Early Renaissance Studies*, Binghamton (New York) 1982, S. 65 - 75). Dols weist darauf hin, dass *Dafʿ an-niqmah* zu einem nicht genauer benennbaren Zeitpunkt zwischen 1362 und 1375 entstanden sei; *Fī aḫbār aṭ-ṭāʿūn* sei in 765/1363-64 wie es scheint unabhängig von *Dafʿ an-niqmah* niedergeschrieben worden. Das frühere Abfassungsdatum der Abhandlung *Fī aḫbār aṭ-ṭāʿūn* und ihre Beziehung zu *Dafʿ an-niqmah* bedürfe allerdings noch weiterer Klärung (daselbst, S. 71).

[105] "Arabic plague chronologies and treatises", S. 73.

Pestopfer, der uns einen tiefen Einblick in eine Facette[106] der vormodernen muslimischen Mentalität des Nahen Ostens gewährt.

Literaturverzeichnis

Quellen

Ibn Hišām, ʿAbd al-Malik, *as-Sīrah an-nabawiyyah*, 2 Bde., hrsg. von Muṣṭafā as-Saqqā, Ibrāhim al-Abyārī & ʿAbd al-Ḥafiẓ Šalabī, Kairo 1936.

Ibn Daqīq al-ʿĪd, *Šarḥ al-arbaʿīn ḥadīṯan an-nawawiyyah li-l-imām Yaḥyā Ibn Šarafaddīn an-Nawawī*, Mekka [o.J.].

Ṣaḥīḥ Muslim bi-šarḥ an-Nawawī, 18 Bde., Kairo 1929-1930.

Yāqūt Ibn ʿAbdallāh al-Ḥamawī ar-Rūmī, *Kitāb muʿǧam al-buldān*, hrsg. von Ferdinand Wüstenfeld, 6 Bde., Leipzig 1866-1877.

Ibn Qayyim al-Ǧawziyyah, Muḥammad Ibn Abī Bakr, *Zād al-maʿād fī hady ḫayr al-ʿibād*, 6 Bde., hrsg. von Muṣṭafā ʿAbd al-Qādir ʿAṭā, Beirut 1998.

Ibn al-Ǧawzī, Abū l-Faraǧ ʿAbd ar-Raḥmān, *al-Mudhiš*, hrsg. von Marwān al-Qabbānī, Beirut [1981].

as-Saḫāwī, Muḥammad Ibn ʿAbd ar-Raḥmān, *al-Qawl al-badīʿ fī ṣ-ṣalāh ʿalā l-ḥabīb aš-šafīʿ*, hrsg. von Bašīr Muḥammad ʿUyūn, Taif, Damaskus 1408/[1988].

Ibn Abī Ḥaǧalah al-Maǧribī, Šihābaddīn Aḥmad, *Dafʿ an-niqmah bi-ṣ-ṣalāh ʿalā nabī ar-raḥmah*, MS Istanbul Laleli 1361, 82 Fol.

Ibn Abī Ḥaǧalah, *Dafʿ an-niqmah bi-ṣ-ṣalāh ʿalā nabī ar-raḥmah*, MS Escorial 1772, 90 Fol.

Sekundärliteratur

Dols, Michael W., *The Black Death in the Middle East*, Princeton 1977.

Dols, Michael, "Al-Manbijī's *Report of the Plague*: A Treatise on the Plague of 764-65/1362-64 in the Middle East", in: Williman, Daniel (Hrsg.), *The Black Death: The Impact of the Fourteenth-Century Plague; Papers of the Eleventh Annual Confer-*

---

[106] Wohlgemerkt scheint die Stoßrichtung der Argumente in *Fī aḫbār aṭ-ṭāʿūn* al-Manbiǧis derjenigen IAHs in einigen Punkten entgegengesetzt zu sein: laut Dols habe al-Manbiǧī seine Abhandlung gegen die unerlaubten Neuerungen geschrieben, welche im Zuge des Pestausbruchs von 764-65/1362-64 aufgekommen seien. Als solche hätten für ihn z.B. das Aufkommen von Bittgebeten zum Feien der Pest gezählt, welche Mohammed einigen Bittenden im Traum mitgeteilt habe – in einem im 6. Kapitel beschriebenen Vorfall dient das einem Muslim im Traum von Mohammed mitgeteilte apotropäische Bittgebet IAH als ein probates Mittel gegen die Pest; ferner habe al-Manbiǧī auch gemeinschaftliche Anrufungen Gottes darum, der Pest ein Ende zu setzen, für eine Neuerung gehalten – auch hier werden in *Dafʿ an-niqmah* solche Praktiken im Zusammenhang mit dem Pestfall Nr. 31 (Fol. 70b f.) ohne jegliche Wertung beschrieben.

ence of the Center for Medieval and Early Renaissance Studies, Binghamton (New York) 1982, S. 65-75.

Conrad, Lawrence I., "Arabic plague chronologies and treatises: social and historical factors in the formation of a literary genre", in: *Studia Islamica* 54 (1981), S. 51-94.

Rāʾid ʿAbd ar-Raḥīm, „Risālat „an-nabaʾ ʿan al-wabaʾ" li-Zaynaddīn Ibn al-Wardī t 749 h – dirāsah naqdiyyah", in: *Maǧallat Ǧāmiʿat an-Naǧāḥ li-l-abḥāṯ (al-ʿulūm as-siyāsiyyah)*, 24,5 (2010), S. 1495 – 1530.

Edition des Traktats
aṭ-Ṭibb al-masnūn fī dafʿ aṭ-ṭāʿūn
des Ibn Abī Ḥaǧalah[1]

Stephan Tölke

Das Traktat *aṭ-Ṭibb al-masnūn fī dafʿ aṭ-ṭāʿūn* (Die bewährte Medizin zum Schutz vor der Pest) ist die geringfügig umstrukturierte Kurzfassung (*muḫtaṣar*) des Traktats *Dafʿ an-niqmah bi-ṣ-ṣalāh ʿalā nabī ar-raḥmah*,[2] die beide aus der Feder von Ibn Abī Ḥaǧalah (1325-1375) stammen. Der Autor stellt mit diesem *muḫtaṣar* seinen Lesern eine kondensierte und ganzheitliche Handhabe gegen die Pest zur Verfügung, in der religiös-spirituelle wie professionell-medizinische Informationen und Handlungsanweisungen zusammengeführt werden. Die vorliegende Edition des arabischen Textes bildet den ersten Teil einer umfassenden Untersuchung des Traktats. Der zweite Teil wird in einer späteren Publikation – neben einer Übersetzung des Werks – sowohl eine Analyse des Inhalts und seiner Provenienz als auch seines Verhältnisses zum längeren Traktat des *Dafʿ an-niqmah* und zur Tradition der Pestschriften der arabisch-islamischen Vormoderne umfassen.

Inhalt

Ibn Abī Ḥaǧalah hat den *muḫtaṣar* zum Schutz vor der Pest in drei strukturelle Abschnitte unterteilt: eine kurzgehaltene Einleitung, einen Zehn-Punkte-Plan und zwei abschließende Hinweise. Die kurze Einleitung dient Ibn Abī Ḥaǧalah einzig dazu, den zentralen medizin-pädagogischen Dreiklang seines Werks zu postulieren, der darin besteht, dass sich der Prophet medizinisch behandeln ließ, die medizinische Behandlung befahl und zur Achtung der ärztlichen Rede anwies. Daran anschließend leitet er über in den zweiten Abschnitt, der zugleich den ersten Hauptteil darstellt, mit der Bekundung, dass er diesen *muḫtaṣar* aufgrund der folgenden zehn Punkte (*li-ʿašarati ašyāʾ*) erstellt habe. Dieser Zehn-Punkte-Plan gibt dem Leser Handlungsanweisungen samt Erläuterung und Referenzangaben an die Hand, um sich ganz konkret gegen die Pest zu schützen. Inhaltlich lassen sich diese Punkte eingedenk gewisser Überschneidungen einteilen in: spirituelle Heilung (Punkte 1-4), prophetische Medizin (Punkte 5-6) und professionelle Medizin (Punkte 7-10). Den dritten Abschnitt respektive den zweiten Hauptteil bilden die beiden ab-

---

[1] Mein Dank gilt dem gesamten ALEA-Team und im Besonderen Alev Masarwa und Hakan Özkan für ihre Hilfe bei der Beschaffung der Handschriften und Samir Mubayd und Andreas Herdt bei der Erstellung der Edition.

[2] Vgl. für ausführlichere Informationen zu Inhalt und Abfassungsanlass des *Dafʿ an-niqmah* den Beitrag von Andreas Herdt im selbigen Band.

schließenden Hinweise. Der erste Hinweis (*tanbīh*) erörtert die beiden Ursachen für das Auftreten der Pest (*sabab ḥudūṯ aṭ-ṭāʿūn*). Als erste Ursache benennt Ibn Abī Ḥaǧalah eklatante Zuwiderhandlungen von Muslimen gegen schariatische (*šarʿī*) Rechts- und Moralvorstellungen. Als zweite Ursache führt er medizinisch-natürliche (*ṭibbī*) Ursachen an, aus denen sich Pestereignisse ergeben können. Der zweite und somit letzte Hinweis behandelt das Wesen der Pest aus etymologischer, medizinischer und religiöser Sicht. Ibn Abī Ḥaǧalahs Kurzfassung endet mit der Versicherung, dass jedem an der Pest verstorbenen Muslim ein Märtyer-Status zukommt.

Edition

Die Edition des Traktats basiert auf den zwei bis dato bekannten Handschriften des *aṭ-Ṭibb al-masnūn fī dafʿ aṭ-ṭāʿūn*. Als Leithandschrift (LH)[3] fungiert das in Kairo befindliche Manuskript Dār al-Kutub al-Miṣriyyah – MS Nr. 102 Maǧāmiʿ mīm, Folio 141a – 146a, datiert auf den 22. Rabīʿ II A.H. 1076, da es zum einen vollständiger ist und zum anderen eine deutlich geringere Anzahl an Fehlern aufweist. Als Vergleichshandschrift (VH)[4] dient das in der Instanbuler Topkapı Museumsbibliothek verwahrte zweite Manuskript Nr. TSMK A. 2336, Folio 79a – 86b, undatiert.

Der Edition liegt die LH zugrunde. Die Lesart der LH wird ausschließlich an den Stellen anhand der VH korrigiert, an denen diese eine semantisch korrektere Lesart aufweist. Die Edition ist angepasst an die moderne Orthographie und eindeutig identifizierbare Verschreibungen – im Sinne von Auslassungen diakritischer Punkte – sind sinngemäß ohne expliziten Verweis berichtigt. Korrekturen, Varianten und Auslassungen sind im kritischen Apparat vermerkt. Da beide Handschriften keine einheitliche Strukturierung der Textabschnitte aufweisen, sind die farblichen Hervorhebungen der LH durch Fettdruck kenntlich gemacht. Die inhaltlichen Textabschnitte und Unterabschnitte (Punkte, Hinweise, Zitate und Ermahnungen) sind basierend auf dem Abgleich der beiden Handschriften – soweit sinnvoll – durch Absätze hervorgehoben.

---

[3] In der Edition angegeben als: أصل .
[4] In der Edition angegeben als: ب .

كتاب الطبّ المسنون في دفع الطاعون

تأليف الشيخ الإمام العالم العلّامة شهاب الدين أبي العبّاس أحمد بن أبي حجلة المغربي الحنبلي

رَحِمَه الله تعالى آمين

بِسْمِ الله ٱلرَّحْمٰنِ ٱلرَّحِيمِ حَسْبي الله وَنِعْمَ ٱلوَكيلُ

أمّا بعد حمد الله القريب المجيب والصلوة والسلام الأتمّانِ الأكملانِ على نبيّه الذي تداوى وأمر بالتداوي وأرشد إلى قبول كلام الطبيب فهذا جزءٌ اختصرْتُه من كتابي دفع النِقْمة وسمّيْتُه بالطِبّ المَسْنون في دَفْع الطاعون وذلك لعشرة أشياء

أحدها أخبرني الشيخ الإمام العلّامة شمس الدين ابن خطيب بيرود قاضي المدينة النبويّة الآن أنّ بعضَ الصالحين أخبره أنّ كثرةَ الصلوة على النبيّ صلّى الله تعالى عليه وسلّم تدفع الطاعون وقد استدلّيْتُ لصحّةِ قول المشار إليه هذا الرجل الصالح بأشياء منها ما روي عن أُبيّ بن كعب رَضِيَ الله تعالى عنه قال كان رسول الله صلّى الله تعالى عليه وسلّم إذا ذهب ثلثا الليل قام فقال يا أيّها الناس أذكروا الله جاءت الراجفة تتبعها الرادفة جاء الموت بما فيه قال أُبيّ بن كعب قلْتُ يا رسولَ الله إنّي أُكْثِر الصلوة عليك فكم أجعل لك من صلوتي قال ما شِئْتَ قلْتُ الربع قال ما شِئْتَ وإنْ زِدْتَ فهو خير لك قلْتُ النصف قال ما شِئْتَ وإنْ زِدْتَ فهو خير لك قلْتُ الثلثين قال ما شِئْتَ وإنْ زِدْتَ فهو خير لك قلْتُ أجعل لك صلوتي كلّها قال إذاً تُكْفَى هَمَّك ويُغْفَر ذَنْبُك رواه الإمام أحمد والحاكم والتِرْمِذي وقال حديث حسن صحيح وفي رواية إذاً يكفيك الله ما أهمّك مـن دنياك وآخرتك فهذا كاد يكون صريحاً في المَسْألة لأنّ الهمّ يشمل الخوف من الطاعون وغيره ولا شكَّ أنّ

1 كتاب] رسالة ب   2 تأليف...الحنبلي] تأليف العلّامة بن حجلة ب   4 رَحِمَه...آمين] رحمة الله عليه ب   6 حَسْبي...ٱلوَكيلُ] ناقص في ب   9 اختصرْتُه] واختصرْتُه ب | كتابي] كتاب ب   10 لعشرة] بعشرة ب   11 ابن] بن ب | بيرود] بيرُوت ب   13 تعالى] ناقص في ب | استدلّيْتُ] كذا في الأصل، ب   14 تعالى] ناقص في ب   15 تعالى] ناقص في ب   16 يا] ناقص في ب | فيه قال] فيه جاء الموت بما فيه قال ب   19 قلْتُ[1]...لك] ناقص في ب   20 إذاً] إذن ب   21 ويُغْفَر ذَنْبُك] ويغفر لك ذنبك ب   22 إذاً] ناقص في ب

الصلوة على النبيّ صلّى الله تعالى عليه وسلّم تدفع كلّ بلاء الطاعون وغيره وقد ثبت في الصحيح أنّ المدينة لا يدخلها الطاعون وذلك لبركة النبيّ صلّى الله تعالى عليه وسلّم وكذلك الصلوة على النبيّ صلّى الله تعالى عليه وسلّم

الثاني ما شاع في سنة أربع وستّين وسبعمائة لمّا حدث الطاعون بالقاهرة أخبر بعض الصالحين بالمحلّة أنّه رأى النبيَّ صلّى الله تعالى عليه وسلّم في المنام وشكا إليه حال الناس فأمره أنْ يدعو بهذا الدعاءِ الآتي ذكره فقال أخاف أنْ أنساهُ يا رسولَ الله فقال اكتُبْه وأشار بإصبعه الشريفة إلى كفّ الرجل الصالح بكتابته فاستيقظ فوجده مكتوباً في كفّه وهو بسم الله الرحمٰن الرحيم وصلّى الله على سيّدنا محمّدٍ وآله اللّهمّ إنّا نعوذ بك من الطعن والطاعون وعظم البلاء في النفس والمال والأهل والولد الله أكبر الله أكبر الله أكبر ممّا نخاف ونحذر الله أكبر الله أكبر الله أكبر عدد ذنوبنا حتّى تغفر الله أكبر الله أكبر الله أكبر وصلّى الله على سيّدنا محمّدٍ وآله وسلّم الله أكبر الله أكبر الله أكبر اللّهمّ كما شفّعْتَ نبيّنا فينا فأمهلنا وعمّر بنا منازلنا ولا تهلكنا بذنوبنا يا أرحم الراحمين وصلّى الله على سيّدنا محمّدٍ وآله وسلّم

الثالث الصلوة فقد ثبت في السنن أنّ النبيّ صلّى الله تعالى عليه وسلّم كان إذا أحْزَنه أمرٌ فزع إلى الصلوة وذلك لأنّ الصلوة يستشفى بها من جميع الأوجاع قبل استحكامها فمن استحسّ بابتداءِ الألم والمرض من الطاعون أو غيره فبادر إلى الوضوء والصلوة وفرّغ قلبه لله تعالى وجمع همّتهُ على الله في صلوته ارتفع عنه ذلك الألم بإذْن الله تعالى أو خفّ فلم يحصل له من ثقله وحمله ما حصل لمن أعرض عن الله تعالى وعن الصلوة هذا ممّا لا يشكّ فيه مسلم

الرابع الدعاء وكثرة الابتهال والتضرّع إلى الله عزّ وجلّ فقد صحّ عن النبيّ صلّى الله تعالى عليه وسلّم أنّه قال لا يُغْني حذرٌ من قدر والدعاء ينفع ممّا

---

1 تعالى] ناقص في ب   2 وذلك] ناقص في ب   3 تعالى[1]] ناقص في ب | على النبيّ] عليه ب تعالى[2]] ناقص في ب   4 أخبر] أخبرني ب   5 تعالى] ناقص في ب   6 يدعو] يدعوا ب 10 ممّا...ونحذر] ناقص في ب   12 أكبر وصلّى] أكبر ممّا نخاف ونحذر وصلّى ب | اللّهمّ... الراحمين] ناقص في ب   15 تعالى] ناقص في ب   16 فزع] فرع ب   17 استحسّ] أحسّ ب | من الطاعون] والطاعون ب   18 همّتهُ] همّهُ ب   19 ارتفع] اندفع ب | تعالى أو] الصواب من ب وفي الأصل: تعالى وعن الصلوة أو | أو خفّ] وخفّ ب   20 هذا] وهذا ب   22 عزّ وجلّ] تعالى ب 23 تعالى] ناقص في ب | والدعاء] الصواب من ب وفي الأصل: إلّا الدعاء

نزل وممّا لم ينزل وإنّ البلاء لينزل فيتلقّاه الدعاءُ فيعتلجان فيعتلجان إلى يوم القيامة رواه الحاكم وقال صحيح الإسناد قوله يتعالجان أي يتصارعان وصحّ عـن النبيّ صلّى الله تعالى عليه وسلّم أيضاً أنّه قال لا يردّ القضاءَ إلّا الدعاء ولا يزيد في العمر إلّا البرّ ومن المعلوم أنّ الدعاء ولا سيّما المشتمل على الرُّقَى والعُوَذ النبويّة أحد نوعي العلاج الذي تأثيره لا يبلغه الدواءُ الحسّيّ وأفاضـل الأطبّاء معترفون بأنّ تأثيره فوق تأثير الأدوية الطبيعيّة وأنّ نسبة طبّهم إليه كنسبة طبّ العجائز إلى طبّهم

الخامس روى ابن السُنّي في كتابه عـن بعـض أزواج النبيّ صلّى الله تعالى عليه وسلّم قالت دخلت على رسول الله صلّى الله تعالى عليه وسلّم وقد خرج في إصبعي بثرةٌ فقال عندك ذريرةٌ فوضعها عليها وقال قولي اللّهمّ مصغّر الكبير ومكبّر الصغير صغّر ما بي فطفئت والـذريرةُ هي فتاتُ قصبٍ مـن قصب الطيب يجاء به من الهند

السادس يجب على القاعد أنْ لا يـجاور المرضى بالطاعون لئلّا يحصل لـه بمجاورته من أمراضهم ما حصل لهم ففي سنن أبي داود مرفوعاً إنّ من القرف التلف قال ابن قتيبة القرف مـداناة الوباء ومـداناة المرضى وقد تصل رائحة العليل بالطاعـون وغيره إلـى الصحيـح فتسقمـه ومـن المعلوم أنّ الرائحة أحد أسباب العدوى ومع هذا فلا بدَّ مـن استعداد البـدن وقبوله لذلك الداء وقد تـزوّج النبيّ صلّى الله تعالى عليه وسلّم امرأةً فلمّا أراد الـدخول بـها وجد بكشحها بياضاً فقال ألحقي بأهْلِكِ

السابع يجب على كلّ محترزٍ من الوباء أنْ يخرج من بدنه الرطوبات الفضلية ويقـلّل الغِـذاء ويـميل إلـى التـدبير المجفّف مـن كلّ وجهٍ ويـجب أنْ يحـذر الرياضة والحمّام لأنّ البـدن غالباً لا يخلو مـن فضل رديٍّ كامـن فيه فتثيرهُ الرياضةُ والحمّامُ فيختلط بالكَيْموس الرديّ وذلك يجلب علّة عظيمة بل يجب

---

1 فيعتلجان] فيتعالجان ب | القيامة] الصواب من ب وفي الأصل: القيمة   2 وقال...الإسناد] ناقص في ب | يتعالجان] يعتلجان ب   3 تعالى] ناقص في ب | أيضاً] ناقص في ب   8 تعالى] ناقص في ب   9 دخلت...وسلِّم2] ناقص في ب   10 عندك] عندكم ب   11 هي] ناقص في ب   15 التلف] التكلّف ب | وقد] فقد ب   18 تعالى] ناقص في ب   19 بكشحها] الصواب من ب وفي الأصل: بمكشحها   20 السابع...كلّ] الصواب من ب وفي الأصل: السابع يجب على السابع على كلّ | من2] عن ب   21 التدبير] تدبير ب   22 يخلو] يخلوا ب | فتثيرهُ] فيتيرهُ ب   23 فيختلط] ويختلط ب يجلب... عظيمة] بحلب عظيمة ب

عند وقوع الطاعون السكون والدعة وتسكين هَيَجان الأُخْلاط وقد ذكر بعض العلماء أنّ سبب نهي النبيّ صلّى الله تعالى عليه وسلّم عن الخروج من أرض الوباءِ ما في السفر من الحركة الشديدة المهيِّجة للأُخْلاط الكامنة وهي مضرّة جدّاً فاعرفه

الثامن رأيت في بعض المجاميع الأدبيّة المصريّة أنّ المسجد المعروف بالتِّنور على جبل المقطّم كان يوقد عليه نارٌ فإذا رآها أهل مصر علموا بركوب فرعون فتأهّبوا له وأنّه كان يوقد فيه بالطرفاء واللبان والصندروس ليدفع عن أهل مصر الوباء

التاسع قال الشيخ شمس الدين الشهير بابن الأكفاني في كتابه غنية اللبيب عند غيبة الطبيب **آس** إذا كان في المنزل دفع ضرر الوباء **كندر** يبخّر به فينفع من ضرر الوباء التابع لعفن جيف القتلى والنقائع الرديّة والمباقل الخبيثة وكذلك **الشمع** الخام **والميعة** السائلة **والعنبر** وقال أيضاً **القطران** إذا شمَّ طرفي النهار ووسطه وفي الليل دفع ضرر الوباء وكذلك **الأترجّ** وسائر أصناف الياقوت إذا علّق أو تختّم به دفع الطاعون **طين مختوم** ينفع الطاعون شرباً وكذلك **الطين الأرمني والمقل** الأزرق ورِيباس أكله ينفع الطاعون وكذلك **جمار النخل** وشرب **كافور** واشتمامه ينفع الطاعون

العاشر قال ابن النفيس في كتابه الموجز وقد ذكر أنّ الوباء وكيفية الاحتراز منه أنْ ينقّى البدن ويعدّل مزاجه ويقلّل الفاكهة والشراب والمـرق ويقتصر على المجفّفات والصحناء الشاميّة نافعة والحوامض كلّها جيدة والتبخير بما يصلح كيفيّة الهواء بالأُدْوية التي لها في ذلك خاصية كالكافور والسعد والصندل

---

2 تعالى] ناقص في ب   **3** ما] لما ب   **6** المقطّم] المقطّب ب   **7** فتأهّبوا] الصواب من ب وفي الأصل: فيتأهّبوا | واللبان] والبان | والصندروس] والسندروس ب الصواب من ب وفي الأصل: ليدفع] فيدفع ب   **10** دفع...كندر] دفع البلاء وصدّ الوباء كندر ب | كندر] من ب، في الأصل باهت   **11** جيف] جثث ب   **12** الشمع] من ب، في الأصل باهت | والميعة] من ب، في الأصل باهت والعنبر] مـن ب، فـي الأصل باهت | وقال] قال ب | القطران] مـن ب، فـي الأصل باهت   **13** ضرر] أضرار ب | الأترجّ] من ب، في الأصل باهت   **14** طين مختوم] من ب، في الأصل باهت   **15** الأرمـني] في الأصل باهت، ناقص في ب | والمـقل] مـن ب، فـي الأصل باهت وريباس] في الأصل باهت، ريباس ب   **16** النخل] من ب، في الأصل باهت | وشرب كافور] كافور شربه ب | كافور] من ب، في الأصل باهت   **17** ابن النفيس] ابن النقيب ب | أنّ] ناقص في ب   **19** والحوامض] الصواب من ب وفي الأصل: والخوامض | والتبخير] والتبخّر ب

والمسك والعود والعنبر والسكّ والأتـرجّ والطرفاء وورق الـغار ورشّ البيت بماء
الـورد وماء الخـلاف وتقـريب الفواكـه العطـرة كالتفّـاح والسفـرجل والكمـثرى
والزعرور وأطراف الأشجار والزهور الباردة

وقال ابن سينا في القانون ويعالج الطاعون في البدء بما يقبّض ويبرّد وبإسفنجة
مغموسة في ماءٍ وخلٍّ أو في دهن الورد أو دهن التفّاح ودهن الآس هذا في
الابتداء ويعالج بالشرط إنْ أمكن ويسيّل ما فيه ولا يترك إلى أنْ يجمد فتزداد
سمّيّته وإنْ أُحتيج إلى محجمةٍ تمصّ فُعِلَ قال أيضاً ويعالج الطاعون
بالاستفراغ بالفصد بما يحتمله الوقت أو يوجب ما يخرج العفن ثمّ يجب أنْ
يقبل على القلب بالحفظ والتقوية بما فيه تبريدٌ وعطريّةٌ مثل حمّاض الأتـرجّ
والليمـون وربـوب التفّـاح والسفـرجل والـرمان الحامض ويشـمّ الـورد والكافـور
والصندل والغذاء مثل العدس بالخلّ ويجب أنْ يجعل على فراش العليل ورق
الخلاف والبنفسج والورد والنيلوفر ونحوه ويجعل على القلب أطلية مبرّدة مقوية
إلى غير ذلك ممّا هو مذكور في كتابه القانون فأعلم ذلك

وأعلم أنّ النبيّ صلّى الله تعالى عليه وسلّم تداوى وأمر بالتداوي وأرشـد إلى
قبـول كـلام الطبيب وأمـر صلّى الله تعالى عليـه وسلّم بالتحـرّز مـن الأدواء
المتعدّية بطبعها وأرشد الأصحاب إلى مجانبة أهلها كما ثبت في الصحيحين
وغيرهما ممّا هو مذكور في الطبّ النبويّ على صاحبه أفضل الصلوة والسلام

تنبيه في سبب حدوث الطاعون

لحدوث الطاعون سببان شرعيّان شرعيٌّ وطبّيٌّ أمّا الشرعيُّ فمنه ما رواه ابن
ماجة في سننه من حديث عبد الله بن عمـر بن الخطّاب رضِيَ الله تعالى
عنهما قال كنتُ عاشر عشرة رهط من المهاجرين عند رسول الله صلّى الله

---

1 بماء] بالماء ب   2 وتقرّب] وتقرّب ب | الفواكه] الفاكهة ب | 4 وقال] قال ب | وبإسفنجة]
إسفنجة ب   5 ودهن] أو دهن ب | هذا] ناقص في ب | 7 تمصّ] مصّ ب | 9 مثل] ومثل ب
حمّاض] الصواب من ب وفي الأصل: خماض   10 الحامض] الصواب من ب وفي الأصل: الخامض
11 والصندل...مثل] والصندل ومثل ب | فراش] فرش ب   12 والنيلوفر] اللينوفر ب | أطلية]
أدوية ب | مبرّدة] الصواب من ب وفي الأصل: مبرودة   14 تعالى] ناقص في ب | وأمر بالتداوي]
ناقص في ب   15 وأمر] وأخبر ب | تعالى] ناقص في ب   18 تنبيه] من ب، في الأصل باهت
سبب...لحدوث] سبب الطاعون أقول لحدوث ب   19 شرعيّان] ناقص في ب   20 تعالى] ناقص في
ب   21 رهط] ناقص في ب

تعالى عليه وسلّم فأقبل علينا رسول الله صلّى الله تعالى عليه وسلّم بوجهه
فقال يا معشر المهاجرين خمس خصالٍ وأعوذ باللّه أنْ تركبوهنّ ما ظهرت
الفاحشة في قومٍ إلّا ابتلوا بالطاعون والأوجاع التي لم تكن في أسلافهم الذين
مضوا الحديث ومن حديث ابن عبّاسٍ مرفوعاً إذا كثر الزنا كان الموت ومن
حديث عبد الرحمن بن عبد الله بن مسعود عن أبيه رضِيَ الله تعالى عنه قال
إذا ظهر الزنا والربوا في قرية عجّل الله بهلاكها أقول والعامّة تقول الزنا يقصف
العمر وجاء في تفسير قوله تعالى أَئِنَّكُمْ لتأتون الرجال وتقطعون السبيل فقيل
سبيل الولد وقيل كانوا يعترضون الناس في الطرق لطلب الفاحشةِ كما هو
شائع في زماننا هذا فيما أخبرني غير واحدٍ أنّهم يأخذون الصبيان ويخطفون
النسوان من الطرقات ويدخلون بهم إلى الاصطبلات لفعل المنكرات فإنّا للّه
وإنّا إليه راجعون أقول وأمّا في هذه الأيّام فإنّهم لا يتوقّفون على أخذ الواقفة
في الطريق بل يدخلون إلى البيوت والحمّامات ويأخذون النساء الأحرار وسط
النهار فوا غوثاه وا إسلاماه بدأ الإسلام غريباً وسيعود كما بدأ غريباً فلا حولَ
ولا قوّةَ إلّا بالله العليّ العظيم أيّ نازلة نزلت بالمسلمين اللّهمّ أصلح أحوال
المسلمين وإذا أردت بقوم فتنة فأقبضنا إليك غير مفتونين آمين وقد قال عمر
بن الخطّاب رضِيَ الله تعالى عنه لمّا كتب إليه أبو عبيدة من الشام أنّ
جماعةً من المسلمين أصابوا الشراب ليحدثنَّ في هذا العام حادث فحدث
القحط والجوع في عام الرمادة المشهور وقال هشام إنّما حدث الطاعون
بالشام لأجل هؤلاء الذين شربوا الخمر وحكى ابن الصابئ في الطاعون
الحادث في سنة تسع وأربعين وأربعمائة أنّ كلّ دارٍ كان فيها الخمر مات
أهلها في ليلة واحدةٍ وأنّ مريضاً طال نزعه سبعة أيّام فأشار بإصبعِهِ إلى بيت
في الدار فدخلناه وفتّشناه وإذا بخابية خمر فأقلبناها فخلّصه الله تعالى من
الموت أقول ومن غريب الاتّفاق أنّ الطاعون في هذه السنة المذكورة التي هي
سنة تسع وأربعين وأربعمائة عمّ سائر البلاد وعمّها أيضاً في زماننا في سنة

---

1 تعالى¹] ناقص في ب | تعالى²] ناقص في ب | فقال...بوجهه] | بوجهه] ناقص في ب | بوجهه الكريم فقال ب 4 عبّاسٍ
مرفوعاً] عبّاسٍ رضِيَ الله عنهما مرفوعاً ب | إذا] إنْ ب 5 رضِيَ...عنه] ناقص في ب
6 والربوا] الربا ب 7 وتقطعون...سبيل] وتقطعو السبيل قيل يعني سبيل ب 9 أنّهم...النسوان]
أنّهم يخطفون الصبيان والنسوان ب 12 والحمّامات] والحمّامين ب 13 كما بدأ] ناقص في ب
16 تعالى] ناقص في ب 17 حادث فحدث] حادث قحطٍ فحدث ب 18 الرمادة المشهور] الصواب
من ب وفي الأصل: الرماد المشهورة | وقال...الخمر] ناقص في ب 19 الصابئ] الصواب من ب
وفي الأصل: الضاني 21 نزعه سبعة] نزعه في سبعة ب 24 وعمّها أيضاً] كما عمّها ب

تسع وأربعين وسبعمائة وقد ذكرت ما ينوف عن ثلاثين طاعوناً في كتابي دفع
النقمة المشار إليه وذكرت فيها الغرائب والعجائب هناك وبالله المستعان وأمّا
سبب حدوث الطاعون الطبّيُّ فهو فساد الهواء الذي هو مادّة الروح على
مذهب الحكماء قال ابن النفيس في الموجز الوباء فساد يعرض لجوهر الهواء
بأسباب سماويّة أو أرضيّة كالماء الآسن والجيف الكثيرة كما في الملاحم إذا
لم تدفن القتلى أو لم تحرق والتربة الكثيرة النزز والكثيرة التعفّن وإذا كثرت
الشهب والرجوم في آخر الصيف وفي الخريف فأنذر بالوباء وكذلك إذا كثر
ريح الجنوب والصبا في الكوانين وإذا كثرت علامات المطر فلم تمطر فخراج
فاسد وكثرة الحشرات والضفادع دليل الوباء وحكى الجاحظ في كتابه تفاضل
البلدان أنّ من عيوب مصر الريح الجنوب التي يدعونها الجنوب المريسيّ فإذا
هبّت ثلاثة عشر تباعاً اشترى أهل مصر الأكفان والحنوط وأيقنوا بالوباء القاتل

تنبيه قال في الصحاح الطاعون الموت من الوباء والجمع الطواعين وفي شرح
المشارق الطاعون المرض العامّ والوباء الذي يفسد له الهواءُ فتفسد به الأمزجة
والأبدان وفي الأحكام النبويّة في الصناعة الطبّيّة الطاعون من حيث الطبُّ
ورم رديّ قتّال يخرج مع تلهّب شديد مؤذٍ جدّاً ما حوله في الأكثر أسود أو
أخضر أو كمد وغير ذلك ويحدث في الأكثر في أحد المواضع الثلاثة التي
هي الإبط وخلف الأذن والأرنبة وبالجملة في اللحوم الرخوة ويؤيّد ذلك ما
روي عن عائشة رضيَ الله تعالى عنها أنّها قالت يا رسولَ الله الطعن قد عرفناه
فما الطاعون قال غدّة كغدّة البعير تخرج في المراقّ والآباط من مات منها
مات شهيداً أخرجه أبو عمر في التمهيد والاستيعاب وقال ابن النفيس في
شرح القانون أمّا تسمية هذه الأورام بالطواعين فيشبه أنْ يكون لأجل أنّ
مادّتها تنفذ إلى العضو الذي يعرض له نفوذ ما يطعن به وهو الرمح ونحوه أو
يكون ذلك كما حكى لي أنّ هذا المرض يعرض في الحبشة كثيراً ويسمّونه

---

1 وسبعمائة وقد] وسبعمائة عمّ سائر البلادِ وقد ب   4 ابن النفيس] ابن النقيب ب | لجوهر] بجوهر
ب   5 أو أرضيّة] وأرضيّة ب | الآسن] الآجن ب   7 كثر] كثرت ب   8 ريح] ناقص في ب
علامات] علامة ب | تمطر] تمطره ب   9 الجاحظ] الصواب من ب وفي الأصل: الحافظ، بعدها
فراغ يتّسع لكلمة   10 المريسيّ] المريس ب   11 القاتل] الصواب من ب ومن هامش الأصل وفي
الأصل: العاجل   13 فتفسد] فيفسد ب | به] ناقص في ب   14 الطبّيّة] الطيبية ب   15 ورم] ودم
ب | ما] إمّا ب   16 أو كمد] ناقص في ب | ويحدث] ويوجد ب | الثلاثة] المثلاث ب
17 والأرنبة] والأنثيين ب   18 تعالى] ناقص في ب   20 ابن النفيس] ابن النقيب ب   22 العضو]
العمر ب | نفوذ] كنفوذ ب   23 كما] لما ب | لي] في ب

هناك جغلة وأنّه إذا عرض في بلدٍ تخيّل لأهلها نزول مقاتلة عليهـم ومـن رأى
منهم في منامه أو في حال تخيّله لذلك أنّ أحداً من أولئك طعنه في موضع
من بدنه عرض له هذا الورم في ذلك الموضع والذي حكى لي هذا هو الفقيه
شمس الدين المعروف بالنشو وهو رجل فقيه أقام بالحبشة مدّة وهو لم يحك
هذا وهو يعتقده تخيّلاً بل كان يظنّه حقيقة وقد حكى هـذه الحكايـة قطـب
الدين الشيرازي في شرح القانون أيضاً فقال وقال القرشي يعنـي ابـن النفيس
حكى لي صديق معتمد القول قد سافر بلاد الحبشـة أنّ أكثر مـوت أهلهـا
بالطاعون وهم يسمّونه هناك جغلة ويحـدث أكثره في اللحـوم الرخوة وغالب
القاتل منه لا يبلغ قدر الجوزة ويعرض معه ألـم شـديد وكـرب مفـرط وقيء
مختلف الألوان والسليم منه وهو قليل جدّاً بعظم وإذا بطَّ خرجت منه قطعةٌ
كأنّها لحم ميّت ويبرأ بسرعة قال وإذا حلّ ببلدة عمّ أهلها وأيّ بيت أصاب
واحداً فيه عمّ أهله وعندما يحدث يشاهد أهل ذلك البلد عسكراً قد نزل بهم
بالطبول والسيوف والحراب والبيارق وغيرها ومن شـاهد ذلك العسكر رأى أنّه
قد رشقه أحدهم بسهمٍ أو بحربةٍ أو غير ذلك فيحدث الطاعون في الموضـع
الذي رشق فيه وإنّ ذلك الذي أُصيب يسمع كلامهم ويشاهد حركاتهم قلت
وهذا من عجيب ما سمعته في أمر الطاعون وحدوثه ومصداق ذلك ما روي
عـن أبـي موسى قال قال رسـول الله صلّى الله تعالى عليـه وسلّـم فناء أُمّتي
بالطعن والطاعون فقيل يا رسولَ الله هـذا الطعـن قد عرفناه فما الطاعون قال
وخز أعدائكم الجنّ وفي كلّ شهداء رواه الإمام أحمد في المسند الوخز طعن
ليس بنافذٍ وقد تواتر في هذه الأيّام رؤية جماعةٍ من الجانّ في المنام بأيديهم
رماحٌ يطعنون بها الناس وقد رأى بعضهم ذلك في اليقظة أخبرني بذلك غير

---

1 جغلة] خعلة ب | تخيّل] يخيّل ب | 2 تخيّله] تخييله ب | لذلك] ذلك ب 3 لي] ناقص في ب
4 أقام] الصواب من ب وفي الأصل: إمام 5 يظنّه] بظنّه ب 6 القانون أيضاً] القانون وحكى أيضاً
ب | ابن النفيس] ابن النقيب ب 8 جغلة] حفلـة ب | وغالب] وغالباً ب 9 الجـوزة] الجوز ب
ويعرض] ثم يعرض ب | وقيء...الألوان] ناقص في ب 10 وهو] ناقص في ب | بعظم] ناقص
في ب 11 أصاب] أمات ب 12 واحداً...وعندما] الصواب من ب وفي الأصل: واحداً عمّ أهلها
وعندما | أهله] الصواب من ب وفي الأصل: أهلها 13 والبيارق] والمبارق ب 14 غير] الصواب
من ب ومن هامش الأصل وفي الأصل: بغير 15 وإنّ] فإنّ ب 16 سمعته] سمعت ب | وحدوثه]
ووجدتـه ب 17 موسى قال] موسى رضِيَ الله قال ب | تعالى] ناقص في ب | فناء] ما ب
18 فقيل] قيل ب 19 الجنّ] ناقص في ب | شهداء] الصواب من ب وفي الأصل: شهادة شهيداً
طعن] الطعن ب 20 بنافذٍ] بنافدٍ ب 21 بعضهم ذلك] ذلك بعضهم ب

واحدٍ ولهذا كان المطعون شهيداً لأنّه قد قتل بطعن أعدائنا من الجنّ ويؤيّد
هذا ما روي عن العرباض بن سارية رضِيَ الله تعالى عنه أنّ رسول الله صلّى
الله تعالى عليه وسلّم قال يختصم الشهداء والمتوفّون في فرشهم إلى ربّنا في
الذين يتوفّون من الطاعون فيقول الشهداء إخواننا قتلوا كما قتلنا ويقول المتوفّون
على فرشهم إخواننا ماتوا على فرشهم كما متنا فيقول ربّنا عزّ وجلّ أنظروا إلى
جراحهم فإنْ أشبهت جراح المقتولين فإنهم منهم فإذا جراحهم قد أشبهت
فيلحقون معهم رواه الإمام أحمد في المسند والنسائي وفي رواية أحمد فإنْ
كانت جراحهم كجراح الشهداء تسيل دماً كريح المسك فهم شهداء
فيجدونهم كذلك وقد ثبت في الصحيحين عن أنس رضِيَ الله تعالى عنه قال
قال رسول الله صلّى الله تعالى عليه وسلّم الطاعون شهادةٌ لكلّ مسلمٍ وثبت
في صحيح البخاري أنّ عائشة رضِيَ الله تعالى عنها سألت النبيّ صلّى الله
تعالى عليه وسلّم عن الطاعون فقال كان عذاباً يبعثه الله على من شاء من
عباده فجعله رحمةً للمؤمنين ما من عبدٍ في بلده يكون فيه ويمكث فيه لا
يخرج من البلدة صابراً محتسباً يعلم أنّه لا يصيبه إلّا ما كتب الله له إلّا كان
له مثل أجر شهيدٍ وقال الشيخ محيي الدين النواوي في شرح مسلم وفي
حديث آخر غير الصحيحين أنّ الطاعون كان عذاباً يبعثه الله على من شاء
الحديث المتقدّم عن عائشة رضِيَ الله تعالى عنها وهذا عجيب من الشيخ
محيي الدين رَحِمَه الله تعالى فإنّ الحديث المذكور في صحيح البخاري كما
تقدّم وهذا وهم منه فأعرفه وقد يعثر الجواد السابق والله تعالى أعلم والحمد
لله وحده وصلّى الله تعالى على سيّدنا محمّدٍ وآله وصحبه وسلّم

---

1 قتل] الصواب من ب وفي الأصل: قيل | قتل...الجنّ] قتل من أعدائنا الجنّ ب   2 العرباض]
العرياض ب | تعالى] ناقص في ب   3 تعالى] ناقص في ب | يختصم] تختصم ب | إلى...في[2]
ناقص في ب   4 يتوفّون...الطاعون] الصواب من ب وفي الأصل: بالطاعون | فيقول] فتقول ب
5 إخواننا...على[2]] الصواب من ب وفي الأصل: إخواننا على   7 أحمد في] أحمد رضِيَ الله عنه في
ب   8 كريح] ريح ب   9 ثبت] روي ب | تعالى] ناقص في ب   10 تعالى] ناقص في ب
11 تعالى] ناقص في ب | النبيّ] رسول الله ب   12 تعالى] ناقص في ب | الله على] الله عزّ وجلّ
على ب | شاء] يشاء ب   13 فجعله رحمةً] فجعله الله تعالى رحمةً ب | بلده] الصواب من ب وفي
الأصل: بلدة | فيه[2]] ناقص   14 البلدة] البلد ب   15 محيي] محي ب
الدين...في] الدين النووي رضِيَ الله عنه في ب   16 غير] عن ب | الله...الحديث] الله تعالى على
من يشاء من عباده الحديث ب   17 تعالى] ناقص في ب | وهذا...هذا] ناقص في ب   20 تعالى]
ناقص في ب | محمّدٍ وآله] محمّدٍ وعلى آله ب

Ein Trauergedicht auf Muḥammad
im Kontext des Werkes *Ǧiwār al-aḫyār*

Syrinx von Hees

Der Verlust des eigenen Kindes ist einer der schmerzlichsten Trauerfälle, der zu Pestzeiten ungewöhnlich häufig eintrat. Es wird vermutet, daß durch die Pest im 8./14. Jahrhundert ungefähr ein Drittel der ägyptischen Bevölkerung dahingerafft wurde – darunter überproportional viele Kinder.[1] Auch Ibn Abī Ḥaǧalah (725-776/1325-1375) ereilte dieses Schicksal. Er verlor seinen minderjährigen Sohn Muḥammad, im Raǧab des Jahres 764, d.h. im April/Mai 1363. Er fiel einem der vielen Pestausbrüche zum Opfer, die nach der gewaltigen Pestepidemie des Jahres 749/1348 über einen längeren Zeitraum immer wieder auftraten.[2]

Aufgrund dieser Erfahrung setzte sich Ibn Abī Ḥaǧalah mit dem Phänomen des Schwarzen Tods in Form von Pestschriften auseinander: In seinem Werk *Dafʿ an-niqmah* endet er seine Auflistung von Pestausbrüchen mit demjenigen des Jahres 764/1363.[3] Ibn Abī Ḥaǧalah beschäftigte sich auch direkt mit dem Thema Kinder-

---

[*] Für die wertvollen Hinweise und Kritiken bei der Edition und Übersetzung bin ich allen Mitgliedern der ALEA-Forschungsgruppe und insbesondere Nefeli Papoutsakis sehr dankbar. Für das Korrekturlesen in verschiedenen Stadien danke ich Ines Weinrich, Alev Masarwa und Thomas Bauer. Mein besonderer Dank gilt Navid Chizari, der mir bei der Suche nach Koran- und Ḥadīṯ-Verweisen großartigen Dienst erwies.

[1] Dols, Michael W., *The Black Death in the Middle East*, Ann Arbor 1971; über die demographischen Auswirkungen der Pest in Ägypten und Syrien siehe 221-256; über die proportional besonders hohe Kindersterblichkeit siehe 195, 197f., 233 und 251; Daten zur hohen Kindersterblichkeit finden sich auch bei Stuart Borsch und Tarek Sabraa, „Plague Mortality in Late Medieval Cairo: Quantifying the Plague Outbreaks of 833/1430 and 864/1460“, in: *Mamluk Studies Review* 19 (2016), 145-146.

[2] Der Pestausbruch des Jahres 764/1363 zog sich laut al-Maqrīzī (766-845/1364-1442) in Ägypten über fünf Monate hin, von Ǧumādā al-Ūlā bis Ramaḍān, wobei zu seinem Höhepunkt im Raǧab nach al-Maqrīzīs Behauptung dreitausend Menschen täglich starben, al-Maqrīzī, *as-Sulūk li-maʿrifah duwal al-mulūk*, ed. Muḥammad ʿAbd al-Qādir ʿAṭā, Beirut 1997, 4:267; laut Ibn Kaṯīr (ca. 700-774/1300-1373), der zu dieser Zeit lebte, erhielten die Leute in Damaskus Nachricht aus Kairo, daß täglich tausend Menschen starben, Ibn Kaṯīr, *al-Bidāyah wa-n-nihāyah*, ed. ʿAbdallāh ibn ʿAbd al-Ḥasan at-Turkī, Gizeh 1998, 18:675; Ibn Abī Ḥaǧalah spricht in seiner Pestschrift *Dafʿ an-niqmah*, MS Istanbul Laleli 1361, fol. 72b, von über zweitausend und erwähnt, daß insgesamt über 40.000 Menschen namens Muḥammad während dieses Pestausbruchs starben, wie er von einer vertrauenswürdigen Person erfahren habe.

[3] *Dafʿ an-niqmah*, MS Istanbul Laleli 1361, fol. 72b-73a; zu dieser Pestschrift siehe Andreas Herdt, „Ibn Abī Ḥaǧalah und sein Traktat ‚Das Feien gegen jedwede Widerwärtigkeit mittels des Bittgebets für den Propheten der Gnade (*Dafʿ an-niqmah bi-ṣ-ṣalāh ʿalā nabī ar-raḥmah*)‘“, in diesem Band; Lawrence I. Conrad, „Arabic Plague Chronologies and Treatises: Social and Historical Factors in the Formation of a Literary Genre“, in: *Studia Islamica* 54 (1981), 51-93; und Dols, *Black Death*, 281-282, der darauf verweist, daß Ibn Abī Ḥaǧa-

tod, und zwar in seinem Werk *Salwat al-ḥazīn fī mawt al-banīn* (Trost für den über Kindertod Trauernden),[4] das er für den *šayḫ aš-šuyūḫ* (Obermystiker) von Ägypten und Syrien verfaßte, als dieser ein Kind verloren hatte.[5] Er führt darin zunächst Überlieferungen an, die versichern, daß nicht nur den jung Verstorbenen, sondern auch deren Eltern das Paradies sicher sei, gefolgt von Überlieferungen über das Unterlassen der Betrübnis und das standhafte Ertragen, dann aber über das Trösten der Hinterbliebenen – nicht nur von Kindern – angereichert mit Gedichtbeispielen, gefolgt von einer Diskussion verschiedener Themen der Trauerdichtung über die Vergänglichkeit der Welt, die Ruinen und das Weinen. Es folgt ein Kapitel über das Kondolieren mit Überlieferungen, Gedichten und Beispielen von Beileids-Briefen. Ibn Abī Ḥaǧalah schließt mit einem Kapitel über Trauerdichtung speziell auf Kinder, darunter die in seiner Zeit herausragenden Kindertotenlieder des at-Tihāmī (gest. 416/1025) und Ibn Nubātahs (gest. 768/1366).[6] Nach weiteren Zitaten einschlägiger Verse auch früherer Dichter führt er noch mehrere Kindertotenlieder des ʿUmārah al-Yamanī (gest. 569/1174) an und beendet sein Werk mit einem eigenen Trauergedicht, das er allerdings nicht auf ein Kind, sondern im Gedenken an den Tod des Propheten verfaßt hat.[7] Dieses Werk ist wohl eines der ersten Kindertod-Trostbücher, von denen bis ins 16. Jahrhundert im Gefolge der Pestausbrüche nach 749/1348 eine ganze Reihe entstanden.[8] Ibn Abī Ḥaǧalah kann also als eine Art Pionier dieser Untergattung der Totenbücher gelten.

Nach diesem ersten Kindertod-Trostbuch verfaßte Ibn Abī Ḥaǧalah das Werk *Ǧiwār al-aḫyār fī dār al-qarār* (Die Nachbarschaft der Rechtschaffenen im Haus der ewigen Ruhe), in dem er den Tod seines eigenen Kindes als Anlaß zur Abfassung

---

lah in diesem Zusammenhang auch seine zweite Pestschrift *Kitāb aṭ-ṭibb al-masnūn fī dafʿ aṭ-ṭāʿūn* verfaßte.

4   Ibn Abī Ḥaǧalah, *Salwat al-ḥazīn fī mawt al-banīn*, ed. Muḥaymir Ṣāliḥ, Amman o.J.; eine kurze Zusammenfassung des Inhalts bietet Beatrice Gründler, „Ibn Abī Hajalah (1325-1375)", in: Joseph E. Lowry & Devin J. Stewart (Hg.), *Essays in Arabic Literary Biography: 1350-1850*, Wiesbaden 2009, 124-125.

5   Ibn Abī Ḥaǧalah verfaßte auch ein Beileidsgedicht für einen *šayḫ aš-šuyūḫ* als dessen Sohn starb, *Dīwān Ibn Abī Ḥaǧalah*, ed. Muǧāhid Muṣṭafā Bahǧat & Aḥmad Ḥamīd Muḫlif, Amman 2010, 133, Nr. 135. Die Herausgeber verweisen in einer Anmerkung darauf, daß es sich bei diesem *šayḫ aš-šuyūḫ* um Fatḥaddīn Ibn aš-Šahīd handle, der das Amt des Geheimsekretärs und das Amt des „Obermystikers" (*mašyaḫat aš-šuyūḫ*) in Damaskus seit 764 innehatte und ein rhetorisch herausragender Redner war, der im Jahr 793 verstarb, vgl. dazu Ibn al-ʿImād, *Šaḏarāt aḏ-ḏahab fī aḫbār man ḏahab*, ed. Maḥmūd al-Arnāʾūṭ, Beirut 1992, 8:563-564; im *Dīwān Ibn Abī Ḥaǧalah*, 260-262, Nr. 388 steht ein Lobgedicht, ebenfalls verfaßt für einen *šayḫ aš-šuyūḫ*, den Qāḍī Nāṣiraddīn *šayḫ aš-šuyūḫ wa-kātib as-sirr aš-šarīf* und dies sei die erste Qaṣīda, die Ibn Abī Ḥaǧalah verfaßt habe.

6   Siehe hierzu Bauer, Thomas, „Communication and Emotion – The Case of Ibn Nubātah's Kindertotenlieder", *MSR 7* (2003), 49-96.

7   *Salwat al-ḥazīn*, 149-153, eingeleitet mit den Worten: *wa-qultu fī qaṣīdatin ḏakartu fīhā wafāti sayyidinā rasūli llāh*.

8   Bauer, Thomas, „Islamische Totenbücher. Entwicklung einer Textgattung im Schatten al-Ġazālīs", in: S. Leder u.a. (Hg.), *Studies in Arabic and Islam. Proceedings of the 19th Congress, Union Européenne des Arabisants et Islamisants, Halle 1998*, Leuven 2002, 421-436, speziell 435 mit einer Auflistung weiterer Kindertod-Trostbücher.

nennt. In diesem Beitrag soll zunächst dieses Werk vorgestellt und in die Tradition der Totenbücher eingeordnet werden. Ibn Abī Ḥaǧalah schließt dieses Werk
mit einem anthologischen Kapitel im Gedenken an Muḥammads Tod. Da Gedichte über den Tod des Propheten Muḥammad eine Seltenheit sind, liegt der
Schwerpunkt dieses Beitrags in einer Gedichtinterpretation eines dieser Trauergedichte von Ibn Abī Ḥaǧalah, das in die Traditionsstränge des Prophetenlobs, der
Trauerdichtung und des Kindertotenliedes eingeordnet werden soll.

1. Vorstellung des Werkes Ǧiwār al-aḫyār fī dār al-qarār
(Die Nachbarschaft der Rechtschaffenen im Haus der ewigen Ruhe)

Das Werk *Ǧiwār al-aḫyār fī dār al-qarār* ist bislang nicht ediert. Für diesen Beitrag
liegen mir vier Handschriften vor: Die Handschrift Yeni Cami 701 in Istanbul
bringt diesen Text auf 107 Seiten mit je 21 Zeilen. Im Kolophon heißt es, daß sie
im Jahr 1007/1598-9 von Šihābaddīn Aḥmad ibn Aḥmad ibn ʿAbd ar-Raḥmān ibn
Muḥammad aš-Šahyī abgeschrieben wurde, und zwar von einer älteren Handschrift, datiert auf den 5. Šaʿbān 822/1419. Diese Handschrift ist spärlich vokalisiert. Eine weitere Handschrift aus Istanbul, Laleli 1358, ist undatiert. Sie bringt
den Text großzügig geschrieben auf 136 Seiten mit je 17 Zeilen und verwendet
häufiger Vokalisationszeichen. Eine dritte Handschrift befindet sich heute in Leipzig, Vollers 282. Sie wurde am Montag der 1. Dekade des Ḏū l-Qaʿdah im Jahr
1065/1655 fertiggestellt und umfaßt 163 Seiten mit je 15 Zeilen. Sie weist keine
Vokalisation auf. Zum Teil ist sie in falscher Reihenfolge gebunden worden. Eine
vierte Handschrift befindet sich heute in Kairo, Dār al-Kutub al-Miṣriyyah, taṣawwuf 893. Sie wurde am 13. Raǧab 1073/1663 von Muḥammad ibn Muḥammad as-
Suwaysī al-Aḥmadī abgeschrieben und umfaßt 169 Seiten mit je 17 Zeilen, wobei
im anthologischen Schlußkapitel immer nur ein Halbvers pro Zeile erscheint. Sie
weist spärlich gesetzte Vokalisationszeichen auf.

Im Hinblick auf die Chronologie der Schriften Ibn Abī Ḥaǧalahs können wir
feststellen, daß er in *Ǧiwār al-aḫyār* (verfaßt nach Raǧab 764, April/Mai 1363) auf
mehrere seiner eigenen Werke verweist, die also bei Abfassung dieses Werkes bereits geschrieben waren: Im fünften Kapitel verweist Ibn Abī Ḥaǧalah auf sein
Buch *Sulūk as-sanan fī waṣf as-sakan*[9] und im neunten Kapitel auf *Ṯamarāt al-
aʿmāl*,[10] ein Werktitel Ibn Abī Ḥaǧalahs, der bislang unbekannt war. Im zwölften
Kapitel verweist er auf seinen bekannten *Dīwān aṣ-ṣabābah*.[11] Seine Pestschrift *Dafʿ
an-niqmah fī ṣ-ṣalāh ʿalā nabī ar-raḥmah* erwähnt er dreimal und verweist darauf, daß

---

[9]   Yeni Cami, 37b; siehe zu diesem Werk Alev Masarwa, „Urban Architecture and Poetry:
Two Medieval Arabic Anthologies as Manuals of Mapping Urban Space", in diesem Band;
(Abfassungsdatum unbekannt, jedoch vor 760/1359).

[10] Yeni Cami, 51a.

[11] Yeni Cami, 64a; siehe dazu Anke Osigus, „Friedrich Rückerts Übersetzungen aus Ibn Abī
Ḥaǧalahs *Dīwān aṣ-Ṣabābah*", in diesem Band; (verfaßt 760/1359).

im Waqf der al-Azhar-Moschee eine Handschrift davon vorhanden sei.[12] Auch sein Kindertod-Trostbuch *Salwat al-ḥazīn fī mawt al-banīn* erwähnt er im fünfzehnten Kapitel, das speziell vom Tod von Kindern handelt.[13] Im letzten Kapitel erwähnt er eine Gedichtsammlung *Nasamat al-qabūl fī madḥ ar-rasūl* mit Prophetenlob, deren Titel bislang unbekannt war.

Ibn Abī Ḥaǧalah beginnt nach seiner Danksagung an Gott mit folgenden Worten:

> „Nun: Als mein Sohn Muḥammad starb, das Kind, das Glückselige, als Märtyrer an der jüngsten Pest in Kairo im Raǧab des Jahres 764 (d.h. im April/Mai 1363), begrub ich ihn auf dem Qarāfah-Friedhof in der Nachbarschaft meines Herrn (*sayyidī*) ʿUqbah ibn ʿĀmir al-Ǧuhanī, dem Prophetengenossen."[14]

Anlaß dieses Werkes ist also der Pesttod des eigenen Kindes Muḥammad. Der Vater begrub seinen Sohn in guter Nachbarschaft, von der er in diesem Werk berichten will.

Wie Christopher Taylor in seiner Studie über den Brauch der Grabbesuche und die Verehrung der Heiligen im spätmittelalterlichen Ägypten feststellt, war es für jemanden wie Ibn Abī Ḥaǧalah so wichtig, seinen Sohn in der Nähe eines Prophetengenossen zu begraben, weil er sich dadurch Segen und Fürsprache und eine gute Zeit im Grab bis zum Tag der Auferstehung erhoffte.[15] Ibn Abī Ḥaǧalah erhofft sich zusätzlichen Segen durch das Verfassen seines Werkes. Auch wenn diese Art der Verehrung von „Heiligen"-Gräbern von Ibn Taymiyyah (gest. 728/1328) angegriffen worden war, kann Christopher Taylor deutlich zeigen, daß sie damals zur weitverbreiteten, allgemein anerkannten Praxis gehörte.

Ibn Abī Ḥaǧalah hat sein Buch in zwanzig Kapitel unterteilt. Kapitel eins bis vier können wir als eine Art Ziyārah-Buch bezeichnen, während der größere Teil des Werkes, Kapitel fünf bis neunzehn, ein Toten-Buch darstellt. Das abschließende Kapitel, verfaßt im Gedenken an den Propheten Muḥammad, ist eine kleine Gedichtsammlung.

Ziyārah-Buch

Im ersten Kapitel (K1) geht es um den Prophetengenossen ʿUqbah ibn ʿĀmir (gest. 58/678), über dessen Leben aber gar nicht so viel zu berichten ist.[16] Ibn Abī

---

[12] Im elften Kapitel: Yeni Cami, 60a; im dreizehnten Kapitel: Yeni Cami, 67b; im achtzehnten Kapitel: Yeni Cami, 95a; (abgefaßt ebenfalls in oder nach 764/1363).

[13] Yeni Cami, 80b; (Gründler, „Ibn Abī Ḥajalah", 118 geht davon aus, daß dieses Werk „nach 1366" verfaßt wurde).

[14] Yeni Cami, 1b.

[15] Taylor, Christopher, *In the Vicinity of the Righteous. Ziyāra and the Veneration of Muslim Saints in Late Medieval Egypt*, Leiden 1999.

[16] Yeni Cami, 3b-8b (5 Seiten). ʿUqbah ibn ʿĀmir al-Ǧuhanī gilt als Prophetengenosse, der bei der Eroberung Ägyptens anwesend war und unter Muʿāwiyah im Jahr 44/664 die Statthalterschaft über Ägypten für zwei Jahre und drei Monate innehatte, bevor er im Jahr

Ḥaǧalah greift hier in erster Linie auf verschiedene Geschichtswerke zurück. Dieses Kapitel wird von ihm auf einen Umfang von fünfzehn Seiten ausgedehnt, indem er einen Exkurs über das Haarfärben einfügt, ausgelöst von dem Bericht, daß der Prophetengenosse ʿUqbah ibn ʿĀmir sein Haar schwarz färbte. Das längste Kapitel überhaupt ist das zweite Kapitel (K2), in dem es um Schilderungen der Begegnung ʿUqbahs mit dem Propheten geht und um dessen Leistung als Überlieferer von Aussprüchen des Propheten.[17] Hier hat sich Ibn Abī Ḥaǧalah die Mühe gemacht, das vorhandene Material so vollständig wie möglich zusammenzutragen. Er verweist darauf, daß an-Nawāwī (gest. 676/1277) 55, sein Lehrer al-Mizzī (654-742/1256-1341) ca. 70, Ibn al-Ǧawzī (gest. 597/1200) 78 und al-Ǧizī (gest. 256/870) ca. 100 solcher Überlieferungen, die mit Sayyid ʿUqbah in Zusammenhang stehen, gesammelt hätten. Er erwähne hier nun 116 an der Zahl. Im sehr kurzen dritten Kapitel (K3) beschreibt er den Ort des Grabes und diskutiert allgemein die Vorzüge des Qarāfah-Friedhofs,[18] bevor er im vierten Kapitel (K4) auf diejenigen zu sprechen kommt, die in unmittelbarer Nähe von Sayyid ʿUqbah herum begraben wurden.[19] Dazu zählen unter anderen die Prophetengenossen ʿAmr ibn al-ʿĀṣ und Ṣafwān Ǧammāl ʿĀʾišah, dessen Grab sich an der Tür des Mausoleums befände, wo nun auch sein Sohn Muḥammad begraben wurde.[20] Außerdem sei dort auch ein malikitischer Rechtsgelehrter begraben, sowie einer der rechtschaffenen Leute, Yūsuf al-Kannās, der „zum Sterben" verliebt in das Fegen der verlassenen Moscheen war. Vor allem aber befindet sich in der Nähe auch das Grab des Mystikers Ḏū n-Nūn al-Miṣrī (gest. 246/861).[21]

Bis hierher handelt es sich um ein spezielles Ziyārah-Werk, ein Buch zum Besuch des Grabes von Sayyid ʿUqbah ibn ʿĀmir mit seiner Umgebung. Aufgrund des langen zweiten Kapitels mit den Ḥadīṯen von und mit ʿUqbah macht dieser Teil des Gesamtwerkes ungefähr ein Drittel aus.

47/667 abgesetzt wurde. Er starb in Ägypten im Jahr 58/678 und soll laut al-Maqrīzī, *al-Mawāʿiẓ wa-l-iʿtibār fī ḏikr al-ḫiṭaṭ wa-l-āṯār*, ed. Ayman Fuʾād Sayyid, London 2003, 4,2:847, der erste gewesen sein, der auf dem Qarāfah-Friedhof begraben wurde. Er ist vor allem wichtig als Überlieferer von Aussprüchen des Propheten, gilt aber auch als guter Koranrezitator und Dichter.

[17] Yeni Cami 8b-27a (37 Seiten); Vollers, 12b-39a, nur bis zum 101. Ḥadīṯ + 41b-42a mit dem 116. Ḥadīṯ.

[18] Yeni Cami, 27a-29a (3 einhalb Seiten); Vollers, 42a -43a + 39b-40b. Zur Lage des Grabes von Sayyid ʿUqbah siehe Taylor, *Vicinity of the Righteous*, 16-17.

[19] Yeni Cami, 29a-33b (10 Seiten); Vollers, 40b-41a + 45b-47a + 43b-45a, + 48b-49a + 47b.

[20] ʿAmr ibn al-ʿĀṣ gilt als der „Eroberer Ägyptens"; Ṣafwān, dessen Grab auch in Šimšāṭ in der Ǧazīrah verehrt wird, ist vor allem bekannt wegen seiner angeblichen Affäre mit ʿĀʾišah, der Lieblingsfrau des Propheten.

[21] Ibn ʿArabī hatte dessen Aussprüche gesammelt, thematisch angeordnet und zusammen mit Informationen über Ḏū n-Nūns Leben als eigenständiges Werk veröffentlicht, Ibn ʿArabī, *al-Kawkab ad-durrī fī manāqib Ḏū n-Nūn al-Miṣrī*, ed. ʿĀṣim al-Kayyālī, Beirut 2005.

Toten-Buch

Der Hauptteil, die restlichen Zweidrittel, beinhalten ein gelehrtes Totenbuch in der Tradition des al-Ġazālī (gest. 505/1111), wie sie von Thomas Bauer dargestellt wurde.[22] Ibn Abī Ḥaǧalah greift hierfür unter anderem auf drei der von Thomas Bauer diskutierten Werke zurück, nämlich auf al-Ġazālīs letztes Kapitel von seinem *Iḥyāʾ ʿulūm ad-dīn*, al-Qurṭubīs (gest. 671/1272) *Taḏkirah* und Ibn al-Ḥarrāts (gest. 581/1180) *al-ʿĀqibah*.[23] Er zitiert häufig auch Ibn al-Ǧawzī und nennt dessen Buch *aṯ-Ṯabāt ʿinda l-mamāt*. Ibn Abī Ḥaǧalah ergänzt das Material immer wieder mit Geschichten, die ihm berichtet wurden, oder auch eigenen Ausführungen. Gedichte kommen nur vereinzelt vor. Zum Teil wird der Inhalt des Totenbuches in eine besondere Reihenfolge gebracht, um es an das vorangegangene Ziyārah-Buch anzuschließen. So diskutiert Ibn Abī Ḥaǧalah im fünften Kapitel (K5), warum es so wichtig ist, in der Nähe von herausgehobenen Personen begraben zu werden, ein Thema, das von al-Qurṭubī und Ibn al-Ḥarrāṭ auch behandelt wird, aber nicht an erster Stelle.[24] Ibn Abī Ḥaǧalah bringt hier z.B. eine eigene Geschichte, die ihm sein Freund Ǧamāladdīn Yūsuf al-Ḫaṭīb an-Nābulusī in Damaskus im Jahr 749 berichtete, der ebenfalls seinen Sohn verloren hatte und ihn bei dessen Mutter außerhalb des Bāb aṣ-Ṣaġīr begrub. Ein paar Tage später sei ihm sein Sohn im Traum erschienen und habe berichtet:

> „Als ich mich auf die Seite des Grabes legte, schaute ich zu meiner Mutter, die mich an die Brust nahm. Mir und ihr geht es sehr gut, und wir sind in der Gnade Gottes. Nur ist es so, daß unser Nachbar dort uns fortwährend stört, weil er dauernd bestraft wird und wir diese Erschütterungen spüren".[25]

Anschaulich zeigt sich hier die Bedeutung der guten Nachbarschaft im Grab. Ibn Abī Ḥaǧalah verweist auf das neunte Kapitel seines Buches *Sulūk as-sanan*, worin er über das Recht des Nachbarn z.B. auf unangenehme Geruchsvermeidung beim Kochen und dergleichen bereits ausführlich eingegangen sei.

Im sechsten und siebten Kapitel (K 6+7) folgt eine Darstellung dessen, was beim Grabbesuch zu tun sei, wie z.B. Almosen zu geben oder den Koran zu rezitieren.[26] Das achte Kapitel (K8) beinhaltet Berichte über die Todesangst.[27] Im neunten Kapitel (K9) zitiert Ibn Abī Ḥaǧalah verschiedene Testamente wie das des Imām Aḥmad ibn Ḥanbal (gest. 241/855) und des Faḫraddīn ar-Rāzī (606/

---

22 Bauer, „Islamische Totenbücher", der dabei dieses Werk nicht erwähnt.
23 Winter, T.J. (Übers.), *Al-Ghazālī: The Remembrance of Death and the Afterlife, Kitāb dhikr al-mawt wa-mā baʿdahu, Book XL of the Revival of the Religious Sciences, Iḥyāʾ ʿulūm ad-dīn*, Cambridge 1989; Al-Qurṭubī, *Kitāb at-Taḏkirah bi-aḥwāl al-mawtā wa-umūr al-āḫirah*, ed. aṣ-Ṣādiq ibn Muḥammad ibn Ibrāhīm, Riyad 2004.
24 Yeni Cami, 33b-37b (8 Seiten); Vollers, 47b-48a + 49b-54a.
25 Yeni Cami, 36b; Vollers, 52b.
26 Kapitel 6: Yeni Cami, 37b-42b (9 einhalb Seiten); Vollers, 54a-61b /
     Kapitel 7: Yeni Cami, 42b-43b (knapp 3 Seiten); Vollers, 61b-63b.
27 Yeni Cami, 43b-45b (3 einhalb Seiten); Vollers, 63b-64a + 65b-66a + 64b-65a.

1209).[28] Das beste Testament (*waṣiyyah*), von dem Ibn Abī Ḥaǧalah gehört habe, sei das von ad-Dašnāwī, einem der verehrten sufischen Persönlichkeiten (*abdāl*), das dieser für seinen Sohn in zehn Punkten verfaßte. Ibn Abī Ḥaǧalah bringt dann seine eigene Ergänzung für seinen Sohn in weiteren zehn Punkten mit eingestreuten Gedichtversen. Eine derartige Diskussion über Testamente findet sich in anderen Totenbüchern der gelehrten Tradition so nicht.

Die folgenden Kapitel handeln über den Todesengel (K10),[29] die Verführung des Teufels (K11),[30] über die Zeichen beim Tod der bösen und der guten Sterbenden (K12+13),[31] und über berühmte Sterbende (K14).[32] Al-Ġazālī zum Beispiel bringt auch einen Abschnitt über berühmte Sterbende, in dem er ausführlich über den Tod des Propheten und der vier rechtgeleiteten Kalifen spricht.[33] Ibn Abī Ḥaǧalah verfährt hier anders, indem er sehr viel mehr Personen recht knapp abhandelt und über den Tod des Propheten überhaupt nur eine Überlieferung anführt. Im Hinblick auf die Trauergedichte über den Tod des Propheten, die er im letzten Kapitel bringt, können also keine inhaltlichen Beziehungen zu diesem Abschnitt hergestellt werden.

Im Kapitel fünfzehn (K15) behandelt Ibn Abī Ḥaǧalah dann den Tod von Kindern der Muslime und der Ungläubigen.[34] Auch dies ist ein gewöhnliches Thema in den gelehrten Totenbüchern. Im Vergleich zu al-Ġazālī trägt Ibn Abī Ḥaǧalah in diesem Kapitel jedoch wesentlich mehr Material zusammen, was darauf hindeutet, daß es ihm ein besonderes Anliegen war, über dieses Thema zu sprechen. Nach einer bekannten Überlieferung soll der Prophet gesagt haben, daß jeder Gläubige, der drei Kinder verloren hat, ins Paradies komme. Eine Variante läßt eine Frau auftreten, die fragt, ob dies auch bei zwei Kindern der Fall sei, was mit Ja beantwortet wird. Diese Variante erwähnt auch al-Ġazālī.[35] Ibn Abī Ḥaǧalah jedoch führt diese Überlieferung in zahlreichen, leicht unterschiedlichen Fassungen an. Darunter erwähnt er auch zwei Überlieferungen, nach denen sogar ein Kind ausreiche, um sicher ins Paradies zu gelangen. Diese Überlieferungen hatte Ibn Abī Ḥaǧalah bereits im ersten Kapitel seines *Salwat al-ḥazīn* zusammengestellt.

---

[28] Yeni Cami, 45b-52a (14 Seiten); Vollers, 65a + 67b-68a + 66b-67a + 69b-70a + 68b-69a + 71b-72a + 70b-71a + 73b-74a + 72b-73a + 75b-76a +74b-75a +77b.

[29] Yeni Cami, 52a-55a (5 Seiten); Vollers, 77b–78a + 76b–77a + 79b-80a + 78b-79a +82b.

[30] Yeni Cami, 55a-60b (11 Seiten); Vollers, 82b-84a + 80b-82a + 86b-88a + 84b-86a + 90b-91a.

[31] Kapitel 12: Yeni Cami, 60b-65b (fast 10 Seiten); Vollers, 91a-92a + 88b-90a + 94b-96a + 92b-94a, Ende fehlt /
Kapitel 13: Yeni Cami, 65b-71a (11 Seiten); Vollers, Anfang fehlt, 96b-97a + 98b-105b.

[32] Yeni Cami, 71a-76b (11 einhalb Seiten); Vollers, 105b-113a + 114b-115a + 113b-114a + 116b.

[33] Al-Ġazālī, *The Remembrance of Death*, 57-84.

[34] Yeni Cami, 76b-81a (9 Seiten); Vollers, 116b-117a + 115b-116a + 118b-119a + 117b-118a +120b-121a + 119b-120a + 122b-123a + 121b-122a.

[35] Al-Ġazālī, *The Remembrance of Death*, 110.

Die nächsten Kapitel handeln von der Waschung bis zum Begräbnis (K16),[36] von den Engeln Munkar und Nakir und ihren Fragen im Grab (K17).[37] Daran schließt sich die Diskussion an, ob auch Kinder befragt werden oder nicht, weil sie für ihr Handeln noch nicht zur Verantwortung gezogen werden können. Es folgt eine Diskussion über die Seele (K18) mit Wiedergabe einer Diskussion von Ibn Taymiyyah (gest. 728/1328), ob nur die Körper oder nur die Seelen oder beide die Grabesstrafen zu erdulden haben.[38] Schließlich werden noch Träume erwähnt, in denen Verstorbene erschienen sind (K19).[39] In diesem Kapitel stammt ungefähr die Hälfte des Materials aus al-Ġazālis Totenbuch.

Insgesamt läßt sich feststellen, daß dieser Hauptteil sein Material im Wesentlichen aus der Tradition des gelehrten Totenbuches schöpft, dabei allerdings Themen umstellt oder auch anders ausführt. Wenn möglich, wird das Thema des Kindertodes hervorgehoben, bleibt aber dem Genre entsprechend am Rande. Wir können nicht von einem speziellen Totenbuch für Kinder sprechen.

Kleine Anthologie

Im letzten Kapitel (K20) stellt Ibn Abī Ḥaǧalah vier eigene Gedichte im Gedenken an den Propheten Muḥammad zusammen.[40]

2. Ein Trauergedicht auf Muḥammad zwischen Prophetenlob, Trauerdichtung und Kindertotenlied

Diese Gedichte, die Ibn Abī Ḥaǧalah im abschließenden Kapitel seines Ziyārah-Totenbuches *Ġiwār al-aḫyār* präsentiert, verfaßte er nicht speziell für diesen Kontext. Sie entstanden nicht etwa in unmittelbarer Reaktion auf den Tod seines eigenen Sohnes, wie ich zunächst aufzeigen will. Wie er selbst formuliert, seien die Gedichte dieses letzten Kapitels „erfüllt von dem Gedenken an den Tod des Propheten und von seinem Lob (*taštamilu ʿalā ḏikri wafāti n-nabī ṢAʿAS wa-madḥihī)".[41] Er unterscheidet also zwischen Trauer- und Lobdichtung. In der Tat

---

[36] Yeni Cami, 81a–84a (5 Seiten); Vollers, 122a + 124b- 125a + 123b-124a + 126b-127a + 125b-126a + 128b.

[37] Yeni Cami, 84a–89b (11 einhalb Seiten); Vollers, 128b-129a + 127b-128a + 131b-133a + 129b-137a + 133b-134a.

[38] Yeni Cami, 89b–95a (11 Seiten); Vollers, 134a-135a + 139b-141a + 137b-142b.

[39] Yeni Cami, 95a–100a (10 Seiten); Vollers, 142b-143a, dann fehlt, + 146b-147a + 145b-146a + 147b-.

[40] Yeni Cami, 100a-107b (15 einhalb Seiten); Laleli, 123a-136b; Vollers, 150a-160a; Kairo, 157a-174a.

[41] Yeni Cami (يج), 100a; Laleli (ل), 123a-123v; Vollers (و) , 150a; Kairo (ق), 157a:

الباب المُوَفّي في عشرينَ من قصائد خَتَمْتُ بها هذا الكتابَ وأرجوا بها حُسْنَ الخاتمة والسعادة الدائمة تشتمل (ل:يشتمل) على ذكر وفاة النبي صلّى الله عليه وسلّم ومدحه صلّى الله عليه وسلّم (ق: وشرف وكرم أبدًا دائمًا)

Das letzte Kapitel Zwanzig mit Gedichten, mit dem ich dieses Buch abschließe und so ein schönes Ende und eine bleibende Glückseligkeit erhoffe. Sie (die Gedichte) sind erfüllt von

handeln die ersten drei Gedichte speziell vom Tod des Propheten, während das vierte und letzte dem bekannten Genre des Prophetenlobs zuzuordnen ist. Im 14. Jahrhundert entwickelte sich das Prophetenlob zu einem sehr beliebten, eigenständigen Genre, unter anderem aufgrund des besonderen Erfolgs des sogenannten Mantel-Gedichts von al-Būṣīrī (gest. ca. 695/1295).[42] Ibn Abī Ḥaǧalah leitet sein Lobgedicht in *Ǧiwār al-aḫyār* mit folgenden Worten ein:

> „Ich verfaßte auch im Metrum des Gedichtes von al-Abūṣīrī [sic.], das *al-Burdah* heißt, ein Gedicht, dem ich folgenden Titel gab: *Naṣr al-wardah fī ṭayy al-burdah* (<u>Das Entfalten/der Duft</u> der Rose aus den Falten <u>des Mantels/der Burdah</u>) und mit dem ich den zweiten Teil meiner Gedichtsammlung *Nasamat al-qabūl fī madḥ ar-rasūl* (<u>Der Hauch des Südwindes/Die Seele des Empfangs</u> beim Lob des Gesandten) eröffnet habe“.[43]

Es ist bekannt, daß Ibn Abī Ḥaǧalah Gedichtsammlungen zum Lob des Propheten verfaßt hat, bislang ist jedoch kein Titel einer solchen Sammlung bekannt gewesen.[44] Ibn Abī Ḥaǧalah erwähnt den Titel *Nasamat al-qabūl fī madḥ ar-rasūl* aber auch in seinem autobiographischen Abschnitt in seinem Werk *Maǧnāṭīs ad-durr an-nafīs*, indem er überhaupt nur vier seiner zahlreichen Werke mit Titelangabe nennt.[45] Ihm scheint also diese Gedichtsammlung besonders am Herzen gelegen zu haben. In *Maǧnāṭīs ad-durr* erwähnt er, daß diese Gedichtsammlung sowohl Lob- als auch Trauergedichte auf den Propheten enthalte (*madḥuhū wa-riṯā'uhū*), und insofern könnten auch die drei Trauergedichte in *Ǧiwār al-aḫyār* daraus stammen. Auf jeden Fall hat Ibn Abī Ḥaǧalah auch die ersten beiden in *Ǧiwār al-aḫyār* zitierten Gedichte bereits früher verfaßt. Das erste dieser Trauergedichte präsentiert er nämlich auch in seiner Pestschrift *Daf' an-niqmah* am Anfang eines ebenfalls anthologischen Kapitels,[46] sowie zum Abschluß seines Kindertod-Trostbuches *Salwat al-ḥazīn*;[47] und aus dem zweiten Trauergedicht in *Ǧiwār al-aḫyār* zitiert er vier Verse bereits in seinem *Dīwān aṣ-Ṣabābah*, den er schon 760/1359 Sultan Ḥasan gewid-

---

dem Gedenken an den Tod des Propheten – Gott segne ihn und schenke ihm Heil – und von seinem Lob – Gott segne ihn und schenke ihm Heil.

[42] Stetkevych, Suzanne Pinckney, *The Mantle Odes: Arabic Praise Poems to the Prophet Muḥammad*, Bloomington 2005, 70-150.

[43] Yeni Cami (يج), 103b; Laleli (ل), 129b; Vollers (و) , 155a; Kairo (ق), 165b-166a:

وقلتُ أيضًا (يج: وقال أيضًا رضي الله تعالى عنه ورحمه ورضي عنا به)

على وزن قصيدة الأبوصيري الموسومة بالبُردة قصيدة وسميتُها نشرَ الوَرْدَة في طيّ البُردة وافتتحتُ بها الجزء الثاني من ديواني نسمة القبول في مدح الرسول صلى الله عليه وسلم (و: تسليما كثيرا إلى يوم الدين) وهي هذه (ل: وهي (فقد))

[44] Die Herausgeber seines Dīwāns gehen davon aus, daß er wohl fünf verschiedene solcher Sammlungen verfaßt habe, *Dīwān Ibn Abī Ḥaǧalah*, Vorwort, 24; siehe auch Gruendler, „Ibn Abī Ḥajalah“, 118, die unter seinen undatierten Werken „Four collections of praise of the Prophet“ listet.

[45] Siehe den Beitrag von Nefeli Papoutsakis, „The Anthologist's Agenda and Concerns in Ibn Abī Ḥaǧalah's *Maǧnāṭīs ad-durr an-nafīs*“, in diesem Band, 433-435, speziell 434.

[46] *Daf' an-niqmah*, MS Istanbul Laleli 1361, 73a-74b.

[47] *Salwat al-ḥazīn*, 149-153.

met hatte.[48] Da Ibn Abī Ḥaǧalah den speziellen Namen *Naṣr al-wardah fī ṭayy al-burdah*, den er seinem Lobgedicht gab, auch in einem Gedicht für Ibn Makkī (st. 766/1364) erwähnt, das von der „Wiedereroberung" von Ṭarāblus al-Ġarb im Jahr 755/1354 handelt,[49] mag es also sein, daß Ibn Abī Ḥaǧalah sein Prophetenlob schon relativ früh verfaßte und möglicherweise diesem nordafrikanischen Herrscher widmete. Bislang sind jedoch keine Handschriften von irgendeiner Gedichtsammlung mit Prophetenlob aus der Feder Ibn Abī Ḥaǧalahs bekannt. Auch die umfangreiche Sammlung von Prophetenlob aus dem Beginn des 20. Jahrhunderts, zusammengestellt von an-Nabhānī, enthält keine Gedichte von Ibn Abī Ḥaǧalah.[50]

Dennoch ist es deutlich, daß er sich mit dem Genre Prophetenlob beschäftigt hat, das zu seiner Zeit so beliebt war. Er kannte nicht nur das herausragende Gedicht von al-Būṣīrī, sondern verfaßte eine *muʿāraḍah* auf dieses Mantel-Gedicht (also Reim und Metrum übernehmend), die er so gut fand, daß er sie in *Ǧiwār al-aḫyār* nochmals anführt.[51] Wie der Beitrag von Emil Homerin zeigt, hat sich Ibn Abī Ḥaǧalah zu einem späteren Zeitpunkt in seinem Leben auch intensiv mit dem Prophetenlob des Ibn al-Fāriḍ (gest. 632/1235) auseinandergesetzt.[52]

Die ersten drei Gedichte, die Ibn Abī Ḥaǧalah in Kapitel Zwanzig bringt, handeln jedoch nicht von Prophetenlob (*madḥ an-nabī*), sondern speziell vom Tod des Propheten (*wafāt an-nabī*). Trauergedichte auf Muḥammad aus den späteren Jahrhunderten, in denen das Prophetenlob so beliebt war, sind eine Seltenheit. Es gibt natürlich einige Trauergedichte auf den Propheten, die dessen Zeitgenossen in unmittelbarer Reaktion auf seinen Tod verfaßten.[53] Unter diesen erlangte ein Gedicht des Ḥassān ibn Ṯābit (gest. vor 40/661) besondere Bekanntheit, so daß es in allen Prophetenbiographien erwähnt wird.[54] Es beginnt:

Bi-Ṭaybata rasmun li-r-rasūli wa-maʿhadū / munīrun wa-qad taʿfū r-rusūmu wa-tahmadū (In Ṭayba finden sich Spuren des Propheten und ein leuchtendes Denkmal, auch wenn Spuren eigentlich verwischen und erlöschen).[55]

---

[48]   *Dīwān aṣ-Ṣabābah*, Beirut 1984, im 20. Kapitel, 195. Zitiert ist der Beginn dieses Gedichtes in leicht veränderter Reihenfolge (Verse 1-2, 4, 3) und Ibn Abī Ḥaǧalah sagt dort, diese Verse stammten aus einer „*qaṣīdah Ḥiǧāziyyah*".

[49]   Siehe Alev Masarwa, „Der Fall Alexandrias in den Städteklagen Ibn Abī Ḥaǧalahs und seiner Zeitgenossen", in diesem Band, 339-345, speziell 343.

[50]   An-Nabhānī, Yūsuf ibn Ismāʿīl, *Al-Maǧmūʿah an-nabhāniyyah fī l-madāʾiḥ an-nabawiyyah*, 4 Bde., Beirut 1996.

[51]   *Ǧiwār al-aḫyār*, Yeni Cami, 103b-107a; Laleli, 129b-136b; Vollers, 155a-160a; Kairo, 165b-174a.

[52]   Siehe Emil Homerin, „Ibn Abī Ḥaǧalah and Sufism", in diesem Band.

[53]   Siehe hierzu etwa die Sammlung bei an-Nabhānī, *al-Maǧmūʿah*, 1:54-60.

[54]   Z.B. Ibn Hišām, *as-Sīrah an-nabawiyyah*, ed. ʿUmar ʿAbd as-Salām Tadmurī , 4 Bde., Beirut 1990, 4:317-320; dt. Übersetzung von Weil, Gustav, *Das Leben Mohammed's nach Muhammed Ibn Ishak bearbeitet von Abd el-Malik Ibn Hischam*, 2. Bde., Stuttgart 1864, 2:356-358; engl. Übersetzung von LeGassick, Trevor, *The Life of the Prophet Muḥammad: Al-Sīra al-nabawiyya, Ibn Kathīr*, 2 vols., Reading 1989, 2:399-401.

[55]   *Šarḥ Dīwān Ḥassān ibn Ṯābit al-Anṣārī*, ed. ʿAbd ar-Raḥmān al-Barqūqī, Kairo o.J., 89-97; Suzanne Stetkevych analysiert dieses Gedicht in *The Mantle Odes*, 66-69; siehe auch Stetke-

Daraus entwickelte sich aber bis in die Zeit des Ibn Abī Ḥaǧalah kein spezielles Genre zum Tod des Propheten, etwa um seines Todes zu gedenken. Es entwickelte sich auch keine zeremonielle Erinnerung an den Todestag des Propheten im Gegensatz zu den Feierlichkeiten zu dessen Geburtstag (*mawlid an-nabī*), und so bleiben Trauergedichte auf den Propheten eine Ausnahme.[56] Wenn nun Ibn Abī Ḥaǧalah überhaupt und dann auch gleich mehrere solcher Trauergedichte verfaßt hat, stellt dies eine Auffälligkeit dar, die es zu erklären gilt. Warum kam er auf diese Idee? Welche Funktion könnten diese Gedichte für ihn gehabt haben? Auf welche Vorbilder greift er zurück? Wie setzt er seine Idee um?

Da ein Trauergedicht als Untergattung der Lobdichtung wahrgenommen wird und natürlich ein Lobgedicht auf den Propheten auch einer bereits verstorbenen Person gewidmet ist, sind hier Genregrenzen fließend zu sehen, und eine gegenseitige Beeinflussung ist naheliegend. So wird z.B. in einem Trauergedicht (*riṯā'*) üblicherweise auf den *nasīb*, die Einleitung mit Liebesthematik, verzichtet.[57] Eine solche Einleitung ist dagegen wichtiger Bestandteil einer Lob-Qaṣīdah, und das Mantel-Gedicht al-Būṣīrīs beginnt mit einem *nasīb*. Aber ebenso beginnt bereits das Trauergedicht des Ḥassān ibn Ṯābit auf den Propheten mit einem *nasīb*, der in der Interpretation von Suzanne Stetkevych Elemente des traditionellen Trauergedichts mit einer Lob-Qaṣīdah so verbindet, daß ein Bitt-Gedicht entsteht, das in der Bitte kulminiert, durch das Lob auf den Propheten sich das Paradies zu sichern.[58]

Es bleibt aber festzuhalten, daß Trauergedichte auf den Propheten Muḥammad etwas Besonderes darstellen. Im Folgenden soll daher exemplarisch das zweite Trauergedicht, das Ibn Abī Ḥaǧalah in seinem letzten Kapitel in *Ǧiwār al-aḫyār* präsentiert, analysiert werden. Auch wenn diese Trauergedichte in einem anderen Kontext entstanden sind, so hat sie Ibn Abī Ḥaǧalah doch ausgewählt und als Abschluß seines Ziyārah-Totenbuches in einen anderen, neuen Kontext gestellt. Da er für dieses Werk ausdrücklich den Tod seines eigenen Sohnes als Anlaß erwähnt, mag die Frage berechtigt sein, inwiefern diese Trauergedichte und damit auch das hier als Beispiel für die detaillierte Analyse ausgewählte Gedicht im Kontext des Kindertodes zu verstehen sein können. Diese Annahme unterstützend ist die Tatsache, daß das erste in *Ǧiwār al-aḫyār* zitierte Trauergedicht von Ibn Abī Ḥaǧalah bereits in seinem Kindertod-Trostbuch *Salwat al-ḥazīn* in den Kontext „Kindertod" gestellt wurde. Wir könnten die Vermutung aufstellen, daß Ibn Abī Ḥaǧalah diese Trauergedichte auf den Propheten in irgendeiner Art und Weise auch als Ersatz für

---

vych, Jaroslav, *The Zephyrs of Najd. The Poetics of Nostalgia in the Classical Arabic Nasīb*, Chicago 1993, 61-63.

56   An-Nabhānī, *al-Maǧmūʿah* schließt in seiner Sammlung von Lobgedichten auf den Propheten zwar die zeitgenössischen Trauergedichte ein (1:54-60), weist darüberhinaus aber keines der zahlreichen Gedichte in seiner Sammlung als Trauergedicht aus.

57   Siehe etwa Wagner, Ewald, *Grundzüge der klassischen arabischen Dichtung. Band 1: Die altarabische Dichtung*, Darmstadt 1987, 128-129.

58   Stetkevych, *The Mantle Odes*, 66-69.

Trauergedichte auf Kinder verstanden haben könnte, die er also auch als Trostgedicht auf das jüngst verstorbene Kind seines Freundes, den *šayḫ aš-šuyūḫ*, wie auch als Ersatz für ein Trauergedicht auf sein jüngst verstorbenes Kind in Anspruch nehmen konnte.

Trauergedichte auf Kinder gibt es in der arabischen Literatur durchaus und Ibn Abī Ḥaǧalah ist sich dieser Tradition sehr bewußt. Er zitiert in seinem Buch *Salwat al-ḥazīn* aus Kindertotenliedern früherer Dichter bis hin zu seinem Zeitgenossen Ibn Nubātah.[59] Wie Thomas Bauer beschreibt, ist es aber ein relativ schwieriges Unterfangen, Trauergedichte auf Kinder zu verfassen, da Trauergedichte als Untergattung zu den Lobgedichten immer die Vorzüge der Person des Verstorbenen lobend erwähnen sollen – der Unterschied liegt gewissermaßen nur darin, daß die Person bereits verstorben ist. Was soll man aber über ein Kind lobend erwähnen, das ja in diesem Sinne noch nichts geleistet hat? Ibn Nubātah löste dieses Problem, indem er Kindheit und die Frühzeitigkeit des Todes selbst zu seinen zentralen Themen macht und mit Bezug auf die literarische Tradition dennoch eine neue Möglichkeit schuf, Emotionen über den Tod des eigenen Kindes mit seinen Zuhörern zu teilen.[60] Ibn Abī Ḥaǧalah kannte dieses Gedicht, und er hatte es bei der Abfassung seines Kindertod-Trostbuches als Tröstung präsentiert. Er hat auch selbst mindestens zwei Qaṣīden verfaßt, die explizit vom Tod eines Kindes handeln und die er in seinen Dīwān aufnahm.[61] Dennoch integriert er diese Gedichte nicht in sein Kindertod-Trostbuch, sondern bringt als eigenes Gedicht zum Abschluß dieses Werkes ein Gedicht auf den Tod des Propheten und auch in dem hier besprochenen Ziyārah-Toten-Buch, das er aus Anlaß des Pesttodes seines eigenen Kindes verfaßte, stellt er eine Serie seiner eigenen Gedichte auf den Tod des Propheten zusammen. Es scheint, daß Ibn Abī Ḥaǧalah es eigentlich für eine ausgezeichnete Idee hielt, anstelle eines Kindertotenliedes ein Gedicht auf den Tod des Propheten zu rezitieren, zu hören oder zu lesen, weil dies aus seiner Sicht sogar in besonderer Weise tröstend wirken könne.

Anhand einer Interpretation des an zweiter Stelle in *Ǧiwār al-aḫyār* präsentierten Trauergedichtes werde ich versuchen zu zeigen, wie Ibn Abī Ḥaǧalah hier Traditionen der Lobdichtung auf den Propheten einerseits und der Trauerdichtung andererseits überlagert, um ein Gedicht zur Erinnerung an den Tod des Propheten zu verfassen. Darüberhinaus soll der Frage nachgegangen werden, ob und inwiefern Ibn Abī Ḥaǧalah in diesem Gedicht einen Ersatz, vielleicht sogar einen hervorragenden Ersatz für ein Trauergedicht auf ein Kind und damit auch auf seinen eigenen Sohn sehen konnte.

---

[59] *Salwat al-ḥazīn*, speziell Kapitel 8, 133-153.
[60] Bauer, „Communication and Emotion".
[61] *Dīwān Ibn Abī Ḥaǧalah*, 133-135, Nr. 135 und Nr. 136.

Interpretation

Das an zweiter Stelle in Kapitel Zwanzig präsentierte Gedicht von Ibn Abī Ḥağalah über den Tod des Propheten besteht aus 47 Versen, endet auf den Reim *fāʾ*, und hat das Metrum *basīṭ*.

Im Hinblick auf eine lineare Organisationsstruktur kann dieses Gedicht thematisch in fünf Teile eingeteilt werden: Zunächst wird in den einleitenden sechs Versen die eigene, aktuelle Trauer evoziert mit Anklängen an Themen eines *nasīb*, bevor im ersten Hauptteil (Verse 7-19) der Tod des Propheten und die sich damals ausbreitende Trauer geschildert werden. Ein sieben Verse umfassender Mittelteil (Verse 20-26) beschreibt, wie damals Trost gespendet wurde, kulminierend in der Aussage, daß der Prophet als Märtyrer starb und das Paradies mit eigenen Augen sah, bevor dann im zweiten Hauptteil (Verse 27-41) das auch jetzt noch wirksame beste Heilmittel gegen die Trauer thematisiert wird: Die Liebe zum Propheten, die sich an seinem Grab manifestiert. Die abschließenden sechs Verse (Verse 42-47) sprechen über das Gedicht selbst als Ausdruck dieser Liebe und damit als Trostspender.

Rahmenstruktur:

Einleitung:	Meine Trauer jetzt (Verse 1-6)	6 Verse
1. Hauptteil:	Trauer damals als der Prophet starb (Verse 7-19)	13 Verse
Mittelteil:	Trost damals als der Prophet starb (Verse 20-26)	7 Verse
2. Hauptteil:	Trost jetzt durch die Liebe zum Propheten, manifestiert am Grab (Verse 27-41)	15 Verse
Schlußteil:	Mein Gedicht als Ausdruck dieser Liebe und damit als Trost jetzt (Verse 42-47)	6 Verse

Einleitung: Meine Trauer jetzt (Verse 1-6)[62]

وقلت أيضًا[63]

1 جفني القريح على الخدّين إن وكفا[64]   فحسبه ما جرى من أدمعي وكفا

---

[62] Im Folgenden werde ich die Edition des Gedichtes (Yeni Cami, 101b-102b; Laleli, 125b-127b; Vollers, 152b-154a; Kairo, 161a-163b) zusammen mit einer Übersetzung abschnittsweise präsentieren. Dabei werden folgende Sigla verwendet: Yeni Cami: (يج), Laleli: (ل), Vollers: (و), Kairo: (ق).
Da das erste in *Ǧiwār al-aḫyār* zitierte Trauergedicht wichtige, inhaltliche Parallelen aufweist, findet sich von diesem Gedicht im Anhang, S. 299-304, eine Übersetzung, die außerdem Korrekturlesungen zur vorhandenen Edition in *Salwat al-ḥazīn* bringt. Im Folgenden wird dieses Gedicht als „Gedicht Nr. 1" bezeichnet.

[63] (يج): وقال رضى الله تعالى عنه ورضى عنّا به ورحمه – (ل): وقال أيضًا.

فـالدّرّ مـا عـزّ حـتّى فـارق الـصدفا   إن عـزّ [65] نظم دمـوعي [66] حـين أنـثره

أن قيل هـذاك مـن عينيه قـد رعفـا   مـا زلـت أبـكي عـلى وادي العقيق إلى

مـن عينـه مـا جرى فالبحر فيه وفا   لا تعجبوا مـن وفا دمعي غداة جرى

لكـنّ دمعي فـوق الخـدّ مـا وقفـا   5 وقفـت أسـأل عـن سكّان كاظمـةٍ

فـترك رقّة دمعي في الحبيب جفـا   يا عـــاذلي لا تـــلم دمعـي لرقّتــه

Ich dichtete auch:

1) Wenn mein wundes Augenlid über den beiden Wangen nur noch tröpfelt, reicht und genügt ihm, was von meinen Tränen floss.[67]

2) Wenn die Perlenschnur/Dichtung meiner Tränen knapp/kostbar geworden ist, nachdem ich sie zerstreute/Prosa schrieb, ist das kein Wunder, denn Perlen erhalten ihren Wert erst, wenn sie von der Muschel getrennt sind.[68]

3) Ich hörte nicht auf über das Wādi al-ʿAqiq/Tal des Agat zu weinen, bis man sagte, dies kommt von seinen Augen, die sich schon blutig geflossen haben.[69]

---

[64] (و): وقفا.

[65] (و): اعز.

[66] (و): عيوني.

[67] Wie für einen einleitenden Vers üblich, weist auch dieser Vers einen Halbversreim (*taṣrīʿ*) auf. Dabei sind die beiden sich reimenden Wörter in Schriftbild und Laut vollkommen identisch, wobei im zweiten Fall aber das Verb mit einem „und" verbunden ist (*al-ǧinās al-mutašābih*): *wakafā / wa-kafā*. Die Worte *ǧafnī* und *wakafā* aus dem ersten Halbvers werden im zweiten Halbvers des überleitenden, 7. Verses wiederholt: *ǧafnī* und *yakifā*, eine Art versübergreifender *taṣdīr*.
Im zweiten Halbvers findet sich eine Anspielung auf die im Koran wiederholt eingesetzte Formel: „… *wa-kafā bi-llāhi ḥasīban*" (z.B. in 4:6; 33:39), übersetzt etwa: Gott genügt als Abrechner (auch 21:47 „*wa-kafā bi-nā ḥāsibīna*"). Diese beiden Begriffe werden auch von al-Būṣiri zu Beginn seiner Burdah aufgegriffen, vgl. Vers 3: „Was ist mit deinen Augen? Wenn du sagst: 'Hört auf (*akfufā*)!', ergießen sie sich. …" und Vers 4: „Denkt denn (*a-yaḥsabu*) der Liebende …", *Dīwān al-Būṣiri*, ed. Muḥammad Sayyid Kilānī, Kairo 1955, 231.

[68] Kontrast (*ṭibāq*): *naẓmu - anṯuruhū*; *tawriyah*: Perlenschnur/Dichtung – zerstreuen/Prosa schreiben.
Vgl. Vers 89 der Burdah: *fa-d-durru yazdādu ḥusnan wa-hwa muntaẓimun / wa-laysa yanquṣu qadran ġayra muntaẓimī*, *Dīwān al-Būṣirī*, 236; engl. Übers. Stetkevych, *The Mantle Odes*, 121: „For pearls increase in beauty when they're strung, Though their value does not diminish if they're loose"; vgl. auch Vers 60 des Gedichts Nr. 1: „Wenn der Gesandte Gottes nicht wäre, wäre die Komposition/Perlenschnur des Gedichtes nicht kostbarer und nicht nützlicher als die wertvollen Perlen".

[69] Unwahrscheinliche, mittlere Übertreibung (*iġrāq*), die durch eine Ableitung aus dem Eigennamen (*ištiqāq*) aktualisiert wird: Das Wādi al-ʿAqiq aufgrund der Bedeutung des Namens, nämlich Tal des Agat, habe sein (rotes) Wasser von den Blutstränen des Trauernden. Vgl. die Blutstränen, die im 1. Vers der Burdah erwähnt werden: „War es die Erinnerung and die, die du bei Ḏū Salam liebtest, die dich so stark weinen ließ, daß deine Tränen sich mit Blut mischten?", *Dīwān al-Būṣirī*, 231.

4) Wundert euch nicht über die Fülle/Aufrichtigkeit meiner Tränen, nach all dem, was von seinen Augen/<u>seiner Quelle</u> geflossen ist, so daß der Nil/<u>das Meer</u> sogar anschwoll/<u>treu blieb</u>.[70]

5) Ich hielt inne, um nach den Bewohnern von Kāẓimah zu fragen, aber meine Tränen über der Wange hielten nicht inne.[71]

6) Oh, mein Tadler, tadle meine Tränen nicht wegen ihrer Schwäche, weil es grausam wäre, nicht länger aus Schwäche Tränen über den Geliebten zu vergießen.[72]

Sein Gedicht eröffnet Ibn Abī Ḥaǧalah ganz einem Trauergedicht entsprechend mit dem Thema Tränen als Ausdruck seiner Trauer – dabei bleibt es noch ganz offen, über wen er trauert. Er fordert jedoch seine Tränen nicht etwa auf, zu fließen, wie es in vielen Trauergedichten der Fall ist,[73] sondern beschreibt einen erschöpften Zustand: Sein Augenlid hat sich bereits wund geweint und läßt immer noch Wasser durchrinnen. Er meint sogar, seine Tränen reichten nun: es genügt! Tränen treten stark hervor, da sie in allen sechs einleitenden Versen präsent sind – im dritten Vers ist in thematischer Erweiterung von „weinen" die Rede. Der Dichter beschreibt hier seine eigenen Tränen und drückt in immer wieder neuen Bildern aus, daß sie einfach nicht aufhören wollen zu fließen (besonders Verse 1, 4, 5 und auch 3). Damit wird die eigene, überquellende, auslaugende, ja geradezu verzweifelte Trauer in diesen einleitenden Versen sehr stark hervorgehoben. Es handelt sich um eine sehr intensive Schilderung der aktuellen Trauer.

Gleichzeitig verweist Ibn Abī Ḥaǧalah in dieser tränenflutigen Einleitung seines Trauergedichtes aber auch auf die Einleitungen mit Liebesthematik (*nasīb*), die in den Gedichten zum Lob des Propheten eine wichtige Funktion einnehmen. Durch das Erwähnen des Wādī al-ʿAqīq (Vers 3), einem Tal in der Nähe von Medina, das von Muḥammad als „das gesegnete Tal" bezeichnet wurde,[74] und erste Wegstation

---

[70] Wortwiederholungen: *wafā – ǧarā – ǧarā – wafā*; *tawriyah*: Auge/<u>Quelle</u>, Nil/<u>Meer</u>; unwahrscheinliche Übertreibung (*iǧrāq*): Der Nil schwoll sogar an durch den Tränenfluß.

[71] Wiederholung des Anfangs am Ende (*taṣdīr*): *waqaftu / waqafā*, zusätzlich unterstrichen durch die lautliche Parallele zu diesen Worten in *fawqa*; Kontrast (*ṭibāq*): Ich hielt inne – aber sie hielten nicht inne.

[72] Wiederholung von Worten in anderer Reihenfolge (*al-ʿaks wa-t-tabdīl*): *damʿī li-riqqatihī – riqqati damʿī*; 3 Kontraste (*ṭibāq*): Tadler – tadle nicht / Schwäche – Unterlassen der Schwäche / Schwäche – Härte.

[73] So etwa auch in dem Trauergedicht des Ḥassān ibn Tābit Verse 33-35, *Šarḥ Dīwān Ḥassān ibn Tābit*, ed. al-Barqūqī, 95; in der Übersetzung von LeGassick, *The Life of the Prophet Muḥammad*, 2:401: „Weep tears, eye, for the Messenger of God, and may I never know you with your tears dried up! – What is wrong with you, eye, that you do not weep for that generous man whose ample robe encompassed the people? – Shed tears copiously and mourn aloud at loss of him the like of whom will never again exist"; vgl. etwa auch den Beginn des berühmten Trauergedichtes der al-Ḫansāʾ auf ihren Bruder, Wagner, *Grundzüge*, 118; Borg beschreibt diese Ansprache an das Auge als „beliebte Weise, den Bann des „*ṣabr*" zu brechen", um „zur Sprechsituation „Marthiya" zu gelangen", Borg, Gert, *Mit Poesie vertreibe ich den Kummer meines Herzens. Eine Studie zur altarabischen Trauerklage der Frau*, Istanbul 1997, 121 und bringt eine ganze Reihe von Beispielen dazu, 122-127.

[74] Ibn Ḥaǧar al-ʿAsqalānī, *Fatḥ al-Bārī bi-šarḥ Ṣaḥīḥ al-Buḫārī*, ed. ʿAbd al-ʿAzīz ʿAbdullāh ibn Bāz, Riyad? o.J., 3:392, Nr. 1534: Nach ʿUmar sagte der Gesandte Gottes: „Bete in diesem

in Richtung Mekka ist, sowie der Nennung des Ortsnamens Kāẓimah (Vers 5), greift Ibn Abī Ḥaǧalah nämlich auf die Tradition zurück, Orte der Pilgerroute im Zusammenhang mit dem Lob des Propheten zu nennen, die ihrerseits die Ortsnennung im altarabischen *nasīb* aufgreift.[75] Hier kommt die Sehnsucht des Dichters nach Orten bei Medina, der Stadt des Propheten zum Ausdruck.[76] Hiermit gibt Ibn Abī Ḥaǧalah also den ersten Hinweis darauf, daß sich sein Trauergedicht auf den Propheten bezieht. Al-Būṣīrī beginnt sein Mantel-Gedicht mit der Erwähnung der Orte Ḏū Salam, Kāẓima und Iḍam, fragend:

> „War es die Erinnerung an die, die du bei Ḏū Salam liebtest, die dich so stark weinen läßt, daß deine Tränen sich mit Blut mischten? – Oder war es der Wind, der aus der Richtung von Kāẓimah wehte und der Blitz, der in der Dunkelheit von Iḍam aufleuchtete?"[77]

Das Wādī al-ʿAqīq wird von al-Būṣīrī zwar nicht erwähnt, ist aber in der arabischen Dichtung sehr häufig ein Symbol für das arabische Arkadien.[78] Außerdem ist das Gedicht von al-Būṣīrī selbst eine *muʿāraḍah* auf ein mystisches Liebesgedicht des ʿUmar ibn al-Fāriḍ,[79] das ebenfalls mit Fragen eröffnet, in denen derartige Ortsnamen genannt werden.[80] Der Ort al-ʿAqīq kommt dort im sechsten Vers vor: „Bei Gott, wenn du am Mittag dann al-ʿAqīq durchquerst, sag ihnen frei, ich bitte dich, daß ich sie grüße".[81]

Ibn Abī Ḥaǧalah greift zwar auf diese Tradition zurück und verweist damit auch auf al-Būṣīrī und auf Ibn al-Fāriḍ, aber er gestaltet das Thema doch ganz anders: Er stellt keine Fragen, sondern verknüpft sein Trauerthema Tränen mit diesen Sehnsuchtsorten.

Es sind aber nicht nur die Ortsnamen, die Konventionen des altarabischen *nasīb* aufgreifen. Üblicherweise verweilt der Liebende im *nasīb* in melancholischen Gedanken über den Spuren des Ortes, um dann aber zu sagen: Es genügt! Ibn Abī Ḥaǧalah greift diesen Gedanken zwar im ersten Vers auf, deutlich markiert durch den *ǧinās* zwischen *wakafa* und *wa-kafā*, invertiert im folgenden jedoch gewissermaßen diese Tradition. Denn im Weiteren beschreibt er, daß er ja

---

gesegneten Tal", und Ibn Ḥaǧar erklärt: „das heißt im Wādī al-ʿAqīq und das ist in der Nähe von al-Baqīʿ, vier Meilen von Medina entfernt".

[75] Vgl. Stetkevych, *The Mantle Odes*, 93-94; siehe auch Jacobi, Renate, *Ibn al-Fāriḍ: Der Diwan – Mystische Poesie aus dem 13. Jahrhundert*, Berlin 2012, 173-174.

[76] Schimmel, Annemarie, *Und Muhammad ist Sein Prophet. Die Verehrung des Propheten in der islamischen Frömmigkeit*, 3. Aufl., München 1995, 166-170.

[77] Al-Būṣīrī, *al-Burdah*, Verse 1-2, *Dīwān al-Būṣīrī*, 231.

[78] Stetkevych, *The Zephyrs of Najd*, 111-114.

[79] Vgl. dazu Stetkevych, *The Mantle Odes*, 88-90; siehe auch Stetkevych, *The Zephyrs of Najd*, 79-102; Jacobi, *Ibn al-Fāriḍ*, 39-40 dt. Übersetzung und 287-289 Kommentar; Homerin, Emil, *From Arab Poet to Muslim Saint: Ibn al-Fāriḍ, His Verse, and His Shrine*, Kairo 2001, 4-10; für den arab. Text siehe Scattolin, Giuseppe, *The Dīwān of Ibn al-Fāriḍ. Readings of its Text throughout History. A Critical Edition*, Kairo 2004, 152-153.

[80] Jacobi, *Ibn al-Fāriḍ*, 39: Vers 1 „Scheint Lailās Lagerfeuer nachts in Dhū Salam, oder leuchten Blitze über Zaurāʾ und ʿAlam?".

[81] Jacobi, *Ibn al-Fāriḍ*, 39.

gerade nicht aufhört zu weinen, so daß sogar das unwahrscheinlich übertriebene Bild (Stilmittel *iġrāq*) entstehen kann (Vers 3), das (rote) Wasser des Wadis al-ʿAqīq – der Name bedeutet Agat (ʿaqīq), also ein roter Edelstein, – stamme von seinen Augen, die sich schon blutig geflossen haben. Im altarabischen *nasīb* findet sich häufig die Formulierung „*waqaftu asʾalu* (Ich hielt inne, um nach so-und-so zu fragen)", die auch Ibn Abī Ḥaǧalah in Vers 5 verwendet. Durch einen betont aufgebauten Gegensatz, eingeleitet durch *lākinna* (aber), folgt daraufhin aber die kontrastive Aussage: „aber meine Tränen hielten nicht inne", zudem noch unterstrichen durch die Wiederholung des Anfangswortes *waqaftu* am Ende des Verses: *waqafā* (Stilfigur *taṣdīr*). Wieder also die Betonung auf das fortwährende Weinen, das gerade kein Ende nimmt, und zwar im Gegensatz zu den Erwartungen an die *nasīb*-Motive.

Zum *nasīb* gehört natürlich auch die geliebte Person, die vermißt wird. Diese taucht bei Ibn Abī Ḥaǧalah überhaupt erst im letzten Vers der Einleitung auf, zusammen mit dem ebenfalls zur Liebesthematik gehörenden Tadler. Dabei fällt auf, daß die geliebte Person nicht weiter bezeichnet oder beschrieben wird, ja sie taucht überhaupt nur in einer allgemeinen Aussage auf, die der Rechtfertigung des Tränenflusses dient: „Oh, mein Tadler, tadle meine Tränen nicht wegen ihrer Schwäche, weil es grausam wäre, nicht länger aus Schwäche Tränen über den Geliebten (*al-ḥabīb*) zu vergießen."

Suzanne Stetkevych hat als zentralen Unterschied zwischen den Gedichten des Ibn al-Fāriḍ und al-Būṣirīs, die sich aufeinander beziehen, überzeugend herausgearbeitet, daß die geliebte Person bei Ibn al-Fāriḍ im gesamten Gedicht die gleiche bleibt, mit der der Prophet (oder auch Gott selbst)[82] gemeint ist. Stetkevych schreibt daher, daß sein Gedicht ein mystisches Liebesgedicht ist, das *nasīb*-Motive verwendet, aber in eine geschlossene *ġazal*-Form bringt.[83] Im Gegensatz dazu entpuppt sich die bei al-Būṣirī in seiner *nasīb*-Einleitung erwähnte geliebte Person in den darauffolgenden Versen als „die Nichtigkeit der Welt", von der sich der reuige Gläubige abwendet, um sich dem Lob des Propheten zuzuwenden, kulminierend in der Bitte um Fürbitte.[84] Im hier diskutierten Trauergedicht des Ibn Abī Ḥaǧalah erfolgt keine derartige Abwendung. Die geliebte Person, um die er so heftig und über die Maßen in der Einleitung trauert, kann also der Prophet Muḥammad sein.

Das ist natürlich auch in dem Trauergedicht von Ḥassān ibn Ṯābit der Fall, der ja seinerseits bereits in seiner Einleitung Konventionen des beduinischen *nasīb* aufgreift und dem Anlaß entsprechend umformt. Er nennt signifikant gleich zu Beginn seines Gedichtes Ṭayba („Duftende", eine Ehrbezeichnung Medinas) als Ort, an dem sich Spuren finden, die jedoch – im Unterschied zur Konvention – in diesem Fall gerade nicht verwischt werden können, sie sind klar und werden

---

82   Siehe die Interpretation von Homerin, *Arab Poet*, 9.
83   Stetkevych, *Mantle Odes*, 89-90.
84   Stetkevych, *Mantle Odes*, 94-95.

bleiben.[85] Das Weinen als Ausdruck der Trauer thematisiert Ḥassān ibn Ṯābit in dieser Einleitung jedoch noch gar nicht.

Ibn Abī Ḥaǧalah leistet hier also eine sehr eigenständige Umformung der Einleitungsmöglichkeiten für sein eigenes Trauergedicht. Was er damit eigentlich erreicht, werden wir noch versuchen zu verstehen.

Die Einleitung läßt sich leicht abgrenzen, da der 7. Vers, in dem der Prophet zum ersten Mal erwähnt wird, eindeutig den überleitenden Vers (taḫalluṣ) darstellt.

إن مـات فيما مـضى المخـتـار مـن مـضرٍ   فكيـــف تمنـــع جفـــني الآن أن يكفــا

> 7) Wo doch der Auserwählte von Muḍar in der Vergangenheit starb, wie willst du mein Augenlid jetzt hindern, zu tröpfeln?

Ibn Abī Ḥaǧalah gelingt es, eine gelungene Verknüpfung dieses taḫalluṣ-Verses mit der Einleitung herzustellen, indem er die Worte aus dem ersten Halbvers des 1. Verses ǧafnī und wakafā im zweiten Halbvers des 7. Verses wieder aufnimmt: ǧafnī und yakifā. Dies erzeugt eine inhaltliche Klammer, ähnlich der Stilfigur taṣdīr.

Wenn wir nun diesen überleitenden Vers 7 noch im Zusammenhang mit der Einleitung betrachten, so fällt auf, daß hier ein starker, zeitlicher Kontrast aufgebaut wird, der andererseits das Thema der Einleitung mit dem des Hauptteils verbindet: „Wo doch der Auserwählte von Muḍar in der Vergangenheit (fīmā maḍā) starb, wie willst du mein Augenlid jetzt (al-āna) hindern, Wasser durchzulassen?". Die in der Einleitung beschriebene eigene Trauer wird also inhaltlich mit dem Hauptteil verknüpft und damit mit dem Tod des Propheten in Zusammenhang gebracht; aber mit den in Opposition gesetzten Zeitworten wird stark betont, daß die in der Einleitung beschriebene, eigene Trauer ein jetziger, akuter Zustand ist, der Tod des Propheten dagegen in ferner Vergangenheit eintraf. Natürlich kann man auch jetzt noch über den Tod des Propheten vor langer Zeit traurig sein. Der stark betonte zeitliche Kontrast scheint mir aber als Verweis darauf interpretiert werden zu können, daß der Dichter im Augenblick eigentlich (oder zumindest auch) um einen akuten Verlust einer geliebten Person trauert, der ihn an den Tod des Propheten denken ließ: Der Tod des Propheten liegt lange zurück, und wir beweinen ihn dennoch; wie soll der Dichter denn da jetzt nicht weinen über den Propheten und noch dazu über jemanden der gerade erst verstorben ist! Durch diesen Kontrast wird es möglich, das Gedicht auch als Ausdruck der Trauer über einen gerade erlebten Verlust zu lesen und damit auch als Ersatz für die Trauer um den eigenen Sohn.

---

[85] Wie oben schon erwähnt, Vers 1, *Šarḥ Dīwān Ḥassān ibn Ṯābit*, ed. al-Barqūqī, 89; in der Übersetzung von LeGassick, *The Life of the Prophet Muḥammad*, 2:399: „At Ṭayba traces remain of the Messenger, and a light-emitting locality, though traces often fade and disappear".

Möglicherweise läßt sich bereits in Vers 4 ein Hinweis finden, daß sich die als so unermeßlich geschilderte Trauer nicht ausschließlich auf den Tod des Propheten bezieht, wie es auch in Vers 7 zum Ausdruck gebracht wird. Ibn Abī Ḥaǧalah verweist in Vers 4 über die Kombination der Worte *al-baḥru* und *wafā* nämlich auf einen Ort seiner Heimat, hervorgehoben durch die wiederholte Verwendung von *wafā*, Aufrichtigkeit, Fülle und Erfüllung, ein Wort, das speziell für den Höhepunkt der Nilschwelle verwendet wurde: *wafā' an-Nīl*, zu deren Anlaß große Feierlichkeiten in der Stadt Kairo üblich waren.[86] Da nun der Nil von den Ägyptern auch als „das Meer" bezeichnet wurde, liegt hier zwar ein versteckter, aber für den zeitgenössischen Rezipienten in Kairo wahrscheinlich verständlicher Hinweis auf den ägyptischen Erinnerungsort par exellence vor. Damit fügt Ibn Abī Ḥaǧalah, wenn auch unaufdringlich, einen ägyptischen Ort den ḥiǧāzischen Sehnsuchtsorten hinzu und eröffnet damit die Möglichkeit, dieses Gedicht nicht ausschließlich auf den Tod des Propheten zu beziehen, sondern gegebenenfalls auch auf einen Trauerfall in der Heimat.

1. Hauptteil: Trauer damals als der Prophet starb (Verse 7-19)

إن مـات فيـما مضى المختار من مضرٍ   فكيـف تمنـع[87] جفـني الآن أن يكفـا

لـمـا قـضى نجبـه خـير الأنام ضحًـى   أمـسى الرّبيـع خريفًـا بعـده خرفـا

وارتـدّ قـوم عـن الإسـلام حـين رأوا   غـصن[88] الهدى بان لمّا مات وانقصفا

10   وقـام فـيهم أبـو بكـر غـداة غـزى   بـني حنيفـة في أصحابـه الحنفـا

واصفرّت الشمس من بعد الأصيل إلى   أن بات حاجبهـا كالبـدر منكـسفا[89]

وانهـلّ دمـع غـمام كان ظلّـله   وخلّـف المـزن يـبكي دائمًـا أسـفا

ومـاج في بحـره المـوج العظـيم إلى   أن غرّقت سفنه والحـوت فيه طفـا[90]

وأظلمـت طيبـةٌ في وجـه سـاكنها   وسـط النهـار خلافـا لـلّذي ألفـا

15   وقـام حـسّان يرثيـه ووافقـه[91]   فيـه[92] أبـو بكـر الـصدّيق ملتهفـا

---

86   Siehe dazu Conermann, Stephan, „Lebensspender, Stätte der Erinnerung, Gedächtnisort: Der Nil während der Mamlūkenzeit (1250-1517)", in: Ulrich Hübner & Antje Richter (Hg.): *Wasser – Lebensmittel, Kulturgut, politische Waffe. Historische und zeitgenössische Probleme und Perspektiven in asiatischen und afrikanischen Gesellschaften*, Hamburg 2004, 15-59, insbesondere „2.1. Das Fest des Pegelhöchststandes (*wafā' an-Nīl*)", 28-33.

87   (ل): يمنع.

88   (ل): عصن.

89   (و): ونكسفا.

90   (و): خفا.

91   (ل): واوقفه.

هـــذا الــرثاء الّذي يــرثى⁹³ لقائله   مـثلي ويكــثر فيه النـوح والأسـفا

هـــذا المــصاب الّذي عمَّ العــزاء بـه   وأيـــتم⁹⁴ الديــن والأشراف والخلفــا

لـولاه مـا ناح في الأيـك الحمـام ولا   سقت دمـوع الغوادي الغور⁹⁵ والنجفا

تـصرّف الحــزن في الدنيـا وساكنها   لمــا رأى أحـمـدًا عنهـا قـد انصرفا

7) Wo doch der Auserwählte von Muḍar in der Vergangenheit starb, wie willst du mein Augenlid jetzt hindern, zu tröpfeln?[96]

8) Nachdem der Beste der Geschöpfe zur Mittagszeit gestorben war, wurde bereits des Abends der Frühling aus Trübsinn wegen seines Hinscheidens zum Herbst.[97]

9) Etliche fielen ab vom Islam, als sie sahen, wie der Zweig der Rechtleitung abgetrennt wurde/deutlich war, als er starb, und zerbrach.[98]

10) Da erhob sich unter ihnen Abū Bakr am Morgen und kämpfte gegen die Banū Ḥanīfah, mit seinen Anhängern, den Rechtgläubigen.[99]

11) Die Sonne erblich vom Nachmittag an, bis sich ihr letzter Strahl wie der Mond verfinsterte.[100]

12) Heftig gossen die Tränen der Wolken, die dem Propheten Schatten gespendet hatten, denn er hinterließ die Wolken weinend, immerfort, sehr betrübt.[101]

---

⁹² ناقص في (ل) (ق).

⁹³ (ق): يُرثا.

⁹⁴ (ل): ويتّم.

⁹⁵ (يج) (ق): والعور.

[96] Kontrast (ṭibāq): in der Vergangenheit – jetzt; klangliches Spiel mit *fīmā maḍā … muḍarin*; am Ende Wortwiederholung mit *ǧafnī – yakifā* vom Anfang des Gedichts (*ǧafnī – wakafā*).

[97] Kontrast (ṭibāq): zur Mittagszeit – am Abend; der Frühling – Herbst; Wiederholung der selben Wurzel mit einer anderen Bedeutung: *ḫarīf* (Herbst) - *ḫaraf* (Geistesschwäche; hier mit Trübsinn übersetzt, da der Frühling aus Kummer den Sinn verlor).

[98] Vergleichsbasierte Metapher (istiʿāra): der Zweig der Rechtleitung; *tawriyah*: sich trennen/deutlich sein, und durch das Wort *ġuṣn* (Zweig) klingt assoziativ auch die botanische Bedeutung „Moringe oder ägyptische Weide" für *bān* an.
Vgl. mit Gedicht Nr. 1, siehe Anhang S. 302: *wa-fāraqat al-islām* (Vers 35) und *rabʿ al-hudā* (Vers 36).

[99] Ableitung aus dem Eigennamen (*ištiqāq*) als Kontrast (ṭibāq) ausgeführt: *Banū Ḥanīfah – al-ḥunafāʾ*; klangliches Spiel im 1. Halbvers mit *ġadāta ġazā*.
Vgl. mit Gedicht Nr. 1: *fa-qāma Abū Bakrin* (Vers 36) und *āl Ḥanīfatin* (Vers 35); vgl. auch Burdah, Vers 77, *Dīwān al-Būṣirī*, 235.

[100] Kontrast (ṭibāq): Sonne – Mond; auch als Kontrast vorhanden: Sonne (hell) – erbleicht (dunkel), sowie Mond (hell) – verfinstert (dunkel); Vergleich (tašbīh): Sonne erbleicht/letzte Strahlen der Sonne (d.h. was man noch sehen kann, wenn die Sonne untergeht: wörtl. Die Augenbraue der Sonne) wie der Mond verfinstert.
Vgl. mit Gedicht Nr. 1, Vers 31: „Das Gesicht der Sonne wurde gelb, traurig/entblößt, wie ein junges Mädchen, dem die Traurigkeit verbietet, sich zu verschleiern".

[101] Kontrast (ṭibāq): heftig gießen – Schatten spenden; Metapher (istiʿāra): Tränen der Wolken.

13) Stark schlugen in ihrem Meer heftige Wellen, so daß die Schiffe dort versanken und der Walfisch darin auftauchte.[102]

14) Finsternis befiel Ṭaybah (die Duftende, Medina) im Angesicht ihrer Bewohner mitten am Tag, anders als sie es gewohnt waren.[103]

15) Ḥassān erhob sich, um ihn zu beweinen, und Abū Bakr, der wahre Freund, tat es ihm seufzend gleich.

16) Ach, eine Totenklage, deren Sprecher beklagenswert ist wie ich, und die besonders viel Klage und Betrübnis über ihn enthält.[104]

17) Oh, der vom Unglück Getroffene, durch den die Trauer alles umfasste, und der die Religion, die Edlen und die Nachfahren verwaisen ließ.[105]

18) Wäre es nicht seinetwegen, klagten die Tauben in ihrem Dickicht nicht laut und die Tränen des Frühregens tränkten nicht die Senke und die Hügel.[106]

19) Die Traurigkeit breitet sich in der Welt und ihren Bewohnern aus, wenn sie sieht, wie sich Aḥmad schon entfernt hat.[107]

Im ersten Hauptteil geht es, im Gegensatz zu der persönlichen Trauer des Dichters in der Gegenwart, nun um die Reaktionen der Natur und der Menschen damals, als der Prophet starb. Diese Beschreibungen basieren zu einem großen Teil auf Informationen, wie sie in den Prophetenbiographien überliefert wurden. In der Trauerdichtung ist es üblich, Trauerrekationen zu beschreiben, über die Todesumstände des Verstorbenen zu sprechen und seine Taten lobend zu erwähnen. In den Lobgedichten auf den Propheten, die ihrerseits selbstverständlich auf Überlieferungen

---

Vgl. mit Gedicht Nr. 1, Vers 29: „Es entfernten sich die Wolken, die ihn in der Mittagshitze beschatteten und ließen Wolken zurück, die die Erde mit Tränen füllen"; vgl. auch Burdah, Vers 74, *Dīwān al-Būṣīrī*, 235.

[102] Kontrast (*ṭibāq*): untertauchen – auftauchen; Schiffe – Fische; verstärkendes Klangspiel: *māǧa ... al-mawǧ*.

[103] Kontrast (*ṭibāq*): verfinstern – mitten am Tag, wird auch noch explizit ausformuliert: im Gegensatz zu dem, woran sie gewohnt sind.
Vgl. Ḥassān ibn Ṯābit, Vers 1, der emblematisch mit der Erwähnung der Stadt Medina unter ihrem Ehrennamen Ṭaybah (Duftende) beginnt.

[104] Wiederholung derselben Wurzel mit derselben Bedeutung zur Betonung: *ar-riṯāʾ, yurṯā*, fortgeführt durch das verstärkende Klangspiel mit *ṯāʾ: miṯlī wa-yakṯuru*.
Vgl. mit Gedicht Nr. 1, Vers 57: „Ich dichte über ihn eine gute Trauerklage wegen der Stärke meines Kummers".

[105] Nominalreihung (*taʿdīd*): die Religion, die Edlen und die Nachfahren.
Vgl. Ḥassān ibn Ṯābit, Vers 15: „Sie schickten die Weisheit, das Wissen und das Erbarmen in jener Nacht fort, als sie ihn ohne Kissen mit Erde bedeckten".
Vgl. auch al-Būṣīrī, Vers 126, indem die muslimischen Kämpfer die Gemeinde nicht verwaisen lassen.
Vgl. auch mit Gedicht Nr. 1, Vers 54: „Der Prophet starb, nachdem er die Welt mit seiner Freigebigkeit ausfüllte (*ʿamma*)".

[106] Kontrast (*ṭibāq*): Senke – Hügel; Metapher (*istiʿāra*): Tränen des Frühregens; Klangspiel mit *al-ġawādī l-ġawra*.

[107] Kontrast (*ṭibāq*): unbeschränkt bewegen – sich entfernen, der gleichzeitig eine defekte Paranomasia (*al-ǧinās al-kāfī*): *taṣarrafa - inṣarafā*, darstellt und auch noch durch die Position am Anfang und Ende des Verses hervorgehoben ist.

über das Leben des Propheten zurückgreifen, werden üblicherweise sein Tod und die Reaktionen darauf nicht erwähnt. Dieses Thema paßt nicht richtig in den Kontext des Lobgedichtes. Das heißt, in diesem ersten Hauptteil kann Ibn Abī Ḥaǧalah gar nicht auf Konventionen oder gar Formulierungen aus dem Prophetenlob zurückgreifen. Es scheint also, als habe er hier durchaus etwas Besonderes geschaffen. Daher mag es verständlich sein, daß sich einige seiner Formulierungen ähnlich auch in dem anderen Trauergedicht auf den Propheten finden, welches er in *Ǧiwār al-aḫyār* diesem voranstellt (Gedicht Nr. 1 im Anhang). Mithin greift er in dieser Passage auf einige seiner eigenen Gedanken und Formulierungen zurück.

Zu Beginn, im überleitenden Vers 7, wird der Prophet als „Auserwählter von Muḍar" vorgestellt, eine lobende Ehrbezeichnung, deren Steigerung „der Beste (Auserwählteste) der Geschöpfe" im darauffolgenden Vers 8 verwendet wird.[108] Zeitbegriffe markieren die erste Hälfte des 1. Hauptteils, der durch seine zahlreichen Kontraste aufwühlend wirkt, entsprechend den beschriebenen Reaktionen auf den Tod dieses besonderen Menschen. Bereits in Vers 7 werden die Zeitworte „in der Vergangenheit" und „jetzt" als Gegensätze aufgebaut, die hier aber die Funktion hatten, Einleitung (meine Trauer jetzt) mit dem 1. Hauptteil (Trauer damals um den Propheten) inhaltlich zu verknüpfen, aber auch voneinander abzusetzen.

Die sich ausbreitende Dunkelheit (Verse 8-14)

Im Folgenden (Verse 8-14) werden die zeitlichen Gegenüberstellungen genutzt, um auf den Gegensatz zwischen Licht und Dunkelheit zu verweisen. In Vers 8 werden gleich zwei Zeitbegriffe in Opposition gesetzt: *aḍ-ḍuḥā* zu *amsā* und *ar-rabīʿ* zu *ḫarīf*. Solange der Prophet noch anwesend ist, bis zu seinem Tod, herrscht die Tageszeit, in der die Sonne noch steigt (*aḍ-ḍuḥā*). Nach seinem Tod setzt die Dunkelheit sehr schnell ein, denn „bereits des Abends (*amsā*) wurde der Frühling zum Herbst", der mit seinen Wolken und Regen eine dunklere Jahreszeit symbolisiert. Dieser Wandel, von dem Licht, das den Propheten zu Lebzeiten umgab, zur Dunkelheit, die sich in Folge seines Todes ausbreitete, wird durch die Gegensatzpaare „Mittag-Abend" und „Frühling-Herbst" stilistisch als *ṭibāq* hervorgehoben. Ibn Abī Ḥaǧalah referiert hier gedanklich ganz selbstverständlich auf die Vorstellung des Lichts Muḥammads, das insbesondere in der islamischen Mystik besonders ausgearbeitet und verehrt wurde.[109] Mit den Zeitangaben verweist er außerdem auf die Überlieferung, in der es heißt, der Prophet sei zur Mittagszeit

---

[108] Siehe z.B. den in Ibn Katir, *as-Sīrah an-nabawiyyah*, ed. Muṣṭafā ʿAbd al-Wāḥid, Kairo 1964, 1:193-194, überlieferten Ḥadīt: „Gott schuf die Schöpfung und wählte darunter die Menschen aus, unter den Menschen die Araber, unter den Arabern die Muḍar, unter den Muḍar die Qurayš, unter den Qurayš die Banū Hāšim und unter den Banū Hāšim mich, so daß ich der Auserwählteste unter den Auserwählten bin".

[109] Schimmel, *Und Muhammad ist Sein Prophet*, 108-123.

(*aḍ-ḍuḥā*) verstorben, und zwar an einem Montag, den 12. Rabīʿ al-Awwal,[110] wobei er aus diesem Monatsnamen das Wort für Frühling extrahieren konnte.

Die folgenden Verse geben ein konkretes Beispiel für die sich ausbreitende Dunkelheit, nämlich die Abwendung vom Islam einiger Gruppen und die Bedeutung von Abū Bakr in der Abwehr dieser Gefahr, wie sie aus den Biographien des Propheten bekannt ist. Die Abwesenheit des Propheten, der das Licht der Rechtleitung verkörpert, führt sofort dazu, daß einige Menschen den Islam verlassen (Vers 9), wobei sie „den Zweig der Rechtleitung" aufgrund der Doppeldeutigkeit des Verbes *bāna* (irrtümlicherweise) für abgetrennt halten, obwohl er doch deutlich ist, wie es im Verlaufe des Gedichts in anderen Worten sehr klar ausgesprochen wird (Vers 22). Doch die Rechtgläubigen (*al-ḥunafāʾ*) – durch einen schönen *ištiqāq* aus den abtrünnigen Banū Ḥanīfah in Kontrast gesetzt –, angeführt durch Abū Bakr, der sich als neuer Anführer erweist, bekämpfen die Abtrünnigen sofort, vom Morgen an (Vers 10).[111] Dieses Thema wird von Ibn Abī Ḥaǧalah in seinem anderen, in *Ǧiwār al-aḫyār* vorangestellten Trauergedicht in den Versen 35-36 ebenfalls bearbeitet.[112] Die Hervorhebung Abū Bakrs als erste genannte Person neben dem Propheten findet sich auch in der Burdah, wenn auch in anderem Zusammenhang.[113] Ibn Abī Ḥaǧalah hebt die Namensnennung hervor durch den Versbeginn *wa-qāma*, der in Vers 15 wiederholt wird, wo eine weitere im Zusammenhang dieses Gedichtes wichtige Persönlichkeit eingeführt wird, was gleichzeitig einen Einschnitt in diesem 1. Hauptteil darstellt.

Wie in Trauerdichtung im Allgemeinen üblich, wird im Folgenden die sich umkehrende Natur mit Rückgriff auf Schilderungen aus den Prophetenbiographien geschildert. In der Trauerdichtung wird dieses Thema verwendet, um zu betonen,

---

[110] Z.B. Ibn Katīr, *as-Sīrah an-nabawiyyah*, 4:465 nach al-Bayhaqī: „… *ṯabata annahū tuwuffiya ḍuḥan yawma l-iṯnayn*", und 4:484 schreibt Ibn Katīr selbst: „*wa-tuwuffiya … ḥīna štadda ḍ-ḍuḥā min ḏālika l-yawm*", verweist allerdings darauf, daß dies nicht die einzige Meinung sei: „*wa-qīla ʿinda zawwāli š-šams, wa-llāhu aʿlam*", vgl. auch 4:498 und 4:506. Siehe z.B. auch al-Ġazālī, *Iḥyāʾ ʿulūm ad-dīn*, Beirut 2005, 1853, nach ʿĀʾišah: „*māta … bayna rtifāʿi ḍ-ḍuḥā wa-ntiṣāfi n-nahār*".

[111] Unter der Leitung des sogenannten „falschen Propheten" Musaylima revoltierten die Banū Ḥanīfah nach dem Tod des Propheten, und Abū Bakr schickte eine große Armee unter Ḥālid ibn al-Walīd. Es kam zu einer Schlacht bei al-ʿAqrabāʾ mit einem von Mauern umgebenen Garten, der „Garten des Todes" genannt wurde, weil so viele auf beiden Seiten starben. Die Muslime waren jedoch siegreich. Vgl. z.B. W. Montgomery Watt: „Musaylima", in: *EI 2*; vgl. auch Ibn al-Fāriḍ, der das gleiche Wortspiel in seinem berühmten Gedicht *Naẓm as-sulūk* (die Ordnung des Weges) verwendet, Vers 616 in Scattolin, *The Dīwān of Ibn al-Fāriḍ*, 128; Vers 622 in dt. Übersetzung bei Jacobi, *Ibn al-Fāriḍ*, 117: „Nach ihm besiegte Abū Bakr, der Kalif, den Stamm Ḥanīfa und half damit, die ḥanafitische Religion zu sichern", und 348-349 Kommentar dazu.

[112] Siehe Anhang, S. 302, vgl. die Verwendung der gleichen Schlagworte *al-islām, āl ḥanīfah, rabʿ al-hudā* und insbesondere den gleichen Versbeginn *fa-qāma Abū Bakr*.

[113] Dort nämlich als Begleiter im Versteck der Höhle unter seiner Ehrbezeichnung *aṣ-Ṣiddīq* erwähnt, siehe Burdah Vers 77, *Dīwān al-Būṣīrī*, 235; engl. Übers. von Stetkevych, *The Mantle Odes*, 117: „So the Truth (*aṣ-ṣidq*; Muḥammad) and the Truthful One (*aṣ-ṣiddīq*; Abū Bakr) stayed stock-still in the cave, While the unbelievers said, 'There is no one in there'".

daß sogar die Natur um den Verstorbenen trauert. In diesem Gedicht (Verse 8-14) schwingt mit, daß die sich ausbreitende Dunkelheit nicht nur von der Trauer stammen mag, sondern auch vom sich ausbreitenden Unglauben. In Vers 11 werden zwar verschiedene Kontraste (Sonne – Mond, Sonne – erbleichen, Mond – verfinstern) verwendet, die sich jedoch inhaltlich auflösen, so daß der obere Teil der Sonne, die, sobald der Prophet starb, „vom Nachmittag an“ erblich, mit der Verfinsterung des Mondes verglichen wird.[114] In den Prophetenbiographien werden Überlieferungen angeführt, die beschreiben, daß es am Tag seines Todes dunkel wurde.[115] In Vers 12 wird die Personifikation der Natur fortgesetzt. Die Wolken regnen metaphorisch Tränen. Es sind die Wolken, die früher den Propheten zuvorkommend behandelten, indem sie ihm Schatten spendeten, wie es in den Prophetenbiographien berichtet und von al-Būṣīrī in seinem Mantelgedicht auch als eines der prophetischen Wunder geschildert wird.[116] Der Prophet hinterläßt sie aber weinend, und zwar immerfort. Die Trauer scheint kein zeitliches Ende zu haben.[117]

Der Abend, der Herbst, die erbleichende Sonne, die weinenden Wolken, alle zusammen verstärken das Bild der sich ausbreitenden Dunkelheit. In Vers 13 greift Ibn Abī Ḥaǧalah ein koranisches Bild auf, um auf die mehrfachen Schichten der Dunkelheit anzuspielen, denn im Koran wird beschrieben, wie der Prophet Jonas von einem Wal verschlungen sich in „Dunkelheiten“ befindet.[118] Die Koranexegeten erklären, daß sich diese Dunkelheiten zusammensetzen aus der Dunkelheit im Bauch des Wals, der Tiefe des Meeres und der Nacht.[119] Zunächst wird in diesem Vers die Personifikation der Natur weiter fortgesetzt: Das Meer bäumt sich auf, heftige Wellen schlagen hoch, und die Natur kehrt sich um, denn die Fische werden durch das tobende Meer an die Oberfläche geworfen. Dies geschieht nun aber nicht in erster Linie aus Trauer, wie dies beim Weinen der Wolken und der Verfinsterung der Sonne vielleicht noch der Fall war, sondern symbolisiert die vorher erwähnten vielschichtigen Dunkelheiten, die in diesem Augenblick unmittelbar nach

---

[114] Vgl. hierzu auch Gedicht Nr. 1, Vers 31, (Anhang, S. 301), indem die erbleichende Sonne mit einem jungen Mädchen verglichen wird, dem die Traurigkeit verbietet, sich zu verschleiern.

[115] Z.B. Ibn Kaṯīr, *as-Sīrah an-nabawiyyah*, 4:544 nach Aḥmad: „*lammā kāna l-yawmu llaḏī qadima fīhi rasūlu llāh … al-Madīnata aḍāʾa minhā kullu šayʾin, fa-lammā kāna l-yawmu llaḏī māta fīhi aẓlama minhā kullu šayʾin*“; siehe auch al-Ḥākim an-Nīsābūrī, *al-Mustadrak ʿalā aṣ-Ṣaḥīḥayn*, ed. Muṣṭafā ʿAbd al-Qārir ʿAṭā, Beirut 1998, 3:604, Nr. 4445.

[116] Vgl. Burdah, Vers 74, *Dīwān al-Būṣīrī*, 235; engl. Übers. von Stetkevych, *The Mantle Odes*, 117: „Like the cloud that followed him wherever he went, Protecting him when the midday heat blazed like a furnace“.

[117] Vgl. auch die sehr ähnliche Formulierung in dem an erster Stelle in *Ǧiwār al-aḫyār* zitierten Trauergedicht, Gedicht Nr.1, Vers 29, siehe Anhang, S. 301: „Es entfernten sich die Wolken, die ihn in der Mittagshitze beschatteten und ließen Wolken zurück, die die Erde mit Tränen füllen“.

[118] Koran, Sure 21, Vers 87: *fa-nādā fī ẓ-ẓulumāt*.

[119] Z.B. aṭ-Ṭabarī, *Ǧāmiʿ al-bayān ʿan taʾwīl āy al-qurʾān*, 15 Bde., Beirut 2001, Bd. 10, Teil 27:95; az-Zamaḫšarī, *al-Kaššāf ʿan ḥaqāʾiq ġawāmiḍ at-tanzīl*, 4 Bde., o.O. 1947, 3:132; al-Qurṭubī, *al-Ǧāmiʿ li-aḥkām al-qurʾān*, 20 Bde., Kairo 1967, 11:333; Ibn Kaṯīr, *Tafsīr al-qurʾān al-ʿaẓīm*, 5 Bde., Beirut 2000, 3:196: *ẓulmatu baṭni l-ḥūt wa-ẓulmatu l-baḥri wa-ẓulmatu l-layl*.

dem Tod des Propheten den Unglauben, hier symbolisiert duch den Walfisch, auftauchen lassen, während der Glaube und/oder die Rechtleitung symbolisch auf
dem Schiff unterzugehen scheinen. Hier wird das Thema des oben bereits angesprochenen Kampfs zwischen den Abtrünnigen und den Rechtgläubigen kontrastiv
und metaphorisch (Schiffe tauchen unter – Fische tauchen auf) nochmals aufgegriffen und dabei in den Kontext der trauernden, sich verfinsternden Natur gestellt.[120]

Im folgenden Vers 14 wird die eintretende Dunkelheit nochmals und abschließend sehr deutlich gemacht, hier am direktesten auf die Überlieferungen aus der
Sīrah des Propheten zurückgreifend, die beschreiben, daß sich alles in der Stadt
Medina durch seinen Tod verfinsterte, nachdem sie sich erleuchtet hatte, als der
Prophet dort eintraf; ja man habe sogar die Hand vor den Augen nicht sehen können.[121] Wieder wird auf den Zeitpunkt des Todes „mitten am Tag" angespielt,
wenn die Sonne am hellsten leuchtet und damit ein Rückbezug zu Vers 8 hergestellt, in dem das Thema der sich ausbreitenden Finsternis begann. Hier nun wird
der Gegensatz zum Gewohnten explizit ausgesprochen, der die Bewohner der
Stadt des Propheten im Augenblick seines Todes, trotz der Mittagszeit, wenn die
Sonne im Zenit steht, in ungewohnte Finsternis und damit in Schrecken und Trauer, in Furcht und Zweifel versetzte. Die Dunkelheit erfaßt letztendlich die ganze
Stadt Medina, die bis dato noch von dem Licht der Rechtleitung des Gesandten erleuchtet wurde. Die Nennung des Ehrennamens Ṭaybah (Duftende) für die Stadt
Medina verweist deutlich auf den Beginn des berühmten Trauergedichts von
Ḥassān ibn Ṯābit, der im folgenden Vers als zweite namentlich genannte Person
seinen Auftritt hat.

Die sich ausbreitende Trauer (Verse 15-19)

Vers 15 beginnt mit *wa-qāma* wie Vers 10, in dem Abū Bakr sich im Kampf gegen
den sich ausbreitenden Unglauben (die Dunkelheit) erhob. Hier erhebt sich
Ḥassān ibn Ṯābit, um seine Trauer über den Tod des Propheten zum Ausdruck
zu bringen (*yarṯīhi*), wobei ihm Abū Bakr darin folgt. Im Folgenden geht es um
den Ausdruck der sich ausbreitenden und schließlich alles umfassenden tiefen
Trauer. Der Aspekt der Dunkelheit, die durch Zweifel und Unglauben entsteht,
spielt keine Rolle mehr. Ibn Abī Ḥaǧalah stellt hier eine ausdrückliche Beziehung
zu dem aus den Prophetenbiographien bekannten Trauergedicht des Ḥassān ibn
Ṯābit her. Der darauffolgende Vers 16 wird durch die Wiederholung der gleichen

---

[120] Mit „ihrem Meer" könnte auch die Stadt Medina gemeint sein, die im folgenden Vers ja
genannt wird. In einem Ḥadīṯ heißt es: „*al-fitnatu llatī tamūǧu ka-mawǧi l-baḥr* (Die Versuchung, die wie Wellen des Meeres kommen wird)", wobei damit wahrscheinlich der Bür-
gerkrieg (*al-fitnah*) nach dem Kalifat von ʿUmar gemeint ist, siehe Ibn Ḥaǧar al-ʿAsqalānī:
Fatḥ al-Bārī, 13:47-53, Kapitel 17 über *al-fitnatu llatī tamūǧu ka-mawǧi l-baḥr*.
[121] Z.B. Ibn Kaṯīr, *as-Sīrah an-nabawiyyah*, 4:544-545 nach al-Kudaymī: „*lammā qubiḍa rasūlu llāh
… aẓlamat al-Madīnatu ḥattā lam yanẓur baʿḍunā ilā baʿḍ, wa-kāna aḥadunā yabsuṭu yadahū fa-lā
yarāhā*"; nach Abu l-Qāsim (4:545), wie auch schon zitiert nach Aḥmad (4:544) in Fn. 115.

Wurzel in derselben Bedeutung *ar-riṯāʾu* und *yurṯā*, hervorgehoben und mit dem Vers davor verbunden, indem das gleiche Verb als *yarṯīhī* ja auch schon vorkam. Mit dieser Clusterung um den Begriff der Trauerdichtung wird diese Stelle im Gedicht stark hervorgehoben, was durch den weiteren wiederholten Gebrauch des *ṯāʾ*-Lautes in den Worten *miṯlī* und *yakṯuru* fortgeführt wird. Ibn Abī Ḥaǧalah stellt nicht nur eine Beziehung zwischen seinem Gedicht und demjenigen des Ḥassān ibn Ṯābit her, sondern vergleicht sich hier als trauernde Person und Dichter direkt mit dem damaligen Trauerdichter des Propheten, und zwar im Hinblick darauf, daß sie beide zu bemitleiden seien. Wie durch die Einleitung und die Überleitung in Vers 7 nahegelegt, ist Ḥassān ibn Ṯābit wohl über den damaligen augenblicklichen Verlust des Propheten zu bemitleiden (vielleicht auch dafür, eine schwierige Aufgabe zu haben) und der Dichter entsprechend über seinen jetzigen Verlust, mit dem dann auch der Verlust seines eigenen Kindes gemeint sein kann, dazu noch über die nie erlebte Präsenz des lebendigen Gesandten Gottes. Hier wird sehr deutlich die damalige Trauer über den Tod des Propheten mit der jetzigen Trauer des Dichters überlagert. Die jetzige Trauer des Dichters kann sich auf Vieles beziehen, und damit unter Umständen auch auf diejenige über einen Kindertod. Weil beide Dichter direkt betroffen sind, so drückt es Ibn Abī Ḥaǧalah aus, enthält ihr Trauergedicht auch besonders starke Klage und Betrübnis.

Die Trauer, die zuerst vom Dichter zum Ausdruck gebracht wird, breitet sich im Folgenden auf andere Menschen wie auch auf die Natur aus. In Vers 17 ist mit dem vom Unglück Getroffenen (*al-muṣāb*) Muḥammad gemeint, durch dessen Tod die Trauer (*al-ʿazāʾ*) alles umfasst und – hervorgehoben durch eine Nominalreihung (*taʿdīd*) – die Religion, die Edlen und die Nachfahren verwaisen läßt. Die Reihenfolge, die Ibn Abī Ḥaǧalah hier wählt, ist erwähnenswert: Er beginnt mit etwas sehr umfassendem, der Religion, gefolgt von den Edlen, womit entweder eine bestimmte Abstammungslinie oder die Muslime allgemein gemeint sein könnten, und nennt dann als letztes die Nachfahren, die eine noch kleinere Gruppe von Menschen umfaßt. Auch die Tiere (Tauben) und die Natur (Frühregen) trauern um den Propheten (Vers 18). In Vers 19 werden Natur, Tiere und Menschen zusammengefaßt: die Traurigkeit (*al-ḥuzn*) verbreitet sich uneingeschränkt auf der Welt und in ihren Bewohnern (*fī d-dunyā wa-sākinihā*). Das alles einschließende, uneingeschränkte Ausbreiten der Trauer (*taṣarrafa*) wird in deutlichen Gegensatz zum Sich-Entfernt-Haben (*inṣarafa*) des Propheten gesetzt.

Mittelteil: Trost damals (Verse 20-26)

عـزا[122] بـه الخـضر المخـضر جانبـه   وردّ مــا قــاله إبلــيس إذ هتفــا   20

قال اغسلوا ظاهر الأردان واحتسبوا   فـإنّ في الله بعـد المـصطفى خلفـا

---

[122] (ل): غزا.

ما فيه كالشمس في وسْط السماء خفا   مــضى وخلّــف ديــن الله متّـضًا [123]

رأى المــسير إلى الفــردوس قــد أزفــا   لمّــا شــكى ألمـاً مــن قطــع أبهــره [124]

دسّته من سمّها إذ أهـدت [126] الكتفا [127]   ودبّ داء عجــوز الــسوء [125] فيــه بمــا

وعــاين العــين والــولدان والغرفــا   25   فمــات منــه شــهيدًا حــين عــاوده

والــراح والــروح والريحــان والتحفــا   وشــاهد الــشهد في الأنهــار منسرحًا

20) Al-Ḫaḍir, der Grünseitige, tröstete wegen ihm und wies zurück, was ihm Iblis zurief.[128]

21) „Wascht das Äußere der Ärmel", sagte er, „und erhofft (Gottes Lohn im Jenseits), denn in Gott gibt es nach al-Muṣṭafā Nachfolger".

22) Der Prophet verging und hinterließ die Religion Gottes offenkundig: Wie bei der Sonne in der Mitte des Himmels, gibt es an ihr nichts Verborgenes.[129]

23) Als er sich über die Schmerzen beklagte, die ihm das Abschneiden seiner Aorta zufügte, sah er den Weg zum Paradies schon näherkommen.[130]

24) Die Krankheit der Alten des Unheils kroch in ihm mit dem (heimlich) von ihr eingeflößten Gift, als sie die Schafsschulter anbot.[131]

25) Als das Gift zurückkehrte, starb er davon als Märtyrer und mit eigenen Augen sah er die Paradiesjungfrauen, die jungen Knaben und die himmlischen Kammern.[132]

---

[123] (و) (ق): منضجعا.

[124] (ل) (و): انهره.

[125] (ق): السمّ.

[126] (ل) (ق): إذا هديت.

[127] (ق): كتفا.

[128] Kontraste (ṭibāq): al-Ḫaḍir – Iblis, zurückweisen – rufen; al-ǧinās al-ištiqāq: al-Ḫaḍiru l-muḫḍarru.

[129] Vergleich (tašbīh); Klangspiele: maḍā - muttaḍiḥan; ḫallafa - ḫafā.
Vgl. Ḥassān ibn Ṯābit, Vers 3: wa-wāḍiḥu āyātin (offenkundig sind (seine) Zeichen).
Vgl. auch al-Burdah, Vers 88: ... āyātin lahū ẓaharat ẓuhūra nāri l-qirā ... (seine Zeichen erscheinen deutlich wie das Nachtfeuer für den Besucher).
Vgl. auch mit Gedicht Nr. 1, Vers 54: ... wa-ḫallafa dīna llāhi li-n-nāsi maḥyaʿā (und hinterließ die Religion Gottes für die Menschen als klaren Weg).

[130] Ǧinās: lammā - ʾalammā; Kontrast (ṭibāq): abschneiden – näherkommen.
Vgl. mit vorangehendem Gedicht Nr. 1, Vers 50: wa-lammā šakā min qaṭʿi abharihī.

[131] Personifikation der Krankheit, die kriecht, hervorgehoben durch Alliteration: dabba dāʾu.
Mit der „Alten des Unheils" wird die Frau von Loth bezeichnet; dieser Begriff kann aber auch allgemein in anderen Situationen eingesetzt werden. Aufgrund des inhaltlichen Zusammenhanges ist hier Zaynab bint al-Ḥāriṯ gemeint, s.u. S. 277f.
Vgl. mit Gedicht Nr. 1, Vers 50: „Als er beim Abtrennen seiner Aorta den Schmerz erlitt, der vom Essen des mit Gift einmarinierten Vorderfußes stammte".

[132] Nominalreihung (taʿdīd): die Paradiesjungfrauen, die Dienstknaben und die himmlischen Kammern; hervorgehoben durch eine defekte Paronomasia (al-ǧinās al-kāfī): ʿayana (mit eigenen Augen sehen) - al-ʿīn (Schwarzäugige, hier: Paradiesjungfrauen).

26) Mit eigenen Augen sah er, wie der Honig in den Flüssen strömte und den Wein, die Erquickung, das Duftbasilikum und die Kostbarkeiten.[133]

In Vers 20 treten zwei „mythische" Figuren auf: Khidr und Iblis, die symbolisch die Gegensätze hell – dunkel, Glauben – Unglauben aus dem ersten Hauptteil wieder aufgreifen, aber auch den Gegensatz Leben und Tod versinnbildlichen. Khidr wendet hier die Trauer (al-ʿazāʾ) hin zum Trost, den er spendet (ʿazzā): Er weist den Einflüsterer des Bösen, den Aufrufer zum Unglauben, die Versuchung durch den Teufel zurück. Der Kampf Abū Bakrs gegen die Abtrünnigen wird hier auf eine mythologische Ebene übertragen und damit auch überhöht. Khidr steht hier zwar einerseits für den Glauben, der den Unglauben besiegt; darüber hinaus ist Khidr, „der Grünseitige", aber auch derjenige, der jung bleibt, dem das (ewige) Leben gegönnt ist, der trockenes Land grün sprießen läßt, der also das Leben symbolisiert und damit auch den Sieg des Lebens über den Tod.[134]

Ibn Abī Ḥaǧalah greift hier und im darauf folgenden Vers auf Überlieferungen zurück, die in den Prophetenbiographien genannt werden und schildern, wie direkt nach dem Tod des Propheten, während die Angehörigen und Anhänger trauerten, Khidr im Haus des Propheten erschien, zumindest seine Stimme gehört wurde, und die versammelten Trauernden (wa-ǧāʾat at-taʿziyah) tröstet: „In Gott gibt es Trost (ʿazā) für jedes Unglück (muṣībah) und einen Nachfolger (ḫalaf) für jeden Verstorbenen".[135] Ibn Abī Ḥaǧalah beginnt Vers 20 mit dem Signalwort ʿazā für Trost und greift im zweiten Halbvers die überlieferten Trostworte direkt auf: „in Gott gibt es nach al-Muṣṭafā Nachfolger (ḫulafāʾ)". Ibn Abī Ḥaǧalah verbindet diese Berichte mit anderen Überlieferungen, die im Zusammenhang der Waschung des Leichnams angeführt werden. Diese berichten, daß ebenfalls nur eine Stimme zu hören war, deren Identität in diesen Fällen allerdings nicht aufgelöst wird, die die Anwesenden aufforderte, den Propheten mit seinen Kleidern

---

[133] Defekte Paronomasia (al-ǧinās al-kāfī): šāhada (er bezeugte) – aš-šahd (Honig); und: ar-rāḥa (der Wein) - ar-rawḥa (die Erquickung) – ar-rayḥān (das Basilikum); Nominalreihung (taʿdīd) mit vier Gliedern: den Wein, die Erquickung, das Duftbasilikum, die Köstlichkeiten.

[134] Zu den Vorstellungen über Khidr, siehe Franke, Patrick, *Begegnung mit Khidr. Quellenstudien zum Imaginären im traditionellen Islam*, Beirut 2000. Insbesondere auch seine Erörterung II.1.a) zu „Khidr und die Vegetation (1) Khidr, der 'Grüne'", 80-83: Khidr belebt trockenes Land: Wenn er darauf tritt, sprießt es überall grün.

[135] Z.B. Ibn Kaṯīr, *as-Sīrah an-nabawiyyah*, 4:550, der hier allerdings kommentiert, dieser Ḥadīṯ sei *mursal*; dann auch 4:550-551 nach al-Bayhaqī und ähnlich 4:551 nach al-Ḥāriṯ ibn Abī Usāmah. In diesen Versionen hören die Leute nur eine Stimme, ohne jemanden zu sehen, die den Trost ausspricht. Es ist ʿAlī, der hinterher weiß, daß dies Khidr war. Nach Abū ʿAbdallāh (4:551) werden diese Trostworte von einem großen, anmutigen Mann mit grauem Bart gesprochen, der bei den Weinenden eintrat (fa-daḫala raǧulun ašhabu l-liḥyati ǧasīmun ṣabīḥ). Abū Bakr und ʿAlī wissen, daß dies „der Bruder des Gesandten Gottes, al-Ḫiḍr" war. Eine weitere Version dieser Überlieferung findet sich auch in al-Ġazālīs Totenbuch im letzten Band von *Iḥyāʾ ʿulūm ad-dīn*, 1855; engl. Übersetzung von Winter, *Al-Ghazālī: The Remembrance of Death and the Afterlife*, 70-71. Siehe auch al-Ḥākim an-Nīsābūrī, *al-Mustadrak*, 3:605, Nr. 4448.

zu waschen.[136] Hinter diesen Berichten, die Ibn Abī Ḥaǧalah in Vers 21 aufgreift, steht die Vorstellung, daß der Prophet rein und erleuchtet war, wie zu seiner Lebenszeit so auch zum Zeitpunkt seines Todes.[137] In Vers 22 wird der vorher in den Mund Khidrs gelegte Trost wiederholt, dabei noch deutlicher gemacht und damit natürlich auch bestätigt. Der Prophet schied zwar dahin (*maḍā*) - wobei hier *maḍā* aus Vers 7 wiederholt wird, indem dieses Zeitwort den starken Gegensatz zwischen jetzt und damals hervorbrachte -, aber kontrastiv dazu hinterließ (*ḫallafa*) Muḥammad die Religion Gottes offenkundig, deutlich (*muttaḍiḥan*). Auch Ḥassān ibn Tābit spricht in seinem Trauergedicht von den Zeichen, die – im Gegensatz zum üblichen Verwischtwerden im beduinischen *nasīb* – deutlich (*wāḍiḥ*) seien.[138] In dem vergleichbaren, in *Ǧiwār al-aḫyār* zuerst präsentierten Trauergedicht formuliert Ibn Abī Ḥaǧalah es so: „Als er starb ... hierließ er die Religion Gottes für die Menschen als klaren Weg".[139] Damit ist auch die Helligkeit wieder ein Thema: Der zwar dunkle Moment des Todes hinterläßt aber die leuchtende Religion. Diesen Aspekt betont, Ibn Abī Ḥaǧalah durch den sich anschließenden Vergleich, daß diese Religion nichts verberge „wie die Sonne in der Mitte des Himmels", also in dem Augenblick, wenn diese am hellsten leuchtet. Mit diesem Vergleich stellt er eine kontrastive Verknüpfung zu den Versen 11 und 14 her, in denen sich die Sonne mitten am Tag, zum Zeitpunkt ihres Höchstandes aus Verzweiflung und Trauer verdunkelte. Damit wird das Bild der sich aufgrund des Todes ausbreitenden Dunkelheit umgekehrt in das Bild des strahlensten Lichtes zum Zeitpunkt seines Todes. Dieses Licht, das Licht der Rechtleitung, hat der Prophet hinterlassen, und diese Erkenntnis spendet natürlich Trost.

In den beiden folgenden Versen erst geht Ibn Abī Ḥaǧalah, wie dies in Trauerdichtung durchaus üblich ist, auf die Todesursache ein. Er bezieht sich hier auf eine Erzählung aus der Prophetenvita, die sich vier Jahre vor dem Tod des Propheten nach der Eroberung Khaybars ereignete, als eine der jüdischen Gefangenen, Zaynab bint al-Ḥāriṯ, dem Propheten eine vergiftete Schafschulter anbot. Der Prophet, so heißt es in den Berichten, habe dies nach dem ersten Bissen gespürt und ihn wieder ausgespuckt. Sein Begleiter, der ebenfalls gekostet hatte, habe den Bissen jedoch geschluckt und verstarb entsprechend kurz darauf.[140]

---

[136] Z.B. Ibn Kaṯīr, *as-Sīrah an-nabawiyyah*, 4:517 nach Abū Bakr ibn Abī Šayba: *a-lā taǧarridū ʿan rasūli llāhi qamiṣahū*; oder nach Ibn Isḥāq: *an ġassilū rasūla llāhi wa-ʿalayhi ṯiyābuhū*; so auch 4:521 unten; oder 4:521 nach Sayf (ibn ʿUmar): *lā taġsilū rasūla llāhi fa-innahū ṭāhiran*. Auch al-Ġazālī referiert zwei dieser Überlieferungen, eine nach ʿĀʾiša und eine nach ʿAlī, al-Ġazālī, *Iḥyāʾ ʿulūm ad-dīn*, 1856. Siehe auch al-Ḥākim an-Nīsābūrī, *al-Mustadrak*, 3:607, Nr. 4454.

[137] Vgl. auch den Bericht über das Ergreifen der Seele des Propheten bei al-Ġazālī, *Iḥyāʾ ʿulūm ad-dīn*, 1848: *ʿan ǧasadihi ṭ-ṭāhir* (von seinem reinen Körper).

[138] Vgl. Ḥassān ibn Ṯābit, Vers 3, *Šarḥ Dīwān Ḥassān ibn Ṯābit*, ed. al-Barqūqī, 89: „*wa-wāḍiḥu āyātin* (offenkundig sind (seine) Zeichen)"; in der Übersetzung von LeGassick, *The Life of the Prophet Muḥammad*, 2:399: „It signs are clear".

[139] Siehe Anhang, S. 303, Gedicht Nr. 1, Vers 54: *qaḍā ... wa-ḫallafa dīna llāhi li-n-nāsi mahyaʿā*.

[140] Z.B. Rotter, Gernot, *Ibn Isḥāq, Das Leben des Propheten*, Stuttgart 1982, 203-204.

Neben diesen Überlieferungen, die im Zusammenhang mit der Eroberung Khaybars genannt werden, wird nur ein Ḥadīt nach ʿĀʾišah überliefert, in dem ein Zusammenhang hergestellt wird zwischen diesem Vergiftungsversuch und dem Tode Muḥammads vier Jahre später.[141] Im Allgemeinen wird angenommen, der Prophet sei eines natürlichen Todes gestorben. Entsprechend wird etwa in der Prophetenvita des Ibn Hišām/Ibn Isḥāq in dem Abschnitt über den Tod des Propheten, wie auch in al-Ġazālīs Bericht in dessen Totenbuch zum Beispiel, auf diesen Zusammenhang gar nicht hingewiesen.[142] Ibn Katīr jedoch, der ein Lehrer Ibn Abī Ḥaǧalahs war, erwähnt in seiner Prophetenvita in dem Abschnitt über „Koranverse und Ḥadīte, die den Tod des Gesandten ankündigen" diese eine Überlieferung nach ʿĀʾišah, die behauptet, der Prophet habe ihr während seiner Krankheit, an der er starb, gesagt, er spüre immer noch die Schmerzen von dem Essen, das er in Khaybar aß, und fühle jetzt gerade, wie seine Aorta von diesem Gift abgeschnitten werde.[143] Ganz deutlich bezieht sich Ibn Abī Ḥaǧalah auf diese Überlieferung. Allerdings steht dieser Bericht auch bei Ibn Katīr nicht im Zentrum. Ḥassān ibn Tābit, als Zeitgenosse, nennt in seinem Trauergedicht in Vers 27 einen „Pfeil des Todes, der das Licht der Gläubigen traf" als Todesursache.[144] Ibn Abī Ḥaǧalah greift hier also auf eine eher randständige Überlieferung zurück, die bei Ḥassān ibn Tābit keine Rolle spielt, geschweige denn im Prophetenlob auftaucht. Es stellt sich also die Frage, warum Ibn Abī Ḥaǧalah ausgerechnet diese Geschichte aufgreift. Er scheint dies auf jeden Fall für eine sinnvolle Idee gehalten zu haben, da auch in seinem anderen Trauergedicht, das er im letzten Kapitel seines *Ǧiwār al-aḫyār* bringt, diese Todesursache Erwähnung findet.[145]

In Vers 23 wird der Schmerz des Sterbenden durch „das Abschneiden seiner Aorta (*qaṭʿi abharihī*)" in Kontrast gesetzt zu dem für ihn in diesem Augenblick wahrnehmbaren und näherkommenden (*azifā*) Weg zum Paradies (*al-firdaws*). Der schmerzhafte Todesaugenblick wird erhellt von der Aussicht auf das Paradies. Ohne Zweifel, dies wird in den Prophetenbiographien wiederholt zum Ausdruck gebracht, erwartet den Propheten nach seinem Tod das Paradies.[146]

---

[141] Siehe Ibn Ḥaǧar al-ʿAsqalānī, *Fatḥ al-Bārī*, 8:131, Nr. 4428 nach ʿĀʾišah; auch in al-Ḥākim an-Nīsābūrī, *al-Mustadrak*, 3:605-606, Nr. 4449.

[142] Weder in Ibn Hišām, *as-Sīrah an-nabawiyyah*, 289-322; Weil, *Das Leben Mohammed's*, 2:340-359; noch al-Gazālī, *Iḥyāʾ ʿulūm ad-dīn*, 1848-1856.

[143] Ibn Katīr, *as-Sīrah an-nabawiyyah*, 4:449 nach al-Buḫārī nach ʿĀʾišah: *yā ʿĀʾišatu mā azālu aǧidu alama ṭ-ṭaʿāmi lladī akaltu bi-Ḫaybar, fa-hādā awān waǧadtu nqaṭaʿa abharī min dālika s-samm*, Ibn Katīr fährt fort und kommentiert, al-Buḫārī habe diese Überlieferung als *muʿallaq* klassifiziert.

[144] Ḥassān ibn Tābit, Vers 27, *Šarḥ Dīwān Ḥassān ibn Tābit*, ed. al-Barqūqī, 94: *sahmun mina l-mawti*; in der Übersetzung von LeGassick, *The Life of the Prophet Muḥammad*, 2:400: „While there in that light an arrow sent by death struck into their light".

[145] Siehe Anhang, S. 303, Gedicht Nr. 1, Vers 50: „Als er beim Abtrennen seiner Aorta den Schmerz erlitt, der vom Essen des mit Gift einmarinierten Vorderfußes stammte".

[146] So etwa bei Ibn Katīr, *as-Sīrah an-nabawiyyah*, 4:427, bereits zu Beginn der Schilderungen des Jahres 11 der Hiǧrah, in engl. Übersetzung LeGassick, *The Life of the Prophet Muḥammad*, 2:309: „Momentous events took place that year, among the most shocking being the death

Vers 25 ist in mehrfacher Hinsicht stilistisch hervorgehoben: durch einen *ǧinās al-kāfī* mit *ᶜāyana* (mit eigenen Augen sehen) und *al-ᶜīn* (die Paradiesjungfrauen), und stärker durch die Nominalreihung: *al-ᶜīna wa-l-wildāna wa-l-ġurafā*, vergleichbar mit der Nominalreihung in Vers 17. Damit wird die Ankunft im Paradies in besonderer Weise betont. Der Vers beginnt mit der Aussage: „Als das Gift zurückkehrte, starb er davon als Märtyrer (*šahīdan*)". Natürlich, ein Märtyrer gelangt sofort ins Paradies; aber daß der Prophet als Märtyrer starb, ist wieder eine unübliche Formulierung – überliefert nur in einem Ḥadīt -[147], auf die Ibn Abī Ḥaǧalah aber Wert legt und die sich aus der von ihm geschilderten Todesursache ergibt. Ibn Katīr erwähnt diese Überlieferung in seiner Darstellung des Todes des Propheten direkt im Anschluß an die bereits erwähnte Überlieferung nach ᶜĀʾišah mit der Aussage Muḥammads, er fühle immer noch die Wirkung des Essens von Kkaybar, das ihm gerade die Aorta abschneide. Ibn Katīr berichtet dort nach al-Bayhaqī, der dies nach al-Ḥākim an-Nīsābūrī anführe, daß ᶜAbdallāh ibn Masᶜūd gesagt habe: „Ich würde lieber neunmal schwören, daß der Gesandte Gottes (*ṢAᶜAS*) ermordet wurde, als einmal, daß er nicht ermordet wurde, und zwar, weil Gott ihn zum Propheten machte und zum Märtyrer."[148] Es scheint, als habe Ibn Abī Ḥaǧalah die Randüberlieferung über den Vergiftungstod aus der Sīrah genau deswegen als Todesursache ausgewählt, um den Propheten als Märtyrer ansprechen zu können. Die Betonung des Märtyrertums ergibt sich aus dem folgenden Vers 26, der mit einem *ǧinās al-kāfī* von *šāhada* (er sah mit eigenen Augen Zeugnis ablegend) und *aš-šahda* (der Honig) auf das Wort *šahīdan* (als Märtyrer) aus dem Vers davor verweist. Hierdurch entsteht wieder eine Clusterung, entsprechend der Hervorhebung des Begriffs der Trauerdichtung (*ar-ritāʾ*) in den beiden Versen 15 und 16. Darüberhinaus betont Vers 26 nochmals durch eine jetzt vierteilige Nominalreihung die Ankunft im Paradies: der Wein, die Erquickung, das Duftbasilikum und die Kostbarkeiten, zusätzlich hervorgehoben durch ein weiteres Wurzel-Klangspiel mit *ar-rāḫ*, *ar-rawḥ* und *ar-rayḥān*.

Neben der Betonung des Märtyrertums unterstreicht Ibn Abī Ḥaǧalah auch relativ stark den Aspekt des Paradieses durch seine zwei Nominalreihen, mit denen er dieses Paradies genauer beschreibt. Er verwendet hierfür koranische Begrifflichkeiten,[149] wobei er jedoch aus stilistischen Gründen das nicht-koranische Wort

---

of the Messenger of God (ṢAAS). However, he was in fact transported by Almighty God from this transient abode away into eternal ease in an elevated place on high, the most exalted and most splendid level of paradise (*al-ǧannah*)".

[147] Siehe z.B. al-Ḥākim an-Nīsābūrī: *al-Mustadrak*, 3:606, Nr. 4450.

[148] Ibn Katīr, *as-Sīrah an-nabawiyyah*, 4:449: *wa-dālika anna llāha ttaḫadahū nabiyyan wattaḫadahū šahīdan*.

[149] *ᶜīn* (Koran 37:48; 44:54; 52:20): großäugige (Huris); *wildān* (Koran 56:17; 76:19): (ewig) junge Knaben; *ġurafan* (Koran 29:58; 39:20): obere Gemächer, hohe Kammern, auch *ġurfah* (Koran 25:75); Honig (*ᶜasal*) (Koran 47:15): Paradiesesgärten mit Bächen auch aus fein gereinigtem Honig und aus Wein (*ḫamar*), köstlich für die Trinkenden; *fa-rawḥun wa-rayḥānun* (Koran 56:89): dieses Begriffspaar wird in den Koranübersetzungen sehr unterschiedlich übersetzt: Glück und Duft (der Seligkeit) / (kühle) Brise und duftende Kräuter / Glückselig-

šahd für Honig und *rāḥ* für Wein verwendet. Im Verhältnis zu den relativ ausführlichen und detailreichen koranischen Paradies-Schilderungen sei gleichzeitig festgehalten, daß die Beschreibung Ibn Abī Ḥaǧalahs eigentlich recht schlicht und bündig ist. Sie fällt dennoch auf, weil die Erwähnung des Paradieses in der arabischen Dichtung äußerst selten vorkommt und selbst in der Trauerdichtung die Aussicht auf ein ewiges Leben im Jenseits kaum je als Trost vorgebracht wird; in der Trauerdichtung ist vielmehr das Argument des Weiterlebens im Diesseits durch die ruhmreichen Taten des Verstorbenen, und noch häufiger und wichtiger, das Argument, alle müßten ja sterben, als Trost vorgebracht worden.[150] All dies ist also außergewöhnlich bei Ibn Abī Ḥaǧalah: die genannte Todesursache, der Prophet als Märtyrer und die Paradiesbeschreibung, die alle zusammenhängen.

Auch wenn Ibn Abī Ḥaǧalah beide Trauergedichte, in denen er dieses Thema ausführt, schon zu einem früheren Zeitpunkt verfaßt hat, aus Anlässen, die wir nicht nachvollziehen können, so paßt diese Darstellung außergewöhnlich gut in den Kontext eines Kindertotenliedes, denn Kinder, so heißt es in zahlreichen Überlieferungen, die Ibn Abī Ḥaǧalah sowohl in seinem Kindertod-Trostbuch als auch in dem hier vorgestellten Ziyārah-Totenbuch ja ausführlich zusammengetragen hat, kommen direkt ins Paradies, weil sie sich noch keiner Sünde haben schuldig werden lassen können. Darüberhinaus kommen auch diejenigen direkt ins Paradies, die an der Pest sterben, da sie als Märtyrer gelten. Ibn Abī Ḥaǧalahs Sohn Muḥammad starb als Kind und als Märtyrer an der Pest. Sofort zu Beginn seines Buches *Ǧiwār al-aḫyār* schreibt Ibn Abī Ḥaǧalah: *„wa-baʿd: fa-lammā māta waladī Muḥammadun-i l-waladu s-saʿīdu š-šahīdu bi-ṭ-ṭāʿūn"*. Ibn Abī Ḥaǧalah schreibt zwar kein Kindertotenlied für seinen Sohn, scheint aber dieses Trauergedicht auf den Propheten Muḥammad für passend zu halten, in diesen Kontext gestellt zu werden. Der Rückgriff auf die Vergiftungsgeschichte, die es erlaubt, den Propheten als Märtyrer darzustellen und damit dessen sofortigen Eingang ins Paradies zu betonen, ermöglicht eine Übertragung auf ein verstorbenes Kind und damit auch auf sein eigenes Kind. Über das Kind kann noch nichts erzählt werden im Hinblick auf seine ruhmreichen Taten, aber genau aus diesem Grund ist es so sicher, daß es bereits im Paradies ist und die genannten himmlischen Dinge mit eigenen Augen bezeugen kann. Im Zusammenhang mit dem Propheten und mit einem Kind, insbesondere einem Kind, das an der Pest verstarb –

---

keit und Düfte / Ruhe, Barmherzigkeit und gute Versorgung; der Koranvers ergänzt noch: *wa-ǧannatu naʿīmin*: und ein Garten der Wonne. Der Korankommentar des al-Qurṭubī, *al-Ǧāmiʿ li-aḥkām*, 17: 232-233, z.B. führt folgende Deutungen für *rawḥun* an: Ruhe von der Welt (*rāḥatu mina d-dunya*); das Erbarmen (*ar-raḥmah*); das Ausruhen (*al-istirāḥah*); oder auch die Schau des Antlitz Gottes (*an-naẓru ilā waǧhi llāh*), und für *rayḥānun*: Lebensunterhalt (*ar-rizq*); oder auch das Paradies (*al-ǧannah*); das Erbarmen (*ar-raḥmah*); oder auch das bekannte Rayḥān (Basilikum), das duftet (*ar-rayḥānu l-maʿrūfu lladī yušammu*); siehe auch Ibn Katīr, *Tafsīr*, 4:292-293.

[150] Vgl. Bauer, Thomas, „Todesdiskurse im Islam", in: *Asiatische Studien* 53,1 (1999), 5-16, hier insbesondere 10-13.

und es starben besonders viele Kinder an der Pest – erscheint dem Dichter der Gedanke an das Paradies doch als ein großer Trost.

2. *Hauptteil: Trost jetzt durch die Liebe zum Propheten, manifestiert am Grab (Verse 27-41)*

فيا جهولًا بمن أمست محبته   أولى وأقرب من ربّ السماء زلفا

دع البكاء على أطلال غانيةٍ[151]   لو أنصفت في الهوى ما أصبحت نصفا

واندب حمًى جدّد التبريح دارسه   ربع اصطباري إذا أذنبت[152] فيه عفا

30   تبيت[153] فيه سهام الشهب ثاقبةً[154]   والبرق يختطف[155] الأبصار إن خطفا

فقائد الليل إن سارت كتائبه   رأيت جيشًا من الظلماء قد زحفا[156]

يستلّ من برقه في[157] كلّ ناحيةٍ   سيفًا ويلبس من زهر الدجى زغفا[158]

يحمي حمًى لم تزل[159] فيه حدائقه   يهدي إلى الطرف من[160] أزهارها طرفا

لا تأنف[161] العيس[162] سيرًا في حمائلها[163]   حتى تشاهد[164] فيها روضةً أنفا

35   فيها النبي العظيم الهاشميّ ومن   حاز العلى والتقى والمجد والشرفا

مطهّرٌ طاهرٌ أزكى وأجود من   أمسى بذيل[165] رداء الجود ملتحفا

يحبّ من حبّه في الجود قاصده   ويكره البخل والتقتير والسرفا

جبال مكّة تهواه[166] وطيبة كم   أبدا بها[167] أحدٌ في حبّه شغفا

---

[151] (ل): غايبةٍ – (ق): عانيةٍ.

[152] (و) (ق): أدنيت.

[153] (و): بكيت.

[154] (يج): ساقبةً.

[155] (ل): يخطف.

[156] (ق): رجفا.

[157] (ل) حذفت كلمة "في".

[158] (يج, ل, ق): زعفا - (و): الدحا رعفا؛ والأنسب زغفا.

[159] (ل) (و) (ق): يزل.

[160] (و): الطرفين.

[161] (و): لانف.

[162] (ل): العيش.

[163] (ل): جمائلها.

[164] (و) (ق): يشاهد.

[165] (يج) (ل) (و): بديل.

[166] (و): يهواه.

والعـيس تـسري ¹⁶⁸ إلى ريّا ¹⁶⁹ حـماه إذا   هـبّ النسيم لهـا كالـريح إنْ ¹⁷⁰ عـصفا

40   كالقـوس تبـدوا وإن أرسـلتها رجعـت   سـهمًا يبيـت له عـالى الـربا ¹⁷¹ هـدفا

فلـو رأيـت مقامًـا فيـه حـضرته   لبـثّ فيـه لـكأس الدمـع مرتـشفا

27) Oh, du, der du nichts weißt über denjenigen, den zu lieben es sich geziemt und zur nächsten Nähe beim Herrn des Himmels führen kann.

28) Lass es sein, über den Spuren (der Wohnstätten) einer schönen Frau zu weinen! Wenn sie gerecht gehandelt hätte in der Liebe, wäre sie nicht (unverheiratet bis) in (ihre) mittleren Jahre (geblieben).[172]

29) Beweine einen heiligen Bezirk, den die Qualen aus der Asche wieder auferstehen lassen (dessen Verwischt-Sein durch die Qualen erneuert wird); Wohnstatt meines geduldigen Ertragens, wenn ich darin sündigte, verzeiht/verschwindet sie.[173]

30) Dort sieht man des Nachts glänzende/durchbohrende Pfeile von Sternschnuppen und einen Blitz, der die Blicke blendet, wenn er aufblitzt.[174]

31) Dann ist da ein Führer in der Nacht: wenn seine Bataillone marschieren, siehst du eine Armee aus Dunkelheit schon davonkriechen.[175]

32) Von seinem Blitz zückt er in alle Richtungen ein Schwert und zieht einen breiten Panzer aus den in der Finsternis Leuchtenden (Sternen) an.[176]

33) Er beschützt einen heiligen Bezirk, in dem Gärten dem Blick aus ihren Blüten unaufhörlich Glanzstücke schenken.[177]

34) Die hellfarbigen Kamele finden die Reise unter ihren Lasten nicht lästig, um darin mit eigenen Augen den unberührten Garten zu sehen.[178]

35) Darin der ruhmvolle Prophet, der Ḥāšimit, derjenige, der allein besitzt die Höhe und die Gottesfurcht, den Ruhm und die Ehre.[179]

---

[167] (يج): أبداتها.

[168] (ل): يسري.

[169] (ق): ربا.

[170] (يج): إذ.

[171] (و): الريا.

[172] *Ǧinās*: *anṣafat* (gerecht handeln) - *naṣafā* (im mittleren Alter).

[173] *Tawriyah*: verzeihen/verschwinden; (neben *darasa*: auswischen und *ʿafā*: verwischen, auslöschen, bedeutet auch *baraḥa* im erste Stamm: weggehen, verlassen); Metapher (*istiʿāra*): Wohnstatt meines geduldigen Ertragens; Kontrast (*ṭibāq*): sündigen – verzeihen.

[174] Vgl. Koran 37:10: *fa-atbaʿahū šihābun ṯāqibun* und Koran 2:20, wobei hier das Zitat so genau ist, daß wir beinahe von einem Koranzitat (*iqtibās*) sprechen können: *yakādu l-barqu yaḫṭafu abṣārahum*; Metapher (*istiʿāra*): Pfeile der Sternschnuppen; Wiederholung derselben Wurzel mit derselben Bedeutung zur Betonung: *yaḫtaṭifu - ḫaṭafā*.

[175] Kontrast (*ṭibāq*): marschieren – kriechen.

[176] Kontrast (*ṭibāq*): Leuchten/Sterne – dunkle Nacht.

[177] Wiederholung derselben Wurzel mit derselben Bedeutung: *yaḥmī - ḥiman*; *ǧinās*: *aṭ-ṭarf* (Blick) - *ṭurafā* (Glanzstücke).

[178] *Ǧinās*: *taʾnafi* (lästig finden) - *unufā* (unberührt).

36) Ein Reiner, Keuscher, ganz und gar Unschuldsvoller, der Vortrefflichste unter denen, die in einer Mantelschleppe aus Freigebigkeit eingehüllt sind.[180]

37) Er liebt aus Liebe zur Freigebigkeit den, der darin das rechte Maß einhält und den Geiz und die Knauserei und die Maßlosigkeit haßt.[181]

38) Die Berge Mekkas lieben ihn und die Duftende (Medina); wie oft bekundete an diesem Ort ein Mensch/der Berg Uḥud brennende Leidenschaft aus Liebe zu ihm.[182]

39) Die hellfarbigen Kamele legen ihren nächtlichen Weg zurück hin zum Wohlgeruch seines heiligen Bezirks, wenn eine leichte Brise zu ihnen weht, wie der Wind, wenn er stürmt.[183]

40) Wie ein Bogen erscheinen sie und wenn du sie aussendest, werden sie zu einem Pfeil, dem der hohe Hügel zum Ziel wurde.[184]

41) Erblicktest du einen heiligen Schrein, an dem er anwesend ist, würdest du dort einen Kelch Tränen leeren.

Der zweite Hauptteil wird deutlich abgesetzt durch die direkte Anrede *fa-yā ǧahūlan* (Oh, du Unwissender), wie auch der Übergang zum ersten Hauptteil durch die direkte Anrede *yā ʿāḏilī* (Oh, mein Tadler) in Vers 6 markiert war. Der Rezipient des Gedichtes wird direkt angesprochen als Unwissender, der ermahnt werden muß und eindringlich darauf hingewiesen wird, daß es die Liebe zum Propheten ist, die ihn ins Paradies gelangen lassen mag, „zur nächsten Nähe beim Herrn des Himmels". Damit wird ein Bezug zum Paradies hergestellt, von dem in den Versen davor so eindringlich die Rede war. Trost bietet zwar das Wissen, daß der Verstorbene, sei es der Prophet in der Vergangenheit oder auch ein Kind heute, direkt die Paradieseswonnen mit eigenen Augen bezeugen kann. Den größeren Trost scheint Ibn Abī Ḥaǧalah jedoch in der Liebe zum Propheten zu sehen, die einen selbst dorthin bringen kann. Der Prophet wird hier als Vermittler dargestellt, denn wer ihn liebt, wird auch von Gott geliebt. Das ist auch das zentrale Anliegen al-Būṣīrīs in seinem Mantelgedicht: Wer den Propheten liebt und ihn lobt, erhält seine Fürsprache und das Paradies. Vor allem ist die Liebe zum Propheten eine Möglichkeit, Trost zu suchen, die sich den Hinterbliebenen auch noch lange nach dem Tod des Verstorbenen anbietet.

---

[179] Zwei Nominalreihungen (*taʿdīd*): der Prophet, der Ruhmvolle, der Hāšimit; und die Höhe, die Gottesfurcht, der Ruhm und die Ehre.

[180] Zwei kurze Nominalreihungen (*taʿdīd*): Ein Reiner, Keuscher; und der Unschuldsvollste und Vortrefflichste; *ǧinās*: *muṭahharun* (Reiner) - *ṭāhirun* (Keuscher); Wiederholung derselben Wurzel mit derselben Bedeutung: *aǧwad – al-ǧūd*.

[181] Wiederholung derselben Wurzel mit derselben Bedeutung: *yuḥibbu - ḥubbihī*; Nominalreihung (*taʿdīd*): den Geiz, die Knauserei und die Verschwendung; Kontrast (*ṭibāq*): Freigebigkeit – Geiz, Knauserei; Geiz, Knauserei – Verschwendung.

[182] Doppeldeutigkeit, aber nur durch unterschiedliche Vokalisation: einer (*aḥad*)/der Berg Uḥud.

[183] Kontrast (*ṭibāq*): leichte Brise – Wind, wenn er stürmt; Vergleich (*tašbīh*): Sturm der Kamele, Sturm des Windes.

[184] Vergleich (*at-tašbīh*).

Vers 28 greift wieder die *nasīb*-Thematik auf, diesmal mit der üblichen Aufforderung, aufzuhören zu weinen über den Spuren einer schönen Frau (*daˁi l-bukāˀa ˁalā aṭlāli ġāniyatin*). Die Abwendung von der Geliebten wird damit begründet, daß sie ungerecht gehandelt habe. Mit dieser Frau ist wahrscheinlich – entsprechend der Geliebten in der *nasīb*-Einleitung der Burdah –, „die Nichtigkeit der Welt" gemeint, von der sich der Gläubige abwenden soll. In Vers 29 wird er dann aber wieder aufgefordert zu weinen! Die Abkehr vom Weinen soll also nicht etwa durch ein Hin zum Lob abgelöst werden, sondern: Durch die Abkehr von der falschen Geliebten soll sich der Gläubige, der zu Tröstende, hinwenden zum wahren Geliebten, der jedoch nicht mehr persönlich aufzusuchen ist, weil er bereits (vor langer Zeit) verstarb, sondern nur noch dessen Grab: „Beweine einen wohlbewachten Ort (*ḥimā*)". Wie im Folgenden sehr deutlich wird, ist hiermit der heilige Bezirk des Grabes des Propheten gemeint. Die Spuren nun dieses Grabes, sein Verwischt-Sein (*dāris*), werden nicht ausgelöscht, wie dies mit den üblichen Spuren des Zeltlagers im alt-arabischen *nasīb* der Fall ist, sondern können durch die Trauer, die Qualen, das Weinen im Gedenken an den Verstorbenen immer wieder neu entstehen (*ǧaddada*) und somit erhalten bleiben. Schon Ḥassān ibn Ṯābit spricht in den ersten zwei Versen seines Trauergedichtes davon, daß die Spuren des Propheten, die Zeichen seines Hauses, in dem er begraben wurde, nicht verlöschen (*wa-lā tanmaḥī l-āyātu*), im Gegensatz zum gewöhnlichen Verwischen und Verlöschen von Spuren. Und in Vers 5 spricht er wie Ibn Abī Ḥaǧalah von Zeichen, die sich erneuern (*taǧaddadu*).[185] Wenn nun der zu Tröstende an diesem besonderen Ort sein Schicksal geduldig erträgt, dann werden seine Sünden verziehen.

Die folgenden drei Verse thematisieren wieder den Gegensatz zwischen Helligkeit und Dunkelheit und damit auch den Kampf zwischen Glauben und Unglauben wie in den Versen 8-14 und nochmals 20-22, diesmal auf einer weiteren Ebene. In Vers 30 wird deutlich auf zwei Koranverse Bezug genommen. Der erste Halbvers bezieht sich auf Koran 37:10 mit der Aussage: „Außer dem, der etwas aufschnappt und den dann eine leuchtende Sternschnuppe (*šihābun ṯāqibun*) verfolgt".[186] Dieser Koranabschnitt (37:6-10) beschreibt, wie Gott die Sterne als Verzierung und als Schutz vor dem Lauschen „all der rebellischen Satane" erschaffen hat.[187] Der zwei-

---

[185] Ḥassān ibn Ṯābit, Vers 5, *Šarḥ Dīwān Ḥassān ibn Ṯābit*, ed. al-Barqūqī, 94: *maˁālimu lam tuṭmas ˁala l-ˁahdi āyuhā / atāha l-bilā fa-l-āyu minhā taǧaddadū*; in der Übersetzung von Le-Gassick, *The Life of the Prophet Muḥammad*, 2:400: „Knowledge that will never be effaced, signs wich, if removed become renewed"; oder in der dt. Übers. von Weil, *Das Leben Mohammed's*, 2:356: „Das sind Kennzeichen, die nie vergehen, so oft sie von Vernichtung bedroht sind, leuchten sie auf's Neue hervor".

[186] In den Koranübersetzungen wird *šihābun ṯāqibun* sehr unterschiedlich wiedergegeben, z.B. Paret, Rudi, *Der Koran*, 8. Aufl., Stuttgart 2001, 312: „blendend heller Feuerbrand"; Khoury, Adel Theodor, *Der Koran*, Gütersloh 1987, 339: „leuchtende Sternschnuppe".

[187] In dieser und vor allem in Sure 72 wird beschrieben, wie die Dschinnen sich zum Himmel begaben, um die Nachrichten der Himmelssphäre zu erlauschen. Doch als die Gesandt-

te Halbvers ist noch näher am Wortlaut des Korans: „Der Blitz raubt ihnen (den Ungläubigen) beinahe das Augenlicht (*yakādu l-barqu yaḫṭafu abṣārahum*), jedesmal, wenn er ihnen leuchtet …". Der zentrale Gegensatz von Dunkelheit und Licht, der in den folgenden Versen ausgeführt wird, wird hier eingeleitet: Auf der einen Seite die Nacht, in der sich die Szene abspielt (*tabītu*) und auf der anderen Seite die Sternschnuppen (*aš-šuhb*) und der Blitz (*al-barq*), die die Nacht im Kampf erleuchten.[188] Vers 31 spricht dann von dem „Führer in der Nacht",[189] mit dem der Engel Gabriel gemeint sein könnte, da dieser eine besondere Position unter den Engeln einnimmt, insbesondere als Offenbarungsengel. Gabriel als „Führer in der Nacht" zu bezeichnen macht auch Sinn, da dieser in der Nacht der Bestimmung (*laylat al-qadr*) mit den Engeln herabgesandt wird.[190] Die Nacht paßt auch zu Gabriel, da dieser bei der Nachtreise des Propheten (*al-isrāʾ*), wie sie in der Sīrah geschildert wird, als Begleiter und Führer des Reittieres al-Burāq fungierte, dessen Namen sich vom Wort für Blitz (*al-barq*) ableiten läßt.[191] Gabriel werden auch Helfer zugeschrieben, die auf der Erde die Kräfte des Zorns und Eifers zur Abwehr des Bösen und Schädlichen hervorrufen können.[192] Im Koran werden die Engel, die Gabriel begleiten, als Armee oder Truppen (*ǧunūd*) bezeichnet: „Und er sandte Truppen, die ihr nicht sehen konntet, herab und peinigte diejenigen, die ungläubig waren" (9:26).[193] Die Engel sind von den Menschen nicht wahrnehmbar, da sie Lichtwesen sind und zur Welt des Verborgenen gehören. Ibn Abī Ḥaǧalah zeichnet nun eine Szene, indem er auf diese Vorstellungen zurückgreift. Die Bataillone (*katāʾib*) im ersten Halbvers bestehen also aus den Engeln, die Gabriel begleiten. Im zweiten Halbvers symbolisiert die „Armee aus Dunkelheit" den Unglauben, der sich auch nach dem Ableben des Propheten ausgebreitet hatte. Diese Dunkelheit wird aber an seinem Grab von Gabriel und seinem Engelheer zurückgedrängt. Deutlich sind mit „seinen Bataillonen" und „der Armee aus Dunkelheit" zwei verschiedene Gruppen gemeint, denen kontrastierende Bewegungsarten zugeschrieben werden:

---

schaft des Propheten Muḥammads begann, war der Himmel gefüllt von Engeln und Sternschnuppen, die das Lauschen nicht mehr zuließen.

[188] Auch Ḥassān ibn Ṯābit spricht in Vers 1 bereits im Zusammenhang mit den Spuren, die vom Gesandten bleiben, von einem leuchtenden Ort (*maʿhadun munīrun*).

[189] Die Genitivkonstruktion ist hier wohl in der Bedeutung von *fī* als *iḍāfah ẓarfiyyah* zu verstehen wie z.B. *sahru l-layl* im Sinne von *sahrun fī l-layl*.

[190] Siehe Koran 97:3-4: „Die Nacht der Bestimmung ist besser als tausend Monate. Die Engel und der Geist (*ar-rūḥ*) kommen in ihr mit der Erlaubnis ihres Herrn herab mit jedem Anliegen". Die Korankommentatoren führen für *ar-rūḥ* in diesem Vers verschiedene Interpretationsmöglichkeiten an, deren gewichtigste jedoch Gabriel ist, siehe dazu z.B. von Hees, Syrinx, *Enzyklopädie als Spiegel des Weltbildes. Qazwīnīs Wunder der Schöpfung – eine Naturkunde des 13. Jahrhunderts*, Wiesbaden 2002, 291-292.

[191] Vgl. etwa Ibn Isḥāq, *Das Leben des Propheten*, 78-79.

[192] Siehe z.B. die Beschreibung des Engels Gabriel bei al-Qazwīnī, von Hees, *Enzyklopädie als Spiegel des Weltbildes*, 306-316.

[193] Vgl. auch Koran 33:9: „Oh ihr, die ihr glaubt, gedenket der Gnade Gottes zu euch, als Truppen zu euch kamen. Da sandten Wir gegen sie einen Wind und auch Truppen, die ihr nicht sehen konntet".

die erstere „marschiert/bewegt sich fort (*sārat*)", während die letztere „kriecht (*zaḥafā*)"[194]. Das Bild ist damit deutlich: Die Engel aus Licht, angeführt von Gabriel, bekämpfen und vertreiben die Dunkelheit. Das Subjekt des folgenden Verses 32 ist naheliegenderweise Gabriel, der Führer in der Nacht, dessen Beschreibung erst an dieser Stelle beginnt, da zunächst von seinen Bataillonen die Rede war. Wieder greift Ibn Abī Ḥaǧalah auf Bilder aus dem Koran und der Sīrah zurück. Als der Engel Gabriel dem Propheten einmal in seiner Gestalt erschien, habe er ihn gesehen, wie er „den Horizont ausfüllte (*sadda l-ufuq*)".[195] Dieses Bild wird in dem ersten Halbvers aufgegriffen, wobei es nicht der Engel ist, der überall am Himmel zu sehen ist, sondern sein leuchtendes Schwert, das von überall her zu sehen ist und mit dem er die Dunkelheit vertreibt, gar zum Leuchten bringt. In der Prophetenbiographie erscheinen die Engel auf dem Kriegsfeld genauso, wie man sich Kämpfer zu jener Zeit vorstellte, sie reiten auf Pferden und kämpfen mit Schwertern.[196]

In Vers 33 wird der Blick wieder auf den Ort des Geschehens gelenkt und der Führer in der Nacht als Beschützer dieses wohlbewahrten Ortes wird durch die Wiederholung der Wurzel in gleicher Bedeutung *yaḥmī ḥiman*, hervorgehoben. Gabriel wird bereits im Koran (66:4) als Beschützer des Propheten genannt: „Wenn ihr euch aber gegen ihn zusammenschließt, dann ist Gott sein Beschützer (*mawlāhū*) und Gabriel und die rechtschaffenen Gläubigen, und außerdem sind die Engel Helfer (*ẓahīr*)". Diese Vorstellung wird hier auf das Grab des Propheten übertragen, das von Gabriel zusammen mit seinen Helferengeln beschützt wird. Dieser Ort wird nun genauer beschrieben. In einer bekannten Überlieferung heißt es, daß Muḥammad gesagt habe, der Weg zwischen seinem Haus und seiner Kanzel sei ein Teil vom Paradiesesgarten, weil er diesen am meisten betreten hat.[197] Mit „seinen Gärten" in diesem Vers wird auf diese Stelle verwiesen, die den Namen *ar-Rawḍah* trägt, der im folgenden Vers ja auch erwähnt wird.[198] Das Grab des Propheten ist mithin ein kleines Stück Paradies auf Erden, das mit seinen Blüten die Blicke verzückt. Mit diesem blühenden und leuchtenden Bild (*zahr* in Vers 32: die Leuchtenden und *azhār* in Vers 33: die Blüten) des Gartens ist endgültig das dunkle und trübe Bild vom eingetretenen Herbst, der Verfinsterung der Sonne, den weinenden Wolken, der sich ausbreitenden Dunkelheit und allumfassenden Trauer, abgelöst.

---

[194] Das Verb *zaḥafa* besitzt, auch wenn es marschieren bedeuten kann, eine negative Konnotation, wie in dem Satz: „*zaḥafa ʿalā baṭnihī*", siehe Lane, E.W., *Arabic-English Lexicon*, reprint, Cambridge 1984, 1:1219.

[195] Siehe dazu von Hees, *Enzyklopädie als Spiegel des Weltbildes*, 309-310.

[196] Vgl. etwa die Berichte über die Schlacht von Badr, Weil, *Das Leben Mohammed's*, 1:335-336.

[197] *Mā bayna baytī wa-minbarī rawḍatun min riyāḍi l-ǧannah*, siehe z.B. in Ibn Ḥaǧar al-ʿAsqalānī, *Fatḥ al-Bārī*, 4: 99-100.

[198] Eine genaue Beschreibung dieses Ortes, der heute innerhalb der Prophetenmoschee liegt, findet sich bei Behrens, Marcel, *„Ein Garten des Paradieses" – Die Prophetenmoschee von Medina*, Würzburg 2007, 133-141.

Dieser Garten nun ist Ziel aller „hellfarbenen Kamele", mit denen hier wohl die Gläubigen gemeint sind,[199] damit sie dort vom Paradiesgarten (*rawḍah*) mit eigenen Augen Zeugnis ablegen können (*tušāhidu*). Durch den wiederholten Gebrauch dieses Verbes wird das Grab in direkten Bezug gesetzt zum Paradies, das der Prophet als Märtyrer mit eigenen Augen sieht (Verse 25-26). Das war der Höhepunkt des damaligen Trostes. Jetzt ist es tröstlich, das Grab des Propheten aufzusuchen und dort einen Vorgeschmack auf die Schönheiten des Paradieses zu erblicken. Denn dort, in diesen Gärten (*fīhā*), ist der Prophet gegenwärtig, wie es im folgenden Vers heißt. Verse 35-37 enthalten nun das Lob dieses Propheten. In Trauergedichten ist es üblich, die Taten des Verstorbenen rühmend zu erwähnen, und das Prophetenlob besteht in erster Linie aus Lob. Ibn Abī Ḥaǧalah bringt hier das Lob an zentraler Stelle, faßt sich mit der Ausführung in drei Versen jedoch relativ knapp. Er beschreibt keine speziellen Taten, sondern beschränkt sich auf die Nennung herausragender Charaktereigenschaften. Er hebt das Lob jedoch deutlich hervor durch Nominalreihungen, die er in allen drei Versen anwendet. Dieses Stilmittel verwendete er bereits, um andere zentrale Verse des Gedichtes hervorzuheben; hier nun – über drei Verse hinweg – am stärksten. Außerdem fällt wieder ein Wortcluster auf, nämlich der Begriff der Freigebigkeit (*al-ǧūd*), wodurch diese Eigenschaft des Propheten ins Zentrum des Lobes gerückt wird. Aus Liebe zur Freigebigkeit liebt er auch die Menschen, die das rechte Maß darin einhalten. Damit ist das Thema Liebe aufgegriffen, das in den folgenden Versen als Liebe zum Propheten ausgeführt wird. Hier ist es der Prophet, der in seiner Großzügigkeit selbst die Gläubigen liebt.

Zu Beginn des zweiten Hauptteils wurde dem Rezipienten des Gedichtes ganz deutlich gesagt: Es ist die Liebe zum Propheten, durch die man die Nähe zu Gott und damit den Eintritt ins Paradies erlangen kann. Wie im ersten Hauptteil die Natur und die Menschen um den Propheten getrauert haben, so wird im Folgenden geschildert, wie sowohl Natur (Berge, Kamele) als auch Menschen (viele, die Gläubigen) in Liebe zum Propheten aufgehen, und zwar insbesondere an den heiligen Orten Mekka und Medina. In Vers 38 schwingt durch die mögliche Vokalisation mit *uḥudun* der Berg Uḥud mit, der so in die Liebe zum Propheten mit eingeschlossen wird, denn in einem Ḥadīṯ heißt es: „Der Berg Uḥud liebt uns, und wir lieben ihn. Er ist ein Berg des Paradieses".[200] In Vers 39 werden wieder

---

[199] Vgl. etwa Vers 105 der Burdah, wo von den Bittstellern die Rede ist, die zum Hof des Propheten hineilen, laufend oder auf dem Rücken von Kamelen, *Dīwān al-Būṣīrī*, 236; engl. Übers. von Stetkevych, *The Mantle Odes*, 127: „O best of those whose courtyard the supplicants seek, hastening on foot, Or on the backs of she-camels whose heavy tread leaves traces on the ground".

[200] „Dieser Berg liebt uns und wir lieben ihn", siehe z.B. in Ibn Ḥaǧar al-ʿAsqalānī, *Fatḥ al-Bārī*, 7:377-378. Auch in der Burdah, Vers 128, wird der Berg Uḥud erwähnt, dort allerdings als Zeuge für das erflogreiche Kämpfen der Muslime in der Schlacht von Uḥud, *Dīwān al-Būṣīrī*, 238; engl. Übers. von Stetkevych, *The Mantle Odes*, 133: „Ask Ḥunayn and Badr and Uḥud about them, they will reply: ʿThe ways they kill the infidel are more deadly than the plague'".

die Kamele genannt, die, vom Wohlgeruch des Grabes angezogen, der in einer leichten Brise zu ihnen weht, kontrastiv dazu wie ein stürmischer Wind dahineilen. Hier stehen die Kamele wohl sinnbildlich für die Gläubigen. Renate Jacobi zeigt im Zusammenhang mit der Dichtung des mystischen Dichters Ibn al-Fāriḍ, wie in dem Kamelritt mehrere Ebenen der Deutung zu finden sind: „1. die poetische Ebene, auf der die Wüstenreise als Grundsituation des menschlichen Daseins gedeutet werden kann, 2. die religiöse Ebene, die Pilgerfahrt nach Mekka, 3. die mystische Ebene, denn die Pilgerfahrt ist zugleich der Weg des Mystikers mit dem Ziel der Erleuchtung.“[201] Auf diese Vorstellungswelt referiert auch Ibn Abī Ḥaǧalah, nur daß sich in diesem Gedicht die Pilgerfahrt, die Liebessehnsucht nach Medina, zum Grab des Propheten richtet.

Die Burdah, die überhaupt nur in einem Vers vom Grab des Propheten spricht, hebt darin ebenfalls dessen Wohlgeruch (ṭīb) hervor.[202] In Vers 40 werden zwar Begriffe verwendet, die zu Kampfszenen gehören (Bogen, Pfeil, Ziel), die hier jedoch umgedeutet werden als Bild für die gespannte Sehnsucht, die einen zum Geliebten streben läßt. Die Bezeichnung des Grabes als „hohen Hügel (ʿālī r-rubā)“ mag man vergleichen mit Vers 11 des Trauergedichts von Ḥassān ibn Ṯābit, der „auf dem Hügel des Grabes (ʿalā ṭalali l-qabri)“ steht. In Vers 40 wird außerdem der Rezipient des Gedichtes wieder direkt angeredet: „Wenn du sie aussendest (arsaltahā)“, und insofern könnten die Kamele hier auch für die Liebessehnsucht stehen, die der Gläubige zulassen möge, um ans Ziel zu gelangen. Vers 42, mit dem der zweite Hauptteil abschließt, fährt in dieser Ansprache fort: Wenn du (durch deine Liebe zum Propheten) wirklich seine Anwesenheit an einem Ort erfahren solltest, würdest du dort weinen, - nun allerdings nicht mehr aus Trauer, sondern vor Rührung. Mit maqām ist hier natürlich das Grab des Propheten gemeint. Es ist durchaus üblich, ein verehrtes Heiligengrab – nicht nur das von Muḥammad – als maqām zu bezeichnen.[203]

Dieser zweite Hauptteil beschreibt also die Wichtigkeit der Liebe zum Propheten und die Bedeutung des Besuches des Grabes des Propheten, um diese Liebe zu verwirklichen. Im Zentrum steht mithin das Grab, an dem sich diese Liebe manifestieren, ja sogar die Gegenwart des Verstorbenen zu spüren sein kann. Damit gelangt man in seine Nähe, und das bietet den größten Trost für seinen Verlust. Im Vergleich zum Prophetenlob wie auch zum Trauergedicht schafft Ibn Abī Ḥaǧalah auch in diesem Abschnitt etwas Besonderes. Wie erwähnt, findet sich in dem Prophetenlobgedicht al-Burdah des al-Būṣīrī nur ein einziger Vers, der vom Grab des Propheten handelt. Er steht zum Abschluß der allgemeinen

---

[201] Jacobi, *Ibn al-Fāriḍ*, 171.

[202] Burdah, Vers 58, *Dīwān al-Būṣīrī*, 234; engl. Übers. von Stetkevych, *The Mantle Odes*, 99: „No perfume is as redolent as the dust that holds his bones; Whoever inhales or kisses it is blessed“.

[203] Der koranische Begriff maqām maḥmūd (17:79) wird allerdings meist gar nicht auf das Grab bezogen, sondern als ein Hügel auf der Ebene der Auferstehung gedeutet, auf dem der Prophet am Jüngsten Tag in grün gekleidet als Fürbitter stehen wird.

Lobpreisung des Propheten, bevor al-Būṣīrī dann genauer auf dessen Geburt und seine Wunder wie den Koran, die Himmelsreise und seine Kämpfe eingeht. Die Vorstellung, daß das Erleben dieses Grabes (riechen und küssen) selig mache, wie sie auch für Ibn Abī Ḥaǧalah im Zentrum steht, ist hier bereits formuliert. Im Trauergedicht des Ḥassān ibn Ṯābit spielt das Grab eine viel größere Rolle, zumindest zu Beginn seines Gedichtes. Wie wir sahen, referiert Ibn Abī Ḥaǧalah wohl auch auf die von Ḥassān ibn Ṯābit hervorgerufenen Vorstellungen, daß sich dieses Grab dadurch auszeichnet, daß seine Spuren gerade nicht verwischen werden, ja sich seine Zeichen sogar erneuern. Dennoch, Ḥassān ibn Ṯābit erfleht (Vers 12-13), wie dies in der Trauerdichtung durchaus üblich ist, sehr intensiv den Segen für das Grab (*fa-būrikat ... wa-būrikat ... wa-būrika*).[204] Zu Ibn Abī Ḥaǧalahs Zeiten war das Grab schon länger selbst zum Segensspender geworden.

Im Kontext von *Ǧiwār al-aḫyār*, dem Ziyārah-Totenbuch, können wir natürlich auch in der Betonung auf das Grab einen Hinweis auf die Grabbesuche des Dichters am Grab des Prophetengenossen Sayyid ʿUqbahs und seines Kindes sehen.

Schlußteil: Mein Gedicht als Ausdruck dieser Liebe (Verse 42-47)

تعانق اللام من شوق بها الألفا   لي كلّ عامٍ قصيدٌ فيــه أرسلها

فكم حوت طرفةً لمّا أتت طرفا   تنشى القوى في[205] القوافي فاء أحرفها[206]

والتاء في تفهها[209] لا تختشي التلفا   فالعين[207] أمسى لها من طرسها[208] حورٌ

45   واو ثنت[210] عطف ظبي الحيّ فانعطفا   والهاء من ولهٍ فيه غدت ولها

سلكت بالمدح فيه مذهب الظرفا   إليّ يعزى[211] سلوك النظم فيه فكم

قصيدةٌ[212] راق فيه بحرها وصفا   صلّى عليه إله العرش ما نظمت

---

[204] Ḥassān ibn Ṯābit, Verse 12-13, *Šarḥ Dīwān Ḥassān ibn Ṯābit*, ed. al-Barqūqī, 91; in der dt. Übers. von Weil, *Das Leben Mohammed's*, 2:356-357: „Sei gesegnet, Grab des Gesandten, sei gesegnet, Du Land, in welchem der Gerechte und Feste gewohnt hat! Gesegnet sei die Gruft, welche durch Dich das Beste umschliesst und über welche sich ein steinernes Monument herhebt!“.

[205] "القوى في" ناقص في (و).

[206] (بج) (ل): فا حرفها.

[207] (ق): العيش.

[208] (بج): طرفها.

[209] (بج) (ل) (ق): تيهها.

[210] (ق): رثت.

[211] (ل): يعرى.

[212] ناقص في (و).

42) Ich mache jedes Jahr ein Gedicht über ihn, das ich aussende; das Lām umarmt darin aus Sehnsucht das Alif.

43) Die Kraft in den Reimen läßt das Fāʾ seiner Buchstaben entstehen: Wie viele Glanzstücke enthält es, wenn es am Ende (des Verses) vorkommt.[213]

44) Denn das ʿAyn/das Auge bekommt von seinem Papier starken Kontrast des Weißen und Schwarzen (im Auge) und das Tāʾ in seiner Kleinheit fürchtet sich nicht vor dem Untergang.[214]

45) Und das Hāʾ hat aus starker Liebe zu ihm ein Wāw erhalten, das die Körperseite der Gazelle des Stammes biegt, so daß sie zugeneigt wird.[215]

46) Mir verdankt man den Weg der Poesie/Anspielung auf Werktitel Ibn al-Fāriḍs über ihn: Wievielmals beschritt ich mit seinem Lob den Pfad der Eleganz.[216]

47) Es segne ihn der Gott des Thrones solange Gedichte geschrieben werden, deren Metrum/Meer rein und klar ist.[217]

Im Schlußteil spricht der Dichter wieder in der ersten Person Singular von sich selbst, wie es auch in der Einleitung der Fall ist. Das Thema ist jetzt aber nicht mehr seine eigene Trauer, sondern sein eigenes Gedicht. In Vers 42 sagt er, daß er jedes Jahr ein Gedicht über den Propheten verfasse und es zu seinem Grab sende. Damit wird der Anlaß des Gedichtes in den Kontext eines sich wiederholenden, jährlich stattfindenden Rituals, wohl zur Zeit der Pilgerfahrt, gestellt. Dies war ein Ritual, das auch andere Dichter seiner Zeit vollzogen.[218] Dadurch wird es ganz deutlich, daß das Gedicht nicht etwa unmittelbar aus Anlaß des Todes des eigenen Sohnes Muḥammads verfaßt worden ist. Dennoch läßt es Ibn Abī Ḥaǧalah nachträglich in diesem Ziyārah-Totenbuch-Kontext erscheinen. Seine jährlich verfaßten Gedichte über den Propheten schickt er aus (*ursiluhā*), wie er den Rezipienten aufforderte, die Kamele auszusenden (*arsaltahā*), mit denen wohl am ehesten die Liebessehnsucht zum Propheten gemeint war. Durch die wiederholte Nutzung dieses Verbes wird das Ende des zweiten Hauptteils mit dem Schlußteil inhaltlich verknüpft. Wie im Folgenden deutlich wird, versteht Ibn Abī Ḥaǧalah in der Tat sein Gedicht als Ausdruck dieser Liebessehnsucht, die er zum Grab

---

[213] Gerundete Paranomasia *(al-ǧinās al-mafrūq al-malfūf)*: *al-quwā fī* (die Kraft in) – *al-qawāfī* (die Reime); *ǧinās*: *ṭurfatan* (Glanzstücke) - *ṭarafā* (Ende).

[214] *tawriyah*: ʿAyn/Auge; Alliteration im zweiten Halvers mit dem Buchstanben *tāʾ*. Die in der HS Vollers überlieferte Variante *tafah* (Kleinheit, Geringheit, Bedeutungslosigkeit) ist inhaltlich treffender und wurde deswegen hier gewählt, auch wenn in den drei anderen HSS *tīh* (Stolz) zu lesen ist..

[215] *Ǧinās*: *walahin* (starke Liebe) – *wa-lahā* (es hat); *ʿaṭfa* (Körperseite) – *inʿaṭafā* (zugeneigt werden).

[216] Weg der Poesie *(sulūk an-naẓm)* verweist auf: „*Naẓm as-sulūk* (Die Ordnung des Weges)“, ein Titel des berühmtesten Gedichts von Ibn al-Fāriḍ; Wiederholung derselben Wurzel mit derselben Bedeutung: *sulūk – salaktu*.

[217] *Tawriyah*: Metrum/Meer.

[218] Z.B. der Literat an-Nawāǧī (ca. 1386-1455), siehe Bauer, Thomas, „al-Nawāǧī", in: Joseph E. Lowry & Devin J. Stewart (Hg.): *Essays in Arabic Literary Biography: 1350-1850*, Wiesbaden 2009, 321-331, zu den jährlich gesendeten Prophetenlobgedichten siehe 330.

aussendet. Im zweiten Halbvers heißt es bereits, daß darin „das Lām aus Sehnsucht das Alif umarmt". Hier, wie in den folgenden drei Versen, werden einzelne Buchstaben genannt, die als pars pro toto für das gesamte Gedicht stehen. Die Buchstabenkombination *lām-alif*, die als Ligatur geschrieben wird, und sogar als ein Buchstabe angesehen werden konnte, wird gerne als Metapher für eine enge Umarmung, eine besonders starke Beziehung verwendet.[219]

Vers 43 fällt stilistisch durch seine gerundete Paranomasia *(al-ǧinās al-mafrūq al-malfūf)* auf zwischen *al-quwā fī* (die Kraft in) und *al-qawāfī* (die Reime). Der hier genannte Buchstabe *fā'* wird in der Morphologie verwendet, um den ersten Radikal eines dreiwurzeligen Verbes zu bezeichnen *(fa-ʿa-la)*. Andererseits stellt er in diesem Gedicht den Reimbuchstaben am Ende einer jeden Zeile dar. Der Dichter lobt nun die Schönheit seines Gedichtes, wobei der Buchstabe *fā'* sowohl für den Anfang *(fā' aḥrufihā)* als auch für das Ende steht *(al-quwā fī l-qawāfī)*. Der zweite Halbvers lenkt unsere Blicke auf sich durch den *ǧinās* mit *ṭurfa* (Glanzstücke) und *ṭaraf* (Ende), wobei die verwandten Bedeutungen Blick *(ṭarafa)* und Auge *(ṭarf)* zum nächsten Vers überleiten. In Vers 44 werden diese Bedeutungen durch die *tawriyah* (ʿAyn/<u>Auge</u>) weitergeführt, sowie durch den Begriff *ḥawar*, der den starken Kontrast des Weißen und Schwarzen im Auge bezeichnet. Darin klingt auch eine Anspielung auf die Schönheiten des Paradieses mit ihren besonders intensiv weiß-schwarz kontrastierenden Augen mit, und damit wird die schwarze Tinte auf dem weißen Papier mit den *ḥūr ʿīn*, den schönäugigen Huris des Korans, in Zusammenhang gebracht: Ihre Schönheit wie auch die Schönheit des Gedichts basiert auf starken Kontrasten. Im zweiten Halbvers ist vom Buchstaben *tā'* die Rede, der aufgrund seiner Kleinheit, wenn er am Beginn oder in der Mitte eines Wortes geschrieben wird, dem Blick entschwinden mag, auf jeden Fall nicht einmal mehr zu hören ist – und damit gänzlich verloren geht, wenn er am Ende eines Wortes als *tā' marbūtah* in Erscheinung tritt. Dennoch muß er sich vor dem Untergang nicht fürchten, weil auch der kleinste Buchstabe seinen Beitrag zum Ganzen leistet.[220]

Vers 45 wiederholt die Aussage aus dem zweiten Halbvers zu Beginn des Schlußteils: Die Buchstaben des Gedichtes sind in Liebe verschlungen und geben damit der Liebe des Dichters zum Propheten ihren Ausdruck, wobei auch hier wieder zwei *ǧinās*-Formen: *walahin* (starke Liebe) – *wa-lahā* (es hat); *ʿiṭf* (Körperseite) – *inʿaṭafā* (zugeneigt), die Aussage unterstreichen. Wie bei der *lām-alif*-Verbindung ist auch hier von einer Buchstabenkombination die Rede. Wenn sich *hā'* mit *wāw* verbindet, ergibt sich daraus das Personalpronomen *huwa*, das in der

---

[219] Schimmel, Annemarie, *Calligraphy and Islamic Culture*, New York 1984, 101 und 140.

[220] Vergleiche hierzu auch den letzten Vers von Ibn Abī Ḥaǧalahs Gedicht über seine Tätigkeit als Sufi *šayḫ* im Ḫānqāh des Emirs Manǧak al-Yūsufī, wo er das Hamzā' als kleinsten Buchstaben nennt, der dennoch deutlich spricht, siehe den Beitrag von Homerin, „Ibn Abī Ḥaǧalah and Sufism", in diesem Band, S. 16-17.

Sufipraxis des *ḏikr* eine wichtige Rolle spielt und auf Gott verweist.[221] In Vers 46 kommt wieder eine Doppeldeutigkeit ins Spiel, da *sulūk an-naẓm* (der Weg der Poesie) auf das berühmteste Gedicht des Mystikers Ibn al-Fāriḍ mit dem Titel *naẓm as-sulūk* (die Ordnung des Weges) verweist, gegen das sich Ibn Abī Ḥaǧalah später so deutlich positioniert hat.[222] Er faßt in diesem Vers das Eigenlob über die eigene Dichtung zusammen. Im abschließenden Vers 47 bittet er um den Segen Gottes für den Propheten, solange derartige Gedichte verfaßt werden. Damit endet Ibn Abī Ḥaǧalah sein Gedicht über den Tod des Propheten gedanklich wie al-Būṣīrī sein Lobgedicht auf den Propheten, indem er ebenfalls eine Gegenseitigkeit formuliert: „the poet prays in a *madīḥ nabawī* for Allāh to rain His blessings down upon the Prophet for as long as the remembrance of the Prophet stirs poets to compose *madīḥ nabawī*".[223] Al-Būṣīrī kleidet diese Aussage in eine Metapher: „solange sich die Zweige des Moringastrauchs im Ostwind biegen und der Kameltreiber mit seinem Singen die weißen Kamele ermuntert!".[224] Ibn Abī Ḥaǧalah drückt diesen Gedanken dagegen in direkter Weise aus.

In seinem Gedicht zum Gedenken an den Tod des Propheten bezieht sich Ibn Abī Ḥaǧalah ausdrücklich auf die Tradition der Trauerdichtung durch die namentliche Nennung des Dichters Ḥassān ibn Ṯābit. Er bezieht sich in einigen Vorstellungen auf dessen bekanntes Trauergedicht, insbesondere im Hinblick auf die gerade nicht vergehenden, sich sogar erneuernden Spuren des Grabes des Propheten. Ibn Abī Ḥaǧalah knüpft ebenso an die Tradition des zu seiner Zeit beliebten Prophetenlobs an, insbesondere in seiner Einleitung und wieder ganz zum Schluß. An eigentlichem Prophetenlob bringt er jedoch überhaupt nur drei Verse. Nicht nur die Prophetenlob-Gedichte, auch das Trauergedicht Ḥassān ibn Ṯābits bringt über viele Zeilen hinweg lobende Beschreibungen des Propheten. Dieses Thema hat Ibn Abī Ḥaǧalah zu Gunsten seiner Trauerschilderungen ganz zurückgestellt. Er hebt aber die Verehrung des Propheten an dessen Grab hervor. Seine Darstellung der Ursache des Todes, verknüpft mit der Formulierung, der Prophet sei als Märtyrer gestorben und seiner Paradiesschilderung, die sowohl in diesem Gedicht, wie auch in dem hier verglichenen, im anthologischen Kapitel von *Ǧiwār al-aḫyār* vorangestellten, ersten Gedicht ausgeführt wird, stechen als besonderes Motiv hervor. Ebenso auffallend ist seine äußerst vehemente Trauer, die als Jetzt-Zustand in starkem Kontrast von der damaligen Situation zum Zeitpunkt des Todes des Propheten abgesetzt wird. Insbesondere diese Besonderheiten ermöglichen es, dieses Trauerge-

---

[221] Schimmel, *Calligraphy*, 99; vgl. auch ein späteres Gedicht von ʿĀʾišah al-Bāʿūniyyah (st. 923/1517), das *yā huwa yā huwa yā llāhū* als Refrain bringt, siehe Homerin, Emil, „'Recalling You, My Lord': ʿĀʾishah al-Bāʿūniyah on *Dhikr*", in: *MSR* 17 (2013), 130-154, speziell 151-154.

[222] Siehe Homerin, „Ibn Abī Ḥaǧalah and Sufism", in diesem Band.

[223] Stetkevych, *The Mantel Odes*, 147.

[224] *Dīwān al-Būṣīrī*, 240; dt. Übersetzung von Thomas Bauer; engl. Übers. von Stetkevych, *The Mantle Odes*, 147: „For as long as the eastern breeze stirs the boughs of the ben-tree, And the camel driver stirs his light-hued beasts with song".

dicht auf den Propheten auch als Ersatz für ein Kindertotenlied zu lesen, das den Dichter/Rezipienten im Augenblick beschäftigt. Die Trauer ist unermeßlich und will gar nicht aufhören. Trost spendet zunächst die Erinnerung, daß selbst der Prophet einmal sterben mußte. Trost damals wie auch heute spendet dann das Bewußtsein, daß damit aber das Licht der Rechtleitung, die Religion Muḥammads nicht verloschen ist, auch wenn sie immer wieder erkämpft werden muß. Besonderen Trost spendet dann das Wissen, daß der Prophet und alldiejenigen, die an der Pest starben, insbesondere die vielen Kinder, auch das eigene Kind, des Paradieses sicher sind. Um sich selbst weiterhin Lebenssinn zu geben, ist dann aber das allerwichtigste, in Liebe zum Propheten zu leben. „Die Liebe zum Propheten" bezeichnet Ibn Abī Ḥaǧalah in seinem Gedicht über seine Tätigkeit als Sufi *šayḫ* im Ḫānqāh des Emirs Manǧak al-Yūsufī, als „seinen Weg".[225] Zentraler Ort für diese Liebe ist für Ibn Abī Ḥaǧalah im Zusammenhang dieses Trauergedichtes nicht Mekka, sondern Medina, insbesondere das Grab des Propheten. Hier kann man ihm bereits auf Erden so nahe wie möglich kommen, seine Gegenwart spüren, einen Vorgeschmack auf das Paradies erleben. Deshalb ist auch der Grabbesuch in der Heimat zu einem Prophetengenossen so wichtig. Auch die Nähe zum verlorenen Kind kann beim Grabbesuch erfahren werden, einem Kind, das als Märtyrer an der Pest starb, und das damit gewiß die Eltern ins Paradies führen wird, wie die zahlreichen von Ibn Abī Ḥaǧalah gesammelten Ḥadīte belegen. Wenn auch der Grabbesuch in Medina nicht persönlich möglich ist, so kann der Dichter doch jedes Jahr ein Gedicht an seinen geliebten Propheten aussenden. Diese Verse zeugen von seiner Liebe und bringen ihrerseits Trost.

Leitmotive und Qaṣīdenthemen

Thomas Bauer hat anhand von mehreren Gedichten Ibn Nubātahs eine neue literarische Ästhetik für die Mamlukenzeit beschrieben.[226] Er zeigt, wie die lineare Organisationsstruktur des Rahmens anhand von Qaṣīdenthemen miteinander verknüpft wird, wobei diese Themen variierend entwickelt und zueinander in Bezug gesetzt werden. Er zeigt, daß sich diese Qaṣīdenthemen über die Verwendung von Leitmotiven entwickeln und erklärt, wie thematische und motivische Verdichtungen Steigerung und klimaktische Effekte hervorbringen. Thomas Bauer betont, daß durch den Gebrauch der *tawriyah* als Stilmittel eine derartige Verknüpfung verstärkt möglich sei, da der Dichter im Idealfall thematische Ketten auf primärer und se-

---

[225] Vgl. Beitrag Homerin, „Ibn Abī Ḥaǧalah and Sufism", in diesem Band, 16-17 (Vers 3): *wa-min maḏhabī ḥubbu n-nabī.*

[226] Bauer, „Communication and Emotion: The Case of Ibn Nubātah's Kindertotenlieder"; ders., „'Der Fürst ist tot, es lebe der Fürst!' Ibn Nubātas Gedicht von der Inthronisierung al-Afḍals von Ḥamāh (732/1332)", in: Marzolph, Ulrich (Hg.), *Orientalische Studien zu Sprache und Literatur. Festgabe zum 65. Geburtstag von Werner Diem*, Wiesbaden 2011, 285-315; ders., „'Ayna hāḏā min al-Mutanabbī!' Toward an Aesthetics of Mamluk Literature", in: *MSR* 17 (2013), 5-22.

kundärer Bedeutung bilden kann, wodurch das Gedicht an Vielschichtigkeit weiter gewinnen kann. Er weist außerdem darauf hin, daß es sinnvoll sei, diese Vorgehensweise anhand anderer Beispiele zu überprüfen, um sicher zu gehen, daß es sich hierbei nicht um eine Eigenart Ibn Nubātahs handelt.[227]

Im Folgenden will ich daher anhand von einigen ausgewählten Beispielen aufzeigen, inwiefern Ibn Abī Ḥaǧalah in der Nachfolge Ibn Nubātahs sich dieser neuen Ästhetik bedient. Es ist in der Tat so, daß auch Ibn Abī Ḥaǧalah in den bislang besprochenen, inhaltlich abgrenzbaren Teilabschnitten, die die Rahmenstruktur dieses Gedichts bilden, in verschiedenem Grade dasselbe thematische Material – von Thomas Bauer als Qaṣīden-Themen bezeichnet - verwendet, hervorgehoben und weitergeführt anhand von deutlich in Erscheinung tretenden Leitmotiven.

Das erste, stark auffallende, wenn auch für ein Trauergedicht naheliegende Leitmotiv sind die Tränen (damʿ), da sie in der Einleitung in 5 von 6 Versen auftreten. Es sind hier die realen Tränen des Dichters, die mit der nasīb-Thematik verbunden werden und aufhören sollten, was sie aber nicht tun. Sie sind blutig, zahlreich und schwach (Vers 1-2, 4-6). Im ersten Hauptteil werden die Tränen dann noch zweimal metaphorisch erwähnt (Vers 12: Tränen der Wolken, Vers 18: Tränen des Frühregens). Hier verwandeln sich die Tränen also in Regen, der die Trauer der Natur zum Ausdruck bringt. Im Verlaufe des Gedichtes wird die Trauer dann aber überwunden und Tränen tauchen nur noch einmal in Vers 41 auf: Jetzt weint der Besucher des Grabs vor Rührung, da er die Gegenwart des Verstorbenen hier spürt. Tränen als Leitmotiv akzentuieren mithin in erhöhtem Maße die Einleitung, vollziehen dann aber auch den entscheidenden Wandel von der Trauer hin zum Trost, den man am Grab erfahren kann.

Das Wort al-baḥr wird dreimal im Gedicht erwähnt und kann als Leitmotiv gedeutet werden, das in seiner Transformation wichtige Stationen des Gedichtes beleuchtet. In Vers 4 wird damit in Form einer Übertreibung die Unmenge der Tränen des Dichters unterstrichen. Darüberhinaus wird dieses Wort als tawriyah hervorgehoben: In diesem Vers ist der Nil gemeint und dadurch birgt al-baḥr hier einen Verweis auf die Situation des Dichters/Rezipienten in Ägypten. In Vers 13 taucht al-baḥr zum zweiten Mal auf, zunächst in seiner naheliegendsten Bedeutung als Meer, das ausführlich beschrieben wird mit so hohen Wellen, daß Schiffe unter- und Fische auftauchen. Durch den Vers davor, in dem von Tränen die Rede ist, kann sich dieses Meer einerseits wieder auf die Menge der Tränen beziehen, oder aber auf Medina, die Stadt des Propheten, die im folgenden Vers genannt wird. Das gesamte Bild, das vom wütenden Meer gezeichnet wird, kann als Metapher gedeutet werden für die in Erscheinung tretende Dunkelheit, als Untergang des Glaubens, der dem Unglauben weicht. Schließlich kommt al-baḥr im allerletzten Vers noch einmal vor, hier wieder als tawriyah hervorgehoben, denn jetzt ist das Metrum gemeint. Dieses Leitwort zieht sich also durch das Ge-

---

[227] Bauer, "Ayna hādhā min al-Mutanabbī!", 21.

dicht und beschreibt den Wandel von Tränenmassen über den angedeuteten Untergang des Glaubens hin zum Trost in Form des Gedichtes selbst.

Auf das abschließende Rahmenthema „Gedicht" wird leitmotivisch bereits im zweiten Vers durch das Wort *naẓm* hingewiesen, das hier als *tawriyah* hervorgehoben, die Perlenschnur meint, die an dieser Stelle metaphorisch für den Tränenguß steht; wobei die zweite Bedeutung „Dichtung" durch die Verwendung des Verbes *naṯara*, zerstreuen, das auch das Verfassen von Prosa bezeichnen kann, deutlich angespielt wird. Am Ende des Gedichtes, in Vers 46 ist dann mit *an-naẓm* die Poesie gemeint, wieder durch eine, allerdings anders geartete *tawriyah* hervorgehoben, da sich zusammen mit dem Begriff *sulūk* darin ein Werktitel Ibn al-Fāriḍs verbirgt. Hier also der Wandel von der Trauer zum Dichten. Darüber hinaus wird das Thema „Gedicht" auch in den Versen 15 und 16 deutlich als Trauerdichtung angesprochen, hervorgehoben durch eine Wiederholung des Verbs *yarṯī* in Vers 15, in dem die Trauerklage des Ḥassān ibn Ṯābit über den Tod Muḥammads erwähnt wird, und *yurṯā* in Vers 16, in dem außerdem noch das dazugehörige Substantiv *ar-riṯāʾ* verwendet wird. Durch diese Clusterung werden diese beiden Verse stark betont, in denen die jetzige Situation des Sprechers mit der damaligen Situation zur Zeit des Propheten in Verbindung gebracht wird – eine zentrale Stelle des Gedichts.

Ein vergleichbares Wortcluster fällt in der Mitte des Gedichtes auf, mit *šahīdan* im Vers 25, in dem erklärt wird, der Prophet sei als Märtyrer verstorben, gefolgt von *šāhada* (mit eigenen Augen sehen) und *aš-šahd* (Honig) im darauffolgenden Vers, in dem der Prophet dem Märtyrerstatus entsprechend sofort das Paradies sieht. Damit wird soweit der höchste Trost gespendet und verbindet nach meiner Interpretation wieder die Situation des jetzigen Ichs mit der Situation des Propheten. Wir können hier nicht von einem das Gedicht durchziehenden Leitmotiv sprechen, aber von deutlich auffallenden Wortclustern, die zentrale Stellen des Gedichtes markieren. Allerdings wird *yušāhidu* sogar in Vers 34 nochmals aufgegriffen: Jetzt sind es die edlen Kamele, deren Lauf nicht aufgehalten werden soll, damit sie mit eigenen Augen den neubepflanzten Garten am Grab sehen können. Dieses Bild kann als Metapher gedeutet werden: Die Gläubigen wollen das Fortleben des Glaubens am Grab bezeugen. Der Verstorbene mag im Paradies sein – das ist ein tröstlicher Gedanke – wichtiger ist jedoch seine Erinnerung am Grab und damit das Bezeugen des Glaubens. Damit ist wieder eine wichtige thematische Entwicklung des Gedichtes durch diese Variation des Leitmotivs festgehalten: Vom verstorbenen Märtyrer, zum Trost durch Eintritt ins Paradies, bis hin zum Trost der Verbliebenen am Grab durch Bezeugen des Weiterlebens.

Diesem Wortcluster können wir erweiternd weitere Begriffe für „sehen" hinzufügen, beginnend mit *ʿāyana*, das neben *šahīdan* im Vers 25 vorkommt, und damit ein allgemeineres Qaṣīdenthema benennen, das sich nun durch das gesamte Gedicht zieht (Verse 9, 11, 13, 14, 19, 22, 23, 25, 26, 30, 31, 33, 34, 38, 40, 41,

43), wenn wir die Erwähnung der Augen in den einleitenden Versen 3 (ʿaynayhi) und 4 (ʿaynihi) hinzunehmen als Einführung dieses Leitmotivs.

Eindrucksvoll ist auch der Wandel von *in ʿazza* in Vers 2 „Wenn (die Perlenschnur/Dichtung meiner Tränen) knapp/kostbar geworden ist" im Hinblick auf die Tränen und die Poesie, zu *al-ʿazāʾ* in Vers 17, der allumfassenden Trauer bis hin zum ersten Vers des zweiten Hauptteils (Vers 20) mit *ʿazā* „es tröstet", hier in Bezug auf die mythologische Figur Khidrs und schließlich *ilayya yuʿzā* „mir verdankt man", und zwar die Dichtung.

Zeitangaben, die den ersten Hauptteil leitmotivisch markieren, werden unauffällig im 4. Vers mit *ġadāta* bereits eingeführt. Sie werden dann kontrastiv einander gegenübergestellt, zunächst den Gegensatz zwischen jetzt und damals (*maḍā – al-āna*) in Vers 7 hervorhebend, im Weiteren dann den Gegensatz zwischen hell und dunkel ausdrückend (Vers 8: *ḍuḥan - amsā* und *ar-rabīʿ - ḫarīfan*; und Verse 10 und 11: *ġadāta – al-aṣīl*), und nochmals Vers 14 mit *wasaṭa n-nahār*. Hier verbreitet sich die Dunkelheit. Im Mittelteil wird dieses Leitmotiv in Vers 22 nochmals aufgegriffen (*maḍā - wasaṭ as-samāʾ*), wobei hier die Bedeutung verändert wurde: Das Licht der Rechtleitung kann nicht verlöschen! Wieder durchzieht dieses Leitmotiv nicht das ganze Gedicht, sondern konzentriert sich im ersten Hauptteil, und dennoch wird es genutzt, um den inhaltlichen Wandel als Aussage des gesamten Gedichtes zu unterstützen. Möglicherweise können wir die Zeitangabe zu Beginn des Schlußteils *kulla ʿāmin* gedanklich damit verbinden: Die Gegensätze sind aufgelöst und Trost spendet das jährliche Ritual des Verfassens von Gedichten über den verehrten Propheten.

Eng verknüpft mit den in Kontrast gesetzten Zeitworten ist der Kontrast zwischen Hell und Dunkel, der als Qaṣīdenthema gelten mag. Er dominiert die erste Hälfte des ersten Hauptteils (Verse 8-14): Die Dunkelheit breitet sich aus, im Mittelteil in Vers 22 dann die Aussage: Die Religion ist deutlich und kann nicht erlöschen; und schließlich im zweiten Hauptteil die Szene am Grab (Verse 30-34), in der das Licht (Sternschnuppen, Blitze, Leuchten) die Dunkelheit vertreibt und schließlich im Bild der leuchtenden Blüten des schönen Gartens übergeht. Einleitung und Schlußteil sind von diesem Thema jedoch ausgeschlossen, es sei denn wir wollten die anfänglich so stark geschilderte Trauer als Dunkelheit deuten, die am Ende in den Schönheiten des Gedichtes einen hell glänzenden Trost findet.

Auch der Einsatz von Stilmitteln kann leitmotivischen Charakter haben. Besonders charakteristisch für dieses Gedicht ist der Gebrauch des Stilmittels *ṭibāq*, der kontrastiven Gegenüberstellung, die insbesondere in den Versen der Gegenüberstellung von Hell und Dunkel ihren Platz hat, aber darüberhinaus insbesondere auch die Einleitung aufwühlend durchzieht und sich auch noch über das Lob des Propheten hinaus erstreckt, und erst im Schlußteil des Gedichtes dann gar nicht mehr angewandt wird.

1 Wasser durchlassen – aufhören; 2 Perlenschnur/<u>Dichtung</u> – zerstreuen/<u>Prosatext schreiben</u>; 5 still halten – nicht still halten; 6 Schwäche – Unterlassen der Schwäche; Schwäche – Härte; 7 in der Vergangenheit – jetzt; 8 zur Mittagszeit – am Abend; Frühling – Herbst; 9 abgetrennt wurde – deutlich war (in einem Wort als *tawriyah*); 10 Banū Ḥanīfah – rechtgläubige Anhänger; 11 Sonne – Mond; (12 Schatten spenden – weinen); 13 untertauchen – auftauchen; 14 verfinstern – im Gegenteil zum Gewohnten; 18 Senken – Hügel; 19 sich verbreiten – sich entfernen; 20 zurückweisen – rufen; 22 offenbar – verschwinden; 23 das Abschneiden – näherkommen; 29 sündigen – verzeihen; 31 marschieren – kriechen; 32 Dunkelheit – Leuchten; 37 Freigebigkeit – Geiz/Knauserei/Maßlosigkeit; 39 leichte Brise – Wind, wenn er stürmt.

Am Ende ist die Trauer überwunden wie auch der Kampf gegen den Unglauben. Der Dichter tröstet sich mit dem vollendeten Ausdruck seiner Liebe zum Propheten. Im Schlußteil wird der Kontrast zwischen schwarz auf weiß durch den einzelnen Begriff *ḥawarun* benannt, was einerseits die Auflösung des Kontrastes unterstreicht, andererseits die Schönheit des Gedichtes durch die Kontraste hervorhebt.

Es sei noch hinzugefügt, daß wir zeigen konnten, wie Ibn Abī Ḥaǧalah an drei markanten Stellen in seinem Gedicht das Stilmittel der Nominalreihung anwendet: In Vers 17 läßt der Verunglückte die Religion, die Edlen und die Nachkommen verwaist zurück, in den Versen 25 und 26 wird dieses Stilmittel zur Beschreibung des Paradieses eingesetzt und dann nochmals, jetzt über drei Verse hinweg (Verse 35-37), zur Lobpreisung des Propheten.

Ibn Abī Ḥaǧalah verwendet Leitmotive, mit denen er zum Teil sehr schön den Gedankengang des Gedichtes veranschaulicht. Er konzentriert jedoch diese Leitmotive in starkem Maße auf thematische Abschnitte, so daß er die Möglichkeiten, die Ibn Nubātah in seinen Gedichten eröffnete, zumindest in diesem Gedicht nur in beschränktem Maße ästhetisch ausnutzt.

Leitmotive /Qaṣīdenthemen

	Tränen Weinen TRAUER	Meer NATUR	Poesie DICHTUNG	Zeuge SEHEN		ZEIT	HELL/ DUNKEL	*aṭ-ṭibāq*
1	أدمعي			جفني				×
2	دموعي		نظم، أنثره		عزّ			×
3	أبكي			عينيه				
4	دمعي	البحر		عينه		غداة		
5	دمعي							×
6	دمعي، دمعي							×
7				جفني		مضى، الأن		×

	Tränen Weinen TRAUER	Meer NATUR	Poesie DICHTUNG	Zeuge SEHEN		ZEIT	HELL/ DUNKEL	aṭ-ṭibāq
8						ضحىً، أمسى الربيع، خريفاً	ضحىً، أمسى الربيع، خريفاً	×
9				رأوا				×
10						غداة		×
11				بات		الأصيل	اصفرت الشمس البدر منكسفا	×
12	دمع، يبكي					دائماً	غمام، ظلّله	×
13		بحر		طفا				×
14				وجه		وسط النهار	أظلمت، النهار	×
15			حسّان يرثيه					
16			الرثاء، يرثي					
17					العزاء			
18	دموع							×
19				رأى				×
20					عزّا			×
21								
22				منتضحًا		مضى وسط السماء	الشمس	×
23				رأى			الفردوس	×
24								
25				شهيدًا عاين العين				
26				شاهد				
27							السماء	
28	البكاء							
29	واندب							×
30				الأبصار			الشهب، البرق	
31				رأيت			الليل، الظلماء	×

	Tränen Weinen TRAUER	Meer NATUR	Poesie DICHTUNG	Zeuge SEHEN		ZEIT	HELL/ DUNKEL	*aṭ-ṭibāq*
32							برقه، زهر الدجى	×
33			الطرف				حدائقه، أزهار	
34			يشاهد				روضة، جمائلها	
35								
36								
37								×
38				أبدا				
39								×
40				تبدوا				
41	الدمع			رأيت				
42			قصيدة، اللام، الألفا			كلّ عام		
43			القوافي، فأء أحرفها	طرفا				
44			العين، التاء	العين، حور				
45			الهاء، واو					
46			النظم، المدح الظرفا	يعزى				
47		بحر	نظمت، قصيدة بحر					

Anhang

Gedicht Nr. 1, ediert in *Salwat al-ḥazīn*, 149-153, hier zum Vergleich in Übersetzung wiedergegeben und in den Fußnoten mit Korrekturlesungen aus den Handschriften von *Ǧiwār al-aḫyār* und *Dafʿ an-niqmah* versehen, wobei folgende Sigla verwendet werden: Yeni Cami: YC; Laleli: L; Vollers: V; Kairo: K; *Dafʿ an-niqmah*, MS Istanbul: Dafʿ; Metrum: *ṭawīl*, Reim: *ʿā*.

   1) Ich öffnete die zweiflügelige Tür meiner Augenlider, um den Hügel des Naǧd zu tränken, wenn die Regenwolken fortziehen.[228]

---

[228] Lies إذا (so in YC, V, K und Dafʿ) anstatt إذ (so auch in L).

2) Meine Augen sind wahrhaftig großzügig mit den Tränen, wenn die Wolken des Frühregens affektiert weinen.[229]

3) Sag zu demjenigen, der mich tadeln will wegen meiner Traurigkeit: Laß ab vom Unrecht, denn das Unrecht stürzt einen ins Verderben.[230]

4) Da war ein Blitz, ähnlich meinem mageren, blassen Körper und meinem heftig zuckenden Herz und den vertränten Augen.[231]

5) Als mir in al-ʿAqiq sein Glanz erschien, trank ich einen Kelch mit Wasser verdünnten Tränenweines.[232]

6) Wundert euch nicht über den Rausch des von Sehnsucht erfüllten, wenn ihm die Abwesenheit einen randvollen Kelch von Tränen zu trinken gab.[233]

7) Als ob meine Tränen in al-ʿAqiq ein anvertrautes Gut hätten, das derjenige, dem es anvertraut war, zusammen mit dem Blut zurückgegeben hat.[234]

8) Oh Tränen, wenn ihr nicht jeden Berghang im Naǧd tränkt, laßt ihr für den Friedensschluß keinen Platz.[235]

9) Die Tränen tränken die Abhänge von al-Muḥaṣṣab, von Minā und Salʿ und Naǧd und al-Ġawir und Laʿlaʿ;[236]

10) Und der Regen macht in al-Aḫšabayn Wohnorte lebendig und er bewässert auch al-Ḥimā und al-Maʾzamayn;[237]

11) Wohnorte – der Aufgangsort ihres Glückssterns hört nicht auf am Horizont dessen, den ich liebe, ein Erscheinungsort des Geliebten/Aufgangsort des Mondes zu sein.

12) Das Festhalten dessen, den ich liebe, an der Winterreise, läßt mich die Sommer- und Frühlingsweiden lieber haben.[238]

13) Ein wohlbeschützter Ort, in dem die Taube ihren Tod nicht fürchtet und die Gazelle keinen Tag in Furcht ist;[239]

14) Und kein Jäger erschreckt den Wiedehopf dort, den der köstliche Tau mit einer juwelenbesetzten Krone bekleidet.[240]

15) Wer bringt mir zurück das Gazellenjunge in seinem wohlbeschützten Ort, mit dem ich vertraut bin, so daß es zum besten Hüter des letzten Lebensodems wird?[241]

16) Das Gazellenjunge hütet in Liebe die Verbindung mit dem, den ich liebe, seitdem es sah, daß die Weideplätze des Herzens eines von Sehnsucht Erfüllten die Bekömmlichsten und Futterreichsten sind.[242]

---

[229] Lies الغوادي (so in YC, V, K) anstatt العوادي (so auch in L).

[230] Lies للبغي anstatt للنعي.

[231] Lies مدمعا anstatt أدمعا.

[232] Lies كأسًا anstatt كان ; (V und Dafʿ haben شعاعة anstatt شعاعه).

[233] Lies فلا anstatt ولا ; lies مترعا anstatt أعدما.

[234] (V hat وديعة anstatt وداعة).

[235] Lies ثنيّة anstatt بنيّة; Dafʿ hat منيّة.

[236] (Dafʿ hat الغنق).

[237] (K hat المأزنين).

[238] Lies يحبّب anstatt تحبّب; (L hat ومربعا anstatt ومرتعا).

[239] Lies الظبي anstatt الضبّ.

[240] (Dafʿ hat الدرّ anstatt الطلّ).

[241] Lies رعا anstatt دعا am Ende des Verses.

[242] Lies في الحبّ anstatt بالحبّ; und أمرى anstatt أمرا.

17) Es übertraf das Antlitz des Mondes in der Nacht, als es vierzehn Jahre überschritt.[243]

18) Mein Entferntsein von ihm bekleidet mich mit einem Hemd aus Siechtum und das Kleid meiner Geduld zerfällt beinahe.[244]

19) Vielleicht kommt von ihm ein Krankenbesuch (ʿāʾid) zu seinem Geliebten, der eine beständige Beziehung zu der Krankheit hat, aber ohne ʿā (d.h. ʾid, gelesen yad = Wohltat)?[245]

20) Selbst wenn sie in der Nacht das Traumgesicht seiner Erscheinung von mir abwenden, wenden sie doch keineswegs die Traurigkeit und den Schmerz von mir ab.[246]

21) Mir zum Trotz ähnelt die Jugend dem Traumbild an Flüchtigkeit, denn sobald sie mich besuchte, da stand sie schon auf und verabschiedete sich.[247]

22) Die Trennung von der Jugend ist für mein Herz schwer zu ertragen. Ich tröste deswegen mein bekümmertes Herz.

23) Ach, welch ein Kummer! Die Jugend geht fort und ich schaffe es nicht, das Strömen des weißen Haars an der Schläfe abzuwehren.[248]

24) Ein Windhauch, in dem sich der Duft des Lavendels ausbreitet, unterrichtet mich in den Erzählungen über den Liebestod.[249]

25) Oh Tod, wenn du immer wieder zu ʿĀd zurückgekommen bist, so hast du ja lange auch Ṯamūd und Tubbaʿ unter den Lebendigen/den Stämmen verfolgt.[250]

26) Welchem Liebenden hast du den Geliebten nicht genommen und ließest ihn zurück über Spuren und Wohnstätten weinend?[251]

27) Du überschreitest bei uns jede Grenze/Körperstrafe und deine Lanzen richten sich gerade gegen die Leute des geraden Weges/Gesetzes.

28) Siehst du nicht, nachdem der Hāšimit, Muḥammad, fortging, Gegenden der Rechtleitung, die verwüstet wurden?

29) Es entfernten sich die Wolken, die ihn in der Mittagshitze beschatteten und ließen Wolken zurück, die die Erde mit Tränen füllen.[252]

30) Am Pilgerlauf Mekkas ist ein großes Ereignis vorbeigezogen; wenn Felsen/aṣ-Ṣafā damit beworfen werden, würden sie sich spalten.[253]

31) Das Gesicht der Sonne wurde gelb, traurig/entblößt, wie ein junges Mädchen, dem die Traurigkeit verbietet, sich zu verschleiern.[254]

---

[243] Lies محيّا anstatt محيا; L hat محبّ.

[244] (YC und L haben درعًا anstatt ذرعًا); lies الضنى anstatt الضنا.

[245] Lies بغير عا anstatt تضرّعا am Ende des Verses; (Dafʿ hat الدمع anstatt السقم).

[246] Lies والتوجّعا anstatt والجرّعا am Ende des Verses; (Dafʿ hat لكن anstatt لئن; K hat فلم anstatt فلن).

[247] Lies شبابٌ anstatt شبابًا; und lies زارني anstatt زادني.

[248] Lies الفود anstatt القلب.

[249] Lies قتل anstatt قبل; (V hat عرفا anstatt عرف); lies الخزامى anstatt الخزامي; YC hat الجوى ما; K hat الجوا ما; V hat الحواما; Dafʿ hat الحراما.

[250] Lies فطالما anstatt مظالما.

[251] (Dieser Vers fehlt in Dafʿ).

[252] (V hat الاجير anstatt الهجير).

[253] Lies يرمى anstatt يرمي.

[254] Lies الحزن anstatt الحسن; Dafʿ hat auch الحسن; (V hat تتبرعا anstatt تتبرقعا).

32) Am Abend erhält die Finsternis der Nacht durch die leuchtenden Sterne immer Rabenflügel (weiß und schwarz gefleckt), die dem Stamm am Morgen eine schlechte Nachricht bringen.[255]

33) Die Dunkelheit erneuert ihr Trauergewand und es erscheint ein mit Sternen geflicktes Hemd.[256]

34) Bei Seitenwind vollendete sich ein gewaltiges Unglück und erregte damit am Horizont einen stauberregenden, orkanartigen Wind.[257]

35) Die Leute der Ḥanīfah verließen den Islam und die gelbweißen Kamele des Irrtums bogen mit ihnen (vom rechten Weg) ab.[258]

36) Da erhob sich Abū Bakr, um seine Religion zu retten und setzte vom Haus (Frühlingslager) der Rechtleitung instand, was zerbrochen war.[259]

37) Wie vortrefflich ist doch der Glaube, der durch den Propheten Muḥammad und seine Gefährten eine uneinnehmbare Festung bleibt.[260]

38) Durch ihn wurde uns Beistand gewährt an all den Tagen, an denen der Schlachtstaub die Stelle der Wolken einnahm, als sie sich entfernten.[261]

39) Siehst du nicht, daß wir, obwohl wir stark sind, mit unseren Reitern noch kräftiger werden in allen Dimensionen?[262]

40) Wenn die von Kopf bis Fuß Gerüsteten des Unglaubens sich eines Tages zum Kriege scharen, schicken wir zu ihnen einen mit Eisenhelm Gerüsteten.

41) Wie vortrefflich sind doch die Menschen, die auf Gottes Weg kämpfen und das tragen können, was die starkgebauten, großen Pferde außer Stand setzt.[263]

42) Wie vortrefflich sind doch die Menschen, die zu Anfang der Nacht aufbrechen Richtung Garten, durch dessen Zweige sich die Religion der Rechtleitung verzweigt hat.[264]

43) Wenn die Schläfrigkeit sie auf der Nachtreise niederdrückt, kommen sie am Morgen an, sich auf dem Sattel niederbeugend und niederkniend.[265]

44) Ihre Sättel sind wie Neumonde: wieviel tragen sie doch an Vollmonden, die an den Horizonten der Reittiere aufgehen.[266]

---

[255] Lies لجنح anstatt بجنح; (V hat لشهب anstatt الجنح); lies بالشهب anstatt للشهب.

[256] Lies مرقعا anstatt مبرقعا.

[257] Lies وزعزعا anstatt ورغرغا am Ende des Vers; (YC hat أسارت anstatt أثارت); lies بها anstatt لها; (L hat ساق anstatt ساف).

[258] Lies حنيفة anstatt خيف; lies وأمست anstatt فأمست; lies عيس anstatt عبس; (L hat hier عيش; Dafʿ hat auch عبس).

[259] Lies ورمّم anstatt ورسّم; (V hat ربع anstatt زبع; Dafʿ hat تضرعا anstatt تصدّعا).

[260] (V hat ممتعا anstatt ممنعا).

[261] Lies يوم غباره anstatt حال غباوة; lies تقشّعا anstatt يقشّعا; (Dafʿ hat hier تشفعا).

[262] Lies العرض anstatt الأرض; (YC, L und V haben تزداد anstatt نزداد; L, K und Dafʿ haben أذرعا anstatt أدرعا).

[263] (L hat أعنا anstatt أعيا).

[264] (L hat أذلجوا anstatt أدلجوا).

[265] Die Lesung سنة in der Edition von *Salwat al-ḥazīn* scheint sinnvoller zu sein, auch wenn in allen Hss von *Ǧiwār al-aḫyār* نسمة steht; (YC und V haben تنتهم anstatt ثنتهم).

[266] Lies كم anstatt قد.

45) Wer bringt mir die Tage zurück, in denen ich sein Grab besuchte und bei seinen Türen demütig verweilte?[267]

46) Wenn meine Tränen paarweise über den Wangen rinnen, empfinde ich Freude, einen einzigen Geliebten zu haben.

47) Die beiden Horizonte (Ost und West) beengen mich, wegen seiner Entfernung, obwohl mein Zustand immer noch weit ist.[268]

48) Mir reicht das Lob des Ḥāšimiten, desjenigen, der der enthaltsamste und treueste der Gesandten ist und der gottesfürchtigste.

49) Versammelt ist alles Schöne in ihm und daher stimmen sie überein, daß er alle Geschöpfe zusammen übertrifft.

50) Als er beim Abtrennen seiner Aorta den Schmerz erlitt, der vom Essen des mit Gift einmarinierten Vorderfußes stammte,[269]

51) Da starb er davon als Märtyrer und kehrte ein in Schlösser und Wohnstätten des wohlbewahrten Ortes, des Gartens der Einkehr.[270]

52) Er sah mit eigenen Augen vor dem Zeitpunkt des Todes seinen Ort im Garten Edens, Ort für Ort.

53) Vor dem Tod wurde ihm die Wahl gelassen zwischen dem Tod und dem Bleiben. Da eilte er zum Rufer des Gartens der Ewigkeit.

54) Der Prophet starb, nachdem er die Welt mit seiner Freigebigkeit ausfüllte und die Religion Gottes für die Menschen als klaren Weg hinterließ.[271]

55) Wieviele leben in seiner Güte nach seinem Tod, so wie nach der Sturzflut das Wadi fruchtbar ist?[272]

56) Seine Ahnen besaßen wie Abraham Tische, die ununterbrochen großzügig waren, aus freien Stücken Wohltaten erweisend.[273]

57) Ich dichte über ihn eine gute Trauerklage wegen der Stärke meines Kummers und meine Dichtung ist ausgezeichnet, wenn sich die wunderbaren Dinge/Stilfiguren darin offen zeigen.[274]

58) Meinem Glücksvogel ist das Gurren von Gedichten zu Eigen; die in vibrierendem Ton singenden Tauben lieben es, sie zu wiederholen.

59) Wenn die Gedichte die Beschreibung von Süßem (wörtl.: Diminutiv von süß)/al-ʿUḏayb (ein Süßwasserbrunnen) enthalten, dann gefällt ihr Metrum/Salzmeer durch seine Fähigkeit, den Durst zu löschen und entzückt das Ohr.[275]

60) Wenn der Gesandte Gottes nicht wäre, wäre ihre Komposition/Perlenschnur nicht kostbarer und nicht nützlicher als die wertvollen Perlen.

---

[267] (YC hat متضلعا anstatt متضرّعا).

[268] Lies الخافقان anstatt الخافقات; (K und Dafʿ haben hier الخافقين).

[269] (L hat أبهرة anstatt أبهره und ذارع anstatt ذراع; V hat أفقعا und K hat أقفعا und Dafʿ hat منفعا anstatt منقعا).

[270] (V hat كلّ anstatt حلّ).

[271] (Dafʿ hat زعم anstatt عمّ).

[272] Lies مرتعا anstatt مربعا am Ende des Verses; (Dafʿ hat فكم من anstatt فكم).

[273] Lies وأباؤه anstatt وأياؤه.

[274] Lies الميمون anstatt المأمون; und lies تهوى anstatt يهوى.

[275] (YC, V und K haben فنحوها anstatt فبحرها).

61) Möge Gott ihn segnen, solange ein Versrezitator seine Hände nach dem Lob auf ihn im Gebet ausstreckt.

Bibliographie

Bauer, Thomas, „Islamische Totenbücher. Entwicklung einer Textgattung im Schatten al-Ġazālīs", in: S. Leder u.a. (Hg.), *Studies in Arabic and Islam. Proceedings of the 19th Congress, Union Européenne des Arabisants et Islamisants, Halle 1998*, Leuven 2002, S. 421-436.

Bauer, Thomas, „Communication and Emotion – The Case of Ibn Nubātah's Kindertotenlieder", in: *MSR* 7 (2003), S. 49-96.

Bauer, Thomas, „'Ayna hādhā min al-Mutanabbī!' Toward an Aesthetics of Mamluk Literature", in: *MSR* 17 (2013), S. 5-22.

Al-Būṣirī, *Dīwān al-Būṣirī*, ed. Muḥammad Sayyid Kilānī, Kairo 1955.

Dols, Michael W., *The Black Death in the Middle East*, Ann Arbor 1971.

Al-Ġazālī, *Iḥyāʾ ʿulūm ad-dīn*, Beirut 2005.

Gründler, Beatrice, „Ibn Abī Ḥajalah (1325-1375)", in: Joseph E. Lowry & Devin J. Stewart (Hg.): *Essays in Arabic Literary Biography: 1350-1850*, Wiesbaden 2009, S. 118-126.

Al-Ḥākim an-Nīsābūrī, *al-Mustadrak ʿalā aṣ-Ṣaḥīḥayn*, ed. Muṣṭafā ʿAbd al-Qārir ʿAṭā, Beirut 1998.

Al-Ḥassān ibn Ṯābit, *Šarḥ Dīwān Ḥassān ibn Ṯābit al-Anṣārī*, ed. ʿAbd ar-Raḥmān al-Barqūqī, Kairo o.J..

Hees, Syrinx von, *Enzyklopädie als Spiegel des Weltbildes. Qazwīnīs Wunder der Schöpfung – eine Naturkunde des 13. Jahrhunderts*, Wiesbaden 2002.

Homerin, Emil, *From Arab Poet to Muslim Saint: Ibn al-Fāriḍ, His Verse, and His Shrine*, Kairo 2001.

Homerin, Emil, „Ibn Abī Ḥaǧalah and Sufism", in diesem Band, 13-44.

Ibn Abī Ḥaǧalah, *Dafʿ an-niqmah*, MS Istanbul Laleli 1361.

Ibn Abī Ḥaǧalah, *Salwat al-ḥazīn fī mawt al-banīn*, ed. Muḫaymir Ṣāliḥ, Amman o.J..

Ibn Abī Ḥaǧalah, *Dīwān Ibn Abī Ḥaǧalah*, ed. Muǧāhid Muṣṭafā Bahǧat & Aḥmad Ḥamīd Muḫlif, Amman 2010.

Ibn Ḥaǧar al-ʿAsqalānī, *Fatḥ al-Bārī bi-šarḥ Ṣaḥīḥ al-Buḫārī*, ed. ʿAbd al-ʿAzīz ʿAbdullāh ibn Bāz, Riyad? o.J..

Ibn Hišām, *as-Sīrah an-nabawiyyah*, ed. ʿUmar ʿAbd as-Salām Tadmurī , 4 Bde., Beirut 1990.

Ibn Kaṯīr, *as-Sīrah an-nabawiyyah*, ed. Muṣṭafā ʿAbd al-Wāḥid, 4 Bde., Kairo 1964-1966.

Jacobi, Renate, *Ibn al-Fāriḍ: Der Diwan – Mystische Poesie aus dem 13. Jahrhundert*, Berlin 2012.

LeGassick, Trevor (Übers.), *The Life of the Prophet Muḥammad: Al-Sīra al-Nabawiyya, Ibn Kathīr*, 2 Bde., Reading 1989.

An-Nabhānī, Yūsuf ibn Ismāʿīl, *Al-Maǧmūʿah an-nabhāniyyah fī l-madāʾiḥ an-nabawiyyah*, 4 Bde., Beirut 1996.

al-Qurṭubī, *al-Ǧāmiʿ li-aḥkām al-qurʾān*, 20 Bde., Kairo 1967.

Rotter, Gernot (Übers.), *Ibn Isḥāq, Das Leben des Propheten*, Stuttgart 1982.

Scattolin, Giuseppe, *The Dīwān of Ibn al-Fāriḍ. Readings of its Text throughout History. A Critical Edition*, Kairo 2004.

Schimmel, Annemarie, *Und Muhammad ist Sein Prophet. Die Verehrung des Propheten in der islamischen Frömmigkeit*, 3. Aufl., München 1995.

Schimmel, Annemarie, *Calligraphy and Islamic Culture*, New York 1984.

Stetkevych, Jaroslav, *The Zephyrs of Najd. The Poetics of Nostalgia in the Classical Arabic Nasīb*, Chicago 1993.

Stetkevych, Suzanne Pinckney, *The Mantle Odes: Arabic Praise Poems to the Prophet Muḥammad*, Bloomington 2005.

Taylor, Christopher, *In the Vicinity of the Righteous. Ziyāra and the Veneration of Muslim Saints in Late Medieval Egypt*, Leiden 1999.

Wagner, Ewald, *Grundzüge der klassischen arabischen Dichtung. Band 1: Die altarabische Dichtung*, Darmstadt 1987.

Weil, Gustav, *Das Leben Mohammed's nach Muhammed Ibn Ishak bearbeitet von Abd el-Malik Ibn Hischam*, 2. Bde., Stuttgart 1864.

Winter, T.J. (Übers.), *Al-Ghazālī, The Remembrance of Death and the Afterlife, Kitāb dhikr al-mawt wa-mā baʿdahu. Book XL of the Revival of the Religious Sciences, Iḥyāʾ ʿulūm ad-dīn*, Cambridge 1989.

Der Fall Alexandrias in den Städteklagen Ibn Abī Ḥaǧalahs und seiner Zeitgenossen

Alev Masarwa

<table>
<tr><td>

Ах, покидаю я Александрию
И долго видеть ее не буду!

Увижу Кипр, дорогой Богине,

Увижу Тир, Ефес и Смирну,

Увижу Афины – мечту моей юности,

Коринф и далекую Византию,

И венец всех желаний,

Цель всех стремлений –

Увижу Рим великий! –

Все я увижу, но не тебя!

Ах, покидаю я тебя, моя радость,

И долго, долго тебя не увижу! [...]

</td><td>

Ach, ich verlasse Alexandria
Und lange werde ich es nicht mehr sehen!

Ich werde Zypern sehen, das der Göttin kostbar ist,

Ich werde Tyrus, Ephesus und Smyrna sehen,

Ich werde Athen, meinen Jugendtraum, sehen,

Korinth und das ferne Byzanz,

und die Krönung aller Wünsche,

– Das Ziel aller Bestrebungen –

Ich werde das erhabene Rom sehen!

All das werde ich sehen, dich aber nicht!

Ach, ich verlasse dich, du meine Freude,

Und werde dich lange, lange nicht sehen! […]

</td></tr>
</table>

Михаил Алексеевич Кузмин (1872-1936),
Александрийские песни: заключение (1906)

Michail Alekseevič Kuzmin (1872-1936),
Alexandrinische Gesänge: Abschluß (1906)

Die nostalgischen Verse Michail Kuzmins lesen sich fünf Jahrhunderte später wie die Rückroute der Franken, als diese im Jahre 767/1365 unter der Führung Peter Lusignans,[1] von Zypern aus, in einem verheerenden Angriff Alexandria plünderten und sich wieder zurückzogen.[2] Die Motivation Kuzmins war geprägt vom

---

*   Für die wertvollen Hinweise und Kritiken bei der Edition der arabischen Gedichte bin ich allen Mitgliedern der ALEA-Forschergruppe und insbesondere Muhammad El-Hrout sehr dankbar. Mein ganz besonderer Dank gilt Anke Osigus und Andreas Herdt, die ohne Zögern die mühevolle Arbeit des Korrekturlesens auf sich genommen haben.

1   Peter I. von Lusignan, in arabischen Quellen auch *Rubir Buṭrus Ibn Ruyūk* (Roi Pierre Peter, der Sohn König Hugos) genannt, lebte 1328-1369, reg. 1359-1369, Titularkönig von Jerusalem und König von Zypern.

2   Grundlegende Studien zu diesem Überfall liefern (für vollständige bibliographische Angaben dieser Werke siehe Literaturverzeichnis): Paul Herzsohn, *Der Überfall Alexandriens durch Peter I., König von Jerusalem und Zypern, aus einer ungedruckten arabischen Quelle mit historischen und kritischen Bemerkungen dargestellt*, Erstes Heft [mehr nicht erschienen]; Georgius J. Capitanovici, *Die Eroberung von Alexandria (Iskanderīje) durch Peter I. von Lusignan, König von Cypern 1365: mit einer Karte von Alexandrien* (mit zahlreichen Angaben zu zeitgenössischen christlichen Quellen, teilw. auch mit arabischen); Nicolae Jorga, *Philippe de Mézières, 1327-1405, et la croisade au XIVe siècle*, S. 273-327; George Hill, *A History of Cyprus II: The Frankish Period, 1192-1432*, insb.

wiedererwachten Interesse russischer Intellektueller am antiken, hellenisch-römischen Erbe zu Beginn des 20. Jahrhunderts.[3] Kuzmin ging alleine nach Alexandria und schrieb in dieser Geisteshaltung seine *Alexandrinischen Gesänge*, während Peter Lusignan, nachdem er zwei Jahre für die Wiederbelebung der Kreuzzugsidee in sämtlichen Herrscherhäusern Europas geworben hatte, mit einer riesigen Flotte kam.[4] Der großangelegte Kreuzzug entpuppte sich als ein kurzer, aber für die Mamluken überraschender und umso schmachvollerer Raubzug. Zudem wurde er in den Augen der Chronisten von einem niederen König einer Insel verübt, der die Schwächen des mamlukischen Reichs aufgezeigt hatte.[5] Die in Schutt und Asche gelegte Stadt sollte sich bis in die Zeiten Kuzmins nicht wieder erholen.[6]

S. 309-369; Steven Runciman, *A History of the Crusades*, 3 Bde., III: S. 445-449; Kenneth Setton, *A History of the Crusades*, Bd. III: The fourteenth and fifteenth Centuries, Hg. Harry Hazard Madison, S. 340-360; Peter Edbury, [u.a.] *The Kingdom of Cyprus and the Crusades 1191-1374*; Tilman Nagel, *Timur der Eroberer und die islamische Welt des späten Mittelalters*, S. 268-271; Vassilios Christides, "Cyprus between East and West. The French Kingdom of Lusignans, an appendage to the Latin Kingdom, vs. Mamluks", S. 98-105; eine neuere Diskussion zur Datierungsproblematik vorwiegend in den arabischen Hauptquellen gibt Jo van Steenbergen, "The Alexandrian Crusade (1365) and the Mamluk Sources: Reassessment of the *Kitāb al-Ilmām* of an-Nuwayrī al-Iskandarānī (d. 1372 ad)", S. 123-137. Die bislang einzige narratologische Studie zu einer der zeitgenössischen arabischen Quellen, das *Kitāb al-Ilmām* von an-Nuwayrī (siehe hierzu Herzsohn und die folgenden Ausführungen, S. 10 ff.), ist die Dissertation von Otfried Weintritt, *Formen spätmittelalterlicher islamischer Geschichtsdarstellung: Untersuchungen zu an-Nuwairī al-Iskandarānīs Kitāb al-Ilmām und verwandten zeitgenössischen Texten.*

3   Nach Wolfgang Kissel verweist der Ägypten-Diskurs russischer Literaten immer auch auf eine Chiffre, die sich auf Rußlands mögliche oder drohende Entfernung aus dem jüdisch-christlichen Geschichtskontinuum bezieht (siehe ders., „Pyramiden in Petropolis. Der ‚Petersburger Text' und das Erinnerungsbild Altägyptens", in: Ders. (Hg.), *Kultur als Übersetzung. Festschrift für Klaus Städtke zum 60. Geburtstag*, Würzburg 1999, S. 141-166, hier S. 163).

4   1362 trat Peter I. zusammen mit seinem Kanzler Philippe de Mézières und dem päpstlichen Legaten Peter Thomas eine Europareise an, um für seine Idee zu werben. Er traf mit Papst Urban V., König Johann II. von Frankreich und Kaiser Karl IV. zusammen und brachte ein großes Heer zusammen. Vor Peter I. hatte der venezianische Händler und Chronist Marino Sanudo Torsello (1270-1343) ebenfalls eifrig für einen großangelegten Kreuzzug gegen Ägypten geworben. In seiner Schrift „Liber secretorum Fidelium Crucis super Terrae Sanctae Recupertione et Conservatione" (geschr. und vielfach rev. im Zeitraum von 1306-1321), befürwortet er, vor einer großangelegten Expedition gegen das Sultanat Handelsembargos und navale Blockaden zur Schwächung der Mamluken zu verhängen. Siehe hierzu Kate Raphael, *Muslim Fortresses in the Levant: Between Crusaders and Mongols*, Routledge 2011, S.109-110 nebst Anm.; Stefan Stantchev, *Spiritual Rationality: Papal Embargo as Cultural Practice*, Oxford 2014, u.a. Kapitel 1 (und S. 151 zum Alexandria-Überfall); Christopher J. Tyerman, "Marino Sanudo Torsello and the Lost Crusade: Lobbying in the Fourteenth Century", in: *Transactions of the Royal Historical Society* 32 (1982), S. 57-73; zur Propaganda-Charakteristik dieser Schrift siehe Eliyahu Ashtor, *Levant Trade in the Middle Ages*, Princeton 1983, S. XIX und S. 23 f.

5   Vgl. Aziz Suryal Atiya, *A Fourteenth Century Encyclopedist from Alexandria: A Critical and Analytical Study of al-Nuwairy al-Iskandarāni's "Kitab al-Ilmām"*, Utah 1977, S. 35.

6   Diesen Eindruck mag man gewinnen, wenn man dem Urteil der Historiker wie Ibn Iyās Glauben schenkt, der nach seinem Bericht über den Überfall Peters I. resümiert, daß sich die Lage der Stadt seitdem verschlechtert habe (Ibn Iyās, *Badāʾiʿ aẓ-ẓuhūr* = *Die Chronik des Ibn*

Zypern kam wegen seiner strategischen Lage eine besondere Bedeutung als Ausgangspunkt für die Kreuzfahrer, Zwischenstation der Pilger, aber auch als Umschlagplatz der Waren zu. Die reiche Insel war ein Tummelplatz der Händler, Pilger und Flüchtlinge verschiedenster Sprach- und Religionsgruppen. Ein ähnliches Bild lässt sich von vielen Hafenstädten entlang der Mittelmeerküste skizzieren.[7] Alexandria war stets eine wichtige Hafen- und Handelsstadt, in der aber vor allem die Emire Geschäfte zu ihren Gunsten abschließen konnten. Allerdings war sie, obwohl sie immer eine Stätte der Bildung blieb, im Gegensatz zu Kairo nicht der Augapfel des Reichs.[8] Insbesondere zur Zeit der Mamluken wurden „in

---

Ijās, hg. von Muḥammad Muṣṭafā, Stuttgart 1974, I, 2: S. 24; dagegen entwirft Halil Ibn Šāhīn az-Ẓāhiri (geb. 813/1410) im Kapitel über Alexandria, das typische *Faḍāʾil*-Elemente enthält, das Bild einer prosperierenden und gutgeschützten Stadt, die nach dem Muster eines Schachbretts aufgebaut sei. Den Überfall Peters auf Alexandria erwähnt er nicht (siehe *Zubdat kašf al-mamālik wa-bayān aṭ-ṭuruq wa-l-masālik*, Hg. Paul Ravaisse, Paris 1894, S. 39-41; zum Autor siehe Jean Gaulmier & Toufic Fahd, "Ibn Shāhīn al-Ẓāhiri", in: *EI²*). Ausführlicher und unter Anführung zahlreicher heroischer Gedichte fällt dagegen sein Bericht über die mamlukische Wiedereroberung Zyperns im Jahre 829/1426 unter Barsbay aus (Ibn Šāhīn, *Zubdat kašf al-mamālik*, S. 136-145); zur Wiedereroberung Zyperns siehe auch Christides, „Cyprus between East and West", S. 104-105. Den Verfallsdiskurs führen moderne arabische Studien weiter, siehe z.B. das Urteil über Alexandria in Ğamāladdin aš-Šayyāl, *Tāriḫ madinat al-Iskandariyyah fī l-ʿaṣr al-islāmī*, al-Qāhirah [1386/1966], S. 116, der den Verfall der Stadt auch auf den erheblichen Rückgang der Bevölkerungszahl zurückführt. Moderne Anthologien zur Stadt Alexandria übergehen allerdings damit die gesamte Kulturgeschichte Alexandrias in islamischer Zeit, indem sie zwischen dem antikenzeitlichen und dem modernen Alexandria nur sehr wenig wiederzugeben wissen. Siehe z.B. der in Alexandria geborene Apostolos Polyzoides (*Alexandria. City of Gifts and Sorrows. From Hellenistic Civilization to Multiethnic Metropolis*, Brighton 2014), der nach dem Untergang des antiken Alexandria (vermutlich mit der islamischen Eroberung?) 1400 Jahre später ansetzt (im 8. Kapitel, ab S. 103) und mit der „Wiedergeburt" seine Stadtgeschichte weiterschreibt. Nicht ganz frei von islamischer Geschichte, dennoch recht spärlich, fallen die Anthologien von Joachim Sartorius (*Alexandria. Fata Morgana*, Stuttgart 2001) und Michael Haag (*An Alexandria Anthology. Travel Writing through the Centuries*, Cairo 2014) aus.

[7] Vgl. David Jacoby, "Western Merchants, Pilgrims, and Travelers in Alexandria in the Time of Philippe de Mézières (ca. 1327-1405)", in: Blumenfeld-Kosinski / Petkov (Hg.), *Philippe de Mézières and his Age. Piety and Politics in the Fourteenth Century*, Leiden 2012, S. 403-425, hier S. 418-422; siehe auch Wilhelm Heyd, „Die mittelalterlichen Handelscolonien der Italiener in Nordafrica von Tripolis bis Marokko", in: *Zeitschrift für die gesamte Staatswissenschaft* 20 (1864), S. 617-660.

[8] Zu den großen Namen gehören z.B. Dichter und vor allem sufische Gelehrte wie Ibn Qalāqis, Ibn Ḥaddād, Ibn ʿAṭāʾ Allāh as-Sakandari und al-Būṣiri. Zur ökonomischen und kulturellen Bedeutsamkeit Alexandrias in jener Zeit siehe Clifford Edmund Bosworth, *Historic Cities of the Islamic World*, Leiden 2007, S. 13-22; Martina Müller-Wiener, *Eine Stadtgeschichte Alexandrias von 564/1169 bis in die Mitte des 9./15. Jahrhunderts: Verwaltung und innerstädtische Organisationsformen*, Berlin 1992, S. 34. Siehe auch die große Anzahl westlicher (andalusischer und maghrebinischer) Gelehrter, die sich für ihre (*Ḥadīt*-)Studien in Alexandria niederließen im zweiten und dritten Bd. von al-Maqqari, *Nafḥ aṭ-ṭib min ġuṣn al-Andalus ar-raṭib*, Hg. ʿAbbās, Iḥsān, 8 Bde., Bayrūt 1388/1968, siehe Index zu al-Iskandariyyah. Zahlreiche Verse und Biographien alexandrinischer Literaten führt ʿImād-addin al-Kātib al-Iṣfahāni (gest. 597/1201) in seinem Werk *Ḫaridat al-qaṣr wa ġaridat al-ʿaṣr* (Hg. Muḥammad Bahğat al-Aṭari und Ğamil Saʿid et. al., 17 Bde., Baġdād 1955-1986) im zweiten Band über ägyptische Dichter (Bd. 15) an.

Ungnade gefallene Emire hierhin verbannt oder verurteilte Emire gefangengesetzt".[9] Dennoch gab es bei all der bewegten Geschichte des Mittelmeerraums in jener Zeit neben religiös-militärischen Expeditionen auch ständige Handelsvertretungen aller Mittelmeer-Autoritäten auf mamlukischem Gebiet. Von der Warenlöschung profitierten Genuesen, Venezianer, Zyprer wie auch die Mamluken.[10] Daß nicht nur Waren ausgetauscht wurden, sondern auch ein intensiver kultureller Austausch stattgefunden hat, liegt auf der Hand. So sollte gerade diese eher mißlungene Expedition einen großen literarischen Nachhall finden, der die politische Bedeutsamkeit des Überfalls um ein Vielfaches überstieg. Dies gilt für den Nachhall sowohl auf Seiten der Kreuzfahrer als auch auf Seiten der Angegriffenen.[11] Die Expedition bescherte dem mamlukenzeitlichen Alexandria – wenn auch in Form von Städteklagen – kurzfristig wieder einen Platz im Pantheon der Städtepanegyrik, den es spätestens seit der Konsolidierung des Islams im literarischen Feld eingebüßt hatte.[12] Unter diesen kommt der Elegie Ibn Abī Ḥaǧalahs (725-776/1325-1375), die im Folgenden im Kontext der Ereignisse und Schriftzeugnisse näher vorgestellt wird, eine bedeutende Rolle zu.[13]

Klagegedichte über gefallene Städte (*marāṯī l-mudun*) sind neben ihrer ästhetischen Gestaltung stets ein Indikator für die kulturelle Bedeutung einer Stadt und den politisch relevanten Herrschaftsdiskurs. Insofern wird bei der Analyse der Gedichte auf das Spannungsverhältnis von poetischer und historischer Narrative

---

[9]   Paul Kahle, „Zur Geschichte des mittelalterlichen Alexandria", in: *Der Islam* 12 (1921), S. 29-83. Über Alexandria als Verbannungsort und Alterssitz für verdiente Veteranen siehe Müller-Wiener, *Eine Stadtgeschichte Alexandrias*, S. 40, S. 107, S. 190. Weitere Beispiele für Inhaftierungen und Verbannungen der Mamluken verzeichnet Gustav Weil, *Das Chalifat unter den Bahritischen Mamlukensultanen von Ägypten*, Stuttgart 1860, IV: S. XIX, 393, 424, 490, 492, 494, 502, 518, 521.

[10] Vgl. zur Bedeutung Alexandrias für die europäischen Seemächte zur Zeit der Mamluken Georg Christ, *Trading Conflicts: Venetian Merchants and Mamluk Officials in Late Medieval Alexandria*, Leiden 2012.

[11] Zu den christlichen Quellen, die diesen Vorfall beschreiben, siehe Anhang I.

[12] Die Städtepanegyrik für Alexandria bleibt nach bisherigem Kenntnisstand relativ übersichtlich. Neben an-Nuwayrīs *Ilmām*, das einige Stadtpanegyriken enthält, sind die wichtigsten Autoren, von denen lobende und tadelnde Verse über Alexandria überliefert sind u.a. Ibn Miknasah, Ẓāfir Ibn Ḥaddād, Ibn Qalāqis, Ibn al-Ǧazzār (siehe ʿAbd al-ʿAlim al-Qabānī, *Šuʿarāʾ al-Iskandariyyah fī l-ʿuṣūr al-islāmiyyah*, s. l. [1964], insb. ab S. 35 und Muḥammad Yūsuf Ġurayb, *Ittiǧāhāt šiʿr al-hiǧāʾ fī miṣr wa-š-šām zamān az-Zankiyyīn wa-l-Ayyubiyyīn (489-648 H.)*, Mag. Univ. al-Ḫalīl 2009). Eine weitere Perspektive auf die Stadt bilden Reiseberichte maghrebinischer Reisender, die auf dem Weg nach Mekka dort gewöhnlich Station machten, siehe hierzu Ralf Elger, „Geldgier und jihâd in Alexandria", in: *Venezia. Incrocio di culture. Percezioni di viaggiatori europei e non europei a confronto*, Hg. Klaus Herbers und Felicitas Schmieder, Rom 2008, 201-224; siehe auch allgemein zur Stadtdichtung Hussein Bayyud, *Die Stadt in der arabischen Poesie, bis 1258 n. Chr.*, Berlin 1988.

[13] Diese Schriftzeugnisse sind überwiegend im *Kitāb al-Ilmām* des an-Nuwayrī enthalten (über ihn und das Werk siehe S. 318 ff. in diesem Aufsatz). Ich benutze vorwiegend das Manuskript *Berlin Wetzstein II 359* und *360* [fortan *Ms. Ilmām*, fol.] mit durchgehender Foliennummerierung. An einigen Stellen ziehe ich die Edition von Etienne Combe und Aziz Suryal Atiya (Muḥammad b. Qāsim an-Nuwayrī, *Kitāb al-ilmām*, Hyderabad 1968-1976, 7 Bde), heran. [fortan an-Nuwayrī, *KI*]

eingegangen. Beide Narrativen eignen sich die Zeit, den Stoff der Vergangenheit, gemäß eigenen Gattungs- und Gestaltungskonventionen der *Umkehrung* an. Gerade die Dichtung muß sich aber stets – zumindest in späterer europäischer Literaturkritik – den Rhetorismusvorwurf gefallen lassen, wonach die Dichtung der nachformativen Periode als allein dem Regelwerk verpflichtet gesehen wird.[14] Die Dichtung wird als epigonenhaft, starr, de-personalisiert, folglich als nicht authentisch bzw. nicht realistisch abgewertet.[15] Diese Beurteilung hat lange Zeit die literaturwissenschaftliche und vor allem -theoretische Beschäftigung mit ihr, die sie in den allgemeinen Diskurs miteinbezogen hätte, wenn nicht gehemmt, so doch erheblich gebremst. Deshalb sollen im Anschluß an die Vorstellung der Motive in den Elegien Form und Funktion dieser Texte allgemein vor dem Hintergrund der Frage nach der *Originalität* und des *Neuen in der Kunst* diskutiert werden.

Überblick über den Fall Alexandrias und die Akteure

Die Landung der Franken in Alexandria geschah im Oktober 1365 (Muḥarram 767) unter der Herrschaft des jungen Sultans al-Ašraf Šaʿbān (reg. 754-778/1363-1377). Die eigentliche Macht lag aber in den Händen des strengen Reichsverwesers Yalbuġā al-Ḥāssakī (zuweilen auch al-Ḥāṣṣakī, d. i. der Vertraute).[16] Der Statthalter in Alexandrien, Ṣalāḥaddīn Ḫalīl Ibn ʿArrām, hatte sich zu jener Zeit die Erlaubnis Yalbuġās geholt, die Pilgerfahrt antreten zu dürfen. An dessen Stelle wurde der Emir Ğanġarā (Šawwāl 766/Juni 1365 im Rang des Emirs von Zehn) eingesetzt. Dieser kümmerte sich jedoch wenig um die Angelegenheiten in der Stadt; er hatte kaum Truppen und vertrieb sich mit Naphta-Feuerspielchen die Zeit.[17]

Geleitet von dem Ehrgeiz, seinem Geschlecht im gesamten Mittelmeerraum Geltung zu verschaffen, einen neuen Orden zu gründen und vermutlich auch in Ägypten einen Kreuzfahrerstaat zu gründen, zog Peter I. von Lusignan mit Franzosen, Johannitern, Venezianern, Genuesen und allerhand Freiwilligen anderer

---

[14]   Zum Rhetorismusvorwurf und dem Authentizitätsideal des Realismus, in dem „*[d]as Authentische und der Abbau bzw. die Problematisierung der darstellenden Mittel und das Konzept der Wirklichkeit als ausschließlicher Fokus [...] ein neues Feld literarischer Reflexion ab[steckt]*", siehe ausführlich in Renate Lachmann, *Die Zerstörung der schönen Rede, rhetorische Tradition und Konzepte des Poetischen*, München 1994, Zitat: S. 287.

[15]   Hinter dieser Kritik an klassischer Dichtung scheint die Vorstellung zu stehen, daß in einem System, das nach innen hin ausgerichtet ist, irgendwann die konstruktiven Verbindungsmöglichkeiten ausgeschöpft sind.

[16]   Beide Schreibweisen mit *sīn* und *ṣād* sind möglich; die Handschrift hat stets al-Ḥās(s)akī, siehe Dozy, *Suppl. I*, 346. Über seinen Aufstieg und Fall siehe van Steenbergen, "The Amir Yalbughā al-Khāṣṣakī (d. 1366), the Qalāwūnid Sultanate, and the Cultural Matrix of Mamlūk Society: A Reassessment of Mamlūk Politics in the 1360s", in: *Journal of the American Oriental Society* 131 (2011), S. 423-443 und den Beitrag von Özkan in diesem Band.

[17]   Müller-Wiener, *Eine Stadtgeschichte Alexandrias*, S. 47 und S. 105.

Mächte gegen Alexandria.[18] Zuvor hatte Peter entlang der kleinasiatischen und syrischen Küste immer wieder Übergriffe gestartet, so daß die Mamluken derlei Angriffe von ihm gewöhnt waren.[19] Doch scheinbar wollte Peter dieses Mal die Mamluken im Kernland besiegen.[20] Alle Parteien, die an dem Kreuzzug teilnahmen,
waren entweder lange Handelspartner der Mamluken oder hatten eigene Interessen
im Kreuzzug vertreten. So musste Peter mit Verrat rechnen und gab der eigenen
Flotte, die er zunächst auf Rhodos versammeln ließ, erst auf See das Ziel Alexandria bekannt.[21] Peters Flottenstärke maß je nach Quellenangabe 70-165 Schiffe, be-
laden mit Pferden, Waffen und allerlei Prominenz.[22] Indessen müssen Informationen über die Bewegungen Peters Yalbuġā zu Ohren gekommen sein.[23] Doch in
Kairo nahm man diese Informationen nicht sehr ernst und unterschätze eventuell
auch die Größe der Flotte. Auf die gute Befestigung der Stadt vertrauend, unter-
schätzte ebenso der unerfahrene und stellvertretende Gouverneur Ǧanġarā die Lage.[24] Als Teile der fränkischen Flotte an einem Mittwoch[25] morgens vor dem Hafen

---

[18]   Machaut gibt an, daß die Flotte am Montag, den 28. September 1367 in See gestochen ist,
       rechnerisch ist dies aber ein Sonntag, vgl. Machaut, *La Prise d'Alixandre*, V. 2089-2091.

[19]   Zu den zahlreichen und relativ kurzlebigen Angriffen der Franken auf Ägypten (1165 und
       1168 Bilbays; 1167 Alexandria, 1168 Kairo, 1169, 1218-1219 Damietta u.a.) siehe Raphael,
       Muslim Fortresses in the Levant, S. 9-10. Dabei betont Raphael eine intensive militärische Auf-
       rüstung und Bautätigkeit in den Befestigungsanlagen der Wehrstädte. Trotz der zahlenmäßi-
       gen Überlegenheit der christlichen Angreifer sei es deshalb nach den Erfolgen während der
       ersten Kreuzzüge nie wieder zum längerfristigen Sieg über die Städte gekommen (*ebd.*).

[20]   Für Peter Edbury überwogen in der Motivation Peters I. die Handelsinteressen Zyperns zu
       sichern und Alexandria als Konkurrenz auszuschalten (siehe Edbury, *The Kingdom of Cyprus
       and the Crusades 1191-1374*, S. 151 f.; siehe auch Palmers Einführung zu Machaut, *La Prise
       d'Alixandre*, S. 22-23).

[21]   Peter I. war über die Verhältnisse Alexandrias durch seinen Kämmerer Perceval de Cologne
       (Coulonges), der dort als Gefangener gelebt haben soll, informiert. Nach Perceval wäre die
       Stadt zwar gut befestigt, aber wenig bewacht, vgl. Capitanovici, *Die Eroberung von Alexan-
       dria*, S. 24 nebst Anm. 2; Machaut, *La Prise d'Alixandre*, V. 1961-2081 [2034-2039: *„The city of
       Alexandria will be laid waste / Through the Old Port, / Destroyed, captured, burned, set afire, / And
       brought down; and I tell you / That this is supposed to happen on a Friday.“*]

[22]   Zu den prominenten Begleitern Peters gehörten missionseifrige Größen wie der Papstlegate
       Peter Thomas, Philippe de Mézières und Familienmitglieder aus dem Hause Lusignan. Die
       Flottenstärke variierte ebenfalls, wobei ein Großteil der arabischen Quellen „70“ oder „70
       und mehr“ angeben (vgl. vorwiegend nach arabischen Quellen Nagel, *Timur*, S. 270; Capi-
       tanovici, *Die Eroberung von Alexandria*, Excurs II (Peters Flottenstärke), S. 38 ff.). Entspre-
       chend variiert auch die Zahl der christlichen Kämpfer, siehe *Ders.*, S. 42 (12000 bei al-
       Maqrizi, 30000 bei Ibn Taġribirdī, bis zu 8000 bei Machaut, 10.000 und zusätzlich 1400
       Reiter bei Mazzerius); siehe auch Weil, *Das Chalifat*, IV: S. 511 und Ibn Šāhin (über 30.000
       Mann bei 70 und mehr Schiffen) in: Ibn Šāhin (gest. 920/1514), *Nayl al-amal fi ḏayl ad-
       duwal*, Hg. ʿUmar ʿAbd as-Salām Tadmūrī, 9 Bde, Ṣaydā 2002, I, 1: S. 374 f.

[23]   Siehe Weil, *Das Chalifat*, IV: S. 511 (nach al-Maqrizi), wonach der Governeur von Alexan-
       drien bereits Monate zuvor über die Angriffspläne informiert war und Yalbuġā seine Be-
       denken mitgeteilt habe. Siehe auch Atiya, *A Fourteenth Century Encyclopedist*, S. 25.

[24]   Über seine Unerfahrenheit als Ursache für die Katastrophe siehe Paul Kahle, „Die Kata-
       strophe des mittelalterlichen Alexandria“, in: *Melanges (Gaston) Mespero* III (1940), S. 137-
       154, hier S. 143-145 und Atiya, *A Fourteenth Century Encyclopedist*, S. 31-32; diese Unerfah-
       renheit wird ihm auch in den Elegien zur Last gelegt (*Ms. Ilmām*, fol. 166a: Vers 18 Ibn Abī

Alexandrias erschien, ließ Peter seine Leute noch nicht landen. Erst am Folgetag Donnerstag gingen sie am Westhafen (*baḥr as- silsilah*) vor Anker. Obwohl das Volk, einige Maghrebiner-Gruppen, die zu Hilfe gerufenen Beduinen und die wenigen Truppen Ğanğarās eifrig die Stadt verteidigten, gelang es den Franken, an einer unbewachten Stelle die Mauer zu erklimmen und von innen her die Tore zu verbrennen.[26] So zogen die überlegenen Franken am Freitag mordend, plündernd

---

Ḥağalahs; fol. 184b; al-Aḥmīmī: *„Doch, Ğanğarā ist der Verantwortliche (der Grund) für die Notlage"* (وَلَكِنْ جنغرا أَصْلُ الضَّرَرْ). Obwohl an-Nuwayrī Ğanğarā ebenfalls als unerfahrenen Stadtherren bezeichnet (fol. 166a: لَكِنَّ الأَمْرَ صَارَ إِلَى غَيْرِ أَهْلِهِ بِوِلاَيَةِ الأَمِيرِ جنغرا وَقِلَّةِ جُنْدِهِ وَجَهْلِهِ بِتَدْبِيرِ الأُمُورِ وَعَدَمِ مَعْرِفَتِهِ بِمَوَاقِعِ الحُرُوبِ), rehabiliert er ihn, indem er seinen kämpferischen Einsatz hevorhebt, siehe dazu Weintritt, *Formen*, S. 114-116, S. 123, S. 178 (Verse an-Nuwayrīs 101-102 darüber).
Ğanğarā habe auf die Verteidigung der Stadt vertraut und auf falschen Rat der *Ribāṭ*-Besitzer auf der Halbinsel gesetzt. Ein maghrebinischer Händler hatte ihm nahegelegt, die *Ribāṭe* außerhalb der Stadtmauern zu räumen und die Stadt innerhalb der Mauer zu verteidigen. Doch die Besitzer der *Ribāṭe* widersetzten sich diesem Plan, indem sie sagten, so an-Nuwayrī, *Ms. Ilmām*, fol. 103a: *„Ihr Maghrebiner! Ihr habt eure Stadt Ṭarāblus al-Ġarb ruiniert, als die Franken sie eingenommen haben. Wollt ihr nun die Ribāṭe der Muslime zerstören, indem die Muslime in die Stadt hineingehen? Nein, auf euch ist kein Verlaß und nichts ergibt Sinn, außer daß man sie (die Franken) daran hindert von ihren Schiffen herunterzukommen damit wir ihnen mit den Pfeilen die ewigen (Höllen-)Leiden kosten lassen.* [Fol. 103b:] Die Antwort Ğanğarās an ʿAbd-allāh, den obengenannten Händler war: *„Ich werde keinem Franken erlauben, daß er an Land geht, selbst wenn mir die Halsschlagader aufgeschnitten wird und die Kämpfer (zugrunde) gehen".* Ja, wenn Gott seinem Diener wohlgesonnen ist, dann schenkt er ihm die richtige Eingebung, Vorsichtsmaß-nahmen zu ergreifen, und wenn er ihn verlässt, so verzweigt sich sich sein Verstand." Mit dem letzten Satz (وَإِذَا أَرَادَ اللهُ أَنْ يَلْطُفَ بِعَبْدِهِ أَلْهَمَهُ حُسْنَ التَّدْبِيرِ وَإِذَا أَخْذَلَهُ شَتَّتَ رَأَيَهُ) formuliert an-Nuwayrī die Verse 33 und 34 aus aš-Šāṭibīs Elegie um und bezieht sie auf Ğanğarās Versagen.

25   Das *Ilmām* gibt relativ konsequent folgende Daten an: am Mittwoch, 20. Muḥarram (rechne-risch ein Dienstag, 7. Oktober) werden erste Schiffe gesichtet und für venezianische Handels-schiffe gehalten, am Donnerstag, 21. Muḥarram (rechnerisch ein Mittwoch, 8. Oktober) steht die gesamte Flotte vor Alexandria und es finden kleinere Scharmützel am Hafen statt, am Freitag, dem 22. Muḥarram (rechnerisch ein Donnerstag, 9. Oktober) wird die Stadt einge-nommen. Wie Capitanovici (*Die Eroberung von Alexandria*, S. 44) und van Steenbergen ("The Alexandrian Crusade", insb. ab S. 129 ff.) herausstellen, kollidieren diese Daten mit dem er-rechneten Datum wie auch mit den Datumsangaben in den Chroniken. Nach Machaut (*La Prise d'Alixandre*, V. 2089-2091) war Peters Flotte am Montag den 28. September 1367 in See gestochen, rechnerisch ist dies aber ein Sonntag. Am Donnerstag morgen um neun Uhr kam er an und wartete, bis der größere Teil seiner Flotte am Donnerstag abend vor den alten Ha-fen kam und erst am nächsten Morgen gelang es ihnen, die muslimische Verteidigung zu überwinden und an Land zu gehen. Die Kampfhandlungen dauerten bis Sonntag, als sich die Franken mit ihrem Beutegut auf ihre Schiffe zurückzogen. (V. 2191-2195). Nach *Philippe de Mézières* geschah die Ankunft Peters in Alexandria am Donnerstag, den 9. Oktober, allerdings zur sechsten Stunde. Die Übernahme der Stadt erfolgte am Freitag, den 10. Oktober in der neuten Stunde (siehe Zitat in Capitanovici, *Die Eroberung von Alexandria*, S. 33 f.); vgl. Jorga, *Philippe de Mézières 1327-1405*, S. 286 nebst. Anm., dagegen übersetzt Angel Nicolaou-Konnari „quasi hora nona" korrekter mit „ca. 15 Uhr", in: "Apologist or Critics? The Reign of Peter I of Lusignan (1359-1369) Viewed by Philippe de Méziéres (1327-1405) and Leontios Makhairas (ca. 1360/80-after 1432)", in: Blumenfeld-Kosinski / Petkov (Hg.), *Philippe de Mézières and his Age*, Leiden 2012, S. 359-401, hier S. 392.

26   Über die Schwachstelle der Befestigungsanlage in Machaut, *La Prise d'Alixandre*, V. 2780 ff., nebst Kommentar, S. 441; vgl. Capitanovici, *Die Eroberung von Alexandria*, S. 6 und Atiya, *A Fourteenth Century Encyclopedist*, S. 32-33. Die Bogenschützen konzentrierten sich auf den *bāb*

und brandschatzend durch die Stadt. Die schwerbewaffneten Franken waren allein durch ihre Rüstungen überlegen. Und die Muslime waren, so an-Nuwayrī, wie „rohes Fleisch auf dem Hackbrett".[27] Als die Alexandriner sahen, daß ihre Lage hoffnungslos war, drängten sie mit ihren schnell ergriffenen Habseligkeiten zu den Landtoren. Bei der massenhaften Panik verloren jedoch viele ihr Leben. Dabei nutzten einige Beduinenstämme die Gunst der Stunde und plünderten ebenfalls, was in Ibn Abī Ḥaǧalahs Elegie thematisiert wird.[28] Der Emir Ǧanǧarā, im Kampf schwer verwundet, konnte noch Einiges aus der Schatzkammer sichern, bevor er sich mit christlichen Händlern als Geiseln aus der Stadt herausrettete.[29] Die Franken erreichten das *Bāb as-Sidrah* an der südlichen Mauer und richteten darauf ihre Kreuze auf. Am Donnerstag, dem 28. (rechnerisch ein Mittwoch) segelten sie mit dem Beutegut der reichen Stadt und 5000 Gefangenen ab.[30] Von der ursprünglichen Kreuzzugsidee war außer den aufgestellten Kreuzen und der zerstörten Stadt kaum etwas übriggeblieben.

Ob die Franken an einem Mittwoch, Donnerstag oder Freitag[31] zuerst landeten und wie lange die Brandschatzung letztlich dauerte, wird in den Chroniken

---

al-aḫḍar, waren aber nicht im Stande, den *bāb al-baḥr* und *bāb al-ǧumruk* zu erreichen, weil Ibn Ǧurab die Tore von innen versperren ließ. Hier konnten die Franken dann die Leitern aufrichten, ohne daß sie unter Beschuß der Bogenschützen kamen; siehe an-Nuwayrī, *KI*, II: 157/ *Ms. Ilmām*, fol. 109b über das Tor und die Bestrafung des Emirs Ibn Ǧurab durch Ibn ʿArrām für die Schließung des Tores (ders., S. 158); Atiya, *The Crusade in the Later Middle Ages*, London 1938, S. 358-60 und Kahle, „Katastrophe", S. 144-146.

27 An-Nuwayrī führt diesen Gedanken erst in Prosa und dann in Versform aus und greift denselben Motiven in den Elegien al-Aḥmimis und an-Nastarāwis vor (*Ms. Ilmām*, fol. 104a):

[...] كَلَحْمٍ عَلَى وَضَمٍ، فَكَيْفَ يُقَاتِلُ اللَّحْمُ الحَدِيدَ، وَكَيْفَ يَبْرُزُ العَارِي لِمَنْ كَسَى الزَّرَدَ النَّضِيدَ [...].

„[Die Muslime waren] wie Fleisch auf einem Hackbrett, wie könnte Fleisch gegen Eisen kämpfen, und wie könnte ein Nackter vor jemanden treten, der mit geschichtetem Panzer bekleidet ist?"

28 Vgl. u.a. *Ms. Ilmām*, fol. 132b. Zum Gedicht siehe Anhang. Die Beduinen plünderten nachts, während sich die Franken auf ihre Schiffe zurückzogen und als die Muslime vor den Franken aus der Stadt flohen; siehe Atiya, *A Fourteenth Century Encyclopedist*, S. 33 und Capitanovici, *Die Eroberung von Alexandria*, S. 27 und S. 29.

29 *Ms. Ilmām*, fol. 105b (Ǧanǧarā flieht mit den fränkischen Geiseln in Richtung Damanhūr); vgl. auch Kahle, „Katastrophe", S. 147.

30 Zum Beutegut siehe *Ms. Ilmām*, fol. 108b-110b; vgl. Kahle, „Katastrophe", S. 148 ff., Atiya, *A Fourteenth Century Encyclopedist*, S. 34 f. Das gut bestückte Arsenal (*qaṣr as-silāḥ*) wurde nicht geplündert, vermutlich weil die Franken seinen Standort nicht kannten, siehe hierzu Kahle nach an-Nuwayrī, „Katastrophe", S. 153.

31 Zur Landung der Franken siehe Anm. 25. Zu den abweichenden Daten in den christlichen und arabischen Quellen siehe Capitanovici mit einer plausiblen Erklärung in *Die Eroberung von Alexandria*, S. 26, S. 32-37, nebst Anm.; mehrheitlich zu den arabischen Quellen siehe van Steenbergen, "The Alexandrian Crusade".
An-Nuwayrīs Narrative konzentriert sich auf die Nennung der Wochentage in der Abfolge Mittwoch, Donnerstag und Freitag – diese Abfolge der Wochentage ist den Datumsangaben stets vorzuziehen –, wobei sich am Freitag der „offizielle" Fall (*waqʿah*) der Stadt ereignet. Der Raubzug durch die Stadt dauerte nach seinen Angaben von Freitag bis Sonntag an und erst am darauffolgenden Donnerstag kamen die Hilfsregimenter mit Yalbuġā an der Spitze in Alexandria an. Er scheint nachdrücklich diese Narrative untermauern zu wollen und streut hier und dort kleinere Sequenzen ein, die seine Narrative über mögliche

(arabischen und „christlichen") unterschiedlich überliefert.[32] Relativ einheitlich wird überliefert, daß Yalbuġā letztlich viel zu spät mit seinen Truppen zu Hilfe kam, die Franken mit reicher Beute und vielen Gefangenen (gleichermaßen Christen, Muslimen und Juden) die Flucht ergriffen, ohne daß es zu größeren Auseinandersetzungen mit den Mamluken kam. Die besondere Hervorhebung der Flucht der Franken in muslimischen Chroniken und Gedichten fungiert hier als ein Topos, die Enttäuschung über die späte Hilfe aus Kairo zu kompensieren und die Schmach auszugleichen.[33]

In Folge dieses für die Mamluken schmachvollen Angriffs wurde der Bau einer größeren Flotte gegen die Zyprioten begonnen.[34] Gegen den Willen einiger Gelehrter wurde zugleich die ansässige christliche Bevölkerung finanziell bestraft. Sie sollten für den Freikauf der muslimischen Gefangenen und die Instandsetzung der Befestigungsanlagen der Stadt zahlen.[35]

Zweifel erhaben scheinen lassen. Siehe z.B. *Ms. Ilmām*, fol. 27a, 110a: zur Gesamtdauer ab Donnerstag gerechnet mit acht Tagen bis 28. Muḥarram; die Freitagsangaben: fol. 97b, 101b, 102b, 103b, 107b, 188b; Digressionen zum Freitagsthema: fol. 36b: Todestag aš-Šāfiʿis; fol. 97b: Märtyrerstatus, desjenigen, der an einem Freitag im Gotteseifer stirbt; fol. 168b: über den Vorzug, den Grenzdienst zu leisten und am Freitag das Schwert zu heben; fol. 219a: Einzug Ṣalāḥaddins in Jerusalem an einem Freitag; fol. 245a: himmlische Versammlung am *sūq al-muʾminīn* wie die Freitagsgebete. Donnerstagsangaben: fol. 102a: fränkische Flotte vor Alexandria, 102b: Nacht zu Donnerstag und der Tag, 110a: Gesamtdauer von Donnerstag bis Donnerstag (rechn. Mittwoch); Komplementäres zum Donnerstagsthema: fol. 110b: anonyme Verse über die Geiselnahme: „*Sie wurden von den Gefährten der Vielgötterei und des Unglaubens gefangen genommen, / die an einem Donnerstag zu den Einheitsgläubigen (Monotheisten) gekommen waren.*" (Vers 2 v. 3); fol. 188b: aš-Šāṭibis zweites Gedicht, 3. Vers: فِي خَمِيسٍ وَافَى لَنَا بِخَمِيسٍ / وَإِلَى الْجُمُعَةِ التَقَى الجَمْعَانِ „*An einem Donnerstag kam zu uns ein (fünfteiliges) Heer und bis zum Freitag trafen beide Truppen zusammen*"; fol. 214b: Abschnitt über gesegnete Monate, darunter der Muḥarram.

32 Die Abfahrt der Franken geschah nach an-Nuwayrī (*Ms. Ilmām*, fol. 110a) am 28. Muḥarram 767 (16. Oktober 1365). Der Wochentag soll ein Donnerstag gewesen sein, wobei aber rechnerisch der 29. Muḥarram ein Donnerstag war. Vgl. auch Capitanovici mit divergierenden Angaben in: *Die Eroberung von Alexandria* S. 29, S. 34-37.

33 Vgl. ʿImādaddin Ibn Katīr (gest. 774/1372) in einem kurzen Abschnitt über Alexandria in seinem „Kitāb al-iğtihād fī ṭalab al-ğihād", in: *Arbaʿa kutub fī-l-ğihād min ʿaṣr al-ḥurūb aṣ-ṣālibiyyah*, Hg. Suhayl Zakkār, Dimašq 2007, S. 424: „*Und als der elende Verfluchte realisierte, daß der Sultan sich näherte, ergriff er die Flucht, wie der Teufel, wenn er den Gebetsruf hört*". In der Reimchronik Machauts hingegen wird erzählt, daß Peter Lusignan seine Leute nicht dazu bewegen konnte, die Stadt zu halten. Als eine Gruppe nach der anderen sich zurückzog, sagte er verbittert: „*[...] Honor, now you lie dead! / Surely we've forfeited you for good; / We'll never regain you – well we know it.*" (Guillaume de Machaut, *La Prise d'Alixandre* (The taking of Alexandria), hg. und übersetzt von Barton Palmer, London 2002, V. 3582-3584).

34 Weil, *Das Chalifat*, IV: S. 513 nach al-Maqrīzī, innerhalb kurzer Zeit wurde eine Flotte von 100 Schiffen bereitgestellt. Zu den Maßnahmen Yalbuġās siehe auch Weintritt, *Formen*, S. 64-66 und S. 115 f.

35 Die kollektive Bestrafung der eigenen Christen wurde durch die Gelehrten kritisiert, zudem waren ansässige Christen und Juden, wie auch katalanische, genuesische, venezianische Handelsvertreter vor Ort ebenfalls Opfer des Überfalls. Ibn Katīr hatte sich, trotz seiner heftigen Kritik am fränkischen Überfall, energisch gegen diese Maßnahme (gegenüber den ansässigen Christen) ausgesprochen und seine Ansichten dem Gouverneur in Damaskus dargelegt. Siehe ʿImādaddin Ibn Katīr, *al-Bidāyah wa-n-nihāyah (701 H.-767 H.)*, Hg.

Obwohl Peter nach der Alexandria-Expedition weitere vergebliche Angriffe gegen mamlukisches Territorium unternahm,[36] waren größere Auseinandersetzungen vor allem durch geschickte handelspolitische Abkommen der Venezianer verhindert worden.[37] Sowohl Yalbuġā als auch Peter waren unnachgiebig und wandten abwechselnd allerlei hinterhältige und taktische Manöver an, um der Gegenseite die eigene Macht zu demonstrieren. Schließich waren es nicht die Feinde, sondern die Leute aus den eigenen Reihen, die der strengen und unbarmherzigen Politik Yalbuġās als auch Peters I.[38] ein Ende setzten.[39] Entgegen

---

Marwah, Ḥasan Ismāʿil, Dimašq 1431/2010, XVI: S. 460-462 (mit einer kurzen Episode über den Überfall auf Alexandria: hier Mittwoch, den 22. Muḥarram 767 H. (rechn. Donnerstag, 9. Oktober 1365)); vgl. auch sein „Kitāb al-iġtihād fi ṭalab al-ǧihād", wie Anm. 33; siehe zu den Maßnahmen der Mamluken Atiya, *A Fourteenth Century Encyclopedist*, S. 34; ders., *The Crusade in the Later Middle Ages*, S. 323, S. 365, S. 377; vgl. die Geschichte einer betroffenen Koptin (an-Nuwayrī, *KI*, IV: 286 f., *Ms. Ilmām*, fol. 359b); Machaut, *La Prise d'Alixandre*, (V. 3800-3945) über die Verhandlungen der Franken mit dem Sultan; Capitanovici, *Die Eroberung von Alexandria*, S. 31; Runciman, *A History of the Crusades*, III: S. 446-448 und van Steenbergen, "The Amir Yalbughā al-Khāṣṣakī (d. 1366)", S. 428 (nach Ibn Ḥaǧar al-ʿAsqalānī).

[36] Atiya, *A Fourteenth Century Encyclopedist*, S. 35 (gegen Tripolis, Tartus und Latakiya 1366 und zwei Mal im Jahre 1367).

[37] Capitanovici, *Die Eroberung von Alexandria*, S. 31; siehe auch Weil, *Das Chalifat*, IV: S. 512 nebst Anm. 2 nach al-Maqrīzī, wonach genuesische und venezianische Händler mit der Übergabe von muslimischen Gefangenen ihr Bedauern über den Vorfall ausdrückten. Die Venezianer waren besonders bemüht, die Handelsbeziehungen wieder zu normalisieren. Sie boykottieren den Handel mit Zypern für Waffen und Pferde und schickten Falken als Geschenk an Yalbuġā (Hill, *A History of Cyprus*, S. 342). Nachdem der Papst seine Machtlosigkeit gegenüber den Venezianern einsah, riet er Peter zu Friendensverhandlungen. Die Ernshaftigkeit der Friedensverhandlungen zwischen Peter und Yalbuġā scheinen jedoch unglaubwürdig, da sie sich in die Länge ziehen (vgl. Hill, *ebd.*, S. 339-348; Weil, *Das Chalifat*, IV: S. 514, Anm. 5 nach Ibn Qāḍī Šuhbah); über die Beziehungen Peters zu Venedig und Genua siehe Edbury, *The Kingdom of Cyprus and the Crusades 1191-1374*, S. 154-155 nebst Anm. Zu den mamlukisch-zypriotischen Beziehungen nach Peter I., siehe Edbury, *ebd.*, S. 166-179; Atiya, *A Fourteenth Century Encyclopedist*, S. 36. Zu den intensiven Beziehungen der Venezianer und Genuesen zu den Mamluken im folgenden Jahrhundert nach dem Überfall, siehe Ashtor, *Levant Trade in the Middle Ages*, und Tyerman, *"Marino Sanudo Torsello and the Lost Crusade"*, wie in Anm. 4.

[38] Die Ermordung Peters I. haben seine beiden Brüder, die ebenfalls Teilnehmer des Alexandria-Kreuzzugs waren, mitangesehen, weshalb Machaut und Froissart sie der Komplizenschaft bezichtigen. Zur Ermordung Peters I., siehe Edbury, *The Kingdom Cyprus and the Crusades 1191-1374*, S. 174 und ders., "The murder of King Peter I of Cyprus (1359-1369)", S. 219-233, in: *Journal of Medieval History* 6 (1980), S. 219-233 hier S. 224-5, S. 231 Anm. 5; Jorga, *Philippe de Mézières*, S. 394, Anm. 5., siehe auch Palmers Einführung zu Machaut, *La Prise d'Alixandre*, S. 19.

[39] Yalbuġā starb am 14. Dezember 1366 (10. Rabīʿ II. 768). Er wurde enthauptet und sein Kopf in Gegenwart des Sultans, der sich an die Spitze der rebellierenden Mamluken gestellt hatte, auf eine brennende Fackel gesteckt; siehe van Steenbergen, "The Amir Yalbughā al-Khāṣṣakī (d. 1366)", hier S. 426 (nach Ibn Taġrībirdī) und Herzsohn, *Der Überfall Alexandriens*, S. 43. Zum Tode Peters I. im Januar 1369 siehe Edbury, "The murder of King Peter I of Cyprus (1359-1369)". Im *Ms. Ilmām* werden die Todesnachrichten beider Regenten recht nüchtern und beiläufig beschrieben: fol. 236a zum Tode Yalbuġās durch seine eigenen Ǧulbān-Schergen und jeweils fol. 89b (siehe Weintritt, *Formen*, S. 57) und fol.

Peters unzufriedenen Untertanen ist Geoffrey Chaucer (ca. 1343-1400) in seinen *Canterbury Tales* dem König milder gestimmt. Aus dem Munde eines Mönches im Abschnitt über das Schicksal berühmter Männer wird Peters – dem Ritterideal entsprechender – heroischer Aufstieg und sein Fall, wie folgt erzählt:[40]

De Petro Rege de Cipro   [Concerning Pierre de Lusignan, King of Cyprus]

2391	O worthy Petro, kyng of Cipre, also,	[O worthy Pierre, king of Cyprus, also,]
2392	That Alisandre wan by heigh maistrie,	[Who won Alexandria by great strength,]
2393	Ful many an hethen wroghtestow ful wo,	[To very many a heathen thou wroughtest great woe,]
2394	Of which thyne owene liges hadde envie,	[Of which thine own lieges had envy,]
2395	And for no thyng but for thy chivalrie	[And for no thing but for thy chivalry]
2396	They in thy bed han slayn thee by the morwe.	[They in thy bed have slain thee in the morning.]
2397	Thus kan Fortune hir wheel governe and gye,	[Thus can Fortune govern and guide her wheel,]
2398	And out of joye brynge men to sorwe.	[And out of joy bring men to sorrow.]

169b f. zur eigentümlich verschachtelten Todesnachricht Peters I., die an-Nuwayrī im Anschluß an sein Beschwörungsgedicht gegen Peter und mit der Notiz anführt, daß im Šawwāl 772/April 1371 die Nachricht in Alexandria ankam, Peter sei durch seinen Bruder al-Brinz (Jean de Lusignan) getötet worden, gleichsam als hätte sich sein Wunsch erfüllt (*al-faʾl muwakkalun bi-l-manṭiq*).

[40] Geoffrey Chaucer, *The Canterbury Tales*, Fragment VII: The Monk's Prologue and Tale. An Interlinear Translation URL: [https://sites.fas.harvard.edu/~chaucer/teachslf/mkt-par.htm]. Wie sehr die Ritterideale in den *Canterbury Tales* mit der Person Peters I. verbunden sind, arbeitet Celia M. Lewis ("History, Mission, and Crusade in the "Canterbury Tales", in: *The Chaucer Review* 42 (2008), S. 353-382) heraus. Ein ähnlich pathetisches Bild über die Tugenden Peters I. gibt Jean Froissart (ca. 1337-1405) wieder: "*And if the noble king of Cyprus, Pierre de Lusignan, a courageous and enterprising man who conquered the great city of Alexandria, and Antalya, had lived longer, he would have given the sultan and the Turks so much to do that they would not have had as much to occupy them since the time of Godefroy de Bouillon.*" (fol. 252 v in Buch III. der Online-Ausgabe, nach Ms. Besançon 865). So sind für Jean Froissart auch die Motive für die Ermordung klar: "*The Turks and Tatars and infidels were well aware of his prowess and enterprise, and that is why in order to bring about his downfall they bargained with his brother Jacques to have him assassinated, and so he had the noble king, his brother, killed before his eyes, even while he slept. It was truly a despicable and coldblooded thing to murder such a valiant man as the king of Cyprus who, day and night, thought of nothing else besides a means of liberating the Holy Land and prising it from the hands of the infidels [...].*" (ebd., fol. 253 r). [Peter Ainsworth and Godfried Croenen / URL: http://www.hrionline.ac.uk/onlinefroissart/index.jsp].

Poetischer Niederschlag dieses Ereignisses in arabischen Quellen

Insgesamt finden sich sechs umfangreichere Elegien auf den Überfall Alexandrias.[41] Sie sind in einer einzigen Schrift verzeichnet, die unter die Kategorie ‚der thematischen Kommentaranthologie' zum Oberthema Alexandria fällt.[42] Es handelt sich um das Werk *Kitāb al-Ilmām bi-l-iʿlām fī-mā ġarat bihī l-aḥkām wa-l-umūr al-maqḍiyyah fī waqʿat al-Iskandariyyah* (Das Buch des vollständigen Berichts über das, was die göttlichen Beschlüsse und die Vorherbestimmungen bei dem Vorfall von Alexandrien herangeführt haben) des Muḥammad b. Qāsim an-Nuwayrī (gest. nach 777/1375).[43] Mit Ausnahme von Ibn Abī Ḥaǧalah, dessen Gedicht in dieser Schrift eine zentrale Rolle einnimmt, scheinen die anderen Dichter Augenzeugen des Vorfalls gewesen zu sein. Die hohe Anzahl poetischer Manifestationen des Unglücks, das Alexandria befiel, verweist nicht unbedingt auf die historische Bedeutung des eigentlich ephemeren Ereignisses, wie Weintritt schreibt.[44] Doch mit einem Mal ist Alexandria Gegenstand der Poetik und kann sich mit Elegien auf Bagdad, Damaskus oder al-Andalus messen lassen.

An-Nuwayrī ließ sich 737/1337 als Grenzwächter und Kopist in Alexandria nieder und schrieb sein Werk in einem Zeitraum von acht Jahren, von März 1366 bis Juni 1374.[45] Er war Augenzeuge bei dem Überfall auf Alexandria, floh einige

---

[41] In der Druckausgabe an-Nuwayrī, *KI*, II: S. 211-219 (an-Nuwayrīs eigene Elegie); III: S. 217-221, 221-222 (aš-Šāṭibī mit zwei Gedichten); III: S. 223-230 (al-Aḥmimī, vorher ein Auszug ohne Nennung des Namens), IV: S. 171-178 (an-Nastarāwī); Ibn Abī Ḥaǧalahs *ritāʾ* erstreckt sich über die Bände II und III (Bd. II Vers 1: 229, 2: 230, 3: 254, 4: 256, 5: 269, 6: 270, 7: 279, 8: 272, 9: 274, 10: 335, 11: 336, 12: 340, 13: 341, 14: 342, 15: 346, 16: 348, Bd. III Vers 17: 1, 18: 64, 19: 68, 20: 88, 21: 88, 22: 174, 23: 202, 24: 208). – Kurz vor Drucklegung machte mich Nefeli Papoutsakis freundlicherweise auf eine *Qaṣīde* über den Vorfall in Alexandria aufmerksam. Eine detaillierte Analyse kann an dieser Stelle nicht mehr erfolgen, daher beschränke ich mich auf die wichtigsten Angaben: Der Verfasser ist Nūr ad-Din al-ʿAsqalānī (Vater Ibn Ḥaǧars), dessen Vater Tuchhändler in Alexandria war. Es handelt sich wohl um ein längeres Gedicht (ebenfalls eine *rāʾiyya*, Versmaß *ramal*), aus dem as-Saḫāwī 19 Verse im Zusammenhang mit Ibn Abī Ḥaǧalah wiedergibt. Al-ʿAsqalānī integriert in drei aufeinanderfolgenden Versen die Jahreszahl (767 H.) und das Datum (23. Muḥarram) mit dem Wochentag Freitag, was eher der Narrative al-Maqrīzis zur Datierung des Vorfalls entspricht. Siehe Šamsaddin as-Saḫāwī, *al-Ǧawāhir wa-d-durar fī tarǧamat šayḫ al-islām Ibn Ḥaǧar*, ed. Ibrāhīm Bāǧis ʿAbd al-Maǧīd, Bayrūt 1999, I: S. 112-113.

[42] Siehe Thomas Bauer, „Literarische Anthologien der Mamlukenzeit", in: Stephan Conermann, u.a. (Hg.), *Die Mamluken. Studien zu ihrer Geschichte und Kultur. Zum Gedenken an Ulrich Haarmann (1942-1999)*, Hamburg 2003, S. 71-122, hier S. 76-78.

[43] Zu den Manuskripten und Lebensdaten siehe Wilhelm Ahlwardt, *Verzeichnis*, Bd. 21, No: 9815 (Wetzstein II 359 und 360); *GAL* II: 35, S II: 34, siehe auch Clifford E. Bosworth, "al-Nuwayrī", in: *EI²*; Herzsohn, *Der Überfall Alexandriens*; Atiya, *A Fourteenth Century Encyclopedist*, S. 6-7, S. 9-12.

[44] Weintritt, *Formen*, S. 169.

[45] *Ms. Ilmām*, fol. 120b (Übers. von Herzsohn, *Der Überfall Alexandriens*, S. XIII f.): *Ich gewann dieselbe damals lieb, nahm sie als Wohnort und verfaßte dieses Buch in ihr. Im Ǧumāda ʾl-āḫir des Jahres 767 (Febr./März 1366) begann ich es und im Dhu ʾl-Ḥiǧǧa 775 (Mai/Juni 1374) brachte ich es zu Ende. Ein fernerer Grund, daß ich sie als Wohnort wählte, war das Verlangen, Grenzwachdienst in ihr zu thun, in Gemäßheit des Ausspruchs von ʿAbd Allāh Ibn ʿOmar, ‚Geboten ist der hei-*

Tage aus der Stadt und kehrte wieder zurück, als die Leichen begraben waren. Sein *Kitāb al-Ilmām* gehört neben Ibn Baṭṭūṭahs *Riḥlah* vielleicht zu den eindrucksvollsten Zeugnissen der arabischen Erzählliteratur des 14. Jahrhunderts. Außer in der umfangreichen und im Schwerpunkt narratologischen Untersuchung Otfried Weitritts war das Werk bislang häufiger nur in Auszügen Gegenstand historischer Forschung für die Rekonstruktion der Ereignisse. Das narratologisch äußerst spannende Textmodell in der vornehmlich beliebig scheinenden Verkettung von Faktualem und Fiktionalem, der ständigen Desorientierung des Lesers durch Digressionstaktiken und Brechungen des Erzählflusses, bremst freilich den unmittelbaren Auswertungsdrang des Historikers.[46] Aus dem Blickwinkel der Historiker fällt die Würdigung des Gesamttextes entsprechend negativ aus: Der Text wäre unsystematisch, labyrinthaft, die einzelnen Sequenzen bizarr aneinandergereiht.[47] Solange der Text einen – nach modernen Maßstäben – Quellenwert für Historiker hatte, war er nützlich und wichtig, ansonsten wurde er wenig beachtet. Entsprechend sind von Historikern die Gedichte meist großzügig

---

lige Krieg, um das Blut der Götzendiener zu vergießen, und die Grenzbewachung, um das Blut der Muslime zu schonen, aber lieber ist mir, das Blut der Muslime zu schonen, als das Blut der Götzendiener zu vergießen'.

[46] Z.B. durch die Einbettung fingierter Dialoge und historischer Dokumente (wie Briefe und Dekrete, z.B. *KI*, IV: S. 146-154), die teilweise einzigartig sind, so Atiya (*A Fourteenth Century Encyclopedist*, S. 25), sowie durch eine in jener Zeit beispiellose Anwendung der digressiven Erzählstrategie (arab.: *istiṭrād* siehe Weintritt, *Formen*, u.a. S. 87-101). Zu Recht verweist Weintritt darauf, daß die Digression ein literarästhetisches Phänomen berührt. Er bezeichnet diese Textstrategie wegen ihrer Systematik im *Ilmām* als ,konzeptionalisierte Digression': *„Da es sich jeweils um Einzelstücke historischer Mitteilung handelt, kann istiṭrād nicht als Abschweifung im Sinne einer Unterbrechung der durchgängigen Narratio verstanden werden, die als willkürliches und unkontrolliertes Zufalls- und Nebenprodukt der Textentstehung zu deuten wäre.“* (*Ebd.*, S. 87 f.). Zum *istiṭrād* im Kontext der Dichtungstheorie siehe insb. Geert Jan van Gelder, *Beyond the Line: Classical Arabic Literary Critics on the Coherence and Unity of the Poem*, Leiden 1997, S. 35 f., darüber hinaus S. 87, 118, 206 und Pierre Cachia, *The Arch Rhetorician or the Schemer's Skimmer: A Handbook of Late badīʿ drawn from ʿAbd al-Ġanī an-Nābulsī's Nafaḥāt al-Azhār ʿalā Nasamāt al-Ashār*, Wiesbaden 1998, No: 144.

[47] Vgl. das Urteil Atiyas zur narrativen Technik: *"His approach to his subject was not direct and straightforward, but rather in the form of a commentary on an elegy on the fate of Alexandria by an obscure contemporary poet, namely ibn Abi Hajalah. So we find the story of the details of that crusade embedded into that commentary. To make things worse, he must have decided to use the tremendous crop of his manuscript excerpts in a haphazard way in the course of his accounts, moving from one subject to another disconnected episode whose link with the theme was a cursory word or a peripheral idea with no real bearing on the matter under review. As a result, we find him ambling from history to legend, or from Islamic tradition to obscenities, or from classical poetry to tales of fantasy, or from ascetic wisdom and scriptural doctrine to folk medicine and flora and fauna, or from the lore of astronomy and geography to seafaring craft to archeological data or even from such petty item as amusing riddles to new poetic forms of rajaz and prosaic artificial compositions. It was these confusing aberrations that deterred serious readers from wading into a vast text without obvious plan or a set system."* (Atiya, *A Fourteenth Century Encyclopedist*, S. 37) Ähnlich ist das Urteil Franz Rosenthals (*A history of Muslim historiography*, Leiden 1968, S. 155). Auch im Urteil arabischer Historiker fällt an-Nuwayris Erzählstrategie negativ aus, wie z.B. bei as-Saḫāwī (gest. 1427/8-1497): *"[…] and he tarried so much that in comparison with the other things he mentioned, the event (of the year 757) is hardly noticeable."* (ebd., S. 458-9).

umgangen worden. Dabei erfüllt die Dichtung mehrere zentrale Funktionen im Erzähltext, indem sie z.B. eine Digression abschließt, eine Argumentation amplifiziert, einen Sachverhalt / Zustand exemplifiziert, abstrahiert oder konkretisiert, die Verinnerlichung des Erlebten gewährleistet und vor allem einen sentimentalen Kontakt des Textes zum Leser herstellt.[48] Diese Motivation verschleiert der Autor nicht, schließlich gibt er explizit an, was ihn dazu bewogen hat, die Geschehnisse aufzuzeichnen, nämlich daß er den nachkommenden Generationen ein umfassendes Bild der Ereignisse geben wolle.[49] Unter das Konzept des umfassenden Bildes fallen unter anderem unsere Alexandria-Elegien, die in keinem anderen Werk in dieser Dichte vorkommen. Jedenfalls ist an-Nuwayrī die bislang einzige und (fast) vollständige Überlieferung von Ibn Abī Ḥaǧalahs Elegie zu verdanken, die soweit derzeit nachvollziehbar, auch in keinem der bislang erschlossenen Werke Ibn Abī Ḥaǧalahs aufgeführt wird.[50] Eine Schrift, die sich explizit auf den fränkischen Überfall bezieht, ist mit dem Titel *Harǧ al-Firanǧ* (Das Wirrwarr der Franken)[51] bekannt, doch vermutlich nicht mehr erhalten. Weitere Textzeugen haben wir in den Schriften Ibn Ḥabībs (gest. 779/1377)[52] und Ibn Iyās (gest. ca. 930/1523).[53] Während Ibn Iyās nur eine auf sechs Verse gekürzte Variante der Elegie, aber gleich mit zwei neuen Versen wiedergibt, erfahren wir

---

[48] Besonders eindrücklich sind z.B. Verse, die an-Nuwayrī anführt, nachdem er die Schicksale von Personen, die den Greueltaten der Franken ausgeliefert waren, bereits prosaisch vorgestellt hat – meist einleitend mit der Phrase *lisān ḥālihī/-hā* (*Ms. Ilmām*, fol. 259a ff.).

[49] Nach dem Anblick des Ausmaßes der Verwüstungen nennt an-Nuwayrī seinen Abfassungsgrund (fol. 121a, Übers. Herzsohn, *Der Überfall Alexandriens*, S. XVI:) „*Da riß der Eifer mich fort, da spornte mich der Enthusiasmus für die Bewohner zur Abfassung dieses Buches in ihr an, damit die Muslime, die nach dieser unserer Zeit kommen, es lesen sollten, um daraus zu erfahren, was sich in vergangener Zeit in Alexandrien zugetragen, und damit die Herrscher von Ägypten, die nach den Herrschern unserer Zeit kommen, die Behütung der Stadt vor den Franken eifrig angelegen sein ließen, indem sie dieselbe mehr am Zaume (unter Obhut) hielten und zu ihrer Wache Besatzung hineinlegten.*“

[50] Im Dīwān (*Dīwān Ibn Abī Ḥaǧalah 725 H.-776 H.*, Hg. Aḥmad Ḥilmī Ḥulwah, al-Qāhirah 1425/2014), der deutlich nach dem Tode Yalbuġās abgefaßt ist (siehe Epigramm auf dessen Tod, *ebd.*, S. 48), führt er seine Elegie nicht auf, wohl aber, daß er einiges zum Thema *ǧihād* verfaßt habe. Diese Verweise finden sich in einer Lobqaṣīde mit reichlichen bibliographischen Referenzen zu seinen eigenen Werken (siehe *ebd.*, S. 178-183).

[51] Siehe Verweise zu diesem Werk im *Dīwān Ibn Abī Ḥaǧalah 725 H.-776 H.*, S. 182 und Ismāʿīl Bāšā Bābānī, *Hadīyat al-ʿārifīn*, Bayrūt 1951, I: S. 113.

[52] ʿUmar Ibn al-Ḥasan Ibn Ḥabīb al-Ḥalabī (gest. 779/1377), *Taḏkirat an-nabīh fī ayyām al-Manṣūr wa-banīh*, Hg. Muḥammad M. Amin und Saʿīd ʿAbd al-Fattāḥ ʿĀšūr, S. 288-291 (über den fränkischen Überfall mit einem Auszug aus der *Maqāme*), und ders., *Durrat al-aslāk fī [mulk] dawlat al-atrāk*, Ms. Ayasofya/Ḥadīǧa Sulṭān 233, (33 Z.), fol. 220a-220b (auf fol. 243b findet sich ein Nekrolog über Ibn Abī Ḥaǧalah). Beide Texte zitieren mit nur wenigen Varianten den gleichen Maqāmentext, unterscheiden sich aber in den Zusätzen Ibn Ḥabīs. Zum Autor siehe *GAL* SII 35 und Thomas Bauer, „Was kann aus dem Jungen noch werden! Das poetische Erstlingswerk des Historikers Ibn Ḥabīb im Spiegel seiner Zeitgenossen“, in: Otto Jastrow (Hg.), *Studien zur Semitistik und Arabistik. Festschrift für Hartmut Bobzin zum 60. Geburtstag*, Wiesbaden 2008, S. 15-56.

[53] Ibn Iyās, *Die Chronik des Ibn Iǧās*, I, 2 (764-815/1363-1412): S. 21-43: Ereignisse der Jahre 767 H.-768 H.; S. 24: Auszug aus dem Alexandria-Gedicht; weitere Gedichte Ibn Abī Ḥaǧalahs in diesem Band: S. 46, S. 60, S. 64, S. 94, S. 106, S. 108, S. 146, S. 149, S. 184, S. 244.

aus den Schriften Ibn Ḥabībs, daß die Auszüge der Elegie Bestandteil einer *Maqāme* des Autors über den Vorfall in Alexandria waren.[54] Alle drei Textzeugen überliefern die verkürzte Form, was vermuten lässt, daß Ibn Abī Ḥaǧalah das Thema Alexandria in zwei formal gesehen konträren Textsorten (*marṯiyah* und *maqāmah*) verarbeitet hat.[55] An-Nuwayrī scheint diese *Maqāme* nicht zu kennen, zumindest scheint er keine Kenntnis von einer zweiten Version zu haben, wie er überhaupt am Leben und Werk Ibn Abī Ḥaǧalahs, trotz seiner derart hervorgehobenen Position innerhalb des *Ilmām*, wenig Interesse zeigt.

Der Reihenfolge ihrer Präsentation im *Kitāb al-Ilmām* entsprechend finden sich folgende Elegien auf Alexandria; alle müssen ihren Inhalten nach zu urteilen unmittelbar nach den Ereignissen oder im Folgejahr verfaßt worden sein.[56]

1. Eine Elegie des Verfassers (an-Nuwayrī, gest. ca. 777/ 1375), eine *mīmiyyah* (-āmī) mit 117 Versen im Versmaß *ḫafīf*, fol. 118a-120a.[57]

2. Die Elegie Ibn Abī Ḥaǧalahs, eine *rāʾiyyah* (-ˣrī), in 24 Versen im Versmaß *ṭawīl*, ab Folio 122b. Diese Elegie wird im *Ilmām* nicht am Stück wiedergegeben,

---

54   Das bibliographische Gedicht (siehe Anm. 50) deutet auf das Oberthema *ǧihād* hin, doch über die Gattung sagt das Oberthema nichts aus. Eine weitere Referenz haben wir in der Handschrift Wetzstein 1803, 2 (Ahlwardt 8379, siehe Beitrag Pomerantz in diesem Band). Sie enthält einige Verse über die Einnahme Alexandrias (zwei Epigramme, Nr. 4 und Nr. 5, fol. 100a) und Auszüge aus einem Maqāmentext (*min maqāmat al-ġirbān*, fol. 124b-125a), der sich auf den Überfall der Franken auf Alexandria bezieht (wie z.B. auf fol. 125a: „*Der Sāǧiʿ Ibn Ḥamām erzählte, was sich in Alexandria zugetragen hatte, die gottlosen Franken richteten in ihr (Alexandria) ein Chaos an (haraǧa fīhā munāfiq al-firanǧ) [...] und die ġirbān stürzten sich wie die Vögel auf ihren Lebensunterhalt/Besitz (arzāq)*"), jedoch keine Überschneidungsmenge mit der bei Ibn Ḥabīb zitierten *Maqāme* hat. Derzeit können wir nicht sicher bestimmen, ob dieser Auszug aus dem *Harǧ al-firanǧ* entnommen wurde, oder tatsächlich Teil des *Manṭiq aṭ-ṭayr* ist und ob die *Maqāme* (zitiert in Ibn Ḥabībs *al-Aslāk* bzw. *Taḏkirah*) ein eigenständiger Text ist, oder ein Teil der *Harǧ*-Schrift.

55   Die Einbettung eines ernsten Themas in eine Gattung, die zu allererst mit fiktiven und elaborierten „Schelmengeschichten" eines al-Hamaḏānī (358-395/967-1008) oder al-Ḥarīrī (446-516/1054-1112) assoziiert wird, ist zwar nicht neu, aber bezeichnend für Ibn Abī Ḥaǧalah (siehe auch Beitrag Özkan, Pomerantz und Kruk). Überhaupt scheint er sehr viele seiner Themen „maqāmisiert" zu haben, was bedeutet, daß Ibn Abī Ḥaǧalah die *Maqāme* als einen formalen Rahmen genutzt hat, um mit ihren (prosimetrischen) Gestaltungsmöglichkeiten sein Thema erneut zu präsentieren und bei dem die maqāmentypischen inhaltlichen Assoziationen und Disputationsgegenstände nicht maßgebend sind. Umgekehrt gilt dies auch für die *marṯiyah*, in der nicht immer ernste Themen Gegenstand der Dichtung sein müssen, vor allem muß sie nicht immer die Qaṣīdenform vorweisen und kann durch andere poetische Formen (wie *zaǧal*) ausgedrückt werden. Siehe hierzu Ibn Quzmāns *zaǧal* für Abū l-Qāsim b. Ḥamdīn, zitiert in Faruk Toprak, „İbn Kuzmān", in: *Diyanet İslam Ansiklopedisi*, Ankara 1999, 20: S. 155 oder das Parodie-Zaǧal Ibn Dāniyāls zur Beerdigung des Teufels in Li Guo, "Paradise Lost: Ibn Dāniyāl's Response to Baybars' Campaign against Vice in Cairo", in: *Journal of the American Oriental Society* 121 (2001), S. 219-235.

56   Vgl. hierzu und zum Folgenden die Übersetzung und Analyse der Gedichte von an-Nuwayrī und Ibn Abī Ḥaǧalah in Weintritt, *Formen*, S. 179-182. Die Elegie Ibn Abī Ḥaǧalahs ediere und übersetze ich neu, weil mir die Handschrift Berlin We II 359 und 360 vorlag. (Siehe Anhang)

57   Übersetzt und zusammengefaßt in Weintritt, *Formen*, S. 173-179.

sondern versweise oder in Doppelversen mit knappen Kommentaren und reichlichen Ausschweifungen des Autors. Somit verteilt sich das ganze Gedicht in der Druckausgabe auf Bd. II und III und nimmt eine zentrale Stellung im Gesamtwerk an-Nuwayrīs ein. [siehe Anhang]

Ein weiteres Gedicht Ibn Abī Ḥaǧalahs außerhalb des Textkorpus' des *Kitāb al-Ilmām* will ich hier als Kontrastgedicht stellenweise heranziehen. Es ist eine *rāʾiyyah* mit 45 Versen, ebenfalls im Versmaß *ṭawīl* aus dem *Dīwān* (Nr. 120) Ibn Abī Ḥaǧalahs und handelt vom Angriff der „Franken" auf Ṭarāblus al-Ġarb durch den Genuesen Filippo Doria.[58]

3. und 4. Zwei Elegien von dem Dichter und Šayḫ Abū ʿAbdallāh Muḥammad b. Ḥasan aš-Šāṭibī. Beide sind *nūniyyah*s, das erste Gedicht in 60 Versen[59] mit dem Reim *-ʾnī*, im Versmaß *ṭawīl*, ab Folio 187b und das zweite Gedicht mit 13 Versen auf *-ānī* im Versmaß *ḫafīf* auf Folio 188b.[60] [siehe Anhang]

5. Die Elegie von Abū ʿAbdallāh Muḥammad b. Ṭāhir al-Aḥmīmī (gest. 3. Šawwāl 776 / 7. März 1375)[61], eine *rāʾiyyah* mit 112 Versen (-ˣr) im Versmaß *ramal*, Folia 188b-190b, die er dem Yalbuġā in einer Audienz persönlich vorgetragen hat und alle Anwesenden sehr bewegt haben soll.[62]

6. Die *muʿāraḍah*-Elegie (i.e. Replik, stilistisches Gegenstück) auf al-Aḥmīmīs *rāʾiyyah* von Abū ʿAbdallāh Muḥammad an-Nastarāwī mit 85 Versen, ebenfalls im Versmaß *ramal*, Folia 236a-238a.[63]

---

[58] *Dīwān Ibn Abī Ḥaǧalah*, Hg. Muǧāhid Muṣṭafā Bahǧat, ʿAmmān 2010, S. 120-122, No: 120 sowie ders. in der Edition von Aḥmad Ḥilmī Ḥulwah, S. 86-88. (Siehe Edition und Übersetzung im Anhang).

[59] Die Druckausgabe enthält 59 Verse.

[60] Dieses Gedicht berücksichtige ich nur stellenweise, dort wo es inhaltlich etwas Neues bietet (zum Text siehe Anhang). Es hat die stilistische Besonderheit, daß es symmetrisch aufgebaut ist (arab. Terminus: *radd al-ʿaǧuz ʿalā aṣ-ṣadr*). Jeder Vers endet mit dem Wort mit dem es beginnt (mit Außnahme des dritten Verses, der diese Figur jeweils am Anfang und Ende der Halbverse verwendet), daher präsentiert das Gedicht verschiedene Formen des *ǧinās*. Vgl. Wolfhart Heinrichs, "Rhetorical Figures" in: Scott Meisami, Julie (Hg.), *Encyclopedia of Arabic Literature*, 2 Bde., Routledge 1998, II: S. 660.

[61] Über die Lebensdaten der aufgeführten Dichter informiert an-Nuwayrī grundsätzlich nicht, dieses Datum gibt Ibn Ḥaǧar al-ʿAsqalānī an (siehe *ad-Durar al-kāminah*, 4 Bde., Hyderabad [Dāʾirat al-Maʿārif al-ʿUṯmāniyyah]1349/1930, III: S. 475, No: 1269).

[62] an-Nuwayrī, *KI*, III: S. 230-231. Über diese Audienz sagt al-Aḥmīmī, daß Yalbuġā von seinen Versen derart bewegt war, daß er sich energischer an die Arbeit gemacht hat, die mamlukische Flotte aufzurüsten. Hierauf folgt im *Ilmām* der Bericht über die Aufrüstung der mamlukischen Armee und Flotte (S. 231 f.); vgl. hier auch Weintritt, *Formen*, S. 64.

[63] an-Nuwayrī, *KI*, IV: S. 171-178. An-Nuwayrī erzählt im Anschluß, daß als er al-Aḥmīmī von dieser *muʿāraḍah* erzählte, al-Aḥmīmī sein Gesicht verzogen habe und seine Bedrückung zum Ausdruck brachte, so als würde er sagen (Metrum *ṭawīl*):

إِذَا مَا ادَّعَى دِينَ الهَوَى غَيْرُ أَهْلِهِ   أَقُــولُ إِذَا قَــالُوا نَــرَاكَ مُقَطِّبَــا

إِذَا جَـاءَ بَيْــتُ العَنْكَبُـوتِ بِمِثْلِـهِ   يَحِــقُّ لِــدُودِ القَــزِّ يَقْتُـلُ نَفْـسَهُ

Wenn man sagt: „Wir sehen, daß du dich grämst (wörtlich zusammenrollst), / wenn sich jemand anmaßt, die Religion der Liebe (Das Geschäft der Leidenschaft) für sich in Anspruch zu nehmen, ohne vom

Alle Elegien bieten unterschiedliche Nuancierungen, doch die zentrale Position, die Ibn Abī Ḥaǧalah im Werk hat, zeugt davon, daß seine Elegie sehr zeitnah und intensiv in den gelehrten Kreisen in Alexandria rezipiert wurde. Wenn es auch nicht das Hauptanliegen an-Nuwayrīs war, sein Werk allein der Ausfaltung und Analyse der Verse Ibn Abī Ḥaǧalahs zu widmen, so nutzt er dessen Verse doch für allerhand Digressionen, um sein eigenes Werk zu komplettieren.

Gattungsspezifische Motive und Formen in Städteklagen

Generell weisen Elegien auf gefallene Städte den gleichen Formenbestand der *riṯāʾ*s[64] für Personen auf, d.h. es finden sich Tränen- und Trauermotive, poetische Beschreibung des Unglücksfalls, vergangene Schönheiten (Taten) verbunden mit Liebesmotiven, Auseinandersetzung mit Gott und dem Schicksalsschlag im Allgemeinen, die Schmähung des Zerstörers und eine mögliche abstrakt-religiöse Begründung für das Unglück.

Mit der Personifizierung der Stadt dringt eine neue lebendige Figur in den Motivhaushalt der Qaṣīde und wird Gegenstand der Liebes-, Spott- und Lobdichtung. Historisch gesehen emanzipiert sich das Stadtmotiv mit zunehmendem Reichsbewußtsein von einzelnen *raḥīl*- und *waṣf*-Versen hin zu eigenständigen Stadtgedichten und es ist nur selbstverständlich, daß sie Gegenstand des Klagelieds geworden ist.[65] Allerdings stirbt die Stadt in den seltensten Fällen den

---

Fache zu sein", sage ich, // *daß es der Seidenraupe zusteht sich umzubringen, / wenn sich eine Spinne mit ihrem Netz anschickt, das gleiche hervorzubringen"*.

64 Zum Trauergedicht (*riṯāʾ* bzw. *marṯiyah*, Pl. *marāṯī*) siehe Charles Pellat, "Marthiya", in: *EI²*; Ignaz Goldziher, „Bemerkungen zur arabischen Trauerpoesie", in: *WZKM* 16 (1902), S. 307-329; Šawqī Ḍayf, *ar-Riṯāʾ*, al-Qāhirah 1955; Ewald Wagner, *Grundzüge der klassischen arabischen Dichtung*, 2 Bde., Darmstadt 1987, hier I: S. 116-134; Emil Homerin, "A Bird Ascends the Night: Elegy and Immortality in Islam", in: *Journal of the American Academy of Religion* 59 (1991), S. 247-279; Arie Schippers, *Spanish Hebrew Poetry and the Arabic Literary Tradition: Arabic Themes in Hebrew Andalusian Poetry*, Leiden 1994, S. 244-287; Pieter Smoor, "Elegies and Other Poems on Death by Ibn al-Rūmī", in: *Journal of Arabic Literature* 27 (1996), S. 49-85; Renate Jacobi, „Bemerkungen zur frühislamischen Trauerpoesie", in: *Wiener Zeitschrift für die Kunde des Morgenlandes* 87 (1997), S. 83-99; Alan Jones, *Early Arabic Poetry: Select Poems*, 2. Aufl.., Reading 2011, S. 33 f., S. 43-142; Gert Borg, *Mit Poesie vertreibe ich den Kummer meines Herzens: Eine Studie zur altarabischen Trauerklage der Frau*, Leiden 1997; Ibrahim Musa al-Sinjilawi, *The ʿAtlal-Nasib in Arabic Poetry: A Study of the Development of the Elegiac Genre in Classical Arabic Poetry*, Irbid 1999; Thomas Bauer, "Communication and Emotion: The Case of Ibn Nubātah's Kindertotenlieder", in: *Mamlūk Studies Review* 7 (2003), S. 49-95.

65 Für einen allgemeinen Überblick siehe Geert Jan van Gelder, "City panegyric, in classical Arabic", in: *EI³*; Ibrahim Musa al-Sinjilawi, *The Lament for Fallen Cities. A Study of the Development of the Elegiac Genre in Classical Arabic Poetry*. Ph. D. Diss., University of Chicago 1983; Bayyud, *Die Stadt in der arabischen Poesie, bis 1258 n. Chr.*; Gustav von Grunebaum, „Städtische Züge in der arabischen Literatur, vornehmlich im neunten und zehnten Jahrhundert", in: ders., *Kritik und Dichtkunst*, Wiesbaden 1955, S. 52-69; ders., „Zum Lob der Stadt in der arabischen Prosa", in: ders., *Kritik und Dichtkunst*, S. 80-86. Elegien über bestimmte Regionen und Städte behandeln z.B. Joseph de Somogyi, "A Qaṣīda on the De-

richtigen Tod und daher erfüllt die Trauerarbeit in den *riṯāʾ al-mudun* neben der Aufzeichnung einer Ruinenästhetik weitere historisch und literarisch relevante Funktionen. Wie die Dichtung in der arabischen Tradition ein gewichtiger Diskursträger ist, so manifestieren sich in diesen Städteklagen im Lob (der Stadt) und Tadel (z.B. der Zerstörer) neben sozialer Kritik und Machtdiskurs gleichzeitig auch Vorstellungen von idealer Ordnung.[66]

Eine der Gattungsnorm entsprechende Anordnung in Städteklagen folgt – hier und dort im Schwerpunkt variierend – üblicherweise folgendem Schema: analog zu den Personenelegien gibt der Dichter einen sentimentalen Einstieg, der seine Betroffenheit verdeutlicht (z.B. durch Tränen-, Wasser- und Augenlid- bzw. Herz-, Schmerz- und Feuer-Motive), die anschließend durch *ṣabr-/ʿazāʾ*-Verse (Geduld, Fassung / Trost) weiter gesteigert werden.[67] Dabei bildet der Dichter Vergleiche, in denen die Korrespondenz des individuellen/persönlichen Leids mit kosmischem Leid hervorgehoben wird – meist durch Bilder der Dunkelheit oder dem Sich-Verhüllen der Gestirne, dem Leiden der Natur. Dann verkündet der Poet, was sich ereignet hat. In diesen formalen Modulen schnürt der Dichter, nachdem er Leid und Kosmos zusammengeführt hat, in der Kontrastierung der Details, wieder die Trauer auf. Neben der Aufzählung der Schandtaten der Feinde und Flüchen[68] auf diese nutzt der Poet den Raum zur Kontrastierung der unschuldigen Bevölkerung (korrespondierend mit der unschuldigen Natur) mit den schuldigen Wüstlingen (korrespondierend mit der transformierten Natur).[69] Den Hauptteil der Elegien bilden mehr oder minder detaillierte Unheilsbeschreibun-

---

struction of Baghdād by the Mongols", in: *BSOAS* 7 (1933), S. 41-48; Cynthia Robinson, "Ubi Sunt, 'Memory and Nostalgia in Taifa Court Culture'", in: *Muqarnas* 15 (1998), S. 20-31 und Alexander Elinson, *Looking Back at al-Andalus. The Poetics of Nostalgia in Medieval Arabic and Hebrew Literature*, Leiden 2013; Beispiele für den Städtetadel im Zeitalter der Kreuzzüge gibt insb. Mašhūr al-Ḥabbāzī, "Šiʿr hiǧāʾ al-mudun wa-l-aqālim fi zamān ḥurūb al-firanǧah: dirāsa mawḍuʿiyyah", in: *Maǧallat Ǧāmiʿat al-Quds al-Maftūḥah li-l-Abḥāṯ wa-d-Dirasāt* 19 (2010), S. 293-327.

[66] Über die rhetorischen Elemente in der Dichtung und ihre Reversion, mit denen diese Entwürfe generiert werden, siehe Alev Masarwa, "Praising Damascus: City Panegyrics as a Literary Genre and a Concept of Urbanity" (2014, eingereicht).

[67] Siehe Ḍayf, *ar-Riṯāʾ*, S. 86-99 und Borg, *Mit Trauer vertreibe ich den Kummer*, S. 111-177.

[68] In unseren Elegien z.B. bei aš-Šāṭibī (Gedicht Nr. 3), Verse 12, 24, 30, 37, 41; ders. (Gedicht Nr. 4), Vers 6: [*sanna li-ṯ-ṯaġri ḏā l-ḥabīṯu sinānan / fa-taʿaddā bihā ʿalā l-asnāni = Der Feind mit den häßlichen Zähnen schleifte die Stadt / und überschritt sie (verletzte sie) mit den Lanzenspitzen (Zähnen)*]; an-Nuwayrī hält sich in seiner Elegie zurück, dafür läßt er im *Ilmām* keine Gelegenheit unausgenützt, Peter I mit Negativ-Epitheta zu belegen, z.B. auf fol. 166a (Z. 7-8): *Rūbir Buṭrus al-kāfir al-laʿīn aḍ-ḍāll al-māriq al-liṣṣ as-sāriq = Der verfluchte König Peter / Buṭrus, der verirrte Renegat, marodierender Einbrecher"* und auf fol. 166b (*KI*, III: S. 65; hier in der Übersetzung Weintritts, *Formen*, S. 77): „*Das Verhalten der Diebe (ʿādat al-luṣūṣ) besteht darin, daß sie nach dem Diebstahl mit dem gestohlenen Gut eiligst fliehen, damit man sie nicht ergreifen, bestrafen und wechselweise Hand und Fuß abschlagen kann. Der verfluchte Zyprer scharte die Diebe des Christentums (luṣūṣ an-naṣrānīya) um sich und kam mit ihnen nach Alexandria.*" Zur Funktion dieser Niedrighaltung Peters siehe ders. S. 76, 78 f. und die folgenden Ausführungen im Abschnitt über Ṭarāblus al-Ġarb (S. 29 ff.).

[69] Siehe z.B. Schippers, *Spanish Hebrew Poetry*, S. 251-255.

gen bei gleichzeitiger Preisung der Schauplätze der nun vergangenen, zerstörten (kollektiv und individuell erfahrenen) Schönheit im Stil der klassischen *vanitas*- und *ubi sunt-Motive*.[70] Im Unterschied zur klassischen Lobqaṣīde, in der das *raḥīl*-Motiv den Auszug des (heroischen) Helden, den Wüstenritt von den Ruinen oder den Erinnerungsorten der einstigen Liebe beschreibt, um ins *faḥr* überzugehen, wird in den Städteelegien eine Art *raḥīl* von einem Anti-Helden parcoursartig zu den Spuren zurück erzählt, um das Stadtlob bzw. die poetische Aussage zu generieren. Während die *raḥīl*-Sektion einer Qaṣīde höchst dynamisch ist, vor allem, weil sie nach einem Moment des Innehaltens an den Spuren (*aṭlāl*) eindrucksvoll entfaltet werden kann, suggeriert die Stadtruine eher ein statisches Moment, das die Elegie jedoch mit ihren eigenen Ausdrucksmöglichkeiten wie z.B. starken Kontrastfiguren, ihrer Dialogizität usw. aufbricht bzw. wieder dynamisiert. Dies ist der Part, in dem am deutlichsten hervortritt, was der Dichter als zur Stadt und städtischer Ordnung zugehörig hervorhebt. Formal-stilistisch sind dies ausgedehnte *aṭlāl*-Motive bzw. ein umgekehrtes *raḥīl*-Modul.[71] Um das Ausmaß der Transformation dessen, was einst gut war und nun zerstört wurde, deutlich zu machen, geschieht der virtuelle Rundgang durch die ruinierte Stadt[72] *chronotopisch*, i.e. topologisch und historisch.[73] Analog zu den *ubi sunt*-Motiven

---

[70]   Als Topos in der Predigt und in der Literatur und seine antiken Ursprünge siehe Carl H. Becker, „Ubi sunt qui ante nos in mundo fuere", in: [Scherman, L. und Bezold, C. (Hg.)], *Aufsätze zur Kultur- und Sprachgeschichte vornehmlich des Orients: Ernst Kuhn zum 70. Geburtstag am 7. Februar 1916 gewidmet von Freunden und Schülern*, Breslau 1916, S. 87-105; Mark Lidzbarski, „[Mitteilung zu dems. „Ubi sunt ..."]", in: *Der Islam* 8 (1918), S. 300; Paul Keseling, „[Mitteilung zu dems. „Ubi sunt ..."]", in: *Der Islam* 17 (1928), S. 97-100; als ein Genre in der arabischen Dichtung mit eigenem Motivrepertoire zur Nostalgie und Vergänglichkeit in den Städteklagen siehe Robinson, "Ubi Sunt, 'Memory and Nostalgia in Taifa Court Culture'", S. 20: *"Ubi Sunt" has, as does any other literary genre, a repertoire of themes and topoi by which it is recognized: nostalgia, comparison of past to present, a consciousness that the past evoked will never return."*

[71]   Zu den *raḥīl*-Versen in der klassischen Dichtung siehe Renate Jacobi, "Raḥīl", in: *EI²*; Wagner, *Grundzüge*, S. 114-115, 139-140 und Index; daß bereits der *raḥīl* ein Thema der Selbstpreisung ist, zeigt die Studie von Nefeli Papoutsakis, *Desert Travel as a Form of Boasting: A Study of Ḏū r-Rumma's Poetry*, Wiesbaden 2009.

[72]   Über die Bedeutung der Ruine im ästhetischen Diskurs und u.a. als literarisches Symbol für Umbrüche, Begrenztheit und Vergänglichkeit siehe „Ruine" in: *Metzler Lexikon literarischer Symbole*, hrsg. von Günter Butzer und Joachim Jacob, 2. Aufl., Stuttgart 2012, S. 555-356; Hartmut Böhme, „Die Ästhetik der Ruinen", in: Kamper / Wulf (Hg.), *Der Schein des Schönen*, Göttingen 1989, S. 287-304.

[73]   Der von Michail Bachtin geprägte und vorwiegend in den literarischen Gattungen der Epik untersuchte Terminus Chronotopos (Raumzeitgefüge) bezeichnet eine Form-Inhalt Kategorie: *„Den grundlegenden wechselseitigen Zusammenhang der in der Literatur künstlerisch erfaßten Zeit-und-Raum-Beziehungen wollen wir als Chronotopos („Raumzeit" müßte die wörtliche Übersetzung lauten) bezeichnen"* (aus: Michail M. Bachtin, *Chronotopos*, hg. v. Michael C. Frank, Kirsten Mahlke, übers. v. Michael Dewey, Berlin 2008, S. 7). Der aus Einsteins Relativitätstheorie entlehnte Terminus wird von Bachtin wie folgt in die Literaturwissenschaft übertragen: *„Im künstlerisch-literarischen Chronotopos verschmelzen räumliche und zeitliche Merkmale zu einem sinnvollen und konkreten Ganzen. Die Zeit verdichtet sich hierbei, sie zieht sich zusammen und wird auf künstlerische Weise sichtbar; der Raum gewinnt an Intensität, er wird in die Bewegung der Zeit,*

werden dabei vergangene Merkmale (*maḥāsin*) nostalgisch vergegenwärtigt und der städtische Raum in einen Erinnerungsraum ausgeweitet. Eine Spannungssteigerung wird erreicht durch Vergeltungswünsche kriegerischer oder metapoetischer Art, z.B. durch *ǧihād*-Aufrufe mit dem Schwert oder Rache mit dem Stift. Ein weiteres wichtiges und organisierendes Modul häufig am Ende sind die Verse, in denen der Poet sich allgemein mit den Wechselfällen des Schicksals, dem vergänglichen Leben, der Unentrinnbarkeit vor göttlicher Vorsehung auseinandersetzt. Mit diesen Versen übergibt der Poet das Geschehen häufig mit einer für das Thema prägnanten Preisung des Propheten dem Urteil Gottes.

Der Grad der Emotionalität ist in solchen Gedichten prinzipiell sehr hoch. Das betrifft allerdings eher die *Lexik* der Trauer. Das Anführen der Tränenverse ist eine Technik zur Einstimmung und Erinnerung, die mitunter signalisiert, auf welche Gattung wir uns einzustellen haben und welchen Grad der Personifizierung der Stadt der Poet vorgenommen hat. Die öffentliche „laute, zur Schau getragene" Trauer ist im Islam verboten bzw. verpönt. Wie Fritz Meier eindrucksvoll dargelegt hat, gilt diese negative Haltung zur lauten Trauer in vielen Kulturen auf der Welt.[74] Standhaft widersetzt sich aber diese Gattung dem religiös-moralischen Gebot. Daher findet man gerade in den Einleitungsversen noch Spuren einer poetischen Scheinrechtfertigung für diese Übertretung:

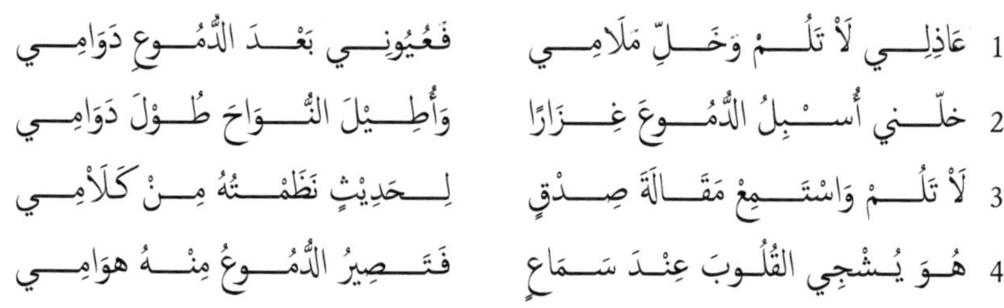

1 عَاذِلِـي لَاْ تَلُـمْ وَخَـلِّ مَلَامِـي   فَعُيُونِـي بَعْـدَ الدُّمُـوعِ دَوَامِـي

2 خَلِّـني أُسْـبِلُ الدُّمُـوعَ غِـزَارًا   وَأُطِـيْلَ النُّـوَاحَ طُـوْلَ دَوَامِـي

3 لَاْ تَلُـمْ وَاسْتَـمِعْ مَقَـالَةَ صِـدْقٍ   لِـحَدِيْثٍ نَظَمْـتُهُ مِـنْ كَلَامِـي

4 هُـوَ يُشْجِي القُلُـوبَ عِنْـدَ سَمَاعٍ   فَتَـصِيرُ الدُّمُـوعُ مِنْـهُ هوَامِـي

des Sujets, der Geschichte hineingezogen. Die Merkmale der Zeit offenbaren sich im Raum, und der Raum wird von der Zeit mit Sinn erfüllt und dimensioniert." (ebd., S. 7). Für die Städteelegien eignet sich das Chronotopos-Modell (in unserem Fall das Chronotopos der Ruine/der zerstörten Stadt) besonders, weil hier Zeit- und Raumdiskurse, wie im englischen Ausdruck „history takes place" zusammenfallen. Weitere Chronotopoi, in denen die Semantisierung des Raums und die Verräumlichung der Zeit besonders deutlich hervortreten (siehe Bachtin, *ebd.*, ins. S. 58-73), wären beispielsweise das Chronotopos der Begegnung, der Gefangenschaft, der Stadt, des Krieges, und der Erinnerung. Mir ist nur eine arabistische Studie bekannt, die sich Bachtins Ansatz widmet, für die klassische Literatur steht eine Untersuchung noch aus. Siehe Granara, "Nostalgia, Arab Nationalism, and the Andalusian Chronotope in the Evolution of the Modern Arabic Novel", in: *Journal of Arabic Literature* 36 (2005), S. 57-73; einen allgemeinen Überblick über die Chronotoposforschung gibt Nele Bomong et. al. (Hg.), *Bakhtin's Theory of the Literary Chronotope: Reflections, Applications, Perspectives*. Proceedings of the workshop entitled "Bakhtin's Theory of the Literary Chronotope: Reflections, Applications, Perspectives" (27-28 June 2008), Gent 2010, introduction.

[74] *„Mohammed verbot auch die trauergedichte (marāṯī, sg. marṯiyah). Diese verbote richteten sich zweifellos gegen bestehende vorislamische sitten. Und an deren Zähigkeit scheiterten sie!"* aus: Fritz Meier, „Ein profetenwort gegen die totenbeweinung", in: *Der Islam* 50 (1973), S. 207-229, hier S. 207.

5 كَـيْفَ لَا أُجْـرِيَ الـدُّمُوعَ كَوْبِلٍ   هَاطِلٍ مُسْبِلٍ كَـهَطْلِ الغَمَامِـي [75]

1. „O mein Tadler, tadle mich nicht, laß ab von den Vorwürfen / denn meine Augen sind nach dem Tränenfluß immer noch voll <Trauer>.

2. Laß mich die Tränen reichlich vergießen / und laß mich wehklagen für immer.

3. Tadle mich nicht, sondern höre die wahre Darstellung / eines Berichtes, den ich mit eigenen Worten in Verse gesetzt habe.

4. Hört man ihn, betrübt er die Herzen / und läßt die Tränen fließen.

5. Wie sollte ich auch nicht die Tränen fließen lassen wie / einen andauernden Regenguß, wie einen Wolkenbruch."[76]

An-Nuwayrī beginnt sein Gedicht mit einem fiktiven Tadler, der ihn nicht tadeln soll. Fünf Verse lang bietet er feine Tränen- und Tadelmotive,[77] die aš-Šāṭibī sogar auf neun erweitert, um der Heftigkeit der eigenen Trauer Ausdruck zu geben und die Adressaten emotional zu erreichen. Dabei ist es schon beachtenswert, was Dichter in dieser Gattung und in dem an sich engen Ausdrucksraum mit beschränkter Lexik seit Jahrhunderten für Variationen leisten können. Al-Aḫmīmī und an-Nastarāwī sind zwar zügelloser und fallen sofort mit der Verkündung des *großen* Unheils auf die poetische Bühne, doch mit dem Verweis auf die Größe des Unglücks, die die Gemeinschaft betrifft, ist es zumindest für die Poeten gerechtfertigt, die Klage öffentlich zu erheben. Ibn Abī Ḥaǧalahs schneidender Einstieg in das Thema bietet im ersten Moment das Gegenteil. Er umgeht die Trauerlexik rigoros, kehrt das Motiv der Größe um und beginnt mit einer ‚kleinen Einheit', um in der Einbettung einer rhetorischen Frage, als zweite Umkehrung, doch auf den allgemeingültigen Charakter des Angriffs zu verweisen (Ibn Abī Ḥaǧalah, V. 1). Alle drei Poeten (al-Aḫmīmī, an-Nastarāwī und Ibn Abī Ḥaǧalah) verbindet, neben ihrem gemeinsamen Reim, daß sie mit einem Mahnbild beginnen. Die Elegien an-Nuwayrīs, al-Aḫmīmīs und an-Nastarāwīs weisen typische Elemente einer ‚klassischen' Städteelegie in einer ausladenden Form auf. Sie monumentalisieren den alexandrinischen Erinnerungsraum, den Ort und das Geschehen, doch sind sie in ihrem Schwerpunkt eher als poetische Chroniken des Ereignisses zu verstehen. Auf der Achse der persönlichen Ergriffenheit und Emotionalität sind von allen im *Ilmām* präsentierten Elegien die Texte von aš-Šāṭibī und Ibn Abī

---

[75] *Ms. Ilmām*, fol. 118a hat die Variante (كَيْفَ لَا أُجْرِي الذُّمُوعَ كَوَيْلٍ مُسْبِلٍ كَهَطْلِ الغَمَامِي), die allerdings metrisch (Versmaß *al-ḫafīf*) defekt ist, daher ist die Edition hier vorzuziehen (*KI*, III: S. 211).

[76] Übersetzung der Elegie an-Nuwayrīs in Weintritt, *Formen*, S. 173.

[77] In der Mitte dieser Einleitung (hier V. 3) baut der Dichter sein Anliegen ein, eine in Verse gefaßte, wahre Darstellung des Berichts geben zu wollen. Weintritt geht daher davon aus, daß es sich um die Versifizierung des Eroberungsberichts handelt. Doch handelt es sich hierbei mehr um eine prosaische Ausfaltung u.a. dieser Elegie, da die Elegie dem Gesamtwerk vorangeht und die Themen im *Ilmām* zeitlich über die Themen der Elegie hinausgehen (siehe Weintritt, *Formen*, S. 170 und die Ausführungen hier S. 35 ff.).

Ḥaġalah am weitesten voneinander entfernt, weshalb im Folgenden Inhalt und
Aufbau dieser beiden Gedichte wiedergegeben werden, stellenweise aber auch die
anderen Autoren für einen Vergleich herangezogen werden.

Elegie Abū ʿAbdallāh aš-Šāṭibīs

Im *Ilmām* erscheinen die beiden Elegien aš-Šāṭibīs (Abū ʿAbdallāh Muḥammad b.
Ḥasan aš-Šāṭibī) nach dem Schlußvers Ibn Abī Ḥaġalahs. Die beiden Elegien trennen kurze Abschnitte über Yalbuġās Eintreffen in Alexandria, dessen und Ibn
ʿArrāms unmittelbare Aufbesserungsarbeiten an den Stadttoren und Befestigungsanlagen, sowie Ibn ʿArrāms Absetzung und seine Wiedereinsetzung im Folgejahr
(Šawwāl 768). Ohne Kommentierung und weitere Informationen zum Autor gibt
an-Nuwayrī dieses Gedicht schlicht als weitere Elegie über Alexandria wieder.

Der Poet richtet seine Verse (V. 1-9) direkt an die Öffentlichkeit. Erst nach diesem ausgiebigen Präludium mit Trauermotiven (Tränen, Schlaflosigkeit, Unruhe,
Finsternis, Tadler etc.) benennt der Poet abstrakt das Unglück, das die Grenzstadt
getroffen hat (V. 10) und im Folgevers sehr konkret das Datum (22. Muḥarram
767) des Ereignisses.[78] Dem folgt zunächst die Beschreibung des Unglücks mit
einigen Details zur Ergreifung der Stadt durch die „Feinde" (V. 12-17), die er
nicht weiter benennt, außer an späterer Stelle (V. 39) als *ar-Rūm* (die Römer). Unter dem Oberthema *širk* vs. *tawḥīd* arbeitet der Autor in diesen Versen bewegende
Kontraste heraus, in denen die Aggressoren (z.B. als Feinde, Ungläubige, Verfluchte) der unschuldigen Stadt und ihrer Bevölkerung (z.B. als edelmütige Gemeinschaft, wohlhabende und wohlgeschützte Stadt) gegenübergestellt werden.

---

[78] Den Wochentag kann der Poet wegen des Metrums nicht einbauen, da Datumsangaben in
Versen recht viel Raum beanspruchen. Sein zweites Gedicht erwähnt den Wochentag, dafür
aber nicht das Jahr (Vers 3, siehe Anm. 31). Noch ist das poetische Chronogramm in jener
Zeit unbekannt, aber an-Nuwayrī kommt diesem in seinen Versen 115-116 formal bereits
sehr nahe, indem er das Signalwort *tāʾrīḫ* benutzt. Er schreibt in eigentlich späterer und
ganz osmanischer Manier einen *maḫlaṣ*-Vers:

115 فَالنُّوَيرِيُّ قَدْ رَثَى الثَّغْرَ حَقًّا   عَـامَ سَـبْعٍ وَيَـا وَيْحَـهُ مِـنْ عَـامِ

116 بَعْـدَ سِـتِّيْنَ بَعْـدَ سَـبْعِمِائَةٍ   وَأَتَـى بِالتَّـارِيخِ لِلإِعْـلاَمِ

*(V. 115) „An-Nuwayrī hat im Jahre sieben – wehe über dieses Jahr! – mit einer Elegie die Hafenstadt
beklagt, (V. 116) nach 60 und 700, und brachte diese Chronik (tāʾrīḫ) den angesehenen Leuten."*
(Übers. Weintritt, *Formen*, S. 179) Rechnerisch ergibt das Wort *lil-iʿlām* aber keine sinnvolle
Jahreszahl. Zu der Zahl sieben und dem literarischen Konzept, das Ibn Abī Ḥaġalah im
Sukkardān as-Sulṭān verwirklicht, siehe (ders.) im Kapitel: „Das Verhältnis von Panegyrik
und Historiographie", S. 183-200. Die Einbettung von Buchstaben und Zahlen in die
Dichtung ist recht typisch in der Zeit. In der Dichtung Ibn Abī Ḥaġalahs kommen sie sogar recht häufig im Prophetenlob wie auch im Ṭarāblus-Gedicht vor. Zur späteren Chronogramm-Dichtung siehe Thomas Bauer, „Vom Sinn der Zeit. Aus der Geschichte des
arabischen Chronogramms", in: *Arabica* 50 (2003), S. 501-531 sowie Masarwa, "Performing
the Occasion: The Chronograms of Māmayya ar-Rūmī (930-985 or 987/1534-1577 or
1579)", in: Stephan Conermann und Gül Şen (Hg.), *The Mamluk-Ottoman Transition: Continuity and Change in Egypt and Bilād aš-Šām in the Sixteenth Century*, Bonn 2016, S. 177-206.

Diesen Kontrasten folgen Verse, in denen der Eigenanteil an diesem Unglück reflektiert wird (V. 18-22). Die Verse 23-27 fungieren als Augenzeugenbericht des Poeten, was er an traumatisierenden Szenen mit eigenen Augen gesehen hat. Mit einem Überleitungsvers (V. 28) wendet er sich an das Mitgefühl seiner Leserschaft, um erneut den Eigenanteil an diesem Vorfall zu reflektieren (V. 28-34). Nun spricht die personifizierte Stadt als Resonanzboden und weitere Zeugin der Geschehnisse; sie ist eine Leidtragende und beklagt ihren schlechten Schutz (V. 35-37). Gestärkt durch die Zeugenschaft der Leidtragenden, wendet sich der Poet an sein Publikum, um das unmoralische Verhalten der „Muslime", die sich am Raub beteiligten, anzuklagen (V. 28-40). Mit einem erneuten Überleitungsvers, worin er sich Gott zuwendet (V. 41), gestaltet der Poet vier Verse mit den Schwurausdrücken (*a-lā bi-abī yā ṯaġru …!*) und vergegenwärtigt mit diesen Anrufungen der geliebten Stadt die erlebte Transformation ihrer einstigen Schönheiten sowie die Klage über den Verlust der Lieben (V. 42-48). Dieser Verlust wird untermauert von der Klage und den Schilderungen eines weiteren Betroffenen, nämlich einer freigelassenen bzw. ausgelösten Geisel, stellvertretend für alle Geiseln (V. 49-53). Die ergreifenden Schilderungen dieses Zeugen treffen den nun von sich selbst abgelösten Poeten so sehr, daß er sich auf die Finger beißen muß und betend zu Boden fällt (V. 54). Der Wehklage über die Geiseln folgen Verse mit Vergeltungs-Motiven persönlicher und metapoetischer Art (mit Weinen die Trauer zu erregen (V. 56) und mit dem Gedicht den Rost des Herzens zu polieren (V. 57)). Mit einem Verweis auf die *sīrah* des Propheten, dem in einem Kampf mit einer Handvoll Staub der Sieg gewährt wurde, beendet der Poet mit diesem Verweis im Aufruf zu Gebeten seine Elegie (V. 58-60).

Zu den markantesten Zügen dieser Elegie gehört die häufige Verwendung der Redefigur des *iltifāt* (wörtl. die Wendung des Gesichts; Hinwendung). In der Gattung der Elegie ist sie naturgemäß besonders prominent, da diese Gattung im Wesentlichen die Aufgabe meistert, die innerlich empfundene Trauer angemessen nach außen zu tragen. Für Städteelegien definiert sich dieses „Außen" allerdings je nach Funktion des Textes vielfältig, zumal es thematisch multiple Kopplungen an Psyche, Person, Religion, Geschichte, Politik und Kultur aufweist. Da aš-Šāṭibī keinen *madīḥ* aufweist, ist davon auszugehen, daß diese Elegie aus einer persönlichen Betroffenheit und einem speziellen Anlaß heraus geschrieben wurde. Die formale Gestaltung des Gedichts stützt diese Annahme. Durch die Figur des *iltifāt* im häufigen Wechsel der Adressaten – hier mit einer graduellen Steigerung im Laufe des Gedichts (Leute, Tadler, Freunde, Alexandria, Muslime und Gott) – und der Einbettung weiterer Sprecherinstanzen neben dem Textsubjekt (Stadt, Geisel, zuhörendes Ich), vergleichbar mit den in Balladen wechselnden Sprechern, bringt der Poet eine Unmittelbarkeit zum Vorschein und spiegelt multiperspektivisch die emotionale Zerrissenheit wieder. Daher bietet sich in diesem Sujet auch nur die personale Erzählweise an, in der der Poet von ,unten' her die erlebte Situation zu umfassen versucht. Erst die Gesamtheit des Gedichts bündelt die Szenerien des

Unglücks, das das „Ich" nicht mehr selber zu bewältigen vermag. Daher übergibt der Poet hoffnungsvoll (in Gebeten und mit einem Beispiel des Propheten) die reale Handlungsoption den Machtträgern, sich dieser Herausforderung zu stellen, den diesseitigen *ordo* wiederherzustellen und das erlittene Leid zu sühnen.

Elegie Ibn Abī Ḥaǧalahs

Ibn Abī Ḥaǧalah nimmt eine distanzierte Position zum Geschehen ein. Mit 24 Versen gehört das Gedicht zu den kürzeren Städteelegien. Es lässt sich in drei Teile teilen, in denen jeweils acht Verse bestimmten Leitaspekten des Unglücks gewidmet sind, die sich durchaus noch weiter nuancieren lassen (s.u.): I. das Was (V. 1-8): Nennung und Beschreibung des Überfalls; II. das Wie (V. 9-16): Kontextualisierung der Heimsuchung mit Rekurrenz auf Geschichte und Koran, insb. Straflegenden und III. das Wäre im Urteil des Poeten (V. 17-24): Kausalisierung, Schuldzuweisungen für die Heimsuchung, Handlungsoptionen des Poeten als Anleitung für die realen Machtträger und als Vorwurf für militärisches Versagen der Verantwortlichen.

Ohne Tränen oder Schmerz, sondern mit einem Gewalt- und Märtyrer-Motiv präsentiert Ibn Abī Ḥaǧalah seine Städteklage. Das ästhetische Prinzip, das er hierbei verfolgt, ist die Differenzästhetik. Vor allem in den ersten acht Versen geht es ihm darum, mit Hilfe rhetorischer Figuren des *ǧinās* und der *muqābalah / muṭābaqah* (multipler / einfacher Kontrast) der Veränderung, die die Stadt durch den Überfall erlitten hat, – und darum geht es überwiegend in Städteelegien – Ausdruck zu verleihen:

(1) أَلاَ فِي سَـبِيلِ اللهِ مَـا حَـلَّ بِالثَّغْـرِ   عَلَى فِرْقَةِ الإِسْلاَمِ مِنْ عُصْبَةِ الكُفْرِ

Ist es denn nicht für die Sache Gottes, was in der Grenzstadt einem Teil des   122b
Islams durch die Legion des Unglaubens widerfahren ist?   [II: 229]

Im Eingangsvers (*maṭlaʿ*) skizziert der Poet bereits den ersten Kontrast (klein zu groß) gleich auf zwei Ebenen: *firqah* zu *ʿuṣbah*[79] und *ʿuṣbah* in Verbindung mit *kufr* (und nicht *kuffār*) wie auch *firqah* in Verbindung mit *Islām* (und nicht *muslimīn*). Mit der rhetorischen Frage ist auch eine Art Begründung für die öffentliche Klage gegeben, was also einem Teil des Islams zustößt, betrifft alle und somit auch den Poeten.[80] Die Stadt Alexandria wird nicht namentlich erwähnt, sondern le-

---

[79] In seinem Kommentar erklärt an-Nuwayrī: „*[al-ʿuṣbah] yaʿnī [...] ǧund al-kilāb al-laʿīn*" (*al-ʿuṣbah: das ist die verfluchte Hundearmee*).

[80] Innerhalb der Narrative an-Nuwayrīs nimmt das *ǧihād*-Motiv (der große und kleine, der individuelle und kollektive *ǧihād*) eine zentrale Stellung ein. So hebt sich z.B. der tapfere und vergebliche Kampf eines Alexandriners gegen die Franken vor dem Hintergrund der massenhaften Flucht und Panik der Alexandriner besonders ab. Als man diesem zurief, er werde sterben, entgegnete er, „*Welcher Tod ist besser als der Tod im Glaubenseifer auf dem Felde Gottes (ǧihād fī sabīl Allāh)* [...]?" (an-Nuwayrī, *KI*, II: S. 149, siehe zu diesem Abschnitt im

diglich ihr Beiname *aṯ-ṯaġr* (Pl. *ṯuġūr*, Schneidezahn, Mund, Bucht, häufig auch Grenz- bzw. Wehrstadt). Diese Entscheidung kann aus Gründen der Prosodie getroffen worden sein, zum einen lautet *ṯaġr* auf dem Reimbuchstaben des Gedichts aus,[81] zum anderen lässt sich das Wort al-Iskandariyyah mit der Silbenabfolge (– – – ⌣ – –) nur in wenigen Metren umsetzen.[82] Darüber hinaus erlaubt die maskuline Form, die auf ein Femininum rekurriert, mehr Freiheit im Ausdruck, im Verb und bei den Personalpronomen. Doch anders als bei allen anderen Elegie-Autoren im *Ilmām* unterstreicht die Nichtnennung des Stadtnamens seine Distanz zur Stadt, zumal Ibn Abī Ḥaġalah, soweit nachvollziehbar, als einziger nicht vor Ort und somit kein Augenzeuge des Überfalls war. Für ihn steht die Stadt Alexandria stellvertretend für viele Wehrstädte. Aber auch die Akteure sind ihm nicht wichtig. Obwohl im engen Raum seiner Qaṣīde doch allerlei Namen fallen, wird Peter Lusignan nicht erwähnt. In gleicher Weise fehlen der Sultan und zumindest namentlich Yalbuġā (vgl. V. 20 und 23), dafür findet aber Ibn ʿArrām, der denominierte Gouverneur der Stadt, Platz im letzten Vers.

(2) أَتَاهَــا مِــنَ الفِــرِنْجِ سَــبْعُونَ مَرْكَبًــا   فَصَاحَتْ بِهَا الغِرْبَانُ[83] في البَرِّ وَالبَحْرِ[84]

Ilmām die Ausführungen Weintritts, *Formen*, S. 140). Der Überfall auf Alexandria und die weiteren Angriffe Peters I. an der syrischen Küste sind auch der Anlaß für Ibn Kaṯīr, eine Abhandlung über den Grenzdienst zu schreiben, in der insbesondere der Märtyrer-Status der Kämpfer im *ǧihād* hervorgehoben wird. Siehe sein *Kitāb al-iǧtihād fī ṭalab al-ǧihād*, S. 413-436 (die Überfälle der Franken mit den üblichen Verfluchungen ihrer Gräueltaten, bes. S. 424-427).

[81] Die *Rāʾiyyah* Ibn Abī Ḥaġalahs verdichtet sich zudem lautlich und evoziert allein auf lautlicher Ebene das Wort *ṯaġr*; der Buchstabe /rāʾ/ kommt 82 Mal, also durchschnittlich über drei Mal in jedem Vers vor; die meisten Häufungen weisen die Verse 2, 3, 14, 22 und 24 mit fünf /rāʾs/ auf.

[82] Eine bekannte Städtepanegyrik auf Alexandria, die auch den Namen der Stadt in sich trägt, ist das Gedicht (أَرَى الإِسْكَنْدَرِيَّةَ ذَاتَ حُسْنٍ) mit 16 Versen im *wāfir*-Metrum von Yaḥyā Abū l-Ḥusayn al-Ġazzār (601-79/1204-81); zu ihm siehe Thomas Bauer, "al-Jazzār, Abū l-Ḥusayn Yaḥyā", in: *EI³*. An-Nuwayrī gibt eine verkürzte Form im *Ilmām*, unmittelbar nach den eignen Versen, wieder (*Ms. Ilmām*, fol. 120b).

[83] *Ġurāb*, Pl. *ġirbān, aġriba*. Agius definiert: "*a Mediterranean decked or undecked war vessel of different sizes operated by oars and sails (see shillīr and ʿukayrī); sixteenth to eighteenth-century Western Indian Ocean war vessel, the galliot type [s.v.] with oars and one mast; also crow; raven*", zit. aus Dionisius Agius, *Classic Ships of Islam. From Mesopotamia to the Indian Ocean*, (HdO 92), Leiden 2008, S. 406. Zu den *ġirbān*, wie auch den Schiffstypen, siehe insbesondere fol. 123b ff. und 127a ff. im *Ms. Ilmām*. Die Druckausgabe des *Ilmām* enthält ein Verzeichnis der im Werk zahlreich genannten Schiffstypen; siehe auch Capitanovici, *Die Eroberung von Alexandria*, S. 38-45 (über die Streitmacht Peters I.); Ferdinand Wüstenfeld, „Die Namen der Schiffe im Arabischen", in: *Nachrichten von der Königl. Gesellschaft der Wissenschaften und der Georg-Augusts-Universität zu Göttingen* (1880), S. 133-143; Gildemeister, „Ueber arabisches Schiffswesen", in: *Nachrichten von der Königl. Gesellschaft der Wissenschaften und der Georg-Augusts-Universität zu Göttingen* (1882), S. 431-448 (vorwiegend nach an-Nuwayrī und Ibn Mammātī); Karl Kemna, *Der Begriff „Schiff" im Französischen. Eine lexikographische Untersuchung*, Marburg 1901; Kindermann „Schiff" im Arabischen: Untersuchung über Vorkommen und Bedeutung der Termini*, Diss. Univ. Bonn 1934 (seine Untersuchung basiert hauptsächlich auf an-Nuwayrī) und Atiya, *A Fourteenth Century Encyclopedist*, S. 14, *afrūṭa* (*Ms. Ilmām*, fol. 27a mit einem Gedicht darüber).

Als von den Franken 70 Schiffe zu ihr (der Stadt) kamen, da kreischten die 123a
Raben (Galeeren) zu Lande und zu Wasser (Meer). [II: 230]

Im zweiten Vers konkretisiert Ibn Abī Ḥaǧalah, wer mit der Legion des Unglaubens gemeint ist (*al-firanǧ*) und gibt die Größe der Flotte mit 70 an.[85] Multipliziert mit der durchschnittlichen Besatzungsgröße eines Kriegsschiffes (250-400 Mann)[86], ergibt sich aus der Benennung des „Geringen" die „Übergröße" der gegnerischen Seite (hier noch mit dem relativ neutral aufzufassenden Wort *markab* für das Schiff verbunden). Das nahende Unheil findet dann in einer klanglichen Figur (Kreischen der Raben / Galeeren) ihren Ausdruck, die der Poet an eine *tawriyah* (*ǧirbān* für Raben und Galeeren[87]; Signalwort für die *tawriyah*: *markab*) koppelt. Die Raben sind zudem das Verbindungsmotiv der Verse 1 und 2. Sie verweisen auf die unheilverkündenden und Trennung vorhersagenden Raben (*ǧurāb al-bayn* oder *ǧurāb al-firāq*), wie sie in Gedichten von ʿAntarah b. Šaddād und al-Mutanabbī[88] vorkommen.[89] Eindrucksvoller und prägnanter hätte die bedrohliche Einfassung der Stadt als Beute („zu Lande und zu Wasser") nicht ausgedrückt werden können.

---

[84] Umkehrung des koranischen Motivs (vgl. *Q* 105: 3-4, *sūrat al-fīl*), worin Gott zum Schutze Mekkas Vogelschwärme gegen das Heer Abrahas schickte.

[85] Obwohl wie Weintritt ausführt (*Formen*, S. 171), diese Zahl symbolisch zu verstehen ist, geben auch viele arabische Quellen die Zahl 70 an, christliche Quellen hingegen sprechen von bis zu 165 Schiffen.

[86] Vgl. Carl Busley, *Geschichte der Segelschiffe: die Entwicklung des Segelschiffes vom Altertum bis zum 20. Jahrhundert*, Leipzig (Repr. von 1920) 2008, S. 132.

[87] Der Vergleich Rabe (*ǧurāb*) mit der Galeere (*ǧurāb/ǧirbān*) bot sich wegen der Erscheinung der Schiffe und ihrer pechschwarzen Farbe an. Das Wort scheint ins Romanische (corvetta/corvette) übergegangen zu sein (siehe Thomas Herzog, *Geschichte und Imaginaire: Entstehung, Überlieferung und Bedeutung der Sīrat Baibars in ihrem sozio-politischen Kontext*, Wiesbaden 2006, S. 109 Anm. 368). Die Bezeichnungen *šīnī* und *qiṭʿah* sowie *qarqūr* wurden teilweise synonym benutzt. Siehe zu den verschiedenen Schiffsbezeichnungen Anm. 83. Während der mamlukischen Wiedereroberung Zyperns prägte Baybars einen Spruch gegen die Franken. Nachdem er ihnen gegenüber die Tugendhaftigkeit des Kampfes zu Schwerte und nicht auf Schiffen (Jagen nach „Raben", hier: *ǧurāb*) pries, sagte er: „*antum ḫuyūlukum al-marākibu wa-naḥnu marākibunā al-ḫuyūl*: Bei euch sind Pferde eure Schiffe, bei uns aber sind die Schiffe unsere Pferde!", so wiedergegeben in David Ayalon, "The Mamluks and Naval Power", *Studies on the Mamlūks of Egypt (1250-1517)*, Variorum Reprints, London 1977, Art. VI: 5-6.

[88] ʿAntarah Ibn Šaddād al-ʿAbsī (ca. 525-608) und al-Mutanabbī (303-354/915-965); für Beispiele für dieses Motiv siehe im *Dīwān Abī ṭ-Ṭayyib al-Mutanabbī*, Hg. ʿUmar Fārūq aṭ-Ṭabbāʿ, 2 Bde., Bayrūt 1418/1997, I: S. 122 nebst Kommentar; siehe auch Charles Pellat, "Ghurāb", in: *EI²*; weitere Beispiele zum Raben-Motiv in Prosa, Dichtung und der Ḥadīṯliteratur gibt Fadime Kavak, „Klasik Arap Edebiyatı Kaynaklarında Karga Motifi", in: *Uludağ Üniversitesi İlahiyat Fakültesi Dergisi* 22 (2013), S. 117-142. Beispiele zum Motiv des Raben in der Dichtung, vorwiegend für das Alter, siehe Hasan Shuraydi, *The Raven and the Falcon: Youth versus Old Age in Medieval Arabic Literature*, Leiden 2014, S. 56 f.: *ǧurāb al-bayn*.

[89] Nach dem Vorbild Ibn Abī Ḥaǧalahs formuliert aš-Šāṭibī in seinem zweiten Gedicht das gleiche Motiv (Vers 4): وَغُرَابُ الفِرَاقِ يَنْعَبُ فِينَا (Die Raben der Trennung krächzten uns zu), siehe *Ms. Ilmām*, fol. 188b; Druckausgabe III: 221.

Was klanglich eingeläutet wurde, findet im dritten Vers durch eine optische Figur (Stilmittel *tadbīǧ*)[90] ihre Fortsetzung:

(3)   وَصَيَّرَ مِنْهَا أَزْرَقَ الْبَحْرِ أَسْـوَدًا   بَنُـو الأَصْفَرِ الْبَاغُونَ بِالْبِـيضِ وَالسُّمْرِ [91]

Die frevlerischen Byzantiner verwandelten mit Schwert (biḍ) und Lanze (sumr) das   128b
Blau des Meeres in Schwarz.   [II: 254]

Das Farbbild, das hier von der Transformation der Umwelt durch die Kreuzfahrer entworfen wird, entspricht einer gewaltsamen Verfärbung, denn die Farblehre wird bewußt aufgebrochen. Ein buntes Chaos an Farben (Blau = Wasser, Gelb = die Byzantiner, Weiß = die Schwerter, Braun = die Lanzen) ergibt das Schwarz, das mit der Pechfarbe ihrer Schiffe und der Raben korrespondiert.[92] Ibn Abī Ḥaǧalah hat diese Figur bereits ausgiebig in seinem Ṭarāblus-Gedicht benutzt. Während es dort in ganzen fünf Versen (Ṭarāblus V. 35-39) mit einem positiven Bild von Parade-Pferden[93] in das Herrscherlob übergeht, mündet hier die unfreiwillige Verfärbung in einen Spottvers:

(4)   أَقَـامُوا عَـلَى التَّثْلِيـثِ فِيهَـا ثَلاَثَـةً   كَمَعْبُـودِهِم فِي النَّهْـبِ وَالْقَتْـلِ وَالأَسْرِ

Sie verrichten in ihr die Trinität, die aus drei Dingen besteht, so wie sie es mit ih-   129a
rer verehrten Gottheit hielten: Raub, Mord und Gefangennahme.   [II: 256]

Ibn Abī Ḥaǧalah entwirft für die religiöse Figur von den Hypostasen Gottes in der Trinitätslehre eine verdrehte Analogie, also einen falschen Parallelismus,[94] in der seine Haltung zur Kreuzzugsidee Peters I. zum Ausdruck kommt, nämlich nichts als Geringschätzung im Vergleich zum Einheitsglauben (*tawḥīd*) des Islams. Anders als im Prosatext an-Nuwayrīs ist aber eine einseitige Beschuldigung

---

90   Cachia, *The Arch Rhetorician*, No: 69 (*tadbīǧ*-coloration).

91   Vers fehlt in Weintritt, *Formen*, S. 180, so daß ab diesem Vers die Nummerierung abweicht. Vermutlich bietet *We 359* mit der angegebenen Vokalisation: [بَنُوا الأَصْفَرَ الْبَاغُونَ] „*und es verwandelte sich das Blau des Meeres in Schwarz] indem sie (dort) den gelbesten Frevel mit Schwert (Weiß) und Lanze (Braun) errichteten*" eine metrisch und grammatikalisch defekte (für den Superlativ müsste *aṣfar* + det. Genitiv stehen), aber bildlich kunstvollere Variante. Diese Schreibweise finden wir ebenfalls im Ms. *Durrat al-aslāk*, fol. 220a wieder.

92   Mischt man die genannten Farben (blau und gelb), ergeben sie grün. Für eine dunkle Farbe benötigt man noch mindestens die dritte Grundfarbe rot, die der Poet nicht ausdrücklich nennt. Berücksichtigt man das blutige Resultat von Schwert und Lanze, bildet Ibn Abī Ḥaǧalah über die metaphorische Verwendung von Weiß (Schwert) und Braun (Lanze) eine *kināyah*, in der auf das Rot verwiesen wird. In seiner *Maqāme* löst Ibn Abī Ḥaǧalah dieses Bild detaillierter auf (siehe S. 38 hier im Text).

93   Zur literarischen Tradition der „Parade" von edlen Pferden vorwiegend in der Jagddichtung der späten Ayyubiden- und Mamlukenzeit siehe ausführlich Thomas Bauer, "The Dawādār's Hunting Party. A Mamluk muzdawija ṭardiyya, probably by Shihāb al-Dīn Ibn Faḍl Allāh", in: A. Vrolijk, J.P. Hogendijk (Hg.), *O ye Gentlemen. Arabic Studies on Science and Literary Culture in Honour of Remke Kruk*, Leiden 2007, S. 291-312, bes. ab S. 302.

94   An-Nuwayrī kommentiert, daß Ibn Abī Ḥaǧalah mit der Dreiteilung auch auf die drei Tage des Raubzugs (Freitag, Samstag und Sonntag) verweist. Die Abfolge: Raub, Mord und Gefangennahme mag zumindest im Resultat die zeitliche Abfolge des Überfalls nachzeichnen.

ohne gleichwertige Selbstreflexion untypisch für Ibn Abī Ḥaǧalah und für die kontrastive Struktur dieses Gedichts. Daß er an dieser Stelle die Dreifaltigkeit bzw. die Zahl Drei erwähnt und sie im Spott ausfaltet, hat daher noch eine weitere Bewandtnis und dies hat mit der Zahl Drei, mit der Zahl 70 vom vorigen Vers (Vers 2) und auch mit dem Wort *firqah* (Vers 1) zu tun. In einer Überlieferung des Propheten heißt es: وَتَفْتَرِقُ أُمَّتِي عَلَى ثَلَاثٍ وَسَبْعِينَ فِرْقَةً (*Und meine ummah wird sich in dreiundsiebzig Gruppen aufteilen*).[95]

Was Ibn Abī Ḥaǧalah horizontal, Vers für Vers, analog zur Abfolge des Unheilgeschehens durch die Christen einführt, diskutiert er für die eigene, islamische Seite vertikal von Vers 1-4. Wir sehen hier eine strukturell und inhaltlich sehr durchdachte Verbindung der Verse 1- 4. Der hier vorgegebene Ton gibt auch generell den Modus der Elegie wieder, allzu viel Sentimentales dürfen wir von ihm nicht mehr erwarten. Die Haltung des Poeten zum Ereignis, die er bereits am Anfang signalisiert, bleibt bis zum Schluß erhalten.

In den nächsten Versen (V. 5-7) intensiviert der Poet den *ṭibāq* (z.B. *firanǧ* und *ʿurbān*) mit dem Verweis auf die Teilnahme der Beduinen an der Plünderung der Stadt, wobei hier noch ein schöner *ǧinās* mit *ʿurbān* und *ǧirbān* gebildet wird. Die Teilnahme der Beduinen am niederträchtigen Raub bestätigt an-Nuwayrī in seinem Kommentar, wie auch aš-Šāṭibī in mahnenden Versen ihr gottloses Tun verurteilt (z.B. Verse 39-41). An-Nastarāwī dagegen verweist darauf, daß die zu Hilfe gerufenen Beduinen wohl herbeieilten, aber mit nackten Pferden, die wie Kühe aussahen, sie also keine Hilfe waren.[96]

Die Einleitungsfloskeln wie *fa-* / *wa-kam* + *xy* amplifizieren, ohne viel sagen zu müssen, das Ausmaß der Verwüstung, wobei die Antithesen, die hierauf folgen (reich-arm, alt-jung)[97] prägnanter ausfallen. Innerhalb des begrenzten Raums in der Qaṣīde sind diese Floskeln auch Strategien zur Kompensation des vielen Nichtgesagten oder deren Materialspuren.

Der achte Vers ist ein Überleitungsvers zum nächsten Modul und zeigt, daß der Zenit der stufenweise aufgebauten Heimsuchung erreicht ist:

---

[95] Es gibt zahlreiche Varianten dieser Überlieferung in den Ḥadīṯwerken. Bezüglich ihrer Authentizität sind sie als schwach (*ḍaʿīf*) bzw. als mittelmäßig-gut (*ḥasan*) klassifiziert. Siehe Theodor Haarbrücker, *Abu-ʾl-Fatḥ Muḥammad asch-Schahrastānī's Religionsparheien und Philosophenschulen*, Halle 1850, S. 3-4.

[96] an-Nastarāwī im *Ms. Ilmām*, fol. 235b = *KI*, IV: S. 173 (Vers 20): *wa-la-qad ǧaʾat ʿarābu naǧdatin bi-ḫuyūlin ʿāriyātin ka-l-baqar*.

[97] Eine ähnliche Formulierung gibt auch an-Nastarāwī in seinen Verse 41, 43 (*KI*, IV: S. 175): „*Sie haben keine Rücksicht genommen, weder auf jung noch alt, / ob klein oder groß war ihnen gleichgültig. // Und wieviele mächtige Menschen sind erniedrigt worden, / und (wie viele) reiche Menschen sind nach Zeiten des Wohlstands verarmt*".

فَصَغِيرٌ وَكَبِيرٌ مُسْتَطِرْ مَا رَعَوْا شَابًّا وَلَأْ ذَا شَيْبَةٍ

وَغَنِيٌّ بَعْدَ مَالٍ افْتَقَرْ كَمْ عَزِيزٍ قَدْ غَدَا فِي ذِلَّةٍ

(5)   فَيَـالَكَ مِـنْ هَـوْلٍ عَظِـيمٍ وَفِتْنَـةٍ   أَضَرَّ عَـلَى الإِنْسَانِ مِـنْ فِتْنَةِ القَـبْرِ

Ach, welch gewaltiges Unheil und welche Prüfung du bist, die für den Menschen   133a
peinvoller ist als die Prüfung des Grabes!   [II: 272]

Ab hier würden die zur Stadtpanegyrik typischen Motive der nostalgischen Vergegenwärtigung alter Zeiten erwartet werden, doch im Gegensatz zu den anderen Elegien fällt dieser Part sehr kurz aus (V. 11-13). Bezeichnend ist, daß Ibn Abī Ḥaǧalah mit einem Orakel-Motiv (V. 10) beginnt und selbst für die nachfolgende historische Sequenz mit der islamischen Eroberung Ägyptens weit ausholt, als gäbe es für ihn keine weiteren Vorzüge der Stadt. An-Nuwayrī greift das Motiv auf und führt zu diesem Thema gleich sechs Träume an, die die Einnahme der Stadt voraussagten, darüber hinaus ein mit Zahlen- und Buchstabensymbolik versehenes Weissagungsgedicht (*malḥamah*) und sprichwörtlich gewordene Prophezeiungen über die Eroberung, die in Ägypten verbreitet waren.[98] Für die Stadt Alexandria soll es eine Prophezeiung gegeben haben, nach der diese an einem Freitag erobert würde. Die Verwirklichung dieser Voraussagung ist ein wichtiger literarischer Topos, den Ibn Abī Ḥaǧalah poetisch einbettet und an-Nuwayrī wiederum zu Gegenstrategien seines Textes bewegt, indem er literarisch gegen sich selbsterfüllende Prophezeiungen schreibt.[99] Doch die Weissagung ist auch – zumindest in den Texten – der literarische *movens* von christlicher Seite her. Machaut bettet in seine epische Verschronik über den Vorfall eben diese Prophezeiung ein, die Peter I. von seinem ominösen Berater Perceval de Cologne nahegelegt worden ist.[100] In den Versen 12 und 13 präsentiert Ibn Abī Ḥaǧalah seine Evaluation der aktuellen Ereignisse vor dem Hintergrund der Geschichte und spannt den Bogen von dem, was geschehen ist zu dem, was hätte sein können (sollen!) optativisch (*fa-law* ...):

(12)   فَلَـوْ كَانَ فِيَـا مِثْـلُ مَـا كَانَ عَـسْكَرٌ   يَصُولُ بِذَاتِ الحَرْبِ فِيهَا مَعَ الصَّقْرِ [101]

---

[98]   Die Verkettung der Ereignisse realisiert an-Nuwayrī u.a. durch das Anführen von *prodigia* (Vorzeichen des Schicksals), die bereits in der römischen Autobiographie (und Biographie) als ein wesentliches Sujetmerkmal dienten, die Verbundenheit von individuell-persönlichen und öffentlich-staatlichen Handlungen darzustellen (siehe Bachtin, *Chronotopos*, S. 65 f.). Ausführlich über die Bedeutung der Traum-Orakelsequenzen als Topos aus dem Bereich des ʿ*ilm al-ǧifr* und als Textstrategie bei an-Nuwayrī, siehe Weintritt, *Formen*, S. 126-134.

[99]   Siehe hierzu Ausführungen auf S. 37 (*al-faʾlu muwakkalun bi-l-manṭiq*).

[100]   Dieser erzählt Peter I. das Orakel, wonach Alexandria an einem Freitag vom alten Hafen her eingenommen werden wird, so Machaut *La Prise d'Alixandre*, V. 1962-2081. Zu den *prodigia* gehört wohl auch, daß Peter Lusignan am 9. Oktober 1329 geboren wurde, so daß seine Ankunft in Alexandria auf seinen Geburtstag fiel, siehe Machaut *La Prise d'Alixandre*, V. 135, nebst Kommentar S. 430. Vgl. Capitanovici, *Die Eroberung von Alexandria*, S. 24 nebst Anm. 2; vgl. *Ms. Ilmām*, fol. 76b; Herzsohn, *Der Überfall Alexandriens*, S. 10 (Excurse) und Atiya, *A Fourteenth Century Encyclopedist*, S. 28-29.

[101]   *Ṣaqr* kann hier eine Reihe von Anspielungen haben. Einige Prophetengefährten, die sich in Kriegen auszeichneten, trugen diesen Beinamen wie z.B. Zayd Ibn al-Ḥaṭṭāb (*ṣaqr yawm al-Yamāma*) oder Ṭalḥa Ibn ʿAbdallāh (*ṣaqr yawm Uḥud*). Naheliegender ist hier aber die Anspielung auf den ruhmreichen umayyadischen Prinzen und Emir von Cordoba ʿAbd ar-

Hätte sie (Alexandria) ein Heer gehabt, das mit dem Falken in jenem Krieg   148b
auf sie gestürzt wäre,   [II: 340]

(13)   لَمَــــا ظَفِــــرَ الغِــــرْبَانُ فِيهَــــا بِنَقْــــرَةٍ   ولاَ نَابَهَــــا خَطْــــبٌ بِنَـــابٍ وَلاَ ظُفْــــرِ

dann hätten sich die Raben nicht eines einzigen Happens (Picken) bemäch-   148b
tigen können, und kein Unglück hätte sie heimgesucht weder mit Schnäbeln   [II: 341]
(Reißzähnen) noch mit Klauen.

Erst im 14. Vers tritt das „Ich" des Poeten explizit sentimental zum Vorschein und kündigt, da er bislang unpersonal erzählte, eine erneute Wende im Gedicht an. Doch zunächst bleibt der Poet ganze drei Verse (14-16) bei seinem Trauermotiv über die Gefangenen.

(14)   وقَــدْ أَسَرَتْ قَلْبِي الأَسَــارَى بِــأَسْرِهِمْ   فَوَاعَجَبًــــا مِــــنْ آسِرٍ وَهْــــوَ فِي الأَسْرِ

Die Gefangenen haben mein Herz gefangen durch ihre Gefangenschaft. Oh,   149a
wie seltsam ist es, von jemandem gefangen genommen zu werden, der selber   [II: 342]
gefangen ist.

Seine Betroffenheit bringt der Poet mit einem multiplen Kontrast zum Ausdruck. Die Kombination der Motivik ist eindrucksvoll gestaltet durch die entgegengesetzten Richtungen der Gefangennahme, die Ibn Abī Ḥaǧalah mit der buchstäblichen Verkettung der Folgen der Gefangennahme (bis hin zur Gefangennahme seines Herzens) wiedergibt. Der Vergleich in Vers 16 bricht aber wieder mit der eingeschlagenen sentimentalen Richtung und signalisiert in der hier unerwarteten Kombination von Gefangenen mit einer koranischen Straflegende, also einer negativen Umkehrung von Mitleid zu Strafe, bereits den Modus der Gestaltung des nächsten und letzten Moduls (*wa-ḥaqqika*-Verse (V. 17-20)).[102]

(16)   خَــلَى رَبْعُهُــمْ مِــنْ أُنْــسِهِمْ وَتَفَرَّقُــوا   أَيَادِي سَبَا بالسَّبْي فِي آخِــرِ الــشَّهْرِ[103]

Raḥmān I. (lebte 731-788). Im Jahre 755 führte er eine Armee an, mit der er Sevilla und Cordoba eroberte, obwohl sie erheblich in der Unterzahl war. Wegen seiner Tapferkeit und Unerschrockenheit soll ihn Kalif al-Manṣūr den Beinamen *ṣaqr al-Qurayš* („Falke der Qurayš") gegeben haben (siehe Lévi-Provençal, "ʿAbd al-Raḥmān I.", in: *EI²*). Ein ausdrucksstarkes Bild zur Klaue des Falken und seiner Kraft, das Ibn Abī Ḥaǧalah bei seiner Vorliebe für Maghrebiner und Andalusier womöglich in diesem Vers ebenfalls vorschwebte, liefert der andalusische Dichter ʿAbbās Ibn Firnās (gest. 887) (siehe Lévi-Provençal, "ʿAbbās b. Firnās", in: *EI²*) in einem Gedicht über den Fall Toledos (240/854): (2 von 3 Versen)

ضحت طليطلةٌ معطّلةً ... من أهلها في قبضة الصقرتركت بلا أهلٍ تؤهّلها ... مهجورة الأكناف كالقبر

"*When morning came, Toledo appeared deserted, and (like a bird) in the claws of a falcon // Its houses uninhabited, its streets without people, the whole city as empty and as silent as a tomb.*" Das Gedicht ist zitiert in al-Maqqari, *Nafḥ aṭ-ṭib*, I: S. 162, übers. von Pascual de Gayangos, *The History of the Mohammedan Dynasties in Spain*, 2 Bde, London 1840, I: S. 47.

[102] Zur Konversion von Gefangenen an-Nuwayrī, *KI*, IV: S. 412.

[103] Im Original in etwa [يَا السَّبْي سَبَا]. Ein grammatikalisch und metrisch defekter Halbvers. Die Handschrift lässt die Lesung سَبَأٍ يَا لَلسَّبْي zu, sie passt allerdings metrisch nicht. Auch die Variante in Weintritt *ayādiya sabāyā* (als Plural von *sabyi*) *s-sabyi fī āḫiri š-šahri* ist metrisch in

Ihre Wohnstätten sind von ihrer Geselligkeit verlassen und durch die Gefan- 150b
genschaft wurden sie (~ wie die Stämme von Sabāʾ b. Yašğub nach der Flut al- [II: 348]
ʿArim)[104] am Ende des Monats in alle Winde zerstreut.

Die Gefangenen von Alexandria wurden gewaltsam weggenommen, ohne ihre Schuld. Die Leute von Sabāʾ (Šeba) dagegen flohen nach der Flut al-ʿArim wegen der Strafe Gottes über sie. Sie wähnten sich stark mit ihrem Heer, ihrem Wohlstand und ihrer Baukunst und zeigten sich undankbar, so der Koran, weswegen Gott sie mit einer katastrophalen Flut bestrafte, bei der die Überlebenden in alle Himmelsrichtungen verstreut wurden, ähnlich den Bewohnern Alexandrias, die durch das Rosetta-Tor in einem großen Gedränge vor den Franken flüchteten. Die Bestrafung von Städten ist ein prominenter Topos im Koran. Im Fall von Alexandrien wäre dies der Untergang der Stadt Iram (*Q* 89: 6 f.), die nach Ansicht einiger Gelehrter mit Alexandrien gleichgesetzt wird.[105] Obwohl es Ibn Abī Ḥağalah nirgendwo im Gedicht explizit ausdrückt, so schwebt dennoch die Straflegende von Iram, weil sie sich einerseits auf Alexandria beziehen kann und andererseits die Sündhaftigkeit der Stadt im Allgemeinen angeprangert wird, über den *wa-ḥaqqika*-Versen. Die implizite Anspielung entgeht an-Nuwayrī nicht, so daß dieser in Folge der Verssequenzen 17-20 ausführlicher auf das Thema Iram eingeht.[106]

Mit diesen koranischen Verweisen leitet Ibn Abī Ḥağalah zu seinem letzten Modul mit Straf- und Anklageversen über:

(17)   وَحَقِّكَ هَـذَا مِـنْ ذُنُـوبٍ تَقَـدَّمَتْ   وَقَرْعٍ كُؤُوسِ الخَمْرِ في الثَّغْرِ بِالثَّغْرِ

---

der zweiten *tafʿilah* nicht möglich (⌣ - ⌣/⌣ ⌣ - -/⌣ - -/⌣ - - -). Nach Lane, *Arabic-English Lexicon*, s.v. „sabā" ist in der Phrase *tafarraqū ayādi sabā* das letzte Wort unflektiert, so daß sich die Lesungen mit *bi-s-sabyi* („~ und durch die Gefangenschaft wurden sie … in alle Winde zerstreut") und mit Vokativ *ayādi sabā yā s-sabyi fī āḫiri š-šahri* („~ und – wehe der Gefangenschaft! – sie wurden am Ende des Monats in alle Winde zerstreut") metrisch und inhaltlich anbieten.

[104] *Q* 34: 15-17. Diese Verse gehören zu den Straflegenden im Koran, die Ibn Abī Ḥağalah, hier noch in der Umkehrung im Mitleid und der Trauer über die Gefangenen als Überleitung zu den eigenen „Strafversen" (die folgenden *wa-ḥaqqika*-Verse) verwendet. Ähnlich ist im religiösen Schrifttum die Bestrafung der Bewohner Maʾribs geschildert, die in ihrer Sorglosigkeit auf Grund ihres Wohlstands u.a. Gottes Gesandte ablehnten, die Mahnungen und Zeichen Gottes ignorierten und dafür mit der großen Flut (*sayl al-ʿarim*) durch einen Dammbruch bestraft wurden. Zu den differierenden koranischen Erzählungen über den Staudamm von Maʾrib siehe Raif Georges Khoury, "al-ʿArim", in *EQ* 1: 60-61 und Alfred Felix Beeston, "Sabaʾ", in: *EI²*.

[105] Yāqūt ar-Rūmī, *Muʿğam al-buldān*, 6 Bde., Leipzig 1866-1873, I: S. 155-157; siehe auch Watt, "Iram", in: *EI²*.

[106] *Ms. Ilmām*, fol. 168a f.: in diesen Passagen zitiert an-Nuwayrī einige Ḥadīṯe über die Belohnung der *Ribāṭ*-Kämpfer im Jenseits und schließt ohne weitere Erklärung mit einem *Hadīṯ* ab, worin das koranische „Iram" auf Alexandria verweist: عَنْ كَعْبِ بْنِ مُحَمَّدٍ قَالَ: أَرَمُ ذَاتُ العِمَادِ الإِسْكَنْدَرِيَّةُ. (انْتَهَى. نَعُودُ) (weitere Iram-Bezüge u.a. fol. 205a, 247a). Im Abschnitt über Ğilliq verweist an-Nuwayrī allerdings auch darauf, daß einige Gelehrte Iram mit Damaskus gleichsetzen (*Ms. Ilmām*, fol. 57a).

Bei deinem Leben (sei dir gewiß)![107] Das kommt von vorangegangenen   154a
Sünden / und dem Anstoßen der Weinkelche an den Mund (an die Zähne)   [III: 1]
in der Grenzstadt.

In seinem Kommentar widerspricht an-Nuwayrī an dieser Stelle zu recht, da diese Formulierung ein schiefes Bild vermittelt: Ein Glas (*kaʾs*) könne zerbrechen, *kaʿb* (Weinkelch mit Henkel) wäre passender gewesen; zudem hätte Ibn Abī Ḥaǧalah statt „*qarʿin*" das Wort „*rašfin*" benutzen sollen, da man nicht an die „Zähne" anstößt und sich das zweite *ṯaġr* auf den Mund beziehe.[108]

Ibn Abī Ḥaǧalah bleibt nicht bei der Anklage. Die Handlungsoption, die der Poet gegen die Übermacht des Unvermögens (Verse 18-19) parat hält, ist seine eigene Kunstfertigkeit. Diese positioniert er an eine Stelle, wo das Rache/*ǧihād*-Motiv kommen könnte. Die Verse 20-22 zeigen die Bandbreite, wie man hätte handeln sollen. Der metapoetische Vers 20 ist typisch für Ibn Abī Ḥaǧalah und in ähnlicher Form in vielen Gedichten in seinem Dīwān zu finden. Selbst oder vielleicht gerade, wenn er seine Gedichte an Herrscher richtet, nutzt er *faḫr*-Verse, die seine eigene Kunstfertigkeit wortgewandt preisen.[109] Es ist nicht unbedeutend, daß Ibn Abī Ḥaǧalah, anstatt die *faḍāʾil/maḥāsin* Alexandrias zu rühmen, hier Beispiele aus dem Maġrib und al-Andalus bringt.[110] Die vom Poeten vorge-

---

[107] Die Beschwörungsformel *wa-ḥaqqiku* ist nach den einschlägigen Lexika als Bekräftigung der nachfolgenden Aussage zu verstehen. Ich ziehe die Übersetzung (*sei dir gewiss!*), wie sie auch Gert Borg ("Love Poetry by Arab Women. A Survey", in: *Arabica* 54 (2007), S. 425-465, hier S. 442) verwendet, vor. *Ḥaqq* umfaßt Recht/Anspruch sowie auch Verpflichtung und Schuld/Anteil für empfangene Wohltaten (siehe Heinrich L. Fleischers [Übers.], *Aliʾs hundert Sprüche* nach dem Werk *Maṭlūb kull ṭālib min kalām ʿAlī b. Abī Ṭālib* von Rašidaddin Waṭwāṭ, Leipzig 1837, S. 122 arabischer Index), daher ist der Anklageton des Poeten in Weintritts Übersetzung mit „dies gebührt dir zu Recht" wiedergegeben.

[108] *Ms. Ilmām*, fol. 166a, Z. 3 ff.

[109] Z.B. in seinen zwei ausladenden Panegyriken für den Ǧalāyiridensultan Uways (756-776/1355-1374), der als großer Patron der Künste und selbst als begabter Poet galt (siehe Clifford E. Bosworth, "Uways", in: *EI²*). Für die Gedichte Ibn Abī Ḥaǧalahs siehe *Dīwān Ibn Abī Ḥaǧalah 725 H.-776 H.*, Hg. Aḥmad Ḥilmi Ḥulwah, S. 186-192. Auch für an-Nuwayrī galt Uways als ein Vorbild unter den Königen. Seine solidarische und strenge Haltung gegenüber den fränkischen Kaufleuten in Bagdad ist Anlaß genug, ihn im *Ilmām* lobend zu erwähnen (siehe hierzu ausführlich Weintritt, *Formen*, S. 31, S. 114 und S. 121, nach an-Nuwayrī, *KI*, V: S. 231-232).

[110] Ibn Abī Ḥaǧalah verweist vermutlich auf den ruhmreichen, aber kurzwährenden Sieg der merinidischen Flotte im Jahre 1279 unter Abū Yāʿqūb in Algeciras gegen die Kastilier. Für diesen Sieg hatte u.a. der Fürst von Ceuta al-Azfi 45 Schiffe und viele Kämpfer geschickt, so viele heißt es, daß nur noch Kinder, Alte und Kranke in der Stadt blieben. Die Chronik *Rawḍ al-Qirṭās* berichtet von der heldenhaften Verteidigung gegen die Überzahl der Feinde: *"For four nights the people of Tangier, El Kaṣar eṣ-Ṣaghīr and Ceuta "prayed on their ramparts with eyes and doors open", and, though the Spanish vessels were crowded with men, "like crows on a hilltop", they were defeated and the town was fortified afresh."* (zitiert aus Budgett Meakin, *The Moorish Empire*, London 1899, S. 97-98). 1344 konnten die Kastilier die Stadt wiedererobern. Wegen der regional losen Bündnispolitik zwischen Aragon und Kastilien sowie zu den islamischen Herrscherhäusern gelangte Algeciras erneut 1369 unter dem Naṣriden-Fürsten Muḥammad V. von Granada (reg. 1354-1359, 1362-1391) unter islamische Hoheit. Doch dieses Ereignis liegt deutlich nach dem Abfassungsjahr des Gedichts. Über die Eroberun-

führten Ruhmestaten der *ahl as-Sabtah* und der *al-Ğazīrah al-ḫaḍrā*' dürften wie ein Schlag ins Gesicht Yalbuġās gewesen sein. Diesem zeigt Ibn Abī Ḥaġalah kurz und bündig, was für ein Kampfgeist hinter dessen Truppen stecken müsste, daß die Stadtbefestigung ausgebaut werden müßte, es an erfahrenen (maghrebinischen!) Seeleuten fehlte und daß religiöser Anstand bzw. ein gottgefälliges Leben wieder in die Stadt einkehren sollte. Mitten in Kairo kann sich ein Dichter erlauben, dem Reichsverweser diese Lektion zu erteilen.

Exkurs: Ṭarāblus al-Ġarb – Lob auf Ibn Makkī

Bevor die letzten Verse vorgestellt werden, soll an dieser Stelle auf einige Aspekte des Kontrastgedichts Ibn Abī Ḥaġalahs eingegangen werden. Das Gedicht bezieht sich auf die Wiedereroberung von Ṭarāblus al-Ġarb,[111] das kurz zuvor von den „Franken" eingenommen worden war. Da sich die Lage zugunsten der Muslime entschied, bettet Ibn Abī Ḥaġalah sein poetisches Anliegen in eine hochstilisierte Panegyrik. Die umfangreiche Qaṣīde mit 45 Versen stellt die entgegengesetzte Richtung zum Versagen in Alexandria dar und ist somit mit einigen formalen Parallelen das Gegenteil dessen, was er später für Alexandria geschrieben hat. Sie dient in unserem Zusammenhang als Beispiel dafür, wie Ibn Abī Ḥaġalah hätte rühmen können, wäre die Stadt siegreich verteidigt worden.

Der historische Kontext dieser Qaṣīde ist der, daß der genuesische Freibeuter Filippo Doria[112] im Jahre 755/1354 eigenmächtig und für die Bewohner überra-

---

gen Algeciras siehe Gustav Diercks, *Geschichte Spaniens von den frühesten Zeiten bis auf die Gegenwart*, 2 Bde., Berlin 1896, II: S. 9-18 und Donald Kagay & Andrew Villalon (Hg.), *Crusaders, Condottieri, and Cannon. Medieval Warfare in Societies Around the Mediterranean*, Leiden 2003, S. 193 ff. und S. 204-234.

[111] Zur Stadtgeschichte siehe Oman, Christides and Bosworth, "Ṭarābulus al-Gharb", in: *EI²* sowie *dies.*, "Tripoli, in Libya", in: Bosworth, *Historic Cities of the Islamic World*, S. 529-535. Eine relativ zeitnahe Städtebeschreibung mit zahlreichen Gedichten findet sich in at-Tīğānī, *Riḥlat at-Tīğānī*, Hg. Ḥasan ʿAbd al-Wahhāb, Tūnis 1981, S. 239-307. At-Tīğānī (Abū Muḥammad ʿAbdallāh b. Aḥmad (670-?/1272-?)) begleitete als *kātib* die Expedition des Prinzen und späteren Sultans Abū Yaḥyā al-Liḥyānī und hielt sich im Zeitraum von 1306-1309 ca. 1,5 Jahre in Tripolis auf; siehe zu ihm Michael Brett, "The Journey of al-Tijānī to Tripoli at the beginning of the fourteenth century A.D./eighth century A.H.", in: *Libyan Studies* 7 (1976), S. 41-51; *ders.*, "Tripoli at the Beginning of the Fourteenth Century A. D./Eighth Century AH.", *Libyan Studies* 9 (1978), S. 55-59; Sébastien Garnier, "Departures in Tiğānī's Riḥla", in: *Annali di Ca' Foscari* XLVIII (2009), S. 127-135.

[112] Ṭarāblus war zu jener Zeit quasi autonom von den Banū Ṯābit beherrscht und stand im losen Bündnis mit dem Ḥafṣidenreich, das mit der Zurückdrängung der Meriniden beschäftigt war. Zudem waren sie durch ihren herrschsüchtigen Minister Ibn Tāfrāğīn in weitere politische Wirren geraten, die sich Doria wohl zunutze gemacht hat. Dorias Schiffe stießen zunächst zu den regulären Handelsschiffen am Hafen der Stadt und seine Leute mischten sich unbemerkt unter die Händler, bevor sie angriffen. Der vom Angriff überraschte Fürst Ṯābit b. Muḥammad gab die Verteidigung nach einigen Kampfhandlungen auf und floh mit seinem Bruder zu einem benachbarten Stamm, von dem sie wegen einer alten Blutfehde getötet wurden. Einer seiner Söhne konnte sich in Alexandria absetzen und organisierte von dort aus die 771/1369 die Rückeroberung der Stadt für die Banū Ṯābit. Siehe

schend Ṭarāblus überfiel.[113] Ähnlich wie es in Alexandria geschah, hatte er die
Stadt verwüstet, reichlich Beute gemacht und mehr als 7000 Gefangene genommen. Doch anders als Peter I. zog Doria nicht wieder aus der Stadt, sondern
blieb. Dies ist Anlaß genug für an-Nuwayrī, gegen die Niedrigkeit Peters I. zu po-
lemisieren und Doria als Gegenbeispiel anzuführen. Dorias Vorgehen hatte unmittelbar Gegenangriffe der Muslime auf italienische und südfranzösische Kü-
stenstädte zur Folge. Die Genuesen befürchteten Repressalien und den Verlust
ihrer vorteilhaften Handelskonzessionen in Nordafrika. Wegen heftiger Kritik
von eigener Seite verkaufte Doria schließlich die Stadt gegen eine Zahlung von
50.000 Gold-Miṯqāl an Abū l-ʿAbbās Aḥmad Ibn Makkī (gest. 766/1364, Emir
von Qābis)[114] und beendete für eine Weile (vorsätzlich?) die Vorherrschaft der
Bānū Ṯābit in Tripolis und damit auch ihre Anbindung an die Ḥafṣiden. Der
Leihgeber für diese Summe war u.a. der damals mächtigere Merinidensultan Abū
ʿInān Fāris (759/1358), der sich im Gegenzug dafür die Loyalität der Banū Makkī
sicherte. Die Hälfte des Geldes soll Falschgeld gewesen sein.[115] Ob Ibn Abī Ḥaǧalah und an-Nuwayrī darüber Kenntnis hatten, geht aus den Texten nicht hervor.
Doch angesichts der nicht besonders tapferen ‚Wiedereroberung' der Stadt, die
im besten Falle ein Freikauf war, der zudem den Herrschaftsbereich der Bānū

---

hierzu Ettore Rossi, *Storia di Tripoli e délia Tripolitania, dalla conquista araba al 1911*, ediz.
postuma, Hg. Maria Nallino, Roma 1968, S. 89-91 (arab. Übers. von Muḥammad at-Tillisī,
Lībiyā mundu l-fatḥ al-ʿarabī ḥattā sanah 1911, Bayrūt 1393-1974, S. 141-143); Aḥmad Bek
an-Nāʾib al-Anṣārī, *al-Manhal al-ʿaḏb fī tārīḫ Ṭarāblus al-Ġarb*, Ṭarāblus al-Ġarb [1899], I:
S. 166-169; Heyd, „Die mittelalterlichen Handelscolonien der Italiener in Nordafrica von
Tripolis bis Marokko", S. 617-660, hier S. 635-636; Robert Brunschvig, *La Berbérie orientale
sous les Ḥafṣides des origines à la fin du XVe siècle*, 2 Bde., Paris 1940-1947, I: S. 172-173; Do-
minique Valérian, "Tripoli dans les réseaux d'échanges intercontinentaux à la fin du
Moyen Âge", in: Rémi Dewière et Güneş Işıksel (Hg.), *Tripoli, port de mer, port de désert*, Paris
2011, S. 353-363, hier S. 354; Sébastien Garnier, "Ibn Tāfrāǧin", in: *EI³* über die tiefe
Feindschaft zwischen den Banū Makkī und Ibn Tāfrāǧin.

[113] Taqiyyaddīn Aḥmad al-Maqrīzī (gest. 845/1442), *Durar al-ʿuqūd al-farīdah fī tarāǧim al-aʿyān
al-mufīdah*, Hg. Maḥmūd al-Ǧalīlī, III: S. 523-524; Abū ʿAbdallāh az-Zarkašī (gest. nach
894/nach 1488), *Taʾrīḫ ad-dawlatayn al-Muwaḥḥidiyyah wa-l-Ḥafṣiyyah*, Hg. Muḥammad
Māḏūr, Tūnis 1962, S. 94-95 (der Überfall dauerte vom 10. R. II. 755 bis 12 Šaʿbān 744/ 4.
Mai.1354-30. August 1354); Muḥammad Ibn ʿAbd ar-Raḥmān as-Saḫāwī (gest. 1427/8 -
1497), *aḏ-Ḏayl at-tām ʿalā duwal al-Islām li-ḏ-Ḏahabī*, Hg. Ḥasan Ismāʿīl Marwah, Bayrūt
1992, I: (Ḥawādiṯ wa-tarāǧim li-s-sanawāt 745-850 H., S. 144. As-Saḫāwī schreibt in einem
kurzen Abschnitt über den Vorfall, daß die „Franken" an einem Freitag im Rabīʿ I. heim-
tückisch Ṭarāblus erobert hätten. So sollen nach fünfzehntägigen Kampfhandlungen
Schreiben in Syrien angekommen sein, in denen um Beistand für den Freikauf gebeten
wurde. Nach Ibn Ḥaldūns Angaben aber, wurde in den *bilād al-ǧarīdiyyah* (*bilād al-ǧarīdah*:
„Das Gebiet der Palmzweige" umfaßt das fruchtbare Gebiet entlang des Atlasgebirges an
seiner Südseite und ist eingeteilt in eine West- und Osthälfte, die sich bis nach Libyen erstreckt) für finanzielle Hilfe aufgerufen (siehe Ibn Ḥaldūn (gest. 808/1432), *Tārīḫ Ibn
Ḥaldūn al-musammā [Kitāb al-ʿIbar] dīwān al-mubtadaʾ wa-l-ḫabar fī ayyām al-ʿarab wa-l-ʿaǧam
wa-l-barbar wa-man ʿāṣarahum min ḏawī š-šaʾn [s-sulṭān] al-akbar*, Hg. Ḥalil Šaḥādah, Bayrūt
1959, VI: S. 615-616).

[114] Vgl. Talbi, "Kābis", in: *EI²*.

[115] Siehe John Wright, *A History of Libya*, London 2012, S. 68-69.

Makkī unverhofft erweiterte, stellt sich die Frage, wie niedrig die Schwelle beider Autoren für ein Herrscherlob war, oder ob das Lob eine weitere Funktion erfüllte.[116] Der Kontrast zum Überfall auf Alexandria zeigt jedoch, daß selbst an diese Schwelle weder Yalbuġā (für Ibn Abī Ḥaǧalah) noch Peter Lusignan (für an-Nuwayrī) heranreichten.

Was hier für die Motivation Ibn Abī Ḥaǧalahs vorerst ungewiß bleiben muss, tritt bei an-Nuwayrī in seinen Kommentaren umso deutlicher hervor, da es sich bei ihm um ein literarisches Verfahren zur Schmähung des Gegners handelt.[117] Hätte er Peter Lusignan mit einem bedeutenderen islamischen Herrscher verglichen, hätte er unter Umständen Peter ikonisiert.[118] Bereits in der Schilderung der Unterhaltung zwischen einem maghrebinischen Händler und Ġanġarā zur Verteidigungstaktik Alexandrias hatte an-Nuwayrī die genuesische Eroberung in Tripolis erwähnt, wobei er hier die polemische Kritik am Vorfall in Tripolis einem der Ribāṭ-Besitzer in den Mund legte.[119] An-Nuwayrī arbeitet textstrategisch stetig daran, mit Geschichten und Gedichten, naheliegenden und weithergeholten Beispielen einen – wie Weintritt herausarbeitet – Eroberungsethos zu normieren, an dessen minimalsten Anforderungen er Peter I. scheitern läßt.[120] Die Eroberung von Tripolis dient ihm als Beispiel dafür. So wird dieser Vorfall ein weiteres Mal im Zusammenhang mit der Geschichte einer alten Frau erwähnt, die ihre Golddinare auf der Flucht einem Mann anvertraute, der später aber abstritt, etwas von ihr angenommen zu haben. Auf die Frage, warum sie das Geld nicht lieber in der Erde gelassen habe, sagte sie: *„Was mich aber veranlaßte, sie mitzunehmen, war der Überfall auf das libysche Tripolis und die Eroberung der Stadt durch die Franken. Sie waren nämlich einen Monat lang dortgeblieben und hatten die Böden der Häuser aufgegraben, weil ihr langer Aufenthalt in der Stadt ihnen Zeit dazu gab. Ich rechnete damit, daß derjenige, der sich Alexandrias bemächtigt, ebenfalls in der Stadt mit sei-*

---

[116] Freilich steht im Lob die fromme Tat Aḥmad Ibn Makkīs im Vordergrund, sich der herrenlosen Stadt angenommen und folglich sie nicht an die Christen verloren zu haben. Darüberhinaus verweist die Panegyrik auch auf weitere persönliche Anliegen Ibn Abī Ḥaǧalahs. In diesem Zusammenhang wäre es sicherlich ergiebig, die Haltung Ibn Abī Ḥaǧalahs zu seiner Heimatstadt Tilimsān und den Meriniden herauszuarbeiten.

[117] In dieser Weise führt an-Nuwayrī an folgenden Stellen die Eroberung von Ṭarāblus an, siehe fol. 75a, 103a, 109a, 166a. In einem fingierten Dialog zwischen den Königen der Christenheit und Peter Lusignan heißt es: *„Du hättest, als du es in Besitz genommen, darin bleiben und es vertheidigen […] sollen, wie die Genuesen […] es mit dem Tripolis des Westens machten! Aber du bist als Räuber hinein und als Räuber hinausgegangen […].“* (Übers. Herzsohn, *Der Überfall Alexandriens*, S. 13, nach fol. 165a [sic]). Namentlich erwähnt an-Nuwayrī Aḥmad Ibn Makkī im Zusammenhang mit dem Freikauf von muslimischen Gefangenen, jedoch nicht im Kontext des Überfalls (*KI*, V: S. 389 – diesen Abschnitt der Druckfassung konnte ich im Berliner Manuskript nicht auffinden).

[118] Was er durchaus an einer Stelle tut, indem er Ašraf Šaʿbān mit Peter I. vergleicht, doch an dieser Stelle arbeitet Weintritt heraus, daß beide Figuren jeweils für ihre Religionen Christentum und Islam stehen, siehe ders., *Formen*, S. 79-81.

[119] Vgl. hier Anm. 24.

[120] Zum Eroberungsethos siehe Weintritt, *Formen*, S. 49, S. 57, S. 77 f., S. 80, S. 83.

nem Heer bleiben könnte, wie es in Tripolis geschehen ist. [...] Wenn ich jedoch gewußt hätte, daß sie als Diebe kommen, als Räuber und Plünderer, und nicht vorhatten, in Alexandria zu bleiben, genausowenig wie ein Dieb dort bleibt, wo er gestohlen hat, hätte ich es an seinem Platz gelassen".[121]

Ibn Abī Ḥaǧalahs *maṭlaᶜ* eröffnet das Gedicht mit einem zu seiner Zeit üblich gewordenen homoerotischen *ġazal*,[122] in dem bereits im zweiten Halbvers auf etwas Wundersames („Vollmond in der Nacht des Neumonds") aufmerksam gemacht wird.[123] Das Wundersame setzt sich in ausgefeilten Kontrasten leitmotivisch durch das ganze Gedicht fort und wird über drei Transformationsfiguren mit dem *mamdūḥ* Ibn al-Makkī verbunden: V. 1a-5 Gazellenjunges → V. 1 b; 5 b Vollmond → V. 7-11 Jüngling → ab V. 13-40[124] der Fürst Ibn al-Makkī, dessen Name erst im 20. Vers genannt wird. Während die ersten Figuren translokal und relativ abstrakt bleiben, konkretisiert sich die Preisung in Richtung Ibn Makkī (Nennung des Herrschernamens, der Stadt Ṭarāblus, konkrete Ereignisse und Taten) immer mehr. Dabei überwiegen zunächst äußere, die Physiognomie betreffenden Schönheiten der Liebesobjekte (*rašīq al-qaddi; muḫtaṣar al-ḫaṣri; lahā waǧhu; wurud al-ḫudūdi, sūd laḥẓihī, qāmatuhū, nabt al-ᶜāriḍayn, naml ᶜiḏārihī, waw aṣ-ṣadǧi ḥawla lāmihī, ...*), die den tugendhaften und herrschaflichen Leistungen eines vorbildlichen Fürsten weichen. Die Überleitung zum *mamdūḥ* geschieht in der beliebten poetologischen Figur des Buchstabenspiels, wie sie in der Dichtung Ibn Abī Ḥaǧalahs und seines Zeitgenossen Burhānaddīn al-Qīrāṭī (781/1379)[125] häufig vorkommen. Allerdings kommen diese Buchstabenspiele nicht unverhofft und holprig daher. Der Poet bereitet sein Publikum hierauf implizit und explizit vor, indem er einerseits bei der Beschreibung des Jünglings, der bereits Bartsprossen trägt, Buchstaben als etablierte Metaphern (*lām* = Backenbart) oder Metonymien (*waw aṣ-ṣudǧ* = die *waw*-Form seiner Schläfenlocke) für die Beschreibung

---

[121] Übers. von Weintritt, *Formen*, S. 168 nach an-Nuwayrī, *KI*, IV: S. 326-330.

[122] Siehe Thomas Bauer, *Liebe und Liebesdichtung in der arabischen Welt des 9. und 10. Jahrhunderts: eine literatur- und mentalitätsgeschichtliche Studie des arabischen Ġazal*, Wiesbaden 1998, S. 19 sowie allgemein das Kapitel über Themen des *ġazal*, S. 185-207 und ders. (Hg.), *Ghazal as World Literature I: Transformations of a Literary Genre*, Würzburg 2005.

[123] Der Vergleich des Gazellenjunges mit dem Vollmond ist vertikal gestaltet, im darauffolgenden Vers („*Sein Antlitz war dem Westen zugewandt, als es um das Meer erschien, / und es erleuchtete mir im östlichen Land* [d.i. der Standort des Dichters], *das was der Fluß verbarg* [das Gebiet bis hinter den Oxus]") erweitert der Poet diesen um eine ausgedehnte horizontale Ebene. Hier markiert der Poet bereits das Raummotiv (West-Ost), auf das er im Schlußvers (Nähe und Ferne, zu Wasser und zu Lande) zurückkommt.

[124] Die hier ausgeklammerten Verse 6 und 12 lese ich als Überleitungsverse (*taḫalluṣ*) zum jeweils nächsten Themenmodul.

[125] Geert Jan van Gelder, *Classical Arabic Literature. A library of Arabic Literature Anthology*, New York 2013, S. 347, nebst. Anm.; zum Poeten siehe Thomas Bauer, "Extremely Beautiful and Extremely Long" Al-Qīrāṭī's Exuberant Letter from the Year 761/1360", in: *Arabic Humanities, Islamic Thought. Essays in Honor of Everett K. Rowson*, Hg. Joseph E. Lowry & Shawkat M. Toorawa, Leiden 2017 (im Druck); Beispiele für die Verwendung von Buchstaben für die Beschreibung des Wangenflaums gibt ders., *Liebe und Liebesdichtung*, S. 264.

des Gesichts verwendet und andererseits mit *Abū ʿAmr*[126] auf einen Lesartendiskurs verweist. Gesteigert wird die spannungsreiche Hinführung zum gelobten Fürsten durch das Motiv des sich nicht Zurückhalten-Könnens[127] vor den Reizen und Vorzügen des Geliebten (V. 11-14).

Die Verse 15-18 entfalten im *faḫr* die Freigebigkeit und Großzügigkeit als Herrscherideal. Über diese Form des potenzierten Lobs leitet Ibn Abī Ḥaǧalah auf Verse über, von denen wir annehmen können, daß sie Aufschluß über den Anlaß des Gedichts geben. Es finden sich nämlich in den Versen 19-21 Hinweise darauf, daß er im gelehrten Austausch mit Ibn Makkī gestanden und diesem sein Prophetenlob geschickt hat.[128]

Mit den Kontrasten der freigebigen Hand zur Falte der *burdah* – hier in einer *tawriyah* (Mantel und Prophetenlob) verwendet –, in der ebenfalls reichliche Gaben enthalten sind, ruft der Poet einen Parallelismus hervor, der auf den Leitaspekt des religiösen Handelns des darauffolgenden Moduls einstimmt. Doch zunächst dient ihm diese Freigebigkeit in einer rhetorischen Frage[129] als Überleitung zum Thema der ‚fränkischen Eroberung' (V. 24-27). Es findet in vier Versen die explizite Erwähnung im Gedicht, um in das gesteigerte Fürstenlob (V. 31-40; Reiterei und kriegerisches Potential) überzugehen.

---

[126] Siehe zu ihm Anm. 176.

[127] Bauer, *Liebe und Liebesdichtung*, S. 255-279, hier bes. S. 262 f.

[128] Die Verse 14, 19-21 verweisen auf das Prophetenlob. Auf den gelehrten Austausch verweist ein Abschnitt in der Handschrift *Wetzstein 1803* [Auszug aus dem *Manṭiq aṭ-Ṭayr*, siehe Beitrag Pomerantz], fol. 121b-122a. Darin gibt Ibn Abī Ḥaǧalah einen Auszug mit Versen und Reimprosaproben aus dem literarischen Schriftwechsel mit dem Fürsten von Ṭarāblus (*ṣāḥib Ṭarāblus*), den wir mit Abū l-ʿAbbās Ibn Makkī identifizieren können. Diese Stelle folgt unmittelbar den Schriftproben zu gleichen Themen Ibn al-Ḫaṭibs (713-776/1313-1374), so daß wir annehmen können, daß Ibn Abī Ḥaǧalah auch über Granada mit den Banū Makkī oder mit den Meriniden verbunden war. Eine solche Kommunikationskette zeigt sich auch im *Dīwān aṣ-ṣabābah* Ibn Abī Ḥaǧalahs, der 760/1359 entstanden und an den Naṣridenhof gesandt wurde. Ibn al-Ḫaṭib antwortete mit einer Replik *„Rawḍat at-taʿrīf bil-ḥubb aš-šarīf* (siehe zu dieser Schrift und die weiteren Parallelen Josef van Ess, *Der Eine und das Andere: Beobachtungen an islamischen häresiographischen Texten*, 2 Bde., Berlin 2011, hier I: S. 1189-1193). Daß die Brüder Abū l-ʿAbbās und Abū Marwān (Fürst von Djerba) kultiviert und sich in religiösen Dingen eifrig zeigten, erfahren wir ebenfalls von Ibn Baṭṭūṭah, der die beiden 750/1349 während des Festes zur Geburt des Propheten [demnach am 12 R. I /31. Mai] auf seiner Rückroute in Gabes besuchte (Ibn Baṭṭūṭah, *Riḥlat Ibn Baṭṭūṭah*, Hg. ʿAbd al-Hādī at-Tāzī, 6 Bde., ar-Rabāṭ 1417/1997, IV: S. 184-186 [4/327]; im Abschnitt über das Lob für Abū ʿInān fügt Ibn Ǧuzayy ergänzend zu den Angaben Ibn Baṭṭūṭahs Dorias Überfall auf Ṭarāblus hinzu und daß der Sultan! sich beeilt habe, die erforderliche Summe für die Befreiung der Stadt „aus der Hand der Ungläubigen" bereitzustellen, und überhaupt geht der Ruhm für die Rettung der Stadt vollends an Abū ʿInān. Ibn Makkī wird nicht erwähnt. Siehe *ders.* IV: S. 201 [4/351]. Der Editor at-Tāzī verweist in diesem Zusammenhang auf ein Gratulationsschreiben aus Granada zu Abū ʿInāns „mutiger Unternehmung", in Lisānaddīn Ibn al-Ḫaṭibs *Rayḥānat al-kuttāb wa-nuǧʿat al-muntāb*, Hg. Muḥammad ʿAbdallāh ʿInān, 2 Bde, al-Qāhirah, 1400/1980-1, hier I: S. 324; siehe auch Brunschvig, *La Berbérie orientale*, I: S. 173, Anm. 3.

[129] Vgl. Alexandria-Gedicht V. 1.

(24) أَلَــمْ يُمْــسِ بَحْــرًا فِي طَــرَابُلُسَ الَّتِــي   جَــرَى لِلْعِــدَى فِيهَــا غَدِيــرٌ مِــنَ الغَــدْرِ

War er nicht (in seiner Freigebigkeit) zu einem Meer in Tripolis geworden, / das für
den Feind ein Tümpel der Heimtücke wurde,[130]

(25) أَبَاحَــثَ بِــهَا الإِفْــرَنْجُ قَتْــلَ رِجَالِهَــا   وَأَسْرَ النِّــسَاءِ الغِيْــدِ وَالطِّفْــلِ وَالبِكْــرِ

wo die Franken in ihr (der Stadt) die Tötung ihrer Männer / und die Gefangennahme
der grazilen Frauen sowie der Kinder und der Jungfrauen für erlaubt erklärten?

(26) فَأَنْــقَذَهَا مِنْــهُمْ جُعِلْــتُ لَهُ الفِــدَا   وَفَكَّ رِقَــابَ المُــسْلِمِينَ مِــنَ الأَسْرِ

Und er (Ibn Makkī) – möge mein Leben seins sein! – / rettete sie und kaufte die Muslime aus der Gefangenschaft frei.

(27) دَنَانِيْــرُهُ فِيْــهَا عِــدَاهُ آسَــــتَفَكَّهَا   شُــمُوسٌ جَلَــتْ أَنْوَارُهَــا ظُلْمَــةَ الكُفْــرِ

Seine Dinare, mit denen er seinen Feind zerschlug, / glänzten wie Sonnen, deren Helligkeit die Finsternis des Unglaubens vertrieb.[131]

(28) لَهُ اللهُ مَــا أَنْــدَاهُ فِــي الــجُودِ رَاحَــةً   يُرِيحُ بِــهَا الإِسْــلَامَ فِي اليُــسْرِ وَالعُــسْرِ

Gott segne ihn, denn wie freigebig sind seine Hände, / mit denen er den Islam in guten und in schwierigen Zeiten erleichtert.[132]

Mit dem Dinar-Motiv (V. 27) ist eine relativ kritische Stelle im Gedicht erreicht,
das ihrem bisherigen Fokus nach vornehmlich die Taten des Fürsten in Kombination mit seiner Frömmigkeit rühmen will. Den Freikauf der Stadt verbindet
der Poet resultativ und in einem Farbkontrast (das Licht der Dinare, das die Finsternis des Unglaubens vertrieb) mit dem Dienst des Fürsten am Islam und an
den Muslimen (V. 28 und 29),[133] doch spätestens an dieser Stelle erwartet der Leser die literarische Kampfhandlung oder die Erwähnung einer kämpferischen,
nicht aber einer taktischen Ruhmestat. Ibn Abī Ḥaǧalah wählt dafür einen Überleitungsvers (V. 30), um in das erwartete Kriegsfeld überzugehen. Dieses Modul
gibt eine exzessive Schlachtszenerie wie in einem Historiengemälde wieder, aus
dessen dampfigen, vom Schlachtstaub aufgewirbelten Hintergrund der heroische
Fürst mit seiner Schwertklinge sowie seine farbigen Paradepferde eindrucksvoll
hervorstechen. Trotz Nennung von Surennamen (V. 32) trennt sich der Poet von
den explizit religiösen Idealen und legt seinen Schwerpunkt auf Tapferkeit und
Kraft. Der Poet setzt übermäßig viel Energie in die Gestaltung dieser Verse ein,
um ein ebenfalls energisches Bild vom Fürsten und seiner Reiterei zu vermitteln.
Fast, so möchte man meinen, gingen die Pferde seiner Gestaltung mit ihm durch.
Da ein solcher Kampf, zumindest mit der Reiterei Ibn Makkīs, nie stattgefunden
hat, kompensiert dieses Modul den fehlenden Kampf im Bild des Potentials zum

---

[130] Vgl. Alexandria-Gedicht V. 11 zur negativen Konnotation von Fluß und Tümpel.

[131] Zum Motiv der Finsternis des Unglaubens vs. Glanz/Helligkeit des Islams vgl. Alexandria-
Gedicht V. 3.

[132] Vgl. z.B. *Q* 2: 185 (يُرِيدُ اللهُ بِكُمُ الْيُسْرَ وَلَا يُرِيدُ بِكُمُ الْعُسْرَ); *Q* 65: 7; *Q* 94: 5-6.

[133] Ibn Abī Ḥaǧalah nutzt für beide Städte, Alexandria und Ṭarāblus, die übliche Lexik der
Wehrstädte (*ṯaġr, baḥr, nahr* bzw. *ġadīr*), wobei er für Ṭarāblus diese noch um die semantischen Felder für „Bauen“ und „Dichtung“ erweitert.

Kampf – ebenso eindrucksvoll, als wäre es geschehen. So bleibt der Poet nicht lange im Hintergrund und gibt sich im Schlußteil (V. 41-45) in poetologischen Versen zur Gestaltungskraft seiner Dichtkunst zu erkennen. Den poetologischen Part trennt Ibn Abī Ḥaǧalah in einem Überleitungsvers (V. 43) durch eine rhetorische Frage in zwei Teile (V. 41-42 → *taḫalluṣ* V. 43→ V. 44-45). Der erste Teil greift in einer äußerst komplexen Weise die Reit- und Pferdelexik (*ǧawād, ṭawīl al-bāʿ, ḥiǧāl*) auf, während der zweite Teil die vorangegangenen Leitaspekte (u.a. *baḥr, banā, al-bayt*), die dem Lob des Fürsten zugeschrieben waren, erneut und abschließend vergegenwärtigt. In beiden Teilen kombiniert der Autor die Figuren des Lobs mit poetologischer Lexik jeweils in einer zweiten semantischen Reihe, nämlich mit seiner Dichtkunst, und dies in einer solch energischen Form, als würde er sich auf eine Kraftprobe mit der Stärke des Gelobten und seiner Pferde einlassen. Allerdings balanciert er seine Kunst in einer Weise, die die Leistung Ibn Makkīs keinesfalls mindert, sondern sogar weiter hervorhebt (sein Lob bis in die Milchstraße und zum Sternbild des Adlers führt, V. 42), weil sie, so der Poet (V. 43 und 44), vom Fürsten selbst inspiriert ist. Was Ibn Abī Ḥaǧalah in drei Transformationsfiguren (Gazelle, Mond, Jüngling) bis zum freigebigen Fürsten hergeleitet hat, transformiert er im *madīḥ* mit stärkeren Figuren wie der edlen Pferde und der Milchstraße zum tapferen Fürsten somit kunstvoll weiter. Und so entpuppt sich das, was der Poet in einer ruhigen idyllischen Momentaufnahme mit einem Gazellenkitz beginnen läßt, in stetiger Steigerung als ein faszinierendes Fürstenlob.

Schlußteil der Elegie Ibn Abī Ḥaǧalahs

Statt eines Herrscherlobs integriert Ibn Abī Ḥaǧalah in einem *ǧinās* (*ʿaramram – Ibn ʿArrām*) das Lob auf den beliebteren Gouverneur der Stadt, der als Vorhut und Unterhändler nach Alexandria geschickt wurde. Yalbuġā ist der eindeutige Adressat dieses Gedichts, aber nicht der *mamdūḥ*. Insofern müssen die letzten Verse im Gedicht auch als Anklage des Poeten für politisches und militärisches Unvermögen gelesen werden, denn er schreibt:

(23) عَلَى أَنَّ فِي مِصْرٍ عَلَى الجَيْشِ قَائِدًا   يَبِيتُ وَلَا يُعْطِي القِيَادَ عَلَى القَسْرِ [134]

Obwohl Ägypten einen Heerführer (Yalbuġā) hat, der nachts wacht um der   184b
Unterwerfung keine Zügel zu überlassen (um nicht einmal unter Zwang die   [III: 202]
Führungsgewalt zu übergeben),

(24) أَقَامَ لَنَا بِالثَّغْرِ جَيْشًا عَرَمْرَمًا   وَفِيهِ ابْنُ عَرَّامَ المُؤَيَّدُ بِالنَّصْرِ

stellte er (Yalbuġā) uns in der Grenzstadt ein gewaltiges (ʿaramram) Heer auf,   185b
worin Ibn ʿArrām zum Sieg verholfen wird.   [III: 208]

---

[134] In seinem Kommentar identifiziert an-Nuwayrī *qāʿid* mit Yalbuġā: يَعْنِي بِالقَائِدِ المَذْكُورِ الأَمِيرَ الأَتَابِكِيَّ يَلْبُغَا الخَاسِكِيَّ قَائِدَ الجِيُوشِ المَنْصُورَةِ.

Obwohl Ibn Abī Ḥaǧalah eine sehr distanzierte Haltung zur Stadt Alexandria zeigt, überrascht er im Gebrauch des Possessivpronomens im allerletzten Vers. In dieser Form des *iltifāts* identifiziert er sich aber nur vornehmlich mit den Alexandrinern, denn er ist um Kairo und um das Mamlukenreich im Ganzen (V. 1 und 19) besorgt und knüpft somit im letzten Vers an das *ǧihād*-Motiv im Eingangsvers an. Vielmehr spottet er aber an dieser Stelle mit der Formulierung *lanā* (uns) über die Maßnahmen Yalbuġās, warum er ein Heer mit Ibn ʿArrām aufstellt, dem zum Sieg (*naṣr*)[135] verholfen werden soll, wo er doch ungern die Zügel aus der Hand gibt. In seiner *Maqāme* formuliert er ähnlich ironisierend in Reimprosa, daß die ‚ehrenvolle Vorhut der (nunmehr) Ašrafiyyah-Garden (Wortspiel mit *šaraf* (Ehre) und dem Namen des Sultans Ašraf Šaʿbān) nur noch die Ehre hatte, den Weggang der Geiseln zu erblicken‘.[136] Wenn an-Nuwayrīs Erzählung das Versagen Peters I. am *Eroberungsethos* herausstellt, so kann man diese Sätze bei Abī Ḥaǧalah als eine Klage über das Versagen am *Verteidigungsethos* verstehen.

Sortierung der Abfassungsdaten der Elegien und der Maqāme

Mit diesen letzten Versen sortiert sich allerdings die Chronologie der Entstehung der Elegien und der *Maqāme*. Ibn Abī Ḥaǧalahs Elegie müßte unmittelbar nach der Entsendung Ibn ʿArrāms nach Alexandria, also um den 25. Muḥarram herum oder bis kurz vor dem Auszug Yalbuġās aus Kairo entstanden sein. Ibn ʿArrām war nämlich nach seiner Pilgerfahrt in Kairo angekommen, als sich der Überfall der Franken ereignete. Yalbuġā sandte ihn in Eile mit einigen Truppen vor, um selbst mit einer größeren Armee nachzuziehen.[137] Ibn ʿArrām soll am vierten Tag

---

[135] Yalbuġās vollständiger Name lautet Sayfaddin Yalbuġā Ibn ʿAbdallāh al-ʿUmarī an-Nāṣirī al-Ḫāssakī. Hier spielt Ibn Abī Ḥaǧalah zusätzlich paronomastisch auf den Patronennamen an, d. i. Sultan an-Nāṣir Ḥasan (r. 1347-1351, 1354-1361).

[136] Ibn Ḥabīb, *Taḏkirat an-nabīh*, S. 292.

[137] *Ms. Ilmām*, fol. 185b: فَلَمَّا قَدِمَ الأميرُ صَلاَحِ الدِّينِ مِنَ الحِجَازِ الشَّرِيفِ إِلَى القَاهِرَةِ حِينَ الوَقْعَةِ أَرْسَلَهُ الأميرُ يَلْبُغَا إِلَى اَلْإِسْكَنْدَرِيَّةَ سرعَةً لِيَتَقَدَّمَهُ إِلَيهَا، فَدَخَلَهَا خَامَسِ عِشْرِينَ المُحَرَّمِ رَابِعِ يَوْمِ الوَقْعَةِ، hier allerdings gegen die Annahme von Weintritt, *Formen*, S. 173, Anm. 254, der die Ansicht vertritt, daß sich der 23. Vers auf die zweite Stationierung Ibn ʿArrāms in Alexandria bezieht und somit logischerweise die Entstehungszeit auf nach Šawwāl 768/ab dem 31. Mai 1367 festlegt. Als Ibn ʿArrām Alexandria erreichte, hatten sich die Franken bereits auf ihre Schiffe zurückgezogen. Er soll einen Juden namens Yaʿqūb auf Peters Schiff geschickt haben, damit dieser ihm sein Schreiben zum Gefangenenaustausch (mit den fränkischen Kaufleuten, die Ǧanġarā nach Damanhūr verschleppt hatte) überbringt. Doch bis sich dies wegen geschickter Auflagen Peters I. realisierte, rückte Yalbuġā bereits mit einem großen Regiment heran und die Franken verließen den Hafen (vgl. *Ms. Ilmām*, fol. 186a und zuvor fol. 110a). – An dieser Stelle ergeben sich jedoch erneut Datierungsdifferenzen. Innerhalb des *Ilmām* wird der Überfall gewöhnlich auf den 21. Muḥarram datiert, der vierte Tag des Übergriffs am 25. Muḥarram aber führt auf den 22. Muḥarram. Vermutlich meint an-Nuwayrī nicht das erste Erscheinen der fränkischen Schiffe, sondern die ersten Kämpfe zu Wasser am Donnerstag. Dagegen informiert al-Maqrīzī, ohne von Ibn ʿArrāms Entsendung zu berichten, daß Yalbuġā die Kunde vom Übergriff am Samstag dem 24. Muḥarram erhielt, aber erst am Folgetag der Nachricht Glauben schenkte und eine Truppe entsandte. So müßte Ibn ʿArrām am

des Übergriffs, dem 25. Muḥarram in Alexandria angekommen sein,[138] Yalbuġās Ankunft ist für den 28. Muḥarram verzeichnet.[139] Dies erklärt vermutlich auch den hohen Abstraktionsgrad und die plötzliche Wende am Ende des Gedichts mit *lanā* (uns), weil ihm zu jenem Zeitpunkt in Kairo noch nicht viele Details bekannt waren. Daher poetisiert er auch nicht im Sinne klassischer Städteelegien die Ruinenlandschaft, in der sicher einige materiale Topoi angeführt wären, sondern bleibt konsequent abstrakt-analytisch. Er ist nicht betroffen als Alexandriner und gibt es auch nicht vor, sondern überblickt aus Kairo heraus das Ereignis. Al-Aḥmīmīs Gedicht ist zur Ankunft Yalbuġās verfasst worden, da er es ihm persönlich vorgetragen hat. Die Elegie an-Nastarāwīs folgt naturgemäß al-Aḥmīmīs Elegie. An-Nuwayrī gibt in seiner Elegie an, daß er sie im Jahr des Überfalls, vermutlich unmittelbar nach seiner Wiederkehr in die Stadt und dem Abzug der Franken abgefaßt hat.[140] Aš-Šāṭibīs Elegie muß als letzte abgefasst worden sein, da sie von den ersten freigelassenen Sklaven erzählt, was erst einige Monate später möglich war.

Was die *Maqāme* Ibn Abī Ḥaǧalahs angeht, so ist sie eine spätere Revision seiner Elegie. Anlaß für diese Revision ist das *Kitāb al-Ilmām* selbst und Indiz dafür ist die inhaltliche Gestaltung der *Maqāme*. Daß in der Rezeption gerade bei den Historikern die Kurzfassung der Elegie zitiert wird und die Langfassung nirgendwo sonst außer im *Ilmām* Erwähnung findet, mag ebenfalls als Indiz für diese Abfolge gewertet werden. An-Nuwayrī zerlegt Ibn Abī Ḥaǧalahs Elegie versweise und schöpft aus dieser als Inspirationsquelle für allerlei weitere relevante Themen, die sein Werk prägen. Auch die anderen Dichter orientieren sich, so zeigen die Parallelen, am Motivgerüst der Elegie Ibn Abī Ḥaǧalahs, unterscheiden sich aber freilich im Modus ihrer Ausführung, der Textmotivation und der Adressierung. Doch in einem Punkt wehren sich an-Nuwayrī und im Vers auch an-Nastarāwī entschieden gegen eine Formulierung Ibn Abī Ḥaǧalahs, weil sie bekanntlich aus einer unmittelbaren Betroffenheit heraus schreiben. Dies ist der Vers über die Sündhaftigkeit der Stadt (Vers 17). In seinem Kommentar kritisiert an-Nuwayrī wie oben beschrieben zunächst das poetische Bild, das nicht durch-

---

Sonntag in Windeseile geritten sein, um am selben Tag in Alexandria angekommen zu sein. Al-Maqrīzī berichtet vielmehr von der Entsendung der Emire Quṭlubuġā al-Manṣūrī, Kūkāndāy und Ḫalil Ibn Qūṣūn (siehe al-Maqrīzī, *Kitāb as-sulūk li-maʿrifāt al-mulūk*, III: 104 f.); an-Nuwayrī (*Ms. Ilmām*, fol. 170a = *KI*, III: S. 86 f.) hingegen berichtet von Quṭlubuġās Entsendung mit vielen anderen Emiren erst im Jahre 772/1371.

[138] Von zwei Befreiungstruppen noch vor dem Eintreffen Yalbuġās spricht Robert Palmer in seinem Kommentar zu V. 3563 ff. der Chronik Machauts (*La Prise d'Alixandre*, V. 3563, nebst Anm. S. 442), allerdings ohne Angabe seiner Quellen und mit einer Differenz von einem Tag zur Narrative an-Nuwayrīs: "*[Lines 3563 ff.] These Saracens were the first elements of the relief army sent by Cairo under the command of the emir Qutlobogha al-Mansuri. The city's governor, who had been on pilgrimage in Mecca, was immediately ordered by Yalbogha to return to Alexandria with another force that likely reached the suburbs of the city by October 13.*"

[139] Vgl. *Ms. Ilmām*, fol. 110a.

[140] Vgl. Anm. 78.

dacht formuliert ist, und fragt anschließend, woher Ibn Abī Ḥaǧalah wissen kann, daß *alle* in Alexandria gesündigt hätten. Er führt Beispiele und Verse an, einerseits darüber, daß Gott stets vergibt und andererseits darüber, wann es jemandem gebührt zu schweigen, um zu folgern: *„Und Ibn Abī Ḥaǧalah hätte in diesem Fall schweigen müssen".*[141] Die Heftigkeit dieser Zurückweisung durch den Verfasser rührt nicht daher, daß er es ablehnt, der Überfall auf Alexandria sei ein gottgewolltes Urteil, schließlich trägt sein Werk bereits im Titel die Behandlung der göttlichen Ratschlüsse *(al-umūr al-maqḍiyyah)*,[142] sondern daher, daß er sich persönlich getroffen fühlt, weil er sich und seine *Ribāṭ*-Genossen gemäß den *Faḍāʾil*-Überlieferungen über die Vorzüge des Grenzdienstes zu den Rechtschaffenen zählt.[143] Die Zurückweisung geht so weit, daß an-Nuwayrī eigens dafür einen literarischen Topos stilisiert, um gegen diesen Vers anzugehen. Er bedient hier eine Redewendung *al-faʾlu muwakkalun bi-l-manṭiq* (die Hoffnung soll man aussprechen, i.e. man soll optimistisch sprechen),[144] als sich selbsterfüllende Prophezeiung oder eine Art Redezauber, damit sich nicht das Schlechte ereigne. So schreibt er unter diesem Motto Verse, mit denen er hofft, daß sich das Schicksal zu deren Gunsten (hier der Geiseln) entscheidet.[145] An-Nuwayrī erteilt auf seine Art Ibn Abī Ḥaǧalah eine Lektion, da es auf der Hand liegt, daß Elegien neben ihrer performativen durchaus in ihrer pragmatisch-funktionalen Dimension erfaßt werden und für ihn in der Stadtklage das Wohl und Interesse der Bewohner nicht hätten derartig entblößt werden sollen.[146]

---

[141] *Ms. Ilmām*, fol. 154a; an-Nuwayrī ergießt sich förmlich in der Zurückweisung einer solchen Anschuldigung, indem er zahlreiche Überlieferungen aneinanderreiht, die das Verdecken von Vergehen und den Vorzug des Schweigens vor der Rede befürworten (bis fol. 161b: mit allerlei Digressionen zu Themen Gnade und Barmherzigkeit, Vergebung und Sünden *(kabāʾir)*); bis hin zur Zeugenschaft bei Anklagen und Schuldzuweisungen. Vermutlich verweist an-Nuwayrī subtil darauf, daß Ibn Abī Ḥaǧalah ohne Zeugenschaft spricht und gleichzeitig darauf, daß er nicht vor Ort war. Auch an-Nastarāwī integriert diese Anschuldigung in Vers 78 (*KI*, IV: S. 177; *Ms. Ilmām*, fol. 238a: *In yakun hāḏā l-ḏanbun sābiqun / qad ǧarā minnā wa-ǧahlun wa-ǧirar* „Und wenn dies alles vorangegangene Sünden sind, / dann geschah (taten wir) es aus Unwissenheit und Gedankenlosigkeit") und verweist im nächsten Vers darauf, daß Gott auf seinem Thron der erste ist, der vergibt. Vgl. hierzu auch Weintritt, *Formen*, S. 172.

[142] Nach an-Nuwayrī habe Peter nicht durch seine vermeintliche Stärke, sondern durch die Bestimmung Gottes *(qaḍāʾ)* gesiegt (*Ms. Ilmām*, fol. 27b; vgl. Herzsohn, *Der Überfall Alexandriens*, S. 8).

[143] Über den Vorzug, in einer Grenzstadt, hier insb. in Alexandria, Dienste zu leisten *(faḍl ar-ribāṭ bi-l-Iskandariyyah)*, siehe die zahlreichen Ḥadīṯe im *Ilmām* unmittelbar nach dem 19. Vers Ibn Abī Ḥaǧalahs, fol. 166b-168b = *KI*, III: S. 68-78.

[144] Diese Redewendung ist zwar nicht belegt, aber nachvollziehbar. Bekannter ist die Redewendung für das Herbeischwören einer negativen Sache: *al-balāʾu muwakkalun bi-l-manṭiq*.

[145] *Ms. Ilmām*, fol. 118a (zwei Gedichte in der Hoffnung auf die Rückkehr von Geiseln, was sich verwirklicht); fol. 169a Beschwörungsverse darüber, daß Peter I. seine gerechte Strafe in der Hölle bekommen möge.

[146] Es ist bezeichnend, daß die Elegien-Schreiber hier kein Problem mit der Loyalität zu dem einen oder anderen politischen Machtträger haben, wohl aber damit, wie ihre Stadt poetisiert bzw. beklagt wird. Al-Aḥmimī preist ausgiebig Yalbuġā und scheut sich nicht, auf das

In der *Maqāme* zeigt sich, daß im verkürzten Gedicht die Straf-Verse (*wa-ḥaqqika …*) fehlen. Doch Ibn Abī Ḥaǧalah ändert nicht die Grundaussage seiner Elegie. Seine zynische Haltung zu der aufgestellten Armee steigert er sogar noch mit einem dreifachen *ǧinās* (*wa-mā a̱šrafat aṭ-ṭalīʿat al-a̱šrafiyyah wa-ḥaḍara arbāb as-sayf al-mu̱šarrafiyyah ḥattā katamat [kutibat] ʿalā l-asāri al-ǧaybah*)[147], aber er kanalisiert die Schuldfrage noch stärker auf die Beduinenstämme: „*Sie sind der Grund für die Niederlage und das Ausbleiben des Sieges, so möge Gott sie nicht weiter vermehren und nicht zufrieden mit ihnen sein*"[148]. Anstelle der Strafen treten nun Prüfungen Gottes an die Gläubigen (*Q* 33:11). Auch ist zwar nicht mehr von Wein die Rede, wohl aber noch von vergangenen Sünden und vom Dattelwein (*dabūs*), von dem der *ṯaǧr* (Mund, Bucht, Alexandria) umgeben (besudelt) war. Das prosaische Eingeständnis an an-Nuwayrī liegt darin, daß Ibn Abī Ḥaǧalah neben dem Fehlen eines gottgefälligen Lebens das Unglück mit kunstvollen Vergleichen und Kontrasten nun u.a. auf das Fehlen der *muǧāhidūn*[149] zurückführt. So lautet der entsprechende Abschnitt in der *Maqāme*: „*[…] das blaue Meer färbte sich schwarz durch die Gelben (Banū l-asfar); das grüne Tor wurde geöffnet und unter jedem weißen qalʿ (Stein; Hügel?) befand sich der rote Tod; und die Menschen nahmen ihr Kriegszeug und rüsteten sich zum Kampf; sie zogen aus wie eine Ameisenkolonie und verbreiteten sich an Land wie Sandkörner; und weil es zu jener Zeit im ṯaǧr (Alexandria) keine Schneidezähne (ṯaǧr, Pl. ṯuǧūr) gab und der Mund (ṯaǧr) vom Honigwein besudelt war, was den muǧāhidūn Geschwüre zufügte, und weil die Sorge um den Glauben verschwand und die Umkreisung (i.e. gottesdienstliche oder militärische) in ihr abnahm, vermehrte sich die Sicherheit in Dingen der Angst.*"[150] Mit diesen Ausführungen knüpft Ibn Abī Ḥaǧalah wieder geschickt an sein *ǧihād*-Thema am Anfang des Gedichts an und beendet es in einer offen formulierten poetologischen Wendung[151] im Ausdruck seiner Trauer über die Gefangenen (*Maqāme* V.

Versagen Ǧanǧarās (Vers. 42) zu verweisen, während die anderen Dichter mit dem Lob auf Yalbuǧā zurückhaltend sind. Die Auslassung Yalbuǧās und die vielen parolenhaften Lobverse (96-114) auf Ibn ʿArrām in an-Nuwayrīs Elegie brennen diesen umso eindrucksvoller und positiver in das Gedächtnis.

[147] Ibn Ḥabīb, *Taḏkirat an-nabīh*, S. 291 und ders., *Durrat al-aslāk*, fol. 220b: „*(wa-ḥaḍarū … kutibat): Und die ehrenvolle Garde konnte sie nicht mehr beehren, so waren die Leute des ehrenvollen Schwerts zugegen, als man die Gefangenen fortschleppte (als den Gefangenen das Verschwinden beschieden war)*".

[148] Ibn Ḥabīb, *Taḏkirat an-nabīh*, S. 290 und ders., *Durrat al-aslāk*, fol. 220a.

[149] Auch Ibn Ḥabīb führt das Fehlen der *muǧāhidūn* in jener Zeit an. Sein in Reimprosa abgefaßter Abschnitt über den Überfall der Franken ist dem Auszug der *Maqāme* Ibn Abī Ḥaǧalahs vorangestellt, doch größtenteils paraphrasiert er die *Maqāme*. Auch in dieser Narrative sind es 70 Schiffe, die am Silsilah-Hafen anlaufen. Nach seinen Angaben dauerte die Belagerung und Brandschatzung drei Tage, bis die Manṣūriyyah-Garden ankamen und die Franken flohen.

[150] Ibn Ḥabīb, *Taḏkirat an-nabīh*, S. 289-290 und *Durrat al-aslāk* fol. 220a.

[151] „*fa-yā layta šiʿrī man yuballiǧuhum naṯrī*": Die Wendung steht hier für eine (vermeintlich!) verkürzte und verdichtete Darstellungsmöglichkeit in der Dichtung für das Mitgefühl des Poeten und sein Wissen um die inneren Dinge gegenüber den Möglichkeiten in Prosa (*naṯr*), was Ibn Abī Ḥaǧalah aber dadurch, daß er den Prosateil dem Gedicht voranstellt, selbst sabotiert.

12). Für Ibn Abī Ḥağalah ist Alexandria ein Ort der Nachlässigkeit und der Vernachlässigung. Der Ort, den er durch seinen konzisen Stil in den Augen an-Nuwayrīs als einen unter vielen offensichtlich degradiert, dient ihm lediglich als Medium zur Veranschaulichung des Nicht-Räumlichen.

Gegenentwürfe und Handlungsoptionen der Städtelegien

Realgeschichtlich war der unerwartete Angriff der Zyprer für die lokale Bevölkerung mit Leid und Verlusten verbunden und für die Mamluken eine Herausforderung. Neben der Verarbeitung der Schmach, von einem „niederen" König überfallen worden und überhaupt überrascht worden zu sein,[152] hatten sie diese Herausforderung mit aufwändigen politischen und militärischen Maßnahmen wie dem Ausbau der ägyptischen Flotte, Handelssanktionen, Neubesetzung von Ämtern, der Kollektivbesteuerung der einheimischen Christen sowie dem Ausbau der Befestigungsanlagen Alexandrias zu bewältigen versucht. Für die Literaten jedoch war sowohl der reale Überfall als auch, – in einem höheren Maße – die poetische Umsetzung dieser „Überraschung" eine Herausforderung. Anders als in der klassischen Tragödie oder in modernen Gattungen wie der Novelle, dem freien Gedicht und dem Kriminalroman bietet der gewöhnlich beschränkte und ästhetisch vordeterminierte Qaṣīdenraum nicht die besten Voraussetzungen, die Unmittelbarkeit der Überraschung darzustellen. Auch wenn der Moment der Überraschung eine plötzliche Durchbrechung der Erwartungshaltung bedeutet – was in Qaṣīden durchaus gegeben ist –,[153] so muß diese an früherer Stelle wirkpoetisch markiert und in den Erwartungshorizont des Lesers gestellt werden, damit sie nicht als Kuriosum wahrgenommen wird.[154]

---

[152] فَعَلِمَ اللِّصُّ مِنْ أَيْنَ يَدْخُلُ يَسْرِقُ، فَدَخَلَهَا سَرَقَهَا وَهَرَبَ عَنْهَا خَوْفًا مِنْ كَبْسَةِ جَيْشِ مِصْرَ عَلَيْهِ يُهْلِكُهُ لَوْ أَدْرَكَهُ بِهَا، فَلَوْ كَانَ مَلِكًا قَوِيًّا شَهْمًا جَرِيئًا أَقَامَ بِهَا وَنَاضَلَ عَنْهَا كَفِعْلِ الْمُلُوكِ حِينَ ظَفَرِهِمْ بِالْمُدُنِ („Und dieser Einbrecher wußte, von wo er eintreten und stehlen konnte, und er überfiel die Stadt, plünderte und floh aus ihr aus Angst vor dem Gegenschlag der ägyptischen Armee, die ihn erledigt hätte, wenn sie ihn erreicht hätte. Wenn er ein starker, ritterlich-tapferer und unerschrockener König gewesen wäre, so hätte er sich der Sache gestellt und die Stadt verteidigt, wie es eben Könige tun, wenn sie eine Stadt erobern." *Ms. Ilmām*, 166a).

[153] Vgl. Burkhard Meyer-Sickendiek, *Affektpoetik: eine Kulturgeschichte literarischer Emotionen*, Würzburg 2005, S. 36, S. 52, bes. S. 55 f. (über die seltene Darstellung von Angst und Überraschung in lyrischer Form, dagegen aber in der Novelle), S. 319-334 (Überraschung in der Novelle); Beispiele für rhetorische Verfahren und textstrategische Kompositionsmöglichkeiten in verschiedenen Gattungen der englischsprachigen Dichtung gibt Michael Teune (Hg.), *Structure & Suprise. Engaging Poetic Turns*, New York 2007; siehe auch Heike Ortner, *Text und Emotion: Theorie, Methode und Anwendungsbeispiele emotionslinguistischer Textanalyse*, Tübingen 2014, Kap. 7 (Emotionslinguistische Textanalyse: Methode).

[154] Für den Moment der *anagnorisis* (als Wiedererkennung nach dem Vergessen (oblivio)) in der Tragödie formuliert Aristoteles: „*Die beste unter allen Wiedererkennungen ist diejenige, die sich aus den Geschehnissen selbst ergibt, indem die Überraschung aus Wahrscheinlichem hervorgeht.*" (Aristoteles, *Poetik*, Griechisch und deutsch, hg. und übers. von Manfred Fuhrmann, Stuttgart 1982, S. 35).

Alle hier vorgestellten Texte präsentieren somit unterschiedliche literarische Bewältigungstechniken der Kontingenzerfahrung der Überraschung und zeigen gleichsam, daß die Poeten nicht hilflos vor der Herausforderung standen. Die Rhetorik und die Gattungsspezifika boten allerhand Mittel, das Element des Unvorhergesehenen eindringlich zu vermitteln und zum Teil *innertextlich* und *außertextlich* zu überwinden. Allerdings ist hierbei zu berücksichtigen, – und dies führt uns auf das zu Anfang besprochene Thema der *Umkehrung* zurück – daß die gebotenen Mittel in der Retrospektive zur Verfügung stehen, in etwa der Weise, wie sie Bachtin als ‚historische Inversion'[155] beschrieben hat. Alle fünf Poeten nutzen rhetorische Mittel wie starke Kontrastfiguren, Exklamativ- und Optativsätze oder die Figur der Wiederholung (*takrār*) als Affirmative. Auf der semantischen Ebene psychologisiert aš-Šāṭibī das Überrascht-Sein, indem er der Orientierungslosigkeit aus der Zeugenschaft mehrerer Instanzen heraus Ausdruck verleiht. Obwohl diese Elegie mit einem größeren zeitlichen Abstand geschrieben ist, vermittelt sie durch die verwendeten Stilmittel und ihren Aufbau mehr Nähe zum Erlebten. Das Textsubjekt ist dem kontingenten Walten externer Kräfte scheinbar machtlos ausgeliefert und aus seiner heilen Welt herausgeworfen. Wie die anderen Elegien, semantisiert aš-Šāṭibī den Überfall literarisch, historisch-nostalgisch und religiös. An-Nuwayrī, al-Aḥmīmī und an-Nastarāwī dehnen dafür die Qaṣīdenlänge um ein erhebliches Maß aus, in der sie der Ausfaltung und Entwicklung des Themas mehr Raum geben können, womit ihre Elegien quasi-epische Züge und den Charakter von motivierten Verschroniken annehmen. Bei dieser Länge müssen sie stets darauf achten, daß sie nicht gleichsam den „Feind", der für viele Kontraste herhalten muss, (mit-)ikonisieren. Dafür wenden die Poeten Einiges auf, um ihn durch Schmähungen und Flüche immer wieder niedrig zu halten. Schließlich ist dies nicht nur ein Problem der längeren Elegien, sondern der umfangreichen Schrift an-Nuwayrīs selbst und ein möglicher Grund für die Digressions- und Montagetechnik, um die Größe des feindlichen Gegenübers, die bei einer en bloc-Darstellung unfreiwillig entsteht, bewußt gering zu halten.[156] Für Ibn Abī Ḥaǧalah scheint das Unvorhergesehene / die Überraschung in der distanzierten Position, die er einnimmt, gar nicht erst zu existieren. Der Überfall ist in der horizontalen Abfolge seiner Verse im höchsten Maße akzidentiell (ähnlich den Schicksalsschlägen), aber auch logische Folge dessen, was er vertikal im Text poetisiert, nämlich die Strafe für vorangegangene Vergehen. Dies ist wiederum die

---

[155] Vgl. Bachtin, *Choronotopos*, Kap. 4 (Das Problem der historischen Inversion und des folkloristischen Chronotopos), S. 74 ff. Die Besonderheit des Zeitempfindens, das auf die literarischen Formen Einfluß ausgeübt hat, bezeichnete Bachtin als historische Inversion: „*Das Wesen einer solchen historischen Inversion besteht darin, daß das mythologische und künstlerische Denken Kategorien wie Ziel, Ideal, Gerechtigkeit, Vollkommenheit, harmonischer Zustand des Menschen und der Gesellschaft u.a. in der Vergangenheit ansiedelt. […] Die Gegenwart und besonders die Vergangenheit wurden dabei auf Kosten der Zukunft angereichert. Nur die Gegenwart und die Vergangenheit – das «ist» und das «war» – verfügen über die Kraft und Stichhaltigkeit des Realen, Wirklichen; […].*" (*ebd.*, S. 75).

[156] Vgl. Weintritt, *Formen*, S. 87 f.

Perspektive eines Poeten, der dem Machtzentrum am nächsten war, nicht vor Ort die Geschehnisse erlebte und die Elegie als erster schrieb.

Weder die Dichtung noch die Dichter stehen der Heimsuchung somit hilflos gegenüber, auch wenn die kulturelle Praxis der Poetik gewissen Regeln und Konventionen unterliegt. Die retrospektive Arbeit der hochstilisierten Elegien bleibt nicht bei der bloßen Erinnerung an ein Unheil und der mahnenden Botschaft stehen. Solche Texte bieten durch die Mittel der ‚Inversion‘ gleichzeitig einen Gegenentwurf und Handlungsoptionen für die prospektive Seite, ohne die eine solche Rückschau absurd wäre. Doch kann diese Prospektivität entsprechend der literarischen Praxis nicht als Utopie oder „das Neue" entworfen werden, sondern durch Rekurrenz auf das Vergangene und dessen Semantisierung vor dem Hintergrund der Tradition und des Bekannten, also in der Differenzqualität. Die Texte liefern hierfür implizite und explizite Handlungsoptionen unabhängig von ihrer Realisierbarkeit, quasi als Vermittlung der Vision von idealer Ordnung in zweierlei Raumbezügen, entweder im Raum der Poetik selbst und/oder im real-historischen Raum ihrer Gegenwart.

Zunächst ist die Gattung der Städteklage eine *causa efficiens* und als solche bereits der erste offenkundige und ästhetische Widerstand gegen Verlust, Heimsuchung und die vorangegangene Handlungsohnmacht. Die Motivauswahl, das Gesagte wie auch das Nichtgesagte geben Aufschluß darüber, was zur Vision des Idealen dazu gehört und was nicht. Darüber hinaus sind es vor allem die metapoetischen Elemente, die die Handlungsoptionen für den Poeten und die Adressaten explizit formulieren.[157] Vor dem Hintergrund der Gesamtkomposition sind somit solche Verse, die z.B. mit *wa- layta* und *wa-law* beginnen oder Schwurformeln wie *a-lā bi-abī yā* keine belanglosen mimetischen Floskeln. Aš-Šāṭibīs emotionaler Duktus äußert mit derlei Formeln den Grad der Subjektivierung des Unglücks und der Identifikation mit dem beklagten Raum. Der iterative Modus ist ein poetologischer Ausdruck für die nachdrückliche Aufforderung zur Wiederherstellung des Equilibriums (z.B. im Wieder-zu-sich-Selbst-Finden, in der Wiedervereinigung mit den Lieben, im Schutz der Stadt und ihrer Bevölkerung), vor allem aber auch Ausdruck für den idealisierten Kodex an Tugenden wie Tapferkeit und Rechtschaffenheit. Die Alternative, die der Poet selbst anbietet, ist durch Weinen und Wehklage (und infolgedessen durch die Elegie) die Trauer zu erregen und den Machtträgern diese seine Trauer zur Handlung ans Herz zu legen (V. 56-60). An-Nuwayrīs Elegie überträgt die Handlungsoption, nachdem der Poet detailliert auf die Verluste eingegangen ist und für sich die Duldsamkeit als adäquate Handlung herausgearbeitet hat (V. 79) in einem umfangreichen *madīḥ* in die

---

[157] Zu frühen Beispielen der selbstreflexiven Poesie im Arabischen siehe Huda J. Fakhreddine, *Metapoesis in the Arabic Tradition. From Modernists to Muḥdathūn*, Leiden 2011, insb. ab Kapitel 2. Zur Metapoetik im europäischen Diskurs siehe Eva Müller-Zimmermann, *Lyrik und Metalyrik. Theorie einer Gattung und ihrer Selbstbespiegelung aus der englisch- und deutschsprachigen Dichtkunst*, Heidelberg 2000.

Figur des abwesenden Statthalters (V. 98-99; 104-114). Dabei ist zu berücksichtigen, daß an-Nuwayrī in seinem gesamten *Ilmām*-Werk auf weitere literarische Verfahren zurückgreifen konnte, seine Vision von idealer Ordnung und ihre Diskurse zu vermitteln. Der Abschnitt über den Redezauber geht der Elegie unmittelbar voran, und in dieser Geisteshaltung mag an-Nuwayrī vielleicht selber sein Gedicht gesehen haben, damit sich seine Hoffnungen realisierten. Al-Aḥmimīs Elegie zeigt sogar die außertextliche Verwirklichung seiner Handlungsoption. Nachdem er in mehr als zehn Versen (z.B. V. 52-62) mit Formulierungen wie *lā wa-lā* das Fehlen militärischer Verteidigung und mit *li-kam* die Folgen der gegnerischen Kampfhandlungen auf die ungeschützten Bewohner eindringlich aufgezeigt hat, geht er in seinen ausgedehnten *madīḥ* auf Yalbuġā (Vers 65-107) über.[158] Die Verwirklichung seiner poetischen Aussage geschieht, – so der Bericht über die Selbstaussage – als er Yalbuġā sein Gedicht persönlich vorträgt und diesen zur Aufrüstung der Flotte bewegen kann.[159] An-Nastarāwīs Elegie, weitschweifig wie sein Bezugstext, nutzt ähnliche rhetorische Mittel, doch ihre weitere Funktion innerhalb des *Ilmām* ist die verwirklichte Handlungsoption gegen al-Aḥmimīs Elegie und somit gegen den innertextlichen Diskurs innerhalb des *Ilmām*. Das auffälligste Element dieser Elegie ist, daß die vielen Ruhmesverse auf Yalbuġā und die politischen Größen entgegen der Machart al-Aḥmimīs auf einen Vers verkürzt werden und der Poet in seiner frommen Haltung die reale Handlungsoption in 24 Versen (V. 62-85) der Vermittlung des Propheten anheimstellt.

Ibn Abī Ḥaġalah ist nicht interessiert daran, einen versifizierten Ereignisbericht zu schreiben. Diese Gelegenheit hätte er bei der *Maqāme* durchaus nutzen können, aber auch dort überwiegt sein künstlerischer und analytischer Anspruch. Das, was er zur idealen Ordnung zugehörig findet, drückt er in der Minimalform aus (i.e. Verteidigung / Befestigung der Stadt, Sicherheit der Bevölkerung vor allem der Kinder und Frauen, Schutz der Reichtümer der Stadt, gottgefälliges Leben), um im letzten Drittel des Gedichts (ab Vers 17) das Raumparadigma der Stadt Alexandria zu überwinden und sich als Kämpfer zu präsentieren. Die Gründe dafür gibt er in den Strafversen an, deren letzter (Vers 20) auch die Handlungsoption des Poeten für die kommenden *wa-man lī*-Verse einleitet:

---

[158] Das Lob auf Yalbuġā kommt in diesem Ausmaß nur in der Elegie al-Aḥmimīs vor. An-Nastarawi verlegt diesen Part (V. 51-59) als Teil des Ereignisberichts vor die ausladenden Beschwörungsverse (V. 62-85), mit denen er sein Gedicht beendet. Ibn Abī Ḥaġalah hatte Yalbuġā allenfalls in der Zeit Sultan Ḥasans gelobt (siehe *Dīwān Ibn Abī Ḥaġalah*, Hg. Aḥmad Ḥilmī Ḥulwah, S. 43 ff.). Dieses Gedicht kommt zudem in seinen *Maqāmen* in verkürzter Form (7 Verse) noch einmal vor (*Ms. Wetzstein 1803*, fol. 94a). An-Nuwayrī hält sich in seiner gesamten Schrift, obwohl er nur wenige Verse auf Yalbuġā dichtet (drei Verse auf fol. 118a), mit einem direkten Tadel zurück und kehrt selbst die kritischen Verse Ibn Abī Ḥaġalahs (z.B. im Kommentar zu den Versen 20 und 21) mit der Anführung einer Allegorie zum Rachemotiv ins Positive um (siehe zu dieser Erzählung und der Textstrategie Weintritt, *Formen*, S. 63 f.).

[159] Vgl. Anm. 62.

فَلَيْتَ وَلِيَّ الأَمْرِ يَدْرِي بِمَا أَدْرِي   وَحَقِّكَ عِنْدِي لِلْفِرِنْجِ مَكَائِدٌ

Bei deinem Leben (sei dir gewiß)! Denn ich hätte gegen die Franken einiges   170b
an Kniffen, / ach, und wüßte der Befehlshaber (Yalbuġā) doch das, was ich   [III: 88]
weiß!

بِغِرْبَانِهِمْ مِثْلَ النُّسُورِ إِذَا تَسْرِي   فَمَنْ لِي بِأُسْطُولٍ بِهِ أَهْلُ سَبْتَةَ   (21)

Hätte ich doch eine Flotte mit den Leuten von Ceuta, / die mit ihren Schif-   170b
fen (Raben) angreifen wie Adler.[160]   [III: 88]

تَعَامَلَ أَهْلَ الكُفْرِ فِي البَحْرِ بِالنَّحْرِ   وَمَنْ لِي بِفُرْسَانِ الجَزِيرَةِ عِنْدَمَا   (22)

Und hätte ich doch die Reiterei von Algeciras, / die die Ungläubigen am   179b
Meer niedermetzelten.   [III: 174]

Die Verweise auf al-Andalus und den Maghreb verdeutlichen, daß es ihm in erster Linie um das Versagen der Machthaber ging, diesen Angriff gemäß dem Kampfgeist der Nordafrikaner vorauszusehen oder ihm entsprechend tugendhaft entgegenzutreten. Ibn Abī Ḥaǧalah plaziert sich im poetischen Raum – und dies ist sein Gegenentwurf und seine Handlungsoption – als derjenige Kundige, erfahrene Seemann und kämpferische Reiter, dessen Fehlen das Gedicht beklagt.

Schlußbetrachtung

Ästhetische Texte müssen in erster Linie, auch wenn sie ein nachvollziehbares Raumparadigma bedienen oder ein Ereignis wiedergeben, nicht nach dem Paradigma der Wahrheit bewertet werden. Sie dürfen, da sie explizit als solche verfaßt wurden, auch als Kunst wahrgenommen werden und Ibn Abī Ḥaǧalah hätte den Kunstcharakter, das „Gemachtsein" seiner Elegie nie geleugnet. Dennoch gibt der Kunstcharakter der Werke dem Dichter keinen Freischein für realitätsferne Phantasie. Wie die Analyse der Elegien herausgestellt hat, hat sich die Poetik immer, sei es am empirisch- oder am subjektiv-diskursiven Realen zu brechen. Die Stadt Alexandria als solche ist Ibn Abī Ḥaǧalah nicht wichtig. Das wird deutlich nicht nur durch das, was er schreibt, sondern hauptsächlich durch das, was er nicht schreibt. Und das, was dort nicht steht, erfordert wiederum die Kenntnis davon, was hätte alles stehen können. Im Falle Alexandrias haben wir durch glückliche Umstände ein beachtliches Spektrum[161] an Textzeugen, Gattungen und Varian-

---

[160] An-Nuwayrī kommentiert (*Ms. Ilmām*, fol. 169b), daß Ibn Abī Ḥaǧalah hier, indem er die Fähigkeit der Maghrebiner als berüchtigte „Reiter des Meeres" (*fursān al-baḥr*) hervorhebt, Yalbuġā anspornt, mehr Maghrebiner in Alexandria für den Grenzdienst einzusetzen.

[161] Beispiele in Dichtung und Prosa, in welcher Form Alexandria gerühmt und getadelt wurde, gibt z.B. Elger („Geldgier und jihâd in Alexandria", S. 201-224). Elger kann anhand der untersuchten Textbeispiele aus der Reiseliteratur (u.a. Muḥammad al-ʿAbdarī (gest. um 736/1336); Ḫālid al-Balawī (lebte noch 755/1354) und Ḥafiẓaddīn al-Qudsī (gest. 1055/1645-6)) herausarbeiten, daß Alexandria bestimmte Merkmale als „Charakterzüge" anhafteten, zu denen solche gehören, die in Teilen in den hier vorgestellten Texten thema-

ten, die uns die verschiedenen Perspektiven auf diesen Überfall vermitteln und somit das Sagbare aus dem Bereich des Nichtgesagten durchaus faßbar ist.[162] Dabei sind freilich die gattungsspezifischen Ausdrucksformen zu berücksichtigen.[163] Bei einer literarischen Kultur wie der arabischen, die, was den Motivhaushalt und den Formenbestand der poetischen Sprache – also in der Kunst – anbelangt, dem *burden of the past* in gleicher Weise wie der Innovation verpflichtet ist, darf man nichts Futuristisches in den Qaṣīden erwarten. Das wäre eine ungerechtfertigte Erwartungshaltung. Die Verfremdung und damit das variantenreiche Spiel poetischer Möglichkeiten ist – mit den Formalisten gesprochen – erst vor dem Hintergrund des Bekannten (i.e. in der Differenzempfindung) wahrzunehmen. Was also Ibn Abī Ḥaǧalahs Poetik besonders gemacht hat, sehen wir viel deutlicher in der Art und Weise, wie er die Dinge, die vor ihm gemacht wurden, verändert und variiert hat und nicht darin, ob er vollständig neue *maʿānī* geschaffen hat. Diese *„liegen doch weggeworfen auf der Straße und ein jeder Nichtaraber und Araber, Beduine und Seßhafter, kennt sie"*,[164] das sagte schon al-Ğāḥiẓ im 9. Jahrhundert und diese

---

tisiert wurden, nämlich Glaubenseifer (*ǧihād*) im Grenzdienst (*ribāṭ*) wegen ihrer geographischen Lage, Sittenverfall, Lasterhaftigkeit und Geiz. Mit dem Geiz der Alexandriner verweist Elger auf einen Topos im Städtediskurs, der seit der späten Abbasidenzeit für Alexandria und keinesfalls nur für sie, prägend ist (vgl. die Dichtung Ibn Ḥaddāds). Dieses Motiv findet sich in unseren Elegien nicht, da der Geiz-Diskurs vornehmlich von Reisenden, Fremden und Bettlern aufgegriffen wird, häufig auch diese betraf und ihre Anprangerung in der Urbanitätsrhetorik eine andere ethisch-moralische Handlungsmaxime berührt. Siehe hierzu z.B. Bayyud, *Die Stadt in der arabischen Poesie*, bes. S. 160 ff. und 215 ff.

[162] Neben den hier besprochenen Texten wären noch solche über die *Faḍāʾil* Alexandrias heranzuziehen. Die *Faḍāʾil* Alexandrias gehen meist in das Lob Kairos oder Ägyptens ein; eigenständige Werke sind nur wenige bekannt, darunter: eine Schrift von Abū l-Muẓaffar Manṣūr b. Salim (gest.?); von Abū ʿAlī b. ʿUmar b. al-Ḥasan (b.) aṣ-Ṣabbāǧ (erste Hälfte des 5./11. Jhds.), vorhanden in Ms. Kairo 1485; diesen erwähnt auch as-Suyūṭī (gest. 911/ 1505) in seiner *Risālah fī faḍl aṭ-ṭaġr al-Iskandariyyah* (Ms al-Azhar, No: 54924); eine *Faḍāʾil al-Iskandariyyah* von Ḫalaf b.ʿAlī al-Maġribī at-Tarwaǧī? as-Sakandarī (gest. 844/1440) und von Ibn Duqmāq (gest. 809/1406) *ad-Durrah al-muḍīʿah fī faḍl Miṣr al-Iskandariyyah* (siehe zu diesen Autoren bzw. Schriften *GAL* II 50 und Rosenthal, *A History of Muslim Historiography*, S. 458 (nach as-Saḫāwīs Iʿlān)).

[163] Zum Vorfall in Alexandria ist ebenfalls ein Beispiel aus der Gattung der Kanzleiliteratur (*al-inšāʾ*) erhalten. Ibn al-Ḫaṭīb (gest. 776/1374) gibt uns aus der Korrespondenz für Ibn Aḥmar sein manieristisch auslandendes (Glückwunsch-) Schreiben an Sultan Ašraf Šaʿbān wieder. Eine vertiefende Analyse könnte die Textstrategien der „Umgehung" (hier des militärischen Fehlschlags) und ihre Umwandlung in „Lob" im epistolaren Stil der diplomatischen Hofkorrespondenz herausstellen. Es ist bezeichnend, daß dieser Brief ausdrücklich an den Sultan adressiert ist (siehe Ibn al-Ḫaṭīb, *Rayḥānat al-kuttāb wa-nuǧʿat al-muntāb*, Hg. Muḥammad ʿAbdallāh ʿInān, I: S. 295-303). Der gleiche Text findet sich ebenfalls im *Ṣubḥ al-aʿšā* (siehe Šihābaddīn Abū l-ʿAbbās al-Qalqašandī, *Ṣubḥ al-aʿšā fī ṣinaʿāt al-inšā*; 14 Bde., [Ausgabe Dār al-Kutub as-Sulṭāniyyah], al-Qāhirah 1334/1915, VIII: S. 107-115). Für den Hinweis auf diese Quellen danke ich Andreas Herdt.

[164] Vollständiges Zitat: *„Der Saih (d.i. Abū ʿAmr) war der Ansicht, daß man den maʿnā schön finden müsse, aber die maʿānī liegen doch weggeworfen auf der Straße und ein jeder, Nichtaraber und Araber, Beduine und Seßhafter, kennt sie. Der Rang (sc. der Dichtung) aber liegt doch nur in der Einhaltung des Versmaßes, der Wahl des Sprachausdrucks, der Leichtigkeit der Artikulation (Euphonie), der Stärke der Begabung und der guten Qualität des Gusses (d.h. der sprachlichen Fügung), denn die*

„sind vorgegeben", *„gehören ‚keinem' und sind ‚Gottes'"*[165] sagte immer noch zu Beginn des 20. Jahrhunderts der russische Formalist Viktor Šklovskij.

Anhang I:

Von den zeitnahen historischen Quellen, die den Vorfall in Alexandria beschreiben, sind auf christlicher Seite vor allem folgende zu erwähnen:

1. *„Vita S. Petri Thomasii"* von Philippus de Mazzerius (Phillippe de Mézières, gest. 1405).

Mit dem Papstlegaten und eifrigen Missionar Peter Thomasius (gest. 1366), dessen Biographie in diesem Werk beschrieben wird, gehört de Mézières zu den prominentesten Begleitern Peter Lusignans während des Angriffs auf Alexandria. Philippe de Mézières war französischer Ritter, Diplomat, Schriftsteller und Kanzler Peters I. Er war erfahrener Krieger und gehörte zu den letzten Befürwortern der Kreuzzugsidee im Mittelalter. Er ist Verfasser der Werke *„Le songe du vieil pèlerin"* (Der Traum des alten Pilgers), geschr. 1386-1389 und *„Nova religio passionis"* (Der neue Passions-Orden), geschr. 1384, unvollendet.[166] *Le Songe* ist eine auf Französisch geschriebene Allegorie und ein Herrschaftsratgeber, worin die verschiedenen Sitten Europas und des Orients beschrieben werden. Er befürwortet darin den Friedensschluß zwischen Frankreich und England als Bedingung für die erfolgreiche Fortsetzung der Kreuzzüge. Auch berichtet er darin von der göttlichen Offenbarung, die er in Jerusalem empfangen hatte, einen neuen christlichen Ritterorden zu gründen und das Heilige Land zu befreien. Das Werk *Nova religio passionis* enthält die „Gesetzestafeln" seines projektierten Ritterordens.[167]

Dichtung ist nichts anderes als ein Handwerk (eine Kunstfertigkeit) (Var. eine Formung), eine Art von Weben und eine Weise der Formung." (aus Heinrichs, *Arabische Dichtung und griechische Poetik. Ḥāzim al-Qarṭaǧannīs Grundlegung der Poetik mit Hilfe Aristotelischer Begriffe*, Beirut 1969, S. 70).

[165] Viktor Borisovič Šklovskij (1893-1984) in *Iskusstvo kak priem* (Kunst als Verfahren, 1919) gegen die Auffassung, Dichtung sei Denken in Bildern. Vollständiges Zitat: *„Es erweist sich aber, daß die Bilder fast unbeweglich sind; unverändert wandern sie von Jahrhundert zu Jahrhundert, von Land zu Land, von Dichter zu Dichter. Bilder gehören „keinem", sind „Gottes". Je tiefer man in eine Epoche eindringt, desto klarer wird einem, daß ein Dichter Bilder, die man für sein geistiges Eigentum gehalten hatte, von anderen übernommen hat und sie fast unverändert verwendet. [...] Die Bilder sind vorgegeben, und in der Dichtung gibt es weit mehr Erinnerung an die Bilder als ein Denken in ihnen."* (aus: Jurij Striedter (Hg.), *Russischer Formalismus. Texte zur allgemeinen Literaturtheorie und zur Theorie der Prosa*, München 1994, S. 5). Siehe auch Viktor Ehrlich, *Russischer Formalismus*, Frankfurt 1955, S. 194 in einer Variante, die mir im Original nicht vorlag: *„Der Dichter, schrieb Šklovskij, schafft keine Bilder; er findet sie [in der gewöhnlichen Sprache – V. E.], oder ruft sie sich ins Gedächtnis zurück."*

[166] Siehe zu seinen Werken Blumenfeld-Kosinski, Renate and Petkov, Kiril (Hg.), *Philippe de Mézières and His Age: Piety and Politics in the Fourteenth Century*, Leiden/Boston 2012 und Jorga, *Philippe de Mézières*.

[167] Siehe Herzsohn, *Der Überfall Alexandriens*, S. VIII, Anm. a.

Im Zusammenhang mit Ibn Abī Ḥaġalah und seiner Liebe zur Buchstaben- und Zahlensymbolik ist erwähnenswert, daß de Mézières den alten Pilger in *Le songe* auch „Ardant Désir" nennt und seine Allegorien auf der Zahl vier und dem Schachspiel basieren, mit denen die Grund- und Handlungsprinzipien eines idealen Königs und die vorbildliche Kriegsführung veranschaulicht werden. Das Vierer-Prinzip, auf das die Schachfigurenallegorie zurückgeht, entspricht bei de Mézières einer idealen Ordnung, vertreten durch Kirche, Rittertum, Bürger (Burgher) und Arbeiter. Die Handlungs- und Bewegungsmuster dieser Gruppen entsprechen denen der Schachfiguren, wobei jede gewählte Bewegung Auswirkungen auf das gesamte Spiel hat.[168]

2. „*La Prise d'Alexandrie*" (Die Einnahme Alexandrias)[169] von Guillaume de Machaut, (1300-1377), Reimchronik, geschr. ca 1370-1371.

Guillaume de Machaut war einer der bekanntesten Komponisten und Lyriker seiner Zeit.[170] Seine Verschronik „La Prise d'Alexandrie" schrieb er zu Ehren des 1369 ermordeten Peter Lusignans. An dem Kreuzzug Peters gegen Alexandria nahm Machaut nicht teil, vielmehr scheint sein Werk eine Auftragsarbeit für Karl V. gewesen zu sein.[171] Er diente als Kleriker und königlicher Beamter am böhmischen Hof. Nach ausgedehnten Reisetätigkeiten kam er ab 1340 nach Reims, wo er bis zu seinem Tode als Kanoniker der Kathedrale Notre Dame tätig war.[172]

3. „*Schilderung der Erlebnisse und Thaten Purchart's von Ellerbach des Alten*" ein Österreicher, der am Kreuzzug teilnahm und 1368 starb; geschrieben als Reimchronik von Peter der Suchenwirth (gewöhnlich Peter Suchem).[173]

---

[168] Joël Blanchard, "A Religion in Its Time: Numerology and Moral Alchemy in Philippe de Mézières' Work", in: Blumenfeld-Kosinski / Petkov (Hg.), *Philippe de Mézières and his Age*, Leiden 2012, S. 225-235 sowie Daisy Delogu, "How to Become the "roy des frans": The Performance of Kingship in Philippe de Mezieres's Le songe du vieil pelerine", in: *Dems.*, S. 147-164, hier S. 154 und S. 156.

[169] Die englische Übersetzung von Barton Palmer weist die Schreibung *d'Alixandre* auf.

[170] Hauptgegenstand seiner Lyrik ist „das Lob der Damen" und die profane Liebe. Sein Meisterstück *Livre dou Voir Dit* (geschr. ca. 1363-5), eine Art Enzyklopädie der poetischen Genres, thematisiert die Leidenschaft ähnlich wie der *Dīwān aṣ-ṣabābah* Ibn Abī Ḥaġalahs. Siehe zu Machauts Liebeslyrik und zum Genre, Jessica Rosenfeld, *Ethics and Enjoyment in Late Medieval Poetry: Love after Aristotle*, Cambridge 2010, S. 86-90.

[171] Siehe Lawrence Earp, *Guillaume de Machaut: A Guide to Research*, London 1996, S. 46-48, nebst Anm. 183.

[172] Machauts Reimchronik ist wenige Jahre nach dem Tode Peters I. verfaßt. Seine Informationen hat er vermutlich von zurückgekehrten französischen Teilnehmern des Alexandria-Überfalls zusammengetragen (siehe Edbury, "Machaut, Mézières, Makhairas and Amadi", in: Blumenfeld-Kosinski / Petkov (Hg.), Philippe de Mézières and his Age. Piety and Politics in the Fourteenth Century, Leiden 2012, S. 349-358, hier S. 350-351).

[173] Siehe Herzsohn, *Der Überfall Alexandriens*, S. VIII, Anm. a.

358 ALEV MASARWA

4. "Recital concerning the Sweet Land of Cyprus", eine im zyprischen Dialekt geschriebene Chronik von Leontios Machairas (ca. 1360 o. 80-nach 1432), Hofsekretär und Chronist, orthodoxer Christ im Dienste der katholischen Herrscher der Insel.[174]

Anhang II: aš-Šāṭibīs Elegie

Handschrift: Berlin We II 359 und 360 [= *Ms. Ilmām*] mit insg. 270 Folia. Das Manuskript ist im *Nasḫī*-Duktus geschrieben, 27-zeilig, Titel und Abschnitte meist mit roter Tinte hervorgehoben. Es enthält einige Vokalzeichen, die *hamzah*-Schreibung kommt vor, doch unregelmäßig, vor allem in den Gedichten häufig durch ein *yāʾ* (*makāyid* statt *makāʾid*) ersetzt (ausführliche Beschreibung in Ahlwardt, Wilhelm: *Verzeichnisse*, Bd. 19 (7865-7866) und Bd. 21 (9815)).

Sigla: (ب) *Ms. Berlin We II 360*, fol. 187a-196b; (ج) Druckausgabe (nach den Mss. Patna/Bankipur (بن), Kairo (أصل) und Berlin (رلٍ)) von ʿAzīz Suryāl ʿAṭiyah und Etienne Combé (Hgg.), *Kitāb al-Ilmām bi-l-iʿlām fī-mā ǧarat bi-hi l-aḥkām wa-umūr al-maqḍiyyah fī waqʿat al-Iskandariyyah* / Muḥammad b. Qāsim b. Muḥammad an-Nuwayrī al-Iskandarānī (baʿd 775/1372), 7 Bde., Hyderabad 1968-1976, III: S. 217-231.

Varianten:

‖ 2 : [مُنَايَ] (ب) : منآىء، (ج) : منآى ‖ 3 : [أبدو] كذا في (ب) وصوابه (أبدى) كما في (ج) ‖ 5

(بن) [الحَشَا] : 10 ‖ لا بنفك : (بن) [لاَ يَكُفُّ] : 9 ‖ لعظم : (بن) [لِكُثْرِ] : 7 ‖ كسا : (ج) [كَسَى] :

خَطَايَا : 19 ‖ [ظَافِرٍ] : 16 ‖ كما في (ج) وصوابه (شيني) كذا في (ب) [شينِ] : 14 ‖ الحَشَى :

: 28 ‖ جراير : (ب) [جَرَائِرٍ] : 20 ‖ آثرت : (ج)و (ب) في [أَثَّرَتْ] ، نقضت خطآ : (بن) [تَقَضَّت

كذا [المن] : 32 ‖ (ج) في كما (حكمت) وصوابه (ب) في كذا [حَلَمَتْ] : 30 ‖ (بن) من ساقطة [لِي]

كذا [الأوْصافِ] : 38 ‖ امروا : (بن) [أُمِدُّوا] : 33 ‖ القآء : (ب) [أَلْقَى] ؛ (ب) من وساقطة (ج) في

كما (ان مسلما) : وصوابه [ان مسلم] كذا في (ب) ولعله أصحّ ؛ [الاوصاب] : (بن)و (ج) في و (ب)

: 42 ‖ خؤون : (ج) [خؤن] : 41 ‖ (ج) في كما الأول الشطر الى [غدَا] نقل الوزن ويقتضى ؛ (ج) في

(يضني) : (ج) في و (ب) في كذا [يصمي] : 48 ‖ (ج) في البيت ترك [الخ ... أَسْكَنْتَ ثَغْرُ يَا بِأَبِي أَلاَ]

---

[174] Die Chronik wurde von Emmanuel Miller und Constantin Sathas 1881 ins Französische übersetzt: *Léonce Machérus, Chronique de Chypre*, Paris 1881; eine englische Übersetzung des Werks unternahm Dawkins, *Recital Concerning the Sweet Land of Cyprus Entitled 'Chronicle'- The chronicle of Makhairas*, (S. 148-149 für den Angriff der Franken am Donnerstag, 9. Oktober). Zum Autor siehe Nicolaou-Konnari, "Machairas, Leontios", in: *EMC*, Hg. Graeme Dunphy, Cristian Bratu. Der Duktus der Chronik weist Ähnlichkeiten mit der an-Nuwayrīs auf. Eine wertvolle narratologische Studie, mit der diese Parallelen genauer nachgezeichnet werden können, gibt Anaxagoru, *Narrative and stylistic structures in the chronicle of Leontios Machairas*, Nicosia 1998.

؛ [شُؤُونِي] في (ب) : شؤني ‖ 50 : [مَضِيقٍ] (بن) : ضِيق ‖ 52 : [ذُلٍّ يذوب وهونٍ] كذا في (ج) وفي (ب) : (ذل بذوب وهين) ‖ 55 : [لِلسُّهَادِ] (بن) : السهاد ‖ 56 : [مسمع] (بن) : (ذي سمع) ؛ ويقتضى الوزن نقل [حِجًّا] الى الشطر الثاني كما في (ج) ‖ 58 : [فَاضْرَعُوا] (بن) : فاسرعو ‖ 59 : [بِنَصْرٍ وَفَتْحٍ لِلْأَنَامِ مُبِينِ] كذا في (ب) و(ج) ؛ وفي (بن) : بفتح قريب للامام مبين.

قَوْلُ الشَّيْخِ الفَاضِلِ أَبِي عَبْدِ اللهِ مُحَمَّدِ بْنِ حَسَنٍ الشَّاطِبِيِّ أَسْعَدَهُ اللهُ تَعَالَى [الطويل]

(1) هَمَـــثْ يَا لَقَـــوْمِي بِالدُّمُـــوعِ عُيُـــونِي   لِمُعْظَـــمِ شَجْـــوِي وَانْبِعَـــاثِ شُجُـــونِي

Mir fließen die Tränen, oh Leute, wegen / der Heftigkeit der Trauer und dem Ausströmen meines Kummers.

(2) وَأَمْـــسَيْثُ صَبًّا شَـــاكِيًا مِـــنْ صَبَابَتِي   وَصَـــارَ مُنَـــايَ اقْـــتِرَابُ مَنُـــونِي

Ich wurde zu einem Liebeskranken, der sich aus Liebeskummer beklagt, / und so
wurde es nunmehr mein Wunsch, mich meinem Ende zu nähern.

(3) أُصَـــعِّدُ أَنْفَـــاسِي وَأَبْـــدو تَـــأَوُّهِي   لِخَطْـــبٍ جَلِيـــلٍ هَـــاجَ مِنْـــهُ أَنِيـــنِي

Ich atmete schneller und begann zu seufzen / wegen eines gewaltigen Unglücks, das
meine Seufzer in Wallung brachte.

(4) \187ب\ إِذَا جَنَّ لَيْلِي أَقْلَقَتْنِي خَوَاطِرِي   كَأَنِّي مُـــصَابٌ فِي الدُّجَى بِجُنُـــونِ

Wenn sich die Nacht verfinsterte, dann beunruhigten mich meine Gedanken, / als
hätte mich in tiefster Finsternis ein Dämon (Wahn) befallen.

(5) هَجَـــرْثُ مَنَامِي مُـذْكَـسَى جِسْمِيَ الأَسَى   وَقَـــدْ ظَـلَّ تَـسْهِيدِي حَلِيــفَ جُفُـونِي

So verließ mich mein Schlaf, seitdem die Trauer meinen Körper bekleidete, / während meine Schlaflosigkeit im Bund mit meinen Augenlidern die Nacht verbrachte.

(6) وَمِـنْ عُظْـمِ مَا بِي لَـوْ رَأَتْـنِي مَعَـارِفِي   لِتَغْيِـــيرِ أَحْـــوَالِي لَمَـــا عَرَفُـــونِي

So groß war das (der Schmerz), was (der) mich traf, daß, wenn meine Bekannten mich
gesehen hätten, / mich wegen meines Zustands nicht wiedererkannt hätten.

(7) وَقَـــدْ لَاَمَـــنِي قَـــوْمٌ لِكُـــثْرِ تَـوَلُّهِي   بِبَـــثِّ خُطُـــوبٍ طَـالَ مَـا دَهَمُـونِي

Ja, die Menschen tadelten mich wegen des Ausmaßes meiner Verwirrtheit / und weil
ich über das Unglück, das mich heimsuchte, offen klagte.

(8) فَلَـــوْ نَالَ عُـــذَّالِي قَلِـــيلاً مِـــنَ الَّذِي   مُنِيـــثُ بِـــهِ فِي الدَّهْـــرِ مَا عَـذَلُونِي

Wenn meine Tadler doch nur ein wenig von dem erlebten, was / mir durch das
Schicksal widerfahren ist, so würden sie mich nicht tadeln.

(9) أَلَا يَا أَخِـــلاَّئِي انْـــدِبُوا وَيْحَـــكُمْ مَعِـــي   وَجُـــودُوا بِـــدَمْعٍ لاَ يُكَـــفُّ هُثُـــونِ

Sodann meine Freunde, weint doch mit mir! / Lasst die Tränen fließen [und] nicht
den Trauerstrom versiegen,

(10) عَلَـــى حَـــادِثٍ فِي الثَّغْـــرِ أَشْعَـــلَ فِي الحَـــشَا   لَظًى لَـــمْ يَكُـــنْ يَهْفُـــو بِعقْـدِ يَقِـــينِ

über das Unglück in der Grenzstadt, das in mir / ein Feuer lodern ließ, das nicht mit Gewißheit zu erwarten war [?].
Anm.: Statt *ʿiqd* ist evtl. *ʿayn* zu lesen (~ das mit einem magischen Knoten nicht zu beirren/abzuwenden war).

(11) لِإثْنَيْ وَعِشْرِينَ مَضَتْ مِنْ مُحَرَّمٍ لِسَبْعٍ وَسِتِّينَ وَسَبْعِ مِئِينِ

22 Tage des Muḥarram waren vergangen im Jahre 767,

(12) أَتَاهُ عَدُوٌّ مَارِدٌ فِي عَوَالِمٍ مُعِدٌّ بِلِقْيَاهُ بِحَرْبٍ زَبُونِ

als plötzlich der teuflische Feind von überall her / (mit Unmengen von Truppen) kam, gerüstet, um ihr (der Stadt) einen grausamen Krieg zu erklären.

(13) كَسَى البَحْرَ جِلْبَابا تَلَوَّنَ صِبْغُهُ وَبَيْرَقُ فِي تَلْوِينِهِ بِفُنُونِ

Er kleidete das Meer in ein Gewand, das seine Farbe verfärbte, / und er beflaggte die Färbung in mannigfaltigen Farben.
Anm.: vgl. V. 3 in Ibn Abī Ḥaǧalahs Elegie

(14) قَرَاقِيرُ فِي آثَارِهِنَّ مَرَاكِبٌ وَكَمْ مِنْ غُرَابٍ كَالطُّيُورِ وشِينِ[ي]

Den Spuren ihrer gewaltigen Flaggschiffe / folgten Galeonen und wie viele Ġirbān-schiffe – rabengleich   und wie viele Galeeren!

(15) عِصَابَةُ كُفْرٍ أَثْرَعَتْ أَكُؤُسَ الرَّدَى مَذَاقَتُهَا تُنْحِلْنَ كُلَّ سَمِينِ

Die Schar des Unglaubens füllte die Becher des Verderbens, / deren Geschmack gar jeden Wohlgenährten abmagern lässt.
Anm.: zur Lexik *ʿuṣbat al-kufr* vgl. V. 1. in Ibn Abī Ḥaǧalahs Elegie

(16) أَمَدَّت خُطَاهَا بِالأَذَى فِي خِلَالِهِ فَيَا عَجَبًا مِنْ ظَافِرٍ بِمَصُونِ

Ihr Durchschreiten erweiterte die Pein, als sie durch die Bresche (im Festungswall) zogen / und wie seltsam ist es doch, daß sich jemand einer Sache bemächtigen kann, die wohlgeschützt ist?

(17) مَعَالِمُ تَوْحِيدٍ أَبَاحَ جَنَابَهُم عَدِيمُو حِجًى بَيْنَ الأَنَامِ وَدِينِ

Die Stätten des *tawḥīd* wurden der Willkür preisgegeben, / von solchen, die frei von rechter Leitung (Einsicht) unter den Menschen wie auch im Glauben sind.

(18) لَقَدْ ظَفِرَ القَوْمُ اللِّئَامُ بِمَعْشَرٍ كِرَامٍ وَلَكِنْ قَدْ سَرَتْ بِظُنُونِ

Ja, das verfluchte Volk siegte über die edelmütige Gemeinschaft, / doch sie waren vornehm nur in der Einbildung. (?)

(19) خَطَايَا تَقَضَّت أَثَّرَتْ بِارْتِكَابِهَا قَذًى قَدْ نَمَا فِي أَشْهُرٍ وَسِنِينِ

Sünden, die nun vorüber sind, doch Spuren (Hälmchen) hinterließen, die von Monat zu Monat und Jahr zu Jahr größer wurden.

(20) إِبَاحَةُ قُبْجٍ وَارْتِكَابُ جَرَائِرٍ وَتَضْيِيعُ أَحْكَامٍ وَخَوْنُ أَمِينِ

Das Schreckliche war erlaubt, der Frevel begangen, die Gesetzte mißachtet und selbst der Sichergeglaubte übte Verrat.
Anm.: oder „das Sichergestellte wurde verraten".

(21) وَبَعْدُ فَأَمْرُ اللهِ مَا مِنْهُ مَهْرَبٌ وَلاَ مَعْقِلٌ مِنْ حُكْمِهِ بِحَصِينِ

Allein, vor dem Willen (Befehl) Gottes gibt es kein Entkommen, / und vor seinem Urteil gibt es selbst in einer Festung keine Zuflucht.

(22) أَرَى ذَاكَ تَمْحِيــصًا لَنَــا مِـــنْ ذُنُوبِنَــا   وَمَـــا أَنَا فِيمَـــا قُلْتُـــهُ بِــــضَنِينِ

Ich glaube, daß diese Heimsuchung eine Prüfung ist, die uns wegen unserer Sünden (Vergehen) befiel, / und in dem, was ich darüber berichtete, war ich noch kärglich (sparsam)!

Anm.: Umkehrung des koranischen Motivs: in Q 81:24 ﴿وَمَا هُوَ عَلَى الْغَيْبِ بِضَنِينٍ﴾ „und er hält nicht aus Geiz das Verborgene zurück". Vgl. zum Sünden-Motiv Vers 17 in Ibn Abī Ḥaǧalahs Elegie.

(23) لَقَـــدْ شَـــاهَدَتْ عَيْنِي العَجَائِـبَ مَا رَأَتْ   كَظَفْـــرِ شِمَــالٍ وَانْهِـــــزَام يَمِــــينِ

Ich (wörtl. mein Auge) war Zeuge von unfassbaren Dingen, die das Auge noch nie gesehen hat, / wie den Sieg des linken Teils und die Niederlage der rechten Seite.

Anm.: kontrastreiches Wortspiel mit *šimāl* (links; Norden) und *yamīn* (rechts; die rechten Glaubens sind; Süden), darüber hinaus auch eine bekannte Lexik aus dem Koran (z.B. *aṣḥāb al-yamīn* und *aṣḥāb aš-šimāl* in der bezeichnenden Sure *al-wāqiʿah* (Q 56:8-9, 38, 41, 90-91).

(24) وَمَـــــدَّ عَـــدُوٌّ كَافِـــــرٌ بَاعَ بَغْيِـــهِ   لِخَـــرْقِ سِـــيَاجٍ وَارْتِـــكَابِ مُتُـــونِ

(Der) ungläubige Feind streckte die Ellen seiner Tyrannei, / bis er durch den Schutzwall einfiel und auf die Festung stieg

Anm.: *irtikāb mutūn* ~ Sünden an dem „Festen" (Festung, Texten, Tradition etc.) verübte.

(25) وَقَتْـــلِ رِجَـــالٍ وَانْتِهَـــــابِ ذَخَـــائِـرٍ   وَهَتْـــكِ حَـــرِيمٍ فِي الْخُـــدُورِ مَـــصُونِ

und die Männer tötete, Schätze raubte / und die Frauen in ihren geschützten Zelten (behüteten Gemächern) schändete.

(26) لَقَـــدْ قُطِعَـــت مِنِّي المَفَاصِـــلُ مُـــذْ رَأَتْ   لِــــكُلِّ فَتِيـــلٍ ظَـــلَّ غَـــيْرَ دَفِيـــنِ

Mir wurden die Gelenke geschnitten (d.h. ich brach zusammen), als sie (meine Gelenke) einen jeden Gefallenen erblickten, der unbegraben blieb.

(27) وَحَرَّمَـــتِ الأَجْفَـــانُ نَـــوْمِي وَحُـــقَّ لِي   عَـــلَى حُـــرَمٍ فَـــارَقْنَ كُلَّ خَـــدِينِ

Meine Augenlider versagten mir den Schlaf und erlaubten mir / nunmehr den Anblick der Unantastbaren (Frauen), die ihre Gefährten (Männer) verloren haben.

(28) حَنَانَيْـــكَ خِـــلِّي كُـــنْ بِحَقِّـــكَ مُـــسْعِدِي   وَوَاصِـــلْ حَنِينًــا مِنْـــكَ لِي بِحَنِــــينِ

Hab Mitleid, Freund, sei mir ein echter Helfer, / und verbinde dein Mitgefühl mit meinem.

(29) فَقَـــدْ حَـــلَّ بِالثَّغْـــرِ المَنَّـــعِ مُعْـــضِلٌ   فَظِيـــعٌ أَتَاحَ العَقْـــلَ أَيَّ فُتُـــونِ

In die unzugängliche Grenzstadt kehrte das abscheulich Starke (das Unheil) ein, / das dem Verstand jeden Unfug (jegliche Bosheit) gewährte.

(30) وَكَمْ حَلِمَـــــتْ فِيـــــهِ المَخَـــازِي بِـــرَأْيِهِمْ   لِفُقْـــــدَانِ ذِي رَأْيٍ هُنَـــاكَ مَتِيـــــنِ

Wie oft walteten (hier besser: *ḥakamat*!) die Dämonen (Schamlosen) dort nach eigenem Gutdünken, / ~ weil dort keine Personen mit Entschlusskraft waren.

(31) \188أ\ تَلَهَّبَ صَدْرِي مِنْ شَوَاظِ حَرِيقِهِمْ   وَمِـــنْ نَهْـــبِ مَالٍ ظَاهِرٍ وَخَزِينِ

Meine Brust entflammte wegen der glühenden Funken ihres Brandes / und wegen des Raubs von offenen und versteckten Gütern.

(32) عَجِبْـتُ [لِمَـنْ] أَلْقَـى السِّـلاَحَ جَبَانَـةً   وَوَلَّى بِوَجْـهٍ كَالِـحٍ وَمَهِـينِ

Ich wunderte mich über den, der durch Feigheit die Waffen ablegte / und sein finsteres und verächtliches Gesicht (von dem Feind) abwendete.

(33) إِذَا دَارَكَ المَـوْلَى بِلُطْـفِ عَبِيـدَهِ   أَمِـدُّوا بِعَقْـلٍ فِي الخُطُـوبِ رَصِينِ

Wenn Gott mit seiner Gnade seine Diener versorgt, / so gibt er ihnen einen unerschütterlichen Verstand in Zeiten des Unglücks.

(34) وَإِنْ خُـذِلُوا فَـالرَّأْيُ مِـنْهُم مُـشَتَّتٌ   وَلَـوْ أَنَّهُـم فِي الحَـرْبِ أُسْـدُ عَـرِينِ

Doch wenn sie (Gottes) Unterstützung nicht erhalten, zerstreut sich ihre Entscheidungskraft, / selbst wenn sie im Krieg wie Löwen im Dickicht (kämpfen).
Anm.: Vgl. an-Nuwayrī, *Ms. Ilmām*, fol. 103b, wo die Verse 33 und 34 ihrer Aussage nach auf die Fehlentscheidung Ğanğarās verweisen.

(35) يُنَـادِي لِـسَانُ الحَـالِ بِالحَـالِ أَنْظُـرُوا   كِلاَبُ النَّـصَارَى وَيْحَـكُمْ أَكَـلُـونِي

Es ist so, als ob die Lage (die Stadt) über die Situation spricht: „Schaut, / die Hunde der Christen, bravo! Dank euch (Schande über euch!) haben sie mich aufgefressen!"

(36) تَحَـكَّمَ أَعْـدَاءُ الهُـدَى فِيَّ بِالـرَّدَى   فَلَـوْ أَنَّ حَـولِي عُـصْبَةً نَـصَرُونِي

Die Feinde der Rechtleitung ordneten (willkürlich) über mich den Untergang an (sie hatten mich in der Hand), / hätte ich doch um mich einen Trupp, der mir geholfen hätte!

(37) حِمَـايَ تَعَـرَّى مِـنْ حِجَـابٍ لِفَاتِـكٍ   ظَلُـومٍ يُنَـادِي أَيْـنَ أَيْـنَ قَـرِينِي

Meine Festung (meine Stadt), die man ihres Schutzschleiers entblößte, / rief wegen des tyrannischen Übeltäters: „Wo, wo ist mein Ebenbürtiger?"

(38) وَمِنْ أَعْظَمِ الأَوْصَافِ أَن مُسْلِمًـا [ا] [غَدَا]   يَحُـوزُ وَيَحْـوِي لاَ يَـدِينُ بِـدِينِ

Zu den härtesten Leiden (lies: *awṣāb*) gehört es (~ am schwierigsten ist es zu ertragen), daß ein Muslim nunmehr der ist, / der plündert und nimmt und nicht die Religion befolgt.

(39) تَجَـرَّأَ بَعْـدَ الـرُّومِ بِالنَّهْـبِ عَـادِيًا   وَلَـمْ يَخْـشَ مَـا يَلْقَـاهُ بَعْـدَ مَنُونِ

Nach den Romäern zeigte er sich (der Muslim / der Araber) kühn im niederträchtigen Raub, / wobei er nicht fürchtete, was ihn nach der Prüfung erwartet.

(40) وَلَـمْ يَرْتَقِـبْ سُـوءَ الحِـسَابِ وَهَـوْلِهِ   وَضَـبْطَ حَفِـيظٍ كَاتِـبٍ وَظَنِـينِ

Er bedachte nicht die Schwere des Tages der Abrechnung und ihre Schrecken / und nicht, daß alle seine Taten, auch die beabsichtigten, vom kundigen Schreiber (in der Tatenliste) offengelegt werden.

(41) إِلَى اللهِ أَشْـكُو جَـوْرَ عَـادٍ وَمُعْتَـدٍ   ظَلُـومٍ أَثِـيمٍ مُفْـسِدٍ وَخَـؤُنِ

Ich richte meine Klage an Gott über den Frevel des Feindes und / die tyrannische Überschreitung (Maßlosigkeit), das sündhafte Unheilstiften und den Verrat.

(42) أَلاَ بِـأَبِي يَا ثَغْـرُ أَسْـكَنْتَ باطِـنِي   خَبَـالاً بِـهِ شَـدِّي اضْمَحَـلَّ وَلِيـنِي

Bei meinem Vater! Oh Alexandria! Du hast mein Inneres / mit Wahn besetzt und damit meine Widerstandskraft und meine Zärtlichkeit vertrieben.

(43) أَلاَ بِـأَبِي يَا ثَغْـرُ قَلْـبِي مُقَلَّـبٌ   عَـلَى جَمَـرَاتٍ قَـدْ أَهْجَـنَ سُـكُونِي

Bei meinem Vater! Oh Alexandria! Mein Herz dreht sich / über den Feuerkohlen, die meine Stille aufgewühlt haben.

(44) أَلاَ بِأَبِي يَا ثَغْرُ هَلْ لاَ تَبَسُّمًا   كَمَا قَدْ عَهِدْنَا وَانْبِسَاطَ فُنُونِ

Bei meinem Vater! Oh Alexandria! Gibt es denn kein Lächeln mehr / und keine Freude an der Kunst, so wie wir es damals kannten?

(45) أَلاَ بِأَبِي يَا ثَغْرُ أَيْنَ أَحِبَّتِي   أَبْعْدَ وِصَالِي مَا لَهُمْ هَجَرُونِي

Bei meinem Vater! Oh Alexandria! Wo sind meine Lieben? / Wie konnten sie mich verlassen, nachdem ich angekommen war?

(46) نَثَرْتُ لآلِئَ الدَّمْعِ حِينَ تَنَاثَرَتْ   لآلِيكَ وَاسْتَحْكَمت عِقْد غُبُونِي

Ich verstreute die Tränenperlen, als man deine Perlen auseinanderriß, / während sich der Knoten meines Sinnesverlustes fester zuschnürte [? ~ im Sinne von „meine Sinne verlor"].

Anm.: Ein eindrucksvoller und kontrastreicher Vers, der jedoch metrisch problematisch ist. Das Metrum erfordert etwa *wa-stahkamta/u* statt *wa-stahkamat*, gram. liest sich das Passiv mit dem Plural von ʿ*iqd* (ʿ*uqad*) besser.

(47) دَعَوْتُ اضْطِبَارِي وَالكَرَى وَتَعَقُّلِي   فَلاَ وَأَبِي يَا صَاحِ مَا قَرِبُونِي

Ich rief meine Geduld, meinen Schlaf und meinen Verstand, / doch nichts, mein Freund, näherte sich mir.

(48) وَكَيْفَ وَفُقْدَانِ الأَحِبَّةِ مُذْهِلِي   وَشَأْنُهُمْ يُصْمِي جَمِيعَ شُؤُونِي

Wie soll es denn sein, wo mich der Verlust der (meiner) Lieben um den Verstand brachte / und ihr Zustand mich in allen Lebenslagen tödlich traf?

(49) يَقُولُ فَقِيدُ الأَهْلِ بِالحَالِ مُعْلِمِي   أَلَمْ تَرَ حِزْبَ الشِّرْكِ قَدْ مَلَكُونِي

Jemand, der von seiner Familie getrennt wurde, sagte über die Lage informierend: / „Siehst du nicht, daß der Verband der Vielgötterei mich bereits beherrscht?

(50) فَهَا أَنَا بَعْدَ العِزِّ فِي ذُلِّ أَسْرِهِمْ   وَبَعْدَ سَرَاحِي فِي مَضِيقٍ سُجُونِي

Da stehe ich nun nach der Zeit des Ruhms in der Schmach ihrer Gefangenschaft / und nach meiner Freilassung in der Enge meiner Gefängnisse.

(51) وَبَعْدَ انْشِرَاحِي فِي هَنَاءِ لَذَّةِ المُنَى   أُقَاسِي قَسِيّ القَلْبِ غَيْرَ حَنِينِ

Und nachdem ich mich am Erlangen meiner süßen Wünsche erfreut hatte, / erdulde ich (nun?) die unbarmherzige Herzenshärte (~ einen unbarmherzigen Hartherzigen).

(52) أَبِيتُ اللَّيَالِي لاَ فُتُورَ لِمَدْمَعِي   وَأُصْبِحُ فِي ذُلٍّ يَذُوب وَهُونِ

Die Nächte verbrachte ich, ohne daß das Fließen der Tränen ermüdete / und am nächsten Morgen verging ich vor (ich verbrachte den Morgen in) Scham und Erniedrigung.

(53) وَكُلُّ أَسِيرٍ كَالَّذِي قُلْتُ قَائِلٌ   فَبِاللهِ مِنْ حُسْنِ الدُّعَاءِ هَبُونِي

Und jeder Gefangene würde dasselbe sagen, wie ich es sagte; / so, im Namen Gottes, schenkt mir die schönsten Gebete (betet für mich!)."

(54) عَضَضْتُ بَنَانِي عِنْدَ ذَا مِنْ تَأَسُّفِي   وَأَسْقَطْتُ حُزْنًا فِي التُّرَابِ جَبِينِي

Da biß ich auf meine Finger wegen meines Bedauerns (~ um mich des Bewußtseins zu vergewissern) / und ließ trauernd meine Stirn auf den Staub (Boden) fallen. (~ ich betete!)

(55) وَوَاصَــلَ نَــوْحِي لِلــسُّهَادِ فَــلاَ أَرَى   مُــصَاحَبَةً بَــيْنَ الكَــرَى وَعُيُــونِي

Meine Wehklage verband sich freundschaftlich mit der Schlaflosigkeit, doch / die Freundschaft zwischen dem Schlaf und meinen Augen sehe ich nicht.

(56) ذَرُونِي أُبـــكِي كُلَّ ذِي مَـــسمَعٍ لَهُ   [حِجًـــا] وَأُثِـــيرُ الحُــزْنَ فِيــهِ ذَرُونِي

Laßt mich einen jeden, der hören kann und Verstand besitzt, / zum Weinen bringen und seine Trauer erregen, laßt mich!

Anm.: deutet auf ein Wortspiel mit dem Monat *ḏū l-ḥiǧǧah* hin, der 767 H. auf den August 1366 fällt; der Poet spricht von freigelassenen Gefangenen (V. 49-V. 53), die in dieser Zeit freigekommen sein dürften.

(57) فَيَــا لَيْــتَ شِعْرِي هَــلْ لِثَــأْرِيَ طَالِــبٌ   يُجَــلِّي صَــدَا قَلْــبِي بِفَــكِّ رُهُــونِي

Ach, wenn doch mein Gedicht Rache für mich fordern / und den Rost meines Herzens durch die Auslösung meiner Geiseln polieren könnte.

Anm.: *layta šiʿrī* (für *layta šuʿūrī*) ist phraseologisch geprägt und bedeutet „ach wüßte ich doch/nur, …"; hier übernehme ich die wörtliche Bedeutung „(~ ach könnte doch mein Gedicht"), die in zweiter semantischer Reihe und in der Dichtung ohnehin impiliziert ist.

(58) \188ب\ أَيَا مَعْشَرَ الإِسْلامَ بِاللهِ فَاضْرَعُوا   بِإِخْــلاصِ قَــصْدٍ وَاصْــطِحَابِ يَقِــينِ

Oh ihr Gemeinschaft des Islams (Muslime)! Bittet demütig / mit aufrichtigem Vorsatz, begleitet von Gewissheit (starkem Glauben),

Anm.: Häufung der Surennamen in diesem und im folgenden Vers: *iḫlāṣ*: 112; *naṣr*: 114; *fatḥ*: 48.

(59) بِتَمْكِــينِ أَرْبَابِ النُّهَــى مِــن عَــدُوِّنَا   بِنَــصْرٍ وَفَــتْحٍ لِلــأَنَام مُبِــينِ

daß den großen Leuten des Verstandes gegenüber unseren Feinden Macht verliehen wird / und Gott ihnen für die Menschen einen klaren Sieg verleiht;

Anm.: s.o.; [*fatḥ mubīn*] siehe *Q* 48:1-3.

(60) بِحُرْمَــةِ مَــنْ بِالرُّعْــبِ أُيِّــدَ وَانْكَفَــا   بِكَــفِّ تُــرَابٍ مِنْــهُ أَيَّ مَكِــينِ

mit der Ehrerbietung demgegenüber, dem Gott die Angst (der Feinde vor ihm) zum Beistand verlieh und der mit einer Handvoll Staub jeden Starken zurückweichen ließ.

Anm.: u.a. eine Überlieferung über die Schlacht von Ḥunayn, in der der Prophet eine Handvoll Staub in die Augen der Gegner warf, woraufhin diese flohen und Gott den Muslimen den Sieg bescherte. Hierauf wird der Koranvers (17) in der Sure *al-Anfāl* (8) bezogen. Zum Ḥadiṯ siehe: *Ṣaḥīḥ Muslim*, Hg. Muḥammad Fuʾād ʿAbd al-Bāqī, Bayrūt 1412/1991, S. 1402: *kitāb al-ǧihād: bāb ġazwat al-ḥunayn*, no. 81 (1777).

Anhang III: aš-Šāṭibīs „Elegie", No:2

وَلِلشَّاطِبِيِّ أَيْضًا مَرْثِيَّةٌ فِي الإِسْكَنْدَرِيَّةِ، وَهِيَ : [الخفيف]

(1)   أَيُّ جَفْـنٍ لَهُ المَنَـامُ يُـدَانِي   عِنْـدَ صَدْمِ العَـدُوِّ بِالأَجْفَـانِ

(2)   عَنْ حَرْبٌ مِـنَ اللِّئَـامِ إلَى الثَّغْـرِ   ظَنَّـاهُ خَائِـبَ الـرَّأْي عَـانِي

(3)   فِي خَمِـيسٍ وَافَى لَنَـا بِخَمِـيسٍ   وَإلَى الجُمْعَـةِ التَّقَـى الجُمْعَـانِ

(4)   وَغُـرَابُ الفِـرَاقِ يَنْعَـبُ فِينَـا   فَرَّقَـا مِـنْ تَفَـرُّقِ الغِـرْبَانِ

(5)   هَـوَّنَ المُـسْلِمُونَ أَمْـرَ لِقَـاهُمْ   فَأُذِيقُوا مِـنْهُمْ أَشَـدَّ الهَـوَانِ

(6)   سَـنَّ لِلثَّغْـرِ ذَا الخَبِيـثُ سِـنَانًا   فَتَعَـدَّى بِهَـا عَـلَى الأَسْـنَانِ

(7)   مُكِّـنَ النَّـذْلُ فِي الحَـرِيمِ وَفِي الـ -   ـمالِ وَأَلْقَـى الأَذَى بِـكُلِّ مَكَانِ

(8)   قَمَـرُ الثَّغْـرِ وَيْـلَهُ فَعَلَيْـهِ   لَعْنَـةُ اللهِ مَـا بَـدَا القَمَـرَانِ

(9)   أَعْـرِبِ القَـوْلَ بَعْـدَ ذَا فِي فَرِيقيـ -   ـنِ رِعَـاع العَـوَامِ وَالعُـرْبَانِ

(10)   طُعِنُـوا فِي كُبُـودِهِم بِالطَّوَاعِيـ -   ـنِ لأَجْـلِ الفِـرَارِ يَـوْمَ الطِّعَـانِ

(11)   وَدَنُـوا لانْتِهَـابِ كُلِّ مَكَـانٍ   فِي النَّـوَاحِي وَكُلِّ قَـاصٍ وَدَانِ

(12)   مَكَّـنَ اللهُ مِـنْهُم كُلَّ دَانٍ   مُـسْتَمِرِّ الدَّوَامِ بِالإمْكَانِ

(13)   وَعَـلاَهُمْ مِـنَ الـضَّنَا وَالـرَّزَايَا   فِي حِمَـاهُمْ فَـوْقَ الَّذِي قَـد عَلاني

Anhang IV: Elegie Ibn Abī Ḥaǧalahs auf Alexandria

Sigla: (ب) Ms. Wetzstein II 359 und 360; (ج) Druckausgabe Atiya, wie in Anhang II. Die Übersetzung orientiert sich in weiten Teilen an der Arbeit Otfried Weintritts, *Formen*, S. 179-182).

Varianten:

3 : [بَنُو الأَصْفَرِ] في (ب) و (أَصل ج) : بنوا الاصفر ‖ 5 : [جَانِبَهَا] في (ب) : جانبها ‖ 7 : [الأَسْرَى] في (ب) : الأسرا ‖ 14 : [آسِرٍ وَهْوَ] كذا في (ب) وفي (ج) :من أسر من هو ‖ 15 : [حِلِئَ] في (ب) : حَلى ‖ 16 : في (ب) : (ايَادى سبا يا للسبى/السبى) ولعله تصحيف صوابه : [أَيَادِي سَبَا بِالسَّبْي] او[أَيَادِي سَبَا يَا السَّبْي] ‖ 19 : [تَسْتَفِقْ] كذا في (ج) وفي (ب) : نستفق ‖ 23 :[قَائِدا] في (ب) : قآيد.

مَرْثِيَةُ الإِسْكَنْدَرِيَّةِ لِابْنِ أَبِي حَجَلَة التِّلْمْسَانِيِّ [بحر الطّويل]

Folio
[Druck]

أَلاَ فِي سَبِيلِ اللهِ مَا حَلَّ بِالثَّغْرِ   عَلَى فِرْقَةِ الإِسْلاَمِ مِنْ عُصْبَةِ الكُفْرِ

122b
[II: 229]   (1)

Ist es denn nicht für die Sache Gottes, was in der Grenzstadt / einem Teil des Islams durch die Legion des Unglaubens widerfahren ist?

أَتَاهَا مِنَ الفِرِنْجِ سَبْعُونَ مَرْكَبًا   فَصَاحَتْ بِهَا الغِرْبَانُ فِي البَرِّ وَالبَحْرِ

123a
[II: 230]   (2)

Als von den Franken 70 Schiffe / zu ihr (der Stadt) kamen, da kreischten die Raben (Galeeren) zu Lande und zu Wasser (Meer).

وَصَيَّرَ مِنْهَا أَزْرَقَ البَحْرِ أَسْوَدًا   بَنُو الأَصْفَرِ البَاغُونَ بِالبِيضِ وَالسُّمْرِ

128b
[II: 254]   (3)

Die frevlerischen Byzantiner verwandelten mit Schwert (*biḍ*) und Lanze (*sumr*) das Blau des Meeres in Schwarz.

أَقَامُوا عَلَى التَّثْلِيثِ فِيهَا ثَلاَثَةً   كَمَعْبُودِهِم فِي النَّهْبِ وَالقَتْلِ وَالأَسْرِ

129a
[II: 256]   (4)

Sie verrichteten in ihr die Trinität, die aus drei Dingen besteht, / so wie sie es mit ihrer verehrten Gottheit hielten: Raub, Mord und Gefangennahme.

لَئِن نَهَبَ الإِفْرِنْجُ جَانِبَ بَحْرِهَا   فَقَدْ نَهَبَ العُرْبَانُ جَانِبَهَا البَرِّ

132b
[II: 269]   (5)

Während nun die Franken von der Meeresseite aus plünderten, / taten es ihnen die Beduinen von der Landesseite aus gleich.

فَكَمْ مِنْ فَقِيرٍ عَاشَ فِيهَا مِنَ الغِنَى   وَكَمْ مِنْ غَنِيٍّ مَاتَ فِيهَا مِنَ الفَقْرِ

133a
[II: 270]   (6)

Wie viele Arme lebten in ihr frei von Not (in Reichtum) / und wie viele Reiche starben in ihr durch Armut!

وَكَمْ قَتَلُوا فِيهَا كَبِيرًا وَنَصَّرُوا   صَغِيرًا مِنَ الأَسْرَى وَلاَ سِيَّمَا البِكْرِ

133a
[II: 270]   (7)

Wie viele alte (Menschen) töteten sie darin und / wie viele Kinder und insbesondere Erstgeborene (Unverheiratete) haben sie unter den Gefangenen zu Christen gemacht!

Anm.: Verben können ebenfalls passivisch gelesen werden.

فَيَالَكَ مِنْ هَوْلٍ عَظِيمٍ وَفِتْنَةٍ   أَضَرَّ عَلَى الإِنْسَانِ مِنْ فِتْنَةِ القَبْرِ

133a
[II: 272]   (8)

Ach, welch gewaltiges Unheil und welche Prüfung du bist, / die für den Menschen peinvoller ist als die Prüfung des Grabes!

وَقَدْ أَخَذُوا فِي أَخْذِهَا الطَّالِعَ الَّذِي   بِهِ أَخْبَرَ الكُهَّانُ فِي سَالِفِ الدَّهْرِ

134a
[II: 274]   (9)

Durch die Einnahme machten sie (die Franken) die Prophezeiung wahr, / die ihnen die Wahrsager in früheren Zeiten verkündet hatten.

فَمَـا فَـازَ مِنْـهَـا غَـيْـرُهُمْ بِـدُخُولِهَا ولاَ فُتِحَـتْ مِـنْ بَعْـدِ فَاتِحِهَا عَمْـرو — 148a (10)
[II: 335]

Niemandem außer ihnen war es gelungen, in sie einzudringen, / noch wurde sie nach ihrem Eroberer ʿAmr (ʿAmr b. al-ʿĀṣ) erobert.

ولاَ نَبَعَـتْ مِنْهَـا القَنَـا مِـنْ دِمَـائِهِمْ إلَى أَنْ أَسَـالُوا الدَّمَ في البَحْـرِ كَالنَّهْـر — 148a (11)
[II: 336]

Noch floß jemals aus ihr Blut (der Bewohner), / bis sie (die Franken) das Blut ins Meer strömen ließen wie einen Fluß.

فَلَـوْ كَانَ فِيهَـا مِثْـلُ مَـا كَانَ عَـسْكَرٌ يَصُولُ بِـذَاتِ الحَـرْبِ فِيهَا مَعَ الصَّقْرِ — 148b (12)
[II: 340]

Hätte sie (Alexandria) ein Heer gehabt, / das mit dem Falken in jenem Krieg auf sie gestürzt wäre,

لَمَـا ظَفِـرَ الغِـرْبَـانُ فِيهَـا بِنَقْـرَةٍ ولاَ نَابَهَـا خَطْـبٌ بِنَـابٍ ولاَ ظُفْـرِ — 148b (13)
[II: 341]

dann hätten sich die Raben nicht eines einzigen Happens (Picken) bemächtigen können, / und kein Unglück hätte sie heimgesucht weder mit Schnäbeln (Reißzähnen) noch mit Klauen.

وقَدْ أَسَرَتْ قَلْبِي الأَسَـارَى بِأَسْرِهِمْ فَواعَجَبًـا مِـنْ آسِرٍ وَهْـوَ في الأَسْرِ — 149a (14)
[II: 342]

Die Gefangenen haben mein Herz gefangen durch ihre Gefangenschaft. / Oh, wie seltsam ist es, von jemandem gefangen genommen zu werden, der selber gefangen ist.

وَصَارَتْ ذَوَاتُ الحُـلَى بِالأَسْرِ عِنْدَهُمْ ولَيْسَ لَهَـا حِلًى سِـوَى المَـدْمَعِ الدُّرِّ — 150a (15)
[II: 346]

Die juwelengeschmückten (Frauen) gerieten bei ihnen in Gefangenschaft, / und nun gibt es darin nichts Schönes, außer den Perlenschnüren der Tränen.

Anm.: Alternativ ist *lahā* im zweiten Halbvers statt auf die Stadt auch auf die Frauen zu beziehen (so in der Übersetzung Weintritts).

خَـلَى رَبْعُهُـمْ مِـنْ أُنْـسِهِمْ وَتَفَرَّقُـوا أَيَادِي سَـبَا بِالسَّبْيِ في آخِـرِ الـشَّهْرِ — 150b (16)
[II: 348]

Ihre Wohnstätten sind von ihrer Geselligkeit verlassen und durch die Gefangenschaft wurden sie (~ wie die Stämme von Sabāʾ b. Yašğub nach der Flut al-ʿArim) am Ende des Monats in alle Winde zerstreut.

Anm.: *Q* 34:15-17; siehe Anm. 103.

وَحَقِّـكَ هَـذَا مِـنْ ذُنُـوبٍ تَقَـدَّمَتْ وقَرْعِ كُؤُوسِ الخَمْرِ في الثَّغْرِ بِالثَّغْرِ — 154a (17)
[III: 1]

Bei deinem Leben (sei dir gewiß)! Das kommt von vorangegangenen Sünden / und dem Anstoßen der Weinkelche an den Mund (Zähne) der Grenzstadt.

Anm.: altern.: ~ dem Entleeren der Weinkelche in den Mund der Grenzstadt.

وَحَقِّـكَ لَـوْلاَ أَنَّ لِلثَّغْـرِ حَافِظًـا مِـنَ اللهِ كَانَ الثَّغْـرُ في حَوْزَةِ الكُفْرِ — 166a (18)
[III: 64]

Bei deinem Leben (sei dir gewiß)! Wenn Gott die Stadt nicht beschützt hätte, / dann wäre sie ein Hort des Unglaubens geworden.

$$\text{وَحَقِّـكَ إِنْ لَـمْ تَـسْتَفِقْ لِقِتَـالِهِمْ} \qquad \text{جَرَى مَا جَرَى مِنْهُمْ عَلَى الثَّغْرِ فِي مِصْرِ}$$

166b
[III: 68]
(19)

Bei deinem Leben (sei dir gewiß)! Wenn du nicht zu Bewußtsein gekommen wärest und sie bekämpft hättest, / wäre durch sie in Kairo das passiert, was in der Grenzstadt passiert ist.

Anm.: Das Manuskript hat *nastafiq*, doch nach *ḥaqqika* wäre ein solcher Personenwechsel nicht nachvollziehbar. An-Nuwayrī scheint ebenfalls nastafiq gelesen zu haben, denn seine Anmerkungen beziehen sich auf die 1. P. Pl.: (يَعْنِي: إِنْ لَمْ نَتَيَقَّظْ وَنَنْتَبِهْ مِنَ الْغَفْلَةِ الَّتِي مَضَتْ ...). Allerdings sind für ihn die eigentlichen Helden des Kampfes die Männer bzw. Bewohner der Stadt, die sich unerschrocken den Franken stellten, um noch einmal auf die besondere Stellung der *Ribāṭ*-Diener, zu denen er sich selbst zählt, in der islamischen Überlieferung überzuleiten: وَاعْلَمْ أَنَّ حِفْظَ الثُّغُورِ يَكُونُ بِالرِّجَالِ الْأَبْطَالِ لَا بِالْأَسْوَارِ الطِّوَالِ (Wisse, daß die eigentliche Stadtwehr durch heldenhafte Männer gewährleistet ist und nicht durch lange Mauern).

$$\text{وَحَقِّـكَ عِنْـدِي لِلْفِـرَنْجِ مَكَائِـدٌ} \qquad \text{فَلَيْـتَ وَلِيَّ الْأَمْـرِ يَـدْرِي بِمَـا أَدْرِي}$$

170b
[III: 88]
(20)

Bei deinem Leben (sei dir gewiß)! Denn ich hätte gegen die Franken einiges an Kniffen, / ach, und wüßte der Befehlshaber (Yalbuġā) doch das, was ich weiß!

$$\text{فَمَـنْ لِي بِأُسْـطُولٍ بِـهِ أَهْـلُ سَـبْتَةَ} \qquad \text{بِغِـرْبَانِهِمْ مِثْـلَ النُّـسُورِ إِذَا تَـسْرِي}$$

170b
[III: 88]
(21)

Hätte ich doch eine Flotte mit den Leuten von Ceuta, / die mit ihren Schiffen (Raben) angreifen wie Adler.

$$\text{وَمَـنْ لِي بِفُرْسَـانِ الْجَزِيـرَةِ عِنْـدَمَا} \qquad \text{تَعَامَـلَ أَهْـلَ الْكُفْـرِ فِي الْبَحْـرِ بِالنَّحْـرِ}$$

179b
[III: 174]
(22)

Und hätte ich doch die Reiterei von Algeciras, / die die Ungläubigen am Meer niedermetzelte.

$$\text{عَلَى أَنَّ فِي مِصْرٍ عَلَى الْجَيْشِ قَائِدًا} \qquad \text{يَبِيـتُ وَلَا يُعْطِي الْقِيَـادَ عَلَى الْقَسْرِ}$$

184b
[III: 202]
(23)

Obwohl Ägypten einen Heerführer (Yalbuġā) hat, / der nachts wacht, um der Unterwerfung unfreiwillig nicht die Zügel zu überlassen (um nicht einmal unter Zwang die Führungsgewalt zu übergeben),

$$\text{أَقَـامَ لَنَـا بِالثَّغْـرِ جَيْـشًا عَرَمْرَمًـا} \qquad \text{وَفِيـهِ ابْـنُ عَـرَّامَ الْمُؤَيَّـدُ بِالنَّـصْرِ}$$

185b
[III: 208]
(24)

stellte er (Yalbuġā) uns in der Grenzstadt ein gewaltiges Heer auf, / worin Ibn ʿArrām zum Sieg verholfen wird.

Anm.: *ǧinās* mit *ʿaramram* und Ibn ʿArrām.

Anhang V: Textzeugen für Ibn Abī Ḥaġalahs Elegie auf Alexandria

Sigla:

(ي) Ms. Aya Sofya 233 auf 287 Folia: *Durrat al-aslāk fī dawlat al-atrāk* des Ba-draddīn Abū Muḥammad Ibn Ḥabīb al-Ḥalabī (710-779/1310-1377) geb. und gest. in Aleppo, lebte in Damaskus, Alexandria und Kairo.[175]

(ت) *Taḏkirat an-nabīh fī ayyām al-Manṣūr wa-banīh* des Badraddīn Abū Muḥam-mad Ibn Ḥabīb al-Ḥalabī, Hg. Muḥammad Muḥammad Amīn (al-Qāhirah 1986), III: S. 291; sehr wahrscheinlich die *muswaddah* für *Durrat al-aslāk*.

(د) *Badāʾiʿ z-zuhūr fī waqāʾiʿ d-duhūr* des Muḥammad Ibn Aḥmad Ibn Iyās (852-930/1448-1523): hier in der Druckausgabe *[Die Chronik des Ibn Ijās]*, hg. von Muḥammad Muṣṭafā, Stuttgart 1974, I, 2: S. 24.

Varianten:

2 ‖ [الفِرِنْج] وفي (ت) ، (د) ، (ي) : الافرنج ؛ [فَصَاحَتْ] في (ت) و(د) : ضاقت ، وفي (ي) : حاطت ؛ [الفُرْسَانُ] (ت) : الغربان ، وفي (ي) : الفرسان ‖ 3 : [بَنُو الأَصْفَرِ] في (د) - بنُوا الاصفر ‖ [د/6] : [فَتْرةٍ] في (ي) : غَفْلَةٍ ‖ 12 : [يَصُولُ بِذَاتِ] (ت) : تعول بزاة ، وصوابه كما في (د) : تصُول بُزاةُ ‖ 16 : [سَبَا يَا السَّبْي ...] في (ت) و(د) : سبا بالسبي في السَّرّ والجهرِ.

		درة الاسلاك [د]	تذكرة النبيه [ت]	بدائع الزهور [ي]	الإلمام
عَلَى فِرْقَةِ الإِسْلاَمِ مِنْ عُصْبَةِ الكُفْرِ	أَلَا فِي سَبِيلِ اللهِ مَا حَلَّ بِالثَّغْرِ	1	1	1	1
فَصَاحَتْ بِهَا الغِرْبَانُ فِي البَرِّ وَالبَحْرِ	أَتَاهَا مِنَ الفِرِنْجِ سَبْعُونَ مَرْكَبًا	2	2	2	2
بَنُو الأَصْفَرِ البَاغُونَ بِالبِيضِ وَالسُّمْرِ	وَصَيَّرَ مِنْهَا أَزْرَقَ البَحْرِ أَسْوَدًا	3	3	3	3
كَمَعْبُودِهِم فِي النَّهْبِ وَالقَتْلِ وَالأَسْرِ	أَقَامُوا عَلَى التَّثْلِيثِ فِيهَا ثَلَاثَةً	4	4	-	4
وَكَمْ مِنْ غَنِيٍّ مَاتَ فِيهَا مِنَ الفَقْرِ	فَكَمْ مِنْ فَقِيرٍ عَاشَ فِيهَا مِنَ الغِنَى	5	5	5	6

---

[175] Zu ihm siehe *EI²*: III, S. 775; *GAL* II/36-37 S II/35; Ḥāǧǧī Ḫalīfah III/199-200, Nr. 4916; Kaḥḥālah III/266-267; Ziriklī II/208-209. Die neuere Druckausgabe in drei (?) Bänden in der Edition v. Muḥammad Muḥammad Amīn (Kairo: Dār al-Kutub wa-l-Waṯāʾiq al-Qawmiyyah, 2014), lag mir nicht vor. Weitere Kopien der Handschrift sind in Istan-bul/Süleymaniye (Yeni Cami, 849), Berlin (Sprenger 63; We II 344), Kairo (235; 659), Lei-den (72), Paris (1719-1721) und Leipzig in Auszügen (Vollers 611) vorhanden (siehe http://www.refaiya.uni-leipzig.de für weitere Manuskriptnachweise). Paris 1719 und 1721 (Epi-tome) konnten gesichtet werden, doch weder die *Maqāme* noch das Gedicht Ibn Abī Ḥaġa-lahs sind in den Pariser Epitomen verzeichnet.

البيت	درة الاسلاك [د]	تذكرة النبيه [ت]	بدائع الزهور [ي]	الإلمام
أَتَـوْا أَهْلَهَا هَجْمًا عَلَى حِينِ فَتْرَةٍ وَبَاعُهُمْ فِي الْحَرْبِ يَقْصُرُ عَنْ فِتْرِ	6	6	4	-

Sie (die Franken) stürmten unvermutet (in dieser Zeitspanne; für den *ǧinās* mit *fatra* und *fitr*) auf ihre Bewohner los, / aber sie vermochten nichts gegen (die Franken) auszurichten (wörtl. im Krieg reichten ihre Ellen nicht an die Handspanne).

البيت	درة الاسلاك [د]	تذكرة النبيه [ت]	بدائع الزهور [ي]	الإلمام
وَقَدْ أَخَـذُوا فِي أَخْـذِهَا الطَّـالِعَ الَّذِي بِهِ أَخْبَرَ الْكُهَّـانُ فِي سَـالِفِ الدَّهْـرِ	7	7	-	9
فَمَـا فَـازَ مِنْهَـا غَـيْرُهُمْ بِـدُخُولِهَا وَلاَ فُتِحَتْ مِـنْ بَعْدِ فَاتِحِهَـا عَمْـرو	8	8	-	10
فَلَـوْ كَانَ فِيهَـا مِثْـلُ مَـا كَانَ عَسْكَرَ يَصُولُ بِذَاتِ الْحَرْبِ فِيهَا مَعَ الصَّقْرِ	9	9	-	12

[nach der Variante in (د): تَصُول بُزاةُ] ..., dann würden die Habichte des Krieges mit den Falken angreifen.

البيت	درة الاسلاك [د]	تذكرة النبيه [ت]	بدائع الزهور [ي]	الإلمام
لَمَـا ظَفِـرَ الْغِـرْبَانُ فِيهَـا بِنَقْـرَةٍ ولاَ نَابَهَـا خَطْـبٌ بِنَـابٍ وَلاَ ظُفْـرِ	10	10	-	13
خَـلَى رَبْعُهُـمْ مِـنْ أُنْـسِهِمْ وَتَفَرَّقُـوا أَيَادِي سَبَا [يَا الدْ]سَبْي فِي آخِرِ الشَّهْرِ	11	11	-	16
نَـثَرْتُ دُمُـوعِي يَـوْمَ فَـرْطِ نِظَـامِهِمْ فَيَا لَيْتَ شِعْرِي مَنْ يُبَلِّغُهم نَثْرِي	12	12	6	-

Ich zerstreute meine Tränen am Tage, als ihre Ordung (ihr Leben) auseinanderbrach; / ach wüßte ich doch (lexikalische Anspielung auf die eigene Dichtung), wer ihnen meine meine Prosa (Zerstreuung) übermitteln wird.

Anhang VI: Lob auf Ibn Makkī – Ṭarāblus

Sigla:

(ب) *Dīwān Ibn Abī Ḥaǧālah*, Hg. Muǧāhid Muṣṭafā Bahǧat, ʿAmmān 2010, S. 120-122; No: 120 unter Zugrundlegung der Handschrift Kairo 1525.

(ج) *Ms. Kairo 1127* (Dār al-Kutub), fol. 27b-29a (wenige Vokalzeichen, lacuna in V. 9).

(د) *Dīwān Ibn Abī Ḥaǧalah (725-776 H.)*, Hg. Aḥmad Ḥilmī Ḥulwah, al-Qāhirah 2014, S. 86-88 unter Zugrundelegung der Handschriften Kairo 1525 und 1127.

Varianten:

‖ [-] (ب) ، (د) : وقال رحمه الله تعالى ؛ (ج) : وقال أيضا في نائب طرابلس ‖ 3 : [جَونَةِ] (ب) ،
(د) : جَوْفِهِ ، (ج) : جو-ه ، ولعله يريد : (جونه) كما ضبطناه ‖ 7 : [إذَا اخْضَرَّ] كذا في (ب) ، (د) ،
في (ج) : إذا ما خضر ‖ 8 :[نَبْتِ] (ب) : (بيت) و صوابه كما ورد في (ج) ، (د) : نبت ‖ 9 : [[...]]

بِوَاوٍ] بياض في النسختين ؛ [يُعَوِّذُهُ] كذا في (ب) ، (د) ، وفي (ج) : (يغوده) 16 : [خِضَمٌّ غَزِيرٌ...]

(ج) : (حضم عزيز) 19 : [تَسْدِيْدِهِ] (د) : تسديسه 22 : [البَحْرِ وَالبَرِّ] كذا في (ب) ولعله أصحّ ،

(ج) : (البَرِّ وَالبَحْرِ) ، قارن أيضا بيت (45) 23 : [بِالفَقْرِ] وفي (ب) : مِنَ الفَقْرِ 24 : [لِلْعِدَى]

وفي (ب) : لِلْعِدَا 29 : [أَهْلِهَا] وفي (ج) : لنها ؛ [جَالِيَةً] وفي (ج) : حاليه 31 : [عَلَى الفُرْسَانِ]

وفي (ب) : (عَنِ الفُرْسَانِ) و صوابه كما في (ج) و (د) : على الفرسان 33 : [تَجَلُّوا] وفي (ج) : تجلوا

35 : [هِلَالَ] وفي (د) : هلاك 37 : [كَعِقْدِ] في (ج) : (عقد) وفي (ب) : (كفد) 38 : [الضَّبِّ]

وفي (ج) و(د) : صب وصوابه كما في (ب) ؛ [ثَوْبًا] في (ب) و (د) : (لَوْنًا) وصوابه كما في (ج) : ثوبا

40 : [ثَارٌ؟] في (ب) : (غَارَ) وفي (ج) : (ترا) ، وفي (د) : (زَيَّنَه جَيش كلما ثَارَ عنتر) ويقول المحقق

في تعليقه هذا الشطر : "ورد هذا الشطر مكسور الوزن غير واضح المعنى." 41 : [قصيدتي] في (ب)

: (قُصَيِّدِي) وفي (ج) : (قصيدتي) و لعله أصحّ ؛ [العُصُورِ] وفي (ب) و(د) : (الغُصُونِ) 42 :

[النَّسْرِ] (ب) : (نشر) 43 : [عَزْمِي] تكررت الكلمة في (ج).

وقال رحمه الله تعالى [من الطويل]

(1) وَظَبْيٍ رَشِيقِ القَدِّ مُخْتَصَرِ الخَصْرِ ⁣   يُرِيْنَا مُحَيَّا البَدْرِ في لَيْلَةِ الفِطْرِ

Ich denke an ein Gazellenjunges von schönem Wuchs und schmaler Taille, / das uns das Antlitz des Vollmonds in der Nacht des Neumonds zeigt.

(2) إِذَا لَاحَ حَوْلَ البَحْرِ بِالغَرْبِ وَجْهُهُ ⁣   أَضَاءَ بِأَرْضِ الشَّرْقِ لِي مَا وَرَا النَّهْرِ

Sein Antlitz war dem Westen zugewandt, als es um das Meer erschien, / und es erleuchtete mir im östlichen Land, das was der Fluß verbarg (das Gebiet bis hinter den Oxus).

(3) عُنِيْتُ بِآسٍ حَوْلَ وَرْدِ خُدُوْدِهِ ⁣   وَعَنْبَرِ مِسْكِ الخَالِ عَنْ جَوْنَةِ العِطْرِ

Ich war hingerissen von der Myrte (Bart) um die Rose seiner Wangen, / und die Ambra des Moschus seines Males lenkte mich von dem Duftfläschchen ab

(4) عَلَى أَنَّهُ يُغْنِي بِسُودِ لِحَاظِهِ ⁣   وَقَامَتِهِ الهَيْفَا عَنِ البِيْضِ وَالسُّمْرِ

Seine schwarzen Augen und seine schlanke Statur machten sogar die Schwerter (Weißen) und die Lanzen (Dunklen) überflüssig.

(5) غَزَالٌ حَوَى نُوْرَ الغَزَالَةِ في الضُّحَى ⁣   وَأَشْبَهَ بَدْرَ التَّمِّ مِن جِهَةِ العُمْرِ

Er ist eine Gazelle, die das Licht der Vormittagssonne in sich trägt, / hinsichtlich des Alters aber dem Vollmond ähnelt.

(6) فَهَبْنِي وَجَدْتُ العُذْرَ في صُغْرِ سِنِّهِ ⁣   إِذَا مَا بَدَا نَبْتُ العِذَارِ فَمَا عُذْرِي

Sei es mir gegönnt, daß ich eine Entschuldigung in seinem jungen Alter fand; / was kann ich dafür (alt.: wie kann ich mich sonst rechtfertigen), wenn ihm der Bart gewachsen ist?

(7)   إِذَا اخْـضَرَّ نَبْـتُ الْعَارِضَيْنِ بِوَجْــهِهِ   قَنَعْتُ مِـنَ الْأَغْـصَانِ بِالْـوَرَقِ الْخُضْرِ

Wenn der Pflanzenwuchs seiner Wangen (schon) Blüten auf seinem Gesicht
treibt, / so begnüge ich mich mit den grünen Blättern der Zweige.

(8)   وَإِنْ حَدَّثُوا عَنْ نَمْلِ نَبْتِ عِذَارِهِ   رَوَيْـتُ حَـدِيْثاً مُـسْنَداً عَـنْ أَبِـي ذَرِّ

Und wenn sie davon erzählen, daß die Ameisen seine Wangen bevölkert haben
(wört.: wenn sie von den Ameisen seines Bartwuches erzählen), / dann überlie-
fere ich den (lückenlos überlieferten) Bericht (*ḥadīt musnad*) des Ibn Abī Ḏarr
(wörtl. der Vater der Ameise).[176]

(9)   [...] بِـوَاوِ الـصُّدْغِ مِـنْ حَـوْلِ لَأمِهِ   يُعَوِّذُهُ الْقَارِي بِـحَرْفِ أَبِـي عَـمْرِو

[...] er trägt das *Wāw* seiner Schläfenlocke um sein *Lām* (Backenbart), / den der
Leser mit der Lesart des Abū ʿAmr[177] Gottes Schutz anheimstellt.

(10)   فَـكَمْ زَالَ مِـنْ لَثْمِـي دُخَـانَ عِـذَارِهِ   كَـمَا زَالَ بِالنَّـفْخِ الرَّمَـادُ عَـنِ الـجَمْرِ

Wieviel Rauch verschwand (stieg hoch) von seinem Wangenflaum durch meine
Küsse (wörtl. Hufenscharren), / genauso wie die graue Asche hochfliegt, wenn
man in die Glut hineinpustet (~ und die Glut roter wird)?

(11)   أَيْنْهَـى عَذُولِـي عَـنْ هَـوَاهُ وَلَـحْظُهُ   لَهُ أَسْـهُمٌ فِـي القَلْـبِ نَافِـذَةُ الأمْـرِ

Will mir denn mein Tadler verbieten, ihn zu lieben, / wo doch seine Blicke
Pfeile haben, die sich mitten in mein Herz bohren (im Herzen ihren Befehl
ausführen)?

(12)   إِذَا مَـا أَمَـرْتُ القَلْـبَ عَنْـهُ بِـسَلْوَةٍ   وَأَفْكَرْتُ فِي نَفْسِي تَحَيَّرْتُ فِي أَمْرِي

Immer wenn ich dem Herzen befahl, mich über ihn hinwegzutrösten / und in
mich ging, dann verwirrte mich dieser Befehl (mich über ihn hinwegzutrösten).

(13)   لَهُ مِيْـمُ ثَغْـرٍ مِـنْ ثَنَـايَاهُ لَـمْ تَـزَلْ   كَـسِينِ أَبِـي العَبَّـاسِ بَاسِـمَةَ الثَّغْـرِ

Er hat einen *Mīm*-Mund, mit Schneidezähnen, / der wie das *Sīn* in Abū ʿAbbās
(wörtl. der Mürrische, der Löwe) fortwährend aus der Bucht (dem Mund) lä-
chelt.

(14)   إِمَـامٌ غَـدَا فِـي الطِّـرْسِ مِحْـرَابُ دَالِهِ   لَنَـا قِـبْلَةً فِـي العِلْـمِ وَالـنَّظْمِ وَالنَّـثْرِ

Er (Abū l-ʿAbbās Aḥmad Ibn Makkī) ist ein Vorbeter, die Gebetsnische seines
Dāls[178] / wurde uns zur Gebetsrichtung auf dem Papier, bezüglich des Wissens,
der Prosa und Dichtung (der gebundenen und der losen Rede).

---

[176]   Abū Ḏarr Ǧundub Ibn Ǧunāda al-Ġifārī war einer der frühesten Prophetengenossen und
Überlieferer von zahlreichen *ḥadīten*. Auf seinem Weg in die Verbannung soll er Ameisen
ausgewichen sein, um sie nicht zu zertreten. Im religiösen Schrifttum werden insbesondere
seine Aufrichtigkeit, Askese und Demut als vorbildlich hervorgehoben (siehe Asma Afsa-
ruddin, "Abū Dharr al-Ghifārī", in: *EI³*.

[177]   Abū ʿAmr Zabbān b. al-ʿAlāʾ al-Baṣrī (gest. 154/770-1) ist einer der sieben anerkannten Ko-
ranleser in der sunnitischen Tradition, der *qirāʾāt as-sabʿ* (die sieben kanonischen Lesarten).
Auf ihn geht die Gründung der Basrensischen Grammatikschule zurück (siehe Asma Afsa-
ruddin, "Abū ʿAmr b. al-ʿAlāʾ", in: *EI³* und dies., *Encyclopaedia of Qurʾān*, u.a. II: S. 355-363
(zu den Grammatikschulen) und IV: S. 356-361 (zu den sieben bzw. vierzehn kanonischen
Lesarten).

(15) بَنَى كُلَّ بَيْتٍ فِي الْـمَدَائِحِ بَـحْرُهُ   إِذَا مَـدَّ يُغْنِـيْهِ عَـنِ الْـمَـدِّ وَالْقَـصْرِ

Seine Freigebigkeit (sein Meer, sein Metrum) hatte allerlei Häuser (Verse) der Lobdichtung errichtet, daß, wenn er das Meer seiner Freigebigkeit ausdehnte (flutete) (auch: sein Versmaß überschritt), er nicht mehr (*a*, *b*, *c*) bedurfte:[179]

a) die Dehnung und Kürzung[180]

b) *al-madd wa l-ğazr*: Flut und ~ Ebbe (eigentl. *ğazr*) / hier: *qaṣr* i. S. v. „Kontraktion"[181] sowie auch *qaṣr* (Palast)[182]

c) die poetischen Lizenzen zur Dehnung und Kürzung.[183]

(16) نَقِـيٌّ تَقِـيٌّ أَرْيَحِـيٌّ حُلَاحِـلٌ   خِـضَمٌّ غَزِيْـرُ الفَـضْلِ مُتَّـسِعُ الـصَّدْرِ

Ein Reiner, ein Frommer, ein Freigebiger, ein Fürst, / ein mächtiger Ozean (Herrscher) voll von Tugenden und mit großem Herzen.

(17) مَلِيْـكٌ أَتَـى بَعْـدَ الـمُلُوكِ فَأَصْـبَحُوا   كَلَامِـعِ بَـرْقٍ بَعْـدَهُ وَابِـلُ القَطْـرِ

Wohl ein Fürst, der nach vielen Fürsten kam, / doch diese sind wie ein kurz aufscheinendes Blitzlicht, nach dem der reichliche Regen fällt.

---

[178] Ein semantisch aufgeladener Vers mit einer mehrfachen *tawriyah* in einer Genitivverbindung. Der Kontext der vorangegangenen Verse mit den Buchstaben ergibt zunächst die naheliegende Bedeutung „die Nische seines *Dāls*" (die Krümmung im Buchstaben *Dāl*), was eventuell auf seinen Namen Aḥmad verweist; *dāl* kann auch Delta heißen. Darüber hinaus kann auch *dāll* (Beweis, Bezeichnendes, Signifikant, Führer, Leitung, Beliebtheit, Mut) gelesen werden. In Kombination mit dem Bedeutungsfeld von *miḥrāb* (Nische, Gebetsnische, Sprechhalle, Krieger, Schlachtfeld und Sprechhalle) vervielfacht Ibn Abī Ḥaǧalah das Lob auf Ibn Makkī und verweist unmerklich auf die Leitaspekte seines Gedichts..

[179] Ein sehr schwieriger und verschachtelter Vers, der mehrere semantische Reihen öffnet. Für die poetische Aussage sind auch Kombinationen der *maʿānī* unter a) bis c) möglich.

[180] a) Dehnung und Kürzung – grammatische Terminologie, die an das „Buchstabstaben-Thema" dieses Gedichts (vgl. Verse 9, 13, 14) anknüpft und an späterer Stelle weiter aufgefächert wird (vgl. Verse 31 und 42).

[181] *Al-Madd wa-l-ğazr* wäre die automatische Erwartungshaltung des Lesers, die der Poet nicht bedient. Die Durchbrechung dieser Erwartungshaltung, um dem „Automatismus" entgegenzuarbeiten, kommt in der Dichtung häufig vor.

[182] Die Anspielung auf Gebäude ist durch *banā* und *bayt* im ersten Halbvers durchaus gegeben, wobei *qaṣr* antithetisch zu *bayt* gebraucht wird, doch ergibt sie im zweiten Halbvers in der Gegenüberstellung zu *madd* keinen adäquaten Kontrast, da *madd* sich kaum topologisch verstehen lässt, ein Palast aber etwas in diese Richtung erfordern würde.

[183] Neben den poetischen Lizenzen sind es vor allem die Regeln der korrekten Koranrezitation (*taǧwīd*), die in den Grammatikschulen von Baṣra und Kūfa diskutiert wurden. In der Dichtung geht es z.B. um die Frage, ob Wörter, die mit *alif mamdūdah* geschrieben werden, verkürzt werden dürfen (z.B. صنعا für صنعاء) oder vice versa mit *alif maqṣūrah* geschriebene Wörter im Vers mit *alif mamdūdah* (z.B. غناء für غنى) geschrieben werden dürfen. Abū ʿAmr, den Ibn Abī Ḥaǧalah zuvor in Vers 9 nicht willkürlich erwähnt hat, war z.B., wie auch die Baṣrensische Schule allgemein, gegen die letztere Form der poetischen Lizenz (*lā yaǧuz madd al-maqṣūr (fī ḍarūrat aš-šiʿr)*). Siehe al-Fawzān, *Dalīl as-Sālik ilā šarḥ Alfiyyat Ibn Mālik*, [ar-Riyāḍ 1432/2010], S. 146-147; al-Anbārī, *al-Inṣāf fī masāʾil al-ḫilāf bayn an-naḥwiyyīn al-Baṣriyyīn wa-l-Kūfiyyīn*, Hg. Muḥammad Muḥyiddin ʿAbd al-Ḥamīd, S. 614-620 (Frage Nr. 109) und Ulrich Haarmann, "An eleventh century précis of Arabic orthography", in: Waddad al-Qadi (Hg.), *Studia Arabica and Islamica. Festschrift for Ihsan Abbas on his Sixtieth Birthday*, Beirut 1981, S. 165-182, S. 165-182.

(18) كَـرِيمٌ لَهُ فِـي رَاحَتَيْـهِ أَنَامِـلُ   كَعَـشْرَةِ خُلْجَـانٍ تُمَـدُّ مِـنَ الْبَحْـرِ

Solch ein Freigebiger, dessen Finger an seinen Händen / wie zehn Buchten sind, die das Meer in das Land hineinschlägt.

(19) يَرُوقُـكَ فِـي تَـسْدِيْدِهِ الْبُرْدَةَ الَّتِـي   حَـوَى طَيُّـهَا مَـدْحاً تَـضَوَّعَ بِالنَّـشْرِ

Er entzückt dich damit, wie er die Burdah (das Gedicht, den Mantel) ausbreitet (zuknöpft), / in deren (dessen) Falte Lobpreisungen enthalten sind, die ausströmen, wenn sie ausgebreitet wird.[184]

(20) غَـدَا لِابْـنِ مَكِّـي في مَـدِيحِ مُحَمَّـدٍ   نِظَـامٌ فَرِيـدٌ كَالْقَلَائِـدِ فِـي النَّحْـرِ

Für Ibn Makki wurde das Prophetenlob / eine kostbare Perlenreihe, die wie eine Kette seinen Hals schmückte.

(21) فَأَيْقَـنْتُ أَنَّ اللهَ رَامَ اصْـطِفَـاءَهُ   بِـمَدْحِ النَّبِـيِّ الْمُـصْطَفَى وَأَبِـي بَكْـرِ

So war ich überzeugt, daß Gott ihn dazu auserkoren hatte, / den Propheten Muṣṭafā (den Auserwählten) und Abū Bakr zu preisen.[185]

(22) شَهِيْـرٌ بِإِكْـرَامِ التَّنْزِيـلِ وَكُلِّ مَـنْ   يَمُرُّ مِـنَ الْـحُجَّاجِ فِي الْبَحْـرِ وَالْبَـرِّ

Er ist bekannt dafür, den Einkehrenden und jeden / Station machenden Pilger, der zu Lande und zu Wasser kommt, gastlich zu empfangen.

(23) عَـلَى كُلِّ حَيٍّ مِـنْ نَـدَاهُ سَحَابَـةٌ   يَعِيْـشُ لَهَا كَالْـحَيِّ مَـنْ مَـاتَ بِالْفَقْـرِ

Über allen Stämmen entstehen Wolken aus dem Tauwasser seiner Freigebigkeit, / mit denen diejenigen wiederbelebt werden, die bereits durch Armut gestorben waren.

(24) أَلَـمْ يُمْـسِ بَـحْراً فِـي طَرَابُلْسَ الَّتِـي   جَرَى لِلْعِدَى فِيهَا غَدِيْـرٌ مِنَ الْغَـدْرِ

War er nicht (in seiner Freigebigkeit) zu einem Meer in Tripolis geworden, / das für den Feind ein Tümpel der Heimtücke wurde,

(25) أَبَاحَـتْ بِـهَا الْإِفْـرَنْجُ قَتْـلَ رِجَالِهَـا   وَأَسْرَ النِّسَاءِ الْغِيْـدِ وَالطِّفْـلِ وَالْبِكْـرِ

wo die Franken in ihr (der Stadt) die Tötung ihrer Männer / und die Gefangennahme der grazilen Frauen sowie der Kinder und der Jungfrauen für erlaubt erklärten?

---

[184] Mit der Auswahl dieser Lexik verweist Ibn Abī Ḥaǧalah auf sein umfangreiches Prophetenlobgedicht mit dem Titel *Našr al-wardah fī ṭayy al-burdah* (Das Entfalten / der Duft der Rose aus den Falten des Mantels / der Burdah) in der Gedichtsammlung *Nasamat al-qabūl fī madḥ ar-rasūl*, das er Ibn Makkī zuvor geschickt haben muß und wohl auch Aufschlüsse über den eigentlichen Anlaß dieser Komposition gibt. Dieses Gedicht ist enthalten in Ibn Abī Ḥaǧalahs *Ǧiwār aḫyār fī dār al-qarār* (siehe *Ms. Laleli* 1358, fol. 121a-a26b und *Ms. Yeni Cami 701*, fol. 103b-107a., sowie ausführlich zum Burdah-Gedicht Beitrag von v. Hees in diesem Band). – Weitere Parallelen finden sich in den Versen 13 (zu *Našr*: V. 134), 33 (zu *Našr*: V. 92) sowie jeweils im Gazellenmotiv beider Gedichte im *nasīb*.

[185] Mit der Nennung Abū Bakrs nach dem Propheten spielt der Poet auf die Befolgung der *sunnah* an.. Für das Auserwähltsein vgl. *Q* 7: 144 (قَالَ يَا مُوسَىٰ إِنِّي اصْطَفَيْتُكَ عَلَى النَّاسِ بِرِسَالَاتِي وَبِكَلَامِي فَخُذْ مَا آتَيْتُكَ وَكُن مِّنَ الشَّاكِرِينَ).

(26)   فَأَنْقَذَهَا مِنْهُمْ جُعِلْتُ لَهُ الفِدَا   وَفَكَّ رِقَابَ المُسْلِمِيْنَ مِنَ الأَسْرِ

Und er (Ibn Makkī) – möge mein Leben seins sein! – rettete sie / und kaufte die Muslime aus der Gefangenschaft frei.

(27)   دَنَانِيْرُهُ فِيْهَا عِدَاهُ اسْتَفَكَّهَا   شُمُوسٌ جَلَتْ أَنْوَارُهَا ظُلْمَةَ الكُفْرِ

Seine Dinare, mit denen er seinen Feind zerschlug, / glänzten wie Sonnen, deren Helligkeit die Finsternis des Unglaubens vertrieb.

(28)   لَهُ اللهُ مَا أَنْدَاهُ فِي الجُودِ رَاحَةً   يُرِيْحُ بِهَا الإِسْلَامَ فِي اليُسْرِ وَالعُسْرِ

Gott segne ihn, denn wie freigebig sind seine Hände, / mit denen er den Islam in guten und in schwierigen Zeiten erleichtert.[186]

(29)   فَكَانَتْ بِهَا يُمْنَاهُ يُمْنًا لِأَهْلِهَا   وَكَانَتْ بِهَا يُسْرَاهُ جَالِبَةَ اليُسْرِ

Während seine rechte (Hand) sein Volk beglückte, / zog er mit seiner Linken Erleichterung herbei.[187]

(30)   فَلَو فُزْتُ فِي الدُّنْيَا بِتَقْبِيْلِ كَفِّهِ   نَسِيْتُ بِهَا مَا قَدْ جَنَتْهُ يَدُ الدَّهْرِ

Wenn es mir[188] im Leben gewährt wäre, seine Hand zu küssen, / würde ich (würdest du) dadurch vergessen, was die Hand des Schicksals angerichtet hat.[189]

(31)   يَزِيْدُ عَلَى الفُرْسَانِ جُودًا وَنَجْدَةً[190]   إِذَا قِيْلَ زَيْدُ الخَيْلِ أَفْرَسُ مِنْ عَمْرِو

---

[186] Vgl. z.B. *Q* 2: 185 (يُرِيدُ اللهُ بِكُمُ اليُسْرَ وَلَا يُرِيدُ بِكُمُ العُسْرَ)؛ *Q* 65: 7; *Q* 94: 5-6.

[187] Alternativ: „Seine rechte Hand beglückte das Volk, während es durch seine Linke eine (sorglose) Gemeinschaft wurde (für: *ǧāliyata l-yusr*)".

[188] (ـ) vokalisiert hier für die 2. P. Sg. (*fuzta* und *nasīta*), was metrisch und grammatikalisch paßt, aber inhaltlich ein nicht nachvollziehbarer Adressatenwechsel (*iltifāt*) wäre.

[189] Vers 30 ist ein Überleitungsvers (*taḫalluṣ*) zum letzten Drittel des Gedichts. Im Lob auf Ibn Makkī berührt der Poet – inspiriert durch dessen Namen (Aḥmad Ibn Makkī) und seine frommen Taten – motivisch die prophetentypischen Genres und Topoi, wie die *šamā'il* des Propheten (sein Lächeln, seine Kleidung/Mantel), seine Radianz (hier West bis Ost), seine Wunder (Spaltung des Mondes; hier mit den Dīnāren die Feinde), sein Auserwähltsein, Empfänger einer Schrift (*burdah*); Vorbild und Imām für die Muslime, die *ġazawāt* des Propheten (hier die fingierte Schlacht mit Paradepferden im letzten Modul des Gedichts) zum Wohle der Muslime (Befreiung der Stadt und ihr Erhalt für den Islam; seine materielle Fürsorge für Bewohner und Fremde/Pilger) und dergleichen mehr.

[190] Lautliche Anspielung auf Yazīd al-Fārisī, einem Schreiber des ʿUbaydallāh b. Ziyād (gest. 67/686), der wiederum der Schreiber von Ibn ʿAbbās z. Z. des Kalifen Yazīd (r. 35-40/655-660) war. Auf beide erstgenannten soll eine weitergehende Pleneschreibung (z.B. *qāla* mit Dehnungs-Alif) anstelle der Defektivschreibung (q+l) zurückgehen. Siehe Theodor Nöldeke, *Geschichte des Qorantexts*, 3 Bde., III: *Geschichte des Qorantexts, von Gotthelf Bergsträsser und Otto Pretzl*, 2. Aufl., Leipzig 1938, S. 255 und Omar Hamdan, "The second Maṣāḥif Project: A Step towards the Canonization of the Qur'anic Text", in Angelika Neuwirth, Nicolai Sinai, and Michael Marx (Hg.), *The Qur'ān in Context: Historical and Literary Investigations into the Qur'ānic Milieu.* Leiden 2010, S. 795-835, hier S. 796-797. Inhaltlich scheint Ibn Abī Ḥaġalah hier auf eine unter den Adressaten und Lesern des Gedichts bekannte literarische Debatte zu verweisen, wie die Verse 9 und 15, die Buchstabenmotive sowie die Korrespondenz mit Ibn al-Ḫaṭīb und Ibn Makkī (in Wetzstein 1803, fol. 121b-122a, siehe Anm. 127 hier im Text) nahelegen. An dieser Stelle kann ich nur auf diese Debatte verweisen, sie konkreter zu erfassen ist mir wegen der anspielungsreichen Lexik und des fehlenden Kontextes zu den fragmentarischen Passagen nicht gelungen.

Wenn es heißt: „Zayd al-Ḥayl (al-Ġifārī) ist behänder als Abū ʿAmr (i.e. ʿAmr b. Kulṯūm)" / dann übertrifft Ibn Makkī selbst diese Ritter an Tapferkeit und Großzügigkeit.[191]

(32) إِذَا اصْطَـــفَّتِ الأَحْـــزَابُ يَـــوْمَ تَغَـــابُنٍ   يُغَـادِرُهُمْ صَرْعَى مِـنَ الـصَّفِّ لِلْحَـشْرِ

Wenn sich am Schlachttag die Truppen aufreihen, / überläßt er sie niedergestreckt aus der Schlachtreihe dem Jüngsten Tag.[192]

(33) وَتَــجْلُو سَـوَادَ النَّقْـعِ بِـيضٌ صِفَاحِهِ   إِذَا مَا تَجَلَّى المَوْتُ فِي الـحُلَلِ الـحُمْرِ

Und die Klinge seines Schwertes glänzt im (aufgewirbelten schwarzen) Schlachtstaub, / wenn sich der Tod in roter Gewandung zeigt.

(34) سَـوَابِقُهُ مِـنْ سُرْعَةِ الـجَرْيِ لَـمْ تَـزَلْ   تَـشُقُّ غُبَـارَ الأَرْضِ وَالأَرْضُ لا تَـدْرِي

Seine Rennpferde rennen so schnell, daß sie mit ihrer Schnelligkeit / den Erdenstaub durchbrechen, wobei die Erde es nicht einmal bemerkt.[193]

(35) لَهُ أَدْهَمٌ كَاللَيْــلِ لَـــونُ جَبِينِــهِ   يُرِيـهِ هِـلَالَ الأُفْـقِ فِـي غُـرَّةِ الـشَّهْرِ

Er hat einen Rappen (einen Schwarzen), schwarz wie die Nacht, dessen Stirnfarbe / die Mondsichel des Horizonts am Monatsanfang zeigt;[194]

(36) وَأَشْهَبُ مِثْلُ الصُّبْحِ يَجْرِي مِنَ الضُّحَى   نَـــهَارًا إِلَى أَنْ يُنْــسَخَ اللَيْـــلُ بِالفَجْـرِ

und einen Grauschimmel, schön wie der Morgenschimmer, der von Tagesanbruch an / über den ganzen Tag hinaus, bis sogar die Nacht vom Morgenlicht aufgelöst wird, rennen kann.[195]

---

[191] Ab hier beginnt das letzte Drittel des Gedichts, mit dem Ibn Abī Ḥaǧalah in einer äußerst dicht gestalteten lexikalischen Verschachtelung von Surennamen und kriegerischen Tugenden auf altarabische „Reiter"-Tugenden und Ḥamāsah-Motive übergeht. Zur Kriegsdichtung siehe Schippers, *Spanish Hebrew Poetry*, S. 217-243.

[192] Vgl. Q 61 ;(فَتَرَى الْقَوْمَ فِيهَا صَرْعَى كَأَنَّهُمْ أَعْجَازُ نَخْلٍ خَاوِيَةٍ) :7 (الحاقة)؛ Q 69 (التغابن)؛ Q 64 (الأحزاب)؛ Q 33 (الحشر) 59 Q ؛(الصف).

[193] In der Gestaltung dieses Abschnitts mit der Aufzählung edler Pferde könnte Ibn Abī Ḥaǧalah, wie die Studie von Bauer zeigt, das Jagdgedicht (*urǧūzah muzdawiǧah ṭardiyyah*) Šihābaddin Faḍlallāhs vor Augen gehabt haben, worin gleich sieben Pferde unmittelbar nacheinander aufgezählt werden (in der Abfolge: *ašhab, adham, aḫḍar, aḥmar, ašqar, asfar, ablaq*), wohingegen es bei *Ibn Abī Ḥaǧalah* namentlich fünf sind (in der Abfolge: *adham, ašhab, aḥmar, asfar, ablaq*). Siehe hierzu Bauer, „The Dawādār's Hunting Party. A Mamluk muzdawija ṭardiyya, probably by Shihāb al-Dīn Ibn Faḍl Allāh", S. 302-312.

[194] Die Variante in (د): هلاك bedeutet Tilgung, Vernichtung etc., was mit dem Verb *yurīhū* nicht recht korrespondiert.

[195] Die Verse 35-39 sind durch den Vers 37 mit einem Weinmotiv vornehmlich zweigeteilt, weisen aber als Einheit eine meisterhaft gestaltete Steigerung in ihrer Abfolge gleich in doppelter Reihe auf. Die Pferde und ihre Eigenschaften korrespondieren mit Farbmotiven, gleichzeitig korrespondieren diese mit den Wortfeldern der Tageszeiten und Gestirne und zwar im zeitlichen Ablauf wie in ihrer räumlich-vertikalen Abfolge, somit ebenfalls chronotopisch. Die Pferde reiten im Raum, durch die (Tages-) Zeit bis in den Himmel und die Farbskala ändert sich und intensiviert sich (von Schwarz, über grauen Morgenschimmer, zum Rot und Gold für den abklingenden Tag bis hin wieder in die Nacht hinein mit ihren funkelnden Sternen). Gleichzeitig erhebt der Poet den Leser mit seiner Reiterschar unmerklich von der Erde (Vers 34) in den nächtlichen Sternenhimmel (V. 39), um daran seine metapoetischen Bilder in Kombination mit der Milchstraße anzuknüpfen (hier Vers 42).

(37) وَأَحْمَرُ مِثْلُ الْوَرْدِ حَلْيُ عِذَارِهِ   كَعِقْدِ حَبَابٍ مُسْتَدِيرٍ عَلَى خَمْرِ

Er hat einen Roten wie eine Rose; sein Zaumzeug (seine Zügel; Wangen) ist (von roten Blumen) rundherum geziert, / als wäre es eine Bläschenkette im Wein (-glas).[196]

(38) وَأَصْفَرُ مِثْلُ الـضَّبِّ لَوْناً كَأَنَّـمَا   كَسَاهُ أَصِيلُ الشَّمْسِ ثَوبًا مِنَ التِّبْرِ

Er hat einen Falben (Gelben), von der Farbe einer Dornschwanzechse[197], / als hätte ihn die Abendsonne in ein Goldgewand gekleidet.

(39) وَأَبْلَقُ مِثْلُ النِّمْرِ لَوْناً وَخِفَّةً   مُنَمْنَمُ أُفْقِ الجِسْمِ بِالأَنْجُمِ الزُّهْرِ

Er hat einen Schecken (Schwarz-Weißen), der einem Leoparden[198] in der Färbung und in seiner Beweglichkeit gleicht, / (und) der mit funkelnden Sternen am ganzen Körper geschmückt ist.

(40) وَلِلَّهِ جَيْشٌ كُلَّـمَا [ثار؟] عَنْتَـرٌ   يُطَالِعُهُ قَبْلَ الطَّلِيعَةِ بِالنَّصْرِ

Welch ein Heer![199] Ein solches, das, wann immer ein ʿAntar rebellierte (?), / ihm vor der Vorhut bereits mit dem Sieg zuvorkam (überraschte).

(41) جَوَادٌ طَوِيلُ البَاعِ بَحْرُ قَصِيدَتِي   يَطُولُ عَلَى مَاضِي العُصُورِ بِهِ عَصْرِي

Wie ein prächtiges Rennpferd (mit weiter Schrittlänge) ist das Metrum meines Gedichts (das im Metrum *ṭawīl* geschrieben ist); / durch ihn (das Gedicht oder das Lob Ibn Makkīs) erstreckt sich meine Zeit bis in die vergangenen Zeiten.[200]

---

[196] Zu den Bläschen als Motiv der Weindichtung siehe Ewald Wagner, *Abū Nuwās: eine Studie zur arabischen Literatur der frühen ʿAbbāsidenzeit*, Wiesbaden 1965, S. 201, 211, 303-304, 389, 390, 401. Bläschen und Blüten werden auch metaphorisch für die Milchstraße verwendet: *wa-lil-maǧarrati fawqa l-ufqi muʿtaraḍun ka-annahā ḥababun yaṭfū ʿalā nahāri* „Die Milchstraße legt sich quer über den Horizont; sie gleicht Wasserbläschen, die auf einem Fluß treiben" (No. 23); Blüten (hier *zahr*): *wa-l-laylu taǧrī d-darārī fī maǧarratihī ka-r-rawḍi taṭfū ʿalā nahrin azāhiruhū* „Die funkelnden Sterne laufen bei Nacht in der Milchstraße, wie es in einem Garten der Fall ist, in dem die Blütenblätter auf einem Fluß treiben" (No: 32), in Manfred Ullman, „Die Milchstraße in der Bildersprache der arabischen Dichter", in: *Sic Itur Ad Astra: Studien zur Geschichte der Mathematik und Naturwissenschaften: Festschrift für den Arabisten Paul Kunitzsch zum 70. Geburtstag*, Wiesbaden 2000, S. 555-571, hier S. 561-562, mit zahlreichen weiteren Beispielen. Das Bild der Kette kann auch eine Anspielung auf die Sterngruppe im Sternbild des Schützen (*al-qilādah*, „die Halskette") sein, sie wird bei Ibn Qutaybah wie folgt definiert: *wa-hiya sittat kawākib mustadīrah ṣiġar tušabbahu bi-l-qaws ...* „das sind sechs kleine schwache kreisförmig angeordnete Sterne, die mit einem Bogen zu vergleichen sind" (zitiert aus Paul Kunitzsch, *Untersuchungen zur Sternnomenklatur der Araber*, Wiesbaden 1961, S. 229, No: 228).

[197] (د) liest an dieser Stelle صب „Guß; heftige Liebe".

[198] Ibn Abī Ḥaǧalah erweitert hier die bekannten Vergleiche der Plejaden mit einem Leoparden (Fell, Körperteile). Solch ein Vergleich war von Abū Hilāl al-ʿAskarī (gest. 395/1005) bereits kritisiert worden, da es eine negative Verkehrung habe „denn die Sterne der Plejaden seien hell, die Tüpfel auf dem Leopardenfell aber dunkel" (aus: Paul Kunitzsch & Manfred Ullmann, *Die Plejaden in den Vergleichen der arabischen Dichtung*, München 1992 S. 107, No: 280 und 281).

[199] Schwer zu lesende Stelle im Manuskript: statt وَلله liest (د) hier زينه, was das Schriftbild der Handschrift (ح) durchaus hergibt. Hier habe ich jedoch die Variante der älteren Druckausgabe gewählt, weil der Vokativ an dieser Stelle die Steigerung besser unterstreicht. Dennoch bleibt der Vers in der Anspielung zu ʿAntarah undurchsichtig.

(42)   حِجَـالُ مَدِيْحِي فِيْهِ بَحْـرٌ قريضُها   يَجُـرُّ عَـلَى نَهْـرِ الـمَجَرَّةِ وَالنَّـسرِ

In den (weißen) Fesseln[201] (in den besten Teilen) meiner Lobdichtung ist ein Metrum (Meer), dessen Verse / die Milchstraße und das Sternbild des Adlers[202] ziehen (oder pass. gezogen werden oder gramm. beugen, i.e. den Genitiv bilden).[203]

(43)   أَيَنْحَـلُّ عَزْمِـي عَـنْ ثَنَـاهُ وَقَـدْ غَـدَا   يَشُدُّ عُـرَى الإِسْـلَامِ فِـي ذَلِكَ الْقُطْـرِ

(Wie) Soll sich denn meine schöpferische Kraft davon befreien, ihn zu loben, / wo er doch die Bande des Islams in jener Gegend noch stärker zusammenzieht?

(44)   وَمَا زِلْتُ أَبْنِي الـمَدْحَ فِي كُلِّ هَادِمٍ   بِقَائِـمِ سَـيْفِ العَـزْمِ قَاعِـدَةَ الكُفْـرِ

So blieb ich dabei, Lobverse über einen jeden Zerstörer zu konstruieren,[204] / der mit dem Schwert der Entschlossenheit das Fundament des Unglaubens niederreißt.

(45)   فَلَا زَالَ مَـمْدُوْحًا عَـلَى القُـرْبِ وَالنَّـوَى   وَلَا زَالَ بَـحْرَ الـجُودِ فِي البَحْرِ وَالبَـرِّ

Möge er aus der Ferne und aus der Nähe immer (dauernd) der Gelobte bleiben, / wie er auch ein Meer der Freigebigkeit zu Wasser und zu Lande bleiben möge.

---

[200] In diesem Vers ist die Lexik des Pferdes in die semantische Reihe der Dichtung übergegangen – ein Motiv, das er bereits markiert hatte. Ibn Abī Ḥaǧalah benutzt hier einen schwer faßbaren *istiḫdām* (eine Art *tawriyah*, in der beide intendierten Konnotationen gleichzeitig gültig sind), weil er die Pferdelexik (in Kombination mit dem *mamdūḥ* Ibn Makkī) mit seinem Gedicht (in Kombination mit dem Metrum) in der Eigenschaft *ṭawīl* („lang sein, erstrecken, mit *ʿalā* auch übertreffen") verbindet. Alternative Übersetzungsmöglichkeiten wären: *„Er ist ein Freigebiger (ein Rennpferd mit mächtiger Schrittlänge im Galopp); mit seinem Lob übertrifft das Metrum meines Gedichts alle anderen Zeiten"*, oder *„Wie ein Freigebiger mit großer Schrittlänge ist das Metrum meines Gedichts, durch ihn (Ibn Makkī / Gedicht) übertrifft meine Zeit alle anderen Zeiten"*.

[201] (*ḥiǧāl*): Ibn Abī Ḥaǧalahs unverwechselbare Überleitung zum metapoetischen Part mit einer Anspielung auf seinen Namen und zugleich ein geschickter Übergang von der Pferdelexik zum *faḫr* und *madīḥ*; hier aber im Sinne von *quyūd* (Fessel) verwendet, siehe z.B. in az-Zabidī, *Tāǧ al-ʿArūs*: (الحِجَالُ: أَي القُيُودُ خَلاخِيلُ الرِّجَالِ، وَالخَلاخِيلُ للنِّساء)؛ vgl. auch Steingass: *ḥaǧǧāl* („splendour, brightness") bietet sich inhaltlich an, jedoch nicht metrisch. Von Ibn ʿUnayn (gest. 630/1233) ist ein solcher Vergleich (hier mit *ḥuǧūl*) überliefert: *al-laylu … ka-anna t-turayyā ġurratun wa-huwa adhamun / lahū min wamīḍi š-šiʿrayayni ḥuǧūlū* „Es ist, als seien die Plejaden eine Blesse, die Nacht aber ein Rappe, dessen Fußfesseln aus dem Glanz der beiden Sirii bestehen" (aus: Kunitzsch & Ullmann, *Die Plejaden in den Vergleichen der arabischen Dichtung*, S. 106, No. 277).

[202] Die Milchstraße zieht durch das Sternbild des Adlers, das im Arabischen verschiedene Namen trägt: fliegender Adler (*an-nasr aṭ-ṭāʾir*) oder fallender Adler (*an-nasr al-wāqiʿ*). Siehe Paul Kunitzsch, *Typen von Sternverzeichnissen in astronomischen Handschriften des zehnten bis vierzehnten Jahrhunderts*, Wiesbaden 1966, S. 18. Über die gebräuchlichsten Metaphern, die in der Dichtung in Kombination mit der Milchstraße vorkommen, siehe Manfred Ullmann, „Die Milchstraße in der Bildersprache der arabischen Dichter", S. 558 (Metapher des Weges und der Schleifspur). Eine weitere Parallele, in der die Pferde-Motivik mit der Milchstraße verbunden wird (vgl. hier Vers 42) bietet ein Vers al-Bahrani's: *„Ein Fuchs [(aš-qaru)] … Es ist, als seien die Sterne an seine Augen geheftet und als sei er mit den Bändern der Milchstraße aufgezäumt"* (aus: ders., S. 569).

[203] Umkehrung des Bildes, in dem ein Fluß (*nahr*) ins Meer (*baḥr*) mündet und die paronomastische Verwendung beider Wörter, wie auch von *ǧarra* und *maǧarrah*.

[204] Der Vers schließt hier an das Bild, das zuvor für den *mamdūḥ* formuliert war, antithetisch an (*banā al-madḥ* zu *hādim*); siehe Vers 15 (بَنَى كُلَّ بَيْتٍ فِي الـمَدَائِح).

Literaturverzeichnis

Benutzte Handschriften

Ms. *Ayasofya/Ḥadīǧa Sulṭān 233*   Ibn Ḥabīb al-Ḥalabī: *Durrat al-aslāk fī dawlat al-atrāk.*

Ms. *Paris 1719*   Ibn Ḥabīb al-Ḥalabī: *Durrat al-aslāk fī dawlat al-atrāk.*

Ms. *Paris 1721*   Ibn Ḥabīb al-Ḥalabī: *Durrat al-aslāk fī dawlat al-atrāk.*

Ms. *Wetzstein II 359*   an-Nuwayrī: *Ms. Ilmām.*

Ms. *Wetzstein II 360*   an-Nuwayrī: *Ms. Ilmām.*

Ms. *Kairo 1127*   Ibn Abī Ḥaǧalah: *Dīwān.*

Ms. *Wetzstein 1803*   Ibn Abī Ḥaǧalah: [Auszug aus] *Manṭiq aṭ-ṭayr.*

Editerte Quellen und Studien

*Für die Artikel in der *Encyclopedia of the Medieval Chronicle* [EMC] sowie in der *Encyclopedia of Islam* [EI² und EI³] wurden jeweils die Online-Ausgaben konsultiert:

EMC: [http://referenceworks.brillonline.com/browse/encyclopedia-of-the-medieval-chronicle]

EI 2nd Edition: [http://referenceworks.brillonline.com/browse/encyclopaedia-of-islam-2]

EI 3rd Edition: [http://referenceworks.brillonline.com/browse/encyclopaedia-of-islam-3].

Agius, Dionisius, *Classic Ships of Islam. From Mesopotamia to the Indian Ocean*, (HdO 92), Leiden 2008.

Ahlwardt, Wilhelm, *Verzeichnis der arabischen Handschriften*, Berlin 1853.

Atiya, Aziz Suryal, *The Crusade in the Later Middle Ages*, London 1938.

Atiya, Aziz Suryal, *A Fourteenth Century Encyclopedist from Alexandria: A Critical and Analytical Study of al-Nuwairy al-Iskandarānī's "Kitab al-Ilmām"*, Utah 1977.

Bachtin, Michail M., *Chronotopos*, hg. v. Michael C. Frank, Kirsten Mahlke, übers. v. Michael Dewey, Berlin 2008.

Bauer, Thomas, "The Dawādār's Hunting Party. A Mamluk muzdawija ṭardiyya, probably by Shihāb al-Dīn Ibn Faḍl Allāh", in: A. Vrolijk, J.P. Hogendijk (Hg.), *O ye Gentlemen. Arabic Studies on Science and Literary Culture in Honour of Remke Kruk*, Leiden 2007, S. 291-312.

Bauer, Thomas, *Liebe und Liebesdichtung in der arabischen Welt des 9. und 10. Jahrhunderts: eine literatur- und mentalitätsgeschichtliche Studie des arabischen Ġazal*, Wiesbaden 1998.

Bayyud, Hussein, *Die Stadt in der arabischen Poesie, bis 1258 n. Chr.*, Berlin 1988.

Blumenfeld-Kosinski, Renate / Petkov, Kiril (Hg.), *Philippe de Mézières and his Age. Piety and Politics in the Fourteenth Century*, Leiden 2012.

Borg, Gert, *Mit Poesie vertreibe ich den Kummer meines Herzens: Eine Studie zur altarabischen Trauerklage der Frau*, Leiden 1997.

Bosworth, Clifford Edmund, *Historic Cities of the Islamic World*, Leiden 2007.

Brunschvig, Robert, *La Berbérie orientale sous les Ḥafṣides des origines à la fin du XVe siècle*, 2 Bde., Paris 1940-1947.

Cachia, Pierre, *The Arch Rhetorician or the Schemer's Skimmer: A Handbook of Late badīꜥ drawn from ꜥAbd al-Ġanī an-Nābulsī's Nafaḥāt al-Azhār ꜥalā Nasamāt al-Ashār*, Wiesbaden 1998.

Capitanovici, Georgius Johannes, *Die Eroberung von Alexandria (Iskanderīje) durch Peter I. von Lusignan, König von Cypern 1365: mit einer Karte von Alexandrien*, Berlin 1894.

Christides, Vassilios, „Cyprus between East and West. The French Kingdom of Lusignans, an appendage to the Latin Kingdom, vs. Mamluks", in: Viguera, Jesús (coord.) et al., *Ibn Khaldun: The Mediterranean in the 14th Century: Rise and Fall of Empires*, Bd.: *Studies*, Granada 2006, S. 98-105.

Dawkins, Richard, *Recital Concerning the Sweet Land of Cyprus Entitled 'Chronicle'- The chronicle of Makhairas*, Oxford 1932.

Ḍayf, Šawqī, *ar-Riṯāʾ*, al-Qāhirah 1955.

Edbury, Peter W., "The murder of King Peter I of Cyprus (1359-1369)", in: *Journal of Medieval History* 6 (1980), S. 219-233.

Edbury, Peter W., *The Kingdom of Cyprus and the Crusades 1191-1374*, paperback ed., Cambridge 1993.

Elger, Ralf, „Geldgier und jihâd in Alexandria", in: *Venezia. Incrocio di culture. Percezioni di viaggiatori europei e non europei a confronto*, Hg. Klaus Herbers und Felicitas Schmieder, Rom 2008, 201-224.

EQ: *Encyclopaedia of Qurʾan*, Hg. Jane Dammen McAuliffe, Leiden 2001-2006.

Froissart, Jean, in: [Peter Ainsworth and Godfried Croenen] URL: http://www.hrionline.ac.uk/onlinefroissart/index.jsp.

GAL: Brockelmann, Carl, *Geschichte der arabischen Litteratur*. Originally published: Leiden: E.J. Brill, 1943. With new introd., Leiden 1996.

Herzsohn, Paul, *Der Überfall Alexandriens durch Peter I., König von Jerusalem und Zypern, aus einer ungedruckten arabischen Quelle mit historischen und kritischen Bemerkungen dargestellt*, Erstes Heft [mehr nicht erschienen], Bonn 1886.

Heyd, Wilhelm, „Die mittelalterlichen Handelscolonien der Italiener in Nordafrica von Tripolis bis Marokko", in: *Zeitschrift für die gesamte Staatswissenschaft* 20 (1864), S. 617-660.

Hill, George, *A History of Cyprus II: The Frankish Period, 1192-1432*, Cambridge 1948.

Ibn Abī Ḥaǧalah, *Dīwān Ibn Abī Ḥaǧalah 725 H.-776 H.*, Hg. Aḥmad Ḥilmī Ḥulwah, al-Qāhirah 1425/2014.

Ibn Abī Ḥaǧalah, *Dīwān Ibn Abī Ḥaǧālah*, Hg. Muǧāhid Muṣtafā Bahǧat, ʿAmmān 2010.

Ibn Ḥabīb al-Ḥalabī, ʿUmar Ibn al-Ḥasan, *Taḏkirat an-nabīh fī ayyām al-Manṣūr wa-banīh*, Hg. Muḥammad Amīn, Saʿīd ʿAbd al-Fattāḥ ʿĀšūr, Bd. 3, al-Qāhirah 1986.

Ibn al-Ḫaṭib, Lisānaddin, *Rayḥānat al-kuttāb wa-nuǧʿat al-muntāb*, Hg. Muḥammad ʿAbdallāh ʿInān, 2 Bde, al-Qāhirah, 1400/1980-1.

Ibn Kaṯīr, ʿImādaddin, „Kitāb al-iǧtihād fī ṭalab al-ǧihād", in: Zakkār, Suhayl, *Arbaʿat kutub fī l-ǧihād min aṣr ḥurūb aṣ-ṣalibiyyah*, Dimašq 2007.

Ibn Kaṯīr, ʿImādaddin, *al-Bidāyah wa-n-nihāyah (701 H.-767 H.)*, Hg. Ḥasan Ismāʿīl Marwah, Dimašq 1431/2010.

Jorga, Nicolae, *Philippe de Mézières 1327-1405 et la Croisade au XIVe Siècle*, Paris 1896.

Kahle, Paul, „Die Katastrophe des mittelalterlichen Alexandria", in: *Melanges (Gaston) Mespero* III (1940), S. 137-154.

Kahle, Paul, „Zur Geschichte des mittelalterlichen Alexandria", in: *Der Islam* 12 (1921), S. 29-83.

Kunitzsch, Paul und Ullmann, Manfred, *Die Plejaden in den Vergleichen der arabischen Dichtung*, München 1992.

al-Maqqari at-Tilimsānī, Aḥmad b. M., *Nafḥ aṭ-ṭīb min ǧuṣn ar-raṭīb*, Hg. Iḥsān ʿAbbās, 8 Bde., Bayrūt 1388/1968.

al-Maqrīzī, Taqiyyaddīn Aḥmad, *Kitāb as-sulūk li-maʿrifāt al-mulūk*, Hg. Bde 1-2: Muḥammad Muṣtafā Ziyādah, al-Qāhirah 1934-1958, Hg. Bde. 3-4: Saʿīd ʿAbd al-Fattāḥ ʿĀšur, al-Qāhirah 1970-1973.

al-Maqrīzī, Taqiyyaddīn Aḥmad, *Durar al-ʿuqūd al-farīdah fī tarāǧim al-aʿyān al-mufīdah*, Hg. Maḥmūd al-Ǧalīlī, 4 Bde., Bayrūt 1423/2002.

Müller-Wiener, Martina, *Eine Stadtgeschichte Alexandrias von 564/1169 bis in die Mitte des 9./15. Jahrhunderts: Verwaltung und innerstädtische Organisationsformen*, Berlin 1992.

Nagel, Tilman, *Timur der Eroberer und die islamische Welt des späten Mittelalters*, München 1993.

an-Nuwayrī, Muḥammad b. Qāsim, *Kitāb al-ilmām*, Hg. Etienne Combe und Aziz Suryal Atiya, 7 Bde., Hyderabad 1968-1976.

al-Qalqašandī, Šihābaddin Abū l-ʿAbbās, *Subḥ al-aʿšā fī ṣinaʿāt al-inšā*, 14 Bde., [Ausgabe Dār al-Kutub as-Sulṭāniyyah], al-Qāhirah 1334/1915.

Raphael, Kate, *Muslim Fortresses in the Levant: Between Crusaders and Mongols*, Routledge 2011.

Rosenthal, Franz, *A history of Muslim historiography*, Leiden 1968.

Runciman, Steven, *A History of the Crusades*, 3 Bde., Cambridge, U.K., 1951-1954.

Schippers, Arie, *Spanish Hebrew Poetry and the Arabic Literary Tradition: Arabic Themes in Hebrew Andalusian Poetry*, Leiden 1994, S. 244-287.

Setton, Kenneth, *A History of the Crusades*, Bd. III: The fourteenth and fifteenth Centuries, Hg. Harry Hazard Madison 1975, S. 340-360.

Steenbergen, Jo van, "The Alexandrian Crusade (1365) and the Mamluk Sources: Reassessment of the *Kitāb al-Ilmām* of an-Nuwayrī al-Iskandarānī (d. 1372 ad)", in: Cigaar, K. & Teule H.G.B. (Hg.), *East and West in the Crusader States. Context-Contacts-Confrontations: Acta of the Congress Held at Hernen Castle in September 2000*, (Series: Orientalia Lovaniensia Analecta, 125), Bd. 3, Leuven 2003, 123-137.

Steenbergen, Jo van, "The Amir Yalbughā al-Khāṣṣakī (d. 1366), the Qalāwūnid Sultanate, and the Cultural Matrix of Mamlūk Society: A Reassessment of Mamlūk Politics in the 1360s", in: *Journal of the American Oriental Society* 131 (2011), S. 423-443.

Tyerman, Christopher J., "Marino Sanudo Torsello and the Lost Crusade: Lobbying in the Fourteenth Century", in: *Transactions of the Royal Historical Society* 32 (1982), S. 57-73.

Ullman, Manfred, „Die Milchstraße in der Bildersprache der arabischen Dichter", in: *Sic Itur Ad Astra: Studien zur Geschichte der Mathematik und Naturwissenschaften: Festschrift für den Arabisten Paul Kunitzsch zum 70. Geburtstag*, Wiesbaden 2000, S. 555-571.

Valérian, Dominique, "Tripoli dans les réseaux d'échanges intercontinentaux à la fin du Moyen Âge", in: Rémi Dewière et Güneş Işıksel (Hg.), *Tripoli, port de mer, port de désert*, Paris 2011, S. 353-363.

Wagner, Ewald, *Grundzüge der klassischen arabischen Dichtung*, 2 Bde., Darmstadt 1987.

Weil, Gustav, *Das Chalifat unter den Bahritischen Mamlukensultanen von Ägypten*, Bd. IV, Stuttgart 1860.

Weintritt, Otfried, *Formen spätmittelalterlicher islamischer Geschichtsdarstellung: Untersuchungen zu an-Nuwairī al-Iskandarānīs Kitāb al-Ilmām und verwandten zeitgenössischen Texten*, Beiruter Texte und Studien; 45, Stuttgart 1992 (Zugl.: Freiburg (Breisgau), Univ., Diss., 1988).

Die Makame *Dawr az-zamān fī ṭaḥn al-ǧulbān* – Eine sehr persönliche Schmähschrift

Hakan Özkan

Ibn Abī Ḥaǧalahs Gedichte mögen manchmal etwas ungelenk daherkommen. Wenn er sich etwa anschickte, Vorbilder von hohem literarischen Raffinement, wie beispielsweise Gedichte von al-Qīrāṭī oder die Siebenzeiler Ibn Nubātahs nachzubilden, traten seine Unzulänglichkeiten zu Tage – in seinen Kontrafakturen wirken die Bilder zuweilen überanstrengt, die Sprache gefesselt von den Vorgaben des gewandteren Dichters und den hohen Ansprüchen, denen Ibn Abī Ḥaǧalah gerecht werden wollte. Ganz anders dagegen seine Reimprosa: In seinen Makamen, die zum größten Teil in der Sammlung *Manṭiq aṭ-ṭayr* vereint sind und an anderer Stelle in diesem Band von Maurice Pomerantz behandelt werden, zeigt er sein wahres Können. Bei der Sammlung handelt es sich im Wesentlichen um Makamen, die ganz ähnlich wie ihr direktes Vorbild, die einschlägigen Makamen von al-Ḥarīrī, als zentrales Thema eine Stadt oder eine Region haben. Die hier zu besprechende Makame hingegen, welche nicht Teil von *Manṭiq aṭ-ṭayr* ist, dreht sich um die unerhörten Ereignisse im Kairo des ausgehenden Jahres 768/1366 und die Monate danach, welche Ungemach und Leid über die Bewohner der Stadt brachten.

Der historische und gesellschaftliche Hintergrund

Im Dezember des Jahres 768/1366 hatten sich Soldaten des Amīrs und de facto Herrschers über das Mamlukenreich, Sayfaddīn Yalbuġā al-Ḥāṣṣakī an-Nāṣirī, gegen ihren Meister aufgelehnt und ihn am 11. Rabīʿ al-Āḫar 768 bzw. dem 14. Dezember 1366 niedergemetzelt. Bei diesen Soldaten, die Ibn Abī Ḥaǧalah *ǧulbān* (vom Stamm *ǧalaba* „ziehen, herführen, herbeiziehen, heranschaffen")[1] nennt, handelte es sich um neuangeschaffte Militärsklaven (im folgenden Neusklaven genannt), die ihrem jeweiligen Meister (*ustāḏ*), der sie rekrutierte und nach dem man sie benannte, in der Regel treu verbunden blieben. Gleichermaßen bildete sich unter ihnen ein Korpsgeist (*ḫūšdāšiyyah*) aus, die sie zusammenschweißte, wobei dieser Korpsgeist einzelnen aufstrebenden Sklaven nie ein Hindernis war, sich gegenüber den anderen Mitstreitern zu profilieren. Außer *ǧulbān* nannte man sie auch *aǧlāb* bzw. *muštarawāt* (von *muštarā* „gekauft"). Letztere Bezeichnung ist der früher – zumindest zu Lebzeiten Ibn Abī Ḥaǧalahs – geläufigere Name für diese Gruppe von Sklaven. Die Bezeichnung *ǧulbān* für die

---

[1] Vgl. dazu auch türk. *çelebi*, das nach einer Interpretation vom gleichen Stamm herrühren soll, Barthold, W. und Spuler, B, „Čelebi", in: EI².

Urheber der Revolte vom Dezember 1366 und die Unruhen in den folgenden Monaten, ist jedoch in der Makame von Ibn Abī Ḥaǧalah zum ersten Mal von einem Zeitzeugen belegt. Der Begriff *aǧlāb* wird zwar von Maqrīzī in seinem *Sulūk* ebenfalls für die Sklaven der Revolte, über die ich hier rede, benutzt, es handelt sich bei ihm aber sehr wahrscheinlich um einen Anachronismus, da sich der Begriff in seiner Zeit (Anfang 9/15. Jhdt.) erst einbürgerte.[2]

Normalerweise war es ein Privileg des Sultans, sich neue Sklaven anzuschaffen und daraus eine Armee zu bilden. Nicht so bei Sayfaddin Yalbuġā al-Ḥāṣṣakī an-Nāṣirī. In der Tat wurde der Name Yalbuġā gleichbedeutend für ein Riesenkorps an *ǧulbān* – noch Jahrhunderte später wird die Zahl seiner Mamluken als Meilenstein in der Geschichte angesehen. Yalbuġā schaffte sich nach den Informationen von Ibn Ḥaǧar al-ʿAsqalānī, und Ibn Qāḍī Šuhbah ganze 3.500 neue Mamluken an, eines der größten privaten Gefolge eines mamlukischen Herrschers überhaupt.[3] Andere Historiker berichten, dass Yalbuġā auch in der Außenwirkung als Sultan angesehen wurde, z.B. durch seine Heirat mit der Witwe Ḥasans Ṭulubāy und der Tatsache, dass nach al-Maqrīzī Gesandte aus Europa ihn als Sultan wahrnahmen.[4]

Er stieg unter seinem Herrn, dem Sultan al-Malik al-Ašraf an-Nāṣir Ḥasan (gest. 762/1361, reg. 735–748/ 1347–1351 und 755–762/ 1354–61) zu bedeutender Macht auf, bis er beim Sultan in Ungnade fiel. Einer bereits legendär gewordenen Darstellung zufolge zwang Sultan Ḥasan Yalbuġā dazu, sich vor seinen Augen und derer anderer Hofangehöriger auszuziehen. Das soll Yalbuġā ihm nie verziehen haben.[5] Es handelte sich demnach um ein angespanntes Verhältnis zwischen beiden und Ḥasan wusste wohl, dass Yalbuġā ihm gefährlich sein könnte.

Bevor Ḥasan ihn jedoch unschädlich machen konnte, kam Yalbuġā ihm zuvor und tötete ihn im Jahr 762/1361. In der Folgezeit bis zu seinem Tod im Jahr 768/1366 versammelte Yalbuġā große Macht in seiner Hand und verschmolz die Finanzen des Sultanats mit seinen. Behilflich war ihm dabei der Schatzmeister, ein konvertierter Kopte namens Faḫraddin Māǧid Ibn Qarawīnah, welcher gleichzeitig die Position des *nāẓir al-ḫāṣṣ* als Verantwortlicher für die Finanzen des königlichen Haushalts bekleidete.[6] Andere Stimmen wie Ibn Katīr behaupten, dass Ḥasan selbst die Schuld an seinem Niedergang trug, da er Misswirtschaft betrieben und sich seinen Lastern hingab; es nähme kaum Wunder, dass Yalbuġā sich gegen ihn wandte, Ḥasan sollte ja nach seinem Leben getrachtet haben.[7]

---

2 Van Steenbergen, Jo, „On the Brink of a New Era? Yalbughā al-Khāṣṣaki (d. 1366) and the Yalbughāwiyyah", in: *Mamluk Studies Review* 15 (2011), S. 117-152; hier S. 142.

3 Van Steenbergen, *Yalbughā*, S. 144.

4 Siehe u.a. al-Maqrīzī, Aḥmad b. ʿAli, *Kitāb as-Sulūk li-maʿrifat duwal al-mulūk*, Hg. M. M. Ziyādah u.a., Bde. 1-12, Kairo, 1934–72, hier Bd. 3, S. 129-30.

5 Van Steenbergen, Jo, „The Amir Yalbughā al-Khāṣṣaki, the Qalāwūnid Sultanate, and the Cultural Matrix of Mamluk Society: A Reassessment of Mamlūk Politics in the 1360s", in: *Journal of the American Oriental Society* 131,3 (2011), S. 423-444; hier S. 433.

6 Al-Maqrīzī, *Sulūk*, Bd. 3, S. 60; Van Steenbergen, *Reassessment*, S. 436.

7 Siehe Ibn Katīr, Ismāʿil b. ʿUmar, *al-Bidāyah wa-n-nihāyah*, Hg. Aḥmad Abū Mulḥim, Bde. 1-14, Beirut 1990, hier Bd. 14, S. 278 und Ibn Taġrībirdi, Ǧamāladdin, *an-Nuǧūm aẓ-*

In vielen historiographischen Quellen gilt Yalbuġā als undankbarer, schlechter, Mensch, der seinen Meister umgebracht und sich darauf des Reichs bemächtigt hat. Er schaltete und waltete und brachte den 14jährigen Enkel Ḥasans, Ṣalāḥaddīn Muḥammad al-Manṣūr (reg. 763–65/1361–63) und später den 10jährigen Ašraf Šaʿbān, einen Neffen Ḥasans (reg. 764–78/ 1363–77) auf den Thron. An-Nuwayrī al-Iskandarānī (d. 774/1372), ein Zeitgenosse aus Alexandria, ist in seinem Urteil viel schärfer als z.B. al-Maqrīzī in seinem *Sulūk*. Es scheint als ob die kritische Haltung zu den *ġulbān* aus frühen Zeiten einer milderen, ausgewogeneren Platz gemacht hat. Grund dafür ist einmal die zeitliche Distanz, andererseits die etwas positivere Sicht gegenüber den rehabilitierten *ġulbān* und Yalbuġā selbst.[8]

Al-Maqrīzī und andere, wie z.B. der syrische Historiker Ibn Ḥabīb und der Ägypter Ibn al-ʿIrāqī bezeugen, dass Yalbuġā auch gute Taten vollbracht hat, so habe er Hilfen nach Mekka geschickt, die Pilger von Steuern enthoben und die Ḥiġāz-Regionen, die durch den Wegfall der Einkünfte durch Pilger benachteiligt wurden, mit Einkünften aus anderen Gebieten in Ägypten entschädigt. Man berichtet weiterhin, er habe Syrien in Zeiten der Hungersnot unter die Arme gegriffen und Nahrungsmittel in die betroffenen Regionen geschickt.[9]

Wie kam es dazu, dass sich die eigenen Sklaven, die überdies nicht ohne weiteres auf eigenen Füßen stehen konnten – man muss sich vor Augen halten, dass sie Fremde in dem Land waren, die noch nicht einmal die Sprache der Bevölkerung sprachen – gegen ihren übermächtigen Meister auflehnten und ihn umbrachten? Noch Wochen vor seinem Tod sah alles danach aus, als stünde seiner absoluten Herrschaft nichts mehr im Wege. Sogar den mächtigen Amīr Ṭaybuġā aṭ-Ṭawīl (d. 768/1368), seinen langjährigen Widersacher, hatte er kaltgestellt. Mit dem Bau einer Flotte von 100 Kriegsschiffen demonstrierte er seine Macht auch den ausländischen Mächten gegenüber und konnte damit die peinliche Plünderung Alexandrias im Jahr zuvor durch Peter I. von Zypern vergessen machen.[10] Diese Flotte sollte jedoch niemals gegen die ungläubigen Feinde eingesetzt werden, sondern verblieb am Nil. Am 8. Dezember diente Yalbuġā ein schnelles Feuerschiff (*ḥarrāqah*) aus der Flotte als Fluchtvehikel, das er benutzte, um von seinem Jagdrevier bei Ġīzah, wo man versucht hatte ihn umzubringen, die andere Seite des Nils zu erreichen.[11] Er hatte nur einen Teil seiner Gefolgschaft mit in sein Jagdlager gebracht, so dass er unbedingt zur Zitadelle, dem Sitz des Sultanats eilen wollte, um sich dort neu aufzustellen. Der Verwalter der Zitadelle, *nāʾib al-ġayba*, der in Abwesenheit des Sultans über die Zitadelle herrschte, verwehrte ihm jedoch den Eintritt, so dass Yalbuġā sich auf seine Festung, Qalʿat al-Kabš, zurückzog.

---

zāhirah fī mulūk Miṣr wa-l-Qāhirah, Hg. Muḥammad Ḥusayn Šamsaddīn, 1-16, Beirut 1992, hier Bd. 10, S. 244.

[8]　Van Steenbergen, *Yalbughā*, S. 144.

[9]　Van Steenbergen, *Reassessment*, S. 438-9.

[10]　Al-Maqrīzī, *Sulūk*, Bd. 3, S. 129-30.

[11]　Die folgende Schilderung stammt aus al-Maqrīzī, *Sulūk*, Bd. 3, S. 132.

Die auf dem anderen Ufer des Nils verbliebenen Neusklaven befanden sich in einer Zwickmühle: Da sich einige von ihnen den Amīren anschlossen, die sich gegen Yalbuġā wandten und den Sultan auf ihre Seite ziehen konnten, mussten sie sich entscheiden – entweder schlugen auch sie sich auf die Seite der Aufständischen oder sie blieben ihrem Meister treu. Die Entscheidung war deshalb so schwierig, da sie nicht wussten, was Yalbuġā im Zentrum der Macht in Kairo an Kräften zusammenziehen konnte. So kam es, dass einige Yalbuġā treu blieben, was jedoch nur dazu führte, dass sie von den anderen geächtet und ausgeraubt wurden. Yalbuġā seinerseits versuchte indessen seine Kräfte zu sammeln, um sie im Kampf gegen seine Gegner, die sich noch auf dem anderen Ufer des Nils befanden, einzusetzen. Trotz seiner Versuche, sie an der Überquerung des Nils zu hindern, gelang es ihnen, zusammen mit dem Sultan auf dem Westufer des Nils zu landen und bis zur Zitadelle vorzudringen. Dies war der entscheidende Schritt für viele der noch unentschiedenen Neusklaven, sich auf die Seite der Gegner Yalbuġās zu schlagen. Yalbuġā konnte nur noch auf eine kleine Streitkraft zählen, so dass er nach aussichtslosen Scharmützeln schließlich auf seine Festung flüchtete. Auf seinem Weg dorthin bewarfen ihn sogar die Menschen auf der Straße mit Steinen. Der Sultan befahl, ihn festzunehmen und einzusperren. Da einige ehemalige Amīre von Yalbuġā fürchteten, er könne irgendwann wieder in den Dienst des Sultans treten, baten sie letzteren, über ihn zu verfügen, worauf dieser einging; man holte ihn aus dem Gefängnis, und als er sich anschickte, auf sein Pferd zu steigen, trat einer hervor und schlug ihm den Kopf ab. Andere kamen nach und zerteilten seinen Körper mit ihren Schwertern.

Die tieferen Gründe für die Ermordung Yalbuġās sind vielschichtig und können nicht nur, wie in einigen historischen Quellen dargestellt, damit erklärt werden, dass er gegenüber seinen Sklaven ein grausamer Herr gewesen war und sie auch folterte. Maqrīzī berichtet, er habe einigen die Zunge abschneiden lassen und bei Ibn Ḫaldūn heißt es, er habe einige Soldaten solange mit einem Stock verprügeln lassen, bis ihre Nasen abgeschnitten und ihre Ohren verstümmelt waren.[12] Wie van Steenbergen zeigt, geht die Revolte nicht einfach auf unzufriedene Neusklaven zurück, die sich von ihrem Herrn schlecht behandelt fühlten, sondern auf ein Zusammentreffen von Interessen hochrangiger Mamluken, die sich die Unzufriedenheit der Neusklaven Yalbuġās zunutze machten. Van Steenbergen schreibt:

> On that occasion, veteran ambitions concurred with junior frustrations to ignite a rebellious spark, and geographical circumstances, including the young sultan's presence on the rebellious side of the river, encouraged that spark to turn into a blaze that even the almighty Yalbughā proved incapable of fighting.[13]

---

[12] Al-Maqrīzī, *Sulūk*, Bd. 3, S. 130, van Steenbergen, *Yalbughā*, S. 123, wo er aus dem *K. al-ʿIbar* zitiert.

[13] Van Steenbergen, *Yalbughā*, S. 150.

Der junge, derweilen auf eigene Macht bedachte Sultan Ašraf Šaʿbān, befand sich in jenen Tagen nicht nur wie vom Zufall gewollt auf dem rebellischen Nilufer, sondern machte nun wie in den Quellen bezeugt auch aus eigenem Antrieb Machtansprüche geltend.

Seit jenem Tag, wurde alles, was mit Yalbuġā in Verbindung gebracht werden konnte, geächtet. Soldaten von niederem Rang, darunter die vielen herrenlosen Neusklaven, aber auch das gemeine Volk, begannen nun, die Häuser der Würdenträger von Yalbuġās Gnaden zu plündern. Es blieb jedoch nicht dabei —bald raubten sie auch Passanten auf der Straße aus, verlangten sogar, dass sie ihnen die Kleider auf dem Leib gäben.[14] Auch wenn die Obrigkeit diese plötzlichen Ausbrüche von Anarchie eindämmen konnte, gaben sie einen Vorgeschmack auf das, was in den Folgemonaten in Kairo passieren sollte.

Die noch nicht voll ausgebildeten Neumamluken Yalbuġās konnten sich zwar kurz daran erfreuen, dass ihr Peiniger keine Bedrohung mehr für sie war, doch hatten sie nun auch keinen mehr, der sie unterhielt; ihr sicheres Einkommen, ihre Karriere, alles ging mit Yalbuġā unter. Im Gegensatz zu den höher gestellten Militärsklaven konnten sie nämlich nicht ohne weiteres auf eine Wiedereingliederung vonseiten des Sultans oder anderer Amire hoffen. Noch im gleichen Monat erreichten die Übergriffe der Neusklaven ungekannte Ausmaße, sie überfielen die Menschen auf den Straßen Kairos, stürmten öffentliche Bäder, wo Frauen gerade badeten und vergewaltigten sie. Sie raubten die Häuser wohlhabender Menschen aus, so dass sich Angst und Schrecken in der Bevölkerung Kairos breitmachte. Damit war es nicht getan, sie gingen auf direkten Konfrontationskurs mit den Ordnungskräften, so dass die Streitkräfte des Sultans schließlich eingriffen, eine Anzahl ihrer Anführer festsetzten und sie außer Landes wiesen.[15]

Währenddessen hatte es ein Amir Yalbuġās, Asandamur, in den folgenden Monaten geschafft, sich als neuer *primus inter pares* zu positionieren. Er lenkte die Staatsgeschäfte so wie sein Vorgänger Yalbuġā, zudem residierte er in der gleichen Festung, Qalʿat al-Kabš, die auch schon Yalbuġā als Residenz gedient hatte. Viele der nach dem Tod Yalbuġās herrenlos brandschatzenden Neusklaven, die sich etwas von einem neuen Meister erhofften, stellte er in seinen Dienst. Das war für beide erst einmal ein gutes Geschäft: Asandamur konnte sich schnell eine Armee aufbauen, und die Neusklaven mussten nicht mehr verloren im fremden Land herumirren.

Dann, am Sonntag, dem 7. Šawwāl 768/ 6. Juni 1367 erfuhr Asandamur, dass der Sultan mit der Unterstützung anderer Amire gegen ihn und seine Truppe mobil machte. In wenigen Tagen konnte Asandamur die Angriffe zurückschlagen und seine Position als wichtigster Sachwalter des Reichs festigen. Es scheint jedoch, dass die Neusklaven Yalbuġās keinen sicheren Rückhalt für Asandamur boten. Noch im selben Monat musste er feststellen, dass er sie nicht mehr kontrollieren konnte

---

[14]　Al-Maqrīzī, *Sulūk*, Bd. 3, S. 137.
[15]　Al-Maqrīzī, *Sulūk*, Bd. 3, S. 141.

oder auch wollte. Entweder lehnten sie sich auf, weil sie nicht mehr zufrieden waren mit ihrer Lage, oder ihre Hoffnung auf eine Besserstellung und Beförderung
wurde nicht erfüllt. Jedenfalls häuften sich wieder Fälle von Raub, Vergewaltigun-
gen und Plünderungen in den Monaten nach Juni 1367 bis der Sultan und seine
Truppen dem Treiben ein Ende setzen konnten, viele aufständische Neusklaven im
Nil ertränkten und deren wichtigste Anführer aus Kairo verbannten:

> On Thursday 14 [October 1367] (19. Safar 769), the sultan drowned a group from the
> Yalbughāwiyah mamluks, who had agreed to kill him, in the Nile. [...] in the morning
> of this Thursday, 100 of the notables of these Yalbughāwiyah ajlāb (al-ajlāb al-
> Yalbughāwiyah) were nailed and cut in two. A group of them were drowned. The re-
> mainder of them were banished to Syria and to Aswan.[16]

Diese Darstellung geht auf Schilderungen zurück, die in den historischen Quellen
verbürgt sind.[17] Was all diesen Schilderungen gemein ist – sie sprechen dem Sultan
eine entscheidende Rolle bei der Niederschlagung der Aufstände zu, wie oben im
Sulūk des al-Maqrīzī oder auch seiner Vorlage, dem *Kitāb al-ʿIbar* des Ibn Ḫaldūn.
Wie wir im Folgenden sehen werden, spielt der Sultan keine derart zentrale Rolle
in der Schilderung der Ereignisse innerhalb der Makame von Ibn Abī Ḥaǧalah.

Ibn Abī Ḥaǧalahs Makame Dawr az-zamān fī ṭaḥn al-ǧulbān

Wann genau Ibn Abī Ḥaǧalah diese Makame geschrieben hat, geht nicht aus den
Angaben in der einzig erhaltenen Kairener Handschrift, Dār al-kutub *adab 5664
hervor*. Im Kolophon steht:

> Angefertigt von ʿUmar ad-Dimyāṭī aš-Šāfiʿī im Jahre 870/1465 [also ungefähr ein Jahr-
> hundert nach Ibn Abī Ḥaǧalahs Tod] – wieder abgeschrieben von Muḥammad b. Zayn
> ad-Dīn al-Ḥamawī, der sie am heiligen Sonntag, dem 6. des Monats Ǧumādā l-Ūlā des
> Jahres 1030/ 29. März 1621 mit seiner vergänglichen Hand kommentiert hat.

Auch in anderen Quellen ließen sich keine Angaben zum Entstehungszeitpunkt
finden, doch ist der Zeitraum, in der die Makame verfasst wurde, recht gut ein-
grenzbar. Da die Unruhen in Kairo bis Anfang des Jahres 769 bzw. bis zum
Herbst des Jahres 1367 andauerten und Ibn Abī Ḥaǧalah im Jahr 1375 starb,
muss er sie in den acht Jahren (769–777/1367–1375) bis zu seinem Tod verfasst
haben, vermutlich eher in den ersten Jahren nach den Aufständen. Dass es sich
zweifellos um eine Makame unseres Autors handelt, geht aus dreierlei Indizien
hervor: In der ersten Zeile wird als Autor Ibn Abī Ḥaǧalah und als Erzähler as-
Sāǧiʿ b. Hamām vorgestellt. Ein sehr bezeichnender Name, da Sāǧiʿ auf der einen Seite „der Gurrende" bedeutet aber auch „der Reimprosa Schreibende" und
Ibn Hamām „Sohn der Taube". Der Makamen-Erzähler hat also wie Ibn Abī

---

[16] Al-Maqrīzī, *Sulūk*, Bd. 3, S. 154-5 in der Übersetzung von van Steenbergen, *Yalbughā*,
    S. 147-8.
[17] Nach al-Maqrīzī, *Sulūk*, Bd. 3, S. 142-3 und den Ausführungen von van Steenbergen (*Yal-
    bughā*, S. 145-51), der hier auch andere Quellen benutzt.

Ḥaǧalah („Sohn des Vaters des Rebhuhns") selbst einen Namen aus dem Vogelreich. Ihm scheint das Spiel mit seinem Namen gefallen zu haben, denn in nicht wenigen Gedichten spielt er auf seine geflügelten Namensgeber an. Ein drittes Indiz ist der angestammte Held seiner Makamen. Auch in der hier zu besprechenden tritt er, wenn auch nur alibiartig, auf. Wie Autor und Erzähler, ist auch der Held dem Vogelreich nicht fremd: Er heißt Abū r-Riyāš („Vater der Federn") oder auch Abū r-Rayyāš („Vater des Federers").

Die fünf Folios, die die Makame enthalten, sind mit weiteren vier Folios zusammengebunden, die sich nach flüchtigem Durchlesen als ein eigenständiges, von anderer Hand geschriebenes Schriftstück zu pharmazeutischen Fragen herausstellten.

Dawr az-zamān fī ṭahn al-ġulbān also Das Zermahlen der *ġulbān* genannten Neusklaven durch eine Drehung des „Mühlrads der Zeit". Ein bezeichnender Titel, da Ibn Abī Ḥaǧalah hier die Hauptdarsteller der Makame, die *ġulbān,* in einer doppelten Bedeutung benutzt: *ġulbān* bedeutet nämlich nicht nur „neuangeschaffte Militärsklaven" wie oben bereits angemerkt, sondern auch „Platterbse" oder mit ihrem lateinischen Namen *Lathyrus Sativus.* Eine Erbsensorte, die vor allem an Tiere verfüttert wurde, die hart und für Menschen mehr schlecht als recht genießbar sind. Und was macht man mit solchen Erbsen? Man zermahlt sie. Daher wundert es kaum, dass Ibn Abī Ḥaǧalah hier den Namen *ġulbān* für diese unseligen Zeitgenossen gewählt hat und nicht *aǧlāb,* was nach *muštarawāt* bzw. im Fall der Neusklaven Yalbuġās *mamālīkuhu al-ašrār* „seine boshaft Sklaven" oder *mamālīkuhu al-aǧlāb* „seine angeschafften Sklaven" der deutlich häufigere Name war.[18]

Ibn Abī Ḥaǧalah, Yalbuġā und seine ġulbān – *das biographische Moment*

Ibn Abī Ḥaǧalah hat die Unruhen der *ġulbān* in Kairo selbst erlebt. Wahrscheinlich konnte auch er keinen Fuß vor die Tür setzen, ohne Angst zu haben, die *ġulbān* stellten ihn auf der Straße und raubten ihn bis aufs letzte Hemd aus. Sein Erzähler, as-Sāǧiʿ b. Ḥamām, beginnt seinen Augenzeugenbericht von den Aufständen wie folgt:

> Ich war in Kairo, als Tumulte herrschten und Aufständische im Inneren und Äußeren des Landes ihr Unwesen trieben * Ich sah, wie hochstehende Würdenträger gestürzt wurden und Dinge passierten, über die noch lange geredet wird * Ich war von Unruhe erfüllt, wenn ich den Aufbegehrenden nur sah * und floh sogar vor den Vögeln, vor denen, die zum Flug ansetzten und denen, deren Federn gestutzt wurden.

Sogar der Anblick von harmlosen Vögeln, zudem solchen, die noch nicht einmal mehr Flügel zum Fliegen hatten, versetzten ihn in Angst und Schrecken.

---

[18] Van Steenbergen, *Yalbughā,* S. 142-3.

Was auf diese Einleitung folgt, ist eine chronologische und genaue Schilderung der Ereignisse um die Aufstände der *ġulbān,* wobei er aber nicht mit diesen beginnt, sondern mit deren eigentlichen Urheber: Yalbuġā al-Ḥāṣṣakī. Ein Grund, warum Ibn Abī Ḥaǧalah einen sehr kritischen Ton gegen Yalbuġā anschlägt, ist wohl, dass Sultan Ḥasan sein größter Wohltäter gewesen war und Yalbuġā nicht an seine Stelle als Mäzen getreten ist. Yalbuġā, den der Sultan maßgeblich gefördert hat, habe ganz im Gegensatz zu ihm selbst Treuebruch begangen und anstatt dem Sultan zu danken ihn aus Machtbesessenheit und Eigennutz umgebracht:

> Dieser [Yalbuġā] war ihr vereinendes Band [das der *ġulbān*] * und jener, der ihre Pfeile mit Federn ausstattete * Der Sultan hatte ihn mit seinen Wohltaten überschüttet * und ihn zum Köcher seiner Pfeile gemacht * Als sein Arm [Yalbuġās] jedoch erstarkt war, hat er ihn beiseite geschoben * „Wer jemandem, der ihm nicht nahesteht etwas Gutes tut, der kriegt nur Undank. Ihm widerfährt das, was auch dem Helfer der Hyäne widerfahren war" [Sprichwort] * denn er brachte darauf Sultan an-Nāṣir um * und bemächtigte sich seines glorreichen Reichs * und raubte [allen Menschen] den Schlaf. Er vergalt Gutes mit Schlechtem * und machte sich eilig dran, ihn [den Sultan] zu vernichten.

Ibn Abī Ḥaǧalahs Erzähler beschreibt nun, wie Yalbuġā die Herrschaft an sich riss, ein Kind als Sultan einsetzte und mit dem Reich verfuhr, wie es ihm beliebte – der Sultan war nur noch dem Namen nach, *bi-l-ism,* ein Sultan. Die Glorifizierung Yalbuġās, ob diese nun von ihm eingefordert wurde oder nicht, ging sogar soweit, dass man bei ihm schwor. Er war es, der bestimmte, wie viele Münzen geprägt wurden und somit war er die letzte Instanz, die die Finanzen des königlichen Haushalts in der Hand hielt.

Für Ibn Abī Ḥaǧalah besteht kein Zweifel daran, dass Yalbuġā durch die Heranschaffung der *ġulbān* sein eigenes Ende besiegelt hat. Mit dem Geld, dass er sich erschwindelt hatte, brachte er dieses „unreine Gesindel" (*al-ġalab an-naǧis*), dieses „Volk von grobschlächtigen Hirten" (*al-ġūbān,* aus türk. *çoban*) ins Land. Türkischen Ursprungs waren die Mamluken zumeist ohnehin; dass diese aber Horden von wilden Ziegenhirten waren, noch dazu unreine und ungläubige, ist wohl übertrieben. In den Quellen wird nämlich sehr wohl vermerkt, dass Yalbuġā hohe Ansprüche an seine Sklaven stellte, und sehr auf ihre Ausbildung, in die zu der auch religiöse Unterweisung gehörte, achtete. In Anbetracht dessen ist die Behauptung, die *ġulbān* wären vom Glauben Abgefallene (*ᶜulūǧ*), die all jenen, welche den *tawḥīd* (*lā ilāha illā llāh*) aussprachen, die Zunge abschnitten, kaum verständlich: Yalbuġā kann schwerlich für diese Taten seiner Sklaven verantwortlich gemacht werden, da er wie auch andere Amīre vor ihm ein beflissener Förderer der Geistlichkeit, in diesem Fall der hanafitischen Rechtsschule, war und zudem den Pilgern ihre Wallfahrt erleichterte.[19]

Ibn Abī Ḥaǧalahs Aversion gegen Yalbuġā war dermaßen groß, dass er ihn selbst nach dessen Tod mit Häme überzog. Es war ein Leichtes und ebenso recht Wohlfeiles für ihn und seine Leser, etwas über die Missetaten Yalbuġās und seiner *ġulbān*

---

¹⁹ van Steenbergen, *Reassessment,* S. 429.

zu schreiben. Ein Epigramm im Diwan, das auch in der Makame vorkommt, ist als Trauergedicht auf Yalbuġā ausgezeichnet, zeugt aber nicht gerade von Trauer, sondern von Ablehnung und liest sich daher gerade im Kontext der Makame wie eine Abrechnung: Wie anders sollte man die folgenden Zeilen sonst verstehen?

> Wegen dem Tod Yalbuġās plündert man in Ägypten / so wie dort geplündert wurde, als er noch am Leben war //
> Die Würfel waren gefallen, er ward durch die Stadt geschleift / vom Unglück verfolgt im Leben wie im Tod

Ibn Abī Ḥaǧalah verhehlt nicht, dass Yalbuġā auch Gutes getan hat; wir haben oben gesehen, dass al-Maqrīzi und andere Historiker wie der Syrer Ibn Ḥabīb und der Ägypter Ibn al-ʿIrāqī bezeugen, dass er Hilfe nach Mekka geschickt hat, dass er die Pilger von Steuern befreit und den Hiǧāz-Regionen durch die Einkünfte anderer Gebiete in Ägypten entschädigt und Syrien in Zeiten der Hungersnot unterstützt hat. Doch in Ibn Abī Ḥaǧalahs Makame rühren diese guten Taten nur von seiner Hybris und seinen wechselnden Launen her.

Immer wieder erinnert Ibn Abī Ḥaǧalah daran, was für ein Übel Yalbuġā ins Land geholt habe. Diese „Skorpione", wie der Erzähler sie an anderer Stelle nennt, sollten eigentlich seinen Machtanspruch unterstreichen und ihn schützen, in Wirklichkeit aber verrieten sie ihn und stürzten ihn schließlich ins Verderben:

> 1. Oh, wie schlimm ist die Brut, die er sich da geholt und herangezogen hatte.
> 2. Er saß somit unter seiner Wand, die einzustürzen drohte * Das Unglück der Dämonen, die er gerufen hatte, zäunte ihn ein.
> 3. Als er nämlich dann das Wasser überquerte und auf dem Festland [dem anderen Ufer] Position bezog * und sich als Sultan gebärdete auf dem Land * verrieten ihn seine Helfer * und es bekrähten seine unheilbringenden Raben die Trennung * es war nunmehr um ihn geschehen.

Die Unruhen, eine zerstörte Synagoge und wie Literatur Geschichte schreiben kann

Ibn Abī Ḥaǧalah lässt nun eine bilderreiche und wortgewaltige, von Unmengen an Koranzitaten, Gedichten und Sprichwörtern untermalte Darstellung der Unruhen, die nach dem Tod Yalbuġās einsetzten, folgen. Von gebrandschatzten Seminarsälen ist die Rede, von Raubzügen mitten in der Stadt am helllichten Tag, von Gelagen in Moscheen, wo die *ġulbān* aus den großen Lampengläsern Wein tranken. Sie stellten Frauen in den Gassen nach, ließen die Richter verstummen, spielten sich selbst als Sultane auf.

Die Bevölkerung Kairos blieb ohne Schutz und musste Monate unter den Übergriffen der *ġulbān* leben, wodurch sogar die Versorgung mit Getreide in Mitleidenschaft gezogen wurde. Als es ihnen zu viel wurde, sahen sie sich gezwungen, die Sache selbst in die Hand zu nehmen, um den *ġulbān* Einhalt zu gebieten. Wo es nur ging, stellten sie sich ihnen in den Weg. Wie Erbsen mischten sie sich unter sie und bewarfen sie von den Hausdächern mit Steinen.

Ibn Abī Ḥaǧalah erzählt außerdem von einer wichtigen Begebenheit, von der jedoch keine Quelle berichtet: Juden hätten bei den Unruhen mitgemischt, weswegen ihre Synagoge schließlich niedergerissen wurde. Diese *al-ġabrā* („erdfarbene") genannte Synagoge konnte ich dabei in keiner Quelle ausfindig machen.

Weiterhin fällt bei den Beschreibungen der Niederschlagung dieser Unruhen auf, dass der Anteil, den das gemeine Volk dabei hatte, unverhältnismäßig hoch eingeschätzt wird. An mehreren Stellen in der Makame beschreibt der Erzähler die entscheidende Rolle, die die gewöhnlichen Menschen bei der Bekämpfung der außer Rand und Band geratenen *ǧulbān* spielen:

1. Als sie sich nun gegen ihn auflehnten und ihre Pfeile des Irrtums gegen ihn kerbten * stürmte das Volk los.

2. Als sie [die ǧulbān] dann von den Gipfeln herunterströmten * und sie wie eine Flut vorpreschten * stellten sich ihnen die Menschen in den Weg * und mischten sich wie Linsen unter die ǧulbān/ Platterbsen * Sie bewarfen diese mit Steinen und Scherben * und durch die herrliche Glückseligkeit des al-Ašraf waren sie auch bald am Rande der Vernichtung.

3. Wie viele Beine haben sie in ihrem Heeresrücken gebrochen * Von überall wurden sie mit Steinen beworfen * So mussten sie [die ǧulbān] dann kehrtmachen (7) * der Allgewaltige zerschlug sie * Ein Gelehrter meldete * dass er eine Heerschar vom Himmel hinunterstürzen sah * ganz wie die Züge von Vögeln aus dem Koran * die sie mit Steinen aus Lehm bewarfen.

Auch in dem folgenden Gedicht wird die große Macht des Volks besungen:

4. Ich sah wie die Steine des Gottesheeres trafen / von den ǧulbān jeden Standhaften // Manch ein Herz haben sie im [Sultans-]Heer damit geflickt / und manch einen Kopf zerschmettert

5. Sie [die ǧulbān] wurden nun müde und schwach, man plünderte sie wie die ahl as-Sabā [Sabäer] * als das Volk unter sie krabbelte wie kleine Ameisen.

Den Sultan findet man hier lediglich als moralische Instanz, der die Kämpfe gegen die *ǧulbān* anführt. Dies steht im krassen Gegensatz zu den auf den Sultan fixierten Chroniken, die sein Einschreiten als maßgeblich für die Niederschlagung der Unruhen ansehen. Oben habe ich als Beispiel ein Zitat von al-Maqrīzī angeführt. Auch der Tod von Yalbuġā geht nicht, auch nicht mittelbar, auf das Wirken des Sultans zurück, sondern Gott ist hier derjenige, der ihn beim Schopf greift und sein Leben verkürzt:

„und Gott erwischte ihn an einer Stelle, in der er sein Vertrauen gesetzt hatte * Denn Er hatte beschlossen, ihn zu vernichten * und sein Leben zu kürzen wegen seiner unendlichen Vergehen."

und schließlich seinen Tod verfügt:

„und der Ewiglebende, Ewigwährende verfügte seinen Tod."

Nur in dem Gedicht des Helden, Abū r-Riyāš und dem folgenden Schlussteil wird die Macht des Sultans beschworen, doch vielfach in Form von Wünschen bzw. Aufforderungen, die an den Herrscher gerichtet sind. Die obigen Beispiele zeigen, dass die Literatur Informationen liefert, die von den Chroniken zugunsten der idealisiert staatstragenden Macht des Sultans vernachlässigt werden. Hierzu eine Anekdote:

In einem Vortrag stellte ich diese Makame einem Publikum von Spezialisten der arabischen Geschichtsschreibung vor. Nachdem ich die Abfolge der Ereignisse wie sie in der Makame vorkamen nacherzählt und den Vortrag abgeschlossen hatte, kam die ungläubige Nachfrage, ob denn der Sultan nicht weiter erwähnt wurde oder seine Rolle nicht deutlicher zu Tage trete. Ich führte die Stellen an, in denen der Sultan erwähnt wird, worauf der Frager noch einmal verblüfft nachhakte, ob es denn nicht noch weitere Stellen gibt, die darauf hindeuten, was der Sultan noch alles gemacht hat, um die Aufständischen zu besiegen. Etwas ratlos, warum man wieder auf den Sultan abhebt, konnte ich abermals nur die Stellen, in denen sein Wirken beschrieben wird, vorweisen. Dagegen strich ich die maßgebliche Rolle des Volks hervor, die sie in der Makame spielen, doch so richtig ließ sich der perplexe Frager auch durch die wiederholte und ausführliche Darlegung des Verlaufs der Ereignisse in der Makame nicht überzeugen. Womöglich passte die Rolle, die das Volk einnahm, nicht in sein Bild, das ihm die Chroniken vermitteln und als Grundlage für die Erforschung der Geschichte der Mamluken dienen.

Form

Bei der Makame handelt es sich um eine historische Makame in dem Sinn, dass sie eine historisch authentische Begebenheit zum Inhalt hat. Ibn Abī Ḥaǧalah folgt dem chronologischen Verlauf der Begebenheiten beginnend mit Yalbuġā, wie er die *ġulbān* ins Land holte bis zu deren endgültigen Vernichtung im Herbst des Jahres 1367 (Safar 769). Es fällt auf, dass er keine genauen Daten angibt, außer der nicht einzuordnenden Angabe eines Sonntags, wobei es nicht klar ist, ob es sich um den Tag, an dem Asandamur und seine übernommenen *ġulbān* bekämpft wurden (7. Šawwāl 768/ 6. Juni 1367), handelt oder um den Tag, an dem die *ġulbān* die Absetzung Sultan al-Ašrafs forderten (19. Raǧab 768/ 21. März 1367).

Die Form einer Makame ist durch mehrere Gesichtspunkte gewahrt: Zum einen haben wir den *isnād* zu Beginn der Makame. Zum anderen die genretypische Erzählperspektive eines Ich-Erzählers, der des Öfteren mit Namen genannt wird. Im Unterschied zu anderen Makamen Ibn Abī Ḥaǧalahs steht der Erzähler hier außerhalb des Erzählgeschehens und greift nicht aktiv ein, sondern er beobachtet von außen, ist also nach Genette ein heterodiegetischer Erzähler.[20] Wie wir weiter unten sehen werden, gliedern diese wiederholten Nennungen des Erzählers

---

[20] Genette, Gérard, *Figures III*, Paris 1972, S. 109 und *passim*.

die Erzählung gleichzeitig in grobe Abschnitte. Ein weiteres Merkmal der Makamen ist der Auftritt eines pikaresken Helden, im Fall Ibn Abī Ḥaǧalahs Makamen, Abu r-Riyāš, der ebenso Augenzeuge der Geschehnisse gewesen war:

> Es sagte as-Sāǧiʿ b. Ḥamām * Abū r-Riyāš war einer von jenen, die loszogen * und sich dran machten, die Nachricht zu verbreiten * als er sah, wie der Staub aufgewirbelt * wie die Lampe auf einem Leuchtturm wurde * und als er mit eigenen Augen die Flüsse ihres Bluts sah * (8) und ihre Flucht von hier nach da * erzählte er, was er mit eigenen Augen gesehen * und hatte dabei keine Hilfe nötig * Ohne Zweifel erzählte er von den Verbrechern * und reihte seine kostbaren Perlen.

An dieser Stelle folgt ein Gedicht von 31 Versen im gleichen Versmaß wie die anderen Gedichte in der Makame. Dem pikaresken Helden Abū r-Riyāšʾ, dem durchtriebenen Hansdampf in allen Gassen, der in den anderen Makamen genretypisch wie aus dem Nichts auftaucht und den Erzähler mit seinem Witz und seiner Eloquenz überrascht, ist hier nur eine marginale Rolle, wenn auch platzmäßig große, beschieden: in Form eines Einschubs am Ende der Makame wo er als Augenzeuge die Geschehnisse in einem langen Gedicht schildert. Auffällig ist, dass Ibn Abī Ḥaǧalah hierbei gleiche oder ähnliche Ausdrücke benutzt wie in seinem übrigen Makamentext.

Es scheint, dass die historisch-authentische Ausrichtung der Makame Ibn Abī Ḥaǧalah daran gehindert hat, einen fiktionalen Handlungsstrang mit einer starken Rolle des Erzählers und des Protagonisten einzubauen. Dass eine Makame nicht unbedingt einen solchen Handlungsstrang benötigt, hat Hämeen-Anttila in seinem Werk über Makamen anhand von mehreren Beispielen gezeigt.[21]

Das formale Hauptmerkmal einer Makame, die Reimprosa, gestaltet Ibn Abī Ḥaǧalah größtenteils in Form von reimenden Doppelkola. Die Länge der Kola kann variieren, wodurch ein rhythmischer Wechsel erzeugt wird, der den Lesefluss auflockert, was in dem folgenden Beispiel deutlich wird; die ersten beiden Kola sind lang, die beiden folgenden hingegen kurz:

> wa-kāna li-s-sulṭāni l-ismu wa-lahu l-fiʿlu wa-l-ḥarf * wa li-l-imāmi l-ḫuṭbatu wa-s-sikkatu wa-lahū ḍ-ḍarbu wa-ṣ-ṣarf * fa-akṯara mina **n-naqdayn** * wa-ltaqafa l-mulka **bi-l-yadayn**

> „Dem Sultan kam der Name, das Verb (die Tat) und der Buchstabe zu * und dem Imam das Recht auf die Freitagspredigt sowie der Name auf den Münzen. Die Prägung aber gehörte nun Yalbuǧā und auch das Inumlaufbringen * (3) Er [Yalbuǧā] ließ die beiden Münzsorten [dīnār und dirham] reichlich prägen * und nahm die Herrschaft in beide Hände.“

Dieses Spiel mit dem Rhythmus findet sich bisweilen auch innerhalb zweier Kola; wie im folgenden Beispiel, wo das erste Kolon aus elf, das zweite hingegen aus fünf Silben besteht:

> fa-akṯara mina l-ǧalabi **n-naǧis** * wa-l-kayli **l-baḫis**

> „dann beschaffte er sich unreines Gesindel * und erwarb mit falschen Gewichten.“

---

21 Hämeen-Anttila, Jaakko, *Maqama. A History of a Genre*, Wiesbaden 2002, S. 179.

In einigen wenigen Fällen erstreckt sich der Reim über drei Kola:

wa-aḫadahu llāhu mina l-ǧānibi llaḏī ya'manu **ilayh** * fa-kāna tadbīruhu fī **tadmī-rih** * wa-qaṣṣara ʿumrahu li-ṭūli **taqṣīrih**

„und Gott erwischte ihn an einer Stelle, in der er sein Vertrauen gesetzt hatte * Denn Er hatte beschlossen, ihn zu vernichten * und sein Leben zu kürzen wegen seiner unendlichen Vergehen."

Inhalt und Gliederung

Die Makame ist grob in drei Hauptteile mit Einleitung, Schluss und eine Art Epilog gegliedert. Von dem eigentlichen Text getrennt sind die vorangestellte *basmalah* und der *isnād* sowie der nachgestellte Kolophon, welche allesamt Paratexte darstellen. Im Folgenden nun übersichtsartig die Gliederung der Makame mit kurzen Erklärungen zum Inhalt:

Basmalah

Isnād „*Es sagte der hochehrwürdige Meister Šihābaddīn b. Abī Ḥaǧalah al-Humām * es erzählte as-Sāǧiʿ b. Ḥamām*"

Einleitung: „*Ich war in Kairo als Tumulte herrschten und Aufständische im Inneren und Äußeren des Landes ihr Unwesen trieben [...].*"

Gedicht, Zweizeiler: über Yalbuġā. Eins von zwei Gedichten im Versmaß *ṭawīl*, alle weiteren sind allesamt im Versmaß *wāfir* geschrieben.

1. Hauptteil: Schilderung dessen, was Yalbuġā mit seinem Herrn gemacht hat. Yalbuġā, der undankbare Sklave, der seine eigene Herrschaft errichtet (indem er die von ihm selbst und seinen Mitstreitern eingesetzten Sultane entmachtet), sich der Finanzen bemächtigt, nach eigenem Gutdünken Geld prägt, und schließlich sein eigenes Grab schaufelt (Vorgriff auf das, was mit ihm im nächsten Hauptteil passiert) durch die Anschaffung von grobschlächtigen türkischen Hirten (*ġubān*) als Sklaven.

Gedicht, Zweizeiler: Das zweite Gedicht im Versmaß *ṭawīl*; zu Yalbuġā und seiner Anschaffung der Sklaven.

2. Hauptteil: Schilderung seines Niedergangs innerhalb von 6 Jahren (entspricht seiner tatsächlichen Herrschaftszeit) unter der übertriebenen Anführung seiner schlechten Eigenschaften. Die *ġulbān* wenden sich von ihm ab und töten ihn. Der Erzähler bringt sich wieder als Augenzeuge ein, ohne dass er als teilhabender Erzähler in Erscheinung tritt. Erwähnung, dass die Juden sich an dem Aufruhr beteiligt haben.

Gedicht, Zweizeiler: Nach dem Tod von Yalbuġā plündert man in Ägypten

3. Hauptteil: *„Die Büchse der Pandora stand nun offen"*, die *ġulbān* wüten in Kairo, der *Marīs*-Wind (aus Nubien/ Oberägypten) bläst. *Ġulbān* plündern und vergewaltigen monatelang. Menschen beginnen sich zu wehren, schlagen sich auf die Seite des Sultans und bewerfen die unreinen Abtrünnigen mit Steinen.

Gedicht, Zweizeiler: Steine werden geworfen, dass die Köpfe der Ġulbān zerspringen.

Vorstellung von Abū r-Riyāš: Dieser hat alles gesehen und tritt nun auf den Plan, um mit seinem Gedicht Kunde davon zu verbreiten.

Abū r-Riyāš' Gedicht: (31 Verse)

Schluss: Zusammenfassung der Geschehnisse, Endbemerkung mit Aufgriff des Titels der Makame: *lammā kān mā kān * min dawri z-zamān * fī ṭaḥni l-ġulbān „als geschah, was geschah * von den Wechselfällen der Zeiten * was die Zermalmung der ġulbān betrifft."*

Gedichte, 2 Zweizeiler: Beschneidung der ungläubigen *ġulbān*, Weiterführung des Gedankens der rituellen Unreinheit.

Epilog: Kurze Schilderung wie wieder Ruhe und Ordnung ins Leben Kairos einzog.

Kolophon

Es fällt auf, dass die mehrheitlich zweizeiligen Gedichte eine veranschaulichende (das zuvor Gesagte wird in Gedichtform in anderer Form erzählt) und gleichzeitig eine gliedernde Funktion (die Gedichte markieren das Ende eines inhaltlichen Teils der Makame) besitzen.[22] Zu der gliedernden Funktion der Gedichte tritt die Wiedereinführung des Erzählers hinzu. Immer wenn der Erzähler mit den Worten *qāla as-Sāǧiʿ b. Ḥamām* neu eingeführt wird, beginnt ein neuer Sinnabschnitt, was insgesamt fünfmal vorkommt. Zwei Mal tritt dieser Satz nach den Gedichten auf, wodurch die gliedernde Eigenschaft der Gedichte unterstrichen wird.

Koranzitate, Sprichwörter, Redensarten und Gedichtzitate

Ein sehr auffälliges Merkmal dieser Makame sind die überaus häufigen Zitate aus dem Koran. Die Verse des Korans, welcher auch ein Werk in Reimprosa ist und in gewissem Sinn auch als Vorbild für die Makamenliteratur gedient hat, bieten sich daher äußerst gut für das Einflechten in die Makame an. Bei Ibn Abī Ḥaǧalah häufen sich diese stellenweise beträchtlich. Ein besonders eindrucksvolles

---

Beispiel mag hier genügen (auf weitere Stellen wird in der Übersetzung gesondert hingewiesen):

Qāla s-Sāǧiʿ b. Ḥamām wa-min hunā futiḥa bābu š-šarr * wa-stamarr * wa-lam tazal ʿaqāribuhum tadubb * wa-rīḥu l-maris tahubb * fa-afšawi l-munkirāt * wa-taṭarraqū ilā n-nisāʾi fi-l-aziqqāt * fa-ʿammati l-muṣībatu l-ʿawāmm * wa-qīla innahum illā ka-l-anʿām **(Furqān: 44)** * yasāqūna ilā l-mawti wa-hum yanẓurūn **(al-Anfāl: 6)** * innā lillāhi wa-innā ilayhi rāǧiʿūn **(Al-Baqara: 156)** * āyu layālihim idlahammat **(Āl ʿImrān, 122)** * wa-mā-ʾidatun **[möglicherweise eine Anspielung auf den Namen der Sure al-Māʾidah]** qaʿadat ʿalayhā š-šayāṭin wa-mā sammat.

„Es erzählte as-Sāǧiʿ b. Ḥamām * Die Büchse der Pandora (das Tor des Bösen) stand nun offen * und blieb auch lange offen * ihre Skorpione krabbelten noch lange herum * und der Wind des Maris zog auf * Sie brachten das Böse hervor * stellten den Frauen in den Gassen nach * das Unglück brach über die Allgemeinheit aus * Es heißt ja auch, dass sie nur wie Vieh sind **(Furqān: 44)** * das sehenden Auges in den Tod getrieben wird **(al-Anfāl: 6)** * so wie es auch im Koran steht: Wir sind Gottes und zu ihm kehren wir zurück **(Al-Baqara: 156)** * als die Zeichen ihrer Nächte finster wurden **(Āl ʿImrān, 122)** und die Teufel sich an den Tisch setzten, ohne den Namen Gottes zu nennen.“

Ähnlich häufig benutzt Ibn Abī Ḥaǧalah Sprichwörter und Redewendungen, die zum jeweiligen Kontext passen. Eine bezeichnende Passage, die viele davon enthält, soll hier der Veranschaulichung dienen:

ṯumma ʿazamū ʿalā nahbi l-balad * wa-aḫaḏa s-sabada wa-l-labad * fa-aḫaḏati n-nāsu fi taḥṣīni l-aziqqah * wa-qaṣura l-amalu li-ṭūli šuqqati l-mašaqqah * fa-yā la-l-ʿaǧab * mina l-ǧalab * wa-min kulli mamlūkin aḥarra mina l-ǧamr * wa-aḥrama mina l-ḫamr * asraʿa t-turku ilā l-ḫaṭā * min qawli qaṭāti qaṭā * aznā min Saǧāḥ * wa-aḥabba min qawwādin fi s-sifāḥ.

„Darauf zogen sie plündernd durchs Land * und nahmen alles, was sie vorfanden, in die Hand * Das Volk begann, die Straßen zu bewehren * Doch konnte ihre Hoffnung lange nicht währen * Oh, wie verwunderlich sind doch diese Herangeschafften * brennender als Kohle noch all ihre Mannschaften * und verbotener als der Wein * Schneller tritt der Türke in den Irrtum ein * als der qaṭā-Vogel ‚qaṭā!‘ sagen kann * selbst Saǧāḥ könnte sündiger [als der Türke] nicht sein * und der Zuhälter nicht eifriger beim Ehebruch.“

Wa aḫaḏa s-sabada wa-l-labad, wörtlich: „sie nahmen das Haar und die Wolle“ bzw. „die Tiere, die Haare haben und solche, die Wolle haben“, kommt der deutschen Redewendung „alles, was nicht niet- und nagelfest ist“ nahe.

Asraʿa min qawli qaṭāti qaṭā, wörtlich „schneller als das Schnattern des qaṭā-Vogels (*Ardea Stellaris*)“ der nach seinem Schrei onomatopoetisch so genannt wurde, ist eine weitere Redewendung.[23]

Aznā min Saǧāḥ ist eine Redewendung, die auf Saǧāḥ Umm Ṣādir bint Aws zurückgeht, eine Seherin und Anführerin der Banū Tamīm zu Zeiten der *ridda*. Aṭ-Ṭabarī beschreibt in frivolen Details wie sie Orgien mit Musaylimah b. Ḥabīb

---

23 Al-Maydānī, Abū l-Faḍl, *Maǧmaʿ al-amṯāl*, Hg. ʿUmar Ḥusayn al-Ḥaššāb, Bde. 1-2, 1896 o.O., hier Bd. 2, S. 313.

feierte, weswegen ihre Sündhaftigkeit sprichwörtlich wurde, darüber hinaus galt sie als sprichwörtliche Lügnerin, da sie behauptete, eine Prophetin zu sein.[24]

Neben seinen eigenen gibt Ibn Abī Ḥaǧalah auch Gedichte anderer Dichter zum Besten, wobei er oft nicht einen kompletten Vers zitiert, sondern nur Halbverse bzw. Anspielungen, die auf ein Gedicht hinweisen. Zu ersteren gehört zum Beispiel der Halbvers *fa-lammā štadda sāʿiduhū ramāh* „als sein Arm erstarkt war, schoss er ihn [Sultan Ḥasan] ab" am Anfang der Makame, der aus der berühmten Kasside *fa-yā ʿaǧaban li-man rabbaytu ṭiflan* des vorislamischen Dichters Maʿn b. Aws stammt. Der vollständige Vers bei diesem lautet *uʿallimuhu r-rimāyata kulla yawmin / fa-lammā štadda sāʿiduhu ramānī* „Ich bringe ihm jeden Tag das Schießen bei / doch als sein Arm erstarkt war, schoss er mich ab".

Textedition

Basierend auf der einzigen erhaltenen Handschrift der Makame folgt nun die Edition des Texts. In Ermangelung anderer Handschriften war ich dazu gezwungen, bei unklaren Stellen interpretierend einzugreifen, was ich jeweils in den Anmerkungen vermerke. Die Zahl in Klammern verweist auf die Numerierung der Folios der Handschrift.

Punkte unter dem *yā*, das Punkt auf dem *dāl* und *ṭā*, sowie das *tā marbūṭah* habe ich nach eigenem Ermessen und den gängigen Schreibkonventionen gesetzt, da der Schreiber hier wie andere in vielen alten Handschriften grundsätzlich willkürlich verfährt. Ebenso wurde das Ende der Kola nach lautlichen Gesichtspunkten modifiziert, was häufig das Hamza betrifft: so wird zum Beispiel *ḫaṭaʾ* ohne *hamza* geschrieben, damit es mit *qaṭā* reimt; ebenso wurde verfahren, wenn *hamza* in der Mitte des Worts steht, wie bei *ḍān* anstelle von *ḍaʾn*. Diese und ähnliche Fälle werden nicht gesondert in den Fußnoten vermerkt.

(٢) بِسْمِ اللَّهِ الرَّحْمَنِ الرَّحِيمِ وبه نستعين

قال الشيخ الإمام شهاب الدين بن أبي جحلة الهُمام * حكى الساجع بن حمام * قال بينا أنا بالقاهرة أيام هرجها * واستيلاء الخوارج على دخلها وخرجها * أعاين قلب الأعيان * وحوادث الحِدثان * فأثور بنظرة[25] الثائر * وأفر من المقصوص والطائر * لا أتوقف عند صورة * ولا أقف بباب مقصورة * خوف الافتتان ودَوَران الزمان * وما الدهر إلا مجنون بأهله * وصادق الوعد والوعيد في قوله وفعله.

---

24 Vacca, V., „Sadjāḥ", in: EI[2] und al-Maydānī, *Maǧmaʿ*, Bd. 2, S. 276.
25 In der Hs. نضرة.

(من الطويل)

فكيف يرى الإنسان مصرع من مضى   ويــركن في الدنيــا إلى ظلــم ظالم

ويأوي إلى جلبـان مصر وقد بغوا   وعمّـوا الـورى فيهـا بخطف العمـائم

وكان واصل حبلهم * ورائش نبلهم * قد عمّه السلطان بإنعامه * وجعله كنانة سهامه * فلما اشتدّ ساعده رماه * ومن يصنع المعروف مع غير أهله * يلاقي كما لاقى مجير أم عامر * ففتك بالناصر * واستولى على ملكه الظاهر * فمنع الوسن * وفعل القبيح بالحسن * فعجّل بهلكه * وشارك المنصور في ملكه * فاستقل بأكثر الأمر * وأقسم بعمره زيد وعمرو * وكان للسلطان الإسم وله الفعل والحرف * وللإمام الخطبة والسكة وله الضرب (٣) والصرف * فأكثر من النقدين * والتقف الملك باليدين * وأخذ في تكثير خِلفِه * والبحث عن حتفه بظلفه * فأكثر من الجلب النجس * والكيل البخس * ولا سيما من الجلبان * ورعيته رُعيان الجوبان

(من الطويل)

فما زال شادّ الملك يرضع ثديه   ويجلبه مـن أرض مصـر إلى حلب

وينشي من الجلبان ما فيه حتفه   فيا بئس ما أنشأ ويا بئس ما جلب

فكان بهم يقوم ويقعد * ويبرق ويرعد * فلمع برق الخلّب * وركب جواد جهله المركب * فاتخذ الجهل علما * وأملى عليه إنما نملي لهم ليزدادوا إثما * فخرق الإجماع * وقطع الإقطاع * وأمر بتلقي الركبان * من الجلبان * ونهى عن طاعة السلطان * فأدبر وتولّى * فيما تولاه * وقطع لسانا يشهد أن لا إله إلا الله * فكم قاده لفعله أذاه * وقال في نفسه وما له واه واه * وأتى في إغراق العامة بالطامه * واهتمّ بفعل كل شيطان وهامّه * فلم يزل ست سنين يخفض ويرفع * ويبدد ويجمع * ويصل ويقطع * ويضر وينفع * ويعطي ويمنع * لا جودا أو كرما * ولا وجودا ولا عَدَما * لكنه خطرات من وساوسه * وتتبعات أذى من هواجسه

قال الساجع بن حمام فلما سعى (٤) في حتفه * وضرب دينار صرفه * أخذ في أخذ أعوانه * ونقض بنيانه * فقعد تحت حائطه المائل * واحتوشته من غيلانه الغوائل * فبينما هو بالجيزة أذ طرقته الطوارق * وفرّ فرار الأوابق * فانساب في البحر كالسمك هاربا * ولاذ بذي النون إذ ذّهب مغاضبا * فلما جاوز²⁶ البحر واستقر * وسلطن سلطانا بهذا البر * خانته أعوانه * ونعقت بالبين غربانه * فسُقط في

---

²⁶ جاور.

يديه * ومالت بسيوف مماليكنا عليه * وأخذه الله من الجانب الذي يأمن إليه * فكان تدبيره في تدميره * وقصر عمره لطول تقصيره

(من الطويل)

إذا لم يكن عون من الله للفتى   فأوَّل ما يجني عليه اجتهاده

فأصبح من المزبلة إلى القبور * ما بين جار ومجرور * قد استوفت فيه عملها العوامل * وأيقن بجنون مماليكه كل عاقل * فسقط نجمه حين تساقطت النجوم * وحكم بموته الحي القيوم * فذبحته التيوس كالضان * ولم ينتطح في الكبش عنزان * ثم نُهبت حواصله * وقطع واصله * وفي أثناء ذلك أخذت الجلبان الجار بالجار * فجاسوا[27] خلال الديار * فكم غرقوا غرفا * وتركوا قاعةً صفوف قاعاً صفصفا * فنهبوا وسَط المدينة وسْط النهار * وشربوا الخمرة في المسجد بالقناديل الكبار * وما بعد هذا المنكر ما نذكر * فمن شاء (٥) فليؤمن ومن شاء فليكفر * وكنت ممن شاهد ذلك هنالك * واستعاذ بالأولياء من أولآئك * فما صحوا من سكرهم * حتَّى ازدادت اليهود كفرا إلى كفرهم * فكان لهدم كنيستهم الغبراء * وقليل في حقهم البصراء * فكفرت اليهود * وربِّكَ المعبود * فكثر السبّ والسلب * والغصب والنهب والضرب

(من الوافر)

لموتــة يبلغـا في مـصرَ نهــبٌ   كــما نُهبـت بـه حالَ الحياة

وبان له وقد شحطوه[28] كعبٌ   مشومٌ في الحيـاة وفي المـمات[29]

قال الساجع بن حمام ومن هنا فُتح باب الشر * واستمر * فلم تزلْ عقاربهم تدُبّ * وريح المريس تهبّ * فأفشوا المنكرات * وتطرَّقوا إلى النساء في الأزقات * فعمَّت المصيبة العوام * وقيل إنهم إلا كلأنعام * يساقون إلى الموت وهم ينظرون * إنا لله وإنا إليه راجعون * آي لياليهم إدلهمَّت * ومائدةٌ قعدتْ عليها الشياطين وما سمَّت * فقلَّت بركتها * وكثرت تَرِكَتُها * فزادت النقمة * وزالت النعمة * وأصبحت المسلمون بلا ذمة كالذمّة * وأتى على ذلك شهر بعد شهر * وحين من الدهر * لا يزداد الأمر * غير استيلاء العِبَر * ويمنع أمر السوء المَيَر

---

[27] فجاشوا.

[28] سخطوه.

[29] Im Diwan führt dieses Gedicht die Nr. 74, Ibn Abī Ḥaǧalah, Šihābaddin, *Dīwān*, Hg. Muǧāhid Muṣṭafā Bahǧat u.a., Amman 2010.

(من البسيط)

فـراح هـذا وراح الـشر يتبعُـه * وجاء هذا وجاء الـشر والنكَد

(٦) ثم عزموا على نهب البلد * وأخذ السَبد واللَبد * فأخذت الناس في تحصين الأزقة * وقصُر الأمل لطول شُقة المشقة * فيا للعجب * من الجلب * ومن كل مملوك أحرّ من الجمر * وأحرم من الخمر * أسرعَ التُرك إلى الخطا * من قول قطاة قطا * أزنى من سَجاح * وأحب من قواد[30] في السِّفاح * لا يفرقون بين الحَيض والطُهر وهم مع ذلك يحكمون على الحكام * ويحجُبون الحجاب عن الأحكام * فهم أجور من سدوم * وأخبارهم كرغيف الحولاء في الشوم

قال الساجع بن حمام * فلما نفذ فيهم السَهْم * ودخلهم الوهْم * وأُسرجت بالليل سروجُهم * وعالجت الرماح علوجهم * فأخذوا في المراء * وأمسكوا بعض الأمراء * فخرجوا عن الطاعة * وتركوا صلاة الجمعة والجماعة * فخلعوا ربقة الإيمان * وتسلطوا على السُلطان * فتسلطوا عليه * وَفَّقوا سهام الخطاء إليه * فبادرت عامة البلد * ولم يتأخر يوم الأحد أحد * فلمّا انصبُّوا من القُلَل[31] * وأقبلوا كالسيْل من الجبل * قعدت لهم العامة بكل مكان * واختلطوا كالعدَس بالجلبان * فرجموهم بالحجارة والشقف * وأشرفوا بسعادة الأشرف * على التلف * وكان شرف الدين خلفهم نعم الخلف * فكم كسروا في ساقتهم من سَاق * ورجموا في الأزقة من الباب إلى الطاق * فأعطوا الأدبار * (٧) وكسرهم الجبار * وقد أخبر بعض العلماء برؤية جند في[32] السماء * كأنهم الطير الأبابيل * ترميهم بحجارة من سجيل * ومصداق هذا الخبر * رؤية هذا الحجر * ونزوله من السماء * وذلك نصرة من الله وحماء

(من الوافر)

أرى أحجـارَ جنـدِ الله تـرمي * مـن الجلبـان كلَّ قـويّ جاش

فكم جبروا بهـا في الجيش قلبًا * وكمْ كسروا بها مـن راس باش[33]

وتوهموا بكرهم النصرُ في كل كرّة * وما كلّ مرة * تسلَم الجرّه * فكُسِرُوا وأُسروا وهَرَبوا انقلبوا[34] * وكلّوا وتعبوا ونُهبُوا * (فذهبوا) كأهل سبا * ودبَّت إليهم العامة كالدَّبا * واستُصحي من مطر نُشَّايهم

---

30 قود.

31 Am Rand steht قلعة الجبل, der Palast des Sultans.

32 Am Rand steht من.

33 Im Diwan führt dieses Gedicht die Nummer 184, Ibn Abī Ḥaǧalah, *Dīwān*, S. 167.

34 انقبوا.

بالأدعية * فأصبحوا على الآكام والظِراب وبطون الأودية * فجيء بهم من الجبال * في الجبال * ومن الآ
كام * كالأنعام * ومن الأودية * في الأرشية * قد بدت سوءاتهم * وتنكرت هيئاتهم * ما بين مَثنىً وثُلاثَ
ورُباعَ * وخمسةٍ سادسُهم * كلُهم السيّءُ الطِباع * قد نتفت العامة رياشَه * وأصبح مع رأس باشهِ في
باشَه * فحلّت دائرة السوء بدُورهم * وهدم ما تطاول مـن قصورهم * ونُبِـت دور البُعد الأقرب
فالأقرب * وكتب على كِسْر أبوابهم * بباب صحيح بحرب[35]

قـال السـاجع ابـن حـمام * وكان أبـو الريـاش ممـن طـار * وانتـصب لرفع الأخبار * فلـما رأى الغبار
ثار * وأصبح كالقنديل في رأس المنار * وأُبْخَر دمِهم بالعين * (٨) وهروبهَم من أين إلى أين * فأخبر عن
مشاهَدَه * ولم يحتج في يدِ ساعدِه * إلى مساعَدَه * لا جرم أنه قال في المجرمين * ونظم من دُرّه الثمين[36]

(من الوافر)

وفاتــــتهم بمــا فعلــوا الـشِطاره	غدا الجلْبان في دست الخساره
سوى خطفُ العمائم والشماره	ولم يُعرف لهـم في مـصر شـيٌ
على ظهر الخيـول من المهاره	يـرون التيــه أن ركبـوا بمـصر
جميعـــا كـارة مــن بعـد كاره	وكم دار بمــــصر كـــــؤّروها
ومـا كتبـوا لإصطبل إجاره	وكم جـــاروا بمنـــع كـــراء دار
وكم شـنّوا على الطرقـات غاره	وكم غارت بهم من عين شخص
وخيـر مـن خيارهم خيـاره	وكم خرقوا السـياج إلى المقاتي[37]
ولكـن بعـدما خربـوا[38] دياره	وكم مـن زرع فـلاح رعـوه
ولكـن بعـدما شربـوا جُراره[39]	وكم من شـارب جرّوه جـرّا
ولا ســيّما إذا ركبـوا حـماره	وكم ركـب المكـاري الذل مـنهم

---

[35] Das *bi-* in *bi-bābin ṣaḥīḥun bi-ḥarb* („frei zum Bekriegen/ Plündern") bezieht sich auf das *kutiba* im Kolon davor. Der dem *bi-* folgende Ausdruck wurde nämlich auf die Seiten der Wände geschrieben, siehe Übersetzung weiter unten.

[36] Das folgende Gedicht hat im Diwan die Nummer 126, Ibn Abī Ḥaǧalah, *Dīwān*, S. 126-7.

[37] Im Diwan المغازي.

[38] حرثوا.

[39] Nicht im Diwan.

وكم فجروا ببنت[40] وابن ناس   إذا انقضّوا وكم فضّوا بكاره

وكم من حاكم حكموا عليه   وكم أخذوا لأنفسهم إماره

فما جاروا على السلطان إلا   وكان الله حافظه وجاره

حماه الله في مصر وأعلى   بها في أفق جامعها مناره

ودار الجيشُ ليلا وهو فيه   كبدر طالع في وسط داره

(٩) مليكٌ بات[41] منه الملك غضا   وليس له نظير في النضاره[42]

لئن ربح الثنا في أهل مصر   فما خسرت لمادحه تجاره

ولا ربحت رؤوس محاربيه   سوى كَسْرُ الجميع على الحراره

فأطفأ نار حربهم جميعا   وما بقيت لجمرهم[43] شراره

لئن شقّوا العصا بغيا عليه   فما شَقّوا وقد ركبوا غباره

وإن طاروا زرافات إليه   فما بلغت صقورهم[44] مطاره

أتوا كالنيل[45] جريا وهو بحر   فما بلغوا بساحله قراره

أشار إلى العوام وقال هيا   فكان النصر في تلك الإشاره

فما[46] حملوا على الأكتاف لمّا   رموهم غير حملات الحجاره

فامسوا بعدما كُسِروا وولّوا   حَيَارَى هاربين بكل حاره

فجيء بهم عراة كلهم ما[47]   عليهم من ستائرهم ستاره

رؤوسهم من الأحجار تدمي   وقد فتحت كما فتحت كِوَاره

فكم من باشة[48] في رأس باشٍ[49]   يرى طول الطريق بها الجراره[50]

---

40 ببيت.

41 مات.

42 Im Diwan وروضة مصرَ كم أبدت زهاره.

43 لجمرتهم.

44 قصورهم.

45 كالسيل.

46 فلما.

47 عرايا ماكليهم.

48 باسة.

49 باس.

50 انجراره.

فصلّب يا مليــك الأرض مـنهم   على أعلى الجسور ذوي الخساره[51]

وطهّــر مــنهم الدنيا جميعًــا   فغــالبهم تــراه بـــلا طهـــاره

فلــو دار الزمــان بهــم[52] أداروا   بهــا دور العلــوم لهــا[53] ديــاره

قال الساجع بن حمام فلمّا كان ما كان * من دور الزمان * في طحن الجلبان (١٠) * وُجد بعضُ أنجاسهم بلا طهارة * وسترت عورته بعد أن رُجم بالحجاره *

فقلت (من الوافر)

أرى الجلبــانَ يا ســلطانُ غُلْفــاً[54]   وفِعْلُهم غــدا فعــلا شــنيعاً

وفي فعــل الختــان لهــم طهــورا   فطَهِّــرْهُم مــن الدنيــا جميعــاً[55]

وقلت (من الوافر)

خــذ الجلبــان يا مــلك البــرايا   فقد خرجوا عن الأمر الشريفِ

وفيــهم مــن كلاب الــروم غلــف   فطهــرهم ولكــن بالــسيوفِ

فأخــذوا أخــذة رابيــة * وفعــل بهــم مــا اقتضته الآراء العاليــة * وأُمر بتوسـيط أوسـاطهم * وأخذ رؤوس بأشـاتهم * وصلــب كل أثنـين على جمـل * فكان جزاؤهم من جنس العمـل * فجرى دمهم كالمـاء في مجاريه * وجعل الأخ يواري * سوأة أخيه * فظهرت علائم النصر وتبيّنت * وأمر بالمدينة فأخذت * زخرفها وزِيّنت[56] * وفرّح الناس * وزال لباس البأس * فأصبحت العامة سالمين غانمين * وقطع دابر القوم الذين ظلموا والحمد لله رب العالمين * تم ذلك على يد الفقير عمر الدمياطي الشافعي عام سبعين وثمانمائة * وعلقه بيده الفانية أقل عباد الله وأحوجهم إلى عفوه * ومغفرته الفقير محمّد بن زين الدين الحموي يوم الأحد المبارك سادس جمادى الأولى سنة ١٠٣٠ * والحمد لله فعله

---

51   الجساره.

52   لهم.

53   لهم.

54   فظيعاً.

55   Im Diwan trägt dieses Gedicht die Nummer 213 auf Seite 178. Vgl. hierzu auch den letzten Vers des langen Gedichts oben.

56   وازينت.

Übersetzung des Texts

Der hin und wieder anzutreffenden *tawriyah* (*double-entendre*) trage ich so Rechnung, dass ich die primäre Bedeutung kursiv setze und die sekundäre, d.h. implizierte, Bedeutung unterstreiche. Die Zahlen in Klammern bezeichnen die Nummer des Folios.

(2) Im Namen Gottes des Barmherzigen des Allerbarmers, Den wir um Hilfe anrufen.

Es sagte der hochehrwürdige Meister Šihābaddīn b. Abī Ḥaǧalah al-Humām * es erzählte as-Sāǧiʿ b. Ḥamām (der Gurrende, Sohn der Taube) * Er sagte: Ich war in Kairo, als Tumulte herrschten * und Aufständische im Inneren und Äußeren ihr Unwesen trieben * Ich sah, wie hochstehende Würdenträger gestürzt wurden * und Dinge passierten, über die noch lange geredet wird * Ich war beunruhigt, wegen des Anblicks des Aufbegehrenden * und floh sogar vor den Vögeln, ob sie nun fliegen konnten oder nicht (ob sie gestutzt waren) * ich blieb bei keiner Gestalt stehen * noch an *einer geschlossenen Tür*/ Bāb Maqṣūrah (Tür des Herrschers für den abgetrennten Betsaal des Herrschers in der Moschee) * aus Angst vor Zwietracht und den Wechselfällen des Lebens * Das Schicksal ist unberechenbar, wenn es um seine Schützlinge geht und erfüllt jedes Versprechen und jede Drohung wegen dem, was er gesagt und getan.

(Gedicht) Wie kann der Mensch den Tod der vergangenen Generationen sehen / und sich trotzdem auf dieser Welt auf das Unrecht eines Tyrannen stützen // und bei den *ġulbān* von Ägypten Zuflucht suchen, wo sie doch gerade ihr Unwesen treiben / und die Menschen in Ägypten bedrängen, indem sie den Religionsgelehrten ihre Turbane rauben?

Dieser [Yalbuġā] war ihr vereinendes Band * er stattete ihre Pfeile mit Federn aus * Dabei hatte der Sultan ihn mit seinen Wohltaten überschüttet * und ihn zum Köcher seiner Pfeilen gemacht * Doch als sein Arm erstarkt war, hat er ihn [Sultan Ḥasan] abgeschossen * So ist es eben. (Gedichtvers:) „Wer jemandem, der ihm nicht nahesteht etwas Gutes tut, der kriegt nur Undank. Ihm widerfährt das, was auch dem Helfer der Hyäne widerfahren war"[57] * denn er brachte darauf den Sultan an-Nāṣir [Beiname Sultan Ḥasans] um * und bemächtigte sich seines glorreichen [*ẓāhir* = mamlukisches Epitheton] Königtums * und raubte [allen Menschen] den Schlaf * Er vergalt *Gutes mit Schlechtem*/ fügte Ḥasan Schlimmes zu * und machte sich eilig dran, ihn [Ḥasan an-Nāṣir] zu vernichten * und al-Manṣūrs [Ṣalāḥaddīn Muḥammad 762–764/1361–1363] Herrschaft zu teilen * so dass er schließlich in vielen Belangen eigenmächtig schaltete und waltete * Hinz und Kunz

---

[57] Sprichwörtliches Gedicht, al-Maydānī, *Maǧmaʿ*, Bd. 2, S. 61.

schworen bei ihm * dem Sultan kam der Name[58], das Verb (die Tat) und der Buchstabe zu * und dem Imam das Recht auf die Freitagspredigt sowie der Name auf den Münzen, die Prägung aber gehörte nun Yalbuġā und auch das Inumlaufbringen * (3) Er [Yalbuġā] ließ die beiden Münzsorten [*dinār* und *dirham*] reichlich prägen * nahm die Herrschaft in seine beiden Hände * vermehrte seine üblen Laster und * suchte den Tod mit seiner Hufe[59] * dann beschaffte er sich unreines Gesindel * und erwarb mit falschen Gewichten * insbesondere brachte er diese *ġulbān* * sein Volk grobschlächtiger Hirten.[60]

(Gedicht:) Dabei ernährte der Verweser [Yalbuġā] sich noch von seinem Busen [des Königtums] / und molk es von Ägypten bis nach Aleppo // wo er *ġulbān* heranzüchtete / die dann schließlich seinen Tod herbeibringen sollten

Er herrschte über sie nach Belieben * und ließ seinen Groll an ihnen mit Blitz und Donner aus * wobei es nur das Aufleuchten eines wirkungslosen verpuffenden Blitzes war * Dann stieg er auf *das mit Steigbügeln versehene Pferd seiner Torheit/* dann bestieg er das Pferd seiner äußersten Torheit * und sah die Dummheit als Klugheit an * Ihm wurde mehr Zeit gegeben, aber nur „damit ihre Sünden vermehrt würden"[61] * So zerriss er den Konsens der Gemeinschaft * schnitt die althergebrachte Lehensvergabe ab * befahl, dass manche *ġulbān* * zu Reitern werden sollten * und verbat, dem Sultan zu huldigen * wandte sich ab[62] * von dem ihm Anvertrauten * Er schnitt die Zungen all jener ab, die den *tawḥīd* aussprachen * Wie oft leitete ihn das Leid, das er [anderen] zufügte * wodurch er sich bereicherte und sagte: Oh wie schön! * Danach begann er, die Menschen in einer Flut des Unheils zu ertränken[63] * und sich wie Teufel und Gewürm zu verhalten[64] * Sechs Jahre lang erniedrigte und erhöhte er * verstreute und versammelte * verband und trennte * schadete und nützte * gab und enthielt anderes vor * doch nicht aus Freigebigkeit noch Großmut * noch aus Reichtum oder Armut * aber aus den Hirngespinsten seiner teuflischen Einflüsterungen * und dem fortdauernden Leid, das seinen inneren Regungen entsprang.

Es erzählte as-Sāǧiʿ b. Ḥamām : Als er dann auf seinen Tod hinstrebte (4) * und den Dinar seines *Abgangs/* seines Inumlaufbringens prägte * fing er an, seine Hel-

---

[58] *Bi-l-ism* gegen *bi-l-bāṭin*, siehe Steenbergen, *Reassessment*, S. 427; basierend auf Ibn Ḥaǧar al-ʿAsqalānī.

[59] Er grub sich, ohne dass er es wüsste, sein eigenes Grab, wie es Schafe tun, die ohne es zu wissen, ein Messer ausgraben (*ḫatfahā tabḥat̲ ḍaʾn bi-aẓlāfihā* „das Schaf scharrt mit seinen Hufen nach seinem Tod", al-ʿAskarī, Abū Hilāl, *Ǧamharat al-amt̲āl*, Hg. Muḥammad Abū-l Faḍl Ibrāhīm, Bde. 1-2, Kairo 1988, Bd. 1, S. 363).

[60] Das Wort *ǧūbān* ist eine Entlehnung aus dem türk. *çoban* „Hirte".

[61] *Āl ʿImrān*, 178.

[62] *Maʿāriǧ*, 15.

[63] Das Wort *aṭ-ṭāmmah* ist möglicherweise eine Anspielung auf *Nāziʿāt*, 34.

[64] Womöglich eine Anspielung auf das *ḥadīt̲* „*lā ʿadwā wa-lā ṭayrah wa-lā hāmmah wa-lā ṣafar*", Muslim b. Ḥaǧǧāǧ, *Ṣaḥīḥ Muslim*, Hg. Naẓar b. Muḥammad al-Fāryābī, Riad 2006, S. 1057, Nr. 2220.

fer zu ergreifen * und das, was er aufgebaut hatte, zu zerstören * Er saß somit unter seiner Wand, die einzustürzen drohte * Das Unglück (*ġāʾila*, Pl. *ġawāʾil*) der Dämonen, die er gerufen hatte, zäunte ihn ein * Und als er dann in Ǧīzah war, ereilte ihn das Unheil * so dass er die Flucht ergriff wie ein Sklave, der sich seinem Meister entzieht * bis er einem entfliehenden Fisch gleich in den Fluss hinabrauschte * und mit all seiner Wut bei dem vom Meer Schutz suchte[65] * Als er nämlich dann das Wasser überquerte, auf dem Festland [dem anderen Ufer] Position bezog[66] * und sich als Sultan gebärdete auf diesem Land * verrieten ihn seine Helfer * und es bekrähten seine Raben die Trennung (*ġurāb al-bayn*) * es war nunmehr um ihn geschehen[67] * Unsere Mamluken wandten sich gegen ihn mit Schwertern * und Gott erwischte ihn an einer Stelle in der er sein Vertrauen gesetzt hatte[68] * Denn Er hatte beschlossen, ihn zu vernichten * und sein Leben zu kürzen wegen seiner unendlichen Vergehen * (Gedicht:) Wenn die Hilfe nicht von Gott kommt für den Recken (*fatā*) / dann ist das erste, was ihm schadet, sein Streben[69] * Denn er ging vom Düngerhaufen ins Grab * *zog und wurde gezogen/ war ein ǧārr und ein maǧrūr* * Die *Faktoren/* Regenten haben mit ihm ihre *Funktion/* die grammatische Funktion voll erfüllt [oder] *die Speerspitzen haben an ihm volle Arbeit geleistet/* die Faktoren [die zu seinem Tod führten] haben ihre Funktion an ihm voll erfüllt[70] * und jeder, der ein bisschen Verstand hatte, konnte sicher sein, dass seine Mamluken des Wahnsinns waren * So stürzte dann sein Stern als die Funken [der gekreuzten Schwerter] fielen (als die Sterne nacheinander herunterfielen) * und Gott, der Ewiglebende und Ewigwährende verfügte seinen Tod * die Böcke schlachteten ihn wie ein Schaf * *über den Widder [wohl Yalbuġā] war der Stab gebrochen/* noch nicht einmal zwei [schwache] Ziegen kämpfen wegen

---

[65]　*Al-Anbiyāʾ*, 87.

[66]　Anspielung auf *al-Aʿrāf*, 138 und *Yūnus*, 90.

[67]　*Al-Aʿrāf*, 149.

[68]　Anspielung auf das Sprichwort *min maʾmanihi yuʾtā al-ḥaḏir*, al-ʿAskarī, *Ǧamharat*, Bd. 2, S. 271.

[69]　Sprichwörtlicher Vers, der ʿAlī b. Abī Ṭālib zugeschrieben wird. Das Wort *fatā* wird im allgemeinen mit ihm in Verbindung gebracht wie in dem Ausspruch *lā fatā illā ʿAlī, lā sayfa illā Ḏū-l-fiqār* = „kein Recke wie ʿAlī kein Schwert wie *Ḏū l-fiqār* (der Name seines Schwerts).

[70]　Die Begriffe *ǧārr* („ins Genitiv setzend"), *maǧrūr* („ins Genitiv gesetzt"), *ʿamal* („grammatische Funktion bzw. Dependenz") und *ʿawāmil* („Regenten") aus den letzten beiden Kola entstammen der Fachsprache der Grammatiker. Es liegt hier demnach ein *double entendre* in der Form eines *tawǧīh* vor, wo mehrere Begriffe, die einem speziellen Bereich (Wissenschaft, Kunst, Handwerk etc.) angehören, in doppelter Bedeutung angewendet werden. Die erste, fachspezifische Bedeutung (in diesem Fall die der grammatischen Begriffe) ist dabei für den Kontext nicht weiter relevant. In dem letzten Kolon liegt ein besonderer Fall vor, da *ʿawāmil* neben der grammatischen Bedeutung als grammatischer Terminus („Regenten") und der allgemeinen Bedeutung („Umstände, Faktoren") auch „Speerspitzen" heißen kann. Zwischen den beiden letzten Bedeutungen besteht also eine Beziehung, wie wir sie von einer einfachen *tawriyah* kennen.

al-Kabš [die Zitadelle Yalbuġās in Kairo][71] * Darauf wurden seine Läger geplündert * und man ließ ihn im Stich * Währenddessen begannen die *ġulbān* ihren Plünderzug * brandschatzten[72] die Häuser * In wie viele Zimmer sind sie doch eingebrochen * und haben leere Flächen hinterlassen, da wo Seminarsäle waren * Sie plünderten mitten in der Stadt, am helllichten Tag * tranken Wein in der Moschee aus den großen Lampengläsern * und anderes Verachtungswürdiges, das über das hinausgeht, was ich hier erwähne * (5) Wer es glaubt, möge es denn glauben, und wer nicht, möge es leugnen * Ich war jemand, der dies an jenem Orte gesehen * und die Heiligen wegen diesen [*ġulbān*] um Hilfe ersucht hat * Diese Leute wachten nicht auf aus ihrem Suff * bis auch die Juden ihrem Frevel weiteren Frevel hinzugefügt hatten * was das Niederreißen ihrer „erdfarbenen"(?) Synagoge zur Folge hatte * und wenige waren jene, die wussten, was es mit ihnen auf sich hatte * So frevelten also die Juden * ja, bei Gott! * Schmähung, Raub * Überfall, Plünderung und Gewalt griffen mehr und mehr um sich.

(Gedicht:) Wegen dem Tod Yalbuġās plündert man in Ägypten / so wie es geplündert wurde, als er noch am Leben war //

Der Würfel war gefallen, man hatte ihn durch die Stadt geschleift / vom Unglück verfolgt war er im Leben wie im Tod

Es erzählte as-Sāǧiʿ b. Ḥamām * Die Büchse der Pandora (das Tor des Bösen) stand nun offen * und blieb auch lange offen * ihre Skorpione krabbelten noch lange herum * und der Wind des Marīs zog auf * Sie brachten das Böse hervor * stellten den Frauen in den Gassen nach * das Unglück brach über die Allgemeinheit aus * Es heißt ja auch, dass sie nur wie Vieh sind[73] * das sehenden Auges in den Tod getrieben wird[74] * so wie es auch im Koran steht: Wir sind Gottes und zu ihm kehren wir zurück[75] * als die Zeichen ihrer Nächte finster wurden[76] und die Teufel sich an den Tisch[77] setzten, ohne den Namen Gottes zu

---

71 Ein geflügeltes Wort *lā yantaṭihu fihā ʿanzāni* „zwei Ziegen kämpfen deswegen nicht", welches auf ein *ḥadīṯ* zurückgeht (al-ʿAskarī, *Ǧamharat*, Bd. 2, S. 403). Es kommt der deutschen Redewendung „es kräht kein Hahn mehr danach" bzw. „das ist Schnee von gestern" nahe. Dass Ibn Abi Ḥaǧalah hier anstatt des *-hā* in *fihā al-kabš* einsetzt, hängt damit zusammen, dass die Zitadelle Yalbuġās al-Kabš stellvertretend für Yalbuġā selbst steht. Diese besondere *tawriyah* findet sich ebenfalls bei Ibn Taġrībirdī mit Bezug auf die Schlacht des Sultans al-Ašraf gegen Asandamur, dem Atabak nach Yalbuġā, in einem Gedicht von Šihābaddin Aḥmad b. al-ʿAṭṭār (geb. ca. 745/1345, gest. 794/1392) mit dem Unterschied, dass al-ʿAṭṭār *šātāni* sagt anstatt *ʿanzāni* (Ibn Taġrībirdī, *an-Nuǧūm*, Bd. 11, S. 39). Wer von beiden der Urheber dieser Umbildung des bekannten Sprichworts ist, konnte ich nicht ermitteln. Im Folgenden der betreffende Vers von al-ʿAṭṭār: *wa-ahlu kabšin ka-ahli l-fīli qad uḫiḏū / raġman wa-mā ntaṭaḥat fi l-kabši šātāni*, „die Leute *des Widders*/ der Zitadelle al-Kabš wurden überwältigt so wie die ‚Leute des Elefanten' (Anspielung auf *al-Fīl*, 1) / keinen Pfifferling gab man mehr auf al-Kabš."

72 *Al-Isrāʾ*, 5.

73 *Furqān*, 44.

74 *Al-Anfāl*, 6.

75 *Al-Baqarah*, 156.

76 *Āl ʿImrān*, 122.

nennen[78] * wodurch er [der Tisch] mehr und mehr an göttlichem Segen verlor * und seine Reste immer mehr wurden * Unsegen nahm zu * von Gottes Segen war keine Rede mehr * Worauf die Moslems ohne Schutz blieben wie die Schutzbefohlenen * So lief dies monatelang * und eine gewisse Zeit * und es wurde nur schlimmer * *unsere Tränen flossen nur reichlicher/* die belehrenden Beispiele vervielfältigten sich nur * die üble Lage unterband die Versorgung mit Getreide.

(Gedicht:) Dieser verging, und auch sein Übel verging / und dieser [die *ġulbān* sind gemeint] kam – und wieder kamen Übel und Widerwärtigkeiten.[79]

(6) Darauf zogen sie plündernd durchs Land * und nahmen alles, was sie vorfanden, in die Hand * Das Volk begann, die Straßen zu bewehren * Doch konnte ihre Hoffnung nicht lange währen * Oh, wie verwunderlich sind doch diese Herangeschafften * brennender als Kohle[80] noch all ihre Mannschaften * und verbotener als der Wein * Schneller tritt der Türke in den Irrtum ein * als der *qaṭā*-Vogel „*qaṭā!*" sagen kann * selbst Saǧāḫ könnte sündiger [als der Türke] nicht sein * und der Zuhälter nicht eifriger beim Ehebruch[81] * Sie machten keinen Unterschied zwischen Unreinheit (Menstruation) und Reinheit * und dennoch herrschten sie über die Richter * und legten einen Schleier über die schützende Macht der göttlichen Gesetze * dabei waren sie schändlicher als [die Leute von] Sodom[82] * und die Nachrichten, die man von ihnen erhielt, waren so schlimm und unheilbringend wie das Brot der Ḥaulāʾ.[83]

Es erzählte Sāǧiʿ b. Ḥamām: * Als der Pfeil in sie eingedrungen war (als ihr Schicksal besiegelt war) * und Wahnvorstellungen sie übermannt hatten * ihre Sättel in der Nacht auf die Pferde geschnallt wurden * und die Lanzen ihre ungläubigen Berserker (*ʿ ulūǧ*)[84] zu durchbohren[85] drohten * schritten sie zum Kampf * hielten sie einige Amire fest * und ließen ab vom Gehorsam * beteten das Freitagsgebet

---

[77] Möglicherweise Anspielung auf den Namen der Sure *al-Māʾidah*.

[78] Ohne *bismillāh* zu sagen, was die Moslems gewöhnlich sagen, bevor sie mit dem Essen anfangen.

[79] Basierend auf dem letzten Vers eines Gedichts von Diʿbil b. ʿAli al-Ḫuzāʿi, das er zum Tod des Kalifen al-Muʿtaṣim gegen diesen geschrieben hat: *fa-marra hāḏā wa-marra š-šuʾmu yatbaʿuhu / wa-qāma hāḏā fa-qāma š-šuʾmu wa-n-nakadu:* al-Ḫuzāʿi, Diʿbil, *Šiʿr Diʿbil b. ʿAli al-Ḫuzāʿi*, Hg. ʿAbdalkarīm al-Aštar, Damaskus 1983, S. 115-6.

[80] *Aḥarru mina l-ǧamri*, Redewendung: al-ʿAskari, *Ǧamharat al-amṯāl*, Hg. Muḥammad Abū-l Faḍl Ibrāhīm, Bde. 1-2, Kairo 1988, Bd. 1, S. 397-8.

[81] Siehe oben zu den Redewendungen und Sprichwörtern in diesem Absatz.

[82] Al-ʿAskari, *Ǧamharat*, Bd. 1, S. 333.

[83] Al-ʿAskari, *Ǧamharat*, Bd. 1, S. 557.

[84] Nach Dozy: „*homme grossier et sans frein qui s'abandonne à ses passions brutales*". Mit dem Begriff werden auch alle bezeichnet, die ihren Glauben gewechselt haben, vom Islam zum Christentum und umgekehrt: Dozy, *Supplément aux dictionnaires arabes*, Bde. 1-2, Leiden 1881, *s.v.* „ʿilǧ".

[85] *ʿālaǧat* = „*tâcher de pénétrer dans une maison; de vaincre la répugnance de qqn*", Dozy, *Supplément*, *s.v.* „ʿālaǧa".

und die gemeinsamen Gebete nimmer * legten das Band des Glaubens ab * und spielten sich gegenüber dem Sultan selbst als Sultane auf * Als sie sich nun gegen ihn auflehnten * und ihre Pfeile des Irrtums gegen ihn kerbten * stürmte das Volk [des Landes] los * Nicht einer versäumte diesen Sonntag[86] * Als sie dann von den Gipfeln [oder wie am Rand steht, vom Qalʿat al-Ǧabal, d.h. von der herrschaftlichen Zitadelle des Sultans am Ǧabal al-Muqaṭṭam] herunterströmten * und wie eine Flut vorpreschten * stellten sich ihnen die Menschen in den Weg * und mischten sich wie Linsen unter die *ǧulbān*/ Platterbsen * Sie bewarfen diese mit Steinen und Scherben * und durch die *herrschaftliche Glückseligkeit*/ Seligkeit des al-Ašraf[87] * waren sie auch bald am Rande der Vernichtung * *Šarafaddīn*/ Die Ehre der Religion verfolgte sie also * und was für ein großartiger Verfolger bzw. Nachfolger [der Qalawuniden] er doch war! * Wie viele Beine haben sie in ihrem Heeresrücken gebrochen * Überall (vom Tür zum Tor- bzw. Fensterbogen) wurden sie mit Steinen beworfen * So mussten sie dann kehrtmachen (7) * der Allgewaltige zerschlug sie * Ein Gelehrter meldete * dass er eine Heerschaar im [vom] Himmel hinunterstürzen sah [mehrfach im Koran] * ganz wie die Züge (*abābīl*) von Vögeln aus dem Koran * die sie mit Steinen aus Lehm (*siǧǧīl*) bewarfen[88] * Beweis für diese Nachricht ist * dass ich diesen Stein gesehen habe * wie er vom Himmel herabfiel * Das ist Gottes Beistand und sein Schutz.

(Gedicht:) Ich sah wie die Steine des Gottesheeres trafen / von den *ǧulbān* jeden Standhaften[89] //

Manch ein Herz haben sie im [Sultans-]Heer damit geflickt / und manch einen *Kopf* Kompanieführer[90] zerschmettert

Jedes Mal wenn sie zum Angriff bliesen, dachten sie, dieser würde ihnen den Sieg bringen * doch nicht jedes Mal * bleibt der Krug heil [nicht immer kommen sie heil davon] * so kam es, dass sie zerschlagen wurden und in Gefangenschaft gerieten, dass sie wie verirrte Hühner die Flucht ergriffen und völlig umgewälzt wurden * sie wurden müde und schwach * man plünderte sie wie die *ahl as-Sabā* [Sabäer] * das Volk krabbelte unter sie wie Ameisen (bzw. Grashüpfer) * es wurde mit

---

[86] Siehe dazu oben.

[87] Al-Ašraf, Zainaddin Šaʿbān, reg. 764–767/1363–1376. Der Sultan, der nur zehnjährig nach Manṣūr eingesetzt wurde, weil er bequemer war für Yalbuġā. Hier helfen ihm die Einwohner Kairos gegen die außer Kontrolle geratenen *ǧulbān* und ihren Anführer Asandamur al-Ḥaṣṣakī, der viele von ihnen übernommen hatte.

[88] *Al-Fīl*: 3.

[89] *Qawiyyi ǧaʾšī*, eigentlich *rābiṭu l-ǧaʾši* = „unerschütterlich", *ǧaʾš*=„Inneres".

[90] *raʾsbāš* = Eher selten anzutreffender Titel von Befehlshabern über Einheiten von ḥalqa-Mamluken, siehe Steenbergen, *Yalbughā*, S. 126 zitiert aus Ḥalil b. Šāhin aẓ-Ẓāhiri, *Zubdat kašf al-mamālik fi bayān aṭ-ṭuruq wa-l-masālik*: "every one hundred from a thousand [ḥalqah troopers] have a chief (*bāsh*) and a superintendent (*naqīb*)." Das arabische Wort *raʾs* bedeutet „Kopf", genauso wie das türkische Wort *bāš*. Es kann durchaus sein, dass Ibn Abi Ḥaǧalah die Grundbedeutung des türkischen Worts bekannt war und diese Doppelbedeutung („Kopf" vs. „Kompanieführer") beabsichtigte.

Bittgebeten um das Ende des Pfeilregens gebetet, der auf sie herniederging * sie gingen auf die Hügel, in die Einöden und Talsohlen[91] * Schließlich wurden sie vom Berg heruntergeführt, * mit Stricken gefesselt * und von den Hügeln * wie Vieh * und von den Tälern hergeholt * mit Seilen geknebelt * Ihre Schamteile traten zu Tage * und ihre Züge verkamen * doppelt und dreifach, vierfach[92] * oder fünf, deren sechster ein Hund war[93] * ein bösartiger * dem das Volk das Fell über die Ohren gezogen hat * und dessen Hals wie auch das seines Kompanieführers ins Joch[94] gelegt wurde * Jetzt waren ihre Häuser dran * Ihre mächtigen, hohen Paläste fielen zusammen * Alle Häuser wurden geplündert, erst die ferneren, dann die näheren und die nächsten[95] * auf die Seiten ihrer Türen wurde geschrieben: * „frei zum Bekriegen/ Plündern"

Es sagte as-Sāǧiʿ b. Ḥamām * Abū r-Riyāš war einer von jenen, die loszogen * und sich dran machten, die Nachricht zu verbreiten * als er sah, wie der Staub aufgewirbelt * wie die Lampe auf einem Leuchtturm wurde * und als er mit eigenen Augen die Flüsse ihres Bluts sah * (8) und ihre Flucht von hier nach da * erzählte er, was er mit eigenen Augen gesehen * und hatte dabei keine Hilfe nötig * Ohne Zweifel erzählte er von den Verbrechern * und reihte seine kostbaren Perlen:

1. Die *ǧulbān* gerieten auf den absteigenden Ast / bei dem was sie getan haben, half ihnen auch Schläue nicht weiter

2. In Ägypten kennt man sie nur vom / Turbanerauben und wütendem Treiben

3. *Sie erdreisteten sich, in Ägypten / auf dem Rücken von Pferdefüllen (al-ḫuyūl min al-mahārah) herumzureiten* [oder] In ihrem Hochmut ritten sie in Ägypten / auf Pferden und meinten es wäre eine Kunst (*mahārah*)

4. Wie viele Häuser haben sie in Ägypten niedergerissen[96]/ Haufen auf Haufen

5. Wie oft haben sie Unrecht geübt, indem sie die Miete für ein Haus verweigert haben / und für keinen Stall Pachtzins geleistet haben

6. Wie viele Augen sind durch sie in ihren Höhlen verschwunden [wie viele Menschen sind gestorben / evtl. Wortspiel mit *ǧāra*=„neiden"] / wie viele Wege haben sie mit Überfällen überzogen

---

91 Dieser Satz geht zurück auf das *ḥadīṯ: Allāhumma ḥawlanā wa-lā ʿalaynā. Allāhumma ʿalā l-ākāmi wa-ẓ-ẓirābi wa-buṭūni l-awdiyati wa-manābiti š-šaǧari*, Muslim, *Ṣaḥīḥ*, S. 397-8.

92 *An-Nisāʾ*, 3. Der Koranvers bezieht sich auf die Heirat von Frauen.

93 *Al-Kahf*, 22.

94 *bāšah*=„anneau garni d'un bouton et d'une boutonnière, qu'on met au bout d'une chaîne et qui entoure le pied de la bête de somme quand on l'attache; collier qu'on met au cou des criminels", Dozy, *Supplément, s.v.* „bāšah".

95 Basiert auf einem *ḥadīṯ*, Muslim, *Ṣaḥīḥ*, S. 1186-7.

96 *At-Takwīr*, 1.

7. Wie oft haben sie die Gartenmauern durchbrochen, um in die Kürbisgärten [wörtl. „Gurkengärten"] zu kommen / dabei ist eine Gurke [was auch „Pestbeule" bedeutet] besser als die Besten von ihnen

8. Wieviel Saaten eines Bauern haben sie abgeweidet / doch davor zerstörten sie sein Haus

9. Wieviel Trinker haben sie [aus den Schankhäusern] gezerrt / doch nicht ohne vorher selbst manch einen Krug getrunken zu haben

10. Wie oft musste der Lasttiervermieter/Eselvermieter sich von ihnen erniedrigen lassen (die Erniedrigung reiten) / und insbesondere, wenn sie einen Esel bestiegen

11. Wie oft haben sie sich an Mädchen und Burschen vergangen / als sie angriffen und wie viele Jungfrauen haben sie geschändet

12. Wie viele Richter haben sie gerichtet / wie oft haben sie sich zu Amīren erklärt

13. Immer wenn sie dem Sultan Unrecht getan haben / war Gott sein Wächter und Helfer

14. Möge Gott ihn in Kairo beschützen und dort / am Horizont ihrer Moschee ein Minarett errichten

15. Das Heer läuft nächtens auf mit ihm in seinen Reihen / wie ein aufgehender Mond in seinem Mondhof

16. Ein König, durch den das Königreich wieder frisch [erneuert] wurde / keiner kommt ihm gleich in Frische

17. Wenn in Ägypten Lobpreis Gewinn brächte / dann blühte das Geschäft seines Preisenden

18. Die Kompanieführer seiner Feinde gewannen nichts / außer das ihre Schädel im hitzigen Gefecht zerschlagen wurden

19. Er hat das Feuer ihrer Wut gelöscht / und so blieb ihrer Glut kein Funken (bzw. keine Bosheit) mehr

20. Wenn sie Unfrieden stiften und sich gegen ihn auflehnen / bekommen sie nichts hin[97]

21. Auch wenn sie ihm in Scharen Zehnertrupps entgegenflogen / ihre Falken konnten gar nicht fliegen

---

[97] Dies ist ein Ausdruck, der an folgende Wendung angelehnt ist: *ṭalaba fulānan wa-mā šaqqa ġubārahu*=„er versuchte jemanden zu kriegen, aber er schaffte es nicht, seinen Staub zu spalten", vgl. Lane, Edward William, *An Arabic-English Lexicon*, Bde. 1-8, Beirut 1968, *s.v.* „ġubār".

22. Sie kamen in Strömen wie ein Fluss, wobei er [der Sultan] aber ein Meer ist, / an dessen Ufer sie keinen Halt finden konnten

23. Er gab dem Volk ein Zeichen und sagte: Los! / der Sieg lag in der Tat in diesem Zeichen

24. Nichts anderes trugen sie auf ihren Schultern / als Ladungen von Steinen die sie auf sie warfen

25. Sie verschwanden, nachdem sie zerschlagen wurden, machten kehrt / verwirrt verzogen sie sich in alle möglichen Viertel

26. Doch zerrte er sie nackt zurück, alle waren sie / entblößt, sie hatten nichts was sie bedecken konnte

27. Ihre Köpfe bluten von dem Einschlag der Steine / die gelöchert waren wie ein Bienenstock

28. Wie viele Joche wurden um den Kopf der Kompanieführer gelegt / der dann den ganzen Weg entlang geschleift wurde

29. Kreuzige, oh Herr dieser Erde, von ihnen / auf die Spitze der Brücken die Übeltäter (die Dreisten)

30. Säubere die Erde von ihnen gänzlich / denn die meisten von ihnen sind ohnehin unrein (unbeschnitten)

31. Auch wenn das Schicksal ihnen mal hold war / die Häuser des Wissens drehen lassen (...)[98]

Es erzählte as-Sāǧiᶜ b. Ḥamām * als geschah, was geschah * von den Wechselfällen der Zeiten * was die Zermalmung der *ǧulbān* betrifft * fand man einen ihrer Unreinen, der unbeschnitten war * so wurde dann seine Scham verdeckt durch die Steine, mit denen er beworfen wurde.

Dann sagte ich:

Ich sah die *ǧulbān*, oh Sultan, unbeschnitten / und ihre Art zu handeln wurde hässlich //

Der Akt der Beschneidung ist eine Reinigung für sie / und die Bereinigung der Welt von ihnen allen

Und ich sagte:

Greif dir die *ǧulbān*, oh Herr der Schöpfung / denn sie missachteten den ehrenvollen Befehl //

unter ihnen sind unbeschnittene Hunde aus Byzanz / beschneiden kann man sie nur mit Schwertern

---

[98] Es ist mir nicht klar, was mit dem zweiten Halbvers gemeint ist.

Da wurden sie dann in großer Zahl ergriffen * und er machte mit ihnen, was die hehren Ansichten so verlangten * er befahl, dass ihre Mitten halbiert werden * und ihre Kompanieführer geköpft * Paarweise wurden sie auf einem Kamel gehängt [?][99] * Denn ihre Strafe entsprach der Art [ihres] Wirkens[100] * ihr Blut floss wie das Wasser in seinen Läufen * ein jeder versuchte * das Schlechte seines Bruders zu verbergen * Doch die Zeichen des Sieges erschienen * Dann befahl er * dass man die Stadt schmückte und verzierte * er erfreute die Menschen * und zog ihnen das dunkle Gewand des Unglücks aus * Die Menschen gingen gesund und mit Gewinn aus der Situation heraus * Derjenige, der die Geschicke der Menschen lenkt, hat die Bösen getötet * dem Gott der Welten sei dafür gedankt

Dies wurde von der Hand des Bedürftigen ʿUmar ad-Dimyāṭī aš-Šāfiʿī im Jahre 870/1465 [also ungefähr ein Jahrhundert nach Ibn Abī Ḥaǧalah] angefertigt, und der Geringste der Diener Gottes, dem seine Gnade und Barmherzigkeit not tut, der Bedürftige Muḥammad b. Zayn ad-Dīn al-Ḥamawī hat es am heiligen Sonntag, dem 6. des Monats Ǧumādā l-Ūlā des Jahres 1030/ 29. März 1621 mit seiner vergänglichen Hand kommentiert * Dank sei Gott, Er hat es vollbracht.

Literaturverzeichnis

al-ʿAskarī, Abū Hilāl, *Ǧamharat al-amṯāl*, Hg. Muḥammad Abū-l Faḍl Ibrāhīm, Bde. 1-2, Kairo 1988.

Dozy, Reinhart, *Supplément aux dictionnaires arabes*, Bde. 1-2, Leiden 1881.

EI²=*Encyclopaedia of Islam, Second Edition*. Hrsg. P. Bearman, Th. Bianquis, W.P. Heinrichs u.a., Brill Online. Letzter Zugriff am 23. September 2016: http:// referenceworks.brillonline.com/browse/encyclopaedia-of-islam-2.

Ibn Abī Ḥaǧalah, Šihābaddīn, *Dīwān*, Hg. Muǧāhid Muṣṭafā Bahǧat u.a., Amman 2010.

Ibn Katīr, Ismāʿil b. ʿUmar, *al-Bidāyah wa-n-nihāyah*, Hg. Aḥmad Abū Mulḥim, Bde. 1-14, Beirut 1990.

Ibn Taġrībirdī, Ǧamāladdīn, *an-Nuǧūm aẓ-ẓāhirah fī mulūk Miṣr wa-l-Qāhirah*, Hg. Muḥammad Ḥusayn Šamsaddīn, Bde. 1-16, Beirut 1992.

al-Maqrīzī, Aḥmad b. ʿAlī, *Kitāb as-Sulūk li-maʿrifat duwal al-mulūk*, Hg. M. M. Ziyādah u.a., Bde. 1-12, Kairo, 1934–72.

al-Maydānī, Abū l-Faḍl, *Maǧmaʿ al-amṯāl*, Hg. ʿUmar Ḥusayn al-Ḥaššāb, Bde. 1-2, 1896 o.O.

Muslim b. Ḥaǧǧāǧ, *Saḥīḥ Muslim*, Hg. Naẓar b. Muḥammad al-Fāryābī, Riad 2006.

---

[99] Diese Praxis ist mir ansonsten unbekannt.

[100] *Fa-l-qiṣaṣu qarībun, wa-l-ǧazāʾu min ǧinsi l-ʿamali* – ein Ausspruch von Ibn al-Qayyim al-Ǧawziyyah (751–691/1292–1350), Hanbalit, Schüler Ibn Taymiyyahs, zu finden bei Ibn Taġrībirdī, *Nuǧūm*, Bd. 11, S. 34.

Van Steenbergen, Jo, „On the Brink of a New Era? Yalbughā al-Khāṣṣakī (d. 1366) and the Yalbughāwiyyah", in: *Mamluk Studies Review* 15 (2011), S. 117-152.

Van Steenbergen, Jo, „The Amīr Yalbughā al-Khāṣṣakī, the Qalāwūnid Sultanate, and the Cultural Matrix of Mamluk Society: A Reassessment of Mamlūk Politics in the 1360s", in: *Journal of the American Oriental Society* 131,3 (2011), S. 423-444.

The Anthologist's Agenda and Concerns in Ibn Abī Ḥaǧalah's *Maǧnāṭīs ad-durr an-nafīs*[1]

Nefeli Papoutsakis

From the point of view of literary history, one of Ibn Abī Ḥaǧalah's most important works was his *Muǧtabā al-udabāʾ* ('The Litterateurs' Pick'), an anthology of contemporary prose and poetry, which he conceived as a chain ring in the long series of anthologies of contemporary literature initiated by aṯ-Ṯaʿālibī's (d. 1039) *Yatīmat ad-dahr*, but which he was destined not to finish. Presumably he was still working on it when he died of the plague in 776/1375. In his *Iktifāʾ al-qanūʿ*, a work on Arabic printed books published in Egypt in 1896, Cornelius van Dyck (1818-95), a nineteenth-century American doctor, missionary and translator of the Bible into Arabic, who spent several years in Syria and Lebanon, notes that *Muǧtabā al-udabāʾ* was printed in Egypt and that it was a highly esteemed work there. Contrary to his usual practice, however, van Dyck does not give the concrete place and date of the print, a fact which casts doubt over his assertion.[2] Indeed, no such print is otherwise known to have existed, nor have any manuscripts of that work come to light so far. The *Muǧtabā* is mentioned only in a couple of late sources, starting with Ḥāǧǧī Ḫalīfah's *Kašf aẓ-ẓunūn*.[3] Ḥāǧǧī Ḫalīfah's wording makes clear that he only knew the work from Ibn Abī Ḥaǧalah's own reference to it in his *Maǧnāṭīs ad-durr an-nafīs* ('The Magnet for Precious Pearls'), a work which has survived and is the subject of the present article.

In essence, the *Maǧnāṭīs* is an open call, or open letter, addressed to contemporary Arabic litterateurs and intellectuals asking them to send Ibn Abī Ḥaǧalah specimens of their literary work, poetry and prose, along with some biographical data, to be included in the *Muǧtabā*, on which he had already started working and from which he quotes extensively in the letter. Apart from a lithographic

---

[1]   I would like to thank Professor Thomas Bauer for drawing my attention to this text.

[2]   Van Dyck, Cornelius, *Iktifāʾ al-qanūʿ bi-mā huwa maṭbūʿ*, Cairo 1896, p. 347: *lahū aydan kitābu Muǧtabā l-udabā[ʾ], ṭubiʿa fī Miṣra wa-yuǧilluhū ahlu l-Miṣr.* This note, which probably relies on Ḥāǧǧī Ḫalīfah (see next footnote), may have been inserted by Muḥammad ʿAlī al-Biblāwī, who published van Dyck's manuscript posthumously adding some notes of his own. Van Dyck's book was apparently Yūsuf Ilyān Sarkīs's source for his entry on Ibn Abī Ḥaǧalah in his *Muʿǧam al-maṭbūʿāt al-ʿarabiyyah wa-l-muʿarrabah*, Cairo ²1968, pp. 28-29: he lists *Muǧtabā al-udabāʾ* as one of his printed works, names Egypt as the place of publication but gives no date of publication.

[3]   Ḥāǧǧī Ḫalīfah, *Kašf aẓ-ẓunūn ʿan asmāʾ al-kutub wa-l-funūn*, 2 vols., Beirut [Dār Iḥyāʾ at-turāṯ al-ʿarabī] n.d., 2:1592, cf. 2:1748. Al-Baġdādī, Ismāʿīl Bāšā, *Hadiyyat al-ʿārifīn: Asmāʾ al-muʾallifīn wa-āṯār al-muṣannafīn*, 2 vols., Istanbul 1951, 1:113.

print made in Cairo in 1305/1887 and which was not available to me,[4] the *Maġnāṭīs* survives in two late manuscripts, one completed on 9 Rabīʿ al-Āḫir 1274 (=27 November 1857) and kept at King Saud University Library in Riyadh and another completed on 19 Šaʿbān 1302 (=3 June 1885) and kept at Yale University Library (Beinecke Library, Carlo Landberg Collection of Arabic Mss, 69). Both manuscripts teem with scribal errors; in the case of the Yale manuscript this is all the more surprising as it was seemingly copied by ʿAbdallāh Fikrī, a renowned late nineteenth-century Egyptian prose writer and statesman.[5]

The *Maġnāṭīs* is made up of six parts (*fuṣūl*), four of which are extracts from the *Muǧtabā*. A short introduction in which the author briefly states the epistle's aim, name and contents in the form of chapter headings is followed by Part One, which is also very brief and explains in more detail the letter's purpose: Ibn Abī Ḥaǧalah composed a book modelled on Ibn Bassām's (d. 1147) *Ḏaḫīrah* and those other anthologies that were conceived as sequels to the *Yatīmah*.[6] Having already gleaned and edited enough material on Egypt, he now invites litterateurs from other regions to contribute to the realization of his project by sending him specimens of their work as instructed in Part Six.[7] Parts Two to Four are excerpts

---

4   Sarkis, *Muʿǧam al-maṭbūʿāt*, pp. 28-29. A copy of this print is preserved in the Manuscripts Institute of the Arab League; see: http://41.32.191.214/cgi-bin/koha/opac-detail.pl?biblio number=3283

5   The several explanatory notes in the margins of this manuscript seem to be by the same hand as the text itself. The name of the copyist is not mentioned in the colophon, but the marginal notes are signed by ʿAbdallāh Fikrī or simply Fikrī (e.g. fol. 3v, 5r, 7v, 8v). In the margin of fol. 19r Fikrī refers to a book by his son titled *Ǧuġrāfiyya Miṣr*. He must therefore be the renowned prose writer and for a short time Minister of Education ʿAbdallāh Pasha Fikrī (Jul 1834-27 Jul 1890), on whom see Jomier, J., "Fikrī", in: *EI²* 2 (1965): 892; El-Sherif, Mona, "Fikrī, ʿAbdallāh", in: *EI Three* (online); Goldschmidt, Arthur, *Biographical Dictionary of Modern Egypt*, Boulder Co. 2000, pp. 58-59; Zirikli, Ḫayraddin, *al-Aʿlām: Qāmūs tarāǧim li-ašhar ar-riǧāl wa-n-nisāʾ min al-ʿarab wa-l-mustaʿrabīn wa-l-mustašriqīn*, 3rd. ed., 12 vols., Beirut 1969-70, 4:113; Brugman, Jan, *An Introduction to the History of Modern Arabic Literature in Egypt*, Leiden 1984, pp. 77-80. The son was Muḥammad Amīn Fikrī (1856-17 Jan 1899) (Goldschmidt, *Biographical Dictionary*, p. 59; Zirikli, *al-Aʿlām*, 6:43). The copyist's handwriting differs somewhat from the specimen of the minister's handwriting given in Zirikli, but what corroborates his identification with him is the fact that the Swedish Orientalist Carlo Landberg (1848-1924) knew both ʿAbdallāh and Muḥammad Amīn Fikrī, whom he met at the Eighth Orientalist Congress at Stockholm in 1889; he hence perhaps acquired the manuscript.
     A large part of the *Maġnāṭīs*, from its beginning to the beginning of the section on *muǧūn* of the entry on al-Qīrāṭī (Part Five, see below), survives also in a manuscript kept at the Library of al-Azhar: no. 7334 – 1186 *Adab*, fol. 62v-74r. I am grateful to Hakan Özkan for bringing this manuscript to my attention and for procuring me copies of the relevant folios.

6   Ibn Abī Ḥaǧalah, *Maġnāṭīs ad-durr an-nafīs*, MS Yale fol. 2r: ...*allafa kitāba adabin fī maʿnā Ḏaḫīrati Bni Bassām*... Ibn Abī Ḥaǧalah's admiration for Ibn Bassām is evidenced by the frequent references to him and the long citations from the *Ḏaḫīrah*'s introduction. In lines 10-13 of fol. 2r he praises the *Muǧtabā* playing with the titles of works from the *Yatīmah* series; he thus reveals his aim to produce a similar work.

7   MS Yale fol. 2r, 13-14: *fa-lammā atraʿtu* (MS Riyadh fol. 2v: *anzaltu*) *min buḥūrihī bi-Miṣra ḫulǧānahā wa-aḫtartu min akuffi sawāǧiʿihī marǧānahā....* (MS Riyadh: *kaṯura... marǧānuhā*).

from his introduction to the *Muğtabā* and touch on the following three points respectively: a. the author's reasons for composing the anthology; b. a refutation of ʿAntarah's famous saying "have poets left anything to darn?", to the effect that contemporary literature can be as excellent as the early canon; c. a justification for including *muğūn* and wine poetry in the *Muğtabā*. Part Five consists of sample entries from this anthology which are meant to exemplify its quality and, of course, to evidence the author's acumen, erudition and good judgment and thus entice the recipients of the *Maġnāṭīs* to respond to his call. Part Six details Ibn Abī Ḥaǧalah's request giving specific instructions as to what material to send.

Given that the *Maġnāṭīs* primarily consists of extracts from the *Muğtabā*, I should here like to address two sets of questions: questions related to the *Maġnāṭīs* itself and questions concerning the *Muğtabā al-udabāʾ*.

The *Maġnāṭīs* itself is all the more interesting since it is – as far as I know – the only extant letter of this sort. As said, *Muğtabā al-udabāʾ* was conceived as a link in the series of anthologies of contemporary literature initiated by aṭ-Ṭaʿālibī's *Yatīmah* and which was aimed at updating and extending the literary canon. This series includes al-Bāḫarzī's (d. 1075) *Dumyat al-qaṣr*, al-Bayhaqī's (d. 1170) lost anthology *Wišāḥ Dumyat al-qaṣr*, ʿImād ad-Dīn al-Iṣfahānī's (d. 1201) *Ḫarīdat al-qaṣr*, and Ibn aš-Šaʿʿār's (d. 1256) *ʿUqūd al-ǧumān fī šuʿarāʾ hāḏā z-zamān*, all of which predate the *Muğtabā*, as well as the later, Ottoman anthologies *Rayḥānat al-alibbāʾ* by al-Ḥafāǧī (d. 1659), al-Muḥibbī's *Nafḥat ar-Rayḥānah* (d. 1699) and Ibn Masʿūm's *Sulāfat al-ʿaṣr* (d. 1692), to name but a few well-known works. These anthologies aspired to cover the Arabic literary production of all Muslim domains and were, with one exception, arranged geographically, as is the case with their prototype, aṭ-Ṭaʿālibī's *Yatīmah*. Anthologies of contemporary litera-ture with a limited geographical scope, such as Ibn Bassām's *Ḏaḫīrah* or Ibn Ḫāqān's (d. 1134) *Qalāʾid al-ʿiqyān*, which focus on al-Andalus, can also be said to belong to the same series in that they followed aṭ-Ṭaʿālibī's example in select-ing contemporary or relatively contemporary literature and publishing original literary work, especially in the case of lesser figures whose work had not been col-lected previously. Besides aspiring to complement aṭ-Ṭaʿālibī's work, they also adopted the format of the *Yatīmah*'s single entries and, to a certain extent, its or-ganizational principles.[8]

More precisely, as can be deduced from a reference to his former patron, Sultan an-Nāṣir Ḥasan (MS Yale fol. 3r, MS Riyadh fol. 4r), he composed a first draft of the introduction to the *Muğtabā*, which he quotes in the *Maġnāṭīs*, after the latter's death in 762/1361. Evi-dently the *Maġnāṭīs*, too, was composed after this date.

[8] See the long list of such anthologies in Ibn aš-Šaʿʿār, *Qalāʾid al-ǧumān fī farāʾid šuʿarāʾ hāḏā z-zamān* (al-mašhūr bi-*ʿUqūd al-ǧumān fī šuʿarāʾ hāḏā z-zamān*), ed. Kāmil Salmān al-Ǧubūrī, 9 vols., Beirut 2005, 1:61-64; cf. Orfali, Bilal, "The Sources of al-Thaʿālibī in *Yatīmat al-Dahr* and *Tatimmat al-Yatīma*", in: *Middle Eastern Literatures* 16/1 (2013), pp. 1-47, 2-3; *idem*, "A Sketch Map of Arabic Poetry Anthologies up to the Fall of Baghdad", in: *JAL* 43 (2012), pp. 29-59, 55-57; Bauer, Thomas, "Literarische Anthologien der Mamlukenzeit", in: Conermann, Stephan, & Anja Pistor-Hatam (eds.), *Die Mamluken. Studien zur ihrer*

Starting with aṯ-Ṯaʿālibī, many of Ibn Abī Ḥaǧalah's predecessors inform us of their sources, oral and written, and how they went about the formidable task of collecting their material; they sometimes also point at the existence of previous drafts of their anthologies in circulation.[9] They normally provide such information in their introductions as well as in various entries throughout the anthologies. For instance, in his introduction to the *Yatīmah*, aṯ-Ṯaʿālibī informs us that the great success of an earlier version of this work had prompted contemporary litterateurs to send him their writings. In addition, in several entries he tells us how he managed to get hold of a *dīwān* or other document, either from the author directly or through some intermediary, and he also names his informants who had provided orally transmitted poetry.[10] ʿImādaddin al-Iṣfahānī gives particularly precise details about how and when he gained access to his data, often noting the exact place, occasion and date on which he had heard or copied a poem or piece of prose. In an equally meticulous way, he names his written sources, from which most of his material on Egypt, the Maghreb and al-Andalus was drawn.[11] Most of the anthologists that engaged in such large-scale projects were well-connected men who managed to amass their material through acquaintances and other informants or enjoyed access to libraries and did so over long periods of time, sometimes during their travels. Ibn Abī Ḥaǧalah apparently collected his Egyptian material in similar ways. The course of action he took with regard to the other areas was rather uncommon. True, Ibn Bassām occa-

---

Geschichte und Kultur. Zum Gedenken an Ulrich Haarmann (1942-1999), Hamburg 2003, pp. 71-122, 84-85; Hamori, Andras, & Thomas Bauer, "Anthologies. A. Arabic Literature", in: *EI Three* 2007/1: 118-28.
On the organizational principle of the *Yatīmah*, see Orfali, *Sources*, p. 2; idem, *Sketch Map*, p. 55.

[9] A pioneer of Quellenforschung concerning these anthologies is Maḥmūd ʿAbdallāh al-Ǧādir: see his "Maṣādir Ibn Bassām fī kitābihi ḏ-Ḏaḫirah", in: *al-Mawrid* 13/3 (1984), pp. 29-62, and his three previous studies on the *Yatīmah* (1981), the *Tatimmah* (1980) and the *Dumyah* (1982) mentioned there, pp. 29, 59 (not available to me).

[10] Orfali, Bilal, "The Works of Abū Manṣūr al-Thaʿālibī (350-429/961-1039)", in: *JAL* 40/3 (2009), pp. 273-318, 276-77; idem, *Sources*, pp. 6-9, 8, 9-11.

[11] Richards, Donald S., "ʿImād al-Dīn al-Isfahānī, Administrator, Litterateur and Historian" in: Shatzmiller, Maya (ed.), *Crusaders and Muslims in Twelfth-Century Syria*, Leiden 1993, pp. 133-46, 135, 140-41. The detailed information ʿImādaddin gives about his sources and informants in the *Ḫarīdah* has been admirably mined by Lutz Richter-Bernburg with the aim of reconstructing the anthologist's broad network of acquaintances among contemporary intellectuals and the political elite and supplementing his biographical data: see his "Funken aus dem kalten Flint: ʿImād ad-Dīn al-Kātib al-Iṣfahānī", in: *Die Welt des Orients* 20-21 (1989-90), pp. 121-66, 22 (1991), pp. 105-41.
On Ibn Bassām's sources, in addition to al-Ǧādir's article, see Soravia, Bruna & Mohamed Meouak, "Ibn Bassām al-Šantarīnī (M. 542/1147): Algunos aspectos de su antología Al-Dajira fī maḥāsin ahl al-Ŷazira", in: *Al-Qantara* 18/1 (1997), pp. 221-32, 227-30.
On Ibn aš-Šaʿʿār's sources, see the editor's introduction in *ʿUqūd al-ǧumān*, 1:31-40 (what enabled him to collect his material, apart from several journeys, was the fact that he spent six years in Arbil at a time when the city was flourishing and managed to attract numerous scholars and litterateurs: *ibid*, p. 36).

sionally quotes from the letters he addressed to contemporary litterateurs requesting that they send him their works, as well as from the letters he received in reply. But these were private letters.[12] The same was apparently true of the letters of Ibn Ḥāqān, whose case is notorious. According to Yāqūt, when Ibn Ḥāqān decided to compile his *Qalāʾid al-ʿiqyān*, he wrote to several prominent Andalusians, who were also reputed to be men of letters, informing them of his project and asking them to send him some of their prose and poetry to include in his book. Those who accepted and sent their documents along with some gift or money were made the subject of panegyrics, while the others were passed over in silence or criticised adversely. This was the treatment meted out to Ibn Bāǧǧah in particular, an extremely derogatory entry on whom Ibn Ḥāqān placed at the very end of the *Qalāʾid*. Ibn Bāǧǧah thereupon sent Ibn Ḥāqān ample gifts and thus received an entirely different albeit very short entry in the latter's second anthology, the *Maṭmaḥ al-anfus*.[13]

To return to Ibn Abī Ḥaǧalah, the *Maǧnāṭis* documents that very practice, but with a crucial difference: it does not address any specific individual. It is worded as an open call,[14] even though, like Ibn Bassām's and Ibn Ḥāqān's letters, it may have been intended to be sent or forwarded to specific recipients. Yet information on how Ibn Abī Ḥaǧalah planned to circulate the *Maǧnāṭis* is entirely lacking. Imaginably, one could circulate such a letter at the *ḥaǧǧ* or entrust it to friends to be carried with them on their travels, but Ibn Abī Ḥaǧalah says nothing on this point. At all events, couching his letter as an open call allowed him to skip the formalities of private correspondence and to focus on and advertise the book he was working on, by way of a prepublication. Evidently his aim was to provide information about the project and his own credentials in such a way as to persuade his addressees to respond positively. Ibn Abī Ḥaǧalah's competence and culture are indeed amply

---

[12] See Ibn Bassām aš-Šantarīnī, * aḏ-Ḏaḫīrah fī maḥāsin ahl al-ǧazīrah*, ed. Iḥsān ʿAbbās, 4 vols., Beirut 1975-79, 2:536-41 (on his correspondence with Abū Bakr Muḥammad b. Ḏī l-Wizāratayn Abī Marwān Ibn ʿAbdalʿazīz; he quotes from his letter to him and the latter's reply); 3:654-55 (on the letters he sent to Abū Ḥātim al-Ḥiǧārī prompting him to send him his work; he quotes from one of them); 3:787-92 (he reports that, having no specimen of Ibn Abī Ḥiṣāl's prose and poetry, he asked a common friend to contact him and ask him to send Ibn Bassām samples of his work, and that he himself did so too; he quotes from Ibn Abī Ḥiṣāl's reply letters to both of them); cf. al-Ǧādir, *Maṣādir*, pp. 47-50.

[13] Bencheneb, M., & Ch. Pellat, "al-Fatḥ b. Muḥammad b. ʿUbayd Allāh b. Khāqān", in: *EI²* 2 (1965): 838; Yāqūt al-Ḥamawī, *Muʿǧam al-udabāʾ: Iršād al-arīb ilā maʿrifat al-adīb*, ed. Iḥsān ʿAbbās, 7 vols., Beirut 1993, 5:2163-65; Ibn Ḥāqān, *Qalāʾid al-ʿiqyān wa-maḥāsin al-aʿyān*, ed. Ḥusayn Ḥaryūš, 2 vols., az-Zarqāʾ 1989, 2:931-47; idem, *Maṭmaḥ al-anfus wa-masraḥ at-taʾannus fī mulaḥ ahl al-Andalus*, ed. Muḥammad ʿAlī Šawābikah, Beirut 1983, pp. 397-99; on this and similar cases cf. the editor's introduction, *ibid*, pp. 38-46.
   Ibn Ḥāqān too refers to his practice of writing to ask for specimens of a litterateur's work: e.g. in *Qalāʾid*, 1:521-25, he quotes Ibn Abī Ḥiṣāl's reply to his request (on this letter, which might originally have been sent to Ibn Bassām, see the editor's comments in Ibn Bassām, *Ḏaḫīrah*, 3:788, note 2); in *Qalāʾid*, 2:614, he cites Abū ʿAbdallāh Ibn Ḥamdīn's reply to his request.

[14] *Maǧnāṭis*, MS Yale fol. 2r: *...an adʿuwa li-maʾdubatihī l-ǧafalā*.

demonstrated throughout the letter, which is also typical of his scintillating rhyming prose. To paraphrase Thomas Bauer, apart from 'fulfill[ing] a purpose in the mode of pragmatic communication' this 'occasional text' was also 'intended to be read as a literary text'.[15] But in this case, the aesthetic/literary qualities of the text were meant to enhance its pragmatic/communicative impact. Hence, besides singing the praises of both the *Maġnāṭīs* and the *Muġtabā* on several occasions, Ibn Abī Ḥaǧalah concludes Part Five – the sample entries section – with a short entry on himself (edited here in the appendix), where he again boasts about his literary output and its excellence. Obviously this was not the place for false modesty; the work had to operate, in accordance to its suggestive title, as a 'Magnet for Precious Pearls'.

If the sample entries were meant to testify to the high quality of the *Muġtabā* and the author's fine literary taste, the extracts from its introduction apparently addressed issues of special importance to the anthologist which stood at the top of his agenda: namely, his reasons for compiling the work, the excellence of contemporary literature, and the permissibility, if not necessity, of including *muǧūn* and wine poetry. The first two points – the reasons for compiling the work and the excellence of contemporary literature – are clichéd topics in introductions to such anthologies. The salvage of contemporary literature, the very best of which risked being lost due to scholars' inattention to it, and the lack of similar anthological endeavours are the reasons which anthologists typically invoke for embarking on projects of this kind. The excellence of contemporary literature, which makes it a subject worthy of attention, preservation and study, is a presupposition of this argument; nevertheless, starting with aṭ-Ṯaʿālibī, most of Ibn Abī Ḥaǧalah's predecessors deemed it necessary to elaborate on this point, too, and even declared contemporary literature superior to that of earlier times.[16] In a way, this was a continuation or recast of an earlier discussion on the poetry of the *muḥdaṯūn*, the early Abbasid poets, and their stylistic innovations.[17] In Ibn Abī Ḥaǧalah's view, the salvage operation was made necessary by the overwhelming quantity of contemporary literary production. Excellent poetry was at risk of

---

[15] Bauer, Thomas, "Mamluk Literature as a Means of Communication", in: Conermann, Stephan (ed.), *Ubi sumus – Quo vademus: Mamluk Studies – State of the Art*, Göttingen 2013, pp. 23-56, 24-25.

[16] See Orfali, Bilal, "The Art of the *Muqaddima* in the Works of Abū Manṣūr al-Thaʿālibī (d. 429/1039)", in: Behzadi, Lale & Vahid Behmardi, *The Weaving of Words: Approaches to Classical Arabic Prose*, Beirut 2009, pp. 181-202, 183; *idem, Sketch Map*, p. 55; Soravia-Meouak, *Ibn Bassām*, p. 228, notes 27 and 28 (on Ibn Bassām and Ibn Ḥāqān respectively); van Gelder, Geert Jan, "Shihāb al-Dīn al-Khafājī", in: Lowry, Joseph E., & Devin J. Steward (eds.), *Essays in Arabic Literary Biography II: 1350-1850*, Wiesbaden 2009, pp. 251-61, 258 ('partisanship for one's time is one of the signs of chivalry'), 260; Lowry, Joseph E., "Ibn Maʿṣūm", in: *ibid*, pp. 174-83, 178; more generally, Freimark, Peter, *Das Vorwort als literarische Form in der arabischen Literatur*, Münster 1967, pp. 68-71.

[17] On this dispute, which has often been compared to the Quarrel of the Ancients and the Moderns, see van Gelder, G.J.H., "*Muḥdaṯūn*", in: *EI²* Supplement 9-10 (2004): 637-40, and *idem*, "Ancients and Moderns", in: *EI Three* 2007/1: 113-14.

being engulfed in its own copious billows / masses (*buḥūr*, also meaning 'metres'), and exquisite prose (*manṯūr*, which also means 'gillyflower') was on the point of vanishing just as flowers are concealed by lush leafage (*waraq*, also meaning 'sheets of paper') – all the more so as contemporary historians did not bother recording this literature systematically.[18]

Already in Part Two Ibn Abī Ḥaǧalah comments that earlier literature has been studied and discussed so extensively that it has become a tedious topic. Part Three,[19] which was aimed at refuting ʿAntarah's maxim that previous poets hadn't left anything unsaid, consists mainly of a series of prose and poetic citations to the effect that wisdom and excellence are not the prerogative of any given time period. After a long citation from Ibn Bassām's introduction to the *Ḏaḫīrah* along this line of thinking, Ibn Abī Ḥaǧalah points to what he sees as a proof of his thesis, to wit, the fact that with his *Maqāmāt* al-Ḥarīrī (1054-1122) outshone Badīʿ az-Zamān al-Hamaḏānī (968-1008), the originator of that genre. A short quotation from Ibn Mālik's (renowned grammarian, 1204-1274) *Tashīl al-fawāʾid*, a manual of grammar, intimates that what is true of literature is true of other disciplines as well. His point is further corroborated by a series of thirteen poetic fragments by Abbasid, Ayyubid and Andalusian poets as well as the author himself, to the effect that late poets are not necessarily less gifted; one's last love is better than the first, just as Muḥammad is the last but most revered prophet; the most beautiful flowers are those that blossom last; thoughts and conceits are inexhaustible. Surprisingly, however, Ibn Abī Ḥaǧalah concludes in a reconciling tone with a couplet of his that acknowledges the input of both earlier and contemporary poets and highlights literary continuity.

Noticeably more space is devoted to the vindication of his choice to also anthologize *muǧūn* and wine poetry. In MS Riyadh this part takes up nine pages as opposed to four and a half and five pages of Parts Two and Three respectively.[20] Here too Ibn Abī Ḥaǧalah's views are underpinned by invoking earlier authorities. His argument is based on the widely circulating saying *rawwiḥū l-qulūba taʿi d-ḏikr* ('rest the hearts so that they [can] understand the lecture/Quran'). Al-Ǧāḥiẓ and some later authors attribute this maxim to Qasāma b. Zuhayr, a 'successor' (*tābiʿī*, i.e. of the Companions of the Prophet) and *ḥadīṯ*-transmitter.[21] Other authors claim that it was a Prophetic *ḥadīṯ*, but this is apparently wrong. At any rate, this adage occurs repeatedly in introductions to *adab* works, especially works on an entertaining subject matter, usually among other similar sayings and reports on the Prophet's Companions and their approval of laughter, humour and amusement as

---

[18] See Part Two, MS Riyadh fol. 3r-5r; MS Yale fol. 2r-3v.
[19] MS Riyadh fol. 5r-7v; MS Yale fol. 3v-5r.
[20] MS Riyadh fol. 7v-12r; MS Yale fol. 5r-7v.
[21] Ibn Ḥaǧar al-ʿAsqalānī, *Tahḏīb at-tahḏīb*, ed. Ibrāhīm Zaybaq & ʿĀdil Muršid, 4 vols., Beirut 2014, 3:440; *idem, al-Iṣābah fī tamyīz aṣ-ṣaḥābah*, ed. ʿĀdil ʿAbdalmawǧūd & ʿAlī Muʿawwaḍ, 8 vols., Beirut 1995, 5:397.

a means to reinvigorate the soul.[22] In Ibn Abī Ḥaǧalah's view *adab* books in general are composed with a view to entertaining and thus relaxing and reviving the mind, which gets weary of serious work and thinking. *Ẓarāfah* ('wittiness, elegance') and the writer's craft itself require this course of action, to which only ignoramuses object. Those who are well-versed in the ways of polite society and in elegant conversation know that an *adīb* adheres to variety and mixes jest with earnest and that for every kind of discourse there is a right time and a right place. Having argued thus, he quotes an array of sayings by various widely respected figures, such as ʿAbdallāh b. ʿAbbās, Abū l-ʿAtāhiya, al-Ǧāḥiẓ, Abū Firās al-Ḥamdānī, ʿAtiq b. Muḥammad (a Maghribī preacher and traditionist, contemporary of Ibn Rašīq)[23] and the thirteenth-century poet al-Isʿirdī,[24] who sanction – by example – the indulgence in joking and frivolous entertainment. Among his citations, there are two remarkably long quotes: the first, from al-Ḫaṭib al-Baġdādī's *Tārīḫ Baġdād*, is a story about al-Mubarrad and his visit to a mental hospital. The gist of this story, it seems, is that even lunatics understand the author's point, for the madman with whom the grammarian conversed outdid al-Mubarrad in honesty (and thus shamed him) by openly declaring his liking for wine and love poetry and implicitly defending their legitimacy.[25] The longest and most important citation, the last of this array, comes from *aṭ-Ṭāliʿ as-saʿīd al-ǧāmiʿ asmāʾ nuǧabāʾ aṣ-Ṣaʿīd*, a biographical work on the prominent men of Upper Egypt, by al-Udfuwī (1286-1347), an early fourteenth-century Egyptian scholar. This is a passage from his entry on the distinguished religious scholar and cadi Ibn Daqīq al-ʿĪd, who to some was the greatest religious authority of the eighth Islamic century. Various reports attest to

---

[22] See al-Ǧāḥiẓ, *al-Bayān wa-t-tabyīn*, ed. ʿAbdassallām Muḥammad Hārūn, 4 vols., Cairo [7]1998, 1:327; *idem, Rasāʾil al-Ǧāḥiẓ*, ed. ʿAbdassallām Muḥammad Hārūn, 4 vols., Cairo 1964-79, 1:290; Isḥāq b. Ibrāhīm al-Kātib, *al-Burhān fī wuǧūh al-bayān*, ed. Ḥifnī Muḥammad Šaraf, Cairo 1969, p. 199 (quoted anonymously); [an-Naysābūrī] Abū l-Qāsim al-Ḥasan b. Muḥammad, *ʿUqalāʾ al-maǧānīn*, ed. ʿUmar al-Asʿad, Beirut 1987, p. 238 (cited as a prophetic *ḥadīt*); Abū Nuʿaym al-Iṣfahānī, *Ḥilyat al-awliyāʾ*, 10 vols., Beirut 1996, 3:104 (cited as a *ḥadīt* transmitted by Qasāma b. Zuhayr on the authority of Abū Mūsā al-Ašʿarī and Abū Hurayrah); al-Ḫaṭib al-Baġdādī, *at-Taṭfīl*, ed. Bassām ʿAbdalwahhāb al-Ǧābī, Beirut 1999, p. 44 (attributed to Qasāma b. Zuhayr); Ibn al-Ǧawzī, *Aḫbār al-ḥamqā wa-l-muġaffalīn*, ed. ʿAbdalamir Muhannā, Beirut 1990, p. 15 (*ʿan* Usāma b. Zayd, a companion of the Prophet); *idem, Ṣayd al-ḫāṭir*, ed. ʿAbdalqādir Aḥmad ʿAṭā, Beirut 1992, p. 97 (quoted anonymously); az-Zamaḫšarī, Muḥammad b. ʿUmar, *Rabīʿ al-abrār wa-nuṣūṣ al-aḫbār*, ed. ʿAbdalamir Muhannā, 5 vols., Beirut 1992, 1:23 (*ʿan* Qasāma b. Zuhayr). In his introduction to *Unmūḏaǧ al-qitāl fī naql al-ʿawāl* (ed. Muʿǧib al-ʿAdwānī, Beirut 2012, p. 5) Ibn Abī Ḥaǧalah refers to this saw (*al-qulūb taʿī ḏ-ḏikr kamā warada fī l-aṯar*) in the context of his justification of writing a book on chess (for chess itself relaxes and reinvigorates the souls).

[23] See al-Kutubī, Muḥammad b. Šākir, *Fawāt al-wafayāt wa-ḏ-ḏayl ʿalayhā*, ed. Iḥsān ʿAbbās, 5 vols., Beirut 1973-74, 2:436-37; aṣ-Ṣafadī, Ḫalīl b. Aybak, *Kitāb al-wāfī bi-l-wafayāt*, ed. Aḥmad Arnāʾūṭ & Turkī Muṣṭafā, 29 vols., Beirut 2000, 19:296-98.

[24] Rosenthal, Franz, "al-Isʿirdī", in: *EI*[2] Supplement 7-8 (2003): 462-63; Ibn Faḍlallāh al-ʿUmarī, Šihābaddīn, *Masālik al-abṣār fī mamālik al-amṣār*, ed. Kāmil Salmān al-Ǧubūrī et al., 27 vols., Beirut 2010, 16:154-75.

[25] MS Riyadh fol. 8v-9v; MS Yale fol. 5v-6r. Cf. al-Ḫaṭib al-Baġdādī, *Taʾrīḫ Madīnat as-Salām*, ed. Baššār ʿAwwād Maʿrūf, 17 vols., Beirut 2001, 4:607-8.

the fact that the amiable and unpretentious scholar never hid his liking for music and poetry, especially those light genres that were composed in the vernacular (*mawāliyā, zaǧal*, etc.) notwithstanding their frequently licentious contents.[26] Ibn Abī Ḥaǧalah rounds up by invoking Quran 26:225 which states that 'poets say what they do not do', and by repeating that the mind needs rest so that it [can] grasp religious teaching, that *adab* books are composed for the refreshment and recreation of bored and weary souls and that only bores and ignoramuses fail to understand this. His arguments were of course not new. Most authors who quote licentious literature discuss it in terms of comic entertainment, instead of obscenity, thus appropriating the arguments that were invoked to legitimize *hazl* ('jesting').[27] Serving as it did a serious purpose, *hazl* was itself serious and useful. *Ẓarf* / *zarāfah* ('wittiness') was a positive quality routinely attributed to the *māǧin*, the 'libertine', as well as to the *adīb* and, more generally, the consumer of licentious literature.[28]

Let me now turn to Part Five, the sample entries:[29] What is very interesting here is the anthology's alphabetic arrangement, for it breaks with the organizational principles of the *Yatīmah* and its sequels. As I have said, these anthologies were arranged geographically. On a lower level, however, that is to say, within the overarching geographical divisions and subdivisions, anthologists also took social criteria into consideration, viz. named rulers first, then viziers, then cadis and other *'ulamāʾ*, then lower bureaucrats and, finally, free-lance litterateurs. Only rarely did literary talent and excellence play a role and upset the purely hierarchical ordering. At-Ṭaʿālibī was the first to apply such social criteria, but his successors seem to have observed them even more strictly. Ibn Ḫāqān even abandoned the geographical arrangement in favour of the hierarchical social one.[30] Ibn Abī Ḥaǧalah notes that in adopting an alphabetic arrangement he followed in the footsteps of al-Udfuwī in his aforementioned work on the prominent men of Upper Egypt.[31] This arrangement brings the work closer to biographical dictionaries. Nevertheless, the author's choice seems to reflect the literary and social realities of the Mamluk era, rather than simply to adopt a

---

26 MS Riyadh fol. 10v-11v; MS Yale fol. 6v-7v. Cf. al-Udfuwī, Ǧaʿfar b. Taʿlab, *aṭ-Ṭāliʿ as-saʿīd al-ǧāmiʿ asmāʾ nuǧabāʾ aṣ-Ṣaʿīd*, ed. Saʿd Muḥammad Ḥasan, Cairo 1966, pp. 583-84.

27 See van Gelder, Geert Jan, "Mixtures of Jest and Earnest in Classical Arabic Literature", in: *JAL* 23 (1992), pp. 83-108, 169-90; Meisami, Julie Scott, "Arabic *Mujūn* Poetry: The Literary Dimension", in: De Jong, Frederick (ed.), *Verse and the Fair Sex: Studies in Arabic Poetry and the Representation of Women in Arabic Literature*, Utrecht 1993, pp. 8-30, 13-5, 24, 29-30; Hämeen-Anttila, Jaakko, "What is Obscene? Obscenity in Classical Arabic Literature", in: Talib, Adam, et al. (eds.), *The Rude, the Bad, and the Bawdy: Essays in Honour of Geert Jan van Gelder*, Oxford 2014, pp. 13-23, 16, 18-19, 22.

28 Szombathy, Zoltan, *Mujūn: Libertinism in Medieval Muslim Society and Literature*, Cambridge 2013, pp. 247-302, 265-79.

29 MS Riyadh fol. 12r-32v; MS Yale fol. 7v-20v.

30 See Orfali, *Sources*, p. 2; *idem, Sketch Map*, pp. 55-57; Soravia-Meouak, *Ibn Bassām*, p. 226 (on social criteria by Ibn Bassām).

31 MS Riyadh fol. 12r; MS Yale fol. 7v.

principle used in biographical literature. The spread of education, 'the increasing participation of traders and craftsmen in literary life' and the 'gradual blurring of the boundaries between "elite" and "popular" literature', are arguably behind the abandonment of the characteristic hierarchical social ordering of the previous anthologies.[32] What we do not know of course is whether Ibn Abī Ḥaǧalah aimed to retain the overarching geographical division, but this is certainly most probable.

The sample entries are of unequal length and include two Ibrāhīms, the poets al-Qīrāṭī (1326-1379)[33] and al-Miʿmār (d. 1349),[34] and three Aḥmads, the lesser figures Aḥmad b. Ismāʿīl Sumaykah (d. 1349)[35] and Šihābaddīn Aḥmad b. Muḥammad al-Ḥāǧibī (d. 1349),[36] and Ibn Abī Ḥaǧalah himself. Al-Miʿmār's entry is the longest (10.5 folia = 21 pages), the second longest being that of al-Qīrāṭī (6 folia = 12 pages). The Aḥmads were given much shorter notes: Sumaykah one folio (2 pages), al-Ḥāǧibī a page and a half, Ibn Abī Ḥaǧalah a folio and a half (3 pages).[37] One should bear in mind that the citations from the *Muǧtabā* may be abridged; apparently the introduction to that work was much longer and perhaps unfinished at the time that Ibn Abī Ḥaǧalah was composing the *Maǧnāṭīs*. The sample entries too may be abridged. The various sections (*fuṣūl*) of al-Qīrāṭī's entry (see below), for example, seem to me to be too short, but of course there is no way of knowing whether they are abridged or not. Ibn Abī Ḥaǧalah's autobiographical entry also gives the impression of having been shortened, all the more so as it contains no specimens of his works.

---

[32] Bauer, *Mamluk Literature as a Means of Communication*, p. 23; *idem*, "Mamluk Literature: Misunderstandings and New Approaches", in: *Mamlūk Studies Review* 9/2 (2005), pp. 105-32, 110-11.

The only other work of the series of *Yatīmah* sequels that is arranged alphabetically is Ibn aš-Šaʿʿār's *ʿUqūd al-ǧumān*, which Ibn Abī Ḥaǧalah most probably did not know of. Ibn aš-Šaʿʿār presumably took over this principle from a previous book of his, *Tuḥfat al-wuzarāʾ*, which no longer exists, but which was a sequel to al-Marzubānī's alphabetically arranged *Muʿǧam aš-šuʿarāʾ* (see Ibn aš-Šaʿʿār, *ibid*, 1:60-61).

[33] Perhaps the best poet of that era after Ibn Nubātah al-Miṣrī (1287-1366); see Ibn Taġrībirdī, Abū l-Maḥāsin Yūsuf, *an-Nuǧūm az-zāhirah fī mulūk Miṣr wa-l-Qāhirah*, ed. Muḥammad Ḥusayn Šamsaddīn, 16 vols., Beirut 1992, 11:160-62; *idem, al-Manhal aṣ-ṣāfī*, ed. Muḥammad Muḥammad Amīn, 13 vols., Cairo 1984-2009, 1:89-95; Ibn Ḥaǧar al-ʿAsqalānī, *Inbāʾ al-ǧumr bi anbāʾ al-ʿumr*, ed. Ḥasan Ḥabašī, 4 vols., Cairo 1969-98, 1:200-1; *idem, ad-Durar al-kāminah fī aʿyān al-miʾah aṯ-ṯāminah*, 4 vols., Hyderabad 1931, 1:31; al-Fāsī, Muḥammad b. Aḥmad, *al-ʿIqd aṯ-ṯamīn fī taʾrīḫ al-balad al-amīn*, ed. Muḥammad Ḥāmid al-Fīqī et al., 8 vols., Cairo [1958]-1969, 3:217-29.

[34] See Bauer, Thomas, "Ibrāhīm al-Miʿmār: Ein dichtender Handwerker aus Ägyptens Mamlukenzeit", in: *ZDMG* 152 (2002), pp. 63-93, and the sources given there.

[35] See Özkan, Hakan, "Ein Fischlein mit Lästermaul: Ibrāhīm al-Miʿmārs liebster Feind, Aḥmad b. Ismāʿīl as-Sumayka" (forthcoming), and the sources given there.

[36] aṣ-Ṣafadī, *al-Wāfī*, 8:106-8; *idem, Aʿyān al-ʿaṣr wa-aʿwān an-naṣr*, ed. ʿAlī Abū Zayd et al., 6 vols., Damascus 1988, 1:366-69; Ibn Ḥaǧar, *ad-Durar al-kāminah*, 1:312-13.

[37] The counting is based on MS Riyadh: al-Qīrāṭī fol. 12v-19r; al-Miʿmār fol. 19r-29v; Sumaykah fol. 29v-30v; al-Ḥāǧibī fol. 30v-31r; Ibn Abī Ḥaǧalah fol. 31r-32v.

The ordering of the entries is strictly alphabetical: Ibrāhīm b. ʿAbdallāh (al-Qīrāṭī) precedes Ibrāhīm b. ʿAlī (al-Miʿmār), etc., but this seems to be a coincidence, given that at the end of Part Two Ibn Abī Ḥaǧalah notes that he arranged litterateurs within each letter according to their closeness to him, placing his acquaintances first:[38] al-Qīrāṭī was his colleague and friend; by contrast, he had not met al-Miʿmār personally.

The format of the entries is typical of the series. As in the *Yatīmah*, the litterateur's full name is followed by flowery praise, with little or no biographical data and/or a listing of his works, whereupon follow samples of his poetry and prose, if he had written any, whereas in longer entries these samples are arranged thematically or generically. Al-Qīrāṭī's entry, for example, starts with florid praise of the man and his poetry by way of an introduction. Thereupon follow eight short *fuṣūl*: 1. a *faṣl* on his works and poetry collections, which consists solely of an array of titles (witty titles were in vogue in Mamluk times); 2. a *faṣl* on his praise of the Prophet consisting of a ten-line excerpt from an ode; 3. a *faṣl* on his epigrams (*maqāṭīʿ*: eighteen examples, mostly love and wine epigrams, plus some verses by other poets and some comments); 4. a *faṣl* on love poetry (an excerpt from a long ode plus some verses by other poets resembling the last verse of the Qīrāṭī quote); 5. a *faṣl* on his praise poetry (*al-madāʾiḥ wa-šukr al-manāʾiḥ*); 6. a *faṣl* on *riṯāʾ*; 7. a *faṣl* on his prose; and 8. a *faṣl* on *muǧūn*, which only comprises a few lampooning epigrams. Similarly, al-Miʿmār's entry contains an introduction and five *fuṣūl*.[39]

Apart from the elegance and wittiness of the anthologist's rhyming prose, typical of the series are also his comments and digressions: the mention of similar verses by other poets – for instance, the series of fifteen epigrams and anecdotes on *ṣifāʿ* (neck-slapping) that follow four epigrams on this topic by al-Miʿmār or the citation of four excerpts by other poets on a motif found in a verse by al-Qīrāṭī –, references to the anthologist's personal relationship to the men whose work he anthologized, if he had any, quotations from their correspondence or *muʿāraḍāt*, etc.

What is not typical of the series, but again reflects the literary developments of the Mamluk era, is the citation of dialectal poetry. Interestingly, Ibn Abī Ḥaǧalah did not deem it necessary to comment on the inclusion of such poetry in the *Muǧtabā* – apparently because the vernacular genres had meanwhile been canonized thanks to Ṣafiyaddīn al-Ḥillī's (ca. 1278-1348) *al-ʿĀṭil al-ḥālī*.[40] Still,

---

38 MS Riyadh fol. 4v-5r; MS Yale fol. 3r: *ṣadartu kulla ḥarfin fī l-ġālibi bi-man ʿāṭaytuhū kuʾūsa l-adabi ṯumma man naẓartuhū min katabin ṯumma man katabtu ilayhi fa-kataba ṯumma man ruwītu ʿanhu, al-aqrabu fa-l-aqrab.*

39 1. Miscellaneous epigrams; 2. epigrams on the *ʿiḏār* (first grow of beard) and on beards, as well as 'Berufsepigramme'; 3. epigrams on *ṣifāʿ* (neck-slapping); 4. *muǧūn wa-nawādir*; 5. *mawāliyā* and *balālīq* (=licentious *zaǧals*).

40 See al-Ḥillī, Ṣafiyaddīn, *Die vulgärarabische Poetik al-Kitāb al-ʿāṭil al-ḥālī wa-l-muraḫḫaṣ al-ġālī des Ṣafiyaddīn al-Ḥillī*, hrsg. und erkl. von Wilhelm Hoenerbach, Wiesbaden 1956.

apart from critical works and thematic anthologies on the new genres, both contemporary and later biographical sources which devote an entry to al-Miʿmār re-
frained from quoting his *zaǧals*; by contrast, Ibn Abī Ḥaǧalah did so uninhibit-
edly. In any case, his must be the first work of the series of *Yatīmah* sequels to
anthologize dialectal poetry.[41]

Finally, in Part Six,[42] Ibn Abī Ḥaǧalah details his request instructing his addressees to send him their personalia (their name, the names of their father and
grandfather, their *nisbah*s and their places of birth and residence), the names of
their masters (*šuyūḫ*) and of those litterateurs (*min ahli hāḏā l-fann*) from and to
whom they transmitted literary material, as well as select poetry and prose of
their own composition: he explicitly mentions the various genres that appear in
al-Qīrāṭī's entry, reckoning that all contemporary litterateurs cultivated at least
some of these, and advises them to also send him dialectal poetry, if they happen
to have composed any. Furthermore, in accordance with the entertaining aspect
of his work, he asks them to send any interesting story or anecdote (*ḥikāyah
laṭīfah wa-nādirah ẓarīfah*) which they had heard about or witnessed and might
wish to publicize.

Concluding Remarks

With the Mamluk period being 'the golden age' of classical Arabic literary anthologies, as Thomas Bauer has shown, it is indeed very remarkable that the series of *Yatīmah* sequels was almost interrupted in this era – as, again, Thomas
Bauer has pointed out.[43] Ibn Abī Ḥaǧalah's assertion that his contemporaries did

---

[41] In *Ḏahabiyyat al-ʿaṣr* (ed. Ibrāhim Ṣāliḥ, Beirut 1432/2011), a similar anthology by Šihābaddin Ibn Faḍlallāh al-ʿUmarī (see below), the author mentions three *zaǧǧāl*s, ʿAlī b. Mu-
qātil al-Ḥamawī (*ibid*, pp. 177-81), Šarafaddīn Ḥusayn b. Sulaymān (*ibid*, pp. 311-14) and
al-Maḥḥār (*ibid*, p. 334, unwritten entry), but does not quote any of their *zaǧal*s. This may
be a coincidence, given that this anthology, too, remained unfinished.
  On the other hand, in his aforementioned work on the prominent men of Upper Egypt al-
Udfuwī extensively cited dialectal poetry; see, e.g., *aṭ-Ṭāliʿ*, pp. 687-89, and the forthcoming study of Hakan Özkan on the Eastern *zaǧal*.

[42] MS Riyadh fol. 32v-33v; MS Yale fol. 20v-21r.

[43] Professor Bauer (*Literarische Anthologien*, pp. 84-85) has suggested that this may be due to
the fact that the percentage of those who participated in literary life had risen so drastically
as to almost invalidate one's participation in literary life as a selection criterion and to blur
the boundaries between literary anthologies and biographical dictionaries of distinguished
contemporaries. Note, however, that Sumaykah and Šihābaddīn al-Ḥāǧibī were minor figures and not scholars or otherwise important men, but, significantly, litterateurs. The same
is true of Šamsaddīn Ibn al-Fuwayh al-Iskandarānī (see aṣ-Ṣafadī, *Aʿyān al-ʿaṣr*, 4:262-66;
Ibn Ḥaǧar, *ad-Durar al-kāminah*, 3:365-66), an entry on whom Ibn Abī Ḥaǧalah announces
in Sumaykah's entry. On the other hand, he also includes men primarily known for their
scholarly merit and activities, such as Ibn Daqīq al-ʿĪd, an entry on whom he announces in
Part Four. To be sure, both the digressional style and the elegance of the anthologists'
prose distinguish the series from biographical literature, but the work does evidence the

not pay due attention to contemporary literature was a false claim and, as I have said, a clichéd reason given by aṯ-Ṯaʿālibī and his continuators for compiling their works. Some thirty years earlier Šihābaddīn Ibn Faḍlallāh (1301-1349) had started working on a similar project. His *Ḏahabiyyat al-ʿaṣr* remained unfinished but a part of it has recently surfaced and been published.[44] Apparently, the reduced importance of this series in Mamluk times was due precisely to the bloom of literary anthologies in general, as contemporary literature was extensively anthologized in other kinds of anthologies, especially thematic ones. Nevertheless, as the cases of *Ḏahabiyyat al-ʿaṣr*, *Muǧtabā al-udabāʾ*, at-Tīǧānī's (ca. 1274-1311) lost anthology *ad-Durr an-nāẓim fī l-adab wa-t-tarāǧim* on poets and prose writers of the Ḥafṣid domains, and perhaps other currently unnoticed works show, the dwindling of the series is also due to purely accidental reasons. As is true of those other anthologies, it is regrettable that *Muǧtabā al-udabāʾ* remained unfinished and its remains have not survived, for to judge from the sample entries cited in the *Maġnāṭīs*, especially those on lesser figures, it would have enhanced our knowledge of the literary life of the period. As to the *Maġnāṭīs*: apart from its literary value, it is a sui generis epistle that offers important insights into the anthologists' methods for collecting their material and advertising their work.

Appendix

The following is an edition of three short extracts from the 'Magnet' as a specimen of the author's style: 1-2. Parts One and Two, stating his reasons for composing the *Maġnāṭīs*, and the *Muǧtabā*, respectively, and 3. the autobiographical entry (from Part Five). I have adapted the text to modern standard Arabic orthographic conventions, adding *hamzah*s, *šaddah*s, dots on *tāʾ marbūṭah*s, and accusative *tanwīn*, when necessary.

Part One, MS Riyadh (=R) fol. 2v-3r; MS Yale (=Y) fol. 2r; MS al-Azhar (=A) fol. 63r-63v

الفصل الأول من هذه الرسالة في السبب الموجب لإثبات فصولها وكتابة[1] وصولها وهو أنّ منشئها أحمد بن[2] يحيى بن[3] أبي بكر بن عبد الواحد المغربي مولدًا الدمشقي منشأ نزيل القاهرة الشهير بابن أبي حجلة ألّف كتاب أدب في معنى ذخيرة ابن بسّام[4] المشتملة على فرسان النثار والنظام يشتمل[5] على غزل ونسيب وذكرى حبيب ومدح وتأبين[6] وبيان وتبيين وابتداء وجواب[7] وتعنيف وعتاب وفوائد وزوائد وأخبار وأسمار[8] ونوادر وبوادر وغير ذلك مما يأخذ بمجامع[9] القلوب ويحبب نفسه كالتغزل بالمحبوب وسمّيته مجتبى

---

blurring of the boundaries between ʿ*ulamāʾ* and *udabāʾ*, which characterizes this period, as Professor Bauer has noted.

[44] See note 41.

الأدبا[ء][10] فهو عند المصريين بالنسبة إلى الذخيرة كالروضة في الجزيرة وعند ناظم القلائد كدرّ بحره الزائد وعند كافل اليتيمة كالدرة اليتيمة وعند صاحب دُمية القَصْر من محاسن أهل العصر فلمّا أُثْرِعُثُ[11] من بحوره بمصر خلجانها وأكثرتُ[12] من أكفّ سواجعه مرجانها والتزمتُ[13] بذكر شعراء الأمصار ومن قطرت سحائب أدبه في سائر الأقطار من أهل هذا القرن وأرباب هذا الفن لزم من ذلك أن أُتَّبع[14] فيه أخبارهم سهلاً وجبلاً وأن أُدْعُوَ لمأدُبَّته[15] الجَفَلَى وأنشأت هذه الرسالة في استدعاء[16] نسبهم ونسيبهم وبعيدهم وقريبهم والتمست من الواقف عليها[17] القعود على مِنَصَّتها والكشف على قصّتها والإصغاء إليها والتوقيع عليها بما يأتي ذكره مفصّلًا في الفصل السادس من هذه الرسالة إن شاء الله تعالى

Variants

1. Y: – لكتابة – 2. Y: – ابن – 3. A: – ابن – 4. R: – هشام – 5. R: – مشتمل – 6. R: – تانين – 7. أُثْرِعَثُ :A, انزلت :R – 11. الأدبآ :A – 10. يؤخذ بجامع :R – 9. أثمار :A – 8. وابتدا واجواب :R – 16. ادعو ما ادبته :R – 15. اتنبع :Y – 14. والزمت :R – 13. كوثر :A, كثر :R – 12. استدعآ :A, استدعا :R – 17. Missing in R.

Part Two, MS Riyadh fol. 3r-5r; MS Yale fol. 2r-3v; MS al-Azhar fol. 63v-65r

الفصل الثاني في ذكر صدر من ديباجة خطبة كتابي مُجْتَبَى الأدبا[ء] الباعث على إنشا[ء][1] هذه الرسالة وطلوع بدر هذه الهالة وهو أما بعد فلمّا كان هذا القرن الثامن والعصر الذي هو بقيام سوق[2] الأدب ضامن مشتملًا حتى من صغاره على[3] كتاب الكتاب[4] وشعراء يغني تشبيبهم بزينب عن الرباب من كل شاعر مفلق وشهاب محرق لا يُصْطَلى لجمر أقلامه بنار[5] ولا يؤخذ[5] لقتيل بنانه[6] بشار إذ منهم شعراء كالكُمَيت فحول وفرسان حماسةٍ تدور رحاهم[7] حولهم وتجول ولم أر إلى يومنا هذا من مؤرخي العصر وواصفي دمية القصر من أفردهم بالذكر ولا أمطر على جمعهم سحابة فكر بيد أنّ تراجم[8] بعضهم في تواريخهم متبددة[9] وديباجة طروسهم أخلقتها الأيام المتجددة فأشرف شعرهم من بحوره على الغرق وضاع منثورهم كالزهر بين الورق فخشيت ضيعة الأدب وما[10] يترتب بترك[11] أهل الرتب فاستخرت الله تعالى في جمع شملهم في هذا المعجم والغوص في بحارهم[12] التي يلزمها من الدرّ ملزم والسكوت عن مثل أمِنْ[13] أمّ أوْفَى دمنةٌ[14] لم تكلّم فرارًا من ذكر ما اشتهر وأخلق ديباجة كتانه[15] القمر ولا أذكر إلّا من[16] تأخّر زمانه وبان في زهر المنثور بانه مما بهر البهار وطلع بدر طرسه وسط النهار لأنّه كان يقال قلّت التعلُّقات بشعر المعلقات وكثرت الملامة في بغلة أبي دلامة وبطل الاحتجاج بسخف ابن[17] حجاج وقدُم طيلسان ابن[18] حرب ومجّت الأسماع ضرطة وهب حتى قيل فيها (بسيط)

قد أكثر الناس في وهب وضرطته * حتى لقد مُلّ ما قالوا وما بردا

لم تعلُ[19] ضرطة هاجيه كضرطته * في الذاكرين ولم يُحسَد كما حُسدا

يا وهبُ[20] لا تكترث للحاسديك بها * فإنّما أنت غيث ربّما رعدا

وقال ابن قلاقس في ألحى (رمل)

هي فـوق الـصـدر قـد سـد * دتـه مـن شرق لغـرب

لحيـة ردّتـه في النـا * س ولا ضرطة وهـب

لا جرم أنّي عدلت عن ورود تلك الحياض واستحليت ما لأبناء عصري من الإحماض كقول بعضهم في حلو الشمائل يلقّب بالحامض (خفيف)

وبـديع الجمـال معتـدل القا * مـة كالغـصن والقنا الأملـود

لقّبـوه بحـامض وَهْـوَ حلـوٌ * قـول مـن لم يـصل ألى العنقود[21]

وقد علم الله ما أودعت هذا الكتاب من محاسن أبناء عصري وجلوته عليهم من بنات فكري وعجائب نظمي ونثري كقولي في خطبة المقامات التي أنشأتُها باسم السلطان الملك الناصر حسن رحم الله شبابه وجعل من الرحيق المختوم شرابه تشتمل على فنون مختلفة ومعان مؤتلفة وقبلة أدب محاريب دالاتها عن المقام الشريف غير منحرفة فأما الأدب وفنونه والأيك وغصونه والبديع وجناسه والظبي[22] وكناسه والشيء وضدّه والعود ونِدّه فلنظمها[23] فيه اليد الطولى ولقرائن سجعها حسن الآخرة والأولى (بسيط)

فـالنظم لي فيـه عقدكلّـه درر * وفي سكردان ولي في النـثر ألـوان

لو كنـت في زمنٍ عبـد الرحيم بـه * مـا بات نـثري لجينًا وهـو عقيـان

إنّي بُليـت بقـومٍ لا خـلاق لهـم * علـيهم مـن ثيـاب اللـؤم خلقـان

في الـشام مـنهم وفي مصر فـذاك وذا * إذا ربطـتـها في النـير نـدّان

وقد علم الله ما أودعتها من مسائل علمية ومنازل علوية وسماء[24] وبروج وأرض ومروج وقطر ونبات ونيل وفرات[25] وفراسة وقيافة وزجر[25] وعيافة وغير ذلك من مُلَح ومِدَح ونسب ونشب وعند الامتحان يكرم المرء أو يهان (بسيط)

  NEFELI PAPOUTSAKIS

لا يكــذب المــرء إلّا مــن مهانتــه   *   أو عــادة الســوء أو مــن قلّــة الأدب

فلو كنت كابن الأثير وغيره ممن يقعقع لمعانيه المبتكرة ويفخر بسحر[26] بيانه على السحرة لفضّلت منشوري على البان وقرّظته إلى أن يؤوب القارظان فدونك كتابًا بنات أفكاره من أُمّهات الأدب وكتبانه تلوح من كثب رعيت[27] فيه لأبناء عصري الذم [28]وتجنبت[28] ما نسب إليهم من كبائر الإثم الفواحش إلّا اللمم فربّ قوم نظرت إلى ذمّهم بعين الإغضاء ورتبت مدحهم على حروف الهجاء[29] لأنّه[30] كان يقال (كامل)

ســامح أخــاك إذا خلــط   *   منــه الإصــابة بالغلــط

اللَّهُمَّ إلّا ما ندر من وصف شاعر كبير الهجاء[29] أو مبتدع قائل بالإرجاء[31] فإنّي أنبّه على حيفه وأقتله بسيفه وصدّرت كلّ حرف في الغالب بمن عاطيته كؤوس[32] الأدب ثم من نظرته من كثب ثم من كتبت إليه وكتب ثم من رويت عنه الأقرب فالأقرب من يومنا هذا إلى سنة سبعمائة ولم أترك من الشعراء[33] الجياد في سائر البلاد إلّا من تخلف في الساقة ولم يكن لوقوفي على بيوته طاقة وربّما ارتبطت بشعر الفقيه المنحلّ وإن قلّ وألحقت من علمه وشعره الوابل بالطلّ رغبة في ذكر سيرته الحميدة [34]وسرد تصانيفه[34] المفيدة

Variants

1. A: انشآ – 2. Y: سوء – 3. Y: عليّ – 4. A: كتاب الكتّاب , probably read: كبار الكتّاب – 5. R: بثار – 6. A: نباله – 7. Y: رجاهم , R: رحالهم – 8. A: ترجم – 9. R: مجددة – 10. R: من – 11. Y: بتزال – 12. Y: بحورهم – 13. R: من – 14. A: زمنة – 15. R: كتابة – 16. R: ما – 17. R: بن – 18. Y, R: بن – 19. A, Y, R: تغل – 20. R: هب – 21. A: the two verses are in reverse order – 22. Y: والظبا – 23. A: لنظمه – 24. R: وسما – 25. R: وحرس – 26. Y, R: بسحره – 27. R: دعيت – 28. Y: تجنبت – 29. Y, R: هجا – 30. Missing in Y – 31. R: بالارجا – 32. A: كؤس – 33. R: الشعر, A: الشعرآ – 34. R: وقيامة وزحر وسود تناصيفه.

Notes

1. The phrase تدور رحاهم حولهم وتجول is the second hemistich of a verse by as-Samaw'al; see *Dīwānā ʿUrwah b. al-Ward wa-s-Samawʾal*, ed. Karam al-Bustānī, Beirut [2]1982, p. 92.
2. أَمِنْ أُمِّ أَوْفَى...تكلّم: the first verse of Zuhayr's *Muʿallaqah*.

3. The three verses on Wahb's fart (*qad akṯara n-nāsu…*) are from a poem by Ibn ar-Rūmī; cf. his *Dīwān*, ed. Ḥusayn Naṣṣār, 6 vols., Cairo 1973-81, 2:735-6 (no. 569).

4. فالنظم لي فيه…: the verses are from a poem by Ibn Abī Ḥaǧalah, see his *Dīwān*, ed. Muǧāhid Muṣṭafā Bahǧat & Aḥmad Ḥamīd Muḫlif, Amman 2010, p. 255.

5. لا يكذب…: Cited anonymously in al-Waššāʾ, *al-Muwaššā*, Cairo ²1953, p. 41.

6. سامح أخاك…: the verse is from al-Ḥarīrī's al-Maqāmah aš-šiʿriyyah; see his *Maqāmāt*, ed. Saḥbān Aḥmad Murūwah, Beirut 2012, p. 267.

Ibn Abī Ḥaǧalah's Autobiographical Entry (MS Riyadh fol. 31r-32v, MS Yale 19v-20v)

ومنهم [١]بن أبي حجلة منشئها أحمد بن يحيى بن أبي بكر بن عبد الواحد المغربي مولدًا الدمشقي منشأ نزيل القاهرة الشهير بابن أبي حجلة مولده بالمغرب سنة خمس وعشرين وسبعمائة بزاوية جدّه الشيخ الصالح الزاهد أبي حجلة عبد الواحد قدس الله ¹سرّه وروحه¹ ونور ضريحه وكنّي جدّه بذلك لصلاح حاله وتعلّق الحجل والوحوش بأذياله وزاوية جدّه بالمغرب مشهورة وأحاديث بركته مأثورة يؤخذ منها التراب لطلب الدوا[ء] والتماس الشفاء² أي والله ‹شعر›³

| (وافـر) | ثُــرابُهُمْ وحـقِّ أبي⁴ ثُــرابٌ | * | أعزُّ عليّ من عيني⁵ اليمين ‹آخر›⁶ |

| (كامـل) | وحِمى يُـداسُ ثُرابُهُ بنعالهمْ | * | مـــنّي بـــأفواهِ الجفـــونِ مقبّـــل |

| (طويل) | ورَبْعُ الذي أهواه يُروي شرابه⁷ الـــــعِطاشَ ويشفي تُرْبه الأعيُن الرمْدا⁸ |

قدم من المغرب⁹ مع أبويه وأخواته وأخويه فبلغوا السول¹⁰ بزيارة الرسول صلّى الله عليه وسلّم ثم تنقّلت به بعد موتهم الأحوال وشاهد بمصر بعد رؤية أبي الهول الأهوال فصنف كتابه غرائب العجائب وعجائب الغرائب وفيه يقول (كامل)

| هـــذا الكتـــاب ذكرتُ فيـــه عجائبًـــا | * | تُغـني النـديم عـن المدامـة والطربْ |

| يهـــتزّ ســـامعها لطيـــبِ حـــديثها | * | إلّا حسـودًا ليـس يعجبـه العجبْ |

فهو ممن¹¹ شاهد العجب وصنف في الحديث والفقه¹² والنحو والأدب ما ينيف على ثمانين مصنفًا وتأليفًا ظريفًا بشهادة شواهدها وكثرة ألوان موائدها مثل كتابه سكردان السلطان الذي امتدّ بحضرة الملوك خوانه وناسبته بحسن التسمية إخوانه وسيأتي من أسمائها المرضية في الإجازة الشعبية ما يطيب الأسماع وتدلّ مطالعته على كثرة الاطّلاع نعم صنف واستهدف وطارح ونافخ وقرأ وقرى ودرى¹³ وسمع ورأى وسار وطار

وأكثر من[14] النظام والنثار[15] وجوّد القصيدة والمقطوع وسلك الطريقة الفاضلية في المنشور والمطبوع وقلّ من أجاد في الثلاثة المذكورة على هذه الصورة لأنّ بحرها زاخر ومن قام بأحدها[16] قعد به الآخر (طويل)

ويا دارهــا بالخيـــف إنّ مزارهـــا   *   قريـــبٌ ولكـــن دون ذاك أهـــوال

واعلم أنّي لم أتّخذ الشعر حرفة[17] ولا سكنت من بيوته غرفة[18] بناء على أنّه[19] صناعتي وجلّ[20] بضاعتي وإنّما دعاني إليه حب الأدب وسجيّة العرب وقول عمر رضي الله عنه لا بأس بالأبيات يقدّمها الرجل أمام حاجته فيستعطف بها الكريم ويستنزل بها اللئيم وقد قلت في كتابي أغاني التهاني وقد اقتضت الحال ذلك على أتّي والحمد لله كالغنيّ[21] لم أكن من طلّاب الرفد بشعري ولكنه كان ما يقال ما بي بطني بي قدري والله تعالى يغنينا من سعة فضله ولا يجعلنا على خوان البخيل خلّ بقله (وافر)

خـــوان لـــيس يحـــضره ضـــيوف   *   وعِــرضٌ مثـــل منـــديل الخـــوان

اللهُمَّ إلّا ما كان في مدح الممدوح بكلّ لسان سيّد ولد عدنان صلّى الله عليه وسلّم ومجّد وكرّم فإنّه وسيلتي الناجحة وبضاعتي الرابحة حيث قلت في ديواني نسمة القبول في مدح الرسول بعد حمد الله الذي ألهمني من مدح نبيّه المختار وجعل لي به[22] قدرًا على المقدار وأطلع عليّ شموسه وأقماره آنآء[23] الليل وأطراف النهار فأنار به قلبي وجعل مدحه ورثا[ء]ه سنّتي وندبي أحمده حمد من[24] منّ عليه بجزيل الطاعة ورفع له بمدح نبيّه الدرجات في الساعة (طويل)

وإنّي لأرجــو الله حـــتى كأنـــني   *   أرى بجميـــل الظـــن مـــا الله صـــانع

Variants

1. Y: روحه – 2. R: الشفا – 3. Missing in R – 4. Y: ابو – 5. Y: عين – 6. Missing in والفقيه – 7. R: ترابه – 8. Y: الرمد – 9. Y: الغرب – 10. R: السؤال – 11. Y: من – 12. R: حروفه – 13. R: ودار – 14. R: في – 15. R: والنشار – 16. R: بأحد – 17. R: حبل – 20. R: حبل – 21. R: كالمعيني – 22. Missing in R – 18. R: غروفه – 19. R: اني – 20. R: حبل – 21. R: كالمعيني – 22. Missing in R – 23. R: انآ – 24. Missing in Y.

Notes

1. ...ثِرابُهُمْ: the verse is by Ibn al-Ḥaǧǧāǧ; see Ibn Faḍlallāh, *Masālik al-abṣār*, 15:265.
2. ...ووَرَبْعُ الذي: Cited anonymously in aṣ-Ṣafadī, *al-Wāfī*, 27:138.
3. ...هذا الكتاب: the verses are not found in Ibn Abī Ḥaǧalah's *Dīwān*.
4. ...وويا دارها: the verse is by Abū l-ʿAlāʾ al-Maʿarrī; cf. *Saqt az-zand*, ed. Dār Ṣādir, Beirut 1957, 229.
5. ...خوان ليس: the verse is by a certain Abū l-Ġanāʾim ar-Ramlī; see aṯ-Ṯaʿālibī, *Tatimmat al-Yatīmah*, ed. Mufīd Muḥammad Qumayḥa, Beirut 1983, p. 82.
6. ...وواني لأرجو: the verse is by Lisānaddīn Ibn al-Ḫaṭīb; see his *Dīwān*, ed. Muḥammad Miftāḥ, 2 vols., Casablanca 1989, 2:650.

Bibliography

Primary Sources

Ibn Abī Ḥaǧalah, *Maǧnāṭīs ad-durr an-nafīs*, MS Yale C. Landberg Collection of Arabic Mss, 69.

Ibn Abī Ḥaǧalah, *Maǧnāṭīs ad-durr an-nafīs*, MS Riyadh King Saud University Library, 2932 zāy.

Ibn Abī Ḥaǧalah, *Maǧnāṭīs ad-durr an-nafīs*, MS al-Azhar Library, 7334 – 1186 *Adab*, fol. 62v-74r.

Ibn Bassām aš-Šantarīnī, *aḏ-Ḏaḫīrah fī maḥāsin ahl al-ǧazīrah*, ed. Iḥsān ʿAbbās, 4 vols., Beirut 1975-9.

Ibn Faḍlallāh al-ʿUmarī, Šihābaddīn, *Ḏahabiyyat al-ʿaṣr*, ed. Ibrāhīm Ṣāliḥ, Beirut 1432/2011.

Ibn Faḍlallāh al-ʿUmarī, Šihābaddīn, *Masālik al-abṣār fī mamālik al-amṣār*, ed. Kāmil Salmān al-Ǧubūrī et al., 27 vols., Beirut 2010.

Ibn Ḥaǧar al-ʿAsqalānī, *ad-Durar al-kāminah fī aʿyān al-miʾah aṯ-ṯāminah*, 4 vols., Hyderabad 1931.

Ibn aš-Šaʿʿār, *Qalāʾid al-ǧumān fī farāʾid šuʿarāʾ hāḏā z-zamān* (al-mašhūr bi-ʿUqūd al-ǧumān fī šuʿarāʾ hāḏā z-zamān), ed. Kāmil Salmān al-Ǧubūrī, 9 vols., Beirut 2005.

aṣ-Ṣafadī, Ḫalīl b. Aybak, *Kitāb al-wāfī bi-l-wafayāt*, ed. Aḥmad Arnāʾūṭ & Turkī Muṣṭafā, 29 vols., Beirut 2000.

aṣ-Ṣafadī, *Aʿyān al-ʿaṣr wa-aʿwān an-naṣr*, ed. ʿAlī Abū Zayd et al., 6 vols., Damascus 1988.

al-Udfuwī, Ǧaʿfar b. Ṯaʿlab, *aṭ-Ṭāliʿ as-saʿīd al-ǧāmiʿ asmāʾ nuǧabāʾ aṣ-Ṣaʿīd*, ed. Saʿd Muḥammad Ḥasan, Cairo 1966.

Modern Studies

Bauer, Thomas, "Literarische Anthologien der Mamlukenzeit", in: Conermann, Stephan, & Anja Pistor-Hatam (eds.): *Die Mamluken. Studien zur ihrer Geschichte und Kultur. Zum Gedenken an Ulrich Haarmann (1942-1999)*, Hamburg 2003, pp. 71-122.

Bauer, Thomas, "Mamluk Literature as a Means of Communication", in: Conermann, Stephan (ed.), *Ubi sumus – Quo vademus: Mamluk Studies – State of the Art*, Göttingen 2013, pp. 23-56.

Al-Ǧādir, Maḥmūd ʿAbdallāh, "Maṣādir Ibn Bassām fi kitābihi ḏ-Ḏaḫirah", in: *al-Mawrid* 13/3 (1984), pp. 29-62.

Orfali, Bilal, "The Sources of al-Thaʿālibī in *Yatīmat al-Dahr* and *Tatimmat al-Yatīma*", in: *Middle Eastern Literatures* 16/1 (2013), pp. 1-47.

Orfali, Bilal, "A Sketch Map of Arabic Poetry Anthologies up to the Fall of Badhdad", in: *JAL* 43 (2012), pp. 29-59.

Sarkīs, Yūsuf Ilyān, *Muʿǧam al-maṭbūʿāt al-ʿarabiyyah wa-l-muʿarrabah*, Cairo ²1968.

Soravia, Bruna & Mohamed Meouak, "Ibn Bassām al-Šantarīnī (M. 542/1147): Algunos aspectos de su antología Al-Ḏajira fi maḥāsin ahl al-Ŷazīra", in: *Al-Qantara* 18/1 (1997), pp. 221-32.